LEARNSMART ADVANTAGE WORKS

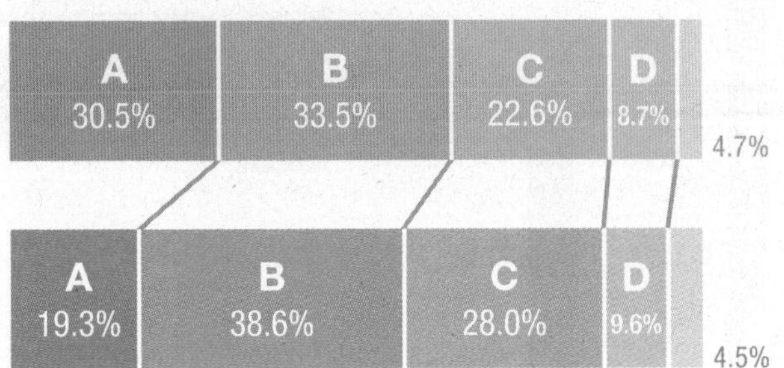

Without LearnSmart

More C students

earn B's

*Study: 690 students / 6 institutions

Over 20%

more students pass the class with LearnSmart

*A&P Research Study

LEARNSMART Pass Rate - 70%

Without LearnSmart Pass Rate - 57%

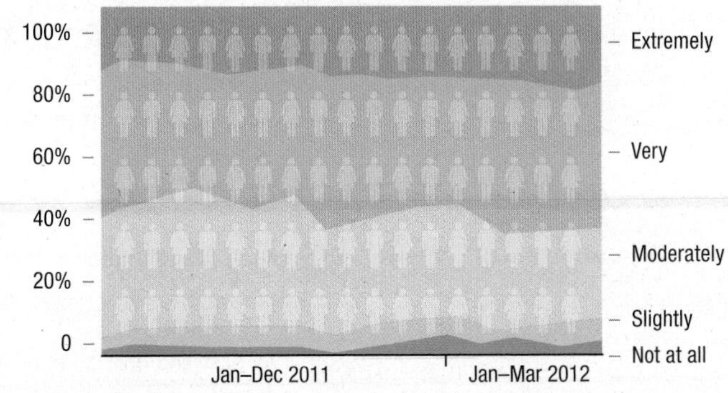

More than 60%

of all students agreed LearnSmart was a very or extremely helpful learning tool

*Based on 750,000 student survey responses

> AVAILABLE ON-THE-GO

http://bit.ly/LS4Apple

http://bit.ly/LS4Droid

advertising 2e

William F. Arens

David H. Schaefer

Michael F. Weigold

advertising
second edition

SENIOR VICE PRESIDENT, PRODUCTS & MARKETS **KURT L. STRAND**

VICE PRESIDENT, CONTENT PRODUCTION & TECHNOLOGY SERVICES **KIMBERLY MERIWETHER DAVID**

MANAGING DIRECTOR **PAUL DUCHAM**

EXECUTIVE BRAND MANAGER **SANKHA BASU**

EXECUTIVE DIRECTOR OF DEVELOPMENT **ANN TORBERT**

DEVELOPMENT EDITOR II **KELLY I. PEKELDER**

DIGITAL PRODUCT ANALYST **KERRY SHANAHAN**

MARKETING MANAGER **DONIELLE XU**

DIRECTOR, CONTENT PRODUCTION **TERRI SCHIESL**

CONTENT PROJECT MANAGER **DANA M. PAULEY**

CONTENT PROJECT MANAGER **SUSAN LOMBARDI**

SENIOR BUYER **DEBRA R. SYLVESTER**

DESIGN **MATTHEW BALDWIN**

SENIOR CONTENT LICENSING SPECIALIST **JEREMY CHESHARECK**

TYPEFACE **10/12 MINION PRO REGULAR**

COMPOSITOR **APTARA®, INC.**

PRINTER **R. R. DONNELLEY**

M: ADVERTISING, SECOND EDITION

This book is printed on acid-free paper.

4 5 6 7 8 9 0 DOW/DOW 1 0 9 8 7 6 5

ISBN 978-0-07-802896-0
MHID 0-07-802896-5

Library of Congress Control Number: 2013955925

www.mhhe.com

brief contents

contents

part one AN INTRODUCTION TO ADVERTISING

CHAPTER 1 THE EVOLUTION OF ADVERTISING 2

CHAPTER 2 THE ENVIRONMENT OF ADVERTISING 26

two all beef patties
i'm lovin' it

SAVE
The Re
COOK
seas
Eating Out
WAITROSE
FOOD
ILLUSTRATED
THE BEST FROM BRITA
Healthy
bon ap

Your Logo & Message Here

CHAPTER 15 IMC: DIRECT MARKETING, PERSONAL SELLING, PACKAGING, AND SALES PROMOTION 366

CHAPTER 16 IMC: PUBLIC RELATIONS, SPONSORSHIP, AND CORPORATE ADVERTISING 396

BONUS CHAPTER PRODUCING ADS (AVAILABLE IN CONNECT AND THROUGH CREATE)

changes to the second edition

chapter one

- Added an opening paragraph describing chapter coverage (in all chapters).
- Updated the opening vignette on 2012 Barack Obama campaign.
- Introduced integrated marketing communications earlier.
- Updated the timetable of advertising history.
- Updated the references to Internet tools that enhance teamwork.
- Updated the table of global marketers.

chapter two

- Updated the opening vignette on celebrity endorsements and the collapse of Lance Armstrong's career.
- Updated the table relating a country's ad spending to its standard of living.
- Added a discussion of the implications of clutter on websites.
- Included fewer chapter "boxes" to reduce chapter length.

chapter three

- Added material on local advertisers and social media.
- Updated the statistics on top advertisers, and top media companies.
- Incorporated the AAAA definition of an advertising agency.
- Updated the trends in the advertising industry, including new material on Google.

chapter four

- Replaced the Toyota opening vignette with an Old Spice vignette.
- Converted the "Commercial Break" chapter boxes to exhibits or deleted them (throughout the text) to improve readability and reduce chapter length.
- Updated three exhibits.
- Enhanced the discussion of geodemographic segmentation.
- Enhanced the discussion of vertical marketing systems.

chapter five

- Added new interactive model of communication that is more relevant to effects of digital media.
- Thoroughly revised and improved coverage of the consumer perception process.
- Revised and improved the discussion of cognition and memory, including consumer memory biases.

chapter six

- Updated the Holiday Inn opening vignette.
- Added a Bill Bernbach quotation in relation to the role of research in advertising.
- Added a discussion of online focus groups.
- Updated the information on Nielsen's research services.

chapter seven

- Revised and updated the Mountain Dew chapter opener.
- Added a new "My Ad Campaign" box on developing brand strategy.
- Incorporated social media examples and references.
- Used more references to chapter opener throughout the chapter.

chapter eight

- Made significant revisions and provided updates to the Target chapter opener.
- Improved coverage of creative resonance, including a reference to Leo Burnett's creative philosophy.
- Incorporated Bill Bernbach's reflections on how creativity enhances advertising.

- Improved coverage of creative thinking, including incorporating the scholarship of Griffin and Morrison.
- Improved coverage of the collaborative nature of advertising creative work.
- Added a new exhibit featuring some of advertising's greatest big ideas.
- Expanded the discussion of ethical issues involved in using sexualized appeals.

chapter nine

- Added a new chapter opener on Sony Bravia.
- Updated material on the use of computers in production.
- Added a new "My Ad Campaign" on choosing the focus of visuals.
- Shortened and added focus on the ethics box on plaigiarism.
- Streamlined and tightened copy throughout the chapter.
- Eliminated coverage of creating for international markets.

chapter ten

- Removed the material on advertising production to reduce textbook length and the number of chapters. Material is still available online and in custom versions.
- Replaced the American Legacy opening vignette with a Levi's GoForth campaign vignette.
- Updated four exhibits and numerous media statistics throughout the chapter.
- Added a discussion of online publications and digital subscriptions.

chapter eleven

- Updated the Hyundai chapter opener.
- Updated content on top network advertisers.
- Added coverage of Netflix and Amazon Prime.
- Updated the exhibit on top cable networks.
- Updated "My Ad Campaign 11–A" on buying TV and radio.
- Added new material on social media use during TV viewing.
- Added a new exhibit on people who begin watching a TV program because of online or social media recommendations.
- Added a new exhibit on how promoted tweets increase brand favorability and purchase intent.
- Updated the exhibit on costs of a 30-second spot in a top-rated TV program.
- Added a new exhibit on the 10-best-recalled product placements of 2012–2013.
- Updated the exhibit on how Nielsen tracks TV viewers.
- Significantly updated coverage of radio.
- Updated the exhibit on top radio advertisers.
- Updated the exhibit on top radio formats.
- Added a new exhibit on reach of terrestrial, satellite, and streaming radio.

chapter twelve

- Added a new opening vignette on Google and digital advertising.
- Added a new exhibit on digital advertising expenditures through 2016.
- Added new content on social media generally and Facebook specifically.
- Added a new exhibit on the most popular social media sites in 2013.
- Tightened the ethical discussion of Facebook Beacon.
- Updated the exhibit on top Internet display advertisers.
- Updated the exhibit on top Internet ad networks.
- Revised and updated information on search engine ads.
- Added a new exhibit on search engine market share as of July 2013.
- Added a new discussion on "banners and buttons" as Internet display advertising.
- Added new material on ad networks and behavioral tracking.
- Added new material on digital advertising dealing with local listings, group buying (Groupon) and affiliate marketing.

chapter thirteen

- Updated five exhibits and numerous statistics throughout the chapter.
- Added an Arbitron study about billboard viewers.
- Added an example of eBay's use of outdoor advertising to attract traffic to its site.
- Added a discussion of mall advertising.
- Enhanced the discussion of guerrilla marketing.

- Simplified the definition of direct-mail advertising and its relationship to direct marketing.
- Updated the discussion of printed catalogs.
- Used "promotional products" to describe the category previously referred to as "specialty advertising," and updated definitions.

chapter fourteen

- Added a new opening vignette on trade desks.
- Updated media spending statistics in Exhibit 14–1.
- Added new material on media-buying agencies.
- Added a new exhibit tracking the inverse relation of TV viewing and costs.
- Added a new ethics box on the media.
- Increased focus on domestic media planning.

chapter fifteen

- Updated the GEICO opening vignette.
- Enhanced the description of database marketing.
- Updated the exhibit on the largest direct-response agencies in the United States and numerous statistics throughout the chapter.
- Added information about the National Do Not Call Registry.
- Clarified the distinction between direct mail that is intended to elicit a direct response (direct-response advertising) and that which is simply intended to communicate information about products and services.
- Added a discussion of direct-response digital interactive media.
- Added an exhibit on the top 10 U.S. trade shows.
- Added a discussion of coupon-to-card (C2C) coupons.
- Enhanced the distinction among contests, sweepstakes, and games.

chapter sixteen

- Replaced the social media opening vignette with a Netflix vignette.
- Updated three exhibits and numerous statistics regarding sponsorships.
- Added a public relations example of working conditions in Apple's Chinese factories.
- Added a reference to *influentials,* a new term to describe "centers of influence."
- Added *online newsroom* as new term.
- Added several examples of sports marketing sponsorships.
- Integrated David Ogilvy's opinions about corporate advertising into the text (formerly in a text box).

bonus chapter (Available in Connect and through Create)

- New opening vignette featuring Jean-Claude Van Damme and Volvo trucks.
- New learning objectives relating to key responsibilities in managing production and explaining how ads are produced for the Web.
- Refocused content to reflect the influence of digital media in electronic production.
- Updated "My Ad Campaign" to offer students new (and free) production tools.

advertising 2e

the evolution of advertising

chapter one

This chapter introduces you to some important themes of this text, including integrated marketing communications (IMC). It also introduces one of the most important components of IMC, advertising, and distinguishes it from other forms of marketing communications. The chapter goes on to explain the functions and effects of advertising in a free economy and traces the evolution of advertising's impact on society.

Advertising pros pay careful attention to the work of others, and they pay extra attention when ads are inspired and effective. One such campaign ran from the end of 2006 through November 2008. But this campaign was not for a soap brand or some other product; it was for a young candidate who, seemingly coming from nowhere, won election to the highest office in the land.

Barack Obama is a natural leader and an exciting speaker. Even so, when he announced that he would run for president, it took audacity, to borrow from an Obama book title, to believe he would win. Just 46 years old, Obama had only two years of experience in national office. Indeed, he was a long shot even for the nomination of his party.

continued on p. 4

LEARNING OBJECTIVES

After studying this chapter, you will be able to:

LO1-1 Define integrated marketing communications.

LO1-2 Define advertising and distinguish it from other forms of marketing communications.

LO1-3 Explain the role advertising plays in business and marketing.

LO1-4 Illustrate the functions of advertising in a free-market economy.

LO1-5 Discuss how advertising evolved with the history of commerce.

LO1-6 Describe the impact of advertising on society.

continued from p. 3

The Obama team's assessment of his situation in late 2006 revealed it would be an uphill climb. In the Democratic primary, polls gave Hillary Clinton three times as many supporters as Obama.[1] Nationally the story was even bleaker. A survey found a matchup with likely Republican nominee John McCain would give McCain every state but two, Illinois and Hawaii.[2]

The situation analysis also revealed some great opportunities. Understanding those opportunities, and developing a strategy for seizing them, proved central to creating Obama's great ads. Obama's team knew that Hillary Clinton, in addition to being ahead in the polls, was well known. Many of her enthusiastic supporters were excited at the prospect that she would become the first female president. But she also had vulnerabilities, chief among them her vote giving President Bush the authority to go to war in Iraq and her association with her husband's administration eight years earlier.

Obama's team decided that he would be positioned as the candidate of change. Every message coming from the campaign, whether in ads, speeches, Web sites, press releases, posters, bumper stickers, or any other medium, would resonate with that theme. As you'll see later in this book, *positioning* is a term marketers use when they create an image of a product, person, organization, or idea in the minds of a group of people.

Creating a campaign around the core idea of change was brilliant. It turned Obama's outsider status and lack of experience into a plus. And it transformed a seeming strength of Clinton into a liability. Obama's message to an electorate that wanted fresh approaches was that electing Clinton would bring more of the old ways of governing. Obama's advisors were right. In 2008, voters were more interested in change than experience.

The election pitted Obama against Republican John McCain. Would the "change" message still work against a self-described "maverick," a candidate known for bucking his own party? Obama's advisors thought so. They would neutralize McCain's maverick status by linking him to President Bush. Obama's ads and

speeches linking McCain to Bush occurred with such frequency that during the final debate an exasperated McCain cried out: "If you want to run against President Bush, you should have run four years ago."

Obama had a solid core strategy: convince voters that he was the candidate of change. Tactically his campaign also made several smart moves. One tactic was to spend heavily on advertising; in fact, a record amount of over $310 million.[3] Television advertising reached large numbers of undecided voters and familiarized them with the candidate.

Another tactic was to effectively use social media as a campaign strategy. They became powerful tools for community building, voter turnout, and fundraising, raising over $500 million from 3 million donors. Nearly 2,000 Obama videos on YouTube were watched more than 80 million times. The McCain campaign could not keep up.

It's hard to believe that when the 2008 campaign started, Twitter had just been launched and the iPhone didn't exist yet. Four years later, during the 2012 presidential campaign, far more social media tools were available and American adults' use of those tools had nearly doubled. Almost half of those in the 18-to-29 age group said they had been lobbied online to vote for one candidate or the other. While the Romney campaign was more social media savvy than McCain's, it couldn't compete with Obama's social media machine. Obama logged twice as many Facebook "Likes" and nearly 20 times as many retweets as Romney. The Obama campaign outspent the Romney campaign 10:1 on digital advertising.[4]

The Obama campaign was also very sophisticated in deciding where to spend its money. In each swing state, the Obama campaign utilized a different media mix, varying the amount of money spent on television, radio, digital, mobile, and social media advertising, based on data about the voters.

Much as John F. Kennedy was considered the first president to effectively use the new medium of television to speak directly to the American people, Barack Obama was the first president to effectively use social media to interact with the populace. It's quite certain that social media will play a key role in future campaigns for politicians, as well as for products.[5] ■

LO1-1 Define integrated marketing communications.

marketing communications The various efforts and tools companies use to communicate with customers and prospects, including newspaper ads, event sponsorship, publicity, telemarketing, digital ads, and coupons, to mention just a few.

The Obama campaigns highlight the importance of having an integrated communications plan. Television played a key role in reaching and informing a vast audience, but messages from digital sources, such as the Internet, may have made the difference in the outcome of the elections. Throughout this text, we will discuss the importance of integrated marketing communications (IMC): the coordination and integration of messages from a variety of sources. Marketers today realize that it is no longer possible to reach and effectively persuade their audiences with traditional media alone—television, radio, magazines, newspapers, direct mail, and outdoor. They need to combine and coordinate those communications tools with public relations, personal selling, sales promotion, and the new digital media to mount an effective marketing campaign.

We will begin by focusing on advertising, since it plays a central role in most marketing campaigns. Advertising is the element of marketing communications over which a company has the greatest control. As such, it is likely to remain an important component of almost every major IMC campaign. But keep in mind that whenever you see the term *advertising*, other communications elements can and should be integrated into a campaign to deliver a coordinated marketing message.

LO1-2 Define advertising and distinguish it from other forms of marketing communications.

WHAT IS ADVERTISING?

You are exposed to hundreds and maybe even thousands of commercial messages every day. They may appear in the forms used by the Obama campaign—television commercials, Web sites, and text messages—or in the form of product placements in TV shows, coupons, sales letters, event sponsorships, telemarketing calls, or e-mails. These are just a few of the many communication tools that companies and organizations use to initiate and maintain contact with their customers, clients, and prospects. You may simply refer to them all as "advertising." But, in fact, the correct term for these various tools is **marketing communications**. And advertising is just one type of marketing communication.

So, then, what is advertising?

At the beginning of the twentieth century, Albert Lasker, generally regarded as the "father" of modern advertising, defined advertising as "salesmanship in print, driven by a reason why."[6] But that was long before the advent of radio, television, or the Internet.

The nature and scope of the business world, and advertising, were quite limited. More than a century later, our planet is a far different place. The nature and needs of business have changed, and so have the concept and practice of advertising.

Definitions of advertising abound. Journalists, for example, might define it as a communication, public relations, or persuasion process; businesspeople see it as a marketing process; economists and sociologists tend to focus on its economic, societal, or ethical significance. And some consumers might define it simply as a nuisance. Each of these perspectives has some

my ad campaign

Overview [1–A]

Welcome to My Ad Campaign, a valuable feature of this text. My Ad Campaign should be useful in any of the following situations:

- Your instructor has asked students in your class to work on part or all of an ad campaign, either individually or in groups.
- You are doing an internship and want practical advice on how to help your company advertise.
- You want to try to apply the concepts and ideas that you are reading about in this book in the real world.

Professors approach advertising projects differently. Some assign students to create ads for a real product, although you never actually contact the company that makes the product. Some assign a fictional brand in a real product category. Perhaps your professor has offered your talents to a client, such as a small local business or firm. You may even have to find a client yourself by making inquiries in your community. Finally, your professor may ask you to help a charity or nonprofit with its advertising. No matter which of these things is true, the good news is that developing an advertising campaign follows a similar path. And the My Ad Campaign feature is designed to help you do it well.

Let's begin with a definition. An advertising campaign involves the creation and placement of a series of strategic communications that are unified by an underlying theme or core message. The communications are intended to help promote a brand, product, service, organization, or idea. The messages are typically designed to resonate with a group called a target audience. Campaigns usually have specific objectives, such as increasing product awareness or persuading people to try a service or donate money to a candidate. And to ensure that the target audience receives them, messages appear in various media, such as newspapers, radio commercials, or Web pages. You may not do all of these activities, especially placing ads in real media. But you will get a chance to do some serious thinking, planning, and brainstorming.

We can make our definition of a campaign a bit more concrete by thinking back to the opening vignette of this chapter. President Obama, of course, is not a "product," but for purposes of winning the election his team had to plan their messages as though he was one. Previously we noted that an ad campaign has an underlying theme or core message. In the Obama campaign this theme was "change," specifically that Obama represented change and his opponents did not. Many years ago, a famous advertising professional named David Ogilvy referred to a great campaign's theme as "the big idea." Deciding what the "big idea" is for your brand will be one of the most important decisions you will make. The big idea of "change" proved central to Obama's victories over Hillary Clinton, John McCain, and Mitt Romney.

Obama's team also did an excellent job identifying target audiences that should receive campaign messages. Two of the most important audiences were undecided voters and young voters, and the campaign developed specific messages for each. It wanted to persuade undecided voters that they could change Washington only by voting for Obama. For young voters, the objective was different. Young voters already liked Obama and wanted him to win. The campaign's challenge with this group was to get them to register to vote, something young voters had not done in large numbers in previous elections. To do all of this, the campaign used a variety of media, both traditional (TV, radio, print) and new (Facebook, Twitter, MySpace).

Hopefully you've inferred from all of this that advertising is very strategic. Lots of planning takes place long before ads are created. For that reason, while you may be itching to create some advertisements for your client, you have lots of work to do before you begin brainstorming ideas for actual ads. Obama's team was successful not only because they created great ads, but because they understood their candidate, his opponents, the audiences that were important to reach, the media that could be used to reach them, and the objectives that were crucial to success. On a much smaller scale and with far less resources, you face similar challenges. My Ad Campaign is designed to help you to meet that challenge.

In subsequent chapters, we'll help you learn to develop a deeper understanding of your brand or client, develop a plan for marketing and advertising activities, conduct research so that you can better understand your target audience, formulate media strategy, and design effective advertisements. Finally, we'll teach you how to implement evaluation programs to test whether your ads have been successful. By the end of the semester, you won't be a top advertising professional. But you'll have some real experience in the art and science of developing an ad campaign.

The My Ad Campaign topics are listed below. You may find it useful or necessary to jump around as you develop your own campaign.

1. Overview/Tools for Teamwork
2. Your Campaign Assignment
3. Understanding What Your Client Wants
4. Segmenting the Audience
5. Understanding Your Customer and Product
6. Conducting Marketing and Advertising Research
7. Situation Analysis, Objectives, and Budgets
8. The Creative Brief
9. Developing the Creative Product
10. Magazine and Newspaper Advertising
11. Television and Radio Advertising
12. Digital Interactive Media
13. Out-of-Home, Direct Mail and Specialty Advertising
14. Developing Media Objectives and Strategies
15. Developing a Plans Book
16. Blogging/The Client Presentation

merit, but for now we'll use the following functional definition:

> **Advertising** is the structured and composed nonpersonal communication of information, usually paid for and usually persuasive in nature, about products (goods, services, and ideas) by identified sponsors through various media.

advertising The structured and composed nonpersonal communication of information, usually paid for and usually persuasive in nature, about products (goods, services, and ideas) by identified sponsors through various media.

consumers People who buy products and services for their own, or someone else's, personal use.

public service announcements (PSAs) An advertisement serving the public interest, often for a nonprofit organization, carried by the media at no charge.

goods Tangible products such as suits, soap, and soft drinks.

Let's take this definition apart and analyze its components. Advertising is, first of all, a type of *communication.* It is actually a very *structured* form of communication, employing both verbal and nonverbal elements that are *composed* to fill specific space and time formats determined by the sponsor.

Even nonprofits use advertising to communicate information.

Second, advertising is typically directed to groups of people rather than to individuals. These people could be **consumers**, who buy products like cars, deodorant, or food for their personal use. Or they might be businesspeople who buy fleets of cars for commercial or government use. The messages are delivered via media, such as television or the Internet, rather than through direct, personal contact between a seller and a buyer. Advertising is, therefore, a kind of nonpersonal, or mass, communication.

Most advertising is *paid* for by sponsors. GM, Walmart, the Obama campaign, and your local fitness salon pay the newspaper or the radio or TV station to carry the ads you read, see, and hear. But some sponsors don't have to pay for their ads. The American Red Cross, United Way, and American Cancer Society are among the many national organizations whose **public service announcements (PSAs)** are carried at no charge because of their nonprofit status. Likewise, a poster on a school bulletin board promoting a dance is not paid for, but it is still an ad—a structured, nonpersonal, persuasive communication.

Of course, most advertising is intended to be *persuasive*—to win converts to a product, service, or idea. Some ads, such as legal announcements, are intended merely to inform, not to persuade. But they are still ads because they satisfy all the other requirements of the definition.

In addition to promoting tangible **goods** such as oranges, iPods, and automobiles, advertising helps publicize the intangible

services A bundle of benefits that may or may not be physical, that are temporary in nature, and that come from the completion of a task.

ideas Economic, political, religious, or social viewpoints that advertising may attempt to sell.

product The particular good or service a company sells.

medium An instrument or communications vehicle that carries or helps transfer a message from the sender to the receiver.

word-of-mouth (WOM) advertising The passing of information, especially product recommendations, in an informal, unpaid, person-to-person manner, rather than by advertising or other forms of traditional marketing.

mass media Print or broadcast media that reach very large audiences. Mass media include radio, television, newspapers, magazines, and billboards.

services of bankers, beauticians, bike repair shops, bill collectors, and Internet providers. Increasingly, advertising is used to advocate a wide variety of **ideas**, whether economic, political, religious, or social. In this book the term **product** encompasses goods, services, and ideas.

An ad *identifies* its sponsor. This seems obvious. The sponsor wants to be identified, or why pay to advertise?

Finally, advertising reaches us through a channel of communication referred to as a **medium**. An advertising medium is any nonpersonal means used to present an ad to its target audience. Thus, we have radio advertising, television advertising, newspaper ads, Google ads, and so on. When you tell somebody how much you like a product, that's sometimes called **word-of-mouth (WOM) advertising**. Although WOM is a communication medium, it has not generally been considered an advertising medium. However, the popularity of social media, such as Facebook and Twitter, is forcing advertisers to reconsider this belief. Historically, advertisers have used the traditional **mass media** (the plural of medium)—radio, TV, newspapers, magazines, and billboards—to send their messages. Modern technology enables advertising to reach us efficiently through a variety of addressable media (like direct mail) and interactive media (like the Internet). Advertisers also use a variety of other nontraditional media such as shopping carts, blimps, and DVDs to find their audience.

check yourself ✓

1. What are the six key components of the definition of advertising?
2. Under what conditions might advertising not be paid for?

LO1-3 Explain the role advertising plays in business and marketing.

THE ROLE OF ADVERTISING IN BUSINESS

In Chapter 5 we discuss in more detail how advertising helps inform and persuade consumers, but first let's consider advertising's role in business. Every business organization performs a number of activities, typically classified into three broad divisions:

- Operations (production/manufacturing)
- Finance/administration
- Marketing

Of all the business functions, marketing is the only one whose primary role is to bring in revenue. Without revenue, of course, a company cannot pay its employees' salaries or earn a profit. So marketing is very important.

What Is Marketing?

Over the years, the concept of marketing has evolved based on the supply of and demand for products. Because we need to understand marketing as it relates to *advertising,* we will use the American Marketing Association's definition:

> **Marketing** is the activity, set of institutions, and processes for creating, communicating, delivering, and exchanging offerings that have value for customers, clients, partners, and society at large.[7]

We will devote all of Part 2 to the subject of marketing and consumer behavior. What's important to understand now is that marketing is a **process**—a sequence of actions or methods—aimed at satisfying consumer needs profitably. These processes are typically broken down into the 4Ps of the **marketing mix**: developing *products, pricing* them strategically, distributing them so they are available to customers at appropriate *places,* and *promoting* them through sales and advertising activities (see Exhibit 1–1). The ultimate goal of the marketing process to earn a profit for the firm by consummating the exchange of products or services with those customers who need or want them. And the role of advertising is to promote—to inform, persuade, and remind groups of customers, or markets, about the need-satisfying value of the company's goods and services.

Advertising and the Marketing Process

Advertising helps the organization achieve its marketing goals. So do market research, sales, and distribution. And these other marketing specialties all have an impact on the kind of advertising a company employs. An effective advertising specialist must have a broad understanding of the whole marketing process in order to know what type of advertising to use in a given situation.

Companies and organizations use many different types of advertising, depending on their particular marketing strategy. The

marketing An organizational function and a set of processes for creating, communicating, and delivering value to customers and for managing customer relationships in ways that benefit the organization and its stakeholders.

process A sequence of actions or methods aimed at satisfying consumer needs profitably.

marketing mix Four elements, called the 4Ps (product, price, place, and promotion), that every company has the option of adding, subtracting, or modifying in order to create a desired marketing strategy.

marketing strategy The statement of how the company is going to accomplish its marketing objectives. The strategy is the total directional thrust of the company, that is, the how-to of the marketing plan, and is determined by the particular blend of the marketing mix elements (the 4Ps), which the company can control.

advertising strategy The advertising objective declares what the advertiser wants to achieve with respect to consumer awareness, attitude, and preference; the advertising strategy describes how to get there. Advertising strategy consists of two substrategies: the creative strategy and the media strategy.

marketing strategy will help determine who the targets of advertising should be, in what markets the advertising should appear, and what goals the advertising should accomplish. The **advertising strategy**, in turn, will refine the target audience and define what response the advertiser is seeking—what that audience should notice, think, and feel. We will discuss the development of marketing, advertising, and media strategies later in the text.

But first, we need to understand the economic dimension of advertising and how advertising has evolved as both an economic and a societal tool.

check yourself ✓

1. What is the ultimate goal of marketing?
2. What are the 4Ps of the marketing mix and under which does advertising fall?
3. What roles does advertising play in helping marketing meet its goals?

L01-4 Illustrate the functions of advertising in a free-market economy.

ECONOMICS: THE GROWING NEED FOR ADVERTISING

Economics has driven the growth of advertising since its earliest beginnings and has made it one of the hallmarks of the free-enterprise system. As English historian Raymond Williams wrote, advertising is "the official art of a capitalist society."

Today, business and advertising are undergoing dramatic changes. To understand the nature of these changes and why they're taking place, we need to look at how advertising has evolved. We'll explain how the changing economic environment has influenced the evolution of advertising through the centuries. Then, in Chapter 2, we'll look at how advertising influences the economy and society and, as a result, is often an object of controversy and criticism.

▼**EXHIBIT 1-1** Advertising is just one of several activities that fall under the promotion component of the marketing mix.

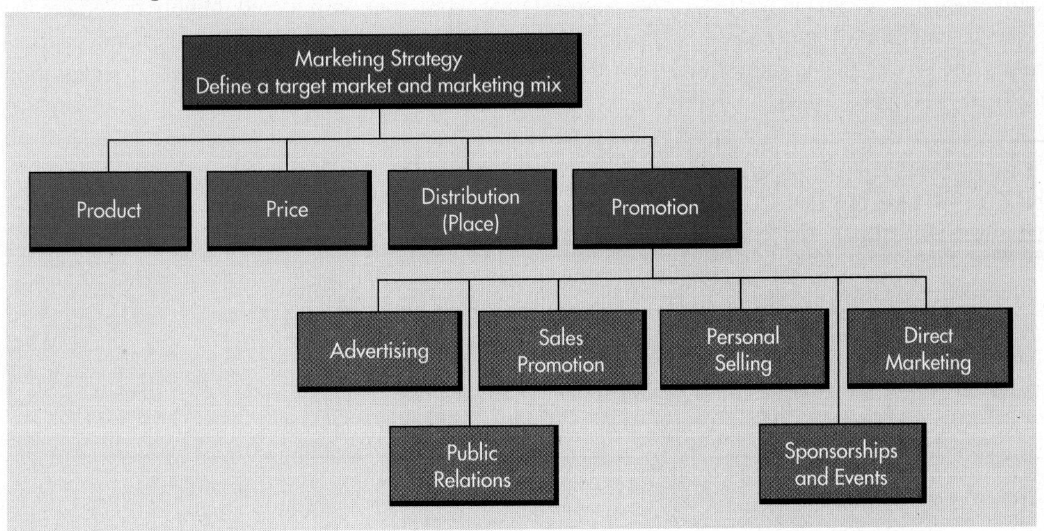

Principles of Free-Market Economics

Our economy is based on the notion of competition. While there is no such thing as *perfect competition,* there are four fundamental assumptions of free-market economics that a market-driven society strives to achieve:

1. *Self-interest.* People and organizations tend to act in their own self-interest. People are acquisitive and always want more—for less. Therefore, open

competition between self-interested sellers advertising to self-interested buyers naturally leads to greater product availability at more competitive prices.

2. *Complete information.* Access by buyers and sellers to all information at all times about what products are available, at what quality, and at what prices, leads to greater competition and lower prices for all. (This is why attorneys are now allowed to advertise.)

3. *Many buyers and sellers.* Having a wide range of sellers ensures that if one company does not meet customer needs, another will capitalize on the situation by producing a more market-responsive product. Similarly, having a wide range of buyers ensures that sellers can find customers who are interested in the unique products they are able to produce at a fair price. (This is why we have antitrust laws.)

4. *Absence of externalities (social costs).* Sometimes the sale or consumption of products may benefit or harm other people who are not involved in the transaction and didn't pay for the product. In these cases, the government may use taxation and/or regulation to compensate for or eliminate the **externalities**. (This is why there are restrictions and requirements placed on tobacco advertisers.)

Now, given these basic assumptions, let's see how advertising fits into the scheme of a free-market economy.

Functions and Effects of Advertising in a Free Economy

For any business, advertising may perform a variety of functions, and, when executed correctly, its effects may be dramatic. To see how this works, let's go back to the beginnings of Coca-Cola, in 1886, when druggist John Pemberton was still mixing the syrup in his lab.

Coca-Cola was first served at a small pharmacy in Atlanta in 1886. The word drink *was added to signs to let people know it was a beverage.*

Pemberton's business partner and bookkeeper, Frank Robinson, suggested the name "Coca-Cola" to identify the two main flavors (coca leaves and kola nuts) and because he thought that "the two Cs would look well in advertising."[8] Robinson wrote down the name in his flowing script, creating a logo that is now instantly recognizable around the world and is one of Coca-Cola's more valued assets. Later, a distinctive bottle shape—purportedly the brainchild of a bored glassblower who based the design on a cacao pod instead of a caca nut, as intended—became the standard throughout the company. The proprietary curvy bottle helped customers differentiate Coca-Cola from other drinks. The creation of the Coca-Cola logo and contour bottle demonstrates one of the most basic functions of **branding** as well as advertising: *to identify products and their source and to differentiate them from others.* (The functions and effects discussed here are listed in Exhibit 1–2.)

When Pemberton first began selling Coca-Cola at Jacobs's Pharmacy, he needed to let people know what it was—although we associate the word *cola* with a cold, bubbly beverage, the people of Atlanta didn't automatically make the same connection. Therefore, Pemberton and Robinson added the suggestion

▼EXHIBIT 1–2 Functions and effects of advertising as a marketing tool.

- To identify products and differentiate them from others.
- To communicate information about the product, its features, and its place of sale.
- To induce consumers to try new products and to suggest reuse.
- To stimulate the distribution of a product.
- To increase product use.
- To build value, brand preference, and loyalty.
- To lower the overall cost of sales.

externalities Benefit or harm caused by the sale or consumption of products to people who are not involved in the transaction and didn't pay for the product.

branding A marketing function that identifies products and their source and differentiates them from all other products.

drink before *Coca-Cola* on the signs that they had painted and placed in front of the drugstore.[9] Ads in the *Atlanta Journal* let readers know why they should drink it (because it is "delicious, exhilarating, refreshing and invigorating," it was the perfect "temperance drink" during Prohibition), how much it cost, and where they could get it. Here is another basic function of advertising: *to communicate information about the product, its features, and its location of sale.*

After Asa Candler gained control of the Coca-Cola Company, he began to develop the market for the drink on a grander scale. With the help of Frank Robinson and a city directory, he mailed thousands of coupons for free drinks to Atlanta residents. Coupons were also handed out on the street and inserted in magazines. To cover the costs of the samples, the company gave free syrup to the soda fountains that offered the beverage. Later, the free sample campaign went along whenever Coca-Cola was introduced in a new market. Candler also distributed promotional items to vendors so that the Coca-Cola logo was visible everywhere both outside and inside the shop. To us, this campaign demonstrates another function of advertising: *to induce consumers to try new products and to suggest reuse.*

Through the early part of the twentieth century, Coca-Cola wasn't the dominant force we know today. Competitors such as Pepsi and the now-defunct Moxie cut into Coca-Cola's market share. Outside forces also threatened the entire industry; sugar rationing during wartimes was especially damaging. Before the United States became involved in World War II, Coca-Cola executives preempted a repeat of the setbacks the company suffered during World War I rationing. They persuaded the government to give troops Coca-Cola instead of alcoholic beverages to boost their morale. The D'Arcy advertising agency gathered endorsements from U.S. officers in training camps to support the company's bid to become an official military supplier—and therefore be exempt from rationing. The War Department agreed to the plan, and Coca-Cola borrowed $5.5 million to establish 64 bottling plants near the front lines. The risky investment had great returns. When the soldiers returned home, a survey showed they preferred Coke by eight to one over Pepsi.[10] Coca-Cola blended patriotism with another of the important functions of advertising: *to increase product use.*

As soft drinks became a staple throughout the United States, Coca-Cola began campaigns outside the country to affect beverage consumption globally. The first international Coca-Cola bottling plants were established in Canada, Cuba, and Panama in 1906; today the company bottles Coke in more than 200 countries. Coca-Cola franchise bottlers around the world can tweak the recipe to match local tastes. Bottlers and distributors also supplement Coke advertising with their own promotions and sponsorships. Through various activities, Coca-Cola has succeeded in accomplishing yet another function of advertising: *to stimulate the distribution of a product,* in this case, on a global level.

In a free-market economy, when one company starts to make significant profits, other companies immediately jump in to compete. Over the years, to battle the constant competitive threat, Coca-Cola has funded ongoing marketing communications campaigns to accomplish yet another function of advertising: *to build value, brand preference, and loyalty.* Although the taste test wars of the 1980s showed that many people liked the taste of Pepsi better than that of Coke, such blind preference has never knocked Coca-Cola out of the top spot. A century of consistently upbeat marketing communications has made its mark. Coca-Cola advertising, such as its current campaign, "The Ahh Effect," has always promoted a common voice and a common theme: Coca-Cola makes life's relaxing moments even better.

For more than 120 years, the Coca-Cola Company has used a variety of media to communicate this message to diverse

For more than 120 years, Coca-Cola has effectively built and maintained strong brand preference and loyalty among its customers. Coke's campaigns confirm that drinking Coca-Cola makes our lives happier.

preindustrial age
Period of time between the beginning of written history and roughly the start of the nineteenth century, during which the invention of paper and the printing press and increased literacy gave rise to the first forms of written advertising.

audiences. Why? To achieve the most significant function of advertising: *to lower the overall cost of sales.* For the cost of reaching just one prospect through personal selling, companies can reach thousands of people through media advertising. The average cost to make a face-to-face field sales call is about $300.[11] Multiply that $300 by the nearly 20 million people who watch a top-rated prime-time TV show, and the cost comes to a mind-boggling $6 billion. However, for only $500,000 Coca-Cola can buy a 30-second TV commercial during a regular season show of *American Idol* and reach the same 20 million people.[12] Through television, advertisers can talk to a thousand prospects for only $25—less than 10 percent of what it costs to talk to a single prospect through personal selling.

[Advertising contributes to a free economy.]

Now, considering this brief synopsis of Coca-Cola history, how does Coke's advertising fit with the basic assumptions of a free-market economy? Has Coke's advertising helped make the soft drink available to more people at lower cost? Has it informed them about where they can buy Coke? Has the freedom to advertise contributed to the competitive environment? What externalities might have had a positive or negative impact on the Coca-Cola Company's efforts to market its beverages?

Perhaps you can see from this one example how advertising contributes to a free economy. But if it's so good, then why didn't advertising take off until the twentieth century? (For a time line of advertising history, see Exhibit 1–3.) Why wasn't it developed and used for the last several thousand years of recorded history?

check yourself ✓

1. What are the seven functions of advertising as a marketing tool?
2. Provide an example of each function from the history of Coca-Cola.

LO1-5 Discuss how advertising evolved with the history of commerce.

THE EVOLUTION OF ADVERTISING AS AN ECONOMIC TOOL

Thousands of years ago, people devoted most of their efforts to meeting basic survival needs: food, clothing, shelter. They lived in small, isolated communities where artisans and farmers bartered products and services among themselves. Distribution was limited to how far vendors could walk and "advertising" to how loud they could shout. Because goods weren't produced in great quantity, there was no need for advertising to stimulate mass purchases. There were also no mass media available for possible advertisers to use. (See Exhibit 1–3.)

The Preindustrial Age

As markets grew larger and became more complex, the demand for products increased, and the need for advertising slowly developed. At first, merchants hung carved signs in front of their shops so passersby could see what products were being offered. Most people couldn't read, so the signs often used symbols, such as a boot for a cobbler. This period was called the **preindustrial age**, and, for Western civilization, it extended from the beginning of recorded history to roughly the start of the nineteenth century.[13]

An early form of advertising. Until the advent of public schooling, most people couldn't read—so signs featured symbols of the goods or services for sale, such as the jerkin on this tailor's sign in Williamsburg, Virginia.

During the preindustrial age, several important developments enabled the eventual birth of modern advertising. The Chinese

EXHIBIT 1–3 Timetable of advertising history.

3000 BC–AD 1	AD 500–1799	1800–1899	1900–1919
3000 BC Written advertisement offering "Whole gold coin" for runaway slave "Shem." **500 BC** Political and trade graffiti on Pompeii walls. **AD 1** First uppercase lettering appears on Greek buildings.	**1455** First printed Bible. **1472** First printed ad in English tacked on London church doors. **1544** Claude Garamond, first "typefounder," perfects a roman typeface that bears his name and is still used today. **1650** First newspaper ad offers reward for stolen horses. **1662** *London Gazette* offers first advertising supplement. **1704** First ads in America published in the *Boston Newsletter.*	**1841** Volney B. Palmer becomes first "newspaper agent" (advertising agent) in America. **1844** First magazine ad runs. **1869** Francis W. Ayer founds ad agency bearing his father's name, N. W. Ayer & Sons, in Philadelphia. He initiates first "for commission" ad contract (1876), first market survey for an ad (1879), and first on-staff creative services (art in 1890, copywriting in 1892). **1888** *Printers' Ink* is first U.S. publication for ad profession.	**1900** Psychologists study the attention-getting and persuasive qualities of advertising. **1900** Northwestern University is first to offer advertising as a discipline. **1903** Scripps-McRae League of Newspapers appoints ad censor, rejects $500,000 in ads in first year. **1905** First national ad plan is for the "Gillette Safety Razor." **1911** First "truth in advertising" codes are established by what is now called the American Advertising Federation (AAF).
1920–1939	**1940–1959**	**1960–1969**	**1970–1979**
1920s Albert Lasker, "father" of modern advertising, calls advertising "salesmanship in print." First ad testimonials by movie stars appear. Full-color printing is available in magazines. **1922** First radio ad solves radio's need for financing. **1924** N. W. Ayer produces first sponsored radio broadcast, the "Eveready Hour." **1930** *Advertising Age* magazine is founded. **1938** Wheeler-Lea amendments to FTC Act of 1938 grant FTC further power to curb false ad practices.	**1946** America has 12 TV stations broadcasting to the public. **1947** Lanham Trademark Act protects brand names and slogans. **1948** 46 TV stations are operating and 300 others are awaiting FCC approval. **1950** First political ads, by Gov. Dewey of New York, appear on TV. **1950s** David Ogilvy's "Hathaway man" and "Commander Whitehead" become popular ad personae.	**1960s** Doyle Dane Bernbach's "Think small" ad for American Volkswagen becomes one of the most famous ads of the decade, establishing a strong market position for the smallest European import. The agency's slogan for Avis, "We're only No. 2, so we try harder," is also very successful. New York's Madison Avenue becomes known worldwide as the center of the advertising world and features the best in advertising creativity.	**1971** Armed services begin first advertising for the new "all-volunteer" military ("Be all that you can be in the Army"). **1972** The *Ad Age* article "Positioning: The Battle for Your Mind" by Al Ries and Jack Trout details the strategy of positioning that dominates the 1970s. **1973** Oil shortages begin period of "demarketing," ads aimed at slowing demand. **1970s (late)** Growth in self-indulgence, signified by popularity of self-fulfillment activities, spurs some agencies into making infomercials.
1980–1989	**1990–1999**	**2000–2009**	**2010–2013**
1980s Ad agency megamergers take place worldwide. **1982** First edition of *Contemporary Advertising* is published. **1984** The Internet (government controlled since 1973) is turned over to the private sector. **1986** *Marketing Warfare* by Al Ries and Jack Trout portrays marketing in terms of classic warfare manual written by General Clausewitz in 1831. **1989** Tim Berners-Lee invents the World Wide Web, allowing surfers to browse the Internet.	**1990s** A recession leads marketers to shift funds from advertising to sales promotion. **1994** Media glut leads to market fragmentation; network TV is no longer sole medium for reaching total marketplace. Ad professions adopt integrated marketing communications (IMC) as the new strategy to build market relationships. **1997** AOL launches Instant Messenger (AIM), allowing online chat and opening the door to social networking. **1998** Google begins answering search queries.	**2000** The Internet is the fastest-growing new ad medium since TV, with 400 million users. **2002** A general economic slump hammers ad spending. **2005** Online advertisers spend $8.32 billion to reach the 170 million wired U.S. residents. **2007** The iPhone takes social media mobile. **2007** U.S. ad agency revenue surges 8.6% to $31 billion, led by double-digit growth in digital advertising. **2009** Broad global recession leads to cutbacks in ad expenditures.	**2010** The Old Spice Guy viral campaign achieves 113 million online views. **2012** Google captures over 30% of the $100 billion digital advertising market. **2013** Growth in global advertising is expected to hit 3.5%, led by mobile advertising, expanding by an estimated 67%. **2013** The *Man of Steel* movie collects $160 million in product placements, paid by 100 promotional partners.

invented paper and Europe had its first paper mill by 1275. In the 1440s, Johannes Gutenberg invented the printing press in Germany. The press was not only the most important development in the history of advertising, and indeed communication, but it also revolutionized the way people lived and worked.

The introduction of printing allowed facts to be established, substantiated, recorded, and transported. People no longer had to rely on their memories. Some entrepreneurs bought printing presses, mounted them in wagons, and traveled from town to town, selling printing. This new technology made possible the first formats of advertising—posters, handbills, and signs—and, eventually, the first mass medium—the newspaper. In effect, the cry of the vendor could now be multiplied many times and heard beyond the immediate neighborhood.

> "With the need for mass consumption came the increasing need for . . . advertising to inform new markets of the availability of products."

In 1472, the first ad in English appeared: a handbill tacked on church doors in London announcing a prayer book for sale. Two hundred years later the first newspaper ad was published, offering a reward for the return of 12 stolen horses. Soon newspapers carried ads for coffee, chocolate, tea, real estate, medicines, and even personal ads. These early ads were still directed to a very limited number of people: the customers of the coffeehouses where most newspapers were read.

By the early 1700s, the world's population had grown to about 600 million people, and some major cities were big enough to support larger volumes of advertising. In fact, the greater volume caused a shift in advertising strategy. Samuel Johnson, the famous English literary figure, observed in 1758 that advertisements were now so numerous that they were "negligently perused" and that it had become necessary to gain attention "by magnificence of promise." This was the beginning of *puffery* in advertising.

In the American colonies, the *Boston Newsletter* began carrying ads in 1704. About 25 years later, Benjamin Franklin, the "father" of advertising art, made ads more readable by using large headlines and considerable white space. In fact, Franklin was the first American known to use illustrations in ads.

THAT the Stage-Waggons, kept by *John Barnhill*, in *Elm-Street*, in *Philadelphia*, and *John Mercereau*, at the *New-Blazing Star*, near *New-York*, continues their Stages in two Days, from *Powles-Hook Ferry*, oppoſite *New-York*, to *Philadelphia*; returns from *Philadelphia* to *Powles-Hook* in two Days alſo; they will endeavour to oblige the Publick by keeping the beſt of Waggons and ſober Drivers, and ſets out from *Powles Hook* and *Philadelphia*, on Mondays and Thurſdays, punctually at Sunriſe, and meet at *Prince Town* the ſame Nights, to exchange Paſſengers, and each return the Day after: Thoſe who are kind enough to encourage the Undertaking, are deſired to croſs *Powles Hook Ferry* the Evenings before, as they muſt ſet off early: The Price for each Paſſenger is *Ten Shillings* to *Prince Town*, and from thence to *Philadelphia*, *Ten Shillings* more, Ferriage free: There will be but two Waggons, but four ſets of freſh Horſes, ſo it will be very ſafe for any Perſon to ſend Goods, as there are but two Drivers, they may exchange their Goods without any Miſtake. Perſons may now go from *New-York* to *Philadelphia*, and back again in five Days, and remain in *Philadelphia* two Nights and one Day to do their Buſineſs in: The Public may be aſſured that this Road is much the ſhorteſt, than any other to *Philadelphia*, and regular Stages will be kept by the Publick's obliged humble Servants,

JOHN MERCEREAU, and
JOHN BARNHILL.

It wasn't until 1729 that Ben Franklin, innovator of advertising art, made ads more readable by using larger headlines, changing fonts, and adding art. This 1767 ad announces the availability of Stage Waggons to carry passengers from Powles Hook Ferry to Philadelphia.

The Industrializing Age

In the mid-1700s, the Industrial Revolution began in England and by the early 1800s it had reached North America. By using machines to mass-produce goods with uniform quality, large companies increased their productivity. For the first time, it cost people less to buy a product than to make it themselves. As people left the farm to work in the city, mass urban markets began to emerge. This further fueled market development and the growth of advertising.

By the mid-1800s, the world's population had doubled to 1.2 billion. Suddenly, producers needed mass consumption to match the high levels of manufactured goods. Breakthroughs in bulk transportation—the railroad and steamship—facilitated the distribution of products beyond a manufacturer's local market. But with the need for mass consumption came the increasing need for mass marketing techniques such as advertising to inform new markets of the availability of products.

During this **industrializing age**, which lasted roughly until the end of World War I (1918), manufacturers were principally concerned with production. The burden of marketing fell on wholesalers. They used advertising primarily as an information vehicle, placing announcements in publications called *price currents* to let retailers know about the sources of supply and shipping schedules for unbranded commodities. Advertising to consumers was the job of the local retailer and the large mail-order catalog companies like Montgomery Ward and Sears Roebuck. Only a few innovative manufacturers foresaw the usefulness of mass media advertising to stimulate consumer demand for their products.

For Americans, the *profession* of advertising began when Volney B. Palmer set up business in Philadelphia in 1841. He contracted with newspapers for large volumes of advertising space at discount rates and then resold the space to advertisers at a higher rate. The advertisers usually prepared the ads themselves.

In 1869, at the ripe old age of 21, Francis Ayer formed an ad agency in Philadelphia and, to make it sound more credible, named it after his father. N. W. Ayer & Sons was the first agency to charge a commission based on the "net cost of space" and the first to conduct a formal market survey. In 1890, Ayer became the first ad agency to operate as agencies do today—planning, creating, and executing complete ad campaigns in

exchange for media-paid commissions or fees from advertisers. In 1892, Ayer set up a copy department and hired the first full-time agency copywriter.

The technological advances of the Industrial Revolution enabled great changes in advertising. Photography, introduced in 1839, added credibility and a new world of creativity. Now ads could show products, people, and places as they really were, rather than how an illustrator visualized them.

industrializing age
The period of time from the mid-1700s through the end of World War I when manufacturers were principally concerned with production.

industrial age
A historical period covering approximately the first 70 years of the twentieth century. This period was marked by tremendous growth and maturation of the U.S. industrial base. It saw the development of new, often inexpensive brands of the luxury and convenience goods we now classify as consumer packaged goods.

consumer packaged goods
Everyday-use consumer products packaged by manufacturers and sold through retail outlets. Generally these are goods such as food and beverages, health and beauty care, cleaning products, and detergents that get used up and have to be replaced frequently.

In the 1840s, some manufacturers began using magazine ads to reach the mass market and stimulate mass consumption. Magazines provided for national advertising and offered the best quality reproduction.

The telegraph, telephone, typewriter, phonograph, and later, motion pictures, all let people communicate as never before. In 1896, when the federal government inaugurated rural free mail delivery, direct-mail advertising and mail-order, selling flourished. Manufacturers now had an ever-increasing variety of products to sell and a new way to deliver their advertisements and products to the public.

Public schooling helped the nation reach an unparalleled 90 percent literacy rate. Manufacturers gained a large reading public that could understand print ads. The United States thus entered the twentieth century as a great industrial state with a national marketing system propelled by advertising. With the end of World War I, the modern period in advertising emerged.

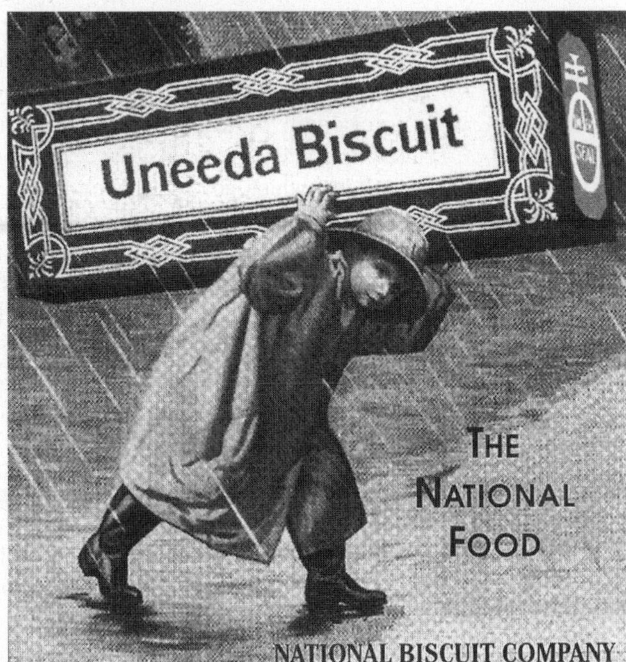

In 1890, N. W. Ayer & Sons became the first agency to operate as agencies do today—planning, creating, and executing complete ad campaigns for advertisers. This 1899 Ayer ad for Uneeda biscuits (catch the play on words) was one of a series of popular ads of the times.

The Industrial Age

The **industrial age** started around the turn of the twentieth century and lasted well into the 1970s. It was a period marked by tremendous growth and maturation of the country's industrial base. As U.S. industry met the basic needs of most of the population, commodity markets became saturated. Fresh mass markets then developed for new brands of consumer luxury and convenience goods we refer to as **consumer packaged goods**.

In the early twentieth century, the Industrial Revolution was in full force. Factories were producing products like Ford automobiles, not just for Americans, but also for overseas markets, as this ad shows.

product differentiation
Manufacturers portraying their brands as different from and better than similar competitive products through advertising, packaging, or physical product differences.

unique selling proposition (USP)
The distinctive benefits that make a product different than any other. The reason marketers believe consumers will buy a product even though it may seem no different from many others just like it.

market segmentation
Strategy of identifying groups of people or organizations with certain shared needs and characteristics within the broad markets for consumer or business products and aggregating these groups into larger market segments according to their mutual interest in the product's utility.

During the industrial age of the nineteenth century, manufacturers changed their focus from a *production* orientation to a *sales* orientation. They dedicated themselves to new product development, strengthened their sales forces, packaged and branded their products, and engaged in heavy national brand advertising. Early brands of this era included Wrigley's spearmint gum, Coca-Cola, Jell-O gelatin, Kellogg's Corn Flakes, and Campbell's soup.

In the 1920s, the United States was rich and powerful. As the war machine returned to peacetime production, society became consumption driven. The era of salesmanship had arrived and its bible was *Scientific Advertising,* written by the legendary copywriter Claude Hopkins at Albert Lasker's agency, Lord & Thomas. Published in 1923, it became a classic and was republished in 1950 and 1980. "Advertising has reached the status of a science," Hopkins proclaimed. "It is based on fixed principles." His principles outlawed humor, style, literary flair, and anything that might detract from his basic copy strategy of a preemptive product claim repeated loudly and often.[14]

Radio was born at about this same time and rapidly became the nation's primary means of mass communication and a powerful new advertising medium. World and national news now arrived direct from the scene, and a whole new array of family entertainment—music, drama, and sports—became possible. Suddenly, national advertisers could quickly reach huge audiences. In fact, the first radio shows were produced by their sponsors' ad agencies.

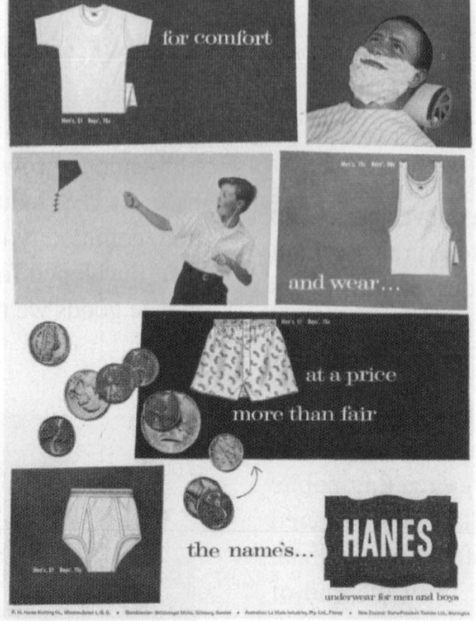

By the middle of the 20th century, advertisers knew it was important to tell consumers why they should prefer a particular brand over its competitors. This 1958 ad for Hanes underwear gives consumers several benefits to think about.

On October 29, 1929, the stock market crashed, the Great Depression began, and advertising expenditures plummeted. In the face of consumer sales resistance and corporate budget cutting, the advertising industry needed to improve its effectiveness. It turned to research. Daniel Starch, A. C. Nielsen, and George Gallup had founded research groups to study consumer attitudes and preferences. By providing information on public opinion, the performance of ad messages, and sales of advertised products, these companies started a whole new business: the marketing research industry.

During this period, each brand sought to sell the public on its own special qualities. Wheaties became the "Breakfast of Champions" not because of its ingredients but because of its advertising. Manufacturers followed this strategy of **product differentiation** vigorously, seeking to portray their brands as different from and better than the competition by offering consumers quality, variety, and convenience.

The greatest expansion of any medium up to that time occurred with the introduction of television in 1941. After World War II, TV advertising grew rapidly, and in time achieved its current status as the largest advertising medium in terms of revenues.

During the postwar prosperity of the late 1940s and early 1950s, consumers tried to climb the social ladder by buying more and more modern products. Advertising entered its golden era. A creative revolution ensued in which ads focused on product features that implied social acceptance, style, luxury, and success. Giants in the field emerged—people such as Leo Burnett, David Ogilvy, and Bill Bernbach, who built their agencies from scratch and forever changed the way advertising was planned and created.[15]

Rosser Reeves of the Ted Bates Agency introduced the idea that every ad must point out the product's **unique selling proposition (USP)**—features that would differentiate it from competitive products. The USP was a logical extension of the Lasker and Hopkins "reason why" credo.

positioning The association of a brand's features and benefits with a particular set of customer needs, clearly differentiating it from the competition in the mind of the customer.

postindustrial age Period of cataclysmic change, starting in about 1980, when people first became truly aware of the sensitivity of the environment in which we live.

demarketing Term coined during the energy shortage of the 1970s and 1980s when advertising was used to slow the demand for products.

But as the USP was used over and over, consumers started finding it difficult to see what was unique anymore.

Finally, as more and more imitative products showed up in the marketplace, all offering quality, variety, and convenience, the effectiveness of this strategy wore out. Companies turned to a new mantra: **market segmentation**, in which marketers searched for unique groups of people whose needs could be addressed through specialized products. The image era of the 1960s was a natural culmination of the creative revolution. Advertising's emphasis shifted from product features to brand image or personality as advertisers sought to align their brands with profitable market segments. Cadillac, for example, became the worldwide image of luxury, the consummate symbol of success.

While this was all going on in the United States, across the Atlantic a new generation of advertising professionals had graduated from the training grounds of Procter & Gamble (P&G) and Colgate-Palmolive and were now teaching their international clients the secrets of mass marketing.

The Postindustrial Age

Beginning around 1980, the **postindustrial age** has been a period of cataclysmic change. People became truly aware of the sensitive environment in which we live and alarmed by our dependence on vital natural resources. During the energy shortages of the 1970s and 1980s, a new term, **demarketing**, appeared. Producers of energy started using advertising to *slow* the demand for their products. Ads asked people to refrain from operating washers and dryers during the day when the demand for electricity peaked. In time, demarketing became a more aggressive strategic tool for advertisers to use against competitors, political opponents, and social problems. For example, many organizations today actively seek to demarket the use of tobacco.

> "What really mattered was how the brand stacked up against the competition in the consumer's mind."

But just as me-too product features killed the product differentiation era, me-too images eventually killed the market segmentation era. With increased competition, a new kind of advertising strategy evolved in the 1970s, where competitors' strengths became just as important as the advertiser's. Jack Trout and Al Ries trumpeted the arrival of the *positioning era* by insisting that what really mattered was how the brand stacked up against the competition in the consumer's mind—how it was positioned.

Positioning proved effective in separating a particular brand from its competitors by associating that brand with a particular set of needs that ranked high on the consumer's priority list. Thus, it became a more effective way to use product differentiation and market segmentation. The most famous American ads of the positioning era were Volkswagen ("Think small"), Avis ("We're #2"), and 7Up ("The uncola"). Product differentiation, market segmentation, and positioning are all very important concepts to understand, so we will discuss them further in Chapter 4.

Demarketing is used to dampen demand for products, especially those that create unwanted costs for society. This public service message uses the metaphor of a fish hook to convey the dangerous addictive qualities of alcohol.

The collapse of the Soviet Union ended the Cold War and with it the need for a defense-driven economy. Companies were anxious to develop the untapped markets in the former Warsaw Pact states. To expand their power globally, big multinational companies and their advertising agencies went on a binge, buying other big companies and creating a new word in the financial lexicon: *megamerger*.

By now European and Asian advertising had caught up with the United States. TV was

Hailed by Jack Trout and Al Ries as "the most famous ad of the 60s," this Volkswagen ad co-opted the "small" position in consumers' minds, giving VW (www.volkswagen.com) a leadership rank for many years.

In recent years, VW has attempted to recapture the style of its 60s advertising.

the hot medium, and agencies focused on growth, acquisitions, and superior creative executions. For several years, Young & Rubicam in New York and Dentsu in Japan alternated as the largest advertising agency in the world. Then two brothers in London, Charles and Maurice Saatchi, started acquiring agencies globally. In rapid succession, a number of high-profile U.S. agencies disappeared under the Saatchi & Saatchi umbrella. Saatchi & Saatchi was suddenly the largest agency in the world. Then followed more buyouts as the big agencies from Europe, the United States, and Japan emulated the merger mania of their huge multinational clients. Names of agency founders disappeared from the doors, replaced by initials and acronyms: WPP Group, RSCG, TBWA, FCA, DDB Needham, and FCB, to mention just a few.[16]

> "These newly affluent consumers concerned themselves more with the quality of their lives."

Then, sparked by unprecedented layoffs in the defense industries, the global economy fell into an economic recession. The mergers temporarily stopped, the business world sucked in its collective belt, and management turned to new theories of Total Quality Management (TQM), reengineering, and downsizing—theories aimed at cutting costs and increasing efficiency. Two related economic factors characterized marketing in this period: (1) the aging of traditional products, with a corresponding growth in competition, and (2) the growing affluence and sophistication of the consuming public, led by the huge baby-boomer generation.[17]

The most important factor was competition, intensified by growing international trade. As high profits lured imitators into the marketplace, each offering the most attractive product features at lower cost, consumers discovered more choices, higher quality, and lower prices.

These newly affluent consumers concerned themselves more with the quality of their lives. With their basic needs met, the baby boomers were interested in saving time and money to spend on products, services, and social causes that represented who they aspired to be.

By the mid-1980s, an avalanche of ads—especially in the toiletry and cosmetics industries—was aimed at the "me" generation ("L'Oréal. Because I'm worth it."). At the same time, the

The recession of the early 90s slammed the advertising industry with over 13,500 layoffs. However, specialists in small, regional creative shops were able to snatch away some large accounts during this period and produce ads for established corporations. This Coca-Cola ad came from the clever minds at Creative Artists Agency in Hollywood (a talent agency).

nation's largest industrial concerns spent millions of dollars on corporate advertising to extol their social consciousness and good citizenship.

As the U.S. economy slowed, many companies were chasing too few consumer dollars. Clients trimmed their ad budgets, and many turned to more cost-effective **sales promotion** alternatives, such as coupons, direct mail, and direct marketing to build sales volume. By 1990, advertising had lost 25 percent of its share of the marketing budget to other forms of marketing communications.[18]

sales promotion
A direct inducement offering extra incentives all along the marketing route—from manufacturers through distribution channels to customers—to accelerate the movement of the product from the producer to the consumer.

As the 1990s unfolded, the traditional advertising industry found itself threatened on all sides and suffering from overpopulation.[19] Clients demanded better results from their promotional dollars; small, imaginative, upstart agencies competed for (and won) some big accounts; TV viewers appeared immune to conventional commercials; and an abundance of new media technologies promised to reinvent advertising. In three short years, the advertising agency business lost over 13,500 jobs. Major clients such as Coca-Cola defected from the big agencies, giving various portions of their business to specialists in small, regional creative shops and media-buying services. But the setback went far beyond the agency business. Throughout the media world, newspapers, magazines, and TV networks all lost advertising dollars. About 40 magazines went out of business during the two-year slump.[20]

By the mid-1990s, U.S. marketers had begun shifting dollars back from sales promotion to advertising to rebuild value in their brands. In 1994, ad budgets surged ahead by 8.1 percent to $150 billion nationally. And throughout the rest of the 1990s, ad spending increased about 7 percent every year until the year 2000, when U.S. advertisers spent $247.5 billion, a whopping 11.3 percent increase over the previous year.[21]

But then the bubble burst. In 2001, the combination of a mild recession, the collapse of the stock market, and the bust of the dot-coms all contributed to a record decline in advertising activity. On September 11 of that year, terrorists attacked the United States and suddenly all marketing and advertising seemed to stop—not just in the United States, but also around the world.[22] Spending in the United States declined 6.5 percent to $231 billion, and overseas spending dropped 8.6 percent to $210 billion.[23]

A year later, though, the economy seemed to be turning around and marketers were again starting to spend money on advertising. By 2005, U.S. advertising expenditures had reached $264 billion, more than completely recovering from the 2001 decline.[24] But hardly anybody thought the problems were over. Technology, evolving lifestyles, new fears over security, and the rising cost of reaching consumers had already changed the advertising business forever. With the explosion of the Internet, we had entered a new electronic frontier—what Tom Cuniff, VP/creative director at Lord, Dentsu & Partners, called "the second creative revolution."[25]

[Technology, evolving lifestyles, new fears over security, and the rising cost of reaching consumers had already changed the advertising business forever.]

The Global Interactive Age: Looking at the Twenty-First Century

In the new millennium, the rest of the world has in many respects caught up to North America, thanks to improved economic conditions and a desire for expansion. Recent estimates of worldwide advertising expenditures outside the United States exceed $400 billion per year. By 2014, half of

the world's media spending will be accounted for by 10 emerging markets. The importance of advertising in individual countries depends on the country's level of development and national attitude toward promotion. Typically, advertising expenditures are higher in countries with higher personal incomes. As Exhibit 1–4 shows, the top 10 worldwide advertisers are based in many different countries.

Although the Communist countries once condemned advertising as an evil of capitalism, eastern European countries now

my ad campaign

Tools for Teamwork [1–B]

Advertising agencies look for at least three qualities in the people they hire: talent, knowledge, and the ability to work well with others. If you are working on your campaign in a group, you'll find those qualities—especially the third—to be important as well.

Your campaign assignment may be the first time you've worked on a group project. If so, you'll discover that working in a team is very different from doing a project on your own.

First, you will need to coordinate everything that you do. That means each person must create schedules that accommodate not only his or her own obligations, but those of the group. Second, you will be sharing work. Tools that help you share documents, calendars, and other files will help you produce better work and do it faster. Third, you should consider the importance of leadership in a group. Your group will usually perform better if someone is formally appointed as leader, at least in the sense of organizing meetings, maintaining a calendar, and keeping track of what has to be done. Finally, everyone is accountable. Talk to your professor about whether he or she expects peer evaluations or some other means to assess differences in group member effort and performance.

Many Internet tools are now available to help improve the coordination of teams. Best of all, they are free. The ones I prefer are those created by Google because they are easy to use, powerful, and integrated (both with each other and with mobile devices). If you would prefer not to use a Google product, I've tried to find equivalents where possible.

Staying Connected

E-mail, of course, remains an essential tool. You may have a school e-mail account, but these can be problematic because (1) your inbox space is limited, (2) spam filters in these accounts are often very aggressive (too much useful mail is moved to the spam folder), and (3) they lack many useful tools for organizing and labeling your mail. Gmail (www.gmail.com) is an excellent free mail service that you will most likely never fill up (which means you never have to delete e-mails and your inbox never gets too full). You can use "labels" to quickly identify mail from people in your group. And with "contacts" you can set up groups of e-mail addresses to message easily and quickly. Use "tasks" to create a to-do list right in your e-mail list. These programs also work well with many mobile devices. Yahoo! (mail.yahoo.com) and Microsoft (outlook.com) offer similar free services.

Creating Documents

Google Docs (http://docs.google.com) offers a free suite of simple yet powerful document creation tools that includes a word processor, a spreadsheet program, and a presentation creator. What makes the programs special is that you can share some or all of the documents you create with others and edit them simultaneously. So if a group member is working on a creative brief, he or she can share it immediately with everyone else for edits and comments. If you would prefer a non-Google solution, Thinkfree "My Office" is similar to Google docs (www.thinkfree.com).

Staying Organized

Many people find that calendars and to-do lists are essential. Google has an excellent calendar program (www.google.com/calendar) that everyone in the team can edit. You can also sync the calendar with many mobile devices. As I indicated before, Google's "task" program is built into gmail. A far more powerful program that is not quite as simple to use is Zoho Project (www.zoho.com/projects/).

Conducting Research

Powerful tools for doing research are also available for free on the Web. For secondary research purposes it is great to have a program that allows you to copy and store documents, Web pages, photos, charts, and other kinds of information. You will find Google Docs very helpful here too. A powerful and popular program is Evernote (www.evernote.com). Your group may also find itself collecting primary data. If you need to administer a survey, consider a useful component of Google docs called "forms." With forms you can easily create a Web-based survey and have your data set up in a Google spreadsheet as it comes in. A non-Google program that does the same thing is SurveyMonkey (www.surveymonkey.com).

Working Well and Staying Accountable

Learning to adapt to group projects is not easy for everyone. Knowing what to expect and developing the skills to work well with others is essential. For guidance, consider these thoughts from experts:

- Brian Tracy: www.myarticlearchive.com/articles/6/079.htm
- Susan Heathfield: http://humanresources.about.com/od/workrelationships/a/play_well.htm
- Arnold Anderson: http://smallbusiness.chron.com/characteristics-effective-teamwork-691.html

If you volunteer to be a team leader (or are appointed one), some helpful tips can be found here:

- Stephen: http://www.stephencovey.com/blog/?p=6
- Jack Welch, former CEO of GE (this is an hour-long video filmed at the MIT School of Management): http://mitworld.mit.edu/video/260/

If you are doing peer evaluations in your class, your professor will likely have a form that you should use. These types of forms can be found throughout the Web. Some examples include these:

- https://courses.worldcampus.psu.edu/public/faculty/PeerEvalForm.html
- www.utexas.edu/courses/kincaid/peerevaltips.html

narrowcasting Delivering programming to a specific group defined by demographics and/or program content, rather than mass appeal. Usually used to describe cable networks. The opposite of broadcasting.

digital video recorders (DVRs) A device (such as TiVo) that is similar to a VCR, but records programs on a hard drive in digital format, providing high-quality image and sound and the ability to "pause live TV."

EXHIBIT 1-4 Top 10 global marketers (2010).

Advertiser	Headquarters	Worldwide Advertising Spending ($ millions)	Measured U.S. Media Spending ($ millions)
Procter & Gamble Co.	Cincinnati, OH	$11,426	$3,341
Unilever	London/Rotterdam	6,620	826
L'Oréal	Clichy, France	4,984	1,153
General Motors Corp.	Detroit, MI	3,592	2,171
Nestlé	Vevey, Switzerland	3,186	931
Toyota Motor Co.	Toyota City, Japan	2,857	1,122
Coca-Cola Co.	Atlanta, GA	2,455	419
Reckitt-Benckiser	United Kingdom	2,429	460
Kraft Foods	Northfield, IL	2,343	886
Johnson & Johnson	New Brunswick, NJ	2,323	1,197

Source: "Top 100 Global Media Spenders," http://marketresearchr.blogspot.com/2012/05/top-100-global-media-spenders.html.

encourage private enterprise and realize the benefits of advertising. And the United States now looks west to find its biggest economic rival. In 2010, China overcame Germany and became the third largest market for media spending. By 2015, China will have surpassed the current number two, Japan.[26] Some estimates suggest the Chinese economy, which is growing at over 10 percent a year, will surpass that of America in 2025.[27]

The explosion of new technologies in the last decade has affected advertising considerably. With cable TV and satellite receivers, viewers can watch channels devoted to single types of programming, such as straight news, home shopping, sports, or comedy. This shift transformed television from the most widespread of mass media to a more specialized, **narrowcasting** medium.[28] Now small companies and product marketers that appeal to a limited clientele can use TV to reach audiences with select interests.

A concurrent change that didn't please advertisers was the growing presence of VCR and remote controls, which allow viewers to avoid commercials altogether by channel surfing during breaks or zipping through them when watching a previously recorded show. Advertisers and TV executives became even more upset with the introduction of **digital video recorders (DVRs)** like TiVo, which allow viewers to pause, fast-forward, and rewind live TV, store programming, and skip commercials altogether.

Ironically, though, within a very short time, TiVo executives were courting marketers and agencies to join its charter advertiser program, which would let viewers opt in to a marketer's "advertainment" show. Best Buy bought in early and so did Sony Pictures, Lexus, Procter & Gamble, and Miller Brewing. One of the major features of TiVo is its ability to target potential customers and measure effectiveness against that target. As *Advertising Age* pointed out, the Holy Grail to advertisers is a one-to-one relationship with consumers, and that becomes increasingly possible with permission-based, opt-in, and two-way interactions with viewers.[29]

Television networks are turning to the Internet to market themselves. Episodes of the most popular shows can be viewed online and there's even an app for iPad owners so they can watch their favorite ABC shows anywhere, anytime. Of course, you have to watch an advertisement first.

Digital technology has also had a huge impact. Personal computers, mobile phones, the Internet, and e-mail give advertisers new media for reaching potential customers. In response to products such as TiVo, and perhaps as a result of the hard lessons learned by the recording industry, which experienced declines in music sales as a result of file-sharing technologies, the broadcast networks realized they would have to adapt to the digital age. In 2006, ABC was the first network to offer hit shows for Internet download just days after the programs aired, posting

episodes of popular series such as *Lost* and *Desperate Housewives* on Apple's iTunes Web site. The broadcast networks also developed Web sites for watching streamed versions of the shows with embedded Web-only advertisements. ABC, NBC, and Fox collaborated to offer Hulu, a site where viewers could watch their favorite shows online, complete with ads different from those shown during live broadcasts. Clearly, TVs and personal computers had melded into something new, vibrant, and exciting: technologies that make custom entertainment schedules available to viewers when and where they want them. TVs, computers, and network advertising will never be the same. A writer's strike that affected the industry for months in late 2007 and early 2008 was motivated partially by compensation issues surrounding digital entertainment.

What we are witnessing is an interactive revolution. Advertising is evolving into a two-way medium where consumers with PCs, Internet connections, and cable TV can choose the information they access and then spend time researching the product information they desire.[30] As we discuss in Chapter 12, this is a revolutionary way for advertisers to reach consumers.

In September of 2008 the global economy began an economic slowdown. Many companies, faced with declining sales and lower revenue, cut back on advertising expenditures. Particularly hard hit was the newspaper industry. Through 2012, print newspapers have seen seven consecutive years of ad revenue decline, and the total decline over the period is 40 percent.[31] Several high-profile papers, including the *Christian Science Monitor* and the *Rocky Mountain News,* already weakened by lower ad sales, shut down their presses.

In truth, despite strong government intervention on behalf of banks, insurers, and auto manufacturers, capitalism is likely to remain the greatest influence on markets in the United States. By 2011, the U.S. economy was growing again, but at a very slow rate and with unacceptably high unemployment. Advertising expenditure growth is predicted to hit 3.5 percent in 2013, followed by 5.1 percent in 2014 and 5.8 percent in 2015. Most of this growth will come from significant increases in Internet advertising.[32] When America's economy does emerge, it is likely that those companies smart enough to continue their advertising through tough times will reap significant benefits.

Advertising has come a long way from the simple sign on the bootmaker's shop. Today it is a powerful device that announces the availability and location of products, describes their quality and value, imbues brands with personality, and simultaneously defines the personalities of the people who buy them while entertaining us. More than a reflection of society and its desires, advertising can start and end fads, trends, and credos—sometimes all by itself.[33]

The endless search for competitive advantage and efficiency has made advertising's journey in the last 100 plus years

Internet networks, such as Hulu, allow viewers to watch full episodes of their favorite shows on the Internet, with embedded Web-only advertisements (www.hulu.com).

New technology has meant new media, manifested largely in the Internet. This has opened new avenues of exposure for advertisers. This Web site for Daum shows that beautiful layout and design is not confined to the traditional medium of print.

fascinating. Now companies are realizing that their most important asset is not capital equipment or their line of products. In the heated competition of the global marketplace, their most important asset is their customer and the relationship they have with that person or organization. Protecting that asset has become the new marketing imperative for the twenty-first century. In an effort to do a better job of *relationship marketing,* companies are now learning that they must be consistent in both what they say and what they do. It's not enough to produce outstanding advertising anymore. They must integrate all their marketing communications with everything else they do, too. That's what *integrated marketing communications* really means. And that is presenting exciting new challenges and opportunities to marketing and advertising professionals.

enterprise society, advertising has encouraged increased productivity by both management and labor.

With just a small amount of money, for instance, you can buy a car today. It may be secondhand, but from advertising you know it's available. If you earn more money, you can buy a new car or one with more luxury features. You can also make a statement about yourself as an individual with the vehicle you purchase. As with many products, advertising has created a personality for each automobile make and model on the market. As a free individual, you can select the product that best matches your needs and aspirations.

Advertising serves other social needs besides simply stimulating sales. Newspapers, magazines, radio, television, and many websites all receive their primary income from advertising.

> Their most important asset is their customer and the relationship they have with that person or organization.

check yourself ✓

1. What are the five identified periods in the history of Western civilization and what key developments characterized each period?
2. Explain how one development during each period impacted the evolution of advertising.

L01-6 Describe the impact of advertising on society.

SOCIETY AND ETHICS: THE EFFECTS OF ADVERTISING

Advertising has been a major factor in improving the standard of living in the United States and around the world. By publicizing the material, social, and cultural opportunities of a free

This facilitates freedom of the press and promotes more complete information. Public service announcements also foster growth and understanding of important social issues and causes. The Red Cross, Community Chest, United Way, and other noncommercial organizations receive continuous financial support and volunteer assistance due in large part to the power of advertising.

However, advertising is certainly not without its shortcomings. Since its beginnings, the profession has had to struggle with issues of truthfulness and ethics. In fact, in the early 1900s, the advertising profession was forced to mend its ethical ways. Consumers suffered for years from unsubstantiated product claims, especially for patent medicines and health devices. The simmering resentment finally boiled over into a full-blown consumer movement, which led to government regulation and ultimately to industry efforts at self-regulation.

In 1906 Congress responded to public outrage by passing the Pure Food and Drug Act to protect the public's health and control drug advertising. In 1914, it passed the Federal Trade Commission Act to protect the public from unfair business practices, including misleading and deceptive advertising.

Advertising practitioners themselves formed groups to improve advertising effectiveness and promote professionalism and started vigilance committees to safeguard the integrity of the industry. The Association of National Advertisers (ANA),

These public service announcements, encouraging people to look for Energy Star ratings on computer equipment, appliances, lighting, and heating and cooling systems, are distributed by the EPA to magazines with a request to insert them in their publications.

the American Advertising Federation (AAF), and the Better Business Bureau (BBB) are today's outgrowths of those early groups. These organizations are the result of a fundamental truth: the biggest opponents of unethical advertisers are advertisers who embrace ethical and truthful communication practices.

But in times of economic crisis, false and misleading advertising has invariably reappeared, perhaps out of advertiser desperation. During the Depression years, several best-selling books exposed the advertising industry as an unscrupulous exploiter of consumers.

In a 1962 message to Congress, President Kennedy asserted, "if consumers are offered inferior products, if prices are exorbitant . . . if the consumer is unable to choose on an informed basis, then his dollar is wasted . . . and the national interest suffers." In his Bill for Consumer Rights, Kennedy gave the American consumer four basic rights, including the right "to be protected against fraudulent, deceitful, or grossly misleading information, advertising, labeling, or other practices, and to be given the facts s/he needs to make an informed choice."

In the 1970s, a new American consumer movement grew out of the widespread disillusionment following the Kennedy assassination, the Vietnam War, the Watergate scandals, and the sudden shortage of vital natural resources—all communicated instantly to the world via new satellite technology. These issues fostered cynicism and distrust of the establishment and tradition, and gave rise to a new twist in moral consciousness. On the one hand, people justified their personal irresponsibility and self-indulgence in the name of self-fulfillment. On the other, they attacked corporate America's quest for self-fulfillment (profits) in the name of social accountability.

Today, corporate America has generally cleaned up many of the inequities in advertising. But now attention has shifted to more subtle problems of puffery, advertising to children, the advertising of legal but unhealthful products, and advertising ethics. We believe ethics in advertising is such an important issue that we have included features on this topic throughout the text.

In short, advertising has had a pronounced effect on society as well as the economy. It has also fostered a host of social attitudes and laws that have dramatically affected advertising itself. We'll take a closer look at these issues in Chapter 2. ■

check yourself ✓

1. What are some of the social needs that are served by advertising in the United States?
2. What are some of advertising's societal shortcomings?

learn about, practice, and apply the functions of advertising in business and the economy!

M: Advertising was developed for students who want information packaged in a concise, easy-to-read, yet interesting format.

Check out the book's website to:

- Learn why some advertisers might want to slow demand for their products. (Exploring Advertising)
- Discover the important roles that advertising plays in a free economy. (Exploring Advertising)
- Explore the ways that new media and technologies are challenging traditional media. (Review Questions)

While you are there, check out the professional resource links, review the PowerPoint presentation, and test your knowledge with the Multiple Choice Quiz. Additionally, Connect® Marketing is available for M: Advertising.

www.mhhe.com/ArensM2e

EB 11799560 I
B2

chapter two

the environment **of advertising**

This chapter identifies and explains the economic, social, ethical, and legal issues advertisers must consider. Society determines what is offensive, excessive, and irresponsible; governments determine what is deceptive and unfair. To be law-abiding, ethical, and socially responsible, advertisers must understand these issues.

Would you be more likely to buy a watch brand if you knew that Jeff Gordon or Brad Pitt wears it? What if it was the preferred brand of Maria Sharapova or Uma Thurman? Swiss luxury watchmaker TagHeuer must think so, since it pays celebrities to appear in ads. Nike spends millions on endorsement contracts and has long partnered with Michael Jordan, Derek Jeter, and Tiger Woods. The athletes agree to wear Nike clothes and use Nike gear during competitions. Many also appear in Nike ads.

Are celebrity endorsements worth the large amounts that companies spend on them? Business professors Jagdish Agrawal and Wagner Kamakura argue that celebrities help make ads believable, enhance ad recall, increase brand recognition, and ultimately influence consumers to choose an endorsed brand.[1] So it should be no surprise that as many as one in five TV commercials features someone famous.

But what happens when brands are linked with celebrities who attract the wrong kind of attention? It happens all the time. The long list of famous individuals who have lost endorsement deals because of controversy includes . . . Madonna (Pepsi), Kobe Bryant (McDonald's and Coke), Mary Kate Olsen (milk), Kate Moss (H&M, Chanel, and Burberry), O.J. Simpson (Hertz), Charlie Sheen (Hanes), Michael Phelps (Kellogg), Tiger Woods (Accenture, AT&T, Gatorade), and many more.

continued on p. 28

LEARNING OBJECTIVES

After studying this chapter, you will be able to:

- **LO2-1** Describe the impact of advertising on the economy.
- **LO2-2** Examine the validity of the various social criticisms of advertising.
- **LO2-3** Explain the difference between social responsibility and ethics in advertising.
- **LO2-4** Describe how government agencies regulate advertising to protect both consumers and competitors.
- **LO2-5** Discuss the activities of nongovernment organizations in fighting fraudulent and deceptive advertising.

continued from p. 27

One of the more recent celebrities to disappoint his fans was Lance Armstrong, winner of the Tour de France, the world's most famous bicycle race, a record seven consecutive times between 1999 and 2005. Armstrong's popularity was once so great that corporate sponsors paid him nearly $20 million in a single year. A cancer survivor himself, Armstrong also founded the Livestrong Foundation with the mission "to inspire and empower" cancer survivors and their families. After a brief retirement, Armstrong returned to competitive racing from 2009 to 2011. Then his career began to unravel.

In 2012, Armstrong was banned from cycling for life by the United States Anti-Doping Agency (USADA) for doping offenses. Its report concluded that Armstrong conducted "the most sophisticated, professionalized and successful doping program that sport has ever seen."[2] In January 2013, he admitted to doping in a television interview with Oprah Winfrey.

In the wake of the USADA's report, Armstrong was dropped by every single major sponsor including Nike, Anheuser-Busch, Radio Shack, 24 Hour Fitness, Oakley, and Trek Bicycle. The loss of these endorsement deals was expected to cost Lance $75 million over the next few years; as much as $200 million over the next decade.[3]

The final straw came in 2013, when Nike cut all ties with Armstrong's Livestrong cancer charity; the foundation will stop making Livestrong apparel after 2013. Nike had stood by Tiger Woods, Kobe Bryant, Ben Roethlisberger, and Michael Jordan during lapses in morality that included behaviors such as infidelity, sexual misconduct, and gambling. Nike even re-signed Michael Vick after he served jail time for his involvement in illegal dog-fighting. But as shocking as some of these behaviors were, none of these guys were dopers. None of them violated the spirit of fair play and competition within their sport.[4]

Companies understand that they take a risk when they associate their brands too closely with a single endorser. Nike has recently moved toward an "ensemble approach" to endorsements,

Views of offensiveness vary a great deal. This advertisement was banned by Britain's Advertising Standards Authority. The agency said the ad was likely to cause widespread offense.

using a pool of athletes to promote its wares rather than one big star. Risk to the brand is reduced, therefore, should any of the athletes stumble. Under Armour, a Nike competitor, uses a similar approach. A company VP notes that Under Armour doesn't "let any one person get bigger than the brand."[5]

Lessons? The same dynamics that can benefit a brand linked to an admired celebrity can damage a brand associated with a controversial one. Mr. Clean, the Maytag Repairman, and the Burger King will never embarrass anyone—these "celebrities" exist only in ads. However, when brands partner with real people, life gets much more complicated. Lance Armstrong earned big endorsement contracts because of his athletic ability and inspirational message. Yet, in the end, his legal and moral transgressions created marketing challenges. The quandaries faced by Armstrong's sponsors helped reinforce a basic truth: ethics and social responsibility are every company's business.[6] ■

THE MANY CONTROVERSIES ABOUT ADVERTISING

Advertising is a highly visible activity. Companies risk public criticism and attack if their advertising displeases or offends or if their products don't measure up to the advertised promises. Proponents of advertising say it's therefore safer to buy advertised products because, when a company's name and reputation are on the line, it tries harder to fulfill its promises.

Advertising is both applauded and criticized not only for its role in selling products but also for its influence on the economy and on society. For years, critics have denigrated advertising for a wide range of sins—some real, some imagined.

John O'Toole, the late chair of Foote, Cone & Belding and president of the American Association of Advertising Agencies, pointed out that many critics attack advertising because it *isn't something else.* Advertising isn't journalism, education, or entertainment—although it often performs the tasks of all three—so it shouldn't be judged by those standards. Sponsors advertise because they hope it will help them sell some product, service, or idea.[7]

Notwithstanding O'Toole's articulate defense, many controversies still swirl around the whole field of advertising. Some focus on advertising's *economic* role. For example, how does advertising affect the value of products? Does it cause higher or lower prices? Does it promote competition or discourage it? How does advertising affect overall consumer demand? What effect does it have on consumer choice and on the overall business cycle?

Other controversies focus on the *societal* effects of advertising. For instance, does advertising make us more materialistic? Does it force us to buy things we don't need? Does it reach us subliminally in ways we can't control? How does it affect the art and culture of our society? Does advertising debase our language?

From these controversies, new questions arise regarding the responsibility for and control of advertising. What is the proper role for participants in the marketing process? How much latitude should marketers have in what products they promote and how they advertise them? Do consumers have some responsibility in the process? Finally, what is the proper role of government? What laws should we have to protect consumers? And do laws sometimes go too far and violate the marketer's freedom of speech?

These are important questions, and there are no simple answers. But debate is healthy. This chapter addresses some of the major questions and criticisms about advertising, both the pros and the cons, and delves into the regulatory methods used to remedy advertisers' abuses.

externalities Benefit or harm caused by the sale or consumption of products to people who are not involved in the transaction and didn't pay for the product.

added value The increase in worth of a product or service as a result of a particular activity. In the context of advertising, the added value is provided by the communication of benefits over and above those offered by the product itself.

Recall from Chapter 1 the underlying principle of free-market economics—that a society is best served by empowering people to make their own decisions and act as free agents within a system characterized by four fundamental assumptions: *self-interest, many buyers and sellers, complete information,* and *absence of* **externalities** *(social costs).*

This framework, derived from the goal of society to promote behaviors that foster the greatest good for the most people, offers a system of economic activity—free enterprise—that has accomplished that goal better than any other economic system in history. This is why societies around the world are increasingly adopting free-enterprise economics.

By using this framework for our discussion of advertising controversies, we have a basis for understanding how advertising may contribute to, or detract from, the basic goal of free enterprise: "the most good for the most people."

L02-1 Describe the impact of advertising on the economy.

THE ECONOMIC IMPACT OF ADVERTISING

Advertising accounts for approximately 2 percent of the U.S. gross domestic product (GDP). In relation to the total U.S. economy, this percentage is small. Still the United States has the highest per capita ad spending in the world. As Marcel Bleustein-Blanchet, the "father" of modern French advertising, pointed out, it's no coincidence that the level of advertising investment in a country is directly proportional to its standard of living.[8] Exhibit 2–1 shows the relationship between advertising spending per capita and standard of living (GDP per capita) around the world. Note that China is the third largest ad-spending country in the world, but its per capita spending is low due to its very large population.

▼EXHIBIT 2–1 A country's level of ad spending is closely related to its standard of living.

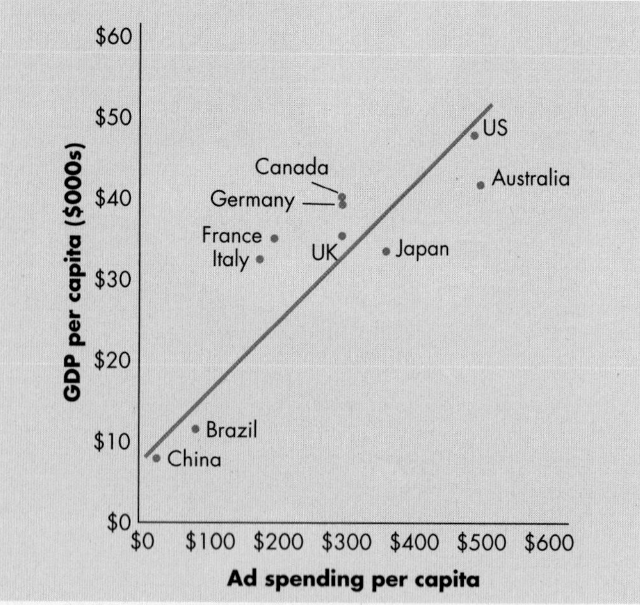

Sources: 2010 data: http://mumbrella.com.au/australia-has-largest-adspend-per-capita-in-the-world-60128; World Bank 2011 data: http://en.wikipedia.org/wiki/List_of_countries_by_GDP_%28PPP%29_per_capita.

The economic effect of advertising is like the break shot in billiards or pool. The moment a company begins to advertise, it sets off a chain reaction of economic events, as shown in Exhibit 2–2.

▼EXHIBIT 2–2 The economic effect of advertising is like the opening break shot in billiards.

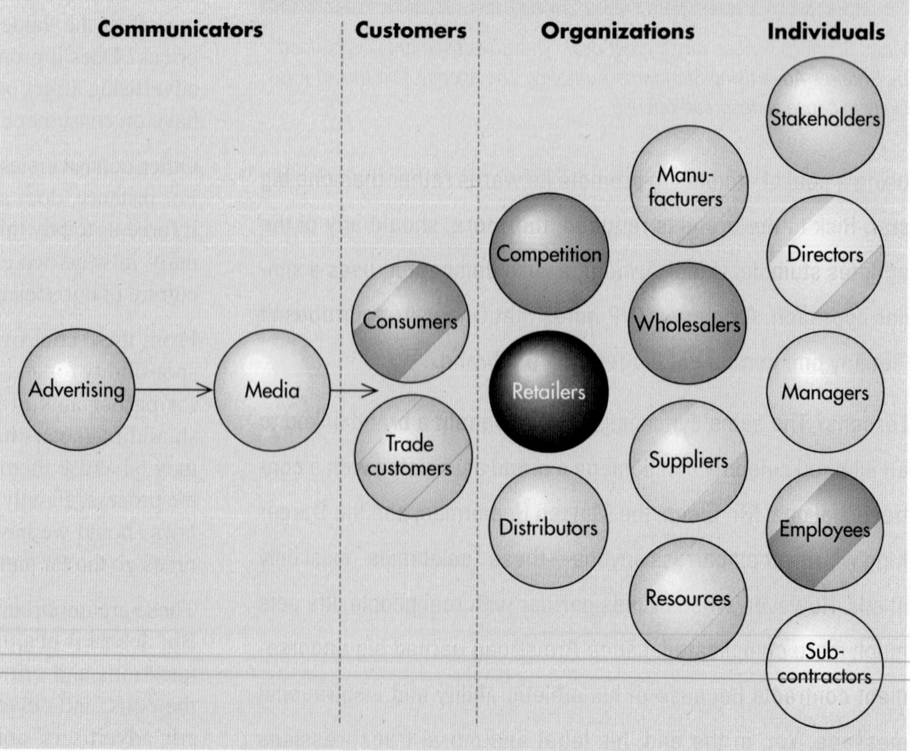

Does advertising lead to higher prices? Economists believe that ads can actually contribute to lower product prices. This ad for Darty, a French retailer, is designed to attract price-sensitive consumers. "Low price or low price with everything included."

Advertising often makes it possible for small businesses to compete effectively against large corporations. Anthony's Pizza's freedom to advertise allows this neighborhood pizza parlor to compete with the national chains.

The extent of the chain reaction, although hard to predict, is related to the force of the shot and the economic environment in which it occurred. Let's consider the economic questions we posed earlier.

> "It's no coincidence that the level of advertising investment in a country is directly proportional to its standard of living.[8]"

Effect on the Value of Products

Why do most people prefer Coca-Cola to some other cola? Why do some people prefer the iPod to some unadvertised brand? Are the advertised products functionally better? Not necessarily. But, in the mind of the consumer, advertising has given these brands **added value**.

Some believe that a product's *image,* created in part by advertising and promotion, is *an inherent feature of the product itself.*[9] While an ad may not address a product's quality directly, the positive image conveyed by advertising may imply quality. By simply making the product better known, advertising can make the product more desirable to the consumer. In this way, advertising adds value to the brand.[10] That's why people pay more for Bayer aspirin than an unadvertised brand displayed right next to it—even though all aspirin, by law, is functionally the same.[11] Advertising also adds value to a brand by educating customers about new uses for a product. Kleenex was originally advertised as a makeup remover, later as a disposable handkerchief. Arm & Hammer baking soda experienced a surge in sales when it was advertised as a refrigerator deodorizer.

In a free-market system, consumers can choose the values they want in the products they buy. If low price is important, they can buy an inexpensive economy car. If status and luxury are important, they can buy a fancy sedan or racy sports car. Many of our wants are emotional, social, or psychological rather than functional. One way we communicate who we are (or want to be) is through the products we purchase and display. By associating the product with some desirable image, advertising offers people the

primary demand
Consumer demand for a whole product category.

selective demand
Consumer demand for the particular advantages of one brand over another.

opportunity to satisfy those psychic or symbolic wants and needs.

In terms of our economic framework, by adding value to products, advertising contributes to self-interest—for both the consumer and the advertiser. It also contributes to the number of sellers. That increases competition, which also serves the consumer's self-interest.

Effect on Prices

If advertising adds value to products, it follows that advertising also adds cost, right? And if companies stopped all that expensive advertising, products would cost less, right?

Not necessarily.

Some advertised products do cost more than unadvertised products, but the opposite is also true. Both the Federal Trade Commission and the Supreme Court have ruled that by encouraging competition, advertising has the effect of keeping prices down. This again serves the consumer's self-interest.

Sweeping statements about advertising's positive or negative effect on prices are likely to be too simplistic. We can make some important points, though.

- As a cost of doing business, advertising is indeed paid for by the consumer who buys the product. In most product categories, though, the amount spent on advertising is very small compared with the total cost of the product.
- Advertising often enables manufacturers to engage in mass production, which in turn lowers the unit cost of products. These savings can then be passed on to consumers in the form of lower prices.
- In regulated industries (agriculture, utilities), advertising has historically had no effect on prices. When industries are deregulated, advertising has affected price—usually downward, but not always.
- In retailing, price is prominent in many ads, so advertising tends to hold prices down. On the other hand, national manufacturers use advertising to stress features that make their brands better; in these cases advertising tends to support higher prices.

The famous "Got Milk" campaign promotes primary rather than selective demand because it promotes consumption of milk in general rather than a specific brand of milk.

Effect on Competition

Some believe advertising restricts competition because small companies or industry newcomers can't compete with the immense advertising budgets of large firms.

Intense competition does tend to reduce the number of businesses in an industry. However, firms eliminated by competition may be those that served customers least effectively. In other cases, competition is reduced because of mergers and acquisitions.

High costs may inhibit the entry of new competitors in industries that spend heavily on advertising. In some markets, the original brands probably benefit greatly from this barrier. However, the investments needed for plants, machinery, and labor are of far greater significance. These are typically greater barriers to entry than advertising.

Advertising by big companies often has only a limited effect on small businesses because a single advertiser is rarely large enough to dominate the whole country. Regional oil companies, for example, compete very successfully with national oil companies on the local level. In fact, the freedom to advertise encourages more sellers to enter the market. And we've all seen nonadvertised store brands of food compete very effectively with nationally advertised brands on the same grocery shelves.

Effect on Consumers and Businesses

The question of advertising's effect on total consumer demand is extremely complex. Numerous studies show that promotional activity does affect aggregate consumption, but they disagree as to the extent of its influence. For example, the demand for flat-panel TVs, cellular phones, and laptop computers expanded at a tremendous rate, thanks in part to advertising but more to favorable market conditions. At the same time, advertising hasn't reversed declining sales of such items as hats, fur coats, and manual typewriters.

Advertising can help get new products off the ground by giving people more "complete information," thereby stimulating **primary demand**—demand for the entire product class. In declining markets, when the only information people want is price information, advertising can influence **selective demand**—demand for a particular brand. But the only effect it will have on primary demand is to slow the rate of decline. In growing markets, advertisers generally compete for shares of that growth. In mature, static, or declining markets, they compete for each other's shares.

Manufacturers who want to beat the competition need to make their product different. For example, look at the long list of car models, sizes, colors, and features designed to attract different buyers. The freedom to advertise encourages

businesses to create new brands and improve old ones. When one brand reaches market dominance, smaller brands may disappear for a time. But the moment a better product comes along and is advertised skillfully, the dominant brand loses out to the newer, better product. Once again, the freedom to advertise promotes the existence of more sellers, and that gives consumers wider choices.

Historically, when business cycles dip, companies cut advertising expenditures. That may help short-term profits, but studies prove that businesses that continue to invest in advertising during a recession are better able to protect, and sometimes build, market shares.[12] However, no study has shown that if everybody just kept advertising, a recessionary cycle would turn around. We conclude that when business cycles are up, advertising contributes to the increase. When business cycles are down, advertising may act as a stabilizing force by encouraging buyers to continue buying.

The Abundance Principle: The Economic Impact of Advertising in Perspective

To individual businesses such as Apple, the local car dealer, and the convenience store on the corner, advertising pays back more than it costs. If advertising didn't pay, no one would use it. But advertising costs less for the consumer than most people think. The cost of a bottle of Coke includes about a penny for advertising. And the $20,000 price tag on a new car usually includes a manufacturer's advertising cost of less than $400.

> Advertising . . . helps create financially healthy consumers who are more informed, better educated, and more demanding.

To the broader economy, the importance of advertising is best demonstrated by the **abundance principle**. This states that in an economy that produces more goods and services than can be consumed, advertising serves two important purposes: It keeps consumers informed of their alternatives *(complete information)*, and it allows companies to compete more effectively for consumer dollars *(self-interest)*. In North America alone, the U.S. and Canadian economies produce an enormous selection of products. The average supermarket carries nearly 40,000 different items.[13] Each automaker markets dozens of models. This competition generally results in more and better products at similar or lower prices.

Advertising stimulates competition *(many buyers and sellers)*. In countries where consumers have money to spend after their physical needs are satisfied, advertising also stimulates innovation and new products. However, no amount of advertising can achieve long-term acceptance for products that people don't want. Despite massive advertising expenditures, fewer than a dozen of the 50 best-known cars developed in the twentieth century are still sold today.

Advertising stimulates a healthy economy. It also helps create financially healthy consumers who are more informed, better educated, and more demanding. Consumers today insist that manufacturers be held accountable for their advertising. This has led to an unprecedented level of social criticism and legal regulation, the subject of our next sections.

abundance principle States that an economy produces more goods and services than can be consumed. In such an economy, advertising serves two important purposes: it keeps consumers informed of their alternatives, and it allows companies to compete more effectively for consumer dollars.

check yourself ✓

1. Why do you think countries with higher advertising spending per capita tend to have a higher standard of living?
2. Explain the effect that advertising has on brands, prices, competition, and primary and selective demand.
3. What beneficial roles does advertising play in a healthy economy?

Despite extensive advertising efforts, some products, like the Edsel automobile, will fail simply because they do not meet the expectations of customers at that particular time. Many of the best-known cars developed in the twentieth century are no longer sold today. Ironically, the Edsel has since become a pricy collector's item for automobile aficionados.

puffery Exaggerated, subjective claims that can't be proven true or false such as "the best," "premier," or "the only way to fly."

LO2-2 Examine the validity of the various social criticisms of advertising.

THE SOCIAL IMPACT OF ADVERTISING

Because it's so visible, advertising gets criticized frequently, for both what it is and what it isn't. Many of the criticisms focus on the *style* of advertising, saying it's deceptive or manipulative. Other criticisms focus on the *social* or *environmental impact* of advertising. Let's look at some of these common criticisms of advertising, debunk some misconceptions, and examine the problems that do exist.

Deception in Advertising

One of the most common criticisms of advertising style is that it is so frequently deceptive. If a product does not live up to its ads, dissatisfaction occurs—something that is as harmful to the advertiser as to the buyer.

For advertising to be effective, consumers must have confidence in it. So deception not only detracts from the complete information principle of free enterprise but also risks being self-defeating. Even meaningless (but legal) puffery might be taken literally and therefore mislead. **Puffery** refers to exaggerated, often subjective claims that can't necessarily be proven true or false, such as "the best hamburger" or "the most comfortable shoe."

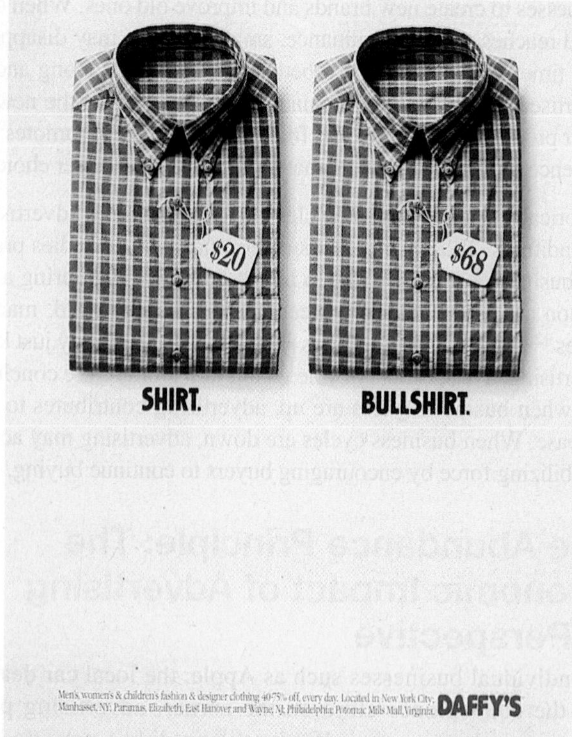

Daffy's (www.daffys.com) uses tongue-in-cheek humor to take a stand against advertising puffery—inflated promises and claims often accompanied by inflated prices. Daffy's beckons smart consumers to shop where they can find the same quality goods with "no bull" price tags.

> Advertising, by its very nature, is *not* complete information. It is biased in favor of the advertiser.

Puffery is rarely so literal as it is in this German advertisement for Tabasco hot sauce. Although the peppery condiment won't actually cause corn kernels to pop off the cob, such puffery is not illegal because it is so unbelievable.

Under current advertising law, the only product claims—explicit or implied—that are considered deceptive are those that are *factually false* or convey a false impression and therefore have the potential to deceive or mislead reasonable people.[14] But puffery is excluded from this requirement because regulators maintain that reasonable people won't believe it anyway.

Of course, advertising, by its very nature, is *not* complete information. It is biased in favor of the advertiser and the brand. People expect advertisers to be proud of their products and probably don't mind if they puff them a little. But when advertisers cross the line and create false expectations, people begin to object. One problem is the difficulty of seeing the line, which may be drawn differently by different people. Papa John's Pizza no doubt thought it was just puffing when it advertised "Better ingredients. Better pizza." Pizza Hut saw it differently, though,

Truth in Advertising: Fluffing and Puffing

In advertising, puffery means exaggerated commendation, or hype. The term comes from the Old English word *pyffan,* meaning "to blow in short gusts" or "to inflate; make proud or conceited." Puffery surely predates recorded history.

The Nature of Puffery

Regardless of its long heritage and current widespread use, we should question puffery's role in advertising. Puffery erodes advertising's credibility as a trustworthy messenger by lowering the public's belief in the advertising they see. People begin to question those who support and create such advertising—the advertisers, ad professionals, and ultimately the media that run such ads.

Defining Puffery

Regardless of the criticisms, puffery remains legal. And in the United States, it's relatively well defined by law.

The Federal Trade Commission, in the late 1950s, confirmed, "Puffery does not embrace misstatements of material facts."

Puffery's legal definition establishes that the characteristics puffed must, in fact, exist. The challenge is defining where puffing crosses over from exaggeration into falsehood and then to deception. Exaggeration is often the starting point of falsehood, but falsehood is not necessarily harmful or injurious—in fact, it may be playful and creative. Deception, however, is potentially injurious to consumers and is therefore illegal.

Take, for example, the case with Papa John's International, which invested millions of dollars over the years in its "Better ingredients, Better pizza" advertising campaign. The vague and subjective claim might be considered puffery. But when it named its rival Pizza Hut in ads, the issue changed from mere puffery to comparison. And comparison advertising requires convincing substantiation; otherwise it may be considered deceptive.

In 1998, Pizza Hut filed a lawsuit in Dallas federal court against Papa John's, alleging that its campaign was "false, misleading, and deceptive." A Texas jury ruled in favor of Pizza Hut, charging that Papa John's "Better ingredients, Better pizza" campaign constituted deceptive advertising. Pizza Hut was awarded $467,619.75. Papa John's was ordered to remove its slogan from ads, pizza boxes, restaurant signage, and delivery trucks.

Later, the decision was reversed by the District Court of Appeals after Papa John's removed the references to Pizza Hut. But the point had still been made: Advertisers have to be careful about the puffery claims they make—they no longer have free rein. Marketers need to be able to substantiate any claims that they make. An indirect comparison, or even the appearance of one, could render them liable.

The Use of Puffery

Common usage portrays puffery as praise for the item to be sold using subjective opinions, superlatives, exaggerations, and vagueness, and generally stating no specific facts.

Puffery often takes the form of "nonproduct facts," information not specifically about the product and therefore not directly testable as true or false. Nonproduct facts are typically about consumers: their personalities, lifestyles, fears, anxieties. An example was the Army's positioning message, "Be all that you can be in the Army" (1981–2001). The claim relied on the potential for what could happen to the ad's readers while they were in the Army. It didn't actually promise any specific benefits such as improved physical fitness or more education. Thus, regardless of what actually happened to readers who joined up, the claim was neither true nor false about the Army.

Puffery can also be "artful display," the visual presentation of a product. Although not well defined by law, visual exaggeration is ever present in ads to enhance moods, excite viewers, and more. The existence of professional models, for example, suggests that some individuals are more visually attractive than others. This factor makes them appealing. But does their appearance in an ad imply that owning the product will make the buyer more physically attractive?

Judging Puffery

We live in exciting times. Populations are more literate, satellites and the Internet keep the world informed instantly, and modern technology speeds up the way we live and play. And part of the glitz of our modern life is puffery, adding pizzazz and stimulating our dreams. On the Internet, small businesses can claim just about anything and who's going to hold them accountable?

So, who should protect consumers from puffery, especially when puffery crosses the line and becomes injurious? Who should evaluate puffery's ethics? The courts may, but only when a consumer challenges an advertiser. The actions and attitudes of the advertising profession can make a huge difference.

subliminal advertising Advertisements with messages (often sexual) supposedly embedded in illustrations just below the threshold of perception.

and sued Papa John's for deceptive advertising. A U.S. District judge agreed and awarded Pizza Hut close to half a million dollars in damages. The judge then ordered Papa John's to stop using its "Better ingredients" slogan.[15] This decision was later overturned on appeal, but the case still goes to show that there are limits on what an advertiser can safely puff. For more on this story and on puffery, see "Ethical Issues: Truth in Advertising: Fluffing and Puffing" on page 35.

The Subliminal Advertising Myth

Wilson Bryan Key promotes the notion that, to seduce consumers, advertisers intentionally create ads with sexual messages hidden in the illustrations. He calls this **subliminal advertising**. His premise is that by embedding dirty words in the ice cubes in a liquor ad, for instance, advertisers can make us want to buy the product. Many academic studies have debunked this theory.[16] In fact, to date no study has proved that such embedding exists or that it would have any effect if it did exist.[17]

The nerve that Key has been able to touch, though, is important. The widespread fear is that advertisers are messing with our heads—manipulating us—without our consent, into buying things we don't want or need. This gets to the heart of the *complete information* principle because the criticism suggests that advertising does not give consumers information but rather manipulates us through brainwashing. Consumers are, therefore, like captured prey, helpless in the jaws of marketing predators.

If you think about all the products you buy, how many involve a choice between different brands and different models? And how many involve a decision based on price or convenience? Probably most. So how many of your purchases can you trace to having been helplessly manipulated? Probably none. You receive information from many different sources: friends and relatives, store displays, ads, packaging, and retail store clerks. At some point, you make a decision. In many cases, your decision is *not* to buy at all—to wait for either more information or more money. As always, the customer, acting in his or her own self-interest, makes the decision.

Status comes in many forms and often vivid imagery can be quite inviting to prospective buyers. This Hermes ad (www.hermes.com) contrasts the warm colors of fall with the cool white of winter to create a unique backdrop for their clothing.

Advertising and Our Value System

An argument, often voiced by critics, is that advertising degrades people's value systems by promoting a hedonistic, materialistic way of life. Advertising, they say, encourages us to buy more cars, iPods, clothing, and junk we don't need. It is destroying the essence of our "citizen democracy," replacing it with a self-oriented consumer democracy.[18]

This manipulation works because ads play on our emotions and promise greater status, social acceptance, and sex appeal. They cause people to take up harmful habits, make poor kids buy $170 sneakers, and tempt ordinary people to buy useless products in the vain attempt to emulate celebrity endorsers.[19] Again, critics claim advertising is so powerful consumers are helpless to defend themselves against it.

Others believe this argument exaggerates the power of advertising. They note that most Americans express a healthy skepticism toward it. One study showed that only 17 percent of U.S. consumers see advertising as a source of information to help them decide what to buy.[20] Perhaps that's why more advertised products fail than succeed in the marketplace.

Still, there's no question that advertisers do indeed spend millions trying to convince people their products will make them sexier, healthier, and more successful. The very amount of advertising we witness every day seems to suggest that every problem we have can be solved by the purchase of some product.

The Proliferation of Advertising

One of the most common environmental complaints about advertising is that there's just too much of it. In the United States alone, the average person may be exposed to 500 to 1,000 commercial messages a day. With so many products competing for attention (nearly 40,000 in the average supermarket), advertisers themselves worry about the negative impact of excessive advertising. An average hour of prime-time network TV programming in 2010 contained over 14 minutes of network commercial messages, plus nearly 11 minutes of in-show brand appearances, resulting in advertising content filling 42 percent of each prime-time hour, according to Kantar Media. Unscripted reality programming was the worst offender, containing over 34 minutes of marketing content, representing over 56 percent of total time.[21] Popular shows are the most cluttered: ABC packed roughly 107 spots—or more than 45 minutes of commercial and promotional time—into the two-and-a-half-hour *Lost* series finale.[22]

But television is not the only offender. Magazines, radio stations, and even the Internet are congested with advertising. Visit a Web site at random and you're likely to be overwhelmed with ads. Ad clutter not only annoys the audience but it also decreases ad effectiveness. A survey by Burst Media found that the majority of

stereotypes Negative or limiting preconceived beliefs about a type of person or a group of people that do not take into account individual differences.

respondents who stay on a Web site they perceive to be cluttered say they pay less attention to advertisements appearing on its pages. Nearly a third immediately leave a site if they think it's cluttered, and over half come away with a less favorable opinion of an advertiser.[23] The Interactive Advertising Bureau (IAB), Google, and others are addressing this issue with new ad formats for digital platforms that "encourage brand engagement with viewers on their terms." The hope is that these more managable, relevant, and visually appealing ads will increase consumer engagement.[24]

While the clutter problem is irksome to viewers and advertisers alike, most people tolerate it as the price for free TV, an information-rich Internet, and a high standard of living. However, with the proliferation of new media choices, this externality is only likely to get worse. In addition to cluttered Web sites, our e-mail boxes are flooded with commercial messages and mobile advertising is still in its infancy. While the Federal Communications Commission exercises no jurisdiction over the Internet, it did consider reinstating commercial time limits on television. But, as of now, the only limits currently in force relate to TV programming aimed at children 12 and under—advertising may not exceed 10.5 minutes per hour on weekends and 12 minutes per hour on weekdays.[25]

Stereotypes in Advertising

Advertising has long been criticized for insensitivity to minorities, women, immigrants, persons who are disabled or elderly, and other groups.[26] Marketing and advertising practitioners sometimes lose touch with the very people they are trying to reach.

In recent years, national advertisers have become more sensitive to the concerns of minorities and women. Latinos, African Americans, Asians, Native Americans, and others are now usually portrayed favorably in ads, not only because of pressure from watchdog groups, but also because it's just good business; these consumers represent sizable target markets. Marilyn Kern-Foxworth, a Texas A&M professor and an expert on minorities in advertising, points out that positive role portrayal in some mainstream ads has had a positive effect on the self-esteem of African American youth.[27] This positive trend has accelerated with the emergence of many ad agencies that specialize in reaching minority markets.

In national advertising, the image of women is also changing from their historic depiction as either subservient housewives or sex objects. This may be partially due to the increasing number of women in managerial and executive positions with both advertisers and agencies. In 2012, nearly 58 percent of women 16 years of age and older were in the labor force and women occupied over half of the management, professional, and related positions.[28] Advertisers want to reach, not offend, this sizable market of upwardly mobile consumers. Some agencies now retain feminist consultants to review ads that may risk offending women.[29] In 2003, Ann Fudge was named CEO of Young and Rubicam and became the first African-American woman to head a major U.S. advertising agency. *Forbes* named Fudge one of the 100 most powerful women in America in 2004. And in 2007, Nancy Hill became the first female head of the American Association of Advertising Agencies (AAAA). The days when sexist practitioners like Don Draper, the central character of AMC's *Mad Men*, defined the culture of ad agencies are now far in the past.

However, problems still exist, especially in local and regional advertising and in certain product categories such as beer and sports promotions. Many advertisers are just not aware of the externalities that their ads can create, and they may perpetuate male and female stereotypes without even realizing it.[30]

Critics have long complained about the way some ads depict women as sex objects. This ad for Hirter Beer created quite a controversy in Austria.

Other advertisers resort to **stereotypes** for convenience. A stereotype is a generalization about a group. Some critics believe ads stereotype women as homemakers or elderly people as weak and frail. And the under representation of minorities in mainstream ads, both local and national, still smacks of tokenism. Observers hope that with increasing numbers of women and minorities joining the ranks of marketing and advertising professionals, and with continuing academic studies of minority and sex-role stereo typing, greater attention will be focused on these issues.

Offensive Advertising

Offensiveness is another style argument that also speaks to externalities. Many parents, for instance, were incensed at Abercrombie & Fitch's ads because they perceived them as pornographic, thereby causing a social cost that extended beyond

the limited scope of merely selling clothes. The fact is, people just don't want their children exposed to messages that they deem immoral, offensive, or strictly adult-oriented.[31]

Taste, however, is highly subjective: What is bad taste to some is perfectly acceptable to others. And tastes change. What is considered offensive today may not be so tomorrow. People were outraged when the first ad for underarm deodorant appeared in a 1927 *Ladies Home Journal;* today no one questions such ads.

Grooming, fashion, and personal hygiene products often use partial nudity in their ads. Where nudity is relevant to the product, people are less likely to regard it as offensive—except when the advertising is targeting kids. In many European countries, in fact, nudity in commercials is commonplace.

Some consumers get so offended by both advertising and TV programming that they boycott sponsors' products.[32] Of course, they also have the option to just change the channel. Both of these are effective strategies for consumers because, ultimately, the marketplace has veto power. If ads don't pull in the audience, the campaign will falter and die.[33]

The Social Impact of Advertising in Perspective

Marketing professionals say advertising encourages the development and speeds the acceptance of new products and technologies. It fosters employment. It gives consumers and business customers a wider variety of choices. By encouraging mass production, it helps keep prices down. And it stimulates healthy competition between producers, which benefits all buyers.[34] Advertising, they point out, also promotes a higher standard of living; it pays for most of our news media and subsidizes the arts; it supports freedom of the press; and it provides a means to disseminate public information about important health and social issues. These benefits, they believe, are important.

Critics might agree with some of these points but certainly not all of them. For example, critics charge that rather than supporting a free press, advertising actually interferes with it. The media, they say, pander to national advertisers to attract the big ad dollars. In the process, they modify their editorial content to suit marketers and shirk their primary journalistic responsibility of presenting news in the public interest.[35]

In summary, we can conclude that while advertising may legitimately be criticized for offering less-than-complete information and, in some instances, for creating unwanted problems, it should also be applauded when it contributes to the benefits of a free economy. In most cases, by being a rich information source (albeit not complete), advertising contributes to the existence of many buyers and sellers and, therefore, to the self-interest of both consumers and marketers.

With tightening markets, advertisers must double their efforts to maintain or expand market share. One way is to expand into minority communities which have enormous buying power and are growing at a faster rate than the rest of the population.

Ultimately, the marketplace has veto power. If ads don't pull in the audience, the campaign will falter and die.[33]

check yourself ✓

1. Describe six common criticisms of advertising and discuss how you might refute them.

Without advertising, public service organizations would be unable to reach a mass audience to educate people about important health and social issues. Here, the Ad Council promotes the adoption of pets from animal shelters.

LO2-3 Explain the difference between social responsibility and ethics in advertising.

SOCIAL RESPONSIBILITY AND ADVERTISING ETHICS

Numerous laws determine what advertisers can and cannot do, but they also allow a significant amount of leeway. That's where ethics and social responsibility come into play. An advertiser can act unethically or irresponsibly without breaking any laws. As advertising professor Ivan Preston says, ethics begin where the law ends.[36]

Ethical advertising means doing what the advertiser and the advertiser's peers believe is morally right in a given situation. **Social responsibility** means doing what society views as best for the welfare of people in general or for a specific community of people. Together, ethics and social responsibility can be seen as the moral obligation of advertisers not to violate our basic economic assumptions, even when there is no legal obligation.

ethical advertising
Doing what the advertiser and the advertiser's peers believe is morally right in a given situation.

social responsibility
Acting in accordance with what society views as best for the welfare of people in general or for a specific community of people.

Advertisers' Social Responsibility

Advertising plays an important role in developed countries. It influences a society's stability and growth. It helps secure large armies, creates entertainment events attracting hundreds of thousands of fans, and often affects the outcome of political elections. Such power places a burden of responsibility on those who sponsor, buy, create, produce, and sell advertising to maintain ethical standards that support the society and contribute to the economic system.

In the United States, the advertising industry is part of a large business community. Like any good neighbor, it has responsibilities: to keep its property clean, participate in civic events, support local enterprises, and improve the community. U.S. advertising professionals meet these challenges by forming local advertising clubs, the American Advertising Federation (AAF), the American Association of Advertising Agencies (AAAA), and the Ad Council. These organizations provide thousands of hours and millions of dollars' worth of *pro bono* (free) work to charitable organizations and public agencies. They also provide scholarships and internships, contributions that serve the whole society. As we discuss later, they even regulate themselves fairly effectively. Still, advertisers are regularly chided when they fail the social responsibility litmus test. Concerned citizens, consumer advocates, and

Non, E. Leclerc ne veut pas être présent partout.

Avec votre aide, mettons fin à la pollution par les sacs en plastique.

Today's consumer is more sophisticated than ever about social issues like environmentalism. Leclerc addresses the issue of "plastic bag pollution" in a beautifully produced campaign, where it tells customers "No, Leclerc does not really want to be seen everywhere." Other ads in the series say, "There are some places we don't want to see our name," and "Some advertising we'll pass up willingly."

"MOST ADVERTISERS TODAY STRIVE TO MAINTAIN FAIR ETHICAL STANDARDS AND PRACTICE SOCIALLY RESPONSIBLE ADVERTISING."

special-interest groups pressure advertisers when they perceive the public's welfare is at risk. The earliest "green advertising" campaigns, for instance, exemplified a blatant effort by some advertisers to cash in on consumers' desire for a cleaner environment. Some promoted nebulous product qualities, such as "environmental friendliness," that had no basis in fact. Finally, when the state attorneys general got together and defined relevant terms for use in green advertising, marketers cleaned up their act.

Ethics of Advertising

Philosophies of ethics span the centuries since Socrates. We can hardly do them justice here. But for practical purposes, let's consider three levels of ethical responsibility and apply them to advertising.

On one level, ethics comprise two interrelated components: the traditional actions taken by people in a society or community, which are customs, and the philosophical rules that society establishes to justify such past actions and decree future actions, which are principles. Customs and principles create the primary rules of ethical behavior in society and enable us to measure how far an individual or company (or advertiser) strays from the norm.

Every individual also faces a second set of ethical issues: the attitudes, feelings, and beliefs that add up to a personal value system. When these two systems conflict, should the individual act on personal beliefs or on the obligation to serve society? When people cannot resolve an ethical dilemma, they must redefine the issue in dispute. Thus, the third level of ethics concerns singular ethical concepts such as good, bad, right, wrong, duty, integrity, and truth. Are these concepts absolute, universal, and binding? Or are they relative, dependent on situations and consequences? People may differ in their answers.

Most advertisers today strive to maintain fair ethical standards and practice socially responsible advertising. Ad agencies rarely force employees to work on accounts they morally oppose. Once a free-swinging, unchecked business, advertising is today a closely scrutinized and heavily regulated profession. Advertising's past shortcomings have resulted in laws, regulations, and regulatory bodies. Consumer groups, governments, special-interest groups, and even other advertisers now review, control, and modify advertising in order to create more *complete information* and reduce unwanted *externalities.*

Your Campaign Assignment [2–A]

You will be working on an advertising/IMC campaign, or part of one, this semester. Few things are more important for you when preparing for a semester-long project than understanding the final product that is expected of you. It is only when you know what is expected at the end that you can plan what happens in between.

What You May Be Working On

Different classes have different projects, but it is likely that you will work on one or more of the following for a brand, service, or firm:

- A campaign audit.
- A research report.
- A marketing or IMC plan, including a SWOT analysis.
- An advertising or IMC budget.
- A media plan.
- A creative brief or creative platform.
- A plans book.

Below we explain each of these in turn and give you guidance about where you can find information in this text and on the Internet.

Campaign Audit

Many classes begin by having teams audit the plans books from prior semesters. This accomplishes several things. First, it gives you an idea about what you will be doing all semester. Second, it introduces you to the importance of seeing how research, strategy, planning, budgeting, and creativity all flow together. If you don't have access to the work of other students, why not look over the work of the very best? Visit the Effie Award Web site (www.effie.org/case_studies/cases), where you can find great ads and a lot of background information about the campaigns.

Research Report

You may be asked to conduct formative research for the brand. This may include secondary research, useful for gathering information for your IMC plan; qualitative primary research, in which you conduct a focus group or series of depth interviews; and quantitative research, in which you administer a survey. You'll find a lot of information in Chapter 6 about these activities. Your school library might have a Web page devoted to secondary marketing research. You can also

check yourself ✓

1. Provide examples of actions that advertisers or their agencies might take that would demonstrate social responsibility and ethical behavior.

L02-4 Describe how government agencies regulate advertising to protect both consumers and competitors.

CURRENT REGULATORY ISSUES AFFECTING U.S. ADVERTISERS

Federal and state courts have made many significant rulings pertaining to advertising issues. The most important of these concern First Amendment rights and privacy rights. We'll review these, while paying special attention to controversies surrounding tobacco advertising and advertising to children.

Freedom of Commercial Speech

The Supreme Court historically distinguishes between "speech" and "commercial speech" (speech that promotes a commercial transaction). But decisions over the last two decades suggest that truthful commercial speech is also entitled to significant, if not full, protection under the First Amendment.

The trend started in 1976 when the Supreme Court held in *Virginia State Board of Pharmacy v. Virginia Citizens Consumer Council* that ads enjoy protection under the First Amendment as commercial speech.[37] The next year the Court declared that the ban by state bar associations on attorney advertising also violated the First Amendment. Now a third of all lawyers advertise, and a few states even permit client testimonials. In 1980 the Court used *Central Hudson Gas v. Public Service Commission* to test whether specific examples of commercial speech can be regulated.[38] The *Central Hudson* test includes the following four parts:

1. *Does the commercial speech at issue concern a lawful activity?* The ad in question must be for a legal product and must be free of misleading claims.
2. *Will the restriction of commercial speech serve the asserted government interest substantially?* The government must prove that the absence of regulation would have a substantial negative effect.
3. *Does the regulation directly advance the government interest asserted?* The government must be able to establish conclusively that regulating advertising would be effective in furthering the government's interest.
4. *Is the restriction no more than necessary to further the interest asserted?* The government would have to establish that there are no other means to accomplish the same end without restricting free speech.[39]

find secondary research sources at www.entrepreneurship.org/en/resource-center/secondary-market-research-resources.aspx.

Marketing or IMC Plan

Many classes require that you create a marketing or IMC plan. We've included lots of information in this text to help. Be sure to read Chapter 7 carefully, as it is your guide to the art and science of planning. Then, to make things more concrete, search for examples of "advertising plan outlines" on the Web. Your instructor may have his or her own outline; if so, use that.

Media Plan

A media plan shows the specific allocations of the budget to different media and promotional activities. It will also specify what vehicles will be used for the campaign, as well as when and how often the ads will run. You will most likely want to use a spreadsheet to show the calendar. We have a sample media plan flowchart in Chapter 14.

The Creative Brief

The creative brief is a fairly short document that is used to inform and guide the people who create the ads. It contains information that has been distilled from some of the documents that we've just reviewed, such as the IMC plan. There are as many different outlines for creative briefs as there are ad agencies, but in many instances the differences are superficial. Chapter 8 provides some examples of a creative brief and shows you the elements of a message strategy. For examples of creative briefs, visit the following sites:

- Emily Cohen: http://emilycohen.com/articles/successful-creative-briefs/
- SmileyCat blog (for a brief written for a Web campaign): www.smileycat.com/miaow/archives/000226.php

The Plans Book

If you are doing a plans book it means you are doing almost everything we've reviewed to this point. A typical plans book will include research findings, an IMC plan, a creative brief, media plans, and, in many cases, mock-ups of real ads. But it puts these things together in a seamless, integrated way, so that the reader has a clear understanding of the entire arc of a planned campaign. In many plans books there will also be a section on campaign evaluation (ways of assessing the campaign).

privacy rights Of or pertaining to an individual's right to prohibit personal information from being divulged to the public.

cookies Small pieces of information that get stored on your computer when you download certain Web sites. These cookies can keep track of whether a certain user has ever before visited a specific site. This allows the Web site to identify returning users and to customize the information based on past browsing or purchase behavior.

Joe Camel appeared in R.J. Reynolds' Camel advertising beginning in 1988. He became a well-known character among children, but R.J. Reynolds denied that Joe Camel was ever targeted at the youth market. In 1997, under pressure from various public-interest groups, R.J. Reynolds replaced Joe Camel with a more traditional, four-legged dromedary.

In 1982, the Supreme Court upheld an FTC order allowing physicians and dentists to advertise. Since then, advertising for medical and dental services has skyrocketed.

In 2011, a Supreme Court ruling had important implications for commercial speech. The case, *Sorrell v. IMS Inc.*, concerned data mining. In this case the Court invalidated a state law that made the practice illegal, at least for drug companies. Many saw this as a broader protection for commercial speech than the one outlined in the *Central Hudson* case.[40]

The issue of freedom of commercial speech is far from settled. Allowing greater freedom of commercial speech enhances the "government interests" of many buyers and sellers and complete information. But critics contend that advertising regulations can help reduce externalities related to controversial products such as tobacco and advertising to children.

Tobacco Advertising

While tobacco is a legal product, the harm created by smoking ends up killing or disabling more than half a million people annually and costing taxpayers billions of dollars every year in health costs—a major externality. To recover these costs, a number of states' attorneys general sued the tobacco industry. In 1998, they reached a historic settlement. It imposed limits on brand-name promotion at events with young attendees, banned the use of cartoon characters (like Joe Camel) in cigarette ads, and created a fund of over $200 billion to be used by the various signatory states. Today, state budgets rely heavily on the money secured in the settlement.[41]

Advertising to Children

Advertising to children presents different challenges. Kids are not sophisticated consumers. Their perceptions of self, time, and money are immature. As a result, they know very little about their desires, needs, and preferences—or how to use economic resources rationally to satisfy them. And the nature of child-oriented advertising can lead to false beliefs or highly improbable product expectations.

More and more children are becoming the sole decision makers about the products they consume. To protect them, and their parents, both critics and defenders agree that advertisers should not intentionally deceive children. The central issue is how far advertisers should go to ensure that children are not misled.

To promote responsible children's advertising and to respond to public concerns, the Council of Better Business

Bureaus established the *Children's Advertising Review Unit (CARU).* The basic activity of CARU is the review and evaluation of child-directed advertising in all media. When children's advertising is found to be misleading, inaccurate, or inconsistent with the *Guidelines,* CARU seeks changes through voluntary cooperation of the advertisers.[42]

In the developed world, other countries are far more strict than the United States about advertising to children. Sweden and Norway, for example, do not permit any television advertising to be directed toward children under 12, and no advertisements at all are allowed during children's programs. While the highest level of advertising to children is in Australia (an average of 34 ads per hour), that country allows no ads on programs aimed at preschool children.[43]

Children are not sophisticated consumers and can easily be misled by advertising that makes unrealistic promises. This advertisement for Gatorade Kids might suggest to children that a sweet, flavored sports drink will give them extraordinary strength (or that they should punch someone).

Consumer Privacy

The second major regulatory issue facing advertisers is privacy. With the increased use of wireless handheld devices, cell phones, and the Internet, all of which can be used for advertising, the issue of **privacy rights** is in the news. The issue deals with people's right to protect their personal information. As we shall see in Chapter 12, privacy is an ethical issue as well as a legal one. It's also a practical issue: Prospective customers who find pop-up ads, telemarketing calls, and e-mail spam annoying and intrusive aren't likely to buy the offending company's products.

> Prospective customers who find pop-up ads, telemarketing calls, and e-mail spam annoying and intrusive aren't likely to buy the offending company's products.

Internet users worry about people they don't know, and even businesses they do know, getting personal information about them. And their concern is not without merit. Many Web sites create profiles of their visitors to get data such as e-mail addresses, clothing sizes, or favorite books. Some sites also track users' surfing habits, usually without their knowledge, to better target ads for products.

To create these user profiles, Web sites use tiny software programs, called **cookies**, that keep a log of where people click, allowing sites to track customers' Web-surfing habits. The cookies are placed on people's computers when they first visit a site or use some feature like a personalized news service or a shopping cart.[44]

Internet companies argue that such tracking is not personal; it's typically performed anonymously and helps them customize content to match users' interests.[45] However, DoubleClick, a leading provider of marketing tools for Web advertisers, direct marketers, and Web publishers, merged with Abacus Direct, a direct-mail company with an extensive offline database of retail and catalog purchasers. This enabled DoubleClick to combine online profiles with offline names, addresses, demographic information, and purchasing data.[46] In turn, DoubleClick was then acquired by the largest Web advertiser, Google. This means that Google has potential access to an enormous amount of information about Web users. Companies like Apple and Facebook do as well.

One survey revealed that only 27 percent of Internet users accept the industry's claim that tracking is helpful. Somewhat more than half, 54 percent, consider it harmful, and 11 percent believe that it both helps and hurts. A large majority of those surveyed, 87 percent, believe sites should ask permission before collecting personal information.[47]

Fortunately, consumers are not completely helpless. They can disable the cookies on their computers. But this may limit their

In 2009, Facebook, the Internet's second largest Web site, came under assault for the amount of personal information it disclosed to third parties. The 50 privacy settings spanning seven pages was considered an onerous task for users seeking to limit disclosure. Facebook responded by reducing this to 15 settings, but many critics of the social networking site are not satisfied that Facebook truly respects the privacy of its users.

Internet access because some Web sites *require* that cookies be accepted. Internet surfers also have the option to "opt in." This feature allows users to set the terms under which they give personal information.[48] Also available is the "opt-out" feature, which allows visitors to specifically inform the site not to gather information by clicking on a button.[49]

Responding to consumer concerns, the Federal Trade Commission together with the Network Advertising Initiative (an organization comprised of leading Internet advertising networks, including 24/7, Google, Microsoft, ValueClick, and Yahoo!) has created a framework for self-regulation of online profiling. The "Fair Information Practice Principles" consist of five core elements:

- *Notice,* which requires that the Web site clearly post its privacy policy.
- *Choice,* which relates to consumers' level of control over being profiled and how their information is used.
- *Access,* the ability for consumers to access information collected about them and make amendments to it.
- *Security,* which requires that network advertisers make reasonable efforts to protect the data they collect from loss, misuse, or improper access.
- *Enforcement,* a requirement that all industry members subject themselves to monitoring by an independent third party to ensure compliance with the Fair Information Practice Principles.[50]

Naturally Internet companies would prefer to avoid government intervention and the layers of laws and regulations that would bring. So it's in everybody's interest for self-regulation to work.

FEDERAL REGULATION OF ADVERTISING IN THE UNITED STATES

The U.S. government imposes strict controls on advertisers through laws, regulations, and judicial interpretations. Among the many federal agencies and departments that regulate advertising are the Federal Trade Commission, the Food and Drug Administration, the Federal Communications Commission, the Patent and Trademark Office, and the Library of Congress. Because their jurisdictions often overlap, advertisers may sometimes have difficulty complying with their regulations.

As a result, every agency and advertiser needs to have a strong understanding of the laws that govern advertising. They also need to retain the services of a good law firm that specializes in advertising and communications law. Reed Smith, a global law firm with an advertising law practice, publishes a blog at www.adlawbyrequest.com to keep clients current on relevant legal developments.

When planning to advertise overseas, companies must be very cautious about the do's and don'ts of other countries. Typically, they retain the services of attorneys familiar with local laws. Many international law firms have Web sites that can be quickly located on the Internet. Reed Smith, a law firm that specializes in advertising and marketing, refers its clients to GALA (www.gala-marketlaw.com), an international network of lawyers to which it belongs.

The U.S. Federal Trade Commission

deceptive advertising According to the FTC, any ad in which there is a misrepresentation, omission, or other practice that can mislead a significant number of reasonable consumers to their detriment.

unfair advertising According to the FTC, advertising that causes a consumer to be "unjustifiably injured" or that violates public policy.

The *Federal Trade Commission (FTC)* is the major regulator of advertising for products sold in interstate commerce. Established by an act of Congress, the FTC is charged with ensuring "that the nation's markets function competitively, and are vigorous, efficient, and free of undue restrictions."[51] The commission enforces a variety of federal antitrust and consumer protection laws and works to regulate the marketplace by eliminating acts or practices that are deceptive or unfair. In other words, it is the FTC's responsibility to maintain the existence of *many sellers* in the marketplace, strive to provide more *complete information* to consumers, and keep the marketing process as free of *externalities* as possible.

The FTC's job is complicated by the fact that the definitions of deceptive and unfair are controversial.

Defining Deception

The FTC defines **deceptive advertising** as any ad that contains a misrepresentation, omission, or any other practice that can mislead a significant number of reasonable consumers to their detriment. Proof that consumers were deceived is not required, and the representation may be either expressed or implied. The issue is whether the ad conveys a false impression—even if it is literally true.[52]

Take the case of the FTC against Office Depot, Buy.com, and Value America. According to the FTC, the companies engaged in deceptive practices in advertising "free" and "low-cost" personal computer (PC) systems because they failed to adequately disclose the true costs and important restrictions on the offers. The low cost of the PCs was tied to rebates that were conditioned on the purchase of long-term Internet service contracts.[53] Exhibit 2–3 lists some common deceptive practices that have been found illegal by the courts.

Defining Unfairness

According to FTC policy, some ads that are not deceptive may still be considered unfair to consumers. **Unfair advertising** occurs when a consumer is "unjustifiably injured" or there is a "violation of public policy" (such as other government statutes). In other words, unfair advertising is due to the inadequacy of *complete information* or some other *externality*. For example, practices considered unfair are claims made without prior substantiation, claims that exploit vulnerable groups such as children and older adults, and cases where the consumer cannot make a valid choice because

EXHIBIT 2–3 Unfair and deceptive practices in advertising.

The courts have held that these acts constitute unfair or deceptive trade practices and are therefore illegal.

False Promises
Making an advertising promise that cannot be kept, such as "restores youth" or "prevents cancer." When Listerine claimed to prevent or reduce the impact of colds and sore throats, the FTC banned the campaign and required the company to run millions of dollars' worth of corrective ads.

Incomplete Description
Stating some but not all of a product's contents, such as advertising a "solid oak" desk without mentioning that only the top is solid oak and the rest is pine.

False and Misleading Comparisons
Making false comparisons, either explicitly or by implication, such as "Like Tylenol, Advil doesn't upset my stomach." That implies that Advil is equal in avoiding stomach upset, though in truth Tylenol is better. To some people, Advil's claim might even suggest that Tylenol upsets the stomach, which is also false.

Bait-and-Switch Offers
Advertising an item at an unusually low price to bring people into the store and then "switching" them to a higher-priced model by claiming that the advertised product is out of stock or poorly made.

Visual Distortions and False Demonstrations
Using trick photography or computer manipulation to enhance a product's appearance—for example, a TV commercial for a "giant steak" dinner special showing the steak on a miniature plate that makes it look extra large. In one classic case, General Motors and its window supplier, Libby Owens-Ford, rigged a demonstration to show how clear their windows were. The GM cars were photographed with the windows down, the competitor's car with the windows up—and Vaseline smeared on them.

False Testimonials
Implying that a product is endorsed by a celebrity or authority who is not a bona fide user, or implying that endorsers have expertise that in fact they don't.

Partial Disclosure
Stating certain facts about the advertised product but omitting other material information. An example is claiming, "Kraft's Singles processed cheese slices are made from five ounces of milk," which give Singles more calcium than the imitators' products without mentioning that processing loses about two ounces of the milk.

Small-Print Qualifications
Making a statement in large print, such as Beneficial's "Instant Tax Refund," only to qualify or retract it in obscure, small, or unreadable type elsewhere in the ad: "If you qualify for one of our loans." To the FTC, if readers don't see the qualification, it's not there.

comparative advertising
Advertising that claims superiority to competitors in some aspect.

substantiation
Evidence that backs up cited survey finding or scientific studies that the FTC may request from a suspected advertising violator.

endorsements
The use of satisfied customers and celebrities to endorse a product in advertising.

testimonials
The use of satisfied customers and celebrities to endorse a product in advertising.

affirmative disclosure
Advertisers must make known their product's limitations or deficiencies.

the advertiser leaves out important information about the product or competitors mentioned in the ad.[54]

In one case, the FTC found that an automaker's failure to warn of a safety problem was not deceptive but was unfair. Advertising organizations have argued that the word "unfair" is so vague it can mean whatever any given individual wants it to. They have lobbied Congress to eliminate the FTC's power to prosecute on unfairness grounds, and Congress did pass a compromise bill requiring the FTC to show that (1) an alleged unfair practice involves substantial, unavoidable injury to consumers; (2) the injury is not reasonably avoidable by consumers themselves; and (3) the injury is not outweighed by benefits to consumers or competition.[55] This legislation suggests that in the future the FTC will have to balance on a far narrower beam in its effort to regulate unfairness.[56]

Comparative Advertising Advertisers use **comparative advertising** to claim superiority to competitors in some aspect. In the United States, such ads are legal (and encouraged by the FTC) so long as the comparison is truthful. In fact, the FTC cracked down on the Arizona Automobile Dealers Association for restricting truthful, nondeceptive comparative price advertising among its members.[57]

Under current law, any advertiser that misrepresents its own or another firm's goods, services, or activities is vulnerable to a civil action. In addition to being truthful, comparative ads must compare on some objectively measurable characteristic. And the greatest scrutiny must be given to the substantiation. Given the potential for sizable damages—up to millions of dollars—for faulty comparative advertising, the greatest care must be exercised in this area.[58]

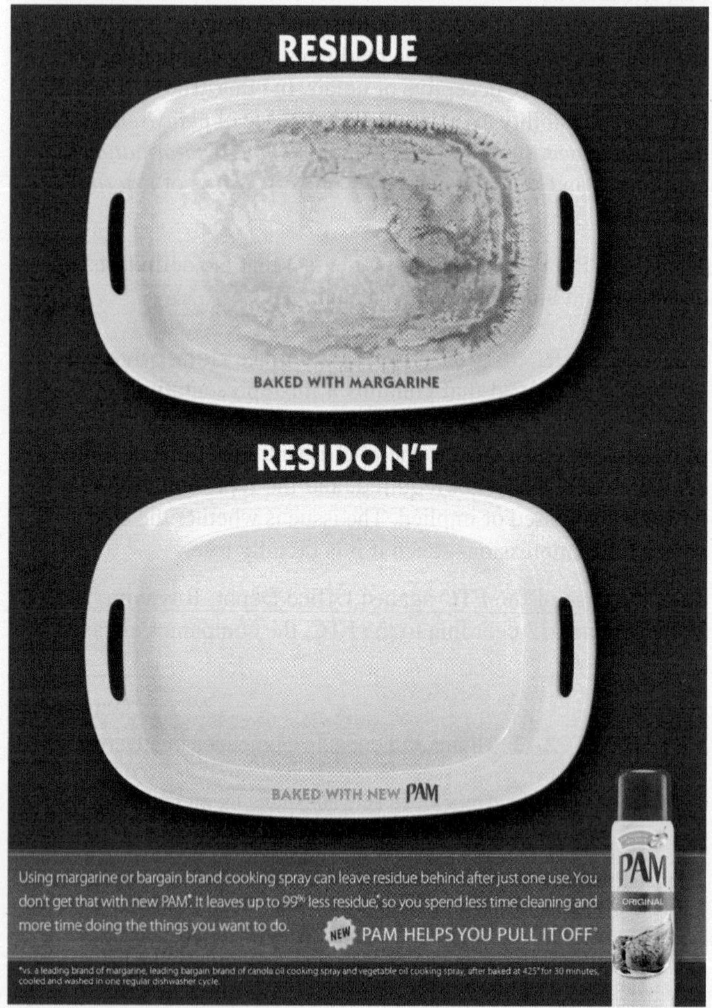

The purpose of comparative ads is to demonstrate the superiority of one product over another. This advertisement makes it clear that PAM cooking spray leaves less residue than the alternatives. And the tagline reinforces that message.

Investigating Suspected Violations If it receives complaints from consumers, competitors, or its own staff members who monitor ads, the FTC may decide to investigate an advertiser. The agency has broad powers to pursue suspected violators and demand information from them. Typically, the FTC looks for three kinds of information: *substantiation, endorsements,* and *affirmative disclosures.*

If a suspected violator cites survey findings or scientific studies, the FTC may ask for **substantiation**. Advertisers are expected to have supporting data before running an ad, although the FTC sometimes allows postclaim evidence.

The FTC also scrutinizes ads that contain questionable **endorsements** or **testimonials**. If a noncelebrity endorser is paid, the ad must disclose this onscreen.[59] The endorsers may not make claims the advertiser can't substantiate. Further, celebrity endorsers must actually use the product or service (if portrayed), and they can be held personally liable if they misrepresent it.[60]

Advertisers must make **affirmative disclosure** of their product's limitations or deficiencies: for example, EPA mileage

ratings for cars, pesticide warnings, and statements that saccharin may be hazardous to one's health.

consent decree A document advertisers sign, without admitting any wrongdoing, in which they agree to stop objectionable advertising.

cease-and-desist order May be issued by the FTC if an advertiser won't sign a consent decree; prohibits further use of an ad.

corrective advertising May be required by the FTC for a period of time to explain and correct offending ads.

Remedies for Unfair or Deceptive Advertising

When the FTC determines that an ad is deceptive or unfair, it may take three courses of action: negotiate with the advertiser for a *consent decree,* issue a *cease-and-desist order,* and/or require *corrective advertising.*

A **consent decree** is a document the advertiser signs agreeing to stop the objectionable advertising without admitting any wrongdoing.

If an advertiser won't sign a consent decree, the FTC may issue a **cease-and-desist order** prohibiting further use of the ad.

> Any advertiser that misrepresents its own or another firm's goods, services, or activities is vulnerable to a civil action.

Advertisers who violate either a consent decree or a cease-and-desist order can be fined up to $11,000 per showing of the offending ad.

The FTC may also require **corrective advertising** for some period of time to explain and correct offending ads. In 1999 the FTC ruled that pharmaceutical giant Novartis advertised without substantiation that its Doan's Pills brand was more effective against back pain than its rivals. Because the deceptive advertising had gone on for more than nine years, the FTC ordered Novartis to run $8 million worth of corrective advertising. The advertising was to include the statement: "Although Doan's is an effective pain reliever, there is no evidence that Doan's is more effective than other pain relievers for back pain." It also ordered Doan's to place the statement on its packaging for a year.[61]

The Food and Drug Administration (FDA)

The *Food and Drug Administration (FDA)* is authorized by Congress to enforce the Federal Food, Drug, and Cosmetic Act and several other health laws. The agency monitors the manufacture, import, transport, storage, and sale of over $1 trillion worth of products annually, about 25 percent of consumer expenditures in the United States. This includes $466 billion in food sales, $275 billion in drugs, $60 billion in cosmetics, and $18 billion in vitamin supplements.[62]

It's the FDA's job to see that the food we eat is safe, the cosmetics we use won't hurt us, and the medicines and therapeutic devices we buy are safe and effective. The FDA requires manufacturers to disclose all ingredients on product labels, in in-store product advertising, and in product literature. The label must accurately state the weight or volume of the contents.

Advertising law requires that celebrity endorsers actually use the product. For example, this ad for Cover Girl makeup (www.covergirl.com) features the actress Queen Latifah. Because the implication is that Cover Girl helps her to "look younger," she would have to be an actual user of the product.

Nutritional Labeling and Education Act (NLEA) A 1994 congressional law setting stringent legal definitions for terms such as *fresh, light, low fat,* and *reduced calorie;* setting standard serving sizes; and requiring labels to show food value for one serving alongside the total recommended daily value as established by the National Research Council.

Labels on therapeutic devices must give clear instructions for use. The FDA can require warning statements on packages of hazardous products. It regulates "cents off" and other promotions on package labels and has jurisdiction over the use of words such as "giant" or "family" to describe package sizes.

To provide consumers with more complete information, the U.S. Food and Drug Administration regulates the content of pharmaceutical ads. It used to require that advertisers include all the information from the package insert in their TV ads. This necessitated lengthy commercials with minuscule copy. In 1997, the rule was changed, allowing pharmaceutical companies to advertise on TV and radio as long as they mentioned any important side effects and directed consumers to other sources for further information, such as their magazine ads or their Web site. Notice how this magazine ad for Animal Health's Revolution (www.revolutionpet.com) complies with the FDA's disclosure requirements.

When consumer-oriented drug ads became common in the mid-1980s, the FDA ruled that any ad for a brand-name drug must include all the information from the package insert.[63] That meant advertisers had to run lengthy commercials or use minuscule type in print ads. In 1997, the FDA changed that rule, allowing pharmaceutical companies to advertise their drugs on broadcast media as long as they mentioned any important possible side effects and directed people to their print ads, their Internet sites, or consumers' own doctors for more information.[64] With that ruling, prescription drug advertising soared on television and radio, tripling over the next five years. It's estimated that in 2011, pharmaceutical companies spent some $4 billion in direct-to-consumer advertising.[65] Although the FDA is responsible for ensuring that these ads are fair and accurate, the agency is so understaffed that many questionable and, unfortunately, deceptive or misleading ads do get through. However, anytime the FDA has sent a letter to marketers citing false advertising claims, the companies have stopped running the misleading ads.[66]

The **Nutritional Labeling and Education Act (NLEA)**, which went into effect in 1994, gave the FDA additional muscle

revolution
(selamectin)

Topical Parasiticide For Dogs and Cats

CAUTION:
U.S. Federal law restricts this drug to use by or on the order of a licensed veterinarian.

INDICATIONS:
Revolution kills adult fleas and prevents flea eggs from hatching for one month and is indicated for the prevention and control of flea infestations (*Ctenocephalides felis*), prevention of heartworm disease caused by *Dirofilaria immitis*, and the treatment and control of ear mite (*Otodectes cynotis*) infestations in dogs and cats. Revolution also is indicated for the treatment and control of sarcoptic mange (*Sarcoptes scabiei*) and for the control of tick *(Dermacentor variabilis)* infestations in dogs, and the treatment of intestinal hookworm (*Ancylostoma tubaeforme*) and roundworm (*Toxocara cati*) infections in cats. Revolution is recommended for use in dogs and cats six weeks of age and older.

WARNINGS:
Not for human use. Keep out of the reach of children.
May be irritating to skin and eyes. Wash hands after use and wash off any product in contact with the skin immediately with soap and water. If contact with eyes occurs, then flush eyes copiously with water. In case of ingestion by a human, contact a physician immediately. The material safety data sheet (MSDS) provides more detailed occupational safety information. For a copy of the MSDS or to report adverse reactions attributable to exposure to this product, call 1-800-366-5288.

Flammable—Keep away from heat, sparks, open flames or other sources of ignition.

PRECAUTIONS:
Use with caution in sick, debilitated or underweight animals (see SAFETY).
Prior to administration of Revolution, dogs should be tested for existing heartworm infections. At the discretion of the veterinarian, infected dogs should be treated to remove adult heartworms. Revolution is not effective against adult *D. immitis* and, while the number of circulating microfilariae may decrease following treatment, Revolution is not effective for microfilariae clearance.

Hypersensitivity reactions have not been observed in dogs with patent heartworm infections administered three times the recommended dose of Revolution. Higher doses were not tested.

ADVERSE REACTIONS:
Following treatment with Revolution, transient localized alopecia with or without inflammation at or near the site of application was observed in approximately 1% of 691 treated cats. Other signs observed rarely (≤0.5% of 1743 treated cats and dogs) included vomiting, loose stool or diarrhea with or without blood, anorexia, lethargy, salivation, tachypnea, and muscle tremors.

DOSAGE:
The recommended minimum dose is 2.7 mg selamectin per pound (6 mg/kg) of body weight.

Administer the entire contents of a single dose tube of Revolution topically in accordance with label directions. (See ADMINISTRATION for the recommended treatment intervals.)

For cats over 15 lbs use the appropriate combination of tubes.

For dogs over 85 lbs use the appropriate combination of tubes.
Recommended for use in animals 6 weeks of age and older.

ADMINISTRATION:
Firmly depress the cap to puncture the seal on the Revolution tube; then remove the cap to administer the product.

Part the hair on the back of the animal at the base of the neck in front of the shoulder blades until the skin is visible. Place the tip of the tube on the skin and squeeze the tube to empty its entire contents directly onto the skin in one spot. Do not massage the product into the skin. Due to alcohol content, do not apply to broken skin. Avoid contact between the product and fingers. Do not apply when the hair coat is wet. Bathing or shampooing the animal 2 or more hours after treatment will not reduce the effectiveness of Revolution. Stiff hair, clumping of hair, hair discoloration, or a slight powdery residue may be observed at the treatment site in some animals. These effects are temporary and do not affect the safety or effectiveness of the product. Discard empty tubes in your ordinary household refuse.

Flea Control in Dogs and Cats
For the prevention and control of flea infestations, Revolution should be administered at monthly intervals throughout the flea season, starting one month before fleas become active. In controlled laboratory studies >98% of fleas were killed within 36 hours. Results of clinical field studies using Revolution monthly demonstrated >90% control of flea infestations within 30 days of the first dose. Dogs and cats treated with Revolution, including those with pre-existing flea allergy dermatitis, showed improvement in clinical signs associated with fleas as a direct result of eliminating the fleas from the animals and their environment.

If the dog or cat is already infested with fleas when the first dose of Revolution is administered, adult fleas on the animal are killed and no viable fleas hatch from eggs after the first administration. However, an environmental infestation of fleas may persist for a short time after beginning treatment with Revolution because of the emergence of adult fleas from pupae.

Heartworm Prevention in Dogs and Cats
For the prevention of heartworm disease, Revolution must be administered on a monthly basis. Revolution may be administered year-round or at least within one month after the animal's first exposure to mosquitoes and monthly thereafter until the end of the mosquito season. The final dose must be given within one month after the last exposure to mosquitoes. If a dose is missed and a monthly interval between dosing is exceeded then immediate administration of Revolution and resumption of monthly dosing will minimize the opportunity for the development of adult heartworms. When replacing another heartworm preventive product in a heartworm disease prevention program, the first dose of Revolution must be given within a month of the last dose of the former medication.

At the discretion of the veterinarian, cats ≥6 months of age may be tested to determine the presence of existing heartworm infections before beginning treatment with Revolution. Cats already infected with adult heartworms can safely be given Revolution monthly to prevent further infections.

Ear Mite Treatment in Dogs and Cats
For the treatment of ear mite (*O. cynotis*) infestations in dogs and cats, Revolution should be administered once as a single topical dose. A second monthly dose may be required in some dogs. Monthly use of Revolution will control any subsequent ear mite infestations. In the clinical field trials ears were not cleaned, and many animals still had debris in their ears after the second dose. Cleansing of the infested ears is recommended to remove the debris.

Sarcoptic Mange Treatment in Dogs
For the treatment of sarcoptic mange (*S. scabiei*) in dogs, Revolution should be administered once as a single topical dose. A second monthly dose may be required in some dogs. Monthly use of Revolution will control any subsequent sarcoptic mange mite infestations. Because of the difficulty in finding sarcoptic mange mites on skin scrapings, effectiveness assessments also were based on resolution of clinical signs. Resolution of the pruritus associated with the mite infestations was observed in approximately 50% of the dogs 30 days after the first treatment and in approximately 90% of the dogs 30 days after the second monthly treatment.

Tick Control in Dogs
For the control of tick *(Dermacentor variabilis)* infestations in dogs, Revolution should be administered on a monthly basis. In heavy tick infestations, complete efficacy may not be achieved after the first dose. In these cases, one additional dose may be administered two weeks after the previous dose, with monthly dosing continued thereafter.

Nematode Treatment in Cats
For the treatment of intestinal hookworm (*A. tubaeforme*) and roundworm (*T. cati*) infections, Revolution should be applied once as a single topical dose.

NADA 141-152, Approved by FDA.

Animal Health
Exton, PA 19341, USA
Div. of Pfizer Inc
NY, NY 10017

TAKE TIME

OBSERVE LABEL DIRECTIONS

www.revolutionpet.com

intellectual property Something produced by the mind, such as original works of authorship including literary, dramatic, musical, artistic, and certain other "intellectual" works, which may be legally protected by copyright, patent, or trademark.

patent A grant made by the government that confers upon the creator of an invention the sole right to make, use, and sell that invention for a set period of time.

trademark Any word, name, symbol, device, or any combination thereof adopted and used by manufacturers or merchants to identify their goods and distinguish them from those manufactured or sold by others.

by setting stringent legal definitions for terms such as *fresh, light, low fat,* and *reduced calories.* It also sets standard serving sizes and requires labels to show food value for one serving alongside the total recommended daily value as established by the National Research Council.[67]

The first time the FDA took severe action against a prominent marketer over a labeling dispute, it seized 2,400 cases of Procter & Gamble's Citrus Hill Fresh Choice orange juice. Fresh Choice was made from concentrate, not fresh-squeezed juice as P&G claimed.[68] Due to increased FDA scrutiny, many advertisers are now more cautious about their health and nutritional claims.

The Federal Communications Commission (FCC)

The seven-member *Federal Communications Commission (FCC)* is an independent federal agency with jurisdiction over the radio, television, telephone, satellite and cable TV industries, and the Internet. Its control over broadcast advertising stems from its authority to license broadcasters (or take away their licenses). The FCC can restrict both the products advertised and the content of ads. For example, the FCC required stations to run commercials about the harmful effects of smoking even before Congress banned cigarette advertising on TV and radio.

In the 1980s, the FCC decided there were enough buyers and sellers that marketplace forces could adequately control broadcast media, so it deregulated both radio and TV stations. The FCC no longer limits commercial time or requires stations to maintain detailed program and commercial logs.

The 1992 Cable Television Consumer Protection and Competition Act gave the FCC additional teeth. It placed new controls on the cable TV industry to encourage a more service-oriented attitude and to improve the balance between rates and escalating ad revenues.[69] The FCC can set subscriber rates for cable TV, so subscription revenues should slow while advertising rates rise.

The FCC's visibility as an arbiter of broadcast decency increased immediately following Janet Jackson's "wardrobe malfunction," which exposed the singer's breast during the 2004 Super Bowl halftime show. A record 500,000 complaints were registered with the FCC. According to FCC rules, over-the-air television channels cannot air "obscene" material at any time. The FCC defines obscene material as describing sexual conduct "in a patently offensive way" and lacking "serious literary, artistic, political or scientific value." The FCC later levied a fine on CBS of $550,000 for the Super Bowl incident. The FCC's fine was voided by the United States Court of Appeals in 2008, a decision that was upheld in 2011. In 2012, the Supreme Court refused to consider an appeal by the FCC.

But Chief Justice John G. Roberts Jr. warned that because of changes in the FCC's rules since then, any similar offense could be punished. "It is now clear that the brevity of an indecent broadcast—be it word or image—cannot immunize it from FCC censure," he wrote in a two-page opinion that put to rest the CBS case, clearing the network of a $550,000 fine.[70]

The Patent and Trademark Office and the Library of Congress

A basic role of government is to promote and protect the economic well-being *(self-interest)* of its citizens. One way the U.S. government does this is by registering and protecting its citizens' **intellectual property**.[71]

"A trademark such as Coca-Cola, AT&T, or Levi's is a valuable asset."

Through the issuance of **patents**, the government provides incentives to invent, invest in, and disclose new technology worldwide. By registering trademarks and copyrights, the government helps businesses protect their investments, promote their goods and services, and safeguard consumers against confusion and deception in the marketplace *(complete information).*

A trademark such as Coca-Cola, AT&T, or Levi's is a valuable asset. According to the Lanham Trademark Act (1947), a **trademark** is "any word, name, symbol, or device or any combination thereof adopted and used by a manufacturer or

copyright An exclusive right granted by the Copyright Act to authors and artists to protect their original work from being plagiarized, sold, or used by another without their express consent.

Coca-Cola's trademark varies from country to country. But the overall look is retained through use of similar letterforms and style, even with different alphabets.

merchant to identify his goods and distinguish them from those manufactured or sold by others."

Patents and trademarks are registered with and protected by the U.S. Patent and Trademark Office. Ownership of a trademark may be designated in advertising or on a label, package, or letterhead by the word *Registered,* the symbol®, or the symbol™. If someone persists in using a trademark owned by another or one confusingly similar to another's mark, the trademark owner can ask for a court order and sue for trademark infringement.

The Library of Congress protects all copyrighted material, including advertising, in the United States. A **copyright** is a form of protection provided to the authors of "original works of authorship," including literary, dramatic, musical, artistic, and certain other "intellectual works."[72] A copyright issued to an individual grants the exclusive right to print, publish, or reproduce the protected material for the life of the copyright owner plus 70 years. If it is the work of corporate authorship, the term is the shorter of 95 years from publication or 120 years from creation.

STATE AND LOCAL REGULATION

Advertisers are also subject to state or local laws. Since the U.S. federal deregulation trend of the 1980s, state and local governments have taken a far more active role.

State legislation governing advertising is often based on the truth-in-advertising model statute developed in 1911 by *Printer's Ink,* for many years the major trade publication of the industry. The statute holds that any maker of an ad found to contain "untrue, deceptive, or misleading" material is guilty of a misdemeanor. Today most states enforce laws patterned after this statute.

All states also have "little FTC acts," consumer protection laws that govern unfair and deceptive business practices. States can investigate and prosecute cases, and individual consumers can bring civil suits against businesses. To increase their clout, some states team up on legal actions—for example, to challenge deceptive ad promotions in the airline, rental car, and food-making industries. As one observer pointed out, "Many of the food manufacturers could litigate some of the smaller states into the ground, but they might not be willing to fight it out against 10 states simultaneously."[73]

Different states have different regulations governing what can be advertised. Some states prohibit advertising for certain types of wine and liquor, and most states restrict the use of state flags in advertising.

This can present a major problem to national marketers. And in some cases, it actually hurts consumers. For example, many companies trying to conduct environmentally responsible marketing programs feel stymied by the different state laws governing packaging materials and recycling.[74]

Many cities and counties also have consumer protection agencies to enforce laws regulating local advertising practices. The chief function of these agencies is to protect local consumers against unfair and misleading practices by area merchants.

In one year alone, the Orange County, California, district attorney's office received more than 1,200 complaint letters from consumers about everything from dishonest mechanics and phony sale ads to a taco stand that skimped on the beef in its "macho" burrito.[75] In a case against Los Angeles–based Closet Factory, Inc., the DA collected $40,000 in fines to settle a false advertising suit. The company was charged with running newspaper ads that gave consumers a false sense of urgency regarding "sales" that actually never end. This type of advertising, known as a *continuous sale,* violates the state's Business and Professions Code. Since the sale is never really over, the sale price becomes the regular price.[76]

check yourself ✓

1. Describe an action that has been taken by a government agency to restrict the activities of advertisers.
2. What is an example of an Internet-related privacy concern?

LO2-5 Discuss the activities of nongovernment organizations in fighting fraudulent and deceptive advertising.

NONGOVERNMENT REGULATION

Nongovernment organizations also issue advertising guidelines (see Exhibit 2–4). In fact, advertisers face considerable regulation by business-monitoring organizations, related trade associations, the media, consumer groups, and advertising agencies themselves.

The Better Business Bureau (BBB)

The largest of the U.S. business-monitoring organizations is the *Better Business Bureau (BBB),* established in 1916. Funded by dues from more than 100,000 member companies, it operates primarily at the local level to protect consumers against fraudulent and deceptive advertising and sales practices. When local bureaus contact violators and ask them to revise their advertising, most comply.

The BBB's files on violators are open to the public. Records of violators who do not comply are sent to appropriate government agencies for further action. The BBB often works with local law enforcement agencies to prosecute advertisers guilty of fraud and misrepresentation. Each year, the BBB investigates thousands of ads for possible violations of truth and accuracy.

The Advertising Self-Regulatory Council (ASRC)

The National Advertising Review Council (NARC), established in 1971, changed its name to the Advertising Self-Regulatory Council (ASRC) in 2012. The objective of the name change was to send a message that it intends to keep government regulators at a distance. NARC's primary purpose is to promote and enforce standards of truth, accuracy, taste, morality, and social responsibility in advertising. The ASRC is one of the most comprehensive and effective mechanisms for regulating

▼**EXHIBIT 2–4** American Association of Advertising Agencies policy statement and guidelines for comparative advertising.

The Board of Directors of the American Association of Advertising Agencies recognizes that when used truthfully and fairly, comparative advertising provides the consumer with needed and useful information.

However, extreme caution should be exercised. The use of comparative advertising, by its very nature, can distort facts and, by implication, convey to the consumer information that misrepresents the truth.

Therefore, the Board believes that comparative advertising should follow certain guidelines:

1. The intent and connotation of the ad should be to inform and never to discredit or unfairly attack competitors, competing products, or services.
2. When a competitive product is named, it should be one that exists in the marketplace as significant competition.
3. The competition should be fairly and properly identified but never in a manner or tone of voice that degrades the competitive product or service.
4. The advertising should compare related or similar properties or ingredients of the product, dimension to dimension, feature to feature.
5. The identification should be for honest comparison purposes and not simply to upgrade by association.
6. If a competitive test is conducted, it should be done by an objective testing source, preferably an independent one, so that there will be no doubt as to the veracity of the test.
7. In all cases the test should be supportive of all claims made in the advertising that are based on the test.
8. The advertising should never use partial results or stress insignificant differences to cause the consumer to draw an improper conclusion.
9. The property being compared should be significant in terms of value or usefulness of the product to the consumer.
10. Comparatives delivered through the use of testimonials should not imply that the testimonial is more than one individual's thought unless that individual represents a sample of the majority viewpoint.

Source:

broadcast standards department
A department at a TV network that reviews all programs and commercials to be broadcast to see that they meet all applicable standards.

consumerism
Social action designed to dramatize the rights of the buying public.

consumer advocate
An individual or group that actively works to protect consumer rights, often by investigating advertising complaints received from the public and those that grow out of their own research.

American advertising. A U.S. district court judge noted in a 1985 case that its "speed, informality, and modest cost," as well as its expertise, give the ASRC special advantages over the court system in resolving advertising disputes.[77]

The ASRC has two operating arms: the *National Advertising Division (NAD)* of the Council of Better Business Bureaus and the *National Advertising Review Board (NARB).* The NAD monitors advertising practices and reviews complaints about advertising from consumers and consumer groups, brand competitors, local Better Business Bureaus, trade associations, and others. The appeals board for NAD decisions is the NARB, which consists of a chairperson and 70 volunteer members (40 national advertisers, 20 agency representatives, and 10 laypeople).

Nothing motivates middle managers like the need to avoid attention.

The case of the leather flight jacket shows how well the NAD process works. Neil Cooper LLC is a company that manufactures a leather jacket. In its print ads it claims that its A-2 leather flight jackets are the "official battle gear of U.S. Air Force Pilots." Avirex, Ltd., a competing company, complained to the NAD since the A-2 jacket currently being purchased by the Department of Defense and worn by U.S. pilots is the jacket manufactured by them, not Neil Cooper. Neil Cooper explained that, while it was not the current supplier, many pilots continued to buy from Neil Cooper directly because they preferred that product. Notwithstanding, the NAD sided with Avirex and recommended that Neil Cooper qualify its claims to make it clear that it is selling a reproduction of an authentic A-2 flight jacket rather than the current official jacket of the U.S. Air Force. Neil Cooper agreed.[78]

Regulation by the Media

Almost all media companies review ads and reject material they regard as objectionable, even if it isn't deceptive.

Television Of all media, the TV networks conduct the strictest review. Advertisers must submit all commercials intended for a network or affiliated station to its **broadcast standards department**. Many commercials (in script or storyboard form) are returned with suggestions for changes or greater substantiation. Some ads are rejected outright if they violate network policies.

The major U.S. broadcast networks base their policies on the original National Association of Broadcasters Television Code. But network policies vary enough that it's difficult to prepare universally acceptable commercials. Cable networks and local stations tend to be much less stringent.

Radio The U.S. radio networks, unlike TV networks, supply only a small percentage of their affiliates' programming, so they have little or no say in what their affiliates advertise. A radio station is also less likely to return a script or tape for changes. Some stations, such as KLBJ in Austin, Texas, look mainly at whether the advertising is illegal, unethical, or immoral.[79] They don't want spots to offend listeners or detract from the rest of the programming.

Every radio station typically has its own unwritten guidelines. KDWB, a Minneapolis–St. Paul station with a large teenage audience, turned down a psychic who wanted to buy advertising time but did allow condom and other contraceptive ads.[80] KSDO in San Diego, a station with a business and information format, won't air commercials for X-rated movies or topless bars.[81]

SiriusXM, or satellite radio, tends to use standards related to its individual channels. Listeners are likely to hear very different spots on the Catholic Channel than they will on Howard Stern's program.

Magazines National magazines monitor all advertising, especially by new advertisers and for new products. Newer publications eager to sell space may not be so vigilant, but established magazines, such as *Time* and *National Geographic,* are highly scrupulous. Many magazines will not accept advertising for certain types of products. The *New Yorker* won't run discount retail store advertising or ads for feminine hygiene or

self-medication products. *Reader's Digest* won't accept tobacco ads.

Some magazines test every product before accepting the advertising. *Good Housekeeping* rejects ads if its tests don't substantiate the advertiser's claims. Products that pass are allowed to feature the Good Housekeeping "Seal of Approval," and the magazine will stand behind those products. The magazine promises a refund or product replacement for defective products within two years of purchase.

Newspapers Newspapers also monitor and review advertising. Larger newspapers have clearance staffs who read every ad submitted; most smaller newspapers rely on the advertising manager, sales personnel, or proofreaders.

The advertising policies set forth in *Newspaper Rates & Data* specify, "No objectionable medical, personal, matrimonial, clairvoyant, or palmistry advertising accepted; no stock promotion or financial advertising, other than those securities of known value." Another rule prohibits ads that might easily be mistaken for regular reading material unless they feature the word *advertisement.*

One problem advertisers face is that newspapers' codes are far from uniform. Handgun ads may be prohibited by one newspaper, accepted by another if the guns are antique, and permitted by a third as long as the guns aren't automatic.

To help consumers make informed decisions, Good Housekeeping *magazine tests the products in its ads and provides a seal of approval to those advertisers, such as Heat & Glo®, who substantiate their claims. This gives the consumer a more authoritative voice to listen to when trying to decide on purchases.*

Regulation by Consumer Groups

Starting in the 1960s, the consumer movement became increasingly active in fighting fraudulent and deceptive advertising. Consumers demanded that products perform as advertised and that more product information be provided for people to compare and make better buying decisions. The consumer movement gave rise to **consumerism,** social action to dramatize the rights of the buying public.

Consumer advocate groups investigate advertising complaints received from the public and those that grow out of their own research. If a complaint is warranted, they ask the advertiser to halt the objectionable ad or practice. If the advertiser does not comply, they release publicity or criticism about the offense to the media and submit complaints with substantiating evidence to appropriate government agencies for further action. In some instances, they file a lawsuit to obtain a cease-and-desist order, a fine, or other penalty against the violator.

Today, with so many special-interest advocacy groups, even the most responsible advertisers feel challenged. To attract attention, advertising must be creative and stand out from competing noise. Yet advertisers fear attention from activists. Calvin Klein ads were attacked by the Boycott Anorexic Marketing group. A Nike ad starring Porky Pig was protested by the National Stuttering Project in San Francisco. An animated public service spot from Aetna Insurance drew complaints from a witches' rights group.[82]

When the protests start, the ads usually get pulled. As Shelly Garcia noted in *Adweek,* "The way things are these days, nothing motivates middle managers like the need to avoid attention.[83]

Self-Regulation by Advertisers and Ad Agencies

Advertisers also regulate themselves. They have to. In today's competitive marketplace, consumer confidence is essential. Most large advertisers gather strong data to substantiate their claims. They maintain careful systems of advertising review to ensure that ads meet both their own standards and industry, media, and legal requirements.

Ad agencies can be held legally liable for fraudulent or misleading advertising claims. For this reason, most major advertising agencies have an in-house legal counsel and regularly submit their ads for review. If any aspect of the advertising is challenged, the agency asks its client to review the advertising and either confirm claims as truthful or replace unverified material.

Several associations monitor industrywide advertising practices. The *American Association of Advertising Agencies (AAAA),* an association of the largest advertising agencies throughout the United States, controls agency practices by denying membership to any agency judged unethical. The *American Advertising Federation (AAF)* helped establish the FTC, and its early vigilance committees were the forerunners of the Better Business Bureau. The *AAF Advertising Principles of American Business,* adopted in 1984, define standards for truthful and responsible advertising (see Exhibit 2–5). The *Association of National Advertisers (ANA)* comprises 370 major manufacturing and service companies that are clients of member agencies of the AAAA. These companies pledge to uphold the ANA code of advertising ethics.

EXHIBIT 2-5 Advertising Principles of American Business of the American Advertising Federation (AAF).

1. *Truth.* Advertising shall tell the truth, and shall reveal significant facts, the omission of which would mislead the public.
2. *Substantiation.* Advertising claims shall be substantiated by evidence in possession of the advertiser and the advertising agency prior to making such claims.
3. *Comparisons.* Advertising shall refrain from making false, misleading, or unsubstantiated statements or claims about a competitor or his products or services.
4. *Bait advertising.* Advertising shall not offer products or services for sale unless such offer constitutes a bona fide effort to sell the advertised products or services and is not a device to switch consumers to other goods or services, usually higher priced.
5. *Guarantees and warranties.* Advertising of guarantees and warranties shall be explicit, with sufficient information to apprise consumers of their principal terms and limitations or, when space or time restrictions preclude such disclosures, the advertisement shall clearly reveal where the full text of the guarantee or warranty can be examined before purchase.
6. *Price claims.* Advertising shall avoid price claims that are false or misleading, or savings claims that do not offer provable savings.
7. *Testimonials.* Advertising containing testimonials shall be limited to those of competent witnesses who are reflecting a real and honest opinion or experience.
8. *Taste and decency.* Advertising shall be free of statements, illustrations, or implications that are offensive to good taste or public decency.

Source: Reprinted with permission of American Advertising Federation.

GOVERNMENT RESTRAINTS ON INTERNATIONAL ADVERTISERS

Now that advertising has become global, many campaigns use similar themes and even the same ads across frontiers. But foreign governments often regulate advertising considerably more than the United States. And while Europe has moved toward uniformity in marketing activities, the laws governing advertising remain largely national.[84] So advertisers need to keep up with the changing legal environments of the countries in which they advertise.

Some governments not only regulate what ads say, show, or do; they often impose severe restrictions or outright bans on advertising specific products. The Swedes ban advertising to children on television. The Greeks ban toy advertising before 10:00 p.m. Throughout Europe, broadcast advertising for tobacco products is prohibited, and liquor ads are sharply restricted, especially in France.[85]

Many countries prohibit puffery. In Germany, for example, advertisers may use only scientifically provable superlatives. McCann Erickson once had to retranslate the old Coca-Cola slogan, "Refreshes you best," because it implied a leadership position that was unprovable. The agency substituted "Refreshes you right" in Germany.

Many European countries also ban coupons, premiums, free tie-in offers, and the like. Companies may advertise price cuts only during "official sales periods," and advertisers often need government approval before publishing a sale ad. Across Europe, advertising on television must be clearly recognizable and kept separate from other programming. Paid *product placements* in programs, therefore, are typically prohibited.[86] In international advertising, the only way to navigate the morass of potential legal problems is to retain lawyers who specialize in advertising law.

check yourself ✓

1. Why do advertisers and ad agencies work so diligently to regulate their own activities?

THE ETHICAL AND LEGAL ASPECTS OF ADVERTISING IN PERSPECTIVE

Unquestionably, advertising offers considerable benefits to marketers and consumers alike. However, there's also no disputing that advertising has been and still is too often misused. As *Adweek* editor Andrew Jaffe says, the industry should do all it can to "raise its standards and try to drive out that which is misleading, untruthful, or downright tasteless and irresponsible." Otherwise, he warns, the pressure to regulate even more will become overwhelming.[87]

Advertising apologists point out that of all the advertising reviewed by the Federal Trade Commission in a typical year, 97 percent is found to be satisfactory.[88] In the end, advertisers and consumers need to work together to ensure that advertising is used intelligently, ethically, and responsibly for the benefit of all. ■

learn about, practice, and apply the economic, social, and regulatory aspects of advertising!

M: Advertising was developed for students who want information packaged in a concise, easy-to-read, yet interesting format.

Check out the book's website to:

- Find out the ways that our privacy rights are perhaps being violated by marketers. (Review Questions)
- Examine the socially accepted line between "erotic suggestiveness" and "explicit sexuality" in advertising. (Exploring Advertising)
- Determine if advertising can manipulate you into buying something you didn't previously want or need. (Exploring Advertising)

While you are there, check out the professional resource links, review the PowerPoint presentation, and test your knowledge with the Multiple Choice Quiz. Additionally, *Connect® Marketing* is available for M: Advertising.

www.mhhe.com/ArensM2e

the business of advertising

chapter three

This chapter introduces the people and groups that sponsor, create, produce, and transmit advertisements. Advertising people may serve in a variety of roles. The chapter discusses the basic tasks of both the client and the advertising agency, the roles of suppliers and the media, the ways agencies acquire clients and are compensated, and the overall relationship between the agency and the client.

Best-selling author Thomas Friedman once wrote that "No two countries that both had McDonald's had fought a war against each other since each got its McDonald's." Friedman's point was that economic development and international trade reduce conflict. Still, who can rule out the possibility that international harmony grows in direct proportion to the availability of Happy Meals?

The foods you can get at McDonald's are the same as those sold in thousands of competing restaurants and chains. Its menu item ingredients—ground beef, French fries, and more recently, salads and yogurt—are widely available. And indeed, there are plenty of competitors out there. But none are so successful. What is McDonald's secret?

continued on p. 58

LEARNING OBJECTIVES

After studying this chapter, you will be able to:

LO3-1 List the various groups in the advertising business and explain their relationships.

LO3-2 Discuss the differences between local, national, and transnational advertisers.

LO3-3 Explain how advertisers organize themselves to manage their advertising both here and abroad.

LO3-4 Define the main types of advertising agencies.

LO3-5 Describe the range of tasks people perform in an ad agency and an in-house advertising department.

LO3-6 Relate how agencies get new clients and how they make money.

continued from p. 57

One could start with the company's value proposition: a tasty, inexpensive meal served quickly.

But it's hard to avoid the conclusion that advertising is part of the equation as well. Throughout its history, McDonald's has spent billions on advertising, both in the United States and around the world. And that investment has paid dividends by helping make the McDonald's brand one of the most valuable in the world.

The slogans are part of advertising lore. "You deserve a break today." "Two all beef patties, special sauce, lettuce, cheese, pickles, onions, on a sesame seed bun." "Have you had your break today?" The ads made the Golden Arches a part of the world's shared culture.

Let's look at how McDonald's uses integrated marketing communications (IMC), including advertising, to maintain its status as the biggest prepared-food seller in the world.

McDonald's has franchises in over 100 countries. But the essence of the McDonald's brand always shines through. Customers can always expect to encounter the Arches, American fast-food items, and fast, friendly service. Employees dress in colorful, clean uniforms.

The unified brand message is reinforced with advertising. McDonald's campaign runs globally, so customers everywhere hear the familiar "ba da ba ba ba," followed by "i'm lovin' it" (naturally translated into the native language).

Another secret to the company's success is its willingness to customize its offerings to suit local preferences. So, for example, McDonald's does not serve pork in predominantly Muslim countries (and it refers to hamburgers as "beefburgers"). In countries where meat is not a big part of the regular diet (such as India), the company offers "veggie burgers." Even in the United States, menu items and food preparation adapt to local preferences.

This willingness to suit local tastes while remaining true to the brand is also reflected in the company's advertising. McDonald's allocates a portion of its advertising budget to co-operative efforts with franchises. Franchise groups make their own decisions about ad agencies and campaign themes.

Even at the national level, McDonald's often runs several campaigns simultaneously. For example, in addition to the "i'm lovin' it" ads, the company runs ads promoting specific menu items, such as its premium salad offerings. Other spots target carefully selected markets, such as Hispanics, African Americans, working moms, or kids.

The strength of the McDonald's brand has propelled it to increased sales and profits through good times and bad. While the U.S. economy was dealing with a crippling recession from 2008 to 2012, McDonald's worldwide sales increased from $23 billion to nearly $28 billion.

Surprising? Not really. In tough times people want value, and McDonald's has shown time and again that a great brand and great advertising are an unbeatable combination. ■

advertisers Companies that sponsor advertising for themselves and their products.

advertising agencies Independent organizations of creative people and businesspeople that specialize in developing and preparing advertising plans, advertisements, and other promotional tools for advertisers. The agencies also arrange for or contract for purchases of space and time in various media.

suppliers People and organizations that assist both advertisers and agencies in the preparation of advertising materials, such as photography, illustration, printing, and production.

media A plural form of *medium,* referring to communications vehicles paid to present an advertisement to their target audience. Most often used to refer to radio and television networks, stations that have new reporters, and publications that carry news and advertising.

LO3-1 List the various groups in the advertising business and explain their relationships.

THE ADVERTISING INDUSTRY

The range of work performed by advertising people goes far beyond what we see daily on TV. Moreover, many people and organizations besides those usually thought of as advertising folks are involved in advertising and IMC. That's because every successful company needs to communicate with customers.

The Organizations in Advertising

The advertising business has has four distinct groups. The two main ones are the *advertisers* and the *agencies.* The **advertisers** (or *clients*) are companies—like Honda, McDonald's, or the local shoe store—that pay to advertise themselves and their products. Advertisers range in size from small independent businesses to huge multinational firms, and in type from service organizations to industrial manufacturers to local charities. The second group, **advertising agencies**, consists of specialists who help advertisers plan, create, and prepare IMC campaigns.

A third group, **suppliers**, includes the photographers, illustrators, printers, digital service bureaus, video production houses, Web developers, and others who assist advertisers and agencies in preparing advertising materials. Suppliers also include consultants, research firms, and professional services. The fourth group, the **media**, sells time (on radio and TV) and space (in print, outdoor) or both (digital media) for delivering the advertiser's message to the target audience.

The People in Advertising

When people think of advertising they imagine the copywriters and art directors who work for ad agencies. But most people in advertising are actually employed by advertisers rather than by agencies. Companies usually have an advertising department, even if it's just one person.

In addition, many other people work for the suppliers and the media. They're in advertising, too. The fact is, advertising is a very broad field that employs a wide variety of people.

In this chapter, we'll see what all these people do at the various places where they work. In the process, we'll get a good understanding of how the advertising industry operates both in the United States and abroad.

1. What are the four distinct groups the ad business has evolved into?
2. What is the difference between an advertiser and an advertising agency?

THE ADVERTISERS (CLIENTS)

While most companies have some sort of advertising department, its importance depends on the company's size, industry, and advertising budget, as well as on the role of advertising in the company's marketing mix and the involvement of top management.

To get a sense of the diversity of companies that advertise, we'll look first at local advertisers to see how they operate. Then, we'll examine regional and national advertisers.

LO3-2 Discuss the differences between local, national, and transnational advertisers.

Local Advertising

When Ralph Rubio opened his first Mexican restaurant, he offered an unusual specialty: fish tacos. At the time, very few other Mexican eateries offered fish tacos. So Rubio found fish tacos hard to sell, even with his secret batter recipe. The first month's sales at the restaurant averaged only $163 a day.

Rubio started using small newspaper ads with coupons to lure courageous customers. As business picked up, he expanded his advertising to radio and TV, targeting his market with ads on Hispanic stations (whose listeners knew what fish tacos were).

Local advertising is critically important because most consumer sales are made (or lost) locally.

And he went after younger, venturesome customers ages 18 to 34 by advertising at local movie theaters. Business picked up some more. Rubio soon opened another restaurant, and then another.

Many local advertisements are for retail stores that sell a variety of branded merchandise or for specialty businesses. This ad for Rubio's promotes the local advertiser's fresh ingredients.

With each new opening, Rubio distributed direct-mail flyers in the area and took free samples to nearby stores. Working with an artist, he created a cartoon character named Pesky Pescado based on the fish taco. He purchased a 15-foot inflatable Pesky to display at his restaurants. Employee T-shirts sported Pesky's picture, and Rubio sold Pesky T-shirts and sweatshirts to enthusiastic patrons. He also offered bumper stickers and antenna balls to add some fun to his promotions. To further integrate his activities, Rubio took an active part in community affairs, including tie-ins with a blood bank, a literacy program, and fund-raising activities for both a Tijuana medical clinic and a local university's athletic program.

As the popularity of the fish taco grew, so did Rubio's revenues, doubling every year for the first five years. He trademarked the phrase "Rubio's, Home of the Fish Taco," and a local restaurant critic, commenting on things San Diegans couldn't do without, called fish tacos "the food San Diegans would miss the most." Today, Rubio's Fresh Mexican Grill has over 180 restaurants in five states. And they still make great fish tacos.[1]

Almost half of the billions of dollars spent each year on advertising in the United States is devoted to **local advertising** by local businesses targeting customers in their geographic area.

Local advertising is sometimes called *retail advertising* because so much is placed by retail stores. But retail advertising isn't always local; Sears and JCPenney advertise nationally. And many businesses besides retail stores use local advertising: banks, movie theaters, auto mechanics, plumbers, radio and TV stations, local politicians, and McDonald's franchises, to name a few.

Local advertising is critically important because most consumer sales are made (or lost) locally. McDonald's may spend billions advertising worldwide, but if it doesn't make a strong effort locally, the dollars may be

wasted. When it comes to making the sale and dealing with customers, local advertising is where the action is—where relationships often start and truly develop.

Types of Local Advertisers

There are four main types of local advertisers.

- Dealers or local franchisees of national companies (Honda, McDonald's, H&R Block).
- Stores that sell a variety of branded merchandise (convenience, grocery, and department stores).
- Specialty businesses and services (banks, restaurants, music stores, remodeling contractors, florists, hair salons, attorneys, accountants).
- Governmental and nonprofit organizations (municipalities, utility companies, charities, arts organizations, political candidates).

A small, local business—say, a hardware, clothing, or electronics store—may have just one person in charge of advertising. That person, the **advertising manager**, performs all the administrative, planning, budgeting, and coordinating functions. He or she may design ads, write copy, and select media. A manager with some digital skills may even produce the ads on a computer.

Chain stores often maintain an advertising department to handle production, media placement, and marketing support services. A typical small advertiser structure is shown in Exhibit 3–1.

EXHIBIT 3-1 Typical department structure for small advertisers with high volumes of work, such as grocery store chains.

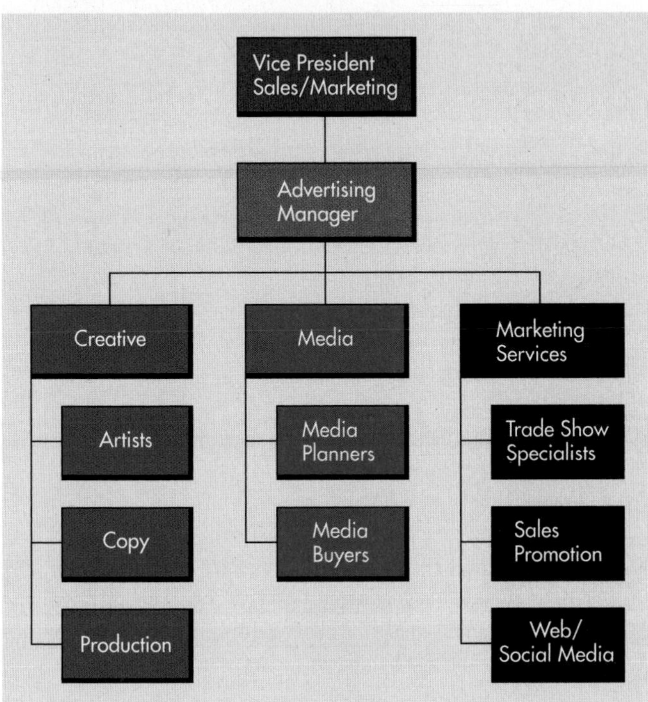

Types of Local Advertising

Most local ads are product, institutional, or classified advertising. Each serves a different purpose.

Product advertising promotes a specific product or service and stimulates short-term action while building awareness of the business. To stimulate sales of merchandise or increase store traffic, local merchants frequently use **sale advertising**, placing items on sale and offering two-for-one specials or other deals.

Institutional advertising attempts to create a favorable long-term perception of the business as a whole, not just of a particular product or service. Many businesses use institutional advertising to promote an idea about the company and build long-term goodwill. It makes the public aware of what the business stands for and attempts to build reputation and image.

Advertisers use **classified advertising** for a variety of reasons: to locate and recruit new employees, offer services (such as those of an employment agency or business opportunity broker), or sell or lease new and used merchandise (such as cars, real estate, and office equipment).

classified advertising Used to locate and recruit new employees, offer services, or sell or lease new and used merchandise.

integrated marketing communications (IMC) The process of building and reinforcing mutually profitable relationships with employees, customers, other stakeholders, and the general public by developing and coordinating a strategic communications program that enables them to make constructive contact with the company/brand through a variety of media.

Local Advertisers and IMC

When Ralph Rubio built his restaurant business, his promotional activities involved a lot more than just running ads. In fact, he did everything he could to build relationships with his customers and to promote word of mouth. That meant using publicity, sales promotion, and direct response as well as media advertising—all integrated with consistently good food, reasonable prices, and excellent service. This combination constitutes **integrated marketing communications (IMC)**—joining together in a consistent manner every element that communicates with customers including the actual delivery of the product or service.

Local Advertisers and Social Media

Social media such as Facebook, Twitter, and LinkedIn have the capacity to dramatically change the strategies of local advertisers. However, a recent survey sponsored by software company Intuit suggests local businesses are not taking full advantage of this opportunity. While nearly half of those surveyed reported they use social media, most spend under $500 a year, and the majority don't employ someone to exclusively manage their social media marketing. The most popular site used by local advertisers is Facebook.[2]

cooperative (co-op) advertising The sharing of advertising costs by the manufacturer and the distributor or retailer. The manufacturer may repay 50 or 100 percent of the dealer's advertising costs or some other amount based on sales.

Joe Morsello, a communications manager at a local business trade association, argues that local advertisers have an advantage over national advertisers in social media because they share a community with their customers. When things happen locally (bad weather, a town festival, a breaking news story), local advertisers can target customers about these shared events. This is exactly what Evie Poitevent did when rain threatened to spoil a jazz festival in New Orleans. The boutique shoe store owner tweeted about her stylish rain boots and quickly sold out her inventory.[3] Ralph Rubio didn't have Facebook or Twitter around to help him when he first launched his small business. But social media are a big part of the way he advertises now (see https://www.facebook.com/Rubios).

Creating Local Advertising The principles for developing good local advertising are really no different than the general principles presented throughout this book. However, given limited budgets and the need to see immediate results, local advertisers have to make every word and every dollar count. To direct and control the creative aspects of their ads and commercials and ensure consistency, local advertisers should adhere to a list of creative do's and don'ts. (See My Ad Campaign 3–B, "Creating Local Advertising," on page 65.)

Local advertisers rely on several sources for creative help, including reps from the local media, local ad agencies, freelancers and consultants, creative boutiques, syndicated art services, and the cooperative advertising programs of wholesalers, manufacturers, and trade associations. McDonald's offers its franchise owners considerable help in designing IMC messages.

Cooperative Advertising Wholesalers and manufacturers often provide local advertisers with ready-made advertising

Understanding Your Client [3–A]

Obtaining a clear understanding of what your client wants from you and what you are prepared to do for your client is essential for a mutually satisfying relationship. From your end it is vital that you be clear about the finished product. In many classes this might be a plans book, which contains research, an advertising plan, a media plan, and even some creative plans. In other classes you might not provide all of that. In either case, make sure your client knows what to expect. If previous classes have done campaign work for other clients, you might wish to show your client that work.

As important as it is that your client understand you, it is equally crucial that you understand your client's expectations. Recognize that some clients may not have a clear set of expectations at first; these may in fact evolve over time. Even in this instance, asking the right questions can get your client thinking about what they hope advertising will do for them.

Below you will find some questions that might prove useful for getting to know your client better. Dr. Debbie Treise, who regularly teaches advertising campaigns at the University of Florida, uses this form. Sending it to the client in advance of a meeting can make your first interaction more useful and informative.

1. Provide a complete description of your product/service:
   What is its current position?
   What is the brand personality as you perceive it?
   Does it need changing?
   Are there seasonal trends for your product?
   Would you be willing to share annual sales trend information?
2. Do you have information on your company to share? Your mission statement? How would you describe the culture of your organization?
3. Do you have a definite target market in mind? Are you targeting consumers, groups, businesses or some combination?
4. Is the market local? Regional? National? International?
5. Would you be willing to share:
   Information on your competition?
   Information on your market?
   Information on market trends? Legal trends?
   Advertising that your competition has used?
   Previous advertising efforts you have undertaken?
6. What is the time period of this campaign? Do you have definite start and stop dates in mind?
7. What is the budget?
8. Do you have any specifications on the budget breakdown in terms of promotion versus advertising? Any other specifications?
9. What are your marketing objectives for this campaign?
10. Please list your advertising/communications objectives for this campaign (that is, to increase knowledge, change attitudes, elicit a specific behavior).
11. Are there media that you would like us to be sure to consider?
12. Are there media that you would prefer we not recommend?
13. Do you have a current, active website? If so, what is its primary purpose? Who accesses it?
14. Do you have any specifications on creative executions? Are you looking to continue current efforts or to come up with something completely different?
15. Are there any current clients/consumers that we could contact?
16. Are there potential clients/customers that we could contact?
17. Who is the individual in your organization we should contact when we have questions? What is the best time to contact this person? How does he or she prefer to be contacted (e-mail, phone, fax)?

In addition to its national campaigns, individual McDonald's franchises also engage in local advertising. One purpose of local ads is to recruit new employees. Another is to announce the opening of new franchises, as in the ads above.

materials and cooperative advertising programs where the costs are shared.

Cooperative (co-op) advertising has two key purposes: to build the manufacturer's brand image and to help distributors, dealers, or retailers increase sales.[4] Every year, national manufacturers give local retailers more than $20 billion for co-op projects. Newspapers, television, and radio are the favored media of co-op spending.[5] Walmart alone benefits from almost $100 million in vendor funding for ads.[6] Exhibit 3–2 demonstrates how important co-op advertising dollars are for certain retail businesses.

On the surface, cooperative advertising seems like a great arrangement for retailers. A manufacturer supplies advertising materials (saving the retailer production costs) and pays a percentage of the media cost. The retailer drops in the store's logo, arranges for the ad to run, and collects the co-op dollars from the manufacturer. The small retail business can stretch its ad budget and associate its business with a nationally advertised product. The retailer receives professionally prepared ads and acquires greater leverage with the local media that carry the co-op ads.

Save on every Hoover® SteamVac™
$20 mail-in rebate on all Hoover® SteamVac™ floorcare $199 and up
Sears

Manufacturers, such as Hoover (www.hoover.com), provide retailers with advertising materials and co-op dollars to encourage dealers like Sears (www.sears.com) to promote the manufacturer's products. If these products are not promoted at the local level, the manufacturer's national advertising efforts will be less effective.

▼EXHIBIT 3–2 The importance of co-op advertising dollars.

Store	Co-op Dollars as a Percentage of Total Ad Budget
Appliance dealers	80%
Food stores	75
Drugstores	70
Department stores	50
Shoe stores	50
Clothing stores	35
Furniture stores	30
Household goods	30
Jewelers	30
Discount stores	20

▼EXHIBIT 3–3 Top 10 advertisers in the United States ranked by total U.S. advertising.

2012 Rank	Company	Total U.S. Ad Spending 2012 (billions)	Percent Change Y2Y	Breakout Spending (millions)					
				Magazine	Newspaper	Outdoor	TV	Radio	Internet
1	Proctor & Gamble	$4,829	−1.50%	$944	$296	$ 5	$1,691	$ 11	$195
2	General Motors	3,067	8.9	137	105	12.6	1189	45.7	166
3	Comcast Corp.	2,989	8.2	119	128	87	923	254	262
4	AT&T	2,910	−7.2	78	107	29	1201	65	112
5	Verizon	2,381	−5.6	27	95	61	983	96	177
6	Ford Motors	2,276	6.3	113	21	2	781	35	113
7	L'Oreal	2,239	5.4	800	41	2	648	0.2	17
8	JPMorgan Chase	2,087	−11.3	53	28	48	249	22	46
9	American Express	2,071	−2.6	33	21	24	143	4.3	124
10	Toyota Motors	2,008	14.8	167	18	22	885	15	138

But as with any marriage, there is give and take.

A retailer may have to sell a lot of merchandise to qualify for significant co-op funds. And sometimes, the retailer and manufacturer have different advertising objectives and different ideas about how the ads should be executed.

The manufacturer often wants total control. It expects co-op ads to tie in with its national advertising promotions. It wants the right product advertised at the right time. Manufacturers prepare guideline pamphlets specifying when and where the ads should appear, what form they should take, and what uses of the name and logo are allowed.

Retailers have their own ideas about which products to feature. They're more concerned with daily volume and with projecting an image of value and variety. An appliance store might prefer to advertise inexpensive TVs even though the manufacturer wants to emphasize its top-of-the-line models.

Manufacturers worry that retailers will place the product in a cluttered, ugly ad or next to inferior products; that the ad will run in inappropriate publications; and that it will not run at the best time. Retailers counter that they know the local market better. In short, manufacturers think they don't have enough control; retailers think manufacturers have too much.

Regional and National Advertisers

Some companies operate in one part of the country—in one or several states—and market exclusively within that region. These are referred to as **regional advertisers**. Typical examples include regional grocery and department store chains, governmental bodies (such as state lotteries), franchise groups (such as the Southern California Honda Dealers), and statewide or multistate banks (Bank of America).

Other companies sell in several regions or throughout the country and are called **national advertisers**. These include consumer packaged-goods manufacturers (such as Procter & Gamble and Johnson & Johnson), national airlines (Delta, JetBlue), media and entertainment companies (Disney, Time Warner), electronics manufacturers (Apple, Hewlett-Packard), and many restaurant chains such as McDonald's. These firms also make up the membership of the *Association of National Advertisers (ANA),* which includes the largest advertisers in the country (see Exhibit 3–3).

How National and Local Advertisers Differ The basic principles of advertising are the same in both local and national advertising. However, local advertisers have special challenges stemming from the day-to-day realities of running a small business (see Exhibit 3–4).

Focus. National companies are concerned about building their *brands,* so their advertising tends to focus on the competitive features of one brand over another. Local merchants or dealers often carry hundreds of different brands, so they focus on attracting customers to a particular *location*—their place of business.

Big companies battle for *market share* against a few competitors, and every share point is worth millions of dollars. Local

▼EXHIBIT 3–4 Differences between local and national advertisers.

	National	Local
Focus	Brand	Location
	Market share	Volume
	Strategies	Tactics
	Markets	Customers
Time	Long-term campaigns	Short-term ads
Resources	$5–$10 million+	Less than $1 million
	Many specialists	A few generalists

regional advertisers Companies that operate in one part of the country and market exclusively to that region.

national advertisers Companies that advertise in several geographic regions or throughout the country.

advertisers compete with many companies, so their focus is on gross sales or *volume:* 60 cars a month, five new insurance policies a week, 55 oil changes a day.

National advertisers plan *strategically* to launch, build, and sustain brands. Local advertisers think *tactically.* Will a new $15,000 sign bring more people into the store? Should we stay open Labor Day? Can we attract more lunchtime customers by reducing our prices or by offering free refills on soft drinks?

> National advertisers plan *strategically*. . . . Local advertisers think *tactically.*

The relationship with the customer may be the greatest difference between national and local advertisers. National advertisers' marketing executives rarely see their customers; instead, they traditionally think of them in terms of segments, niches, or target *markets.* They design their strategies and campaigns to appeal to these large groups. But local advertisers deal with individual *customers* every day. The local advertiser gets regular feedback on the company's advertising, prices, product performance, customer service, store decor, and the new sign out front.

Time orientation. National companies think long term. They develop five-year strategic plans and budget for annual advertising campaigns. Local advertisers worry that this week's ad didn't

Creating Local Advertising [3–B]

Is your client a local business or service? Use these time-tested practices to guide your thinking about how local advertising can help.

- *Stand out from the competition.* Make your ads easily recognizable. Ads with unusual art, layout, and typefaces have higher readership. Make the ads distinctive but keep their appearance consistent.
- *Use a simple layout.* The layout should carry the reader's eye through the message easily and in proper sequence from headline to illustration to explanatory copy to price to store name. Avoid too many typefaces.
- *Use a dominant element.* A large picture or headline ensures quick visibility. Photos of real people and action pictures win more readership, as do photos of local people or places. Color attracts more readers.
- *Stress the benefits.* Present the emotional reason to buy or the tangible performance element customers seek.
- *Make the headline count.* Use a compelling headline to feature the main benefit.
- *Watch your language.* Make your writing style active, lively, and involving. Make the readers feel they already own the product. Avoid negativism and profanity.
- *Let white space work for you.* White space focuses the reader's attention and makes the headline and illustration stand out.
- *Make the copy complete.* Emphasize the benefits most appealing to customers.
- *Make your visual powerful and eye-catching.* Focus on the benefit. The main visual is often more important than the headline. Photos work better than artwork.
- *Specify branded merchandise.* If the item is a known brand, say so.
- *Include related items.* Make two sales instead of one by offering related items along with a featured one.
- *Urge readers to buy now.* Ask for the sale. Stimulate prompt action by using "limited supply" or "this week only."
- *Don't forget the business name and address.* Check every ad to be certain the business name, address, phone number, and hours are included.
- *Don't be too clever.* Many people distrust or misunderstand cleverness.
- *Don't use unusual or difficult words.* Everyone understands simple language. Use it.
- *Don't generalize.* Be specific. Shoppers want all the facts before they buy.
- *Don't make excessive claims.* Advertisers lose customers when they make claims they can't back up.
- *Plan ad size carefully.* Attention usually increases with size.
- *Consider your target customers.* People notice ads more if they are directed at their own gender or age group.
- *Use tie-ins* with local or special news events.

centralized advertising department
A staff of employees, usually located at corporate headquarters, responsible for all the organization's advertising. The department is often structured by product, advertising subfunction, end user, media, or geography.

pull (a term rarely used by national marketers) as well as last week's; a New York advertiser may have months to develop a network TV campaign; the little market on Main Street may have to churn out a new newspaper ad every week.

Resources. Finally, national advertisers have more resources—both money and people. The national advertiser has millions of dollars and an army of *specialists* dedicated to the successful marketing of its brands. The local advertiser may have a small staff of *generalists* or just one person—the owner—to market the business. So the local entrepreneur has to know about every facet of IMC.

check yourself ✓

1. Almost half of advertising dollars are spent on local advertising. Why is local advertising so important?
2. What are the three types of local advertising and what purposes do they serve?

LO3-3 Explain how advertisers organize themselves to manage their advertising.

How Large Companies Manage Their Advertising

In large companies, many people are involved in advertising. Company owners and top corporate executives make key advertising decisions; sales and marketing personnel often assist in the creative process, help choose the ad agency, and evaluate proposed ad programs; artists and writers produce ads, brochures, and other materials; product engineers and designers give input to the creative process and provide information about competitive products; administrators evaluate the cost of ad campaigns and help plan budgets; and clerical staff coordinate various promotional activities, including advertising.

A large company's advertising department may employ many people, led by an advertising manager who reports to a marketing director or marketing services manager. The exact department structure can vary. Most large advertisers tend to use some mix of two basic management structures: *centralized* and *decentralized.*

Centralized organization. Some companies are concerned with cost efficiency and continuity in their communications programs. Thus, many embrace the **centralized advertising department** because it gives the greatest control and offers both efficiency and continuity across divisional boundaries. In centralized departments, an advertising manager typically reports to a marketing vice president. The advertising department may be organized in any of five ways:

- By product or brand.
- By subfunction of advertising (copy, art, digital media, media buying).
- By end user (consumer advertising, trade advertising).

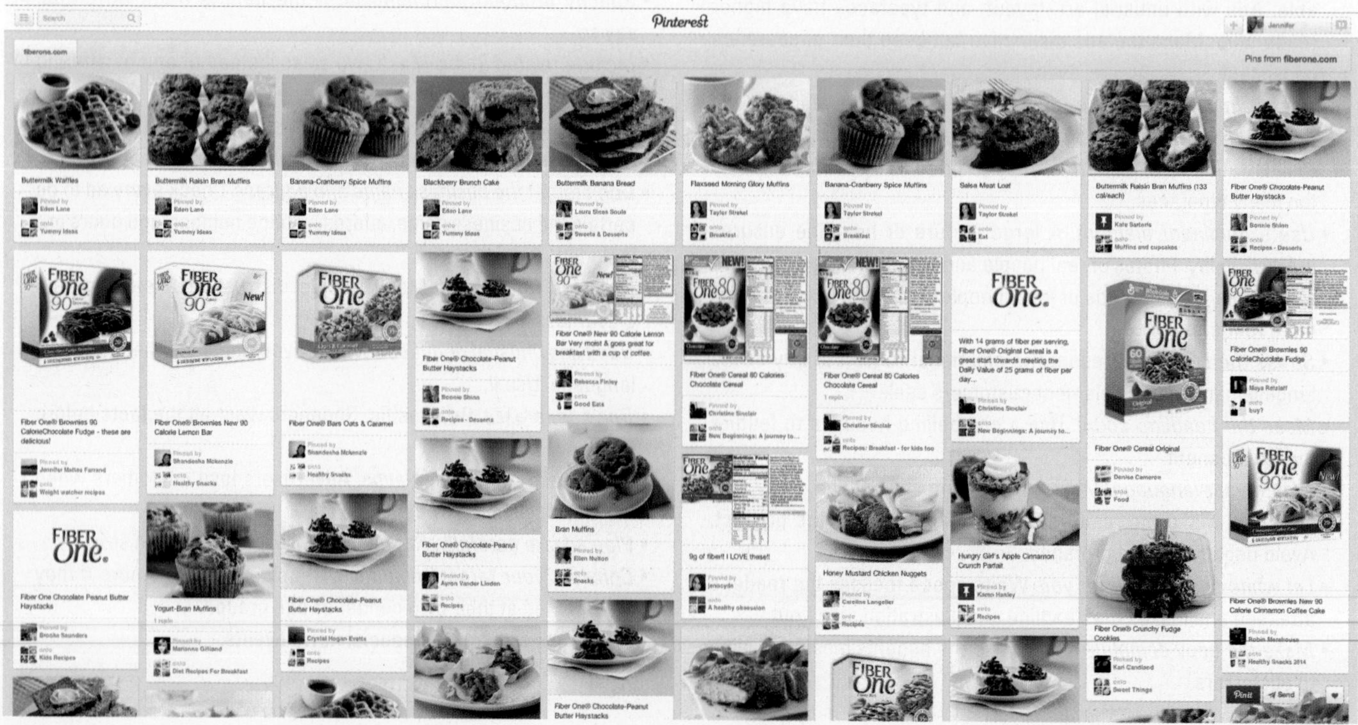

Large agencies working on national campaigns often blend advertising and sales promotion efforts. This Pinterest site for Fiber One is an example.

brand managers The individual within the advertiser's company who is assigned the authority and responsibility for the successful marketing of a particular brand.

decentralized system The establishment of advertising departments by products or brands or in various divisions, subsidiaries, countries, regions, or other categories that suit the firm's needs, which operate with a major degree of independence.

- By medium (radio, TV, digital, outdoor).
- By geography (western advertising, eastern advertising, international advertising).

General Mills, for example, is one of the nation's largest advertisers. It operates a vast advertising and marketing services department with some 350 employees. It spends nearly $1 billion annually in media advertising and other promotional activities.[7]

General Mills's Marketing Services is really many departments within a department. Its centralized structure (see Exhibit 3–5) enables it to administer, plan, and coordinate the promotion of more than 60 brands. It also supervises outside ad agencies and operates its own in-house agency for new or smaller brands.

Organized around functional specialties (market research, media, graphics), Marketing Services helps General Mills's **brand managers** consolidate expenditures for maximum efficiency. Of course, even a traditional company like General Mills has to engage consumers in new and exciting ways. The company is investing heavily in blogs, Facebook, podcasts, and iPhone apps. Digital efforts and campaigns that target fast-growing minority segments are a particular priority.[8]

A recent example of social media use at General Mills is its use of Pinterest to communicate with women in support of Fiber One Chewy Snacks. The goal is to reach "moms who are pinning fun and creative snacking ideas on their Pinterest boards," said Julia Travis, a marketing manager for Fiber One.[9]

Decentralized organization. As some companies become larger, diversify their product line, acquire subsidiaries, and establish divisions in different regions or even different countries, a centralized advertising department often becomes impractical.

In a **decentralized system**, the company sets up separate ad departments for different divisions, subsidiaries, regions, brands, or other categories that suit the company's needs. The general manager of each division or brand is responsible for that group's advertising. A brand manager, who oversees each individual brand, typically works under a marketing manager. This system gives significant authority to the individuals responsible for each brand.

For large companies with many divisions, decentralized advertising is more flexible. Campaigns and media schedules can be adjusted faster. New approaches and creative ideas can be introduced more easily, and sales results can be measured independently of other divisions. In effect, each division has its own marketing

▼EXHIBIT 3–5 General Mills has a centralized advertising department like this model.

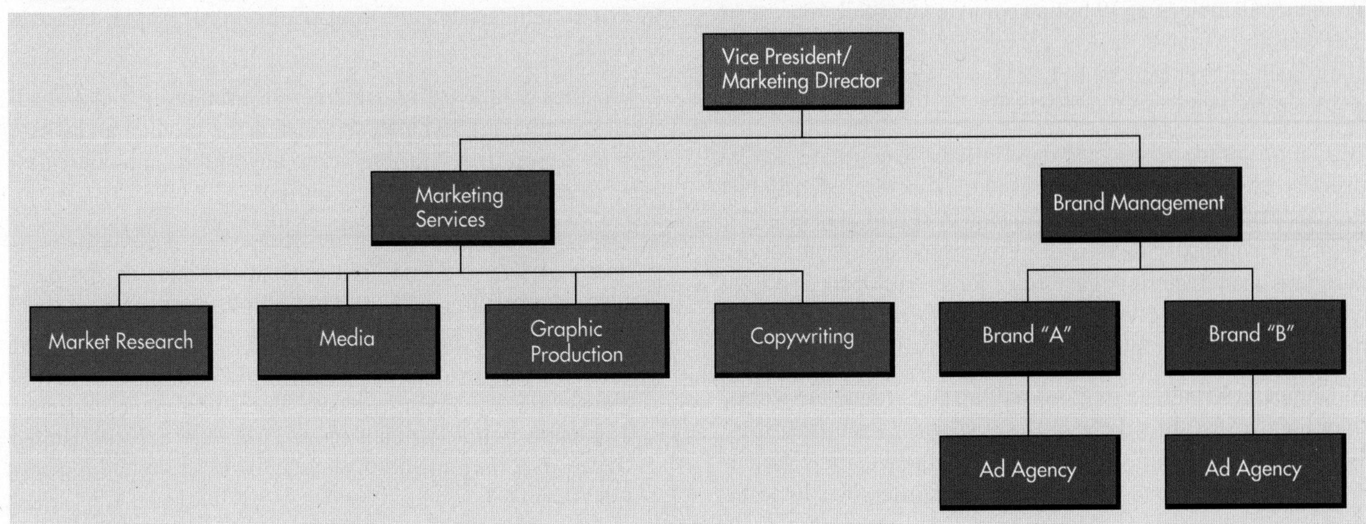

multinational corporations Corporations operating and investing throughout many countries and making decisions based on availabilities worldwide.

global marketers Multinationals that use a standardized approach to marketing and advertising in all countries.

department, with the marketing manager reporting to the division head (see Exhibit 3–6).

EXHIBIT 3–6 In a decentralized structure, each division has its own marketing department.

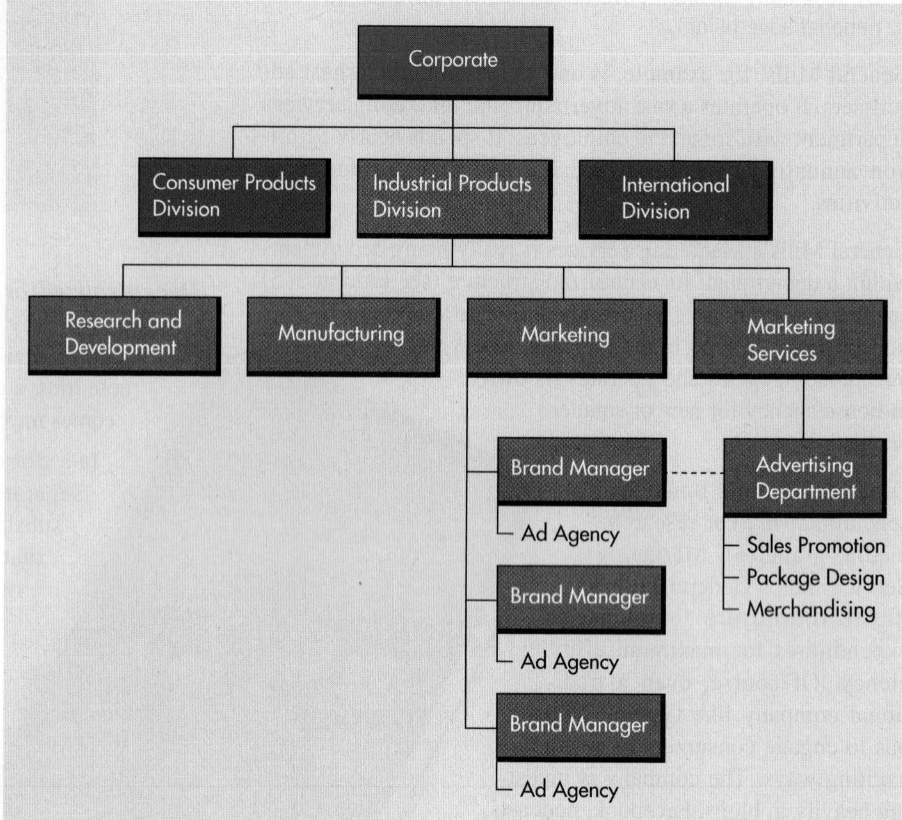

A drawback, though, is that decentralized departments often concentrate on their own budgets, problems, and promotions rather than the good of the whole company. Across divisions, ads may lack uniformity, diminishing the power of repetitive corporate advertising. Rivalry among brand managers may even escalate into unhealthy competition.

Transnational Advertisers

Companies advertising abroad typically face markets with different value systems, environments, and languages. Their customers have different purchasing abilities, habits, and motivations. Media customary to U.S. and Canadian advertisers may be unavailable or ineffective. The companies will therefore likely need different advertising strategies. But they face a more basic problem: How should they manage and produce the advertising? Should their U.S. agency or in-house advertising department do it? Should they use a foreign agency or set up a local advertising department?

Procter & Gamble is a $79 billion company that sells more than 300 consumer brands in over 180 countries. These brands include such market leaders as Tide, Ivory soap, Pampers, Folgers, Pringles, and Crest toothpaste.[10]

P&G is one of the biggest and most influential consumer advertisers in the world; its expenditures worldwide exceeded $9 billion in 2012.[11] Each overseas division is set up almost like a separate company with its own research and development department, manufacturing plant, sales force, and finance and accounting staff. Each division also has an advertising department to help coordinate programs across brands within that division.

As companies continue to grow and prosper around the world, they may invest directly in many countries. True **multinational corporations** strive for full, integrated participation in world markets.[12] Foreign sales often grow faster than domestic sales. In 2002 global, U.S.-based companies derived about 33 percent of all sales from other countries. By the end of the decade global customers accounted for almost half of all sales.[13]

Multinationals that use a *standardized approach* to marketing and advertising in all countries are considered **global marketers**, and they create global brands. Their assumption is that the way the product is used and the needs it satisfies are universal. McDonald's "I'm lovin' it" campaign, first begun in 2003, runs in all 118 countries where the company sells food.[14] Other global advertisers include Coca-Cola, Ford, Apple, GE, and L'Oréal.[15]

Companies do a lot of research before attempting a global advertising strategy. So much depends on the product and where they try to sell it. A "no" answer to any of the following questions means the attempt will be difficult.

1. *Has each country's market for the product developed in the same way?* A Ford is a Ford in most markets. On the other hand, many Europeans use clotheslines, so they don't need fabric softeners for dryers.
2. *Are the targets similar in different nations?* Japanese consumers like jeans, running shoes, and game consoles. The same is true for consumers in Europe and the United States. But they might not share a liking for certain foods or other fashions.

“COMPANIES DO A LOT OF RESEARCH BEFORE ATTEMPTING A GLOBAL ADVERTISING STRATEGY.”

In Canada, all packages and labels must be printed in both English and French, and most major companies also run their ads in both languages. The layout of the French version of this HP (www.hp.com) ad is modified to accommodate the slightly longer text.

3. *Do consumers share the same wants and needs?* Breakfast in Brazil is usually a cup of coffee. Kellogg's Corn Flakes won't be served the same way as in the United States, where people commonly eat cereal for breakfast.[16]

Advertisers who cannot answer yes to the above questions will often take a *localized approach* to international marketing and advertising. They will consider differences in product use, economic development, media options, local laws, technology, and customs. The outcome will often be the adaptation of products, packages, and advertising campaigns to suit each market.

The secret to success in global advertising may be knowing how to tap into basic human emotions and uncover universal appeals that don't depend solely on language. In addition, social media can help global advertisers capitalize on the universal appeal of word of mouth.[17]

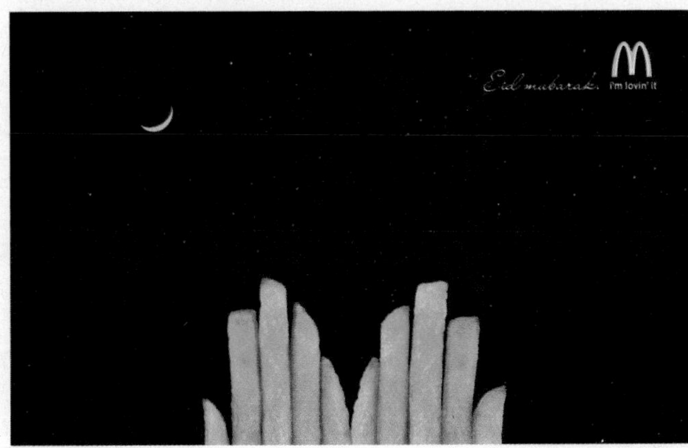

This ad for McDonald's helps celebrate an Islamic observance. Sensitivity to the infinite diversity of worldwide cultures and beliefs is important for a global advertiser's success.

international media Media serving several countries, usually without change, that is available to an international audience.

foreign media The local media of each country used by advertisers for campaigns targeted to consumers or businesses within a single country.

advertising agency An independent organization of creative people and businesspeople who specialize in developing and preparing advertising plans, advertisements, and other promotional tools for advertisers.

local agencies Advertising agencies that specialize in creating advertising for local businesses.

regional agencies Advertising that focuses on the production and placement of advertising suitable for regional campaigns.

Media around the World

In the United States, if you want to promote a soft drink as a youthful, fun refresher, you might use television. In some parts of Europe, Asia, South America, and Africa you may not be able to. Around the world, broadcast media are sometimes owned and controlled by the government, and many governments do not allow commercial advertising. In Egypt, one creative medium used by Coca-Cola and others is the fleet of boats plying the Nile with corporate logos emblazoned on their sails.[18]

Where TV ownership is high, it cuts across the spectrum of income groups. In less-developed countries, though, TV sets may be found only among upper-income groups. This means advertisers may need a different media mix in foreign markets.

Virtually every country has access to radio, television, newspapers, magazines, outdoor media, and direct mail. However, the legalities of different media forms vary from country to country. Generally, the media available to the international advertiser can be categorized as either *international* or *foreign media,* depending on the audience they serve.

International Media

In the past, **international media**—which serve several countries, usually without any change in content—have been limited to newspapers and magazines. Several large American publishers such as Time, McGraw-Hill, and Scientific American circulate international editions of their magazines abroad. Usually written in English, they tend to be read by well-educated, upper-income consumers and are therefore good vehicles for advertising high-end, brand-name products. Television is also a viable international medium. CNN and MTV can be found in many parts of the world, while the Middle Eastern channel Al Jazeera can now be found on U.S. cable systems, such as *OMedia vehicles.*

Foreign Media

Advertisers use **foreign media**—the local media of each country—for large campaigns targeted to consumers or businesses within a single country. Because foreign media cater to their own national audience, advertisers must produce their ads in the language of each country. In countries such as Switzerland, Belgium, and Canada, with more than one official language, ads are produced in each language.

check yourself ✓

1. What factors determine the type of organizational structure that advertisers use?
2. What additional challenges are faced by companies that advertise internationally?
3. What determines whether a multinational advertiser is a global marketer or not?

THE ADVERTISING AGENCY

The American Association of Advertising Agencies (AAAA) defines an **advertising agency** as an independent organization of creative people and businesspeople who specialize in developing and preparing marketing and advertising plans, advertisements, and other promotional tools. Agencies also purchase advertising space and time in various media on behalf of different advertisers (clients) to find customers for their goods and services.[19]

Why does a company such as McDonald's hire ad agencies in the first place? Couldn't it save money by hiring its own staff and creating its own ads? How does an advertising agency, such as Leo Burnett, one of McDonald's agencies, win such a large account? Must an agency's accounts be that big for it to

> Agencies don't work for the media or the suppliers. Their ethical, financial, and legal obligation is to their clients.

make money? This section sheds some light on these issues and gives a clearer understanding of what agencies do and why so many advertisers use agencies.

The agency provides yet another service by researching, negotiating, arranging, and contracting for commercial space and time with different print, electronic, and digital media. Because of its *media expertise,* Burnett saves its clients time and money.

Agencies don't work for the media or the suppliers. Their ethical, financial, and legal obligation is to their clients. Just as a well-run business seeks professional help from attorneys, accountants, bankers, or management specialists, advertisers use agencies out of *self-interest,* because the agencies can create more effective advertising and select more effective media than the advertisers can themselves. Today, almost all sizable advertisers rely on an ad agency.

Finally, a good agency serves its clients' needs because of its daily exposure to a broad spectrum of marketing situations and problems both here and abroad. As technology has enabled companies to work across borders with relative ease, the advertising business has boomed worldwide. Most large U.S. agencies maintain offices abroad.

L03-4 Define the main types of advertising agencies.

Types of Agencies

Advertising agencies are typically classified by their geographic scope, the range of services they offer, and the type of business they handle.

Geographic Scope Every community of any size has reputable **local agencies** that offer expert assistance to local advertisers. Unfortunately, local advertisers use ad agencies less extensively than do national advertisers. Many local advertisers simply don't spend enough money on advertising to warrant hiring an agency. And some large agencies don't accept local advertisers because their budgets are too small.

Every major city has numerous ad agencies that can produce and place the quality of advertising suitable for national campaigns. **Regional** and **national agencies** typically participate in either the 4As (American Association of Advertising Agencies) or some similar trade group such as the Western States Advertising Agency Association (WSAAA). The *Standard Directory of Advertising Agencies* (the Red Book) lists these agencies geographically, so they're easy to find.[20]

The largest national agencies are also **international agencies**. That is, they have offices or affiliates in major communications centers around the world and can help their clients market internationally or globally as the case may be. Likewise, many foreign-based agencies have offices and affiliates in the United States. For example, the largest advertising agency organization in the world today, WPP Group, is based in London. But it owns several top U.S. agencies, including Ogilvy & Mather and J. Walter Thompson.

Range of Services The modern **full-service advertising agency** supplies both advertising and nonadvertising

Arnoldworldwide

Arnold Worldwide is one of the agencies that McDonald's relies on most for its national campaigns.

national agencies Advertising agencies that produce and place the quality of advertising suitable for national campaigns.

international agencies Advertising agencies that have offices or affiliates in major communication centers around the world and can help their clients market internationally or globally.

full-service advertising agency An agency equipped to serve its clients in all areas of communication and promotion. Its advertising services include planning, creating, and producing advertisements as well as performing research and media selection services. Nonadvertising functions include producing sales promotion materials, publicity articles, annual reports, trade show exhibits, and sales training materials.

general consumer agency An agency that represents the widest variety of accounts, but it concentrates on companies that make goods purchased chiefly by consumers.

business-to-business B2B agency Represents clients that market products to other businesses.

creative boutiques Organizations of creative specialists (such as art directors, designers, and copywriters) that work for advertisers and occasionally advertising agencies to develop creative concepts, advertising messages, and specialized art. A boutique performs only the creative work.

services in all areas of communications and promotion. *Advertising services* include planning, creating, and producing ads; performing research; and selecting media. *Nonadvertising services* run the gamut from packaging to public relations to producing sales promotion materials, annual reports, and trade-show exhibits. With the trend toward IMC, many of the largest agencies today are in the forefront of *interactive media.*[21]

Full-service agencies may specialize in certain kinds of clients. Most, though, can be classified as either *general consumer agencies* or *business-to-business agencies.*

General consumer agencies. A **general consumer agency** represents the widest variety of accounts, but it concentrates on *consumer accounts*—companies that make goods purchased chiefly by consumers (soaps, cereals, cars, pet foods, toiletries). Most of the ads are placed in consumer media (TV, radio, magazines, and so on) that pay a *commission* to the agency. General agencies often derive much of their income from these commissions.

General agencies include the international superagency groups headquartered in communication capitals such as New York, London, Paris, and Tokyo, as well as many other large firms in Chicago, Los Angeles, Minneapolis, Montreal, and Toronto. A few of the better-known names in North America are Ogilvy & Mather; Draft FCB; BBDO; DDB Needham; Young & Rubicam (Y&R); and Cossette Communication Group (Canada). But general agencies also include the thousands of smaller *entrepreneurial agencies* located in every major city across the country (Martin Agency, Richmond, Virginia; RPA, Los Angeles; MMB, Boston; and Wieden + Kennedy, Portland, Oregon).

Profit margins in entrepreneurial agencies are often slimmer, but these shops are typically more responsive to the smaller clients they serve. They offer the hands-on involvement of the firm's principals, and their work is frequently startling in its creativity. For these reasons, many large agencies are spinning off smaller subsidiaries. Gotham Advertising, for example, is a hot creative shop in New York that was spun off by the Interpublic Group of Companies to do work for a variety of clients its bigger sister agencies couldn't serve.[22] Some entrepreneurial agencies, such as Zubi Advertising in Coral Gables, Florida, carve a niche for themselves by serving particular market segments.

Some advertising agencies specialize in business-to-business advertising. In this ad from 2004, DHL (www.dhl.com) is promoting its shipping services to small businesses.

Business-to-business agencies. A **business-to-business agency (B2B)** represents clients that sell to other businesses. Examples are electronic components for computer manufacturers, equipment used in oil and gas refineries, and MRI equipment for radiology. High-tech advertising requires some technical knowledge and the ability to translate that knowledge into precise and persuasive communications. While you may be a customer for McDonald's food, the company is itself a customer, and thus an advertising target, for suppliers of soft drinks, eggs, beef, napkins, employee uniforms, and so on.

Most B2B advertising is placed in trade magazines or other business publications. These media are commissionable, but their circulation is smaller, so their rates are far lower than those of consumer media. Because commissions usually don't cover the cost of the agency's services, business agencies typically charge their clients service fees. They can be expensive, especially for small advertisers, but failure to obtain a business agency's expertise may carry an even higher price in lost marketing opportunities.

Specialized Service Agencies

Many agencies assist their clients with a variety of limited services. There has been a continuing trend toward specialization, giving impetus to many of the small agencies called *creative boutiques* and other specialty businesses such as *media-buying services* and *interactive agencies.*

Creative boutiques. Some talented artists—such as graphic designers and copywriters—have set up their own creative services, or **creative boutiques**. They work for advertisers and occasionally subcontract to ad agencies. Their mission is to develop exciting creative concepts and produce fresh, distinctive advertising messages. In the 1990s, Creative Artists Agency (CAA), a Hollywood talent agency, caused a stir by taking on the role of a creative boutique, using its pool of actors, directors, and cinematographers to create a series of commercials for Coca-Cola. McCann Erickson Worldwide remained Coke's *agency of record,* but the majority of the creative work came from CAA. Since then, Coke has allowed numerous other smaller shops to work on its account.[23]

media-buying service An organization that specializes in purchasing and packaging radio and television time.

interactive agency An advertising agency that specializes in the creation of ads for a digital medium.

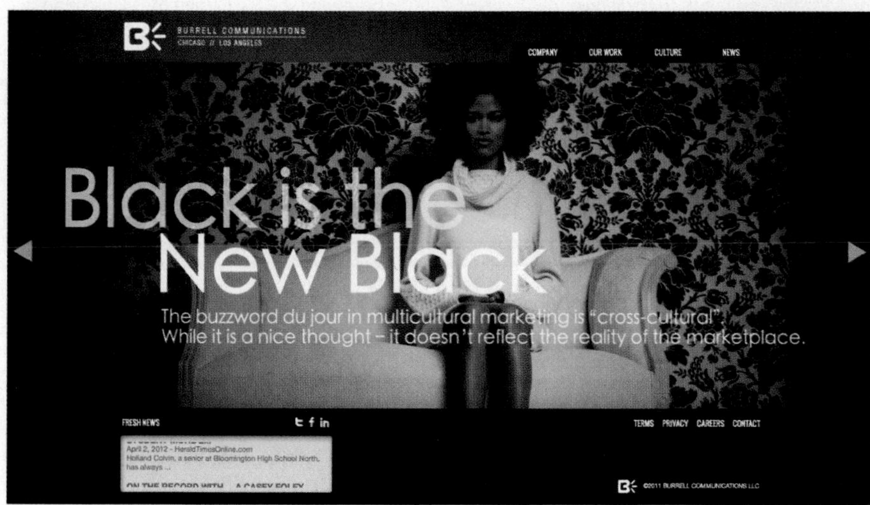

The Internet offers advertisers yet another medium for building brands. An interactive agency helped the advertiser create its Web messages.

Advertising effectiveness depends on originality in concept, design, and writing. However, while boutiques may be economical, they usually don't provide the research, marketing, sales expertise, or deep customer service that full-service agencies offer. Thus, boutiques tend to be limited to the role of creative suppliers.

Media-buying services. Some years ago, a few experienced agency media people started setting up organizations to purchase and package radio and TV time. The largest **media-buying service** (or *media agency*) is Initiative Media. Based in Los Angeles, it is owned by the Interpublic Group, has 99 offices in 58 countries around the world, and places more than $20 billion worth of advertising annually for a wide variety of clients.[24]

Media time and space is perishable. A 60-second radio spot at 8 p.m. can't be sold later. So radio and TV stations presell as much time as possible and discount their rates for large buys. Media-buying services negotiate a special discount with the media and then sell the time or space to agencies or advertisers.

Media-buying firms provide customers (both clients and agencies) with a detailed analysis of the media buy. Once the media package is sold, the buying service orders spots, verifies performance, sees that stations "make good" for any missed spots, and even pays the media bills.

Media agencies have experienced so much growth in the last decade that they have become major players on the advertising stage. Today, even large agencies like BBDO no longer provide media services. Instead, big clients use media firms to plan and place buys.

Interactive agencies. A heightened interest in IMC and digital advertising has led to a new breed of specialist—the **interactive agency**. Agency.com and Tribal DDB are some of the many firms that have sprung up within the last few years with specialized experience in designing Web pages mobile apps, and social media campaigns. The biggest digital agencies in 2011 included SapientNitro, based in Boston, and New York's Wunderman.[25]

Other specialists, such as *direct-response* and *sales promotion agencies,* are also growing in response to client demands for greater expertise and accountability as advertisers add new marketing approaches.

check yourself ✓

1. Why do so many advertisers hire ad agencies?
2. What are the main types of advertising agencies?

L03-5 Describe the range of tasks people perform in an ad agency and an in-house advertising department.

WHAT PEOPLE IN AN AGENCY DO

An agency's purpose is to interpret to desired segments of the public information about a legally marketed product or service. How does it do this? First, it studies the client's product to determine its strengths and weaknesses. Next, it analyzes the product's present and potential market. Then, using its knowledge of product distribution and media alternatives, the agency formulates a plan to carry the advertiser's message to consumers or businesses. Finally the agency writes, designs, and produces ads; contracts for media space and time; verifies media insertions; and bills for services and media used.

The agency also works with the client's marketing staff to enhance advertising's impact through package design and the production of sales literature and displays. To understand these functions, consider the people who were involved, directly and indirectly, in the creation, production, and supervision of McDonald's advertising.

account executives (AEs) The liaison between the agency and the client. The account executive is responsible both for managing all the agency's services for the benefit of the client and for representing the agency's point of view to the client.

management (account) supervisors Managers who supervise account executives and who report to the agency's director of account services.

account planning A hybrid discipline that bridges the gap between traditional research, account management, and creative direction whereby agency people represent the view of the consumer in order to better define and plan the client's advertising program.

media planning The strategic identification and selection of media vehicles for a client's advertising messages.

copy The words that make up the headline and message of an advertisement or commercial.

Account Management The **account executives (AEs)** at Leo Burnett are the liaison between the agency and the client. Large agencies have many account executives, who report to **management** (or **account**) **supervisors**. They in turn report to the agency's director of account (or client) services.

Deena Di Stefano is McDonald's account executive at Burnett. Like many AEs, she can find herself caught in the middle of the fray, as she is responsible for formulating advertising plans (discussed in Chapter 7), mustering the agency's services, representing the client's point of view to the agency, and the agency's point of view to the client. To succeed today, an AE needs to be more of a strategist than an advocate. She must be well versed in an extraordinary range of media and demonstrate how her agency's creative work satisfies both her client's marketing needs and the market's product needs. That means she must be enterprising and courageous, demanding yet tactful, artistic and articulate, meticulous, forgiving, perceptive, persuasive, ethical, and discreet—all at once. And she must always deliver the work on time and within budget.

> "To succeed today, an AE needs to be more of a strategist than an advocate."

Research and Account Planning Clients and agencies give their creatives (artists and copywriters) a wealth of product, market, and competitive information because, at its core, advertising is based on information. Therefore, before creating any advertising, agencies research the uses and advantages of the product, analyze current and potential customers, and try to determine what will influence them to buy. After the ads are placed, agencies use more research to investigate how the campaign fared. Chapter 6 discusses some of the many types of research ad agencies conduct.

Account planning is a hybrid discipline that uses research to bridge the gap between account management and creatives. The account planner also defends the consumer's point of view and the creative strategy in the debate between the agency's creative team and the client.

Account planners study consumer needs and desires through a variety of methods. They help the creative team translate their findings into imaginative, successful campaigns. Not attached to either account management or creative, the account planner balances both elements to make sure the research is reflected in the ads.[26] More about this in Chapter 6.

When McDonald's wanted to attract kids to its Kiddie Crew Workshop in the Philippines, DDB account planner Lester Obice helped guide the creative team to a brilliant execution that merged images of McDonald's fries and yellow crayons.

Media Planning and Buying Ad agencies perform a variety of media services for their clients: research, negotiating, scheduling, buying, and verifying. **Media planning** is critical, because the only way advertisers can communicate is through some medium. Changes over the last decade have made the media function even more important.

With the unprecedented fragmentation of audiences from the explosion of new media options and the trend toward IMC and relationship marketing, the media task has taken on added significance. Tightening budgets demands ingenious thinking, tough negotiating, and careful attention to detail. Media planners must understand how advertising works in coordination with other marketing communication tools and come up with creative media solutions to tough marketing challenges. Today, many products owe their success more to creative media planning and buying than to clever ads.

Creative Concepts Most ads rely heavily on **copy**, the words that make up the headline and message. The people who create these words, **copywriters**, condense all that can be said about a product into a few pertinent, succinct points.

Ads also communicate through layout and design. That is the job of the **art directors**, graphic designers, and production artists, who determine how an ad's verbal and visual symbols will fit together. (The creative process is discussed in Part 4.) A copywriter and an art director work as a creative team under a **creative director**. Each team is usually assigned a particular client's business.

One award-winning ad for McDonald's focuses on the Ronald McDonald House Charities. Titled "First Step," the ad tells the story of a young toddler whose medical care was made more affordable by the company. The beautiful spot was developed by an experienced DDB Chicago team, including creative director Bill Cimino, copywriter Geoff McCartney, and art director Gordon West.

copywriters People who create the words and concepts for ads and commercials.

art directors Along with graphic designers and production artists, individuals who determine how the ad's verbal and visual symbols will fit together.

creative director Head of a creative team of agency copywriters and artists who is assigned to a client's business and who is ultimately responsible for the creative product—the form the final ad takes.

production department The department in an advertising agency that is responsible for managing the steps that transform creative concepts into finished advertisements and collateral materials.

Advertising Production: Print and Broadcast An ad approved by the client is then turned over to the agency's print production manager or broadcast producers.

For print ads, the **production department** buys type, photos, illustrations, and other components and works with printers, engravers, and other suppliers. For a broadcast commercial, production people work from an approved script or storyboard. Actors, camera operators, and production specialists (studios, directors, editors) help produce a commercial on audiotape (for radio) or on film or videotape (for TV). The "First Step" commercial described above was helmed by a famous commercial director named Joe Pytka and was filmed at Pytka's studio.

Some McDonald's advertising is devoted to specific menu items. These ads give existing customers a reason to visit the restaurant chain more often, and may attract new customers who are unaware of the variety of offerings at McDonald's.

But production work is not limited to just ads and commercials. Dealer kits and direct mailings are just two examples of other materials that may be created as part of a campaign.

Traffic Management One of the greatest sins in an ad agency is a missed deadline. If an agency misses a deadline for a monthly magazine, for example, the agency will have to wait another month before it can run the ad, much to the client's displeasure.

The agency **traffic department** coordinates all phases of production and makes sure everything is completed and approved before client and/or media deadlines. Traffic is often the first stop for entry-level college graduates and an excellent place to learn about agency operations.

Additional Services The growth of IMC has caused many agencies to employ specialists who provide services besides advertising. Larger agencies may have a fully staffed **sales promotion department** to produce dealer ads, window posters, point-of-purchase displays, and dealer sales material. Or, depending on the nature and needs of their clients, they may employ public relations people and direct marketing specialists, digital designers, social media experts, or package designers.

Agency Administration In small agencies, administrative functions may be handled by the firm's principals. Large agencies often have departments for accounting, human resources, data processing, purchasing, financial analysis, legal issues, and insurance.

How Agencies Are Structured

An ad agency organizes its functions, operations, and personnel according to the types of accounts it serves, its size, and its geographic scope.

The owner or general manager usually supervises daily business operations, client services, and new-business development. Account executives (AEs) generally handle day-to-day client contact. In smaller agencies, AEs may also do some creative work. Artwork may be produced by an art director or purchased from an independent studio or freelance designer. Most agencies have production and traffic departments or an employee who fulfills these functions. They may have a media buyer, but in very small agencies account executives also purchase media time and space. Exhibit 3–7 shows how a typical advertising agency might be organized.

Medium and large agencies are usually structured in a *departmental* or *group system.* In the **departmental system**, the agency organizes its various functions—account services, creative services, marketing services, and administration—into separate departments.

In the **group system**, the agency is divided into a number of "little" agencies or groups. Each group may serve one large account or, in some cases, three or four smaller ones. An account manager heads each group's staff of account executives, copywriters, art directors, a media director, and any other necessary specialists. A very large agency may have dozens of groups with separate production and traffic units.

▼EXHIBIT 3–7 Typical departmental advertising agency organization.

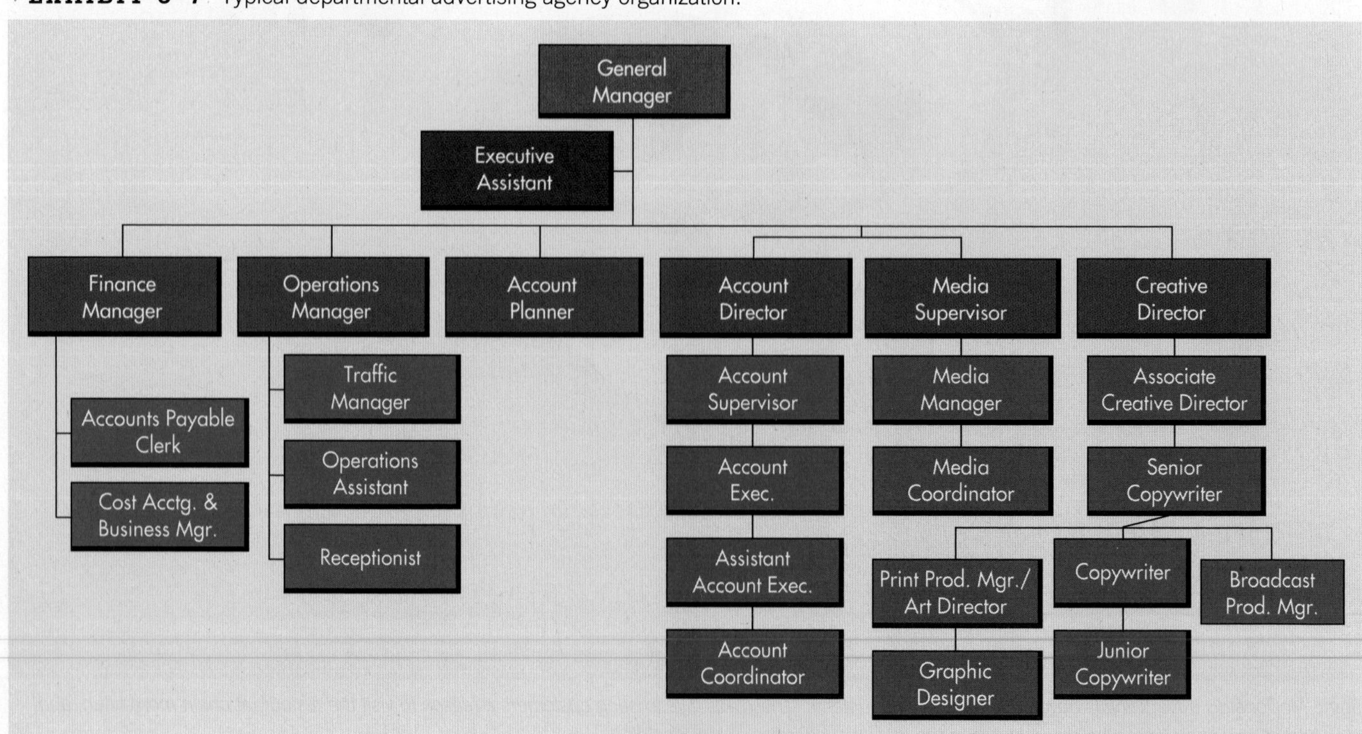

traffic department The department in an advertising agency that coordinates all phases of production and makes sure everything is completed before the deadline.

sales promotion department In larger agencies, a staff to produce dealer ads, window posters, point-of-purchase displays, and dealer sales material.

departmental system The organization of an ad agency into departments based on function: account services, creative services, marketing services, and administration.

group system The organization of an ad agency into a number of little agencies or groups, each with the various people required to meet the needs of the particular clients being served by the group.

media commission Compensation paid by a medium to recognized advertising agencies, traditionally 15 percent (16⅔ percent for outdoor), for advertising placed with it.

markup A source of agency income gained by adding some amount to a supplier's bill, usually 17.65 percent.

fee–commission combination A pricing system in which an advertising agency charges the client a basic monthly fee for its services and also retains any media commissions earned.

straight-fee (retainer) method A method of compensation for ad agency services in which a straight fee, or *retainer,* is based on a cost-plus-fixed-fees formula. Under this system, the agency estimates the amount of personnel time required by the client, determines the cost of that personnel, and multiplies by some factor.

check yourself ✓

1. In what ways does the role of an account planner differ from that of an account executive?
2. What do people in an ad agency do?

L03-6 Relate how agencies get new clients and how they make money.

How Agencies Are Compensated

To survive, agencies must make a profit. But recent trends in the business—mergers of superagencies, shifts in emphasis from advertising to sales promotion and direct marketing, increased production costs, and the fragmentation of media vehicles—have all cut into agency profits.[27] Moreover, different clients demand different services, forcing agencies to develop various compensation methods. Still, there are really only three ways for agencies to make money: *media commissions, markups,* and *fees* or *retainers.*

Media Commissions As we saw in Chapter 1, when ad agencies first came on the scene more than 100 years ago, they were really space brokers, or reps, for the newspapers. Because they saved the media much of the expense of sales and collections, the media allowed the agencies to retain a 15 percent **media commission** on the space or time they purchased on behalf of their clients. That started a tradition that endures to this day, although it is now changing rapidly. Let's see how it works.

Say a national rate-card price for a full-page color magazine ad is $100,000. The magazine bills the agency, and the agency in turn bills the client for the $100,000. The client pays that amount to the agency, and the agency sends $85,000 to the magazine, keeping its 15 percent commission ($15,000). For large accounts, the agency typically provides extensive services (creative, media, accounting, and account management) for this commission. With dwindling profits, though, and clients negotiating smaller commissions, many agencies now must charge a fee for services that used to be included for free.[28]

Markups In the process of creating an ad, the agency normally buys a variety of services or materials from outside suppliers—for example, photos and illustrations. The agency pays the supplier's charge and then adds a **markup** to the client's bill, typically 17.65 percent of the invoice (which becomes 15 percent of the new total).

For example, a markup of 17.65 percent on an $8,500 photography bill yields a $1,500 profit. When billing the client, the agency adds the $1,500 to the $8,500 for a new total of $10,000. When the client pays the bill, the agency keeps the $1,500 (15 percent of the total) and sends $8,500 to the photographer.

$$\$8{,}500 \times 17.65\% = \$1{,}500$$

$$\$8{,}500 + 1{,}500 = \$10{,}000$$

$$\$10{,}000 \times 15\% = \$1{,}500$$

Some media—local newspapers, for example—allow a commission on the higher rates they charge national advertisers but not on the lower rates they charge local advertisers. So, to get their commission, local agencies have to use the markup formula above.

Fees Clients today expect agencies to solve problems rather than just place ads, so fees are becoming more common. In fact, one study shows that only about one-third of national advertisers still rely on the traditional 15 percent commission system. An equal number now use some fee-based system. The rest use some modified commission or incentive system.[29]

There are two pricing methods in the fee system. With the **fee–commission combination**, the agency charges a basic monthly fee for all its services to the client and retains any media commissions earned. In the **straight-fee** or **retainer method**, agencies charge for all their services, either by the hour or by the month, and return any media commissions earned to the client. This latter method addresses a common objection to the commission system, namely that commissions lead agencies to recommend more media spending, rather than

incentive system A form of compensation in which the agency shares in the client's success when a campaign attains specific, agreed-upon goals.

in-house agency Agency wholly owned by an advertiser and set up and staffed to do all the work of an independent full-service agency.

McDonald's uses the creative talent of its partner agencies to develop clever executions like this interactive out-of-home ad.

looking for ways to spend the client's money more efficiently. The fee method also addresses the fact that many clients are now using media buying services to purchase space and time.

Accountability is a major issue in client–agency relationships. With the **incentive system** (sometimes called *pay-for-performance*), the agency earns more if the campaign attains specific, agreed-upon goals. DDB Needham, for example, offers its clients a "guaranteed results" program. If a campaign is successful, the agency earns more; if it fails, the agency earns less. Kraft General Foods rewards its agencies based on their performance. An A grade gets an extra 3 percent commission; C grades are put on review.[30]

The In-House Agency

Some companies set up a wholly owned **in-house agency** (or *house agency*) to save money and tighten control over their advertising. The in-house agency may do all the work of an independent full-service agency, including creative tasks, production, media placement, publicity, and sales promotion.

Advertisers with in-house agencies hope to save money by cutting overhead, keeping the media commission, and avoiding markups on outside purchases. Small, local advertisers in particular seek this goal.

Advertisers also expect more attention and faster turnaround from their house agencies, which know the company's products and markets better and can focus all their resources to meet its deadlines. Management is often more involved in the advertising when it's done by company people, especially in "single-business" companies.

But usually companies sacrifice more than they gain. In-house flexibility is often won at the expense of creativity. Outside agencies typically offer greater experience, versatility, and a larger talent pool. In-house agencies have difficulty attracting and keeping the best creative people, who tend to prefer the variety and challenges offered by independent agencies.

The biggest risk for in-house agencies may be a loss of objectivity. In the shadow of internal politics, linear-thinking policymakers, and criticism from management, ads may become bland and self-serving, rather than imaginative messages relevant to customers. In advertising, that's the kiss of death.

Just as you may like some ads better than others, advertisers sometimes choose an agency based on the quality of their work for other clients. Any advertiser who encountered this creative out-of-home ad (the billboard actually has plants growing on its surface to highlight McDonald's salads), might be tempted to hire the agency that created it.

Is Ronald McDonald Bad for Kids? Are Parents?

Deborah Lapidus has found the "person" responsible for the childhood obesity epidemic that is sweeping the United States. While the culprit can often be found visiting children's hospitals and performing at other charity events, Lapidus is unmoved. She wants him gone for good, or, in her words, "retired." Anyone interested in joining Ms. Lapidus's quest should be on the lookout for an easily recognized, flamboyantly dressed individual with flaming red hair and a bright round nose. Because Deborah Lapidus wants to retire Ronald McDonald.[i]

To make her point, in 2010 she traveled all the way to Oak Brook, Illinois, the location of McDonald's annual meeting, to protest Ronald's prominence in the company's advertising. Her trip was funded by her 30,000-member advocacy group, named "Corporate Accountability."

Does McDonald's market to children? The evidence is pretty compelling. Like any smart family-oriented eatery, McDonald's knows that kids exercise enormous influence in family dining decisions. In response, it has created Happy Meals and playgrounds that make its restaurants fun places for kids to eat and play (and for mom and dad to relax). And, of course, kids love Ronald, one of the world's most recognized brand symbols.

And it is undeniable that America has a health problem, and food is a big part of it. Obama Secretary of Health and Human Services Kathleen Sebelius suggests that one in three kids in the U.S. is overweight, a number that has grown 400 percent in just 20 years. Sebelius recently urged the U.S. Conference of Mayors to join a program initiated by First Lady Michelle Obama called "Let's Move," aimed at encouraging healthier lifestyles among children.[ii]

So the problem that Lapidus is calling attention to is real. What is in question is her proposed solution. Will retiring Ronald make America's children skinnier?

Interestingly, McDonald's may be way ahead of Lapidus. The company has developed a broader line of healthy menus for its Happy Meals, ones that include fresh fruits and veggies. Playgrounds are slowly being phased out at McDonald's in favor of coffee bars. Ads that feature Ronald are difficult to find anymore, part of a recent trend toward reducing McDonald's ads that target children. In fact, while the company's overall ad spending in the first quarter of 2010 was up 30 percent from 2009, ads directed at kids were down 23 percent.[iii]

So McDonald's seems to be doing its part. Lapidus should be thrilled.

But one commentator, Courier News writer Julia Doyle, thinks Lapidus has missed the real source of childhood obesity: moms and dads.[iv]

> If our kids are fat, it automatically has to be because there's a goofy, smiley-faced clown telling them to eat cheeseburgers and French fries, right? It can't possibly have anything to do with Mom or Dad stopping for fried chicken, tacos or burgers every night rather than cooking a healthy dinner when they get home. And if our kids are fat, it has everything to do with the pizza, chicken fingers and hot dogs served in their school cafeterias and nothing to do with the fact that their parents can't be bothered to pack them a healthy lunch to take to school each day. I think it's high time these so-called watchdog groups get off their high horses and stop blaming corporate America for everything they think is wrong with us.

The ethical issues here are complex. Is it right for McDonald's, or any company, to advertise to children? Is it morally acceptable for a fast-food chain to feature playgrounds and brand symbols that kids find appealing? Would these activities be more ethically permissible if the company exclusively sold healthy food? Can the obesity problem affecting American children (and adults) be blamed on a single company? McDonald's has been using Ronald in its ads since the 1960s, a time when children were generally fitter and slimmer than they are today. So how can he be the root cause, or even a significant factor, of the problem? What about Doyle's points regarding the role of parents, both as role models for good eating and as gatekeepers for the types of foods their children eat? Does she have a fair point or not? America's children have a health problem. How significant is advertising as a cause?

[i] www.metrowestdailynews.com/opinion/x1218688656/Chesto-Boston-group-pushes-for-Ronald-McDonalds-retirement.

[ii] www.google.com/hostednews/ap/article/ALeqM5h_6x0AU_CynNNRPSPbTlu_pPzemgD9G9EGE80.

[iii] www.chicagobusiness.com/cgi-bin/article.pl?articleId=33474.

[iv] www.suburbanchicagonews.com/couriernews/news/talk/2311466,3_1_EL25_02TALK_S1-100525.article.

THE CLIENT–AGENCY RELATIONSHIP

Many factors affect the success of a company's advertising program, but one of the most important is the relationship between the advertiser and its agency.

How Agencies Get Clients

To succeed, advertising agencies need clients. New clients come from personal contact with top management, referrals from satisfied clients or advertising consultants, publicity on recent successful campaigns, trade advertising, direct-mail solicitation, or an agency's general reputation.[31] The three most successful ways to develop new business are having clients who strongly champion the agency, having superior presentation skills, and cultivating a personal relationship with a network of top executives.

Referrals Most good agencies get clients by referral—from existing clients, friends, review consultants, or even other agencies. The head of one company asks another who's doing

speculative presentation An agency's presentation of the advertisement it proposes using in the event it is hired. It is usually made at the request of a prospective client and is often not paid for by the client.

her ads, and the next week the agency gets a call. If a prospective client presents a conflict of interest with an existing client, the agency may decline the business and refer the prospect to another agency.[32]

Independent *agency review consultants* often help arrange marriages between agencies and clients. In fact, independent advisors were involved in many important account shuffles on Madison Avenue: Domino's Pizza, DirecTV, Burger King, Compaq computers, and Monster.com, to name just a few.[33]

Sales reps for media and suppliers frequently refer local advertisers to an agency they know. So it's important for agencies to maintain good relations with the media, suppliers, other agencies, and, of course, their existing clients.

Presentations An advertiser may ask an agency to make a presentation (a pitch)—anything from a simple discussion of the agency's philosophy, experience, personnel, and track record to a full-blown audiovisual presentation of a proposed campaign. Successful agencies, therefore, need excellent presentation skills.

Some advertisers ask for or imply that they want a **speculative presentation**, meaning they want to see what the agency intends to do for them before they sign on. But most agencies prefer to build their presentations around the work they've already done, to demonstrate their capabilities without giving away ideas for a new campaign. Invariably, the larger the prospective client, the bigger the presentation. Some agencies now spend upwards of $500,000 to stage a new business presentation.

The presentation process also allows the agency and the advertiser to get to know each other before they agree to work together. Advertising is a people business, so human qualities—mutual regard, trust, and communication—play an important role.

Some companies such as Benetton (www.benetton.com) prefer to create ads using their own in-house agencies. Advertisers may hope to save money and gain more attention by using their house agencies, but they can lose the greater experience, objectivity, and talent of an outside agency.

Soliciting and Advertising for New Business Lesser-known agencies must be more aggressive. An agency may solicit new business by advertising, writing letters, making cold calls, or following up leads from sources in the business. An agency principal usually takes the responsibility for soliciting new business.

Today, more agencies are advertising themselves. Many agencies submit their best ads to competitions around the world to win awards and gain publicity and professional respect for their creative excellence.[34]

Factors Affecting the Client–Agency Relationship

Many forces influence the client–agency relationship. Generally they can be grouped into the four Cs: *chemistry, communication, conduct,* and *changes.*

> Most good agencies get clients by referral—from existing clients, friends, review consultants, or even other agencies.

Networking and Community Relations Agencies frequently find that the best source of new business is the people their employees know socially in the community. Some agencies work *pro bono* (for free) for charities or nonprofit organizations. Matt Freeman, the young CEO of Tribal DDB, McDonald's digital agency, volunteers for the Ad Council and a hunger charity. Leo Burnett is a partner with Global Giving, an organization that matches donors with good causes.

The most critical factor is the personal *chemistry* between the client and people in the agency.[35] Agencies are very conscious of this factor and agency people work hard to establish a good personal connection with potential clients. This is crucial because in the end, effective working relationships are built on trust.[36]

Poor *communication,* a problem often cited by both agencies and advertisers, leads to misunderstandings about objectives,

"ADVERTISING IS A PEOPLE BUSINESS, SO HUMAN QUALITIES—MUTUAL REGARD, TRUST, AND COMMUNICATION—PLAY AN IMPORTANT ROLE."

strategies, roles, and expectations—and to poor advertising. Constant, open communication and an explicit agreement on mutual contribution for mutual gain are key to a good relationship.[37]

Dissatisfaction with agency *conduct,* or performance, is the most commonly cited reason for agency switches in every country.[38] The service the agency gave two years ago may not be valued by the client in the same way today.[39] Or perhaps the agency doesn't understand the client's marketing problems. And clients change, too. Does the client give the agency timely, accurate information? Does it appreciate good work, or does it treat the agency like a vendor?[40]

Changes occur in every relationship. Unfortunately, some of them damage the agency–client partnership. The client's market position or policies may change, or new management may arrive. Agencies may lose key staff people. Client conflicts may arise if one agency buys another that handles competing accounts. Legally, an ad agency cannot represent a client's competition without the client's consent.[41] Saatchi & Saatchi was forced to resign Helene Curtis under pressure from Saatchi's biggest client, Procter & Gamble.[42]

Perhaps the best way to improve understanding between clients and agencies would be to have staff members change places for a while. A Foote, Cone & Belding account executive did just that with great success, filling in temporarily as marketing manager at Levi's Jeans for Women. It gave her a whole new perspective on her agency job and the daily challenges faced by her client.[43]

my ad campaign

Agency Review [3–C]

What will your client look for in your agency team? This agency review should give you an idea. To use this scale, an advertiser would rate each agency on a scale from 1 (strongly negative) to 10 (strongly positive).

General Information

____ Size compatible with our needs.
____ Strength of management.
____ Financial stability.
____ Compatibility with other clients.
____ Range of services.
____ Cost of services; billing policies.

Marketing Information

____ Ability to offer marketing counsel.
____ Understanding of the markets we serve.
____ Experience dealing in our market.
____ Success record; case histories.

Creative Abilities

____ Well-thought-out creativity; relevance to strategy.
____ Art strength.
____ Copy strength.
____ Overall creative quality.
____ Effectiveness compared to work of competitors.

Production

____ Faithfulness to creative concept and execution.
____ Diligence to schedules and budgets.
____ Ability to control outside services.

Media

____ Existence and soundness of media research.
____ Effective and efficient media strategy.
____ Ability to achieve objectives within budget.
____ Strength at negotiating and executing schedules.

Personality

____ Overall personality, philosophy, or position.
____ Compatibility with client staff and management.
____ Willingness to assign top people to account.
____ Ability to articulate rationale behind work.

References

____ Rating by current clients.
____ Rating by past clients.
____ Rating by media and financial sources.

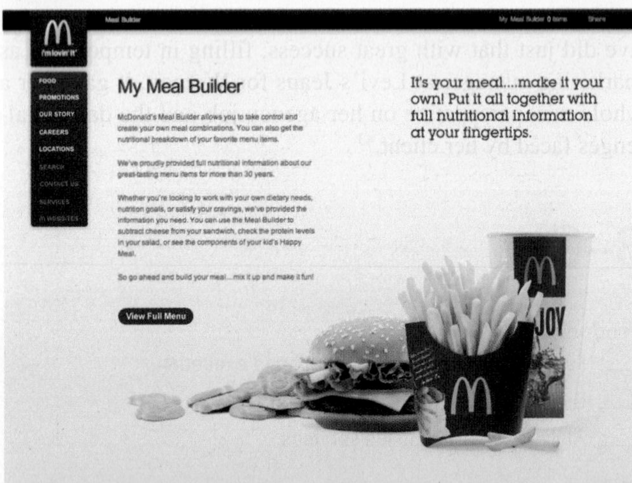

As the Internet continues to grow at an alarming speed, so does the demand for Web design houses that understand both the intricacies of programming languages and the various elements of good Web design. This website for McDonald's uses streaming multimedia technologies to provide rich content. At the same time, its elegance and crisp design complement the brand's strong image.

check yourself ✓

1. How have accountability concerns affected agency compensation?
2. What do you think is the best way to compensate an agency? Explain your answer.
3. What are the most important things an advertiser should consider when selecting an agency?

THE SUPPLIERS IN ADVERTISING

The people and organizations that provide specialized services to the advertising business are called **suppliers**. Without their services it would be impossible to produce the billions of dollars' worth of advertising placed every year. Important suppliers include *art studios and Web design houses, printers, film and video production houses,* and *research companies.*

Art Studios and Web Designers

Art studios design and produce artwork and illustrations for advertisements. They may supplement the work of an agency's art department or even take its place for small agencies. Art studios are usually small with as few as three or four employees. Some, though, are large enough to employ several art directors, graphic designers, layout artists, production artists, and sales reps.

Most studios are owned and managed by a graphic designer or illustrator, who calls on agencies and advertising managers to sell the studio's services, takes projects back to the office to be produced, and then delivers them for the client's approval. The work is time-consuming and requires a talent for organization and management as well as a core competency in art direction and computer graphics.

Similar to art studios, **Web design houses** employ specialists who understand the intricacies of Internet programming languages and can design ads and websites that are both effective and cost efficient.

Printers and Related Specialists

The printers who produce brochures, stationery, business cards, sales promotion materials, and point-of-purchase displays are vital to the advertising business. Ranging from small instant-print

suppliers People and organizations that assist both advertisers and agencies in the preparation of advertising materials, such as photography, illustration, printing, and production.

art studios Companies that design and produce artwork and illustrations for advertisements, brochures, and other communication devices.

Web design houses Art/computer studios that employ specialists who understand the intricacies of HTML and Java programming languages and can design ads and Internet Web pages that are both effective and cost efficient.

printers Businesses that employ or contract with highly trained specialists who prepare artwork for reproduction, operate digital scanning machines to make color separations and plates, operate presses and collating machines, and run binderies.

production houses Companies that specialize in film or video production.

research suppliers Companies that conduct and analyze marketing research.

media A plural form of *medium,* referring to communications vehicles paid to present an advertisement to their target audience. Most often used to refer to radio and television networks, stations that have news reporters, and publications that carry news and advertising.

shops to large offset operations, **printers** employ or contract with highly trained specialists who prepare artwork for reproduction, operate digital scanning machines to make color separations and plates, operate presses and collating machines, and run binderies. Their sales reps must be highly skilled, and they often earn very large commissions.

Film and Video Houses

Few agencies have in-house TV production capabilities. Small agencies often work with local TV stations to produce commercials. But the large agencies normally work with independent **production houses** that specialize in film or video production or both.

Research Companies

Advertisers are concerned about the attitudes of their customers, the size of potential markets, and the acceptability of their products. Agencies want to know what advertising approaches to use, which concepts communicate most efficiently, and how effective past campaigns have been.

The media are concerned with the reading and viewing habits of their audiences, the desired markets of their advertiser-customers, and public perceptions toward their own particular medium.

Research, therefore, is closely allied to advertising and an important tool for marketing professionals. But most firms do not maintain a fully staffed research department. Instead, they use independent **research suppliers** or consultants. Research firms come in all sizes and specialties, and they employ statisticians, field interviewers, and computer programmers, as well as analysts with degrees in psychology, sociology, and marketing. We discuss research in Chapter 6.

THE MEDIA OF ADVERTISING

The *medium* that carries the advertiser's message is the vital connection between the company that manufactures a product or offers a service and the customer who may wish to buy it. Although the plural term **media** commonly describes channels of mass communication such as television, radio, newspapers, and magazines, it also refers to other communications vehicles such as direct mail, out-of-home media (transit, billboards, etc.), specialized media (aerial/blimps, inflatables), specialty advertising items (imprinted coffee mugs, balloons), and newer communication technologies such as digital media, interactive TV, and satellite networks. (Exhibit 3–8 shows the largest U.S. media companies.)

It is important to understand the various media, their role in the advertising business, and the significance of current media trends. For a person seeking a career in advertising, the media may offer the first door to employment, and for many they have provided great financial rewards.

We classify advertising media into six major categories: print, electronic, digital, out-of-home, direct mail, and other media. Due to recent media trends, there is some overlap. These media categories are discussed in Chapters 10 through 13.

CURRENT TRENDS

The ad agency business continues to go through many transitions. We mention just a few of the most important ones here: *industry consolidation,* the *decline of the commission system, changes resulting from new media,* and *the economic downturn that began in 2008.*

In the 1990s a consolidation left most of the famous agencies from decades earlier merged, dissolved, or absorbed, so that advertising was dominated by four enormous conglomerates. These were Omnicom and the Interpublic Group, both headquartered in New York; Publicis, based in Paris; and London's WPP Group. Together these companies account for over half of all advertising spending in the world. Structurally, the conglomerates act as giant holding companies for an assortment of agencies that specialize in different promotional activities (advertising, public relations, sales promotion, direct-response, media buying, etc.) and audiences (general consumer, B2B, minorities, etc.).

Why did this consolidation happen? One important factor is globalization and the emergence of global brands. The conglomerates offer big advertisers services in markets around

▼EXHIBIT 3-8 Top media companies in 2011, by category and percentage change from 2010.

Broadcast TV		Net Revenue ($ millions)		Digital		Net Revenue ($ millions)	
Rank	Media Company	2011	% Chg from 2010	Rank	Media Company	2011	% Chg from 2010
1	CBS Corp.	$5,637	−3.1	1	Google	$11,961	28.7
2	News Corp.	4,734	−0.9	2	Yahoo	2,955	−10.9
3	Comcast Corp. 1	4,256	−11.6	3	Facebook	2,067	69
4	Walt Disney Co.	4,099	2.5	4	Microsoft Corp.	1,676	5.9
5	Univision Communications	1,777	1	5	IAC/InterActiveCorp. 1	1,538	14.1

Cable Networks		Net Revenue ($ millions)		Magazine		Net Revenue ($ millions)	
Rank	Media Company	2011	% Chg from 2010	Rank	Media Company	2011	% Chg from 2010
1	Walt Disney Co.	$11,154	10.9	1	Time Warner	$3,043	−0.9
2	Time Warner	9,983	6.9	2	Advance Publications	2,943	−0.6
3	Viacom	7,111	10.7	3	Hearst Corp. 1	2,223	−2
4	News Corp.	6,406	9.9	4	Meredith Corp.	778	1.9
5	Comcast Corp. 1	6,073	2.1	5	Wenner Media	626	3.7

Newspapers		Net Revenue ($ millions)		Out of Home		Net Revenue ($ millions)	
Rank	Media Company	2011	% Chg from 2010	Rank	Media Company	2011	% Chg from 2010
1	Gannett Co.	$3,050	−5.3	1	Clear Channel Communications	$1,190	3.6
2	Tribune Co.	2,009	−4.7	2	Lamar Advertising Co. 1	1,136	3.3
3	The New York Times Co. 1	1,818	−1.5	3	CBS Corp.	1,039	5.8
4	Advance Publications	1,504	−5.7	4	National CineMedia	421	2.5
5	News Corp.	1,114	−6.2	5	JCDecaux	250	0.1

Radio		Net Revenue ($ millions)	
Rank	Media Company	2011	% Chg from 2010
1	Clear Channel Communications 1	$3,038	0.1
2	CBS Corp.	1,331	0.7
3	Cumulus Media 1	1,142	−3.3
4	Entercom Communications Corp.	383	−2.2
5	Cox Enterprises	350	−5.7

Source: Reprinted with permission (Oct. 1, 2012, *Advertising Age*, p. 43). Copyright Crain Communications Inc.

the world and in whatever promotional channels such clients might require. A second factor is the decline in importance of traditional media and the growing interest in IMC. Profitable agencies have found they need to offer a menu of services rather than rely on income from only one part of the promotional mix. Third, the conglomerates can save their clients money, both because they have substantial power in negotiating favorable media rates for their clients and because they've reached new heights in efficiency by reducing administrative overhead and expenses.

But bigger is not always better, and in recent years the ad industry has witnessed a countervailing trend toward small specialty shops and boutiques. This is because some advertisers are not happy with the quality of the creative work that comes out of the conglomerate agencies. They also question whether the giants

have too much power over media spending. And clients have sometimes been hesitant to give their account to an agency within a conglomerate where a separate agency serves a competitor.

As noted earlier, another industry trend has been the slow death of the commission system. While still used, a number of influential advertisers no longer pay commissions and instead insist on an incentive approach. From the perspective of many clients, commissions have at least two significant problems: First, they provide a powerful incentive for agencies to select media that are expensive and commissionable (like television) instead of media that might be more likely to reach and persuade consumers. Second, commissions encourage agencies to focus on the ad budget rather than on strategy and ideas. Pat Fallon and Fred Senn of Fallon Worldwide have suggested that some agencies have fallen into the trap of thinking that advertisers should "outspend rather than outthink" competitors. They argue that agencies can better serve their clients by focusing on "creative leverage," not "media leverage."[44]

Ways to Be a Better Client [3–D]

These are some ideas your client may wish to keep in mind as they think about working with you.

Relationships

- *Cultivate honesty.* Be truthful in your meetings and in your ads.
- *Be enthusiastic.* When you like the ads, let the agency know.
- *Be frank when you don't like the advertising.* Always cite a reason when turning down an idea.
- *Be human.* React like a person, not a corporation. Laugh at funny ads even if they don't work.
- *Be willing to admit you're unsure.* Don't be pressured. Let your agency know when you need time.
- *Allow the agency to feel responsible.* Tell the agency what you feel is wrong, not how to fix it.
- *Care about being a client.* Creative people work best for clients they like.

Management

- *Don't insulate your top managers from creative people.* Agency creatives work best when objectives come from the top, not filtered through layers.
- *Set objectives.* For timely and quality service from your agency, establish and openly share your marketing objectives.
- *Switch people, not agencies.* When problems arise, agencies often prefer to bring in fresh talent rather than lose you as a client.
- *Be sure the agency makes a profit on your account.* Demanding more services from your agency than fees or commissions can cover hurts relationships.

Production

- *Avoid nitpicking last-minute changes.* Perfection is important, but waiting until the last moment to make minor changes can damage the client–agency relationship. Agencies see such behavior as indecisive and/or arrogant and lose respect for the client.
- *Be aware of the cost of changes (both time and money).* The cost of making major changes at the production stage may be five times greater than in the earlier stages.
- *Don't change concepts during the production stage.* Late changes can inadvertently alter product positioning and image.

Media

- *Understand the economics (and economies) of media.* Be prepared to deal with costs per thousand (CPMs), costs per ratings point (CPP), and other key elements of media planning and buying so that you can evaluate and appreciate your agency's media strategy.
- *Understand the importance of lead time.* Early buys can eliminate late fees, earn discounts, make you eligible for special promotions, strengthen your agency's buying position, and reduce anxiety.
- *Avoid interfering with the agency's media relationship.* The stronger your agency's buying position, the greater the discounts available to you. Refrain from cutting deals with media reps directly and plan media use well in advance.
- *Avoid media arrogance ("they need us").* Some media will deal with clients, and some won't. Misinterpret this relationship and you may either pay more than you should or be too late to get into a medium you need.
- *Avoid insularity.* Be willing to let your mind travel beyond your immediate environment and lifestyle.
- *Suggest work sessions.* Set up informal give-and-take sessions with creatives and strategists.
- *Keep the creative people involved in your business.* Agency creatives do their best work for you when they're in tune with the ups and downs of your business.

Research

- *Share information.* Pool information to create new and bigger opportunities.
- *Involve the agency in research projects.* An agency's creative talent gets its best ideas from knowledge of your environment.

Creative

- *Learn the fine art of conducting the creative meeting.* Deal with the important issues first: strategy, consumer benefits, and reasons why.
- *Look for the big idea.* Concentrate on positioning strategy and brand personality. Don't allow a single ad—no matter how brilliant—to change the positioning or personality of the product.
- *Insist on creative discipline.* The creative process stimulates concepts and actions. Discipline helps keep focus on those that count the most.
- *Don't be afraid to ask for great advertising.* Agencies prefer the high road, but as the client you must be willing to accompany them. If the agency slips, be strong and ask it to try again.

> **Another industry trend has been the slow death of the commission system.**

Throughout its history, advertising has experienced dramatic changes in the face of new media technologies. This is just as true today. Among the important trends here are the growth of media options, the empowerment of consumers as content creators, and reorganization in the ranks of media companies as new upstarts replace established firms in importance.

Media options are exploding with technologies such as TV and video on demand, social media, the Internet, computer games, smartphones, personal digital assistants (PDAs), computer tablets, iPods, GPS systems, and so on. Even older technologies like radio and television are experiencing rapid change (digital cable, interactive TV, satellite radio). These technologies present real opportunities, but also significant challenges, to the knowledge and skills of people who work in agency media and creative departments.

No change wrought by the new media is of greater importance than audience empowerment. The days of expecting media consumers to follow the dictates of content creators, whether they be newspapers, television networks, or magazines, are over. Today people watch what they want, when they want, and expect it for free. Netflix fits this trend perfectly. In addition, social media such as Facebook and YouTube offer seemingly infinite content created by and for ordinary users. Older consumers may still watch network TV, but younger ones are often found elsewhere. These young consumers frequent popular websites like LinkedIn and Pinterest where there is little difference between those who create the content and those who consume it. Agencies know how important these sites are to many consumers, and they have responded by trying to create "viral" ads that social site users can find and recommend to friends. This may or may not ultimately prove effective. But for the foreseeable future the consumer is in charge as never before.

One of the biggest successes in the recent history of advertising is Google. With revenues that dwarf the combined incomes of ABC, NBC, and CBS, Google's revenue growth is the envy of the industry. In Chapter 12 you'll find out more about how a company that is barely more than 15 years old succeeded so greatly. For now it is enough to know that Google's profits come from the company's belief that relevance is the most important factor in effective advertising.

Finally, the entire advertising industry has been affected by the economic downturn that started in 2008 and was still affecting Americans and much of Europe in 2011. The downturn has transformed entire industries (such as the U.S. auto industry) and even led to some grumbling about capitalism, the engine of American prosperity for much of the twentieth century. History says that when companies face a recession they cut back on marketing. And despite a few exceptions, this decline has been no different. Having to do more with less, the agency landscape has been changed, perhaps forever. ■

learn about, practice, and apply the functions of advertising in the business of advertising!

M: Advertising was developed for students who want information packaged in a concise, easy-to-read, yet interesting format.

Check out the book's website to:

- Learn whether you have what it takes to land a job in an ad agency. (Exploring Advertising)
- Show how to bill a client for your agency work. (Exploring Advertising)
- Describe the things agencies will need to do to adapt to the media options created by new technologies. (Review Questions)

While you are there, check out the professional resource links, review the PowerPoint presentation, and test your knowledge with the Multiple Choice Quiz. Additionally, *Connect® Marketing* is available for M: Advertising.

www.mhhe.com/ArensM2e

chapter four

segmentation, targeting, **and the marketing mix**

This chapter describes the role that advertising plays in facilitating transactions and satisfying needs and wants. To accomplish this, marketers must direct advertising to the most appropriate audiences. Because no product or service pleases everybody, marketers need to select specific target markets that offer the greatest potential. They can then fine-tune their mix of marketing elements (the four Ps) to match the needs or wants of the target market.

Advertising success is not just about what you say, but to whom you say it. Case in point, perhaps the best campaign of 2011, the Old Spice "Man Your Man Could Smell Like" promotion. A key secret to the campaign's success? Addressing male body wash ads—to women. Targeting ads for a male brand to a female target audience was unusual, but then, just about everything about this campaign was. To fully appreciate the ads, let's see why Old Spice needed to produce a game-changing campaign in the first place.

Old Spice was first sold in the 1930s. Owned by consumer giant Procter & Gamble (P&G), Old Spice initially became a consumer staple as a men's aftershave lotion. Later, as male consumers showed interest in other grooming products, including lotions and liquid soaps, Old Spice introduced brand extensions to meet those demands.

In 1983, P&G's global archrival, Unilever, introduced Axe. As a younger product, Axe had credibility in positioning itself as a sexy alternative. While Old Spice ads over the years had tended to be safe and conventional, Axe used provocative spots suggesting the simple application of Axe makes men irresistible to beautiful women.[1] However implausible the "irresistibility" appeal may seem, it worked. By the 2000s, Axe established a healthy lead in market share.

continued on p. 90

LEARNING OBJECTIVES

After studying this chapter, you will be able to:

L04-1 Explain the role of advertising in facilitating satisfying exchanges.

L04-2 Illustrate the various methods advertisers use to segment and aggregate consumer and business markets.

L04-3 Discuss how defining a target market enhances a product's marketing strategy.

L04-4 Describe the elements of the marketing mix and the role advertising plays in each element of the mix.

continued from p. 89

By 2010, Procter & Gamble had to consider whether to invest in a mature brand or abandon it. P&G decided to assign the challenge of reinvigorating Old Spice to one of the world's greatest agencies, Wieden+Kennedy. W+K built its reputation by making Nike a world leader in footwear. Its new challenge would be making Old Spice fresh, relevant, even hip.[2]

Before starting, the agency and client made a big decision. They would create ads that appealed to both men (who use body wash) and women (who often buy it for them). The campaign slogan would be "the man your man could smell like."

In the first commercial, former NFL player Isaiah Mustafa, standing in front of a running shower dressed only in a bath towel, addressed the intended audience right from the start. "Hello ladies," he confidently intoned. "Look at your man, now back to me, now back at your man, now back to me. Sadly, he isn't me. But if he stopped using lady-scented body wash and switched to Old Spice, he could smell like he's me."[3] The fast-paced and somewhat absurd style of the ad, along with Mustafa's charm and humor, made the ad an immediate hit. Old Spice was back.

But now what? Advertising is filled with "one-hit wonder" campaigns that quickly fizzle. Perhaps the most famous example was Budweiser's "Whassup" campaign. Funny the first few times maybe. Not the tenth or twentieth.

So W+K changed the game. After the Old Spice television campaign drew national attention, the agency began using Mustafa in social media, developing dozens of different, personalized executions for key influencers like Ellen DeGeneres. Naturally Ellen was flattered and invited Mustafa on her show. More buzz for Old Spice. And a Cannes Grand Prix for the campaign.[4]

W+K still wasn't done. It decided to create a viral story line for Mustafa's "Old Spice guy." Jason Bagley, creative director at

exchange The trading of one thing of value for another thing of value.

target market The market segment or group within the market segment toward which all marketing activities will be directed.

target audience The specific group of individuals to whom the advertising message is directed.

Thus, we can think of marketing as the process companies use to make a profit by identifying and satisfying their customers' needs and desires. This chapter defines and outlines marketing issues to clarify advertising's proper role in the marketing function. As we shall see, the relationship between advertising and marketing is critical.

check yourself ✓

1. What is the value of discovering the needs and wants that exist in the marketplace?
2. In what ways does advertising facilitate exchanges?
3. Why do marketers care if customers are satisfied after they buy products?

L04-2 Illustrate the various methods advertisers use to segment and aggregate consumer and business markets.

THE MARKET SEGMENTATION PROCESS

Marketing and advertising people constantly scan the marketplace to see how consumers and businesses might be better satisfied. The process of market segmentation involves two steps: *identifying groups of people* (or organizations) with certain shared needs and characteristics and *aggregating* (combining) these groups into larger market segments according to their interest in the product's utility. This process should result in market segments large enough to target and reachable through a suitable mix of marketing activities—including advertising.

Markets often consist of many segments. A company may differentiate its products and marketing strategy for every segment, or concentrate its marketing activities on only one or a few segments. Either task is far from simple. Procter and Gamble markets at least five different body washes to appeal to multiple segments. We saw that Old Spice body wash is going after women who want their men to smell like men (and certainly attracts male buyers in the process). At the other extreme, Herbal Essence body wash appeals to women who desire irresistible, natural fragrances. Ivory seeks out everyday women who want a clean, simple, and affordable body wash. Olay targets women who care about moist, healthy skin, and Gillette focuses on men who want a "powerful clean." Catering to all these needs on a global level requires a sophisticated marketing and communications system. In this

Old Spice is a mature brand. But with the use of clever, witty, even somewhat absurd advertising, the brand rebounded strongly. Wieden+Kennedy's great work suggests that, with the right message, brands can find their own Fountain of Youth.

chapter, we look first at how marketers identify and categorize *consumer markets* and second at the techniques they use to segment *business markets.* Then we discuss various strategic options companies use, including advertising, to match their products with markets and create profitable exchanges.

Types of Markets

A firm's marketing activities are always aimed at a particular segment of the population—its **target market**. Likewise, advertising is aimed at a particular group called the **target audience**. When we see an ad that doesn't appeal to us, it may be because the ad is not aimed at any of the groups we belong to. For example, a TV commercial for denture cream isn't meant to appeal to youngsters. They're not part of either the target market or the target audience. There are two main types of target markets, consumers and businesses.

This ad for Virgin Airlines helps to identify the target audience and convey a "personality" for the brand. This ad resonates with the company's young target audiences.

Consumer Markets Most of the advertising we see daily in the mass media—TV, radio, newspapers, and magazines—falls under the broad category of consumer advertising. Usually sponsored by the producer (or manufacturer) of the product or service, these ads are typically directed at consumers, people who buy the product for their own or someone else's personal use. The consumer market is huge, spending over $10 trillion every year on products and services in the United States alone.[7]

In the end, customers are people. So advertising professionals must understand how people act and think—and why they buy what they buy. This requires great skill. In fact, this area of study is the province of another specialty in marketing, consumer behavior, a topic we'll discuss in Chapter 5.

Business Markets Companies use business advertising to reach people who buy goods and services for resale, for use in their own business, or for manufacturing other products. It tends to appear in specialized business publications or professional journals, in direct-mail pieces sent to businesses, at trade shows, or on company Web sites. Since business advertising (also called business-to-business, or B2B, advertising) rarely uses consumer mass media, it is typically invisible to consumers. However, some business-to-business ads, by firms such as computer manufacturers or overnight parcel shippers, do appear on TV and in consumer magazines.

In addition to general business advertising, there are three specialized types of business advertising: trade, professional, and agricultural. Companies aim trade advertising at resellers (wholesalers, dealers, and retailers) to obtain greater distribution of their products. For example, Sunkist places trade advertising in publications such as *Progressive Grocer* to develop more grocery outlets and to increase sales to existing outlets. Advertising aimed at teachers, accountants, doctors, dentists, architects, engineers, lawyers, and the like is called professional advertising and typically appears in official publications of professional societies (such as the *Archives of Ophthalmology*). Companies use agricultural (or farm) advertising to promote products and services used in agriculture to farmers and others employed in agribusiness. FMC Corp., for example, might advertise its plant nutrition products to citrus growers in *Farm Journal Magazine.*

Business customers are often very knowledgeable and sophisticated, and they may require extensive technical information before buying. So people who work in business-to-business advertising often need more specialized product knowledge and experience than their consumer advertising colleagues.

Segmenting the Consumer Market: Finding the Right Niche

The concept of *shared characteristics* is critical to market segmentation. Marketing and advertising people know that, based on their needs, wants, and mental files, consumers leave "footprints in the sand"—the telltale signs of where they live and work, what they buy, and how they spend their

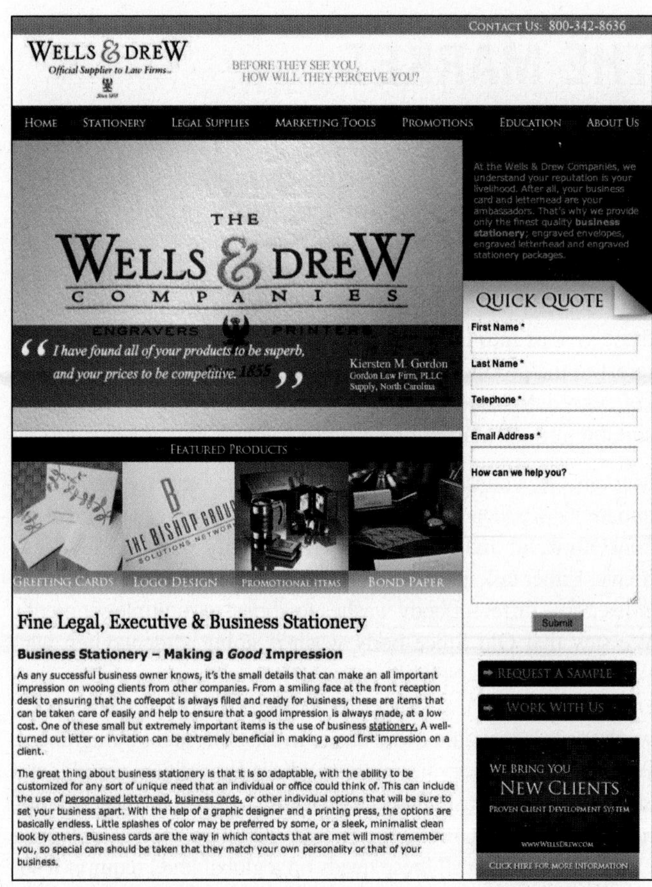

Professional advertising targets audiences in fields such as accounting, medicine, and education. Law firms are the intended target of this ad.

> The goal is to find that particular niche (or space) in the market where the advertiser's product or service will fit.

leisure time. By following these footprints, marketers can locate and define groups of consumers with similar needs and wants, create messages for them, and know how and where to send those messages. The goal is to find that particular niche (or space) in the market where the advertiser's product or service will fit.

Marketers group these shared characteristics into categories *(behavioristic, geographic, demographic,* and *psychographic)* to identify and segment consumer markets (see Exhibit 4–2). The marketer's purpose is twofold: first, to identify people who are likely to be responsive; and second, to develop rich descriptions of them in order to better understand them, create marketing mixes for them, and reach them with meaningful advertising or other communications.

The term *1to1 marketing* was introduced by Don Peppers and Martha Rogers in their 1994 book *The One to One Future* to illustrate the importance of treating different customers differently. The principle is that potential customers can be segmented so specifically that a different marketing message can be sent to each one based on his or her individual demographic, behavioristic, and psychographic characteristics. It is not typically feasible to achieve true 1to1 customization, but the more narrowly defined a customer segment the more accurately it can be targeted.[8] In the past, achieving 1to1 marketing required the use of a direct sales force, where a sales representative could customize an approach for a limited number of individual customers. Today, data gathered from Internet interactions are allowing marketers to conceive of 1to1 customization on a large scale. We'll discuss this further in Chapter 12.

EXHIBIT 4–2 Methods for segmenting consumer markets.

Variables	Typical Breakdowns
Geographic	
Region	Pacific; Mountain; West North Central; West South Central; East North Central; East South Central; South Atlantic; Middle Atlantic; New England
County size	A, B, C, D
Climate	Dry, humid, rain, snow
City or SMSA size	Under 5,000; 5,000–19,999; 20,000–49,999; 50,000–99,999; 100,000–249,000; 250,000–499,999; 500,000–999,999; 1,000,000–3,999,999; 4,000,000 or over
Density	Urban, suburban, rural
Behavioristic	
Purchase occasion	Regular occasion, special occasion
Benefits sought	Economy, convenience, prestige
User status	Nonuser, ex-user, potential user, first-time user, regular user
Usage rate	Light user, medium user, heavy user
Loyalty status	None, medium, strong, absolute
Readiness stage	Unaware, aware, informed, interested, desirous, intending to buy
Marketing-factor sensitivity	Quality, price, service, advertising, sales promotion
Psychographic	
Societal divisions	Upper crust, movers and shakers, successful singles, Social Security, middle of the road, metro-ethnic mix
Lifestyle	Strivers, achievers, actualizers
Personality	Compulsive, gregarious, authoritarian, ambitious

Variables	Typical Breakdowns
Demographic	
Age	Under 6, 6–11, 12–19, 20–34, 35–49, 50–64, 65+
Gender	Male, female
Family size	1–2, 3–4, 5+
Family life cycle	Young, single; young, married, no children; young, married, youngest child under 6; young, married, youngest child 6 or over; young, unmarried, with children; older, married, with children; older, unmarried, with children; older, married, no children under 18; older, single; other
Income	Under \$10,000; \$10,000–20,000; \$20,000–30,000; \$30,000–40,000; \$40,000–60,000; \$60,000–100,000; \$100,000–150,000; \$150,000 and over
Occupation	Professional and technical; managers, officials, and proprietors; clerical, sales; craftspeople, supervisors; operatives; farmers; retired; students; homemakers; unemployed
Education	Grade school or less; some high school; high school graduates; some college; college graduates
Religion	Catholic, Protestant, Jewish, other
Race	White, Black, Asian
Nationality	American, British, French, German, Scandinavian, Italian, Latin American, Middle Eastern, Japanese

> **"[BEHAVIORAL SEGMENTATION TELLS] US WHO OUR CUSTOMERS ARE NOW, WHEN AND WHY THEY BUY, AND HOW MUCH THEY CONSUME."**

Behavioristic segmentation is one of the best ways to organize consumer markets. Purchase behavior variables, such as the benefits sought by the consumer, determine how the segments are defined. In this ad, Porsche (www.porsche.com) appeals to enthusiasts for whom performance is everything.

Behavioristic Segmentation One of the best ways to segment markets is to group consumers by purchase behavior. This is called **behavioristic segmentation.** Behavioral segments are determined by many variables, but the most important are *user status, usage rate, purchase occasion,* and *benefits sought.* These categories tell us who our customers are now, when and why they buy, and how much they consume.

User-status variables. Many markets can be segmented by the **user status** of prospective customers. Researchers Stephan and Tannenholz have identified six categories of consumers based on user status.

Sole users are the most brand loyal and require the least amount of advertising and promotion. *Semisole* users typically use Brand A but have an alternate selection if it is not available or if the alternate is promoted with a discount. *Discount users* are the semisole users of competing Brand B. They don't buy Brand A at full price but perceive it well enough to buy it at a discount. *Aware nontriers* use competitive products in the category but haven't taken a liking to Brand A. A different advertising message could help, but these people rarely offer much potential. *Trial/rejectors* bought Brand A's advertising message, but didn't like the product. More advertising won't help; only a reformulation of Brand A will bring them back. *Repertoire users* perceive two or more brands to have superior attributes and will buy at full price. They are the primary brand switchers and respond to persuasive advertising based on their fluctuating wants and desires. Therefore, they should be a primary target for brand advertising.[9]

Usage-rate variables. It's usually easier to get a heavy user to increase usage than a light user. In **volume segmentation**, marketers measure people's **usage rates** to define consumers as light, medium, or heavy users of products (see Exhibit 4–3). Often, 20 percent of the population consumes 80 percent of the product. Marketers want to define that 20 percent and aim their advertising at them. Hardee's, a fast-food hamburger chain owned by CKE Restaurants, Inc., even has a pet name for its prized 17- to 34-year-old male market segment: the HFFU (pronounced who-foo). According to Andrew Puzder, CKE's CEO, "That's the 'heavy fast-food user,' someone who eats there four or five times a week. . . . It is the sweet spot of the industry and what appeals to him is drippy, messy burgers. He is not interested in little 99-cent burgers or low-carb anything."[10]

By finding common characteristics among heavy users of their products, marketers can define product differences and focus ad campaigns more effectively. For example, independent businesspeople who travel at their own expense, the group that

While Apple is best known for its Macs, iPods, and iPhones, it uses its strong brand name to promote newer products like the iPad. For sole users, this ad reinforces their brand loyalty, and for repertoire users—those most likely to switch brands—it persuades them that Apple products are the superior choice.

behavioristic segmentation Method of segmenting consumers based on the benefits being sought.

user status Six categories into which consumers can be placed, which reflect varying degrees of loyalty to certain brands and products. The categories are *sole users, semisole users, discount users, aware nontriers, trial/rejectors,* and *repertoire users.*

volume segmentation Defining consumers as light, medium, or heavy users of products.

usage rates The extent to which consumers use a product: light, medium, or heavy.

purchase occasion A method of segmenting markets on the basis of *when* consumers buy and use a good or service.

▼EXHIBIT 4–3 Usage rates vary for different products.

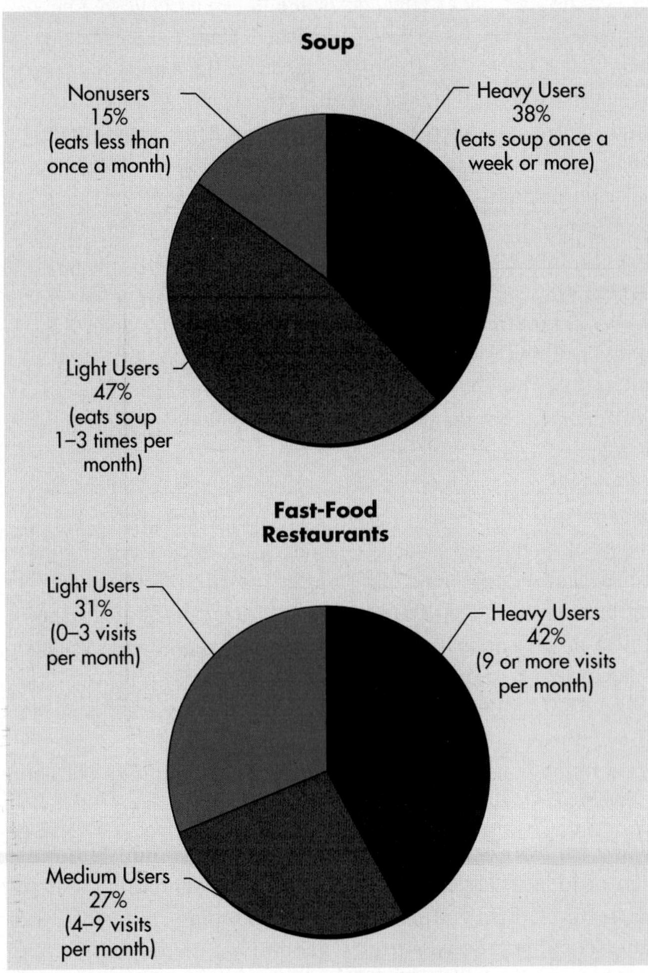

Fallon Worldwide describes as "road warriors," are heavy users of budget hotel chains, with some spending over a hundred nights a year on the road. In creating a campaign that targeted this group for Holiday Inn Express, Fallon also discovered that road warriors make their travel plans at the beginning of the week and like to watch ESPN, CNN, and the Weather Channel. Such knowledge was vital in helping Fallon media people schedule messages when and where the target audience would be most responsive.

Marketers of one product sometimes find that their customers are also heavy users of other products and can define target markets in terms of the usage rates of the other products. For example, upper-income households are overrepresented among buyers of Infinitis, Samsung mobile phones, Starbucks coffee, and Tom's of Maine toothpaste. Conversely, low-income households are more likely to buy Kias, prepaid mobile phones, and Pepsodent toothpaste.[11]

Purchase-occasion variables. Buyers can also be distinguished by when they buy or use a product or service—the **purchase occasion**. Air travelers, for example, may fly for business or vacation so one airline might promote business travel while another promotes tourism. The purchase occasion might be affected by frequency of need (regular or occasional), a fad (candy, computer games), or seasons (water skis, raincoats). The Japan Weather Association tracked buying patterns on 20,000 items and correlated them to the outside temperature. Not surprisingly, when the temperature goes up, people buy

Crest is a leader in identifying the benefits sought by consumers. This ad addresses whiter teeth. How many other dental-hygiene benefits can you think of? And how might these be addressed in a different ad?

Brand Niching May Cause Brand Switching

Advertisers recognize that offensive advertisements don't pay. They know that alienating or stereotyping minorities and other groups causes serious controversy and bad PR for their clients. And, in addition to avoiding the negative effects, there are benefits to being culturally sensitive in advertising: Hispanics, African Americans, Asian Americans, gays, and other minority groups are all sizable target markets with considerable buying power—so much buying power, in fact, that many marketing campaigns are designed specifically to appeal to these consumers.

Unfortunately, even advertisements that are designed to be sensitive can sometimes backfire. During the 2000 Olympics, John Hancock Financial Services made a sudden revision to a commercial set to air during the events. In the spot, two women were shown together in an airport holding an Asian infant whom they presumably had just adopted. Although the ad never specifically identified the child's nationality, international adoption agencies pressured Hancock to amend the ad to avoid offending the Chinese government, which would be opposed to the evident homosexuality of the American parents. Hancock was lucky—the ad was caught before it aired. This isn't always the case, and the results can be disastrous when a controversial ad is aired.

To counter accusations that it favored white clientele over its African American patrons, Denny's created some ads that attempted to resolve the issue—badly. The three-spot television campaign featured black customers being "welcomed back" to Denny's and having the time of their lives. However, 100 percent of the people Denny's "welcomed back" were black, affluent, well-dressed, and apparently aristocratic and successful. One would think that if Denny's were going to solely feature African American customers in the ad, it would do so with a fair representation of the group. Instead of creating an ad that proved Denny's was racially unbiased, as intended, the company had displayed the same behavior it was trying to resolve. Although the company later worked to improve its image, the damage was done.

Not only businesses and retailers have these problems; nonprofit and government organizations also have to watch their step. During the 2002 Super Bowl, the White House introduced a new series of antidrug public service announcements. The campaign tried to link the money spent on drugs to the funding of terrorist activities. Print and television ads in muted black-and-white traced teens' use of drugs for recreation through the supply chain back to tragic, violent episodes in drug-producing regions. To say that the guilt-trip method did not go over well with teenagers would be putting it mildly. Teens felt that the ads were deliberately manipulative and misrepresented the facts in an attempt to support President George W. Bush's war on terrorism. As a result, studies showed that, over time, teens exposed to the ads shifted to a significantly more "prodrug" attitude than those of kids who did not view the ads. In short, the ads fostered enough resentment among their target audience that teens deliberately defied the message being sent.

Advertising sensitivity is a difficult issue. What is politically correct enough? When is something *too* politically correct? And what should be done when a conflict cannot be avoided? Some groups simply cannot be targeted without excluding, and thereby offending, other groups. When this happens, a choice must be made, and it must be made carefully, with serious consideration of all potential consequences.

more sunshades, air conditioners, watermelons, and swimwear. When there's a chill in the air, sales of suits, sweaters, and heaters take off.[12] A marketer who discovers common purchase occasions for a group has a potential target segment and can better determine when to run specials and when to promote certain product categories.

Benefits-sought variables. Consumers seek various **benefits** in the products they buy—high quality, low price, status, sex appeal, fragrance, natural. Procter and Gamble identified the most important benefits sought by body wash users and developed products to meet their needs. In addition to tangible benefits, consumers are motivated by *symbolism*—what the brand name means to them, to their friends, or to some social reference group. **Benefit segmentation** is the prime objective of many consumer attitude studies and the basis for many successful ad campaigns.

Some product categories are characterized by substantial *brand switching* from one purchase occasion to the next. Researchers have determined that switching occurs in response to different *need states* that consumers may experience from one occasion to another.

Using behavioristic segmentation, we can accomplish the first step of identifying likely prospects for our marketing and advertising efforts. The next step in developing rich profiles of these customers makes use of geographic, demographic, and psychographic characteristics.

Geographic Segmentation One simple way to define markets is by using **geographic segmentation**. People in one region of the country (or the world) have needs, wants, and purchasing habits that differ from those in other regions. People in Sun Belt states, for example, buy more suntan lotion. Canadians buy special equipment for dealing with snow and ice—products many Floridians have never seen in stores.

When marketers analyze geographic data, they study sales by region, country size, city size, specific locations, and types of stores. Many products sell well in urban areas but poorly in

benefits The particular product attributes offered to customers, such as high quality, low price, status, speed, sex appeal, good taste, and so on.

benefit segmentation Method of segmenting consumers based on the benefits being sought.

geographic segmentation A method of segmenting markets by geographic regions based on the shared characteristics, needs, or wants of people within a region.

demographic segmentation Based on a population's statistical characteristics such as gender, age, ethnicity, education, occupation, income, or other quantifiable factors.

geodemographic segmentation Combining demographics with geographic segmentation to select target markets in advertising.

suburban or rural ones, and vice versa. As we'll see in Chapter 14, this type of information is critical in developing advertising media schedules because, with limited budgets, marketers want to advertise in areas where their sales potential is best.

Even in local markets, geographic segmentation is important. For example, a local progressive politician might send a mailer only to precincts where voters typically support liberal causes, and a local retail store rarely draws customers from outside a fairly limited *trading area.*

Demographic Segmentation

Demographic segmentation is a way to define groups by their statistical characteristics: gender, age, ethnicity, education, occupation, income, and other quantifiable factors. For example, research shows that people who identify themselves as "strongly Hispanic" tend to be very loyal to certain brands. And, as Exhibit 4–4 reveals, the number of Americans with Hispanic ancestry is expected to grow at a rate much faster than the overall population well into this century. This has meant a surge in advertising dollars allocated to Hispanic media. The Hispanic advertising industry is outpacing all other sectors of advertising, growing four times faster and recently topping \$5 billion.[13] Many blue-chip advertisers, such as Procter & Gamble, AT&T, McDonald's, and General Motors, now aim a significant portion of their advertising specifically at this trillion-dollar market.

Demographics are often combined with geographic segmentation to select target markets for advertising. This is called **geodemographic segmentation**.

▼EXHIBIT 4–4 Projected U.S. Hispanic population and Hispanic media spending growth rates.

Year	Hispanic (thousands)	Total U.S. (thousands)	Hispanic % of Total
2015	\$ 57,075	\$321,363	17.8%
2020	63,784	333,896	19.1
2025	70,973	345,407	20.5
2030	78,655	358,471	21.9
2035	86,659	369,662	23.4
2040	94,876	380,016	25.0
2045	103,259	389,934	26.5
2050	111,732	399,803	27.9
2055	120,242	409,873	29.3
2060	128,780	420,268	30.6

Source: U.S. Census Bureau.

Hispanic media ad spending growth rates versus all media first quarter 2013 vs. first quarter 2012.

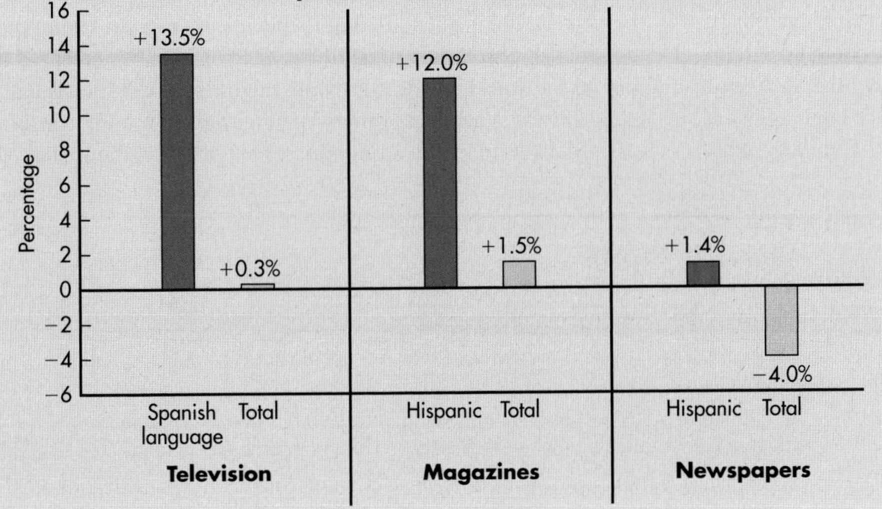

Source: Michael Sebastian, "First-Quarter Ad Spending Comes in Flat," June 25, 2012, www.adage.com/article/media/ad-spending-flat-quarter/242829. Reprinted with permission (June 25, 2013, *Advertising Age* Media News). Copyright Crain Communications Inc.

This Hardee's ad is clearly using behavioristic segmentation. Marketing of the Thickburger is directed at heavy users who seek the benefit of large, meaty burgers.

including values, attitudes, personality, and lifestyle.

personality, and lifestyle.

An understanding of the primary motivation of individuals helps advertisers promote and sell goods and services.

capacities that consumers can draw upon. The resource axis includes education, income, self-confidence, health, eagerness to buy, and energy level.

Geodemographic segmentation is based on two simple principles:

- People who live in the same neighborhood tend to be demographically similar.
- Neighborhoods can be categorized in terms of the characteristics of their populations and two or more neighborhoods can be placed in the same category (i.e., they contain similar types of people), even though they are geographically separated.[14]

Mosaic, Experian's geodemographic segmentation tool, classifies the population into groups or segments, according to their demographic and lifestyle traits right down to individual households. This provides advertisers with a complete picture of their audience based on their offline traits and online behavior, providing the insights needed to direct their advertising in a much more targeted way.[15]

JCPenney, for example, discovered that its Sandra Salcedo line of clothing for Hispanic women sold well in Texas and Northern California stores but not in heavily Mexican American Los Angeles, where urban influences hold greater sway. In other words, people's lives are influenced by their environment as well as by their ethnicity.[16]

As people grow older, their responsibilities and incomes change, and so do their interests in various product categories (see Exhibit 4–5). The auto industry didn't forget that over half of America's consumers are now young adults; the 63 million children of baby boomers are now potential car buyers. To reach out to this group, Toyota promoted its Yaris sedan with a campaign that includes a mobile phone series, a profile page on MySpace.com, and skits featuring the Yaris on the TV show *MADtv*.[17] Similarly, Ford targeted 25- to 35-year-olds with a series of "rockumentary" films about its Fusion sedan. The films, which featured the Norwegian rock group Hurra Torpedo, are available online and represent an attempt by the automaker to reach younger consumers.[18]

Demographic segmentation has long been understood in the fast-food industry. Once stigmatized as unsanitary meat fit only for poor people, chains like White Castle and McDonald's used advertising to change the hamburger's image, fashioning it into the national cuisine by the 1950s.[19] Now, children are McDonald's primary target consumers. Decades of ads for Happy Meals have made an impression. Among fictional characters, Ronald McDonald's cultural penetration is surpassed only by Santa Claus: 96 percent of schoolchildren in the United States can identify the yellow-jumpsuited clown.[20] Against this giant's brand value and advertising expenditures, competitors have returned to the hamburger's traditional consumer, the young male. In the segment where McDonald's is slightly weaker, Hardee's and Carl's Jr. intend to be strong.

In international markets, the demographics of many populations are changing rapidly. From India to Brazil to Poland, middle-class life is becoming available to more people in former Third World countries. This emerging middle class has an apparently insatiable appetite for consumer goods—everything from color TVs and computer tablets to smart phones, cars, and refrigerators.[21] In India, for example, the average salary increased 14 percent in 2005. Spending habits have shifted from buying necessities to purchasing lifestyle products. China has emerged as one of the world's fastest-growing advertising markets as companies try to reach that country's increasingly wealthy consumers. Market research company eMarketer predicts that ad

▼**EXHIBIT 4–5** Heavy usage patterns of various age groups.

Age	Name of Age Group	Merchandise Purchased
0–5	Young children	Baby food, toys, nursery furniture, children's wear
6–19	Schoolchildren and teenagers	Clothing, sporting goods, smart phones, iTunes, school supplies, fast food, soft drinks, candy, cosmetics, movies
20–34	Young adults	Cars, furniture, housing, food and beer, clothing, diamonds, home entertainment equipment, recreational equipment, purchases for younger age segments
35–49	Younger middle-aged	Larger homes, better cars, second cars, new furniture, computers, recreational equipment, jewelry, clothing, food and wine
50–64	Older middle-aged	Recreational items, purchases for young marrieds and infants, travel
65 and over	Senior adults	Medical services, travel, pharmaceuticals, purchases for younger age groups

Changing demographics in many international markets open up new opportunities for advertisers. In Spain, the growing upper middle class and the availability of good expressways enable Mercedes-Benz (www.mercedesbenz.com) to promote its navigation system in this very creative ad.

spending in China will exceed $52 billion in 2013, putting it ahead of Japan and second only to the United States.[22]

Geographic and demographic data provide information about markets but little about the psychology of individuals. People in the same demographic or geographic segment may have widely differing product preferences and TV viewing habits. Rarely can demographic criteria alone predict purchase behavior.[23] That's why marketers developed the study of *psychographics.*

Psychographic Segmentation For certain products, appeals to emotions and cultural values may be persuasive. So some advertisers use **psychographic segmentation** to define consumer markets. With **psychographics**, marketers group people by their values, attitudes, personality, and lifestyle. Psychographics enables marketers to view people as individuals with feelings and inclinations. Then, they can classify people according to what they feel, what they believe, the way they live, and the products, services, and media they use.[24]

Perhaps the best-known psychographic classification system is VALS™, a product of Strategic Business Insights (SBI), a spin-out of SRI International. VALS assigns consumers to one of eight groups based on two dimensions: **primary motivation** and **resources**. According to SBI, individuals are primarily motivated to buy by one of three things: ideals (or basic principles), achievement (tangible markers of success or accomplishment), or self-expression (a desire for experiences or to take risks). In addition, people possess varying levels of resources, which include money, education, or self-confidence. Those with the fewest resources are placed near the bottom of the VALS typology, while those with the most are at the top (see Exhibit 4–6).[25]

According to SBI, the purpose of VALS is to help marketers identify whom to target, uncover what the target group buys and does, locate where concentrations of the target group live, identify how best to communicate with them, and gain insight into why the target group behaves the way it does. The system has been applied to a variety of areas: new product development and design, target marketing, product positioning, advertising message development, and media planning, to name a few.[26] In one case, for example, a foreign car manufacturer used VALS to reposition its sports utility vehicle after its award-winning but ineffective television campaign failed to result in higher sales. Using VALS, the company targeted a new "rebellious" consumer group with a new campaign using a "breaking the rules" theme. Nothing changed but the advertising. But sales increased 60 percent in six months.[27]

Several other classification systems have been developed to help marketers in the United States and worldwide target consumers based on their values, motivations, and lifestyles. These psychographic segmentation schemes include ValueScope from GfK Roper Consulting, BehaviorGraphics from Experian Simmons, and MindBase, a

▼EXHIBIT 4-6 The VALS™ (www.strategicbusinessinsights.com/VALS) classification system places consumers with abundant resources—psychological, physical, and material means and capacities—near the top of the chart and those with minimal resources near the bottom. The chart segments consumers by their basis for decision making: ideals, achievement, or self-expression. The boxes intersect to indicate that some categories may be considered together. For instance, a marketer may categorize Thinkers and Believers together.

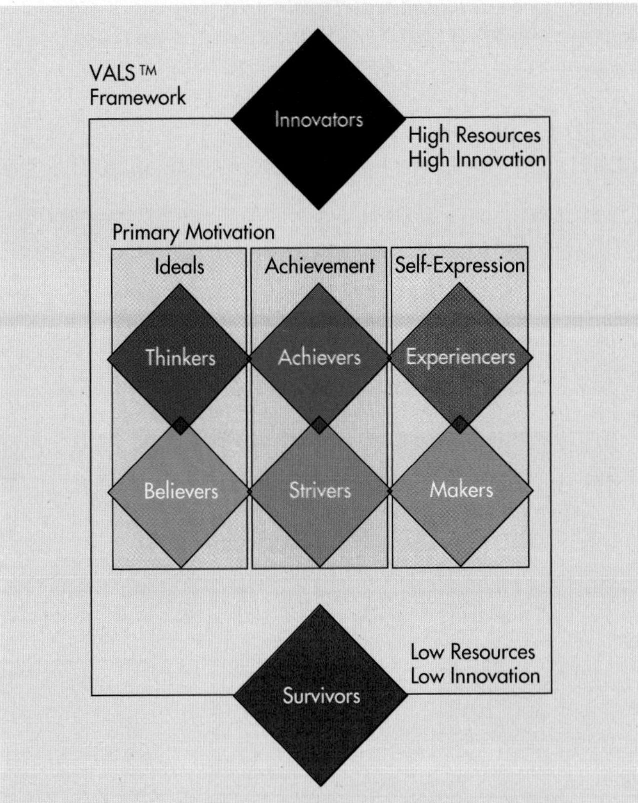

Source: Reprinted with permission of Strategic Business Insights (SBI); www.strategicbusinessinsights.com.

Ads for adidas (www.adidas.com) capture the attitude and lifestyle of its target market: athletic young people around the world who define themselves by their athletic achievements. This series of ads, placed at intervals throughout the Boston Marathon, was intended to simultaneously motivate runners as they hit certain points in their progress as well as to reinforce key values shared by all athletes, which adidas hopes to embody.

product offered by The Futures Company. The MindBase consumer groups are described in Exhibit 4–7.

How might marketers use psychographic segmentation schemes such as these? Recall our discussion about product utility. We argued that people often buy products in an effort to satisfy functional needs and psychological wants. Psychographic tools like VALS attempt to group people in terms of shared needs and wants. Advocates of this approach believe that doing so provides both a more precise way of target marketing and a deeper understanding of what the target market is like. As an example, consider a company that markets high-end motorcycles. A demographic profile of the company's target market might suggest that prospects are males between the ages of 30 and 50. A psychographic profile could extend this analysis by noting that the best prospects are experiencers: men motivated by self-expressive needs who also have sufficient resources to buy an expensive bike. Understanding the motivations of experiencers not only helps the company realize they are a good target market; it also suggests benefits of the product that the marketer should advertise. VALS is thus very useful in a variety of areas, including new product development and design, target marketing, product positioning, advertising message development, and media planning.

An influential book, *The Tipping Point* by cultural observer Malcolm Gladwell, suggests another reason why advertisers may wish to psychologically segment consumers: identifying those who are important social influences on others. Gladwell argues that certain types of people are involved in creating what he calls *social epidemics,* typified by the almost overnight increase in the popularity of a product, fashion, or idea. Gladwell believes that social epidemics are traceable to the actions of

▼EXHIBIT 4–7 The Futures Company's MindBase finds shared patterns of behavior.

Source: The Futures Company; website, http://thefuturescompany.com/what-we-do/mindbase.

business markets Organizations that buy natural resources, component products, and services that they resell, use to conduct their business, or use to manufacture another product.

three types of people, which he labels *Connectors, Mavens,* and *Salesmen.* Connectors are people with very wide social circles; they have the ability to bridge different social groups that would not ordinarily interact with each other. Mavens are people who spend the time and energy accumulating knowledge that most people simply can't be bothered to find out for themselves. Connectors and Mavens are sources of information about new products, trends, and ideas, but the job of persuading people to embrace these things falls to Salesmen. Salesmen are people whom most individuals find credible, trustworthy, and authoritative. Gladwell's analysis suggests that relatively small groups of people are very influential in affecting the consumption habits of much larger segments of society.[28]

Limitations of Consumer Segmentation Methods

Advocates of psychographic systems claim they help address the emotional factors that motivate consumers. However, for some products psychographics may offer little real value—especially since it oversimplifies consumer personalities and purchase behavior. Some typologies, such as VALS, are also criticized for being too complicated.[29]

Still, it's important for marketers to monitor and understand their customers. It helps them select target markets, create ads that match the attributes and image of their products with the types of consumers who use them, develop effective media plans, and allocate their advertising dollars wisely.

Segmenting Business and Government Markets: Understanding Organizational Buying Behavior

Business markets (or industrial markets) include manufacturers, government agencies, wholesalers, retailers, banks, and institutions that buy goods and services to help them operate. These products may include raw materials, electronic components, mechanical parts, office equipment, vehicles, or services used in conducting their businesses. Many business marketers sell to resellers, such as retailers that resell to consumers. For example, much of Hardee's food is supplied by Siméus Foods International, a processing, production, and distribution conglomerate. Siméus's two plants produce and freeze menu items, such as hamburger and chicken patties, to the specifications of customers like Hardee's and Denny's. The end product is resold by Hardee's with no mention of Siméus. Hardee's reselling contract with Coca-Cola, however, is a much more visible *brand partnership;* Coke products are often featured in Hardee's advertising.

Identifying target markets of prospective business customers is just as complex as identifying consumer markets. Many of the variables used to identify consumer markets can also be used for business markets—for example, geography and behavior (purchase occasion, benefits sought, user status, and usage rate).

Business markets also have special characteristics. They employ professional buyers and use systematic purchasing procedures. They may be concentrated geographically. And in any single market there may be only a small number of buyers.

Business Purchasing Procedures

When businesspeople evaluate new products, they use a process far more complex and rigid than the consumer purchase process we will describe in Chapter 5. Business marketers must design their advertising programs with this in mind.

Large firms have purchasing departments that act as professional buyers. They evaluate the need for products, analyze proposed purchases, weigh competitive bids, seek approvals from users and managers, make requisitions, place orders, and supervise all product purchasing. This structured purchase decision process implies a rational approach. Research, however, shows that professional buyers often exhibit a willingness to pay a substantial premium for their favorite brand. This suggests that advertising may play a larger role in business-to-business marketing than previously thought.[30]

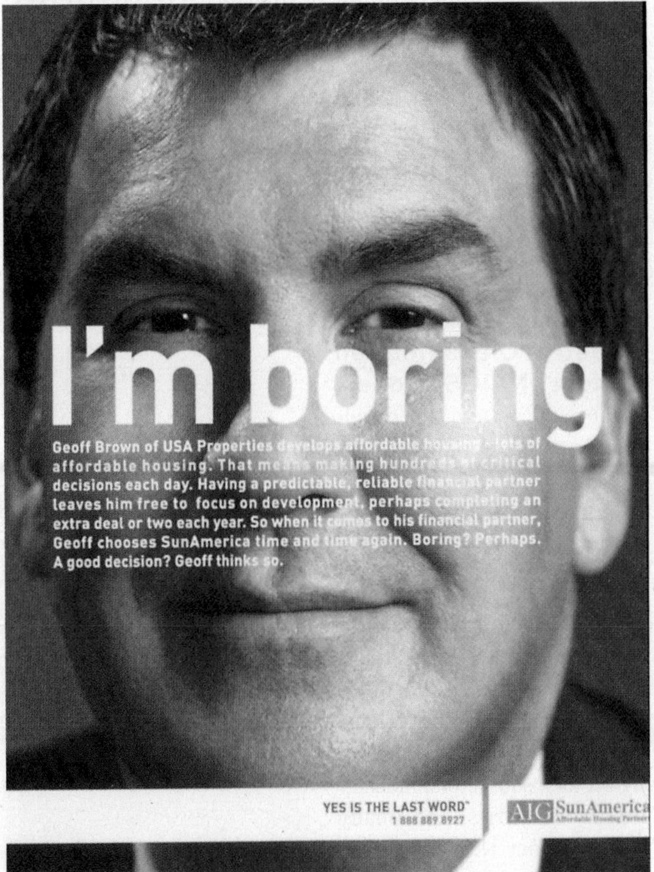

Although business purchases are often made according to a company's well-defined needs and policies, the actual purchasers are people who might be persuaded by traditional forms of product branding. For this reason, business-to-business advertising, as shown in this older AIG Sun-America ad (www.sunamerica.com) places emphasis on establishing and reinforcing the SunAmerica name.

North American Industry Classification System (NAICS) codes Method used by the U.S. Department of Commerce to classify all businesses. The NAICS codes are based on broad industry groups, subgroups, and detailed groups of firms in smaller lines of business.

Making a sale in business markets may take weeks, months, or even years, especially to government agencies. Purchase decisions often depend on factors besides price or quality, among them product demonstrations, delivery time, terms of sale, and dependability. Marketers often emphasize these issues in advertising and promotional appeals.

Before deciding on a target market, business marketers should consider how the purchase decision process works in various segments. New companies, for instance, may want to target smaller firms where the purchase decision can be made quickly. Or they may use commissioned reps to call on the larger prospects that require more time. These decisions will dictate where advertising should be placed.

> Professional buyers often exhibit a willingness to pay a substantial premium for their favorite brand.

Industrial Classification System

Industrial customers need different products, depending on their business. For example, apparel manufacturers such as Levi's are the main customers for buttons and zippers. Marketing managers need to focus their sales and advertising efforts on those firms that are in the right business for their products.[31] The U.S. Census Bureau classifies all U.S. businesses—and collects and publishes industry statistics on them—using the **North American Industry Classification System (NAICS) codes**. Because the system was developed in cooperation with Canada and Mexico, consistency throughout North America is guaranteed.

NAICS organizes industries into 20 broad sectors such as mining, manufacturing, wholesale trade, and information. These are then subdivided into four hierarchical levels of classification, including sectors, subsectors, industry groups, industries, and finally 1,170 distinct U.S. industries. (See Exhibit 4–8 for a breakdown of NAICS codes in the information and wireless telecommunications industry.) The Census Bureau uses NAICS to offer marketers an abundance of information, such as the number of firms, sales volumes, and number of employees by geographic area. Thus, the NAICS codes help companies segment markets and do research, and advertisers can even obtain lists of companies in particular NAICS divisions for direct mailings.[32]

EXHIBIT 4–8 NAICS hierarchy and codes. A business marketer selling goods or services to firms in the paging industry can use the NAICS codes to locate prospective companies in directories or in subscription databases.

Level	Code	Sector
Sector	51	Information
Subsector	513	Broadcasting and telecommunications
Industry group	5133	Telecommunications
Industry	51332	Wireless telecommunications carriers (except satellite)
U.S. industry	513321	Paging

Market Concentration Many countries' markets for industrial goods are concentrated in one region or several metropolitan areas. In the United States, for example, the industrial market is heavily concentrated in the Midwest, the South, and California (see Exhibit 4–9).

EXHIBIT 4–9 The states in this map are represented in proportion to the value of their manufactured products.

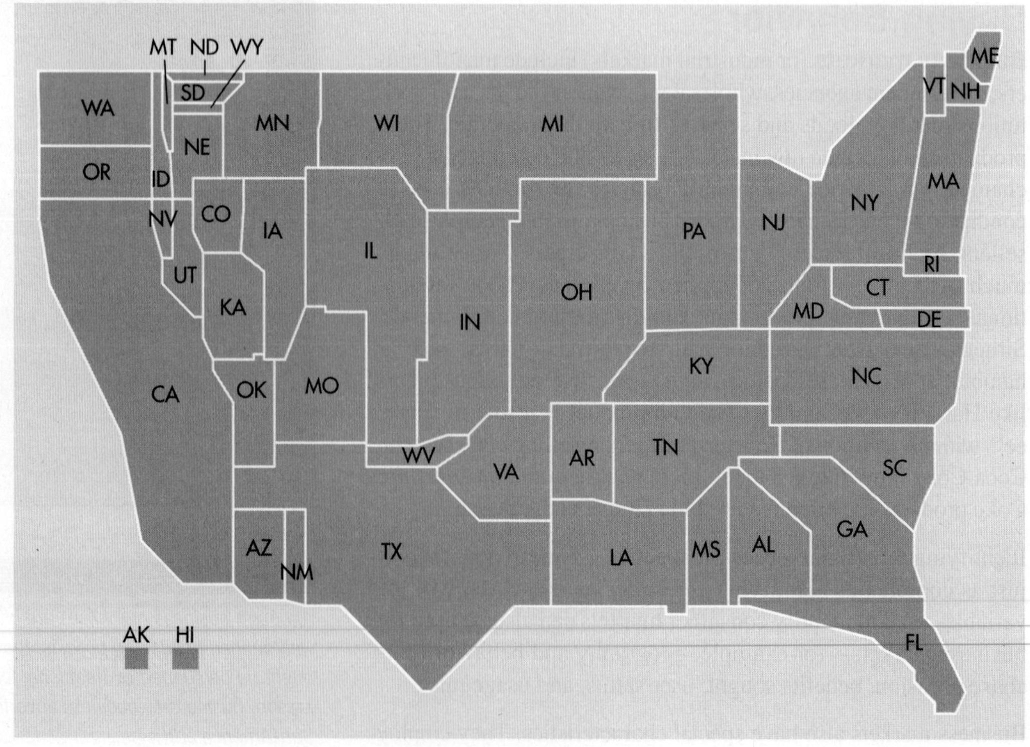

Market concentration reduces the number of geographic targets for an advertiser.

Moreover, business marketers deal with fewer buyers than consumer marketers. Less than 7 percent of U.S. manufacturing establishments employ nearly 75 percent of all production workers and account for almost 80 percent of all manufacturing dollars.[33] Customer size is a critical issue for market segmentation. A firm may concentrate its marketing and advertising efforts on a few large customers, many smaller ones, or both.

Levi Strauss markets through three channels: independent department stores; specialty stores (such as Urban Outfitters); and

my ad campaign

Segmenting the Audience [4–A]

What is the target market for your product? The answer to this question is rarely simple; thus your choices again will require the application of strategic thinking. To make the decision you will need to gather as much information from your client and from secondary sources as you can, focusing on the product's market, users, and the competition. The information you gather about the consumer in the My Ad Campaign from Chapter 6 will be important as well. And in some instances it may make sense to conduct primary research with current customers or with individuals who use competing products.

You may have the opportunity to offer counsel to your client about whether it is pursuing the right target market. Check to be sure before offering such advice; some clients may not wish to receive it. If the client is interested, consider whether there are underserved segments that offer sales or profit potential. For example, if your client is a local pizzeria located near campus, it may be focusing on attracting students. This is to be expected since students normally represent a sizable market in any college town. In addition, your client is doubtless using the timeworn strategy of attracting hungry, cash-strapped undergrads with messages that emphasize low prices, large servings, and coupons. But while students may represent a large market for pizza, there are probably dozens of other food businesses competing for this segment. If so, it might be smarter to refocus on a smaller but underserved segment, especially one that offers great profit potential. If your town lacks an upscale pizzeria that serves specialty pies, the client might be better served by improving its offerings and dining facility, raising prices, and promoting to nonstudents who would be willing to pay more for quality pizzas.

Of course, to evaluate opportunities in a market you will need to segment. Many advertisers find that it makes sense to segment on the basis of standard demographic characteristics such as age, gender, ethnicity, location, social class, or income level. Dividing your market according to product loyalty or product usage levels is also worth strongly considering. Understanding your market with respect to psychographics and lifestyles can be incredibly valuable, especially later when you begin to develop your creative brief. Such data can be more difficult to obtain, however.

Defining the Target Market

	Your Client's Customers	The Competition's Customers	Nonusers
Demographics			
Age			
Gender			
Ethnicity/race			
Location/region			
Social class			
Income			
Education			
Behaviors			
Product usage (light, medium, heavy)			
Brand loyalty (loyal, switchers)			
Psychographics			
Principle-oriented			
Status-oriented			
Action-oriented			
Benefits Sought			
Low price			
Quality			

primary demand trend The projection of future consumer demand for a product category, based on past demand and other market influences.

target marketing The process by which an advertiser focuses its marketing efforts on a target market.

target market The market segment or group within the market segment toward which all marketing activities will be directed.

chain stores (such as Walmart and JCPenney). Its top 100 accounts provide 80 percent of the company's annual sales and are made through 13,000 retail outlets. Its remaining accounts (20 percent of sales) represent another 13,000 stores. Major accounts are served by sales reps from Levi's various divisions, smaller accounts by telemarketers and companywide sales reps.

Business marketers can also segment by end users. For example, a firm may develop software for one industry, such as banking, or for general use in a variety of industries. That decision, of course, affects advertising media decisions.

Aggregating Market Segments

Once marketers identify and locate broad markets with shared characteristics (behavioristic, geographic, demographic, or psychographic), they can proceed to the second step in the market segmentation process. This involves (1) selecting groups that have a mutual interest in the product's utility and (2) reorganizing and aggregating (combining) them into larger market segments based on their potential for sales and profit. Let's take a look at how this process might work for Levi Strauss & Co. in the U.S. market.

First, the company's management needs to know the **primary demand trend** of the total U.S. market for pants. This is the market potential for jeans and casual pants in various market areas across the country. To do this it uses a variety of *marketing research techniques* (discussed in Chapter 6). Then management must identify the needs, wants, and shared characteristics of the various groups within the casual apparel marketplace who live near the company's retail outlets. It may use the services of a large marketing information company such as Claritas, which collects data on purchasing behaviors and creates profiles of geographic markets across the country.

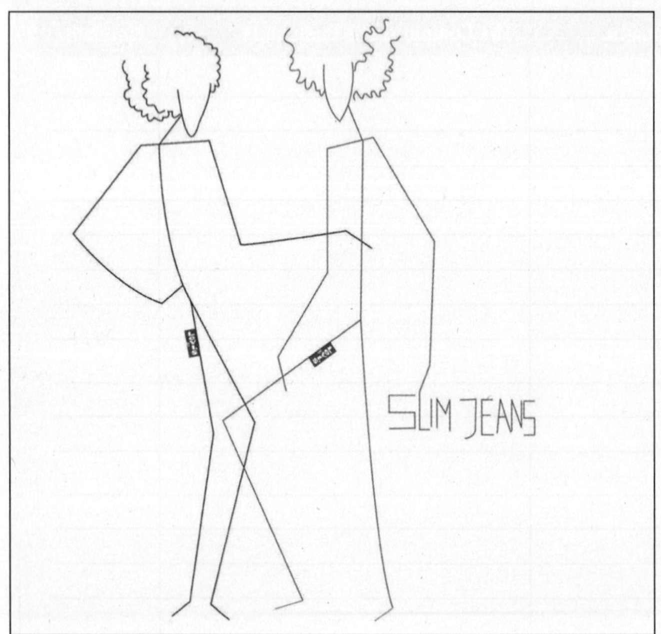

Levi's has introduced several product lines in an effort to satisfy the needs and wants of different consumer segments. In this seemingly simple ad, the style of slim jeans is communicated to a younger, more contemporary market segment.

The company finds many prospective customers throughout the United States: students, blue-collar workers, young singles, professionals, homemakers, and so on. It then measures and analyzes households in each major retail area by demographic, lifestyle, and purchasing characteristics, sorts them into 66 geodemographic segments, and labels them with terms such as those in Exhibit 4–10: Big City Blues, Movers & Shakers, Country Squires, Pools & Patios, and the like. All of these people have apparel needs and many may be interested in the style, cachet, and durability of the Levi's brand.

Selecting Groups Interested in Product Utility

Levi Strauss next selects groups that would like and be able to afford the benefits of Levi's apparel—suitability for work or play, comfort, style, reasonable cost, durability, and so on. Groups interested in all these features make up the total possible market for Levi's clothes.

Part of the challenge of market segmentation is estimating the profits the company might realize if it (1) aims at the whole market or (2) caters only to specific segments. Apparel is a highly competitive market, but 10 percent of 1,000 is always larger than 90 percent of 100. So for a company such as Levi Strauss, the target market must be a large mass market or it won't be profitable.[34]

Combining Groups to Build Target Market Segments The company needs to find groups that are relatively homogeneous (similar) and offer good profit potential. Market data turn up many demographic and lifestyle groups, including middle-aged couples, seniors, and ethnically diverse young singles, as well as groups labeled New Empty Nest, Park Bench Seniors, and Low Rise Living, respectively. These groups, each constituting just over 1 percent of consumer households, have minimal retail or credit activity, and they are thus not prime targets for premium-branded department store products.

Other segments offer greater potential—young to middle-aged households with medium to high incomes and average to high retail activity. These include groups like Movers & Shakers, Bohemian Mix, and Home Sweet Home, each constituting nearly 2 percent of all households. By combining these groups

▼**EXHIBIT 4–10** This exhibit shows how Claritas's Prizm NE system classifies prospective customers in the Louisville area by census tract and labels each area by the residents' shared characteristics.

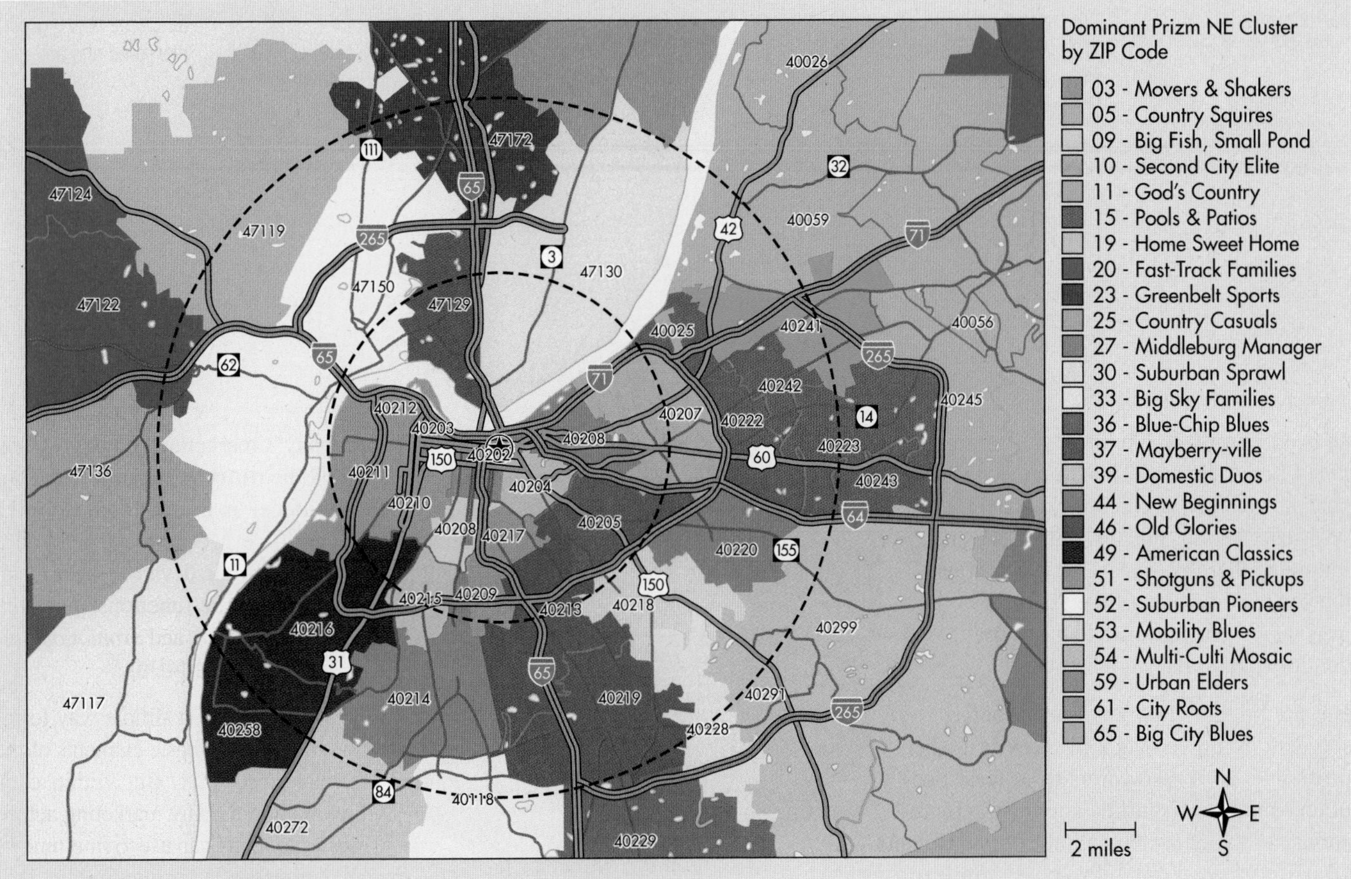

with the young professionals in the Young Influentials and New Beginnings segments, Levi Strauss can target young to middle-aged people on their way up. Nationally, that amounts to nearly 20 million households. That's not everybody, but it's a large and potentially very profitable mass-market segment. These prospects might like the style and comfort of Levi's 550s as well as the tradition of a brand they know and trust. Levi's can expect that a well-conceived campaign will appeal to their particular needs, wants, and self-images.

check yourself ✓

1. What is the marketer's goal in segmenting markets?
2. What characteristics are used in psychographic segmentation?
3. Why do marketers aggregate market segments?

LO4-3 Discuss how defining a target market enhances a product's marketing strategy.

THE TARGET MARKETING PROCESS

Once the market segmentation process is complete, a company can proceed to the **target marketing** process. This will determine the content, look, and feel of its advertising.

Target Market Selection

The first step in target marketing is to assess which of the newly created segments offer the greatest profit potential and which can be most successfully penetrated. The company designates one or more segments as a **target market**—those consumers the company wishes to appeal to, design products for, and tailor its marketing activities toward.[35] It may designate another set of segments as a secondary target market and aim some of its resources at it.

Let's look at the most likely target market for loose-fitting jeans: young to middle-aged customers with moderate to high income

[The target market is] those consumers the company wishes to appeal to, design products for, and tailor its marketing activities toward.

and education who like the style, comfort, and fashion of Levi's apparel. This group represents a large percentage of the apparel market, and if won, will generate substantial profits. Levi's offers what these prospects need and want: the style and fashion of the jeans they grew up with, updated to be more comfortable for the adult body.

But the middle-class, comfort-oriented segment is not enough for Levi's to be profitable, so it also caters to at least two other important market segments. In response to the enormous number of consumers who shop at giant, low-cost retailers like Walmart and Target, Levi's has developed a value-priced line, Levi's Signature. The Signature collection appeals to budget-conscious families with children such as Family Thrifts and Big Sky Families. And at the top end, Levi's met the needs of young, twenty-something, image-conscious consumers with its Warhol Factory X Levi's jeans. This line retailed for $250 and was sold at high-end retailers such as Nordstrom.

The Marketing Mix: A Strategy for Matching Products to Markets

Once a company defines its target market, it knows exactly where to focus its attention and resources. Marketers and advertisers generally try to shape their basic product into a total **product concept**: the consumer's perception of a product or service as a bundle of utilitarian and symbolic values that satisfy functional, social, psychological, and other wants and needs. Companies have many strategic options they can employ to enhance this product/service concept and effect marketing exchanges (make sales). The company can design special features for its target market (such as certain colors or special sizes). It can establish proper pricing. And it can determine the criteria for locating stores or dealers and prepare the most convincing advertising messages.

Marketers categorize these options under four headings: (1) *product,* (2) *price,* (3) *distribution,* and (4) *communication.*[36] The way the marketer mixes and blends these different elements creates the company's marketing strategy—often called the **marketing mix**. For convenience, marketing educator E. Jerome McCarthy developed a mnenomic device to help recall these four functions: *product, price, place,* and *promotion*—or the **four Ps (4Ps)**.[37]

The 4Ps are a simple way to remember the basic elements of the marketing mix. But within each element are many marketing activities a company can use to fine-tune its product concept and improve sales. Advertising, for example, is one instrument of the communication (promotion) element. The remainder of this chapter focuses on the relationship between advertising and the other elements of the marketing mix.

check yourself ✓

1. What is the relationship between the target market and the 4Ps?

L04-4 Describe the elements of the marketing mix and the role advertising plays in each element of the mix.

ADVERTISING AND THE PRODUCT ELEMENT

In developing a marketing mix, marketers generally start with the **product element**. Major activities typically include the way the product is designed and classified, positioned, branded, and packaged. Each of these affects the way the product is advertised.

early adopters Prospects who are most willing to try new products and services.

primary demand Consumer demand for a whole product category.

introductory phase The initial phase of the product life cycle (also called the *pioneering phase*) when a new product is introduced, costs are highest, and profits are lowest.

pull strategy Marketing, advertising, and sales promotion activities aimed at inducing trial purchase and repurchase by consumers.

push strategy Marketing, advertising, and sales promotion activities aimed at getting products into the dealer pipeline and accelerating sales by offering inducements to dealers, retailers, and salespeople.

growth stage The period in a product life cycle that is marked by market expansion as more and more customers make their first purchases while others are already making their second and third purchases.

maturity stage That point in the product life cycle when the market has become saturated with products, the number of new customers has dwindled, and competition is most intense.

selective demand Consumer demand for the particular advantages of one brand over another.

Product Life Cycles

Marketers theorize that just as humans pass through stages in life from infancy to death, products (and especially product categories) also pass through a **product life cycle** (see Exhibit 4–11).[38] A product's position in the life cycle influences the target market selected and the marketing mix used. There are four major stages in the product life cycle: *introduction, growth, maturity,* and *decline.*

When a company introduces a new product category, nobody knows about it. Through market segmentation, the company will try to identify those prospects who are known to be **early adopters**—willing to try new things—and begin promoting the new category directly to them. The idea is to stimulate **primary demand**—consumer demand for the whole product category, not just the company's own brand.

During the **introductory phase** of any new product category, the company incurs considerable costs for educating customers, building widespread dealer distribution, and encouraging demand. It must advertise heavily at this stage to establish a position as a market leader and to gain a large share of market before the growth stage begins.

When cell phones were introduced in the late 1980s, advertisers had to first create enough consumer demand to pull the product through the channels of distribution (called **pull strategy**). Advertising educated consumers about the new product and its category, explained what cellular phones are, how they work, and the rewards of owning one. Promotional efforts aimed at retailers (called **push strategy**) encouraged distributors and dealers to stock, display, and advertise the new products.

When sales volume begins to rise rapidly, the product enters the **growth stage**. This period is characterized by rapid *market expansion* as more and more customers, stimulated by mass advertising and word of mouth, make their first, second, and third purchases. Competitors jump into the market, but the company that established the early leadership position usually reaps the biggest rewards. As a percentage of total sales, advertising expenditures should decrease, and individual firms will realize their first substantial profits.

▼EXHIBIT 4–11 A product's life cycle curve may vary, depending on the product category, but almost every product or service passes through these stages. Marketing objectives and strategies change as the product proceeds from one stage to the next.

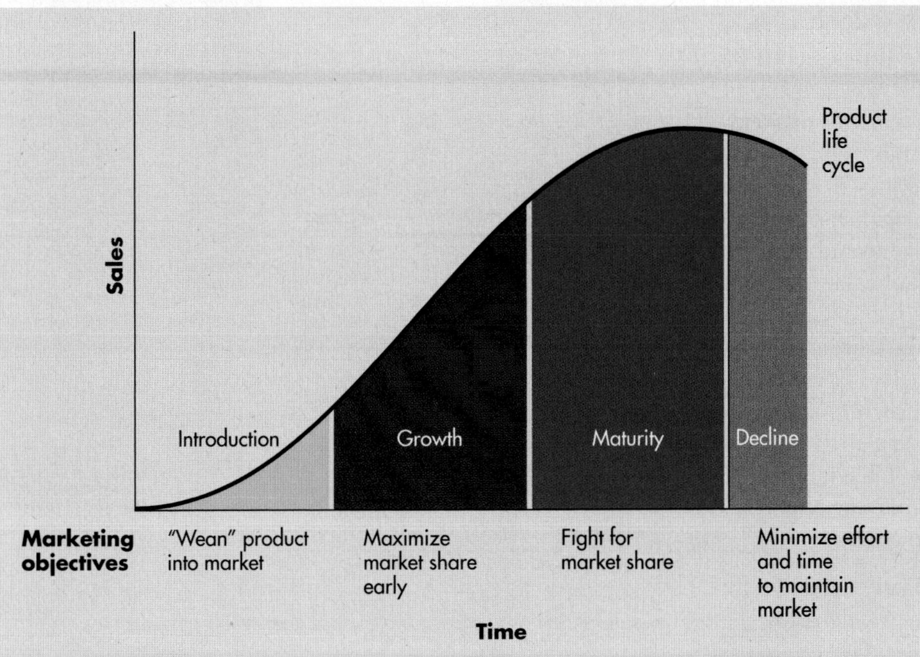

During the early 1990s, the demand for cell phones exploded, and category sales quadrupled every year. Many competitors suddenly appeared. With increased production and competition, prices started to fall, which brought even more consumers into the market. By 2013, 91 percent of all U.S. families owned cell phones.[39]

In the **maturity stage**, the marketplace becomes saturated with competing products and the number of new customers dwindles, so industry sales reach a plateau. Competition intensifies and profits diminish. Companies increase their promotional efforts but emphasize **selective demand** to impress customers with the subtle advantages of their particular brand. At this stage, companies can increase sales only at the expense of competitors. The strategies of market segmentation, product positioning, and price promotion become more important during this shakeout

Glide dental floss exists in a mature product category. To differentiate itself from competing floss products, the brand emphasizes its smoothness and ease of use in tight spaces between teeth.

period as weak companies fall by the wayside and those remaining fight for market share.

By the mid-1990s, for example, cellular phones that once sold for $1,500 were suddenly advertised regularly for $100 to $200. Ads emphasized features and low prices, and the product became a staple of discount merchandisers. Today, of course, one can get a cell phone for free, just by signing up for the service.[40]

Late in the maturity stage, companies may have to scramble to extend the product's life cycle. Without innovation or marketing support, name brands eventually see their sales erode. For example, BlackBerry devices, once market leaders, are struggling to compete with Apple and Android phones. If the advertised brand has no perceived advantage, people will buy whatever's cheapest or most convenient. Professor Brian Wansink, who directs the Brand Lab at the University of Illinois Urbana–Champaign, suggests that the reason many old brands die is less for life cycle reasons and more for marketing neglect. He points out that aging brands often pack plenty of brand equity. The challenge for marketers is to determine which brands can be revitalized and then decide how to do it. With today's high price tag on introducing new products (often $100 million or more), revitalization should be the strategy of choice whenever possible. Marketers may try to find new users for the brand, develop new uses for the product, change the size of packages, design new labels, improve quality, or use promotions to increase frequency of use.[41] One such revitalization effort in the portable computer category is Apple's iPad, which is attracting attention for its multiple uses, including reading books, viewing photos, watching movies, playing music, and surfing the Web on a touch screen for under $400.

If they're not revitalized, products will finally enter the **decline stage** because of obsolescence, new technology, or changing consumer tastes. At this point, companies may cease all promotion and phase the products out quickly, as in the case of record turntables and albums, or let them fade slowly away with minimal advertising.

Product Classifications

The way a company classifies its product is important in defining both the product concept and the marketing mix. As Exhibit 4–12 shows, there are many ways to classify tangible goods: by markets, by the purchasing habits of buyers, by the consumption rate or degree of tangibility, or by physical attributes.

Product Positioning

Once an advertising person understands the product's stage in the life cycle, how it's classified, and how it's currently perceived by the marketplace, the first strategic decision can be made: how to **position** the product. The basic goal of positioning strategy is to own a word

At a time when sport utility vehicles were so popular that competing companies all seemed to be offering the same benefits, Jeep (www.jeep.com) positioned itself as the "only one" to go anywhere on the planet. Positioning is important in tight markets to help differentiate similar products.

decline stage The stage in the product life cycle when sales begin to decline due to obsolescence, new technology, or changing consumer tastes.

position The way in which a product is ranked in the consumer's mind by the benefits it offers, by the way it is classified or differentiated from the competition, or by its relationship to certain target markets.

perceptible differences Differences between products that are visibly apparent to the consumer.

that establishes the product in the prospect's mind. Levi's owns "jeans" (or at least they did for a long time). BMW owns "performance," Maytag owns "reliability," Apple owns "easy to use," and Volvo owns "safety." By developing a unique position for the brand in the consumer's mind, the marketer helps the consumer remember the brand and what it stands for.

Products may be positioned in different ways. Xerox repositioned itself as "the Document Company," moving from the narrow, crowded copier market to the broader, growing document-handling market. With one stroke, Xerox redefined the business it is in, differentiated itself from competition, and created a new number one position for itself.[42]

Product Differentiation

Product differentiation creates a product difference that appeals to the preferences of a distinct market segment. In advertising, nothing is more important than being able to tell prospects truthfully that your product is different. Unfortunately, in response to increased competitive pressures, burgeoning innovation and technology, and various constraints on distribution, new-product development cycles have shortened dramatically. As a result, many brand managers find themselves launching new products that are "only 85 percent there." So it's not surprising that many "new" products fail to impress consumers. (See Exhibit 4–13.)

Differences between products that are readily apparent to the consumer are called **perceptible differences**. Snapple, for example, received its initial impetus because of its unique ingredients and taste, and the company now spends millions of

▼**EXHIBIT 4–12** Product classifications.

By Market	By Rate of Consumption and Tangibility	By Purchasing Habits	By Physical Description
Consumer goods Products and services we use in our daily lives (food, clothing, furniture, cars). Industrial goods Products used by companies for the purpose of producing other products (raw materials, agricultural commodities, machinery, tools, equipment).	Durable goods Tangible products that are long-lasting and infrequently replaced (cars, trucks, refrigerators, furniture). Nondurable goods Tangible products that may be consumed in one or a few uses and usually need to be replaced at regular intervals (food, soap, gasoline, oil). Services Activities, benefits, or satisfaction offered for sale (travel, haircuts, legal and medical services, massages).	Convenience goods Purchases made frequently with a minimum of effort (cigarettes, food, newspapers). Shopping goods Infrequently purchased items for which greater time is spent comparing price, quality, style, warranty (furniture, cars, clothing, tires). Specialty goods Products with such unique characteristics that consumers will make special efforts to purchase them even if they're more expensive (designer clothes, luxury cars, fancy restaurants). Unsought goods Products that potential customers don't yet want (life insurance, funeral services, fire extinguisher) or don't know they can buy (new products), so they don't search them out.	Packaged goods Cereals, soft drinks, cleaning products, and so forth. Hard goods Furniture, appliances. Soft goods Clothing, bedding. Services Intangible products.

▼**EXHIBIT 4–13** What's new? Not much. Consumers didn't think these products were as new as they claimed to be, as indicated by the grades awarded.

Product	New and Different	Purchase Probability	Price/Value	Overall Grade
Airwick Botanicals	F	A	A	B
Mr. Clean Glass & Surface Cleaner	F	A	A	B
Spic & Span with Bleach	F	A	B	B
Aspirin-Free Bayer Select	F	B	B	C
Sugar Twin Plus low-calorie sweetener	F	B	A	C
Lady Power Clear Roll-On antiperspirant	F	B	A	C

hidden differences Imperceptible but existing differences that may affect the desirability of a product.

induced differences Distinguishing characteristics of products effected through unique branding, packaging, distribution, merchandising, and advertising.

branding A marketing function that identifies products and their source and differentiates them from all other products.

brand That combination of name, words, symbols, or design that identifies the product and its source and distinguishes it from competing products—the fundamental differentiating device for all products.

individual brand Assigning a unique name to each product a manufacturer produces.

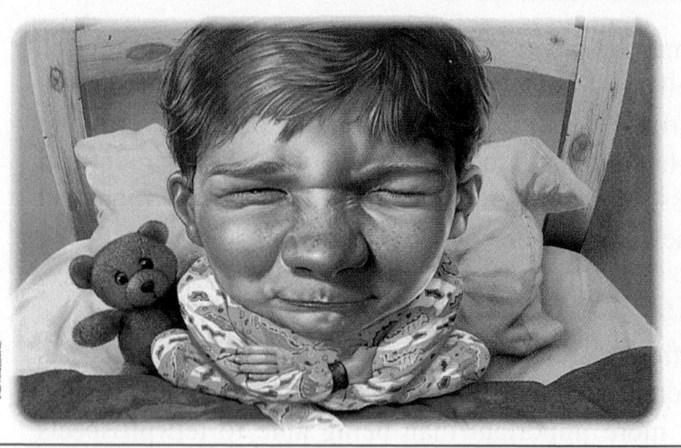

Most of us might stick a thermometer in our mouths when we come down with a fever, but the Braun Thermoscan (www.braun.com) isn't just any thermometer. The company's product concept, using the ear rather than the mouth, differentiates its thermometer as one that is gentle yet effective for the temperament of children.

[Nothing is more important than being able to tell prospects truthfully that your product is different.]

dollars annually to advertise this difference to consumers nationwide.[43] **Hidden differences** are not so readily apparent. Trident gum may look and taste the same as other brands, but it is differentiated by the use of artificial sweeteners. While hidden differences can enhance a product's desirability, advertising is usually needed to let consumers know about them.

For many product classes, such as aspirin, salt, gasoline, packaged foods, liquor, and financial services, advertising can create **induced differences**. Banks, brokerage houses, and insurance companies, for example, which offer virtually identical financial products and services, use advertising and promotion to differentiate themselves. However, few have yet discovered the image asset of **branding** as used by the national packaged-goods marketers. That is created through the accumulation of consistent advertising campaigns, favorable publicity, special-event sponsorship, and good word of mouth.[44]

Chanel is one of the top perfume brands in the world. To reinforce its image of luxury and glamor, Chanel ads feature stars such as Nicole Kidman and Keira Knightley.

Product Branding

The fundamental differentiating device for all products is the **brand**—that combination of name, words, symbols, or design that identifies the product and its source and distinguishes it from competing products. Without brands, consumers couldn't tell one product from another, and advertising them would be nearly impossible.

A manufacturer may establish an **individual brand** for each product it makes. Procter and Gamble, for example, markets its laundry detergents under the individual brand names Tide, Gain, Cheer, and Era. Such companies designate a distinct target market for each product and develop a separate personality and image for each brand. However, this strategy is very costly.

On the other hand, a company might use a **family brand** and market different products under the same umbrella name. When Heinz promotes its ketchup, it hopes to help its relishes too. This decision may be

family brand The marketing of various products under the same umbrella name.

national brands Product brands that are marketed in several regions of the country.

private labels Personalized brands applied by distributors or dealers to products supplied by manufacturers. Private brands are typically sold at lower prices in large retail chain stores.

licensed brands Brand names that other companies can buy the right to use.

brand equity The totality of what consumers, distributors, dealers, and competitors feel and think about a brand over an extended period of time; in short, it is the value of the brand's capital.

> "Advertising . . . is much more effective if it exploits the brand's positioning."

cost-effective, but one weak product in a line can hurt the whole family.

Because it is so expensive for manufacturers to market **national brands** (also called *manufacturer's brands*), some companies use a *private-labeling* strategy. They manufacture the product and sell it to resellers (distributors or dealers) who put their own brand name on the product. **Private labels** are typically sold at lower prices in big retail stores and include such familiar names as Kenmore, Craftsman, and DieHard (Sears), Kirkland (Costco), 365 (Whole Foods), Lucerne (Safeway), and Great Value (Walmart). They now account for over 23 percent of the grocery items purchased.[45] The responsibility for creating brand image and familiarity with private label brands rests with the distributor or retailer, who is also the principal benefactor if the brand is successful. Recent trends have moved toward premium private labels, such as Safeway Select, and healthy labels, such as Eating Right. These products feature better packaging, superior quality, and a higher price, often comparable to national brands.

Product packaging is important around the globe. Kern's uses colorful, attention-grabbing labels to increase sales of its Nectar line and reinforce its familiar brand name.

Branding decisions are critical because the brands a company owns may be its most important capital asset. Imagine the value of owning a brand name such as Coca-Cola, Nike, Porsche, or Levi's. *Bloomberg Businessweek*'s annual brand-value report ranks Coca-Cola as the most valuable brand in the world, followed by Microsoft, IBM, GE, Nokia, and Toyota (see Exhibit 4–14).[46] Some companies pay a substantial fee for the right to use another company's brand name. Thus, we have **licensed brands** such as Sunkist vitamins, Coca-Cola clothing, Porsche sunglasses, and Mickey Mouse watches.

The Role of Branding

For consumers, brands offer instant recognition and identification. They also promise consistent, reliable standards of quality, taste, size, or even psychological satisfaction, which adds value to the product for both the consumer and the manufacturer. In a survey conducted by TWICE/Campaigners, 44 percent of consumers ranked brand name as the most important factor when making a major electronics purchase. Price, by the way, ranked second.[47]

Brands must be built on differences in images, meanings, and associations. It's up to manufacturers to differentiate their products clearly and deliver value competitively. The product has to taste better, or get clothes cleaner, or be more environmentally friendly.[48] Advertising for an established brand, particularly a well-differentiated one, is much more effective if it exploits the brand's positioning.[49] Ideally, when consumers see a brand on the shelf, they instantly comprehend the brand's promise and have confidence in its quality. Of course, they must be familiar with and believe in the brand's promise (a function of advertising effectiveness). The goal is *brand loyalty*—because it serves both the consumer and the advertiser. For the consumer, it reduces shopping time. For the advertiser, it builds **brand equity**, the totality of what

EXHIBIT 4–14 World's most valuable brands.

Rank	Brand	2013 Brand Value ($ billions)
1	Apple	$185
2	Google	114
3	IBM	113
4	McDonald's	90
5	Coca Cola	78
6	AT&T	76
7	Microsoft	70
8	Marlboro	69
9	Visa	56
10	China Mobile	55

Source: Millward Brown Optimor, "BrandZ Top Most Valuable Global Brands," www.millwardbrown.com/brandz/2013/Top100/Docs/2013_BrandZ_Top100_Chart.pdf.

copy points Copywriting themes in a product's advertising.

network marketing A method of direct distribution in which individuals act as independent distributors for a manufacturer or private-label marketer.

reseller Businesses that buy products from manufacturers or wholesalers and then resell the merchandise to consumers or other buyers; also called *middlemen.* The most common examples of resellers are retail stores and catalog retailers.

price element In the marketing mix, the amount charged for the good or service—including deals, discounts, terms, warranties, and so on. The factors affecting price are market demand, cost of production and distribution, competition, and corporate objectives.

psychological pricing Using price as a means of influencing a consumer's behavior or perceptions; for example, using high prices to reinforce a quality image, or selling at $2.99 instead of $3.00 to make a product appear less expensive.

place (distribution) element How and where customers will buy a company's product; either direct or indirect distribution.

direct distribution The method of marketing in which the manufacturer sells directly to the customers without the use of retailers.

Consumers frequently associate higher prices with higher quality. Volvo (www.volvo.com) capitalizes on this by reinforcing that the safety value of its automobiles is worth a higher cost.

consumers, distributors, dealers—even competitors—feel and think about the brand over an extended period of time. In short, it's the value of the brand's assets.

High brand equity offers a host of blessings to a marketer: customer loyalty, price inelasticity, long-term profits. A loyal customer can be nine times as profitable as a disloyal one.[50] But building brand equity requires time and money. Brand value and preference drive market share, but share points and brand loyalty are usually won by the advertisers who spend the most. Charlotte Beers, the former head of J. Walter Thompson, believes companies must maintain consistency in their message by integrating all their marketing communications—from packaging and advertising to sales promotion and publicity—to maintain and reinforce the brand's personality and avoid mistakes such as changing the distinctive color of a Ryder rental truck.[51]

Product Packaging

The product's package is a component of the product element that can determine the outcome of retail shelf competition. In fact, packaging may be a particular brand's one differential advantage—and it's the marketer's last chance to communicate at the point of sale. Package designers (who sometimes work in agencies) must make the package exciting, appealing, and at the same time functional. The four considerations in package design are *identification; containment, protection, and convenience; consumer appeal;* and *economy*. These functions may even become **copy points**—copywriting themes—in the product's advertising.

ADVERTISING AND THE PRICE ELEMENT

As we all know, the **price element** of the marketing mix influences consumer perceptions of a brand. Companies that don't compete on price typically use image advertising to create a particular perception of the company or personality for the brand. Companies that are more price-competitive may regularly use sale advertising, clearance advertising, or loss-leader advertising.

Key Factors Influencing Price

Companies typically set their prices based on market demand for the product, costs of production and distribution, competition, and corporate objectives. Interestingly, though, a company often has relatively few options for determining its price strategy, depending on the desired product concept.

Marketers believe that consumers are often less concerned with a product's actual price than with its perceived price relative to competitors. Many premium-priced brands, such as L'Oréal,

Toyota dealers, like dealers for many other auto manufacturers, share the cost of their advertising through regional cooperatives. For example, the 176 dealerships that fall under the Southeast Toyota Distributors (www.jmfamily.com/Newsroom/Articles/PressKits/Southeast-Toyota-Distributors) umbrella would have split the expenses for this print ad.

are touted for the very fact that they cost more. Setting a high price to make a product seem more valuable is an example of **psychological pricing**. Image advertising may be used to justify the higher price. The important thing is that the price be consistent with the brand image; you can't charge a Rolex price for a Timex watch. And similarly, the brand's advertising must be consistent with its pricing strategy.

ADVERTISING AND THE DISTRIBUTION (PLACE) ELEMENT

Before the first ad can be created, the **place**, or **distribution**, **element** must be decided. It is important for marketers to understand that the method of distribution, like the price, must be consistent with the brand's image. People will not pay Nordstrom prices at Target.

Companies use two basic methods of distribution: *direct* or *indirect.*

distribution channel The network of all the firms and individuals that take title, or assist in taking title, to the product as it moves from the producer to the consumer.

Direct Distribution

When companies sell directly to end users or consumers, they use **direct distribution**. Avon, for example, employs sales reps who sell directly to consumers. Medical equipment suppliers and insurance companies often sell and distribute their products and services directly to customers without the use of wholesalers or retailers. In these cases, the advertising burden is carried entirely by the manufacturer.

An interesting method of direct distribution today is **network marketing** (also called *multilevel marketing*), in which individuals act as independent distributors for a manufacturer or private-label marketer. These people sign up friends and relatives to consume the company's products and recruit others to join. Through a gradual, word-of-mouth process, they form a "buying club" of independent distributors who buy the products wholesale direct from the company, use them, and tout them to more and more friends and acquaintances.

The Internet may be the ultimate direct distribution vehicle. As we will discuss in Chapter 12, Web sites allow marketers like Dell computers to make direct contact with their customers, develop interactive relationships, and consummate the sale of their products or services, all at a lower cost than any other method. The Internet is not appropriate for the distribution of all products, but its acceptance is rapidly spreading.

Indirect Distribution

Manufacturers usually don't sell directly to end users or consumers. Most companies market their products through a *distribution channel* that includes a network of *resellers.* A **reseller** (also called a *middleman*) is a business firm that operates between the producer and the consumer or industrial purchaser. It deals in trade rather than production.[52] Resellers include both wholesalers and retailers, as well as manufacturers' representatives, brokers, jobbers, and distributors. A **distribution channel** comprises all the firms and individuals that take responsibility for the product as it moves from the producer to the consumer.

The advertising a company uses depends on the product's method of distribution. Much of the advertising we see is not prepared or paid for by the manufacturer, but by the distributor or retailer.

An important part of the marketing strategy is determining the amount of coverage necessary for a product. Procter & Gamble, for example, distributes Crest toothpaste to virtually every supermarket and discount, drug, and variety store. Other

intensive distribution A distribution strategy based on making the product available to consumers at every possible location so that the consumers can buy with a minimum of effort.

selective distribution Strategy of limiting the distribution of a product to select outlets in order to reduce distribution and promotion costs.

cooperative (co-op) advertising The sharing of advertising costs by the manufacturer and the distributor or retailer. The manufacturer may repay 50 or 100 percent of the dealer's advertising costs or some other amount based on sales.

exclusive distribution The strategy of limiting the number of wholesalers or retailers who can sell a product in order to gain a prestige image, maintain premium prices, or protect other dealers in a geographic region.

products might need only one dealer for every 50,000 people. Consumer goods manufacturers traditionally use one of three distribution strategies: *intensive, selective,* or *exclusive.*

Intensive Distribution Soft drinks, candy, Timex watches, and other convenience goods are available at every possible location because of **intensive distribution**. In fact, consumers can buy them with a minimum of effort. The profit on each unit is usually very low, but the volume of sales is high. The sales burden is usually carried by the manufacturer's national advertising. Ads in trade magazines *push* the product into the retail "pipeline," and in mass media they stimulate consumers to *pull* the products through the pipeline. As a manufacturer modifies its strategy to more push or more pull, special promotions may be directed at the trade or at consumers to build brand volume.

Selective Distribution By limiting the number of outlets through **selective distribution**, manufacturers can cut their distribution and promotion costs. Many hardware tools are sold selectively through home-improvement centers and hardware stores. Automobile manufacturers limit the number of dealers that can sell their cars in each market. Levi Strauss sells through better department and chain stores. Manufacturers may use national advertising, but the sales burden is normally carried by the retailer. The manufacturer may share part of the retailer's advertising costs through a **cooperative (co-op) advertising** program, as we discussed in Chapter 3. For example, a Levi's retailer may receive substantial allowances from the manufacturer for advertising Levi's clothing in its local area. In return, the retailer agrees to advertise and display the clothing prominently.

Exclusive Distribution Some manufacturers grant **exclusive distribution** rights to a wholesaler or retailer in one geographic region. For example, a small city is not likely to have more than one Jaguar dealer. This is also common in high fashion, major appliances, and furniture lines. What is lost in market coverage is often gained in the ability to maintain a prestige image and premium prices. Exclusive distribution agreements also force manufacturers and retailers to cooperate closely in advertising and promotion programs.

Vertical Marketing Systems: The Growth of Franchising

To be efficient, members of a distribution channel need to cooperate closely with one another. This need gave rise to the **vertical marketing system (VMS)**, a system in which the main members of a distribution channel—producer, wholesaler, and retailer—work together as a cooperative group to meet consumer needs. This contrasts with conventional marketing systems in which producers, wholesalers, and retailers are separate businesses that are all trying to maximize their profits.[53]

There are three types of vertical marketing systems: corporate, administered, and contractual. In a corporate VMS, one company owns multiple levels of the distribution or production channel. An example would be a company such as Apple, which has its own retail stores as well as designing and manufacturing the products sold in those retail stores. An administered VMS is one in which one member of the production and distribution chain is dominant and calls the shots. An example of this type of system would be a large retailer such as Walmart, which dictates terms to its suppliers.[54]

A contractual VMS involves a formal agreement between the various levels of the distribution or production channel to coordinate the overall process. One type of contractual VMS is a **retail cooperative**, in which a group of independent retailers buy from a jointly owned wholesaler. ACE Hardware is an example of a retail cooperative. Another type of contractual VMS is a *franchise*. For the last quarter century, the greatest growth has been in **franchising**—such as McDonald's or Supercuts—in which retail dealers (or *franchisees*) pay a fee to operate under the guidelines and direction of the parent company or manufacturer (the *franchisor*). It's estimated that over 40 percent of all retail sales in

vertical marketing system (VMS) A system in which the main members of a distribution channel—producer, wholesaler, and retailer—work together as a cooperative group to meet consumer needs.

retail cooperative A group of independent retailers who establish a central buying organization (a wholesaler) to acquire discounts from manufacturers and gain economies from joint advertising and promotion efforts.

franchising A type of vertical marketing system in which dealers pay a fee to operate under the guidelines and direction of the parent company or manufacturer.

promotion (communication) element Includes all market-related communications between the seller and the buyer.

marketing communications The various efforts and tools companies use to initiate and maintain communication with customers and prospects, including advertising, personal selling, sales promotion, direct marketing, public relations, and social media.

> "IT IS CRITICAL THAT [ADVERTISING PEOPLE] UNDERSTAND HOW TO BLEND ALL THE TOOLS INTO AN INTEGRATED MARKETING COMMUNICATIONS PROGRAM."

the United States are made through franchise outlets. There are over 1,500 franchise companies operating more than 320,000 retail units in the United States today.[55]

Franchising and other vertical marketing systems offer both manufacturers and retailers numerous advantages, not the least of which are centralized coordination of marketing efforts and substantial savings and continuity in advertising. Perhaps most important is consumer recognition: The moment a new McDonald's opens, the franchisee has instant customers. Moreover, a single newspaper ad can promote all of a chain's retailers in a particular trading area.

Many marketers find that franchising is the best way to introduce their services into global markets. Subway sandwich shops, for example, is one of the fastest-growing franchise operations in the world with a total of nearly 40,000 stores in 102 countries.[56]

The vertical marketing system gave rise to a number of successful business plans, like franchising, in which franchisees pay a fee and operate under the guidelines of a parent company. For instance, the nearly 4,700 The UPS Store locations are franchised and provide greater access to UPS shipping services in addition to packing services and supplies, copying, digital printing, and more.

ADVERTISING AND THE PROMOTION (COMMUNICATION) ELEMENT

Once it determines product, price, and distribution, a company is ready to plan its marketing communications, of which advertising is just one component. The **promotion**, or **communication**, **element** includes all marketing-related communications between the seller and the buyer.

Marketing communications (often called *marcom*) refers to all the planned messages that companies and organizations

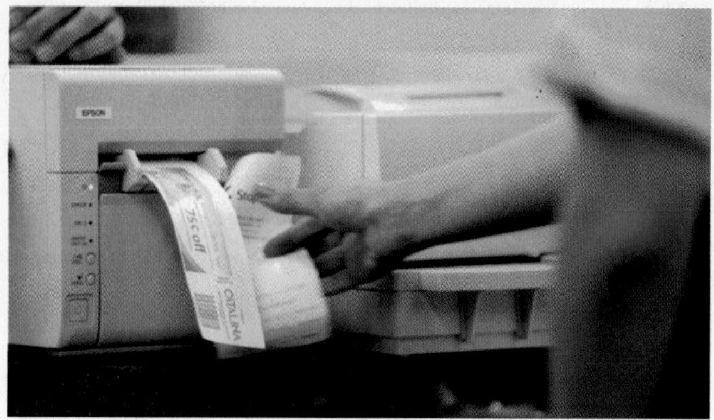

Catalina's personalized digital in-store media delivers incentives to shoppers at the checkout counter, based on what they buy. It integrates the point-of-sale system with the world's largest database of shopper purchase history. Catalina's network (www.catalinamarketing.com) influences more than 350 million households every month in more than 31,000 major retail stores.

create and disseminate to support their marketing objectives and strategies. In addition to advertising, major marketing communication tools include *personal selling, sales promotion, direct marketing,* and *public relations activities.* The extent to which an organization uses any or all of these tools depends on its marketing needs.

Each marketing communication tool offers particular opportunities and benefits to the marketer. In Chapters 15 and 16 we will discuss how these tools can best be integrated into the *marketing mix.* Since advertising people are frequently called on to solve a variety of marketing problems, it is critical that they understand how to blend all the tools into an integrated marketing communications program.

For creating brand awareness, familiarity, and image, as well as for reinforcing prior purchase decisions, advertising is the communications tool of choice for many products. The following factors are particularly important for advertising success:

- Strong primary demand trend.
- Potential for significant product differentiation.
- Hidden qualities highly important to consumers.
- Opportunity to use strong emotional appeals.
- Substantial funds available to support advertising.

Where these conditions exist, companies spend large amounts on advertising, and the ratio of advertising to sales dollars is often quite high. For completely undifferentiated products, such as sugar, salt, and other raw materials or commodities, advertising is usually less important and the other marketing mix elements play a more significant role.

THE MARKETING MIX IN PERSPECTIVE

With the target market designated and the elements of the marketing mix determined, the company has a complete product concept and a strategic basis for marketing to that target. Now it can formalize its strategies and tactics in a written marketing and advertising plan. As part of the planning process, companies use marketing and advertising research. We will discuss this in Chapter 6 before dealing with the formal planning process in Chapter 7. But first we'll examine the process of human communication and some theories of consumer behavior. ■

check yourself ✓

1. How does a product's stage in the product life cycle affect the way the product is advertised?
2. What are the benefits of a strong brand name?
3. Why do advertisers need to be concerned with a product's price?

learn about, practice, and apply segmentation, targeting, and the marketing mix!

M: Advertising was developed for students who want information packaged in a concise, easy-to-read, yet interesting format.

Check out the book's website to:

- Determine why it's so important to define the target market. (Review Questions)
- Understand the role of the product life cycle in determining a company's marketing strategy. (Review Questions)
- Learn how to define a market segment using behavioristic, demographic, psychographic, and geographic variables. (Exploring Advertising)
- Describe a product's positioning. (Exploring Advertising)

While you are there, check out the professional resource links, review the PowerPoint presentation, and test your knowledge with the Multiple Choice Quiz. Additionally, *Connect® Marketing* is available for M: Advertising.

www.mhhe.com/ArensM2e

chapter five

communication and **consumer behavior**

The focus of this chapter is to underline the importance of the marketing process in business and define the role of advertising and other marketing communications tools in presenting the company and its products to the market. The successful advertising practitioner must understand the relationship between marketing activities and the way consumers behave. Ideally, it is this relationship that shapes the creation of effective advertising.

What is a great ad?[1] It could be argued that a campaign that can turn an unknown actor into an overnight sensation qualifies as great. From 1997 to 2003, Taco Bell's "spokesman" was perhaps America's favorite advertising icon. Although technically, this celebrity was not a man. Or a woman either. It was a small dog whose catchphrase "Yo quiero Taco Bell!" became an instant classic. The dog was so popular that many were stunned when the restaurant chain discontinued the campaign and severed its relationship with the agency that created it.

Does liking an ad translate into liking the advertised product? In academic jargon, the issue is whether a favorable attitude toward an ad creates a favorable attitude toward the brand.[2] In many cases, the research literature suggests that the answer is yes.[3]

But the situation is complicated, because consumers tend to like the ads for their preferred brands. This relationship gets it backward: attitude toward the brand creates attitude toward the ad.

And confusing matters even more, sometimes we love ads that fail to arouse interest in the advertised product. The Taco Bell Chihuahua was a case in point. People did love the ad. But those positive emotions failed to generate consumer interest in eating at Taco Bell.[4]

The history of advertising is sprinkled with cases in which agencies did a better job of creating love for the ad than love for the brand. Case in point: The first Internet superstar was a sock puppet created as the advertising mascot for Pets.com. People liked the puppet, but the company went under fairly quickly when sales failed to materialize. An Alka-Seltzer spot from the early 1970s created another phrase that entered the popular jargon, "Mamma mia, that's-a *spicy* meat ball-a!" This "ad within an ad" spot featured an actor appearing to flub takes for a fictitious brand of meatballs. His increasing heartburn was finally alleviated by Alka-Seltzer. Despite the ad's popularity, the spot stopped running after sales remained flat.[5] And America's favorite campaign from 1990 featured the newly introduced "Energizer Bunny." An *Ad Age* survey confirmed that consumers loved the ads. But research suggested that viewers were confused as to whether the pink toy was a symbol of Energizer or rival Duracell, so liking again failed to translate into sales.[6]

continued on p. 122

LEARNING OBJECTIVES

After studying this chapter, you will be able to:

LO5-1 Explain how advertising differs from the basic communication process.

LO5-2 Outline the consumer perception process and explain why advertising people say "perception is everything."

LO5-3 Explain how a consumer's level of involvement with a product influences the decision-making process and the advertising approach.

LO5-4 Describe the fundamental motives behind consumer purchases.

LO5-5 Discuss the various influences on consumer behavior.

source The party that formulates the idea, encodes it as a message, and sends it via some channel to the receiver.

message In oral communication, the idea formulated and encoded by the source and sent to the receiver.

continued from p. 121

All of which suggests that creating great advertising involves more than creating likable advertising. Certainly from an advertiser's perspective, a truly great ad is one that engages consumers with the featured brand. Taco Bell is not in the business of selling Chihuahuas. It sells Mexican-themed fast food. The Taco Bell ads that run today may not feature a cute dog. But they do give consumers a "reason-why" they should consider Taco Bell restaurants when they are looking for an inexpensive break from the hamburgers.

In the end, it is not that difficult to interest people in a cute dog, a funny puppet, or a feisty plush toy. Getting people interested in visiting a fast-food brand? That is helped by great advertising. ■

> "McCann Erickson, the ad agency for Coca-Cola and MasterCard, says that advertising is 'Truth well told.'"

COMMUNICATION: WHAT MAKES ADVERTISING UNIQUE

In the last chapter, we learned that communication is a key element of the marketing mix. However, for communication to be effective, the marketer must construct a message that is meaningful to consumers and will elicit the desired behavior.

In Chapter 1, we defined advertising as "the structured and composed nonpersonal communication of information." Advertising is a special kind of communication. McCann Erickson, the ad agency for Coca-Cola and MasterCard, says that advertising is "Truth well told." This means that ethical advertisers and their agencies work as a team to discover the best methods possible to tell their story truthfully and creatively. To succeed, they must understand the elements of the advertising communication process, which is derived from the basic human communication process.

LO5-1 Explain how advertising differs from the basic communication process.

The Human Communication Process

From our first cry at birth, survival depends on our ability to inform others or persuade them to take action. As we develop, we learn to listen and respond to others' messages. The traditional model in Exhibit 5–1 summarizes the series of events that take place when people share

encoded Translating an idea or message into words, symbols, and illustrations.

semiotics The study of how humans use words, gestures, signs, and symbols to convey feelings, thoughts, ideas, and ideologies.

channel Any medium through which an encoded message is sent to a receiver, including oral communication, print media, television, and the Internet.

personal channels Means of communication that involve direct contact between the parties, such as personal selling.

nonpersonal channels Means of communication that don't involve interpersonal contact between the sender and the receiver. Examples would include advertising, publicity, and sales promotion.

▼**EXHIBIT 5-1** The human communication process.

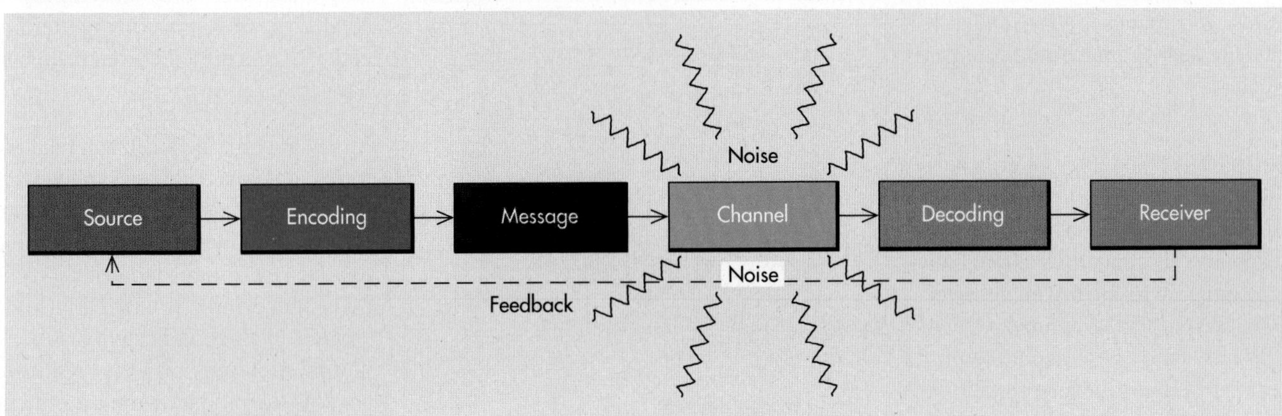

ideas in informal oral communication. The process begins when one party, the source, formulates an idea, encodes it as a message, and sends it via some channel to another party, the receiver. The receiver must decode the message in order to understand it. To respond, the receiver formulates a new idea, encodes it, and then sends the new message back through some channel. A message that acknowledges or responds to the original message constitutes feedback, which also affects the encoding of a new message.[7] And, of course, all this takes place in an environment characterized by noise—the distracting cacophony of many other messages being sent at the same time by other sources.

Applying the Communication Process to Advertising

Applying this model to advertising, we could say that the source is the sponsor, the message is the ad, the channel is the medium, the receiver is the consumer or prospect, and the noise is the din of competing ads and other distractions. A good deal of advertising today is a one-way process, with the message moving from the sponsor to the consumer. However, interactive forms of marketing—personal selling, telemarketing, digital advertising—let consumers participate in the communication by extracting the information they need, manipulating what they see and hear, and responding in real time. This model may not capture such communications well, a point we return to in a moment. For now, let's take a closer look at the traditional model.

The Source The ultimate **source** of a marketing message is the organization that has information it wishes to share with others. However, within the context of an advertisement, a real or imaginary spokesperson actually lends voice or tone to the communication. Because the receiver's perception of the source influences the effectiveness of the communication, the spokesperson must appear to be knowledgeable, trustworthy, and relevant to the audience.

The Message The information contained in a **message** must be **encoded** so that the receiver understands what is being communicated. This involves using words or symbols that are familiar to the intended audience. Depending on the medium used, the message may be verbal or nonverbal. **Semiotics** is the study of how humans use words, gestures, signs, and symbols to convey feelings, thoughts, ideas, and ideologies.[8] For example, the cowboy in Marlboro advertisements symbolizes ruggedness and individualism. The Energizer Bunny communicates reliability and persistence.

The Channel The **channel** is the means by which the encoded message travels from the source to the receiver. Communications channels can be categorized as personal or nonpersonal. **Personal channels**, such as personal selling, involve direct contact between the parties. **Nonpersonal channels** of communication are those that rule out interpersonal contact between the sender and the receiver. Mass

receiver In oral communication, this party decodes the message to understand it.

decode To interpret a message by the receiver.

noise The sender's advertising message competing daily with hundreds of other commercial and noncommercial messages.

feedback A message that acknowledges or responds to an initial message.

interactive media Media such as the Internet and interactive television that permit consumers to give instantaneous, real-time feedback on the same channel used by the original message sender.

communications, such as television, websites, magazines, radio, and billboards, are sent to many individuals at one time.

The Receiver The **receiver** is usually the consumer who receives the advertiser's message. The advertiser must always be concerned about how the consumer will **decode**, or interpret, a message. The last thing an advertiser wants is to be misunderstood. Unfortunately, message interpretation is only partially determined by the words and symbols in the ad. The advertising medium may have an effect as well. As Marshall McLuhan said, "The medium is the message." The unique characteristics of the receivers are also very important, and the sponsor may know little or nothing about them. We'll see later in this chapter that attitudes, perceptions, personality, self-concept, and culture are just some of the many influences that affect the way people receive and respond to messages and how they behave as consumers.

Symbols are often used in advertising to encode messages. In this ad, Evian (www.evian.com) uses a flower to symbolize water's ability to restore, revitalize, replenish, and hydrate. Evian would like you to think of its spring water as a beauty product.

> With interactive media such as the Internet, [consumers] can give instantaneous, real-time feedback.

Complicating this problem is the fact that the sponsor's advertising message must compete with hundreds of other commercial and noncommercial messages every day. This is referred to as **noise**. So the sender doesn't know how the message is received, or even if it is received, unless a consumer acknowledges it.

Feedback and Interactivity That's why **feedback** is so important. It completes the cycle, verifying that the message was received. Feedback employs the sender-message-receiver pattern, except that it is directed from the receiver back to the source.

In advertising, feedback can take many forms: redeemed coupons, phone inquiries, visits to a store, requests for more information, increased sales, responses to a survey, e-mail inquiries, or clicks on a banner ad. Dramatically low responses to an ad indicate a break in the communication process. Questions arise: Is the product wrong for the market? Is the message unclear? Are we using the right media? Without feedback, these questions cannot be answered.

In the past, the consumer's feedback used different channels than the original message. But now, thanks again to technology, the audiences of advertising are no longer just passive receivers of impersonal mass messages. They are now active decision makers who can control what communications they receive and choose the information they want about a particular product. With **interactive media** such as the Internet, they can give instantaneous, real-time feedback on the same channel used by the original message sender. In fact, in interactive media, consumers can be the source and advertisers the receiver, blurring the lines completely.

Exhibit 5–2 presents an interactive model of communication. In this model, no single entity operates as a source or receiver. Instead, two entities serve both roles in an ongoing process. This model better represents marketers' understanding of their

EXHIBIT 5-2 The interactive model of communication.

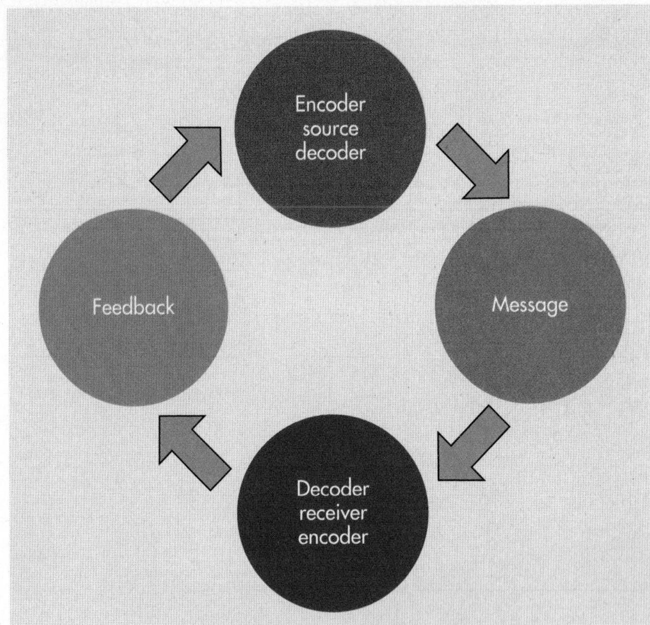

relationships with consumers today. Marketers no longer dominate the exchange of messages. Rather, they are engaged in a conversation with consumers who send their own messages, both to the marketer and to other consumers. The interactive model helps remind companies that they do not have as much control over messages as the traditional model seems to suggest. It also reminds companies that listening to their customers is important, because it ultimately determines whether the company will succeed.

CONSUMER BEHAVIOR: THE KEY TO ADVERTISING STRATEGY

Effective communication happens when the marketer selects a relevant source, develops an appropriate message, encodes it correctly, and then finds a suitable medium that will best reach the target audience. All of these steps rely upon the marketer knowing the receiver of the message and understanding how that individual might respond.

Take a look at your friends in class, or the people you work with. How well do you know them? Could you describe their lifestyles and the kinds of products they prefer? Do they typically eat out or cook for themselves? Do they ski? Play tennis? If so, what brands of equipment do they buy? Do you know which radio stations they listen to? What TV programs they watch? What websites they visit? If you were Sony's advertising manager and wanted to advertise a new laptop to these people, what type of appeal would you use? What media would you use to reach them?

consumer behavior The activities, actions, and influences of people who purchase and use goods and services to satisfy their personal or household needs and wants.

consumer decision process The series of steps a consumer goes through in deciding to make a purchase.

The Importance of Knowing the Consumer

Advertisers spend a lot of money to keep individuals and groups of individuals (markets) interested in their products. To succeed, they need to understand what makes potential customers behave the way they do. The advertiser's goal is to get enough relevant market data to develop accurate profiles of buyers—to find the common ground (and symbols) for communication. This involves the study of **consumer behavior**: the mental and emotional processes and the physical activities of people who purchase and use goods and services to satisfy particular needs and wants.[9]

The Consumer Decision Process: An Overview

Social scientists have many theories of consumer behavior to explain the process of making a purchase decision. Let's look at this information from the viewpoint of the advertiser.

Advertising's primary mission is to reach prospective customers and influence their awareness, attitudes, and buying behavior. To succeed, an advertiser must make the marketing communications process work very effectively.

The moment we receive an advertising message, our mental computer runs a rapid evaluation called the **consumer decision process**. The conceptual model in Exhibit 5–3 presents the basic steps we go through in making a purchase decision. As you can see, the full process involves a rather lengthy sequence of activities: *problem recognition* (which may occur as

personal processes The three internal, human operations—perception, learning, and motivation—that govern the way consumers discern raw data (stimuli) and translate them into feelings, thoughts, beliefs, and actions.

interpersonal influences Social influences on the consumer decision-making process, including family, society, and cultural environment.

nonpersonal influences Factors influencing the consumer decision-making process that are often out of the consumer's control, such as time, place, and environment.

evaluation of alternatives Choosing among brands, sizes, styles, and colors.

postpurchase evaluation Determining whether a purchase has been a satisfactory or unsatisfactory one.

▼ **EXHIBIT 5-3** The basic consumer decision process is a set of steps that the consumer experiences during and after the purchase. Advertising and other influences can affect the consumer's attitude at any point in this process.

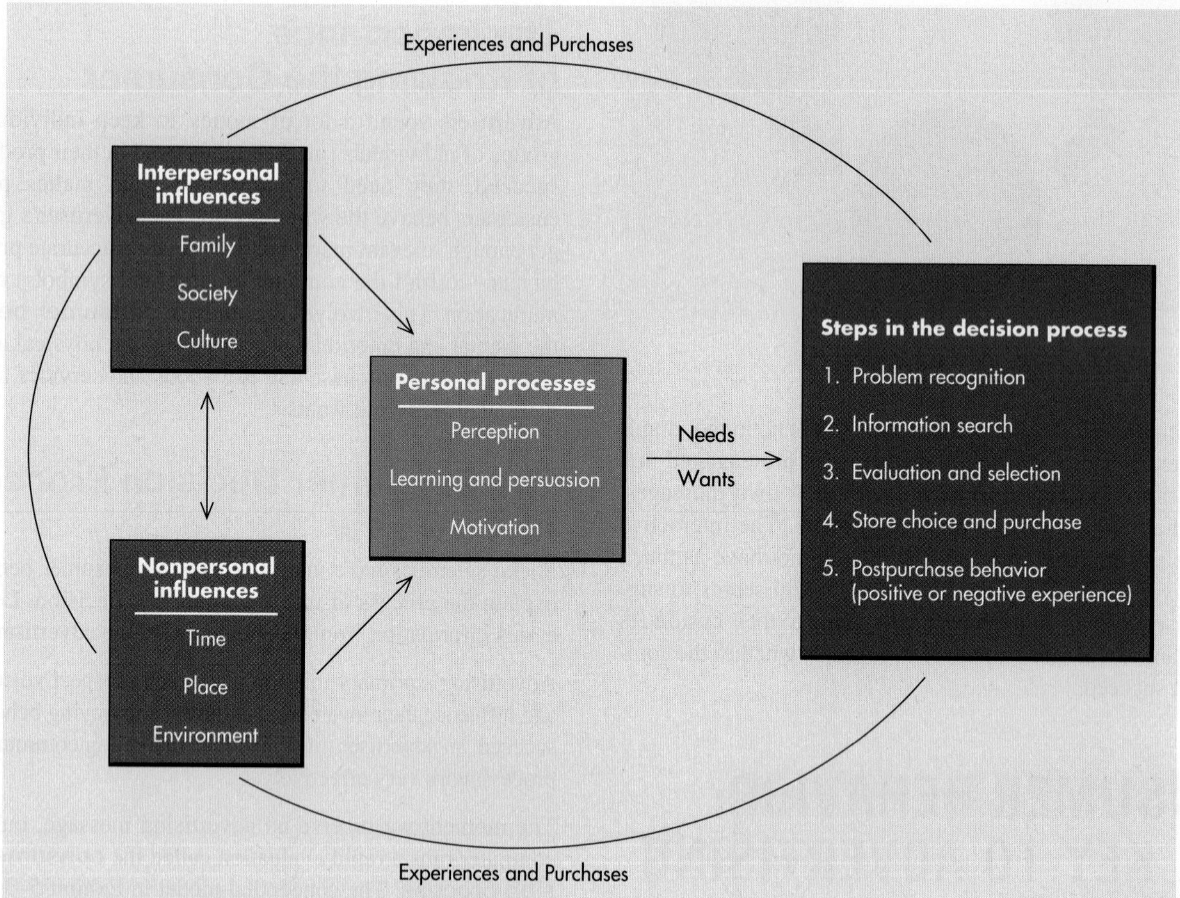

a result of seeing an ad), *information search, evaluation and selection* of alternative brands, *store choice and purchase,* and finally *postpurchase behavior.* For simple, habitual, everyday purchases with low levels of involvement, the decision-making process is typically very abbreviated. But in those situations where we are highly involved in the purchase, it's not at all unusual for us to substantially extend the decision process.

Whether the process is limited or extended, though, numerous sociological and psychological factors invariably play a role in the way we behave. These include a series of personal subprocesses that are themselves shaped by various influences.

The three **personal processes** govern the way we discern raw data *(stimuli)* and translate them into feelings, thoughts, beliefs, and actions. The personal processes are the *perception,* the *learning and persuasion,* and the *motivation* processes.

Second, our mental processes and behavior are affected by two sets of influences. **Interpersonal influences** include our *family, society,* and *culture.* **Nonpersonal influences**—factors often outside the consumer's control—include *time, place,* and *environment.* These influences further affect the personal processes of perception, learning, and motivation.

After dealing with these processes and influences, we face the pivotal decision: to buy or not to buy. But taking that final step typically requires yet another process, the **evaluation of alternatives**, in which we choose brands, sizes, styles, and colors. If we do decide to buy, our **postpurchase evaluation** will influence our subsequent purchases.

Like the communications process, the decision process is circular in nature. What we learn from one experience influences our behavior the next time. The advertiser who understands this

process can develop messages more likely to reach and make sense to consumers.

check yourself ✓

1. What is meant by noise and how might it affect an advertiser's efforts?
2. What are the key differences between human communication and advertising communication?

PERSONAL PROCESSES IN CONSUMER BEHAVIOR

Assume you are the advertising manager preparing to launch a new high-tech, vitamin-laden beverage brand for athletes and sports participants. We'll call it MonsterMalt. What's your first objective?

The first task in promoting any new product is to create awareness *(perception)* that the product exists. The second is to provide enough compelling information *(learning and persuasion)* about the product for prospective customers to become interested and make an informed decision. Finally, you want your advertising to stimulate customers' desire *(motivation)* to satisfy their needs and wants by trying the product.

If they find MonsterMalt satisfying, they likely will continue to purchase it. These three personal processes of consumer behavior—perception, learning and persuasion, and motivation—are extremely important to advertisers. By studying these, advertisers can better evaluate how their messages are perceived.

perception Our personalized way of sensing and comprehending stimuli.

stimulus Physical data that can be received through the senses.

L05-2 Outline the consumer perception process and explain why advertising people say "perception is everything."

The Consumer Perception Process

Perception is important.[10] The average adult may be exposed to thousands of ads each day but notices only a handful and remembers even fewer.[11] How does this happen? The answer lies in the principle of perception.

The term **perception** refers to the information we receive through our five senses. This definition suggests it refers to the first two elements in the consumer perception and cognition model shown in Exhibit 5–4.

Stimulus

A **stimulus** is something (light, sound, a scent) we can perceive through our senses. It may originate within our bodies, as when we notice that we feel hungry at lunchtime. Or it may originate from outside our bodies, as when we see an ad for an iPhone and decide it looks beautiful.

> "The average adult may be exposed to thousands of ads each day but notices only a handful."

EXHIBIT 5–4 The model of the consumer perception and cognition processes portray how consumers perceive, accept, and remember an ad.

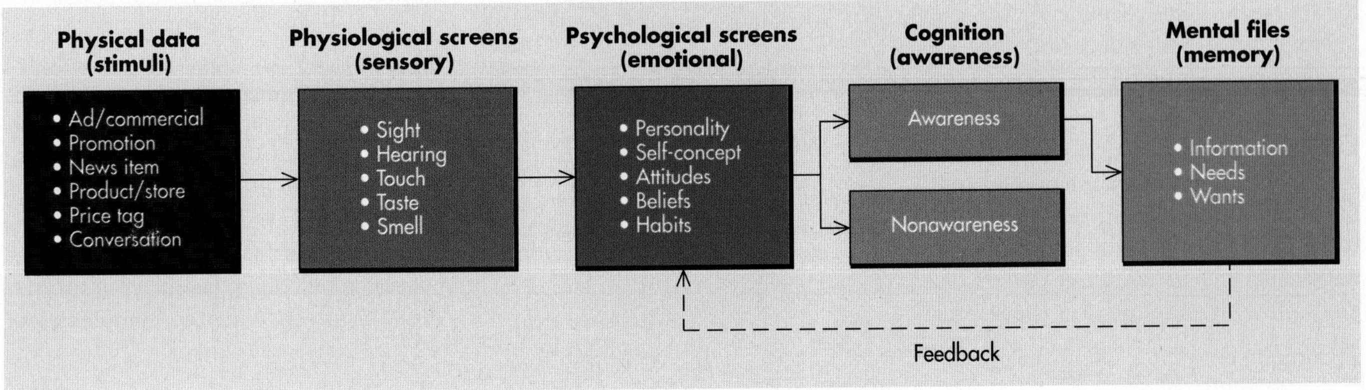

perceptual screens The physiological or psychological filters that messages must pass through.

physiological screens The perceptual screens that use the five senses—sight, hearing, touch, taste, and smell—to detect incoming data and measure the dimension and intensity of the physical stimulus.

cognition The point of awareness and comprehension of a stimulus.

self-concept The images we carry in our minds of the type of person we are and who we desire to be.

mental files Stored memories in consumers' minds.

IMC messages are external stimuli that can appear in a variety of forms: a window display at a local department store, the brightly colored labels on cans of Campbell's tomato soup, or even the red price tag on a pair of skis at REI. These objects are all physical in nature; they stimulate our senses (with varying degrees of intensity) in ways that can be measured.

Screens are barriers that ads must penetrate. This is acknowledged in this ad for the IFAW, which suggests that how you see the tiger depends on the screen you are looking through.

Perceptual Screens The second key element in perception is the personalized way of sensing and interpreting the stimulus data. Before any data can be perceived, they must first penetrate a set of **perceptual screens**, the subconscious filters that shield us from unwanted messages.

The **physiological screens** comprise the five senses: sight, hearing, touch, taste, and smell. They detect incoming data and measure the dimension and intensity of the stimuli. A sight-impaired person can't read an ad in *Sports Illustrated.* And if the type in a movie ad is too small for the average reader, it won't be read, and perception will suffer. Similarly, if the music in a TV commercial for a furniture store fails to complement the message, the viewer may tune out, change channels, or turn off the TV. The advertiser's message is effectively screened out when the viewer can't interpret it; perception does not occur, and the furniture goes unsold.[12]

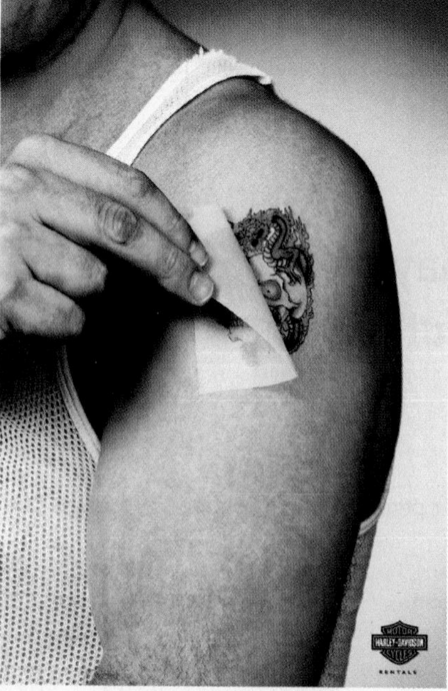
Advertisers frequently capitalize on consumers' concepts of themselves to generate attention and interest in a particular product. This ad takes the next step: It shows consumers that they can temporarily identify with their wilder sides by renting a Harley-Davidson (www.harleydavidson.com).

Cognition When a stimulus is perceived, we must make sense of it by relating it to the things we already know. That is the role of **cognition**: comprehending the stimulus. Once we detect the stimulus and allow it through our perceptual screens, we have the opportunity to understand and accept it.

Just as we saw that there are screens at the level of perception, so too do screens exist at the level of cognition. Each consumer uses psychological screens to evaluate, filter, and personalize information according to subjective standards. These screens evaluate data based on the consumer's personality and instinctive human needs, and learned factors, such as the **self-concept**, interests, attitudes, beliefs, experiences, and lifestyle. They help consumers summarize complex data. For example, perceptual screens help us accept or reject symbolic ideas, such as the sexy commercial for Levi's Dockers in which a man and a number of women seductively dance in a nightclub.

Of course, each of us has his or her own reality. For example, you may consider the tacos advertised by Taco Bell to be "Mexican" food. That perception is your reality. But someone from Mexico might tell you that a fast-food taco bears little resemblance to an authentic one. That person's reality, based on another perception, is considerably different. As much as possible, advertisers seek commonly shared perceptions of reality as a basis for their advertising messages.

Mental Files Cognition is not just about how we respond to things we perceive; it is also about how we store information for later use. Many promotional messages rely on consumers making a purchase long after they are exposed to a brand message. Information in memory is not stored randomly, but rather in **mental files.** To cope with the complexity of

learning A relatively permanent change in thought processes or behavior that occurs as a result of reinforced experience.

cognitive theory An approach that views learning as a mental process of memory, thinking, and the rational application of knowledge to practical problem solving.

conditioning theory The theory that learning is a trial-and-error process.

stimulus-response theory Also called *conditioning theory.* Some stimulus triggers a consumer's need or want, and this in turn creates a need to respond.

stimuli such as advertising, we rank products and other data in our files by importance, price, quality, features, or a host of other descriptors.

Memory is a limited resource, and one susceptible to some well-known biases. As an example, pause for a moment and consider whether there are more words that begin with the letter *k* (i.e., *kangaroo*) versus words that have *k* in the third position (i.e., *Arkansas*). What is your guess? Many people are surprised to discover there are nearly three times more words (*ask, askance, ark*) with *k* in the third position. But when we search through memory, our mental files make it easier to retrieve words by their first letter. We then confuse this ease of retrieval with the frequency of occurrence. This "availability" heuristic is just one example of how the structure of our cognitive system influences what we recall and how we decide.

L05-3 Explain how a consumer's level of involvement with a product influences the decision-making process and the advertising approach.

Learning, Persuasion, and the Role of Involvement in the Ways That Consumers Process Information

By definition, **learning** is a relatively permanent change in thought process or behavior that occurs as a result of experience. Learning, in turn, affects behavior. Learning that a food tastes delicious leads to eating more. Learning that a hot stove burns leads to keeping a distance in the kitchen.

[Learning is a relatively permanent change in thought process or behavior.]

Because screens are such a major challenge to advertisers, it's important to understand what's in the consumer's mental files and, if possible, modify them in favor of the advertiser's product. That brings us to the second process in consumer behavior: *learning and persuasion.* Perceptions can rarely be changed through advertising alone.[13] But once a new perception does enter our mental files, the information alters the database on which our psychological screens feed.

check yourself ✓

1. Why do we use perceptual screens to filter the ads to which we are exposed?
2. What does the term *consumer behavior* refer to, and why is it important to advertisers?

Theories of Learning There are numerous theories of learning, but advertisers classify most into two broad categories—*cognitive theory* and *conditioning theory*—depending on the level of consumer involvement (high or low) required to make a purchase. **Cognitive theory** views learning as a mental process of memory, thinking, and the rational application of knowledge to practical problems. This theory may be an accurate description of how we learn from the experience of others, such as our parents, and how we evaluate a complex purchase such as insurance, stocks and bonds, or business products. **Conditioning theory**—also called **stimulus-response theory**—treats learning as a trial-and-error process. Some stimulus (perhaps an ad) triggers the consumer's need or want, and this in turn creates the drive to respond. If the consumer's response reduces the drive, then satisfaction occurs, and the response is rewarded or reinforced. And that produces repeat behavior the next time the drive is aroused, demonstrating that learning has taken place. Exhibit 5–5 shows simple diagrams of these two theories.

▼**EXHIBIT 5–5** Cognitive theory views learning as a mental process; conditioning theory treats learning as a trial-and-error process.

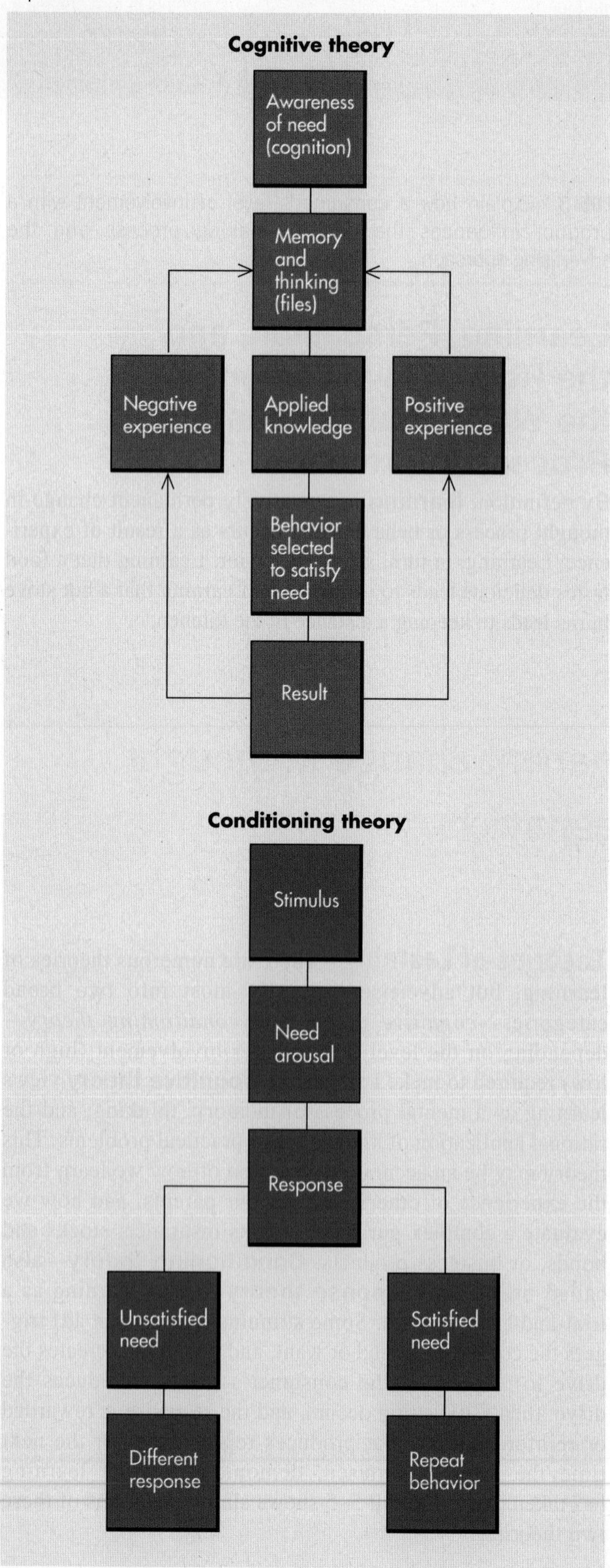

What determines which type of process, conditioning or cognitive, consumers are likely to use when learning information? **Consumer involvement** appears to play an important role. Involvement refers to how important or relevant a decision is to a consumer. More important and personally relevant decisions result in greater involvement.

Conditioning theory is more applicable to the simple, basic, low-involvement purchases consumers make every day, such as soap, cereal, toothpaste, and paper towels. And it is here that reinforcement advertising plays its most important role—along with superior product performance and good service. If learning is reinforced enough and repeat behavior is produced, a purchasing habit may result. Cognitive theories seem most applicable in highly involving situations, as when a consumer buys a car or an expensive TV. In these situations, people search for information from memory, carefully consider new evidence, and often resist the strong urges of emotion.

Learning and persuasion are closely linked. **Persuasion** occurs when the change in belief, attitude, or behavioral intention is caused by promotion communication (such as advertising or personal selling).[14] Naturally, advertisers are very interested in persuasion and how it takes place.

The Elaboration Likelihood Model The fact that learning can happen through a relatively thoughtful way (cognition) or a relatively simple way (conditioning) has direct implications for how marketers should try to persuade consumers to try or use a product. This is because, according to theorists, there are two different routes to persuasion: the central and the peripheral routes. Like learning theory, how persuasion takes place depends on the consumer's level of involvement with the product and the message. When the consumer's level of involvement is higher, the central route to persuasion is more likely. On the other hand, the peripheral route to persuasion predominates when consumer involvement is low.[15]

We can see how this works by looking at the **Elaboration Likelihood Model** in Exhibit 5–6. In the **central route to persuasion**, consumers have a higher level of involvement with the product or the message, so they are motivated to pay attention to the central, product-related information, such as product attributes and benefits or demonstrations of positive functional or psychological consequences. Because of their high involvement, they tend to learn cognitively and comprehend the ad-delivered information at deeper, more elaborate levels. This can lead to product beliefs, positive brand attitudes, and purchase intention.[16]

Suppose you are in the market for a significant purchase, say, a new phone. Because the purchase is relatively expensive, your level of involvement is higher. Perhaps you ask for advice from some friends or family members. You may shop different stores to compare models and prices. And you probably read ads for these products thoroughly to understand the variety of product features and benefits. That's central processing. And in that

consumer involvement How important or relevant a decision is to a consumer.

persuasion A change in thought process or behavior that occurs when the change in belief, attitude, or behavioral intention is caused by promotion communication (such as advertising or personal selling).

Elaboration Likelihood Model A theory of how persuasion occurs. It proposes that the method of persuasion depends on the consumer's level of involvement with the product and the message.

central route to persuasion One of two ways communication can persuade consumers. When a consumer's level of involvement is high, the central route to persuasion is more likely. In the central route to persuasion, consumers are motivated to pay attention to product-related information, such as product attributes and benefits. Because of their high involvement, they tend to learn cognitively and comprehend the ad-delivered information at deeper, more elaborate levels.

peripheral route to persuasion When consumers have low involvement with a product or message, they have little reason to pay attention to or comprehend the central message of the ad. However, these consumers might attend to some peripheral aspects of an ad for its entertainment value. Consistent with stimulus-response theory, consumers may respond to the message at a later date, when a purchase occasion arises.

EXHIBIT 5-6 The Elaboration Likelihood Model.

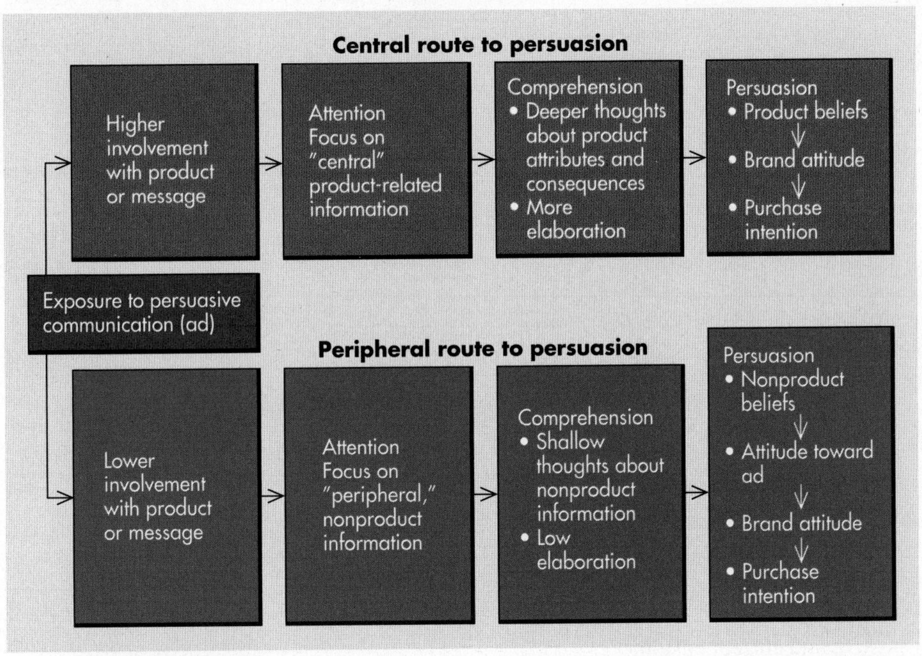

situation, a well-written, informative ad that provides compelling reasons to buy can be very persuasive.

The **peripheral route to persuasion** is very different. It's more like stimulus-response learning. People who are not in the market for a product typically have low involvement with the product message. They have little or no reason to pay attention to it or to comprehend the central information of the ad. As a result, direct persuasion is also low, and consumers form few if any brand beliefs, attitudes, or purchase intentions. However, these consumers might attend to some peripheral aspects—attractive sources, up-tempo music, exciting editing—for their entertainment value. And whatever they feel or think about these peripheral, nonproduct aspects can be integrated into a positive attitude toward the ad. At some later date, if a purchase occasion does arise and the consumer needs to make some brand evaluation, these ad-related meanings could be activated to form a brand attitude or purchase intention.

> "Because very few people are actually in the market at any given time, most mass media advertising receives peripheral processing."

Because very few people are actually in the market at any given time, most mass media advertising receives peripheral processing. We all know that most of the ads we see have little relevance to our immediate goals or needs, so we are not motivated to think about them. Our involvement is very low. That's why we also have very little recall of ads we saw yesterday. In cases where there is little product differentiation, advertisers may actually *want* us to engage in peripheral processing. Their ads focus more on image or entertainment than product features.

But when a product has a distinct advantage, the advertiser's goal should be to encourage central route processing by increasing consumers' involvement with the message. This is often the purpose of comparative advertising.[17]

Whichever route an ad targets, a key to learning and persuasion is repetition. Just as a student prepares for an exam by repeating key information to memorize it, an advertiser

Evian relies on a humorous image and an association with Wimbledon in this clever attempt to persuade via the peripheral route.

must repeat key information to prospective and current customers so they remember the product's name and its benefits. Repeat messages penetrate customers' perceptual screens by rekindling memories of information from prior ads. To see for yourself how important repetition is, identify the sponsors that feature these slogans: "I'm lovin' it," "15 minutes can save you 15 percent or more," and "Just do it."

Learning Produces Attitudes and Interest An **attitude** is our evaluation of some idea or object. An important advertising objective is developing messages that foster positive consumer attitudes.

In Japan, for instance, dishwashers are not a common household appliance. Not only is there very little space for them; Japanese housewives feel guilty about using the labor-saving device. As a result, dishwasher manufacturers have had to change attitudes by designing smaller, space-saving machines and then promoting them using good hygiene themes rather than convenience appeals.[18]

For mature brands in categories with familiar, frequently purchased products, *brand interest* is even more critical for motivating action. **Brand interest** is an individual's openness or curiosity about a brand.[19] Enjoyable, entertaining advertising can enhance interest in the brand and reduce the variety-seeking

For the high-involvement consumer, information is everything. Schwab offers useful facts to its prospects because strong arguments are important in central route processing.

tendencies of consumers who become bored with using the same old product.[20]

Learning Leads to Habits and Brand Loyalty

Attitude is the mental side and *habit* the behavioral side of the same coin. **Habit**—the acquired behavior pattern that becomes nearly or completely automatic—is the natural extension of learning. We really are creatures of habit.

Most consumer behavior is habitual for three reasons: It's safe, simple, and essential. First, regardless of how we learned to make our purchase decision (through either central or peripheral route processing), if we discover a quality product, brand, or service, we feel *safe* repurchasing it.

Second, habit is *simple*. To consider alternatives we must evaluate, compare, and then decide. This is difficult and time-consuming. Habits allow us to skip those steps.

Finally, because habit is both safe and easy, we rely on it for daily living. Imagine rethinking every purchase decision you make. It would be virtually impossible, not to mention impractical. So it's really *essential* to use habit in our lives.

Brand loyalty and interest are two important components of marketing automobiles. Mini USA (www.miniusa.com) has successfully maintained an image of fun and cleverness, as demonstrated by this installation in Toronto's Union Station.

attitude The acquired mental position—positive or negative—regarding some idea or object.

brand interest An individual's openness or curiosity about a brand.

habit An acquired or developed behavior pattern that has become nearly or completely automatic.

brand loyalty The consumer's conscious or unconscious decision—expressed through intention or behavior—to repurchase a brand continually. This occurs because the consumer perceives that the brand has the right product features, image, quality, or relationship at the right price.

The major objective of all brand marketers is to produce *brand* loyalty, a direct result of the habit of repurchasing and the reinforcement of continuous advertising. **Brand loyalty** is the consumer's conscious or unconscious decision, expressed through intention or behavior, to repurchase a brand continually.[21] It occurs because the consumer *perceives* that the brand offers the right product features, image, quality, or relationship at the right price.

In the quest for brand loyalty, advertisers have three aims related to habits:

1. *Breaking habits.* Get consumers to unlearn an existing purchase habit and try something new. Advertisers frequently offer incentives to lure customers away from old brands or stores. Or they may use comparative advertising to demonstrate their product's superiority. As Pets.com discovered, it is very difficult to get consumers to change their habits. Even coupons and discounts couldn't lure customers from their traditional pet products suppliers.
2. *Acquiring habits.* Teach consumers to repurchase their brand or repatronize their establishment. To get you started, Columbia House advertises free CDs when you sign up, tied to a contract to purchase more later on.
3. *Reinforcing habits.* Remind current customers of the value of their original purchase and encourage them to continue purchasing. Many magazines, for example, offer special renewal rates to their regular subscribers. Hotels offer loyalty programs and airlines award frequent flyer miles for the same reason.

Developing brand loyalty is much more difficult today due to consumers' increased sophistication and the legions of habit-breaking activities of competitive advertisers.[22] Only recently have advertisers come to realize that their years of habit-breaking activities have undermined their own *habit-building* objectives. In the quest for instant results, they shifted much of their advertising budgets to sales promotions (deals, coupons, price cuts). But advertising, unlike sales promotion, is an integral part of what makes a brand desirable. It's advertising that reinforces brand loyalty and maintains market share.[23] We revisit this topic in our discussion of sales promotion in Chapter 15.

Learning Defines Needs and Wants The learning process is both immediate and long term. The moment we file a perception, some learning takes place. When we see a succulent food ad, we may suddenly feel hungry; we *need* food. As we collate the information in our mental files, comparing new perceptions with old ones, further learning takes place. The need may become a *want.* This leads to the next personal process, motivation.

check yourself ✓

1. What is the difference between the central route and the peripheral route to persuasion?
2. What is the difference between the cognitive theory and the conditioning theory of learning?
3. What is the role of involvement in learning and persuasion?

LO5-4 Describe the fundamental motives behind consumer purchases.

The Consumer Motivation Process

Motivation refers to the underlying forces (or motives) that contribute to our actions. These motives stem from the conscious or unconscious goal of satisfying our needs and wants. **Needs** are the basic, often instinctive, human forces that motivate us to do something. **Wants** are "needs" that we learn during our lifetime.[24]

Motivation cannot be observed directly. When we see people eat, we assume they are hungry, but we may be wrong. People eat for a variety of reasons besides hunger: They want to be sociable, it's time to eat, or maybe they're nervous or bored.

People are usually motivated by the benefit of satisfying some combination of needs, which may be conscious or unconscious, functional or psychological. *Motivation research* offers insights into the underlying reasons for certain observed consumer behavior. The reasons *(motives)* some people stop shopping at Ralph's Supermarket and switch to Trader Joe's may be that Trader Joe's is closer to home, it has a wider selection of fresh produce, and (most likely) they see other people like themselves shopping there. Any or all of these factors might make a shopper switch even if prices are lower at Ralph's. It's possible that Pets.com did not provide sufficient motives for pet owners to change their behavior.

To better understand what motivates people, Abraham Maslow developed the classic model shown in Exhibit 5–7 called the **hierarchy of needs**. Maslow maintained that the lower, physiological and safety needs dominate human behavior and must be satisfied before the higher, socially acquired needs (or wants) become meaningful. The highest need, self-actualization, is the culmination of fulfilling all the lower needs and realizing one's true potential.

The promise of satisfying a certain level of need is the basic promotional appeal for many ads. In such affluent societies as the United States, Canada, Western Europe, and Japan, most individuals take for granted the satisfaction of their physiological needs. So advertising campaigns often portray the fulfillment of social, esteem, and self-actualization needs, and many offer the reward of satisfaction through personal achievement.

In focus groups for Nabisco SnackWells, for example, it became apparent that middle-aged women today have a high sense of self-worth. Wellness, to them, is no longer about looking good in a bathing suit, but rather celebrating what they do well. The advertiser wondered if it could use women's positive attitude about themselves to change their attitude toward the concept of snacking. Nabisco's agency capitalized on the idea in a new campaign aimed at boosting women's self-esteem. The message: "Snacking is not about 'filling' yourself, but 'fulfilling' yourself."[25]

We all have needs and wants, but we are frequently unaware of them. Before the advent of the desktop computer, people were

> **We all have needs and wants, but we are frequently unaware of them.**

▼ EXHIBIT 5–7 The hierarchy of needs suggests that people meet their needs according to priorities. Physiological and safety needs carry the greatest priority. In advertising, the message must match the need of the market or the ad will fail. Advertisers use marketing research to understand the need levels of their markets and use this information in determining the marketing mix.

Need	Product	Promotional appeal
Self-actualization	A graduate degree	"Realize your full potential"
Esteem	Luxury car	"The pursuit of perfection"
Social	Jewelry	"Show her you care"
Safety	Tires	"Bounces off hazards"
Physiological	Breakfast cereal	"The natural energy source"

completely unaware of any need for it. But the moment a consumer consciously recognizes a product-related want or need, a dynamic process begins. The consumer first evaluates the need and either accepts it as worthy of action or rejects it. Acceptance converts satisfaction of the need into a goal, which creates the motivation to make a purchase. In contrast, rejection removes the necessity for action and thereby eliminates the goal and the motivation to buy.

informational motives The negatively originated motives, such as problem removal or problem avoidance, that are the most common energizers of consumer behavior.

positively originated motives Consumer's motivation to purchase and use a product based on a positive bonus that the product promises, such as sensory gratification, intellectual stimulation, or social approval.

transformational motives Positively originated motives that promise to "transform" the consumer through sensory gratification, intellectual stimulation, and social approval.

Modern researchers translated Maslow's theory about needs and motives into more strategic concepts for use by marketers and advertisers. Rossiter and Percy, for example, identify eight fundamental purchase and usage motives (see Exhibit 5–8). They refer to the first five as *negatively originated (informational) motives* and the last three as *positively originated (transformational) motives.*[26]

Negatively Originated (Informational) Motives

The most common energizers of consumer behavior are the **negatively originated motives**, such as problem removal or problem avoidance. Whenever we run out of something, for instance, we experience a negative mental state. To relieve those feelings, we actively seek a new or replacement product. Thus, we are temporarily motivated until the time we make the purchase. Then, if the purchase is satisfactory, the drive or motivation is reduced.

Negative motivation is a powerful tool for affecting human behavior. This ad for Kids and Cars speaks to the potential danger of power windows and attempts to scare readers into adopting safe habits around children.

These are also called **informational motives** because the consumer actively seeks information to reduce the negative mental state. In fact, Rossiter and Percy point out, these could also be called "relief" motives because consumers work to find relief from a problem.

Positively Originated (Transformational) Motives

From time to time, we all want to indulge ourselves by buying some brand or product that promises some benefit or reward. With the **positively originated motives**, a positive bonus is promised rather than the removal or reduction of some negative situation. The goal is to use positive reinforcement to increase the consumer's motivation and to energize the consumer's investigation or search for the new product.

The three positively originated motives—sensory gratification, intellectual stimulation, and social approval—are also called **transformational motives** because the consumer expects to be transformed in a sensory, intellectual, or social sense. They could also be called "reward" motives because the transformation is a rewarding state.[27]

▼EXHIBIT 5–8 Rossiter and Percy's eight fundamental purchase and usage motives.

Negatively Originated (Informational) Motives
1. Problem removal 2. Problem avoidance 3. Incomplete satisfaction 4. Mixed approach–avoidance 5. Normal depletion
Positively Originated (Transformational) Motives
6. Sensory gratification 7. Intellectual stimulation or mastery 8. Social approval

For some consumers, the purchase of a particular product (say, a new suit) might represent a negatively originated motive (they have to have it for work). But for other consumers, it might be positively originated (they think a suit will lead people to view them as more professional and competent). This suggests two distinct target markets that advertisers must understand and that may call for completely different advertising strategies.

Before creating messages, advertisers must carefully consider the goals that lead to consumer motivations. Denny's Restaurants would make a costly mistake if its ads portrayed

interpersonal influences Social influences on the consumer decision-making process, including family, society, and cultural environment.

social classes Traditional divisions in societies by sociologists—upper, upper-middle, lower-middle, and so on—who believed that people in the same social class tended toward similar attitudes, status symbols, and spending patterns.

the reward of a romantic interlude if the real motive of most Denny's customers is simply to satisfy their hunger with a filling, low-priced meal.

check yourself ✓

1. What are the various approaches that advertisers use to develop brand loyalty among consumers?
2. What type of motive is related to being transformed in a sensory, intellectual, or social sense?

Often purchases are made by a group rather than an individual. In many families, everyone must be happy with a brand, a fact acknowledged by Brazilian retailer BH in this ad.

LO5-5 Discuss the various influences on consumer behavior.

INTERPERSONAL INFLUENCES ON CONSUMER BEHAVIOR

For advertisers, it's not enough just to know the *personal* processes of perception, learning and persuasion, and motivation. Important **interpersonal influences** affect—sometimes even dominate—these processes. They also serve as guidelines for consumer behavior. These influences can best be categorized as the *family,* the *society,* and the *cultural environment* of the consumer.

Family Influence

From an early age, family communication affects our socialization as consumers—our attitudes toward many products and our purchasing habits. This influence is usually strong and long-lasting. A child who learns that the "right" headache relief is Bayer aspirin and the "right" name for appliances is General Electric has a well-developed adult purchasing behavior.

Ads that make use of positively originated motives promise to reward consumers in some way. This Minute Maid Light ad (www.minutemaid.com) addresses two positively originated motives—sensory gratification and social approval—by promising the consumer both great taste and an attractive figure.

From 1970 to 1990, married couple households with children declined sharply—from 40 to 26 percent of all households. Since 1990, that decline has been slower—such households represent 20 percent as of 2011. This suggests that family influence has greatly diminished in the United States over the last 35 years as working parents take a less active role in raising their children and youngsters look outside the family for social values.[28] As this happens, the influence of the social and cultural environments intensifies.

Societal Influence

Our community exerts a strong influence on us all. When we affiliate with a particular societal division or identify with some reference group or value the ideas of certain opinion leaders, it affects our views on life, our perceptual screens, and eventually the products we buy.

Societal Divisions: The Group We Belong To Sociologists traditionally divided societies into **social classes**: upper, upper-middle, lower-middle, and so on. They believed that people in the same social class tended to have similar attitudes, status symbols, and spending patterns.

But today this doesn't apply to most developed countries. U.S. society, especially, is extremely fluid and mobile—physically, socially, and economically. Americans, regardless of their social class, believe strongly in getting ahead, being better than their peers, and winning greater admiration and self-esteem.

Because of this mobility, dramatic increases in immigration, and the high divorce rate, social-class boundaries have become quite muddled. Single parents, stockbrokers, immigrant shopkeepers, retired blue-collar workers, and bankers all see themselves as part of the great middle class. So "middle class" doesn't mean anything anymore. From the advertiser's point of view, social class seldom represents a functional or operational set of values.

To deal with these often bewildering changes, marketers seek new ways to classify societal divisions and new strategies for advertising to them. We discussed some of these in Chapter 4. Exhibit 5–9 outlines some of the classifications marketers use to describe society today: for example, Upper Crust; Brite Lites, Li'l City; Young Influentials; and Urban Achievers. People in the same group tend to have similar patterns of behavior and product usage.

Reference Groups: The People We Relate To

Most of us care how we appear to people whose opinions we

EXHIBIT 5–9 The societal divisions described in this exhibit represent just 8 of the 66 Prizm NE (New Evolution) segments defined by Claritas. Marketers believe that consumers in each segment have a great deal in common.

Upper Crust	Blue-Chip Blues
The nation's most exclusive address. Upper Crust is the wealthiest lifestyle in America—a haven for empty-nesting couples over 55 years old. No segment has a higher concentration of residents earning over $200,000 a year or possessing a postgraduate degree. And none has a more opulent standard of living.	Blue-Chip Blues is known as a comfortable lifestyle for young, sprawling families with well-paying blue collar jobs. Ethnically diverse—with a significant presence of Hispanics and African Americans—the segment's aging neighborhoods feature compact, modestly priced homes surrounded by commercial centers that cater to child-filled households.
Brite Lites, Li'l City	**Old Glories**
Not all of America's chic sophisticates live in major metros. Brite Lights, Li'l City is a group of well-off, middle-aged couples settled in the nation's satellite cities. Residents of these typical DINK [double income, no kids] households have college educations, well-paying business and professional careers, and swank homes filled with the latest technology.	Old Glories are the nation's downscale suburban retirees. Americans aging in place in older apartment complexes. These racially mixed households often contain widows and widowers living on fixed incomes, and they tend to lead home-centered lifestyles. They're among the nation's most ardent television fans, watching game shows, soaps, talk shows, and newsmagazines at high rates.
Young Influentials	**City Startups**
Once known as the home of the nation's yuppies, Young Infuentials reflects the fading glow of acquistitive yuppiedom. Today, the segment is a common address for young middle-class singles and couples who are more preoccupied with balancing work and leisure pursuits. Having recently left college dorms, they now live in apartment complexes surrounded by ball fields, health clubs, and casual dining restaurants.	In City Startups, young, multi-ethnic singles have settled in neighborhoods filled with cheap apartments and a commercial base of cafés, bars, laundromats, and clubs cater to twenty-somethings. One of the youngest segments in America—with 10 times as many college students as the national average—these neighborhoods feature low incomes and high concentrations of Hispanics and African Americans.
Urban Achievers	**Low-Rise Living**
Concentrated in the nation's port cities, Urban Achievers is often the first stop for up-and-coming immigrants from Asia, South America, and Europe. These young singles and couples are typically college educated and ethnically diverse; about a third are foreign-born, and even more speak a language other than English.	The most economically challenged urban segment, Low-Rise Living is known as a transient world for young, ethnically diverse singles and single parents. Home values are low—about half the national average—and even then less than a quarter of residents can afford to own real estate. Typically, the commercial base of Mom-and-Pop stores is struggling and in need of a renaissance.

> AMERICANS, REGARDLESS OF THEIR SOCIAL CLASS, BELIEVE STRONGLY IN GETTING AHEAD, BEING BETTER THAN THEIR PEERS, AND WINNING GREATER ADMIRATION AND SELF-ESTEEM.

value. We may even pattern our behavior after members of some groups we affiliate with. This is the significance of **reference groups**—people we try to emulate or whose approval concerns us. Reference groups can be personal (family, friends, co-workers) or impersonal (political parties, religious denominations, professional associations). A special reference group, our peers, exerts tremendous influence on what we believe and how we behave. They determine which brands are cool and which are not.[29] To win acceptance by our peers (fellow students, co-workers, colleagues), we may purchase a certain style or brand of clothing, choose a particular place to live, and acquire behavioral habits that will earn their approval.

Often an individual is influenced in opposite directions by two reference groups and must choose between them. For example, a college student might feel pressure from some friends to join a Greek house and from others to live independently off campus. In ads targeted to students, a local apartment complex might tap the appeal of reference groups by showing students interacting in the complex's pool.

Opinion Leaders: The People We Trust

An **opinion leader** is some person or organization whose beliefs or attitudes are respected by people who share an interest in some specific activity. All fields (sports, religion, fashion, politics) have opinion leaders. An opinion leader may be some expert we find credible. We reason, "If LeBron James thinks Nike makes the best athletic shoes, then it must be so. He knows more about the sport than I do." Thus, the purchasing habits and testimonials of opinion leaders are important to advertisers.

When choosing an opinion leader as a spokesperson for a company or product, advertisers must understand the company's target market thoroughly. Even if executives in the company do not relate to the spokesperson, they must follow market tastes and interests. A spokesperson out of sync with the market undermines his or her credibility—and the company's. On the other hand, an internal person such as the late Thomas, the founder of Wendy's, might turn out to be a highly credible spokesperson without the risks associated with outside celebrities and athletes.[30]

Of course, using a superstar spokesperson such is extremely expensive. Before losing slews of endorsers to a personal scandal, it is estimated that Tiger Woods's annual endorsement income exceeded $100 million. In comparison, Woods earned just under $12 million from his golf victories.[31]

Cultural and Subcultural Influence

Culture has a tenacious influence on consumers. **Culture** refers to the whole set of meanings, beliefs, attitudes, and ways of doing things that are shared by some homogeneous social group and typically handed down from generation to generation.[32] Americans love hot dogs, peanut butter, corn on the cob, and apple pie. Canada, Russia, Germany—every country has its own favorite specialties. And advertisers find it much easier to work with these tastes than try to change them.

Reference groups are those individuals or groups whose opinions matter to us. Sports stars are often role models for fans, which makes superstar LeBron James worth every penny that Nike pays him.

reference groups People we try to emulate or whose approval concerns us.

opinion leader Someone whose beliefs or attitudes are respected by people who share an interest in some specific activity.

culture A homogeneous group's whole set of beliefs, attitudes, and ways of doing things, typically handed down from generation to generation.

subculture A segment within a culture that shares a set of meanings, values, or activities that differ in certain respects from those of the overall culture.

Global marketers are especially concerned with the purchase environment. Of all business functions, marketing activities are the most susceptible to cultural error.[33]

When creating ads for foreign consumption, marketers must consider many environmental factors: cultural trends, social norms, changing fads, market dynamics, product needs, and media channels.[34]

In countries where people earn little income, demand for expensive products is low. So the creative strategy of an automobile advertiser might be to target the small group of wealthy, upper-class consumers. In a country with a large middle class, the same advertiser might be better off mass-marketing the car and positioning it as a middle-class product.

The United States and Canada embrace many subcultures, some of them quite large. They may be based on race, national origin, religion, language, or geographic proximity. The advertiser must understand these subcultures, for differences among them may affect responses to both products and advertising messages.

Many consider the United States to be a colorful tapestry of subcultures. A **subculture** is a segment within a culture that shares a set of meanings, values, or activities that differ in certain respects from those of the overall culture.[35] According to the U.S. Census, 41 million African Americans, 53 million Hispanics, and 14.7 million Asians live in the United States (plus an unknown number of undocumented foreign nationals). These three minority groups alone account for more than 36 percent of the American population.[36] Canada has two major subcultures, anglophones and francophones, based on language (English and French), plus a mosaic of many other cultures based on ethnic and national origins.

Subcultures tend to transfer their beliefs and values from generation to generation. Racial, religious, and ethnic backgrounds affect consumers' preferences for styles of dress, food, beverages, transportation, personal care products, and household furnishings, to name a few. As we saw in Chapter 3, many ad agencies now specialize in minority markets as more advertisers realize that tailoring their appeals to minorities makes good business sense. Recognizing the rapid growth of the Hispanic population, for example, Procter & Gamble spends $170 million per year to understand and tap this

[Many consider the United States to be a colorful tapestry of subcultures . . . groups whose shared meanings differ from that of the overall culture.]

Advertisers realize that English speakers are not the only market in the United States. Subcultures exist and offer enormous markets for the culturally savvy. Here, the U.S. Army (www.goarmy.com) suggests to the Spanish-speaking audience that the soldier pictured followed his heart, and now "others follow it."

evoked set The particular group of alternative goods or services a consumer considers when making a buying decision.

evaluative criteria The standards a consumer uses for judging the features and benefits of alternative products.

market. Other major marketers that develop messages specifically for Hispanic consumers include Ford Motor Co., AT&T, and Sears.[37]

The social environments in countries from Italy to Indonesia, from Sweden to Surinam are also based on language, culture, literacy rate, religion, and lifestyle. Advertisers who market products globally can't ignore these distinctions.

Is It Marketing or Is It Exploitation?

Commercial sponsorship is one way to help fund primary and secondary schools. San Francisco–based School Properties, Inc., offers various sponsorship programs—including licensing school names and mascots, fundraising catalogs, and affinity credit cards—to national and regional marketers. They test products and hold focus groups at schools, display banners at events, and use former student athletes for company appearances. School Properties, aware that budget cuts jeopardize extracurricular school activities, feel this program is a natural outgrowth of existing athletic and special-event sponsorships. Supporters feel it will help mobilize resources for schools, but opponents say that school funding is the government's problem and commercial product logos don't belong in education. Others wonder if this allows advertisers to take unfair advantage of captive kids.

The ethical dilemma concerns promoting products for advantage or profit at the unreasonable expense of the customer. Commercial products work only if they meet consumer needs, and advertising must appeal to those needs. But what happens if advertisers overstep a need, in a crisis situation, for example, and edge into exploitation?

Look at the public concern about the commercialization of children. In response to complaints about Saturday morning advertising to kids, broadcasters of children's TV are now banned from advertising toys during shows that feature those toys and they must clearly separate commercials from the program by announcing commercial breaks. In a different arena, most baby formula companies don't yet advertise directly to consumers because many doctors think breast-feeding is preferable to using formula. The companies don't want to be accused of exploitation; instead, they market their products through health care professionals, hospitals, and new-mother clubs.

Drastic changes in particular market segments may make new fields fertile for exploitation. For example, the emerging Third World middle class seems to have an insatiable appetite for buying things. While tradition and culture play a big role in what people buy and why, the evolving role of women, a burgeoning youth culture, and a middle class with higher expectations and more money than ever before make whole groups of consumers ripe for new products.

Some critics believe China is especially vulnerable to exploitation. A couple living in a cramped Beijing apartment may have a $270 refrigerator, a $700 foreign-made color TV, a telephone that came with a $600 installation charge, a $600 Panasonic VCR, a $1,200 Toshiba air conditioner, and a $1,200 piano—all purchased on a salary of $300 a month. In Mexico, companies pitch credit cards to people earning as little as $650 a month. The National Association of Credit Card Holders estimates 5 million Mexicans carry credit cards, but 1 million of them can't pay their bills. In the United States, older adults and people with mental disabilities are targeted and exploited by sweepstakes promoters, misleading them into believing they've won contest monies and prizes. Older people are bilked out of thousands of dollars in fees and merchandise they don't need and can't afford. State lotteries also prey on the hopes of low-income people in their advertising, underplaying the long odds of winning significant prizes and exploiting gambling addictions.

Critics say that companies act irresponsibly when they target these groups for marketing and advertising activities because the average consumer can't afford the products being advertised.

However, researchers have investigated how advertising messages influence people to act. One finding, known as the third-person effect, holds that people generally believe others are more influenced by the media than they are. Perhaps the critics need to consider this. While they themselves can resist advertising appeals, they seem to believe the average consumer lacks their sophistication. So where do you draw the line between what is ethical (marketing) and what is not (exploitation)?

Questions

1. Do you think playing on people's desire for material possessions has a place in advertising? When does this become exploitation?
2. Is it the advertiser's responsibility to determine whether prospective customers can afford a product or service? Why or why not?
3. Are marketers enhancing the quality of life in developing countries, or are they exploiting vulnerable consumers? Is this an example of the third-person effect?

In North America, advertising encourages us to keep our mouths clean, our breath fresh, and our teeth scrubbed. But people in some southern European countries consider it vain and improper to overindulge in toiletries. Consumers in the Netherlands and the United Kingdom use three times as much toothpaste as those in Spain and Greece. To communicate effectively with Spanish consumers, who view toothpaste as a cosmetic product, advertisers use chic, creative executions rather than dry, therapeutic pitches.[38]

Clearly, many interpersonal factors influence consumers. They have an important effect on our mental files, screens, and subsequent purchase decisions. Awareness of these interpersonal influences helps marketers, both domestic and international, create the strategies on which much advertising is based.

People will go to great lengths to avoid cognitive dissonance. For example, if someone just spent a lot of money for new Goodyear tires (www.goodyear.com), he or she is more likely to be interested in ads like this one that reinforce the decision.

check yourself ✓

1. What is a reference group and why is it important?
2. What is culture? How does it differ from a subculture?

THE PURCHASE DECISION AND POSTPURCHASE EVALUATION

Now that we understand the elements in the consumer purchase decision process, let's examine how it might work in a typical situation. A hypothetical consumer named Chris is thinking about buying a smartphone.

> Chris is enrolled at a state university and financed in part by a small scholarship. He also has a part-time job but must act conservatively when it comes to spending money because tuition, books, and other expenses are costly.
>
> One day, thumbing through a magazine, Chris sees an exciting ad for a new, top-of-the-line smartphone. A beautiful photograph shows the phone's modern, yet understated design. The ad copy highlights the phone's special features. They exude high-tech class—it's just the right style. The ad's signature: "Exclusively at Tech Depot."
>
> In a split-second Chris leaps from perception to motivation. Got to have it! He is highly involved and he wants this personal reward for all his hard work.
>
> The next day Chris visits Tech Depot. While looking for the advertised smartphone, he encounters a variety of alternative styles and models by well-known manufacturers.

The ad has already done its work; the purchase decision process is well under way. At the point of making a purchase decision, though, consumers typically search, consider, and compare alternative brands.

Consumers evaluate selection alternatives (called the **evoked set**). To do this, they establish **evaluative criteria**, the standards they use to judge the features and benefits of alternative products. Not all brands make it to the evoked set. In fact, based on their mental files, most consumers usually consider only four or five brands—which presents a real challenge to advertisers. If none of the alternatives meets the evaluative criteria, the consumer may reject the purchase entirely or postpone the decision.

> Chris finally finds the advertised phone. But it looks less stylish on the shelf than it did in the ad. Two other phones are

cognitive dissonance The theory that people try to justify their behavior by reducing the degree to which their impressions or beliefs are inconsistent with one another.

FCB grid A two-dimensional model that categorizes consumer products into four quadrants based on "high involvement" or "low involvement," and "think" or "feel." By positioning brands in the grid, an agency can determine the type of advertising that would be most appropriate.

also displayed; both are attractive, both expensive. While trying out the devices, Chris considers other unique qualities of style and design. "This one may be a little too bulky." "This one would fit in my pocket." "This one has a better camera, but less memory."

Using central route processing, Chris compares the phones, considering their style, technology, possible advantages, and price (the models are all within $50 of each other). The advertised phone really is the best buy and would be the most satisfying. None of Chris's friends has one like it. The purchase decision is complete when Chris writes out a check.

On the way home, the postpurchase evaluation begins. Chris suddenly envisions some friends' possible negative reactions to the purchase. Maybe it wasn't wise to spend so much money on a top-of-the-line device. Perhaps his friends made better choices. Chris starts to worry—and to plan.

"It's really a great smartphone. It's excellent quality and worth the money. I'll get a lot of use out of it."

A key feature of the postpurchase evaluation is *cognitive dissonance*. The theory of **cognitive dissonance** holds that people strive to justify their behavior by reducing the dissonance, or inconsistency, between their cognitions (their perceptions or beliefs) and reality.[39] In fact, research shows that, to combat dissonance, consumers are more likely to read ads for brands they've already purchased than for new products or competing brands.[40]

Back at the dorm, Chris puts the magazine on the desk with a Post-it note marking the ad (for his roommate to discover). Then he uses his new phone to post his purchase on Facebook

Understanding What Consumers Look For in a Product [5]

Your client's hope is that you can offer helpful advice on creating promotional messages that will get people to do something. In most cases, that something will be buying the client's product or using the service. If your client is a nonprofit, it might involve donating time and/or money.

This seems like common sense, but in fact persuading people to do something they are not already doing can be quite difficult. To help you organize your approach, it may be useful to review what marketing and psychology scholars have learned about consumers and how they are persuaded.

Your challenge at this point in the campaign is to understand the consumer and to get a sense of how the product or service your client offers relates to the consumer's life. Doing this well will require at least two things: a complete understanding of the product and its possible benefits, and a thorough understanding of the consumer.

Maslow's hierarchy of needs suggests that individuals have a range of needs they seek to satisfy in life.

Here is Maslow's hierarchy and some examples that involve food. Consider whether your client's product or service might have benefits that relate to one or more needs:

Need	Examples Involving Food
Self-actualization	Culinary arts degree
Esteem	Cooking lessons
Social	What everyone is eating
Safety	Healthful, organic foods
Physiological	Something that satisfies your hunger

Informational motives involve eliminating a problem, whereas transformational motives involve getting a reward. Consider the possible informational and transformational motives that exist in your consumers that might be addressed by your product.

Informational Motives	
Motive	**Solution**
Problem removal	"Eliminates your headache fast"
Problem avoidance	"Stay out in the sun—you're protected"
Incomplete satisfaction	"The diet drink that doesn't taste like a diet drink"
Mixed approach-avoidance	"Pain-free dental care"
Normal depletion	"Last gas station for 20 miles"

Transformational Motives	
Sensory gratification	"These headphones sound like you are at the show"
Intellectual stimulation	"Hours of fun with challenging puzzles"
Social approval	"Your spouse will love the way you look"

The Foote, Cone & Belding grid was developed to classify how consumers learn about different types of products. Although it was originally designed with the idea that different products would fit in

and describes the purchase, emphasizing its technology, its great design, the enjoyment it will bring, and how great a deal it was. Later he checks back to see comments and likes to his post.

During the postpurchase period, the consumer may enjoy the satisfaction of the purchase and thereby receive reinforcement for the decision. Or the purchase may turn out to be unsatisfactory for some reason. In either case, feedback from the postpurchase evaluation updates the consumer's mental files, affecting perceptions of the brand and similar purchase decisions in the future.

This story is common for a high-involvement purchase decision. Of course, if Chris's decision had merely involved the purchase of a pack of gum, the process would have been significantly simpler.

Chris may typify a particular group of consumers, and that is important to marketers. As we saw in Chapter 4, marketers are interested in defining target markets and developing effective marketing strategies for groups of consumers who share similar characteristics, needs, motives, and buying habits.

DIFFERENT RESPONSES FROM DIFFERENT PRODUCTS

In the 1980s, Richard Vaughn at Foote, Cone & Belding took the fact that different kinds of products typically evoke different *levels* of consumer involvement (either high or low) and different *types* of involvement, either *cognitive* (think) or *affective* (feel) and concluded therefore that different products called for different kinds of advertising. He created a two-dimensional model known as the **FCB grid**, which categorized consumer products into four quadrants based on "high involvement" or "low involvement," and "think" or "feel." By positioning brands in the grid based on the degree and type of involvement consumers brought to the purchase decision, the agency could determine which type of advertising would be most appropriate.

As shown in Exhibit 5–10, a product's location on the grid also indicates how the product is purchased and how advertising copy

different quadrants, some believe that the quadrants can also be used to classify competing brands within a product category (for example, luxury brands versus discount brands). Where would you place your client's brand? What does that suggest for how you might persuade consumers?

The following guides can help you determine where your client's brand belongs in the FCB grid:

Involvement

1. Is the decision to buy or use the product an important one or an unimportant one?
2. Does the consumer stand to lose a great deal or very little if he or she chooses the wrong brand?
3. Does the decision require a great deal of consideration or very little?

Think versus Feel

Think

1. The decision is based on objective criteria.
2. The decision is based primarily on factual information.

Feel

1. The decision is based on a feeling.
2. The decision is closely related to the consumer's personality.
3. The decision is based on the senses (taste, touch, etc.).

FCB Grid

	Think	Feel
High Involvement	I. Informative Learn-Feel-Do (products: major purchases such as insurance, appliances, computers) Strategy: Follow steps of the creative pyramid, beginning with awareness.	II. Affective Feel-Learn-Do (products: expensive car, jewelry, high end apparel) Strategy: Focus on self-esteem and ego benefits of product purchases.
Low Involvement	III. Habitual Do-Learn-Feel (products: car fuel, detergents, razor) Strategy: Focus on offering samples and creating habits in consumer purchasing.	IV. Satisfaction Do-Feel-Learn (products: experiential products such as beer, chewing gum, greeting cards, pizza) Strategy: Focus on social factors and peer use of the product.

Kim-Lord grid A variation of the FCB grid, which allows for the fact that the level of consumer involvement in a product does not have to be high "think" and low "feel" (or vice versa) but can be high (or low) in both categories.

▼**EXHIBIT 5–10** The Foote, Cone & Belding (FCB) grid.

	Thinking	Feeling
High involvement	**1. Informative (thinker)** Car-house-furnishing-new products model: Learn-feel-do (economic?) **Possible implications** Test: Recall, Diagnostics Media: Long copy format, Reflective vehicles Creative: Specific information, Demonstration	**2. Affective (feeler)** Jewelry-cosmetics-fashion apparel-motorcycles model: Feel-learn-do (psychological?) **Possible implications** Test: Attitude change, Emotional arousal Media: Large space, Image specials Creative: Executional, Impact
Low involvement	**3. Habit formation (doer)** Food-household items model: Do-learn-feel (responsive?) **Possible implications** Test: Sales Media: Small space ads, 10-second I.D.s, Radio; POS Creative: Reminder	**4. Self-satisfaction (reactor)** Cigarettes-liquor-candy model: Do-feel-learn (social?) **Possible implications** Test: Sales Media: Billboards, Newspapers, POS Creative: Attention

should be written (more emotional or more rational).[41] High involvement/thinking products lend themselves to logical explanations and consumers will probably follow the traditional learn-feel-do model. At the other extreme, high involvement/feeling products are more likely to stress emotional motives and consumers may follow a feel-learn-do sequence. In the case of low involvement products, which are associated with routinized or impulse purchase behavior, *learning* and *feeling* may not occur until after *doing*. In such cases, simply gaining exposure or awareness may be the primary advertising objective.

More recently, Kim and Lord recognized that people can be both cognitively and affectively involved at the same time. So they developed a variation of the FCB grid, shown in Exhibit 5–11. The **Kim-Lord grid** also depicts the degree and the kind of involvement a consumer brings to the purchase decision for different products. Some purchases, like cars, require a high degree of personal involvement on both the cognitive and affective levels.[42] For others, like detergent, involvement is low on both axes. Sometimes a marketer uses an advertising strategy aimed at shifting the product to higher involvement on either axis. ■

▼**EXHIBIT 5–11** The Kim-Lord grid.

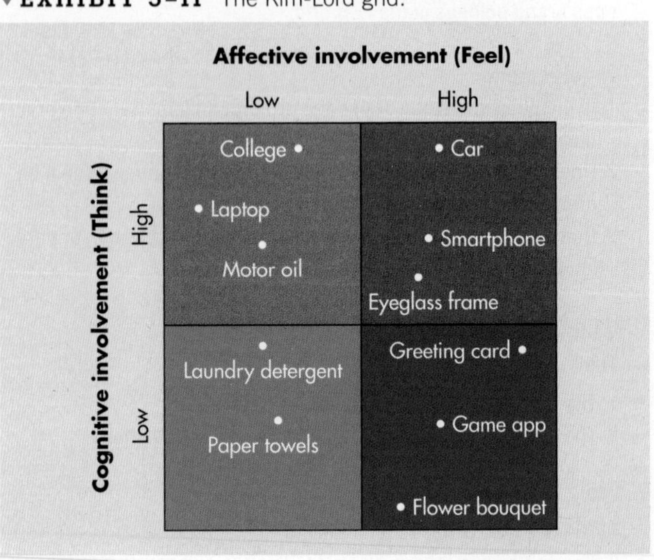

learn about, practice, and apply communication and consumer behavior to advertising!

M: Advertising was developed for students who want information packaged in a concise, easy-to-read, yet interesting format.

Check out the book's website to:

- Find out if you know what consumer behavior process presents the greatest challenge to advertisers. (Review Questions)
- Demonstrate the role of semiotics in advertising. (Exploring Advertising)
- Map brands on the FTC grid. (Exploring Advertising)

While you are there, check out the professional resource links, review the PowerPoint presentation, and test your knowledge with the Multiple Choice Quiz. Additionally, *Connect® Marketing* is available for M: Advertising.

www.mhhe.com/ArensM2e

account planning and research

chapter six

This chapter examines the important role that research plays in the development and evaluation of advertising. It discusses the various sources of research information and the methodologies used to collect and interpret it. We start the chapter examining the important role that account planning plays in cultivating effective advertising strategies and executions.

continued on p. 148

LEARNING OBJECTIVES

After studying this chapter, you will be able to:

LO6-1 Describe the role of account planners in advertising agencies.

LO6-2 Discuss how research can help advertisers select target markets, media vehicles, and advertising messages.

LO6-3 Explain the basic steps in the marketing research process.

LO6-4 Explain the common methods used in qualitative and quantitative research.

LO6-5 Evaluate the challenges of pretesting and posttesting advertising.

LO6-6 Identify issues that can affect the accuracy and usability of quantitative research.

continued from p. 147

Limited-service hotels have proven increasingly effective in capturing business from the nearly two and a half million travelers seeking a room each night in America. By sacrificing some luxuries common to bigger hotels, travelers typically get a clean room, breakfast, and a lower bill at chains such as Hampton Inn, Fairfield Inn, Four Points by Sheraton, and Holiday Inn Express®. Holiday Inn opened its first three Holiday Inn Express hotels in 1991. The Holiday Inn Express concept was intended to target the "upper economy" market segment, offering limited-service, low-price lodging. But it wasn't until 1998 that Holiday Inn Express promoted that positioning in its first TV campaign, developed by Fallon McElligott, Minneapolis (now Fallon Worldwide).

To ensure that Holiday Inn Express did not cannibalize (take) customers from its sister hotel, the agency focused its efforts on a completely different target audience from that of Holiday Inn, a group known as *road warriors.* Road warriors are independent businesspeople who spend as many as a hundred nights or more per year on the road. Predominantly male, road warriors usually foot their own travel bills. Initial discussions with this target made it clear that Holiday Inn Express had a good opportunity because warriors believed that competitor hotel chains were ignoring them.

Fallon knew that creating effective messages for warriors meant account planners and creatives would have to deeply understand their audience, not just in terms of their hotel preferences, but also their personalities and lifestyles. So the planners paired up with some warriors and ventured out on the road. As summarized in Pat Fallon and Fred Senn's book, *Juicing the Orange,* "Our planners videotaped the road warriors while they drove cross-country. We talked to them about their work, their families, and their daily experiences. One account planner barreled down Highway 70 with a guy who was like John Candy's character in the movie *Planes, Trains and Automobiles.*"[1]

The research revealed that road warriors found it deeply rewarding to save on their travel budgets by forgoing unneeded luxuries, and the good feelings from making a "smart choice" remained with the customers long after they had checked out of the hotel. Fallon captured the emotional benefits of Holiday Inn Express with the simple slogan "Stay Smart™." Ads developed for the campaign were funny, unexpected, and centered on the theme of how staying at a Holiday Inn Express was proof that the traveler was smart (see these ads and others by Fallon at www.juicingtheorange.com). In one spot, a man with no medical knowledge offers an intricate diagnosis to a fallen bicyclist. In another, a woman with no knowledge of structural engineering tells a concerned bus driver that a rickety bridge will support his overloaded bus. The protagonist assures the skeptical onlookers that she "stayed at a Holiday Inn Express last night."[2]

Posttesting research showed that the ads increased brand awareness by 40 percent and Holiday Inn Express became the fastest-growing hotel in its category. Attitudinal research showed that Holiday Inn Express easily beat industry averages for key image considerations that drive hotel business such as "good hotel for the money" and "good hotel for business travelers."

The "Stay Smart" campaign was intended to run for five months; 10 years later, the campaign was still on the air and had become part of pop culture. Vice president Al Gore even claimed he had "stayed at a Holiday Inn Express last night" during his presidential campaign. In 2007 the Holiday Inn brand did not take priority—the entire Holiday Inn brand family took priority (Holiday Inn, Holiday Inn Express, and the two newest additions at the time, Holiday Inn Resort and Holiday Inn Club vacations). We brought the brands together with regards to advertising and marketing because that is when we announced and launched the Holiday Inn Brand Family's $1 Billion Global Brand Relaunch, the largest relaunch in hospitality history and so the focus was on the changes happening across the brand family as a whole. During the years following, the midprice hotel

The success of "Got Milk?" and many other notable campaigns is often attributed to the ability of account planners to get into the heads of their prospects. This approach enables brands to develop meaningful relationships with their customers.

market became more competitive and Holiday Inn Express lost its unique positioning as a smart choice for budget-conscious travelers.[3]

Now a newly hired ad agency, Ogilvy & Mather, is attempting to revive the "Stay Smart" campaign with new executions. Not many advertising campaigns achieve such long-term success. And much of that success could be attributed to gaining a clear understanding of the target consumer through research.[4] ■

LO6-1 Describe the role of account planners in advertising agencies.

account planner
The individual at an advertising agency primarily responsible for account planning.

THE ACCOUNT PLANNER AS CONSUMER ADVOCATE

Jeff Goodby, cochair at Goodby, Silverstein & Partners, is famous for award-winning television ads including the Budweiser Lizards and the "Got Milk?" campaign. He believes that everything an agency does should be geared toward getting into people's heads to figure out what they currently think and understand how best to influence them.[5]

This task is shared by many individuals during the process of planning advertising, but has, in recent years, been focused on the **account planner**, described in Chapter 3. The account planner's primary role is to represent the consumer in this process. The late Stanley Pollitt of the London agency Boase Massimi Pollitt is considered by some to be the "father" of account planning. He described planners as "the architects and guardians of their clients' brands, the detectives who uncovered long-hidden clues in the data and gently coerced consumers into revealing their inner secrets."[6]

By putting the consumer, instead of the advertiser, at the center of the process, account planning changes the task from simply creating an advertisement to nurturing a relationship between consumer and brand. That requires tremendous understanding, intuition, and insight. But when performed properly, planning provides that mystical leap into the future—the brilliant, simplifying insight that lights the client's and the creative's way. Interestingly, the U.S. agencies that have embraced account planning are the very ones now considered to be the hottest shops. They're performing the best work, getting the biggest accounts, and winning all the awards.

In large agencies, account planners work side-by-side with account managers. They share a common goal but with different orientations. Where the account planner brings a research perspective and represents the consumer, the account manager brings more of a business perspective and represents the client. In smaller agencies without account planning departments, the consumer's advocate would typically be someone from account management.

Whoever plays this role is responsible for ensuring that the advertising strategy and executions are relevant to the target audience. The account planner is responsible for injecting a wealth of information into the planning process, monitoring the creative development, and testing the finished product to determine if it has achieved its goal of communicating with the intended audience.

Jon Steel summarizes the account planner's mission as follows: "They need to be able to take information of all sorts,

shuffle it around, and rearrange it in new patterns until something interesting emerges."[7] One does not necessarily need to conduct research to get that information. Some questions can be answered without research, or the answers may have been uncovered in previous explorations. But in all cases, the advertiser must understand what is happening in consumers' heads.

Bill Bernbach, considered by many to be the single most influential creative force in advertising's history, was never a strong advocate of research, but recognized how important it is to be familiar with your audience: "At the heart of an effective creative philosophy is the belief that nothing is so powerful as an insight into human nature, what compulsions drive a man, what instincts dominate his action, even though his language so often can camouflage what really motivates him."[8]

In this chapter we will examine various types of research and the role that research plays in the development of advertising.

check yourself ✓

1. What do you think Jon Steel means when he states that the account planner serves as the "conscience" of the agency?

LO6-2 Discuss how research can help advertisers select target markets, media vehicles, and advertising messages.

THE NEED FOR RESEARCH IN MARKETING AND ADVERTISING

Every year companies spend millions of dollars creating ads and promotions that they hope their customers and prospects will notice and relate to. Then they spend millions more placing their communications in print and electronic media, hoping their customers will see and hear them and eventually respond.

Advertising is expensive. In the United States the cost of airing a single 30-second commercial on prime-time network TV averages around $120,000.[9] Likewise, a single, full-page color ad in a national magazine can cost over $340,000.[10]

That's too much money to risk unless advertisers have very good information about who their customers are, what they want and like, where they spend their media time, and whether the ads are effective. And that's why advertisers need research. Research provides the information that drives marketing and advertising decision making. Without that information, advertisers are forced to use intuition or guesswork. In today's fast-changing, highly competitive, global economy, that invites failure.

TNS delivers precise plans for growth

Many research companies can give you interesting insights, but this alone doesn't help you to grow your business. TNS applies world-class expertise and a deep understanding of the human attitudes and emotions that drive behaviour, to uncover insights that lead to business growth.

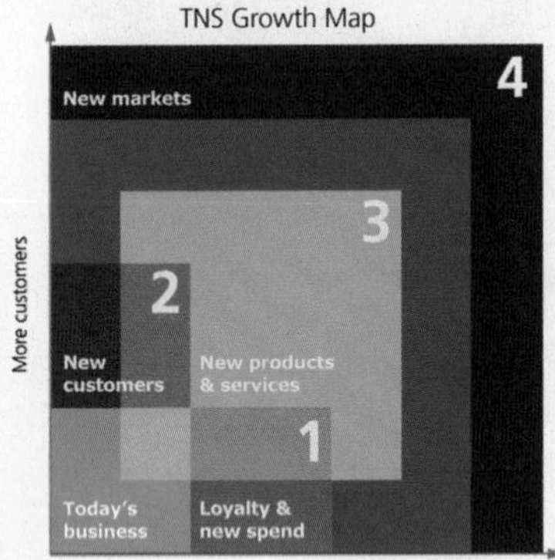

1. Loyalty and new spend
Driving growth through deeper relationships with existing customers

2. New customers
Increasing penetration by attracting the most profitable new customers

3. New products and services
Portfolio extension to drive incremental growth

4. New markets
Extending reach through geographic or category expansion

About TNS
TNS advises clients on specific growth strategies around new market entry, innovation, brand switching and stakeholder management, based on long-established expertise and market-leading solutions. With a presence in over 80 countries, TNS has more conversations with the world's consumers than anyone else and understands individual human behaviours and attitudes across every cultural, economic and political region of the world. TNS is part of Kantar, one of the world's largest insight, information and consultancy groups.

Please visit www.tnsglobal.com for more information.

TNS

Marketing research is the important process of gathering, recording, and analyzing information about customers and prospects. Companies such as TNS Global (www.tnsglobal.com) collect data for their clients and provide critical insight into current and potential markets.

marketing research The systematic gathering, recording, and analysis of information to help managers make marketing decisions.

advertising research The systematic gathering and analysis of information specifically to facilitate the development or evaluation of advertising strategies, ads and commercials, and media campaigns.

Advertisers need to know who their customers are and what they want. Research indicated that Holiday Inn Express customers like to feel "smart" by saving money, as evidenced by this Panini delivery man who is now smart enough to perform accupuncture.

What Is Marketing Research?

To help managers make marketing decisions, companies develop procedures for gathering, recording, and analyzing new information. This is called **marketing research**. Marketing research does a number of things: It helps identify consumer needs and market segments; it provides the information necessary for developing new products and devising marketing strategies; and it enables managers to assess the effectiveness of marketing programs and promotional activities.

What Is Advertising Research?

Before developing any advertising campaign, a company needs to know how people perceive its products, how they view the competition, what brand or company image would be most credible, and what ads offer the greatest appeal. To get this information, companies use *advertising research.* While marketing research provides the information necessary to make marketing decisions, **advertising research** uncovers the information needed for making advertising decisions. By definition, it is the systematic gathering and analysis of information to help develop or evaluate advertising strategies, individual ads, and entire campaigns.

In this chapter, we consider the importance of information gathering to the development of advertising plans and strategies; we look at how companies use research to test the effectiveness of ads before and after they run; and we explore a number of specific research techniques.

Applying Research to Advertising Decision Making Advertising research serves various purposes, most of which can be grouped into four categories: *strategy research, creative concept research, pretesting,* and *posttesting.*

1. *Advertising strategy research.* Used to help define the product concept or to assist in the selection of target markets, advertising messages, or media vehicles.
2. *Creative concept research.* Evaluates the target audience's acceptance of different creative ideas at the concept stage.
3. *Pretesting of ads.* Used to uncover and diagnose possible communication problems before a campaign begins.
4. *Posttesting of ads.* Enables marketers to evaluate a campaign after it runs.

As Exhibit 6–1 shows, marketers use the different categories of advertising research at different stages of ad or campaign development. The techniques they use at each stage also vary considerably. We'll examine each of these categories briefly before moving on to discuss the research process.

> [The advertiser must understand what is happening in the consumers' heads.]

Advertising Strategy Research

As we will discuss in the next chapter, an advertising strategy is comprised of the *creative strategy* and the *media strategy.* Developing these strategies requires a clear understanding of the *product concept,* the *target audience,* the *media* alternatives,

STRATEGY RESEARCH IS ESSENTIAL TO DEVELOP A BLUEPRINT FOR CREATIVES TO FOLLOW.

EXHIBIT 6–1 Categories of research in advertising development.

	Advertising Strategy Research	Creative Concept Research	Pretesting	Posttesting
Timing	Before creative work begins	Before agency production begins	Before finished artwork and photography	After campaign has run
Research problem	Product concept definition Target audience selection Media selection Message-element selection	Concept testing Name testing Slogan testing	Print testing TV storyboard pretesting Radio commercial pretesting	Advertising effectiveness Consumer attitude change Sales increases
Techniques	Consumer attitude and usage studies Media studies Qualitative interviews	Free-association tests Qualitative interviews Statement-comparison tests	Consumer juries Matched samples Portfolio tests Storyboard test Mechanical devices Psychological rating scales	Aided recall Unaided recall Attitude tests Inquiry tests Sales tests

and possible *message elements.* To gain this understanding, companies use **advertising strategy research**.

Product Concept As we saw at the beginning of this chapter, advertisers need to know how consumers perceive their brands. They also want to know what qualities lead to initial purchases and, eventually, to brand loyalty.

Using this information, they try to establish a unique *product concept* for their brand—that bundle of values we discussed in Chapter 4 that encompasses both utilitarian and symbolic benefits to the consumer.

From its research, Fallon knew that road warriors were interested in the kind of value that a stay at a Holiday Inn Express afforded. They also knew that value translated emotionally as feeling good about being "smart" by saving money by forgoing unnecessary luxuries.[11]

It's this kind of information that can lead to an effective positioning strategy for the brand. Advertising can shape and magnify a brand's position and image over time. In fact, this is one of the most important strategic benefits of advertising. But to use media advertising effectively, strategy research is essential to develop a blueprint for creatives to follow.[12]

Advertising works differently for different product categories and, often, even for different brands within a category. This means that each brand must develop a template for the creative based on an understanding of its particular consumers' wants, needs, and motivations. Only if this is done

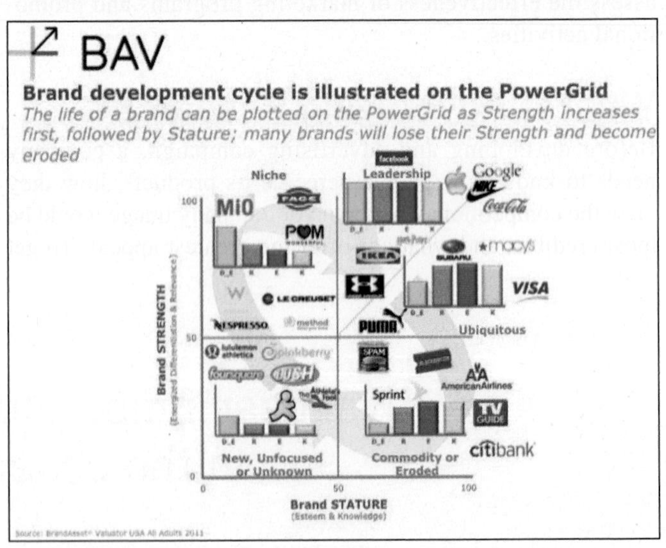

Young & Rubicam's BrandAsset® Valuator is a model to statistically ascertain how brands are built and the assets from which they derive their market strength. BrandAsset® Valuator has to date surveyed more than 800,000 consumers about 40,000 brands. Data have been collected since 1993.

correctly over time (say, one to two years) can brand equity be built.[13]

To determine how brands are built and how they derive their strength, the Young & Rubicam ad agency developed a model called the BrandAsset Valuator. It measures brands in terms of differentiation, relevance, esteem, and familiarity, in that order. According to Y&R's theory, a brand must first develop

No Nonsense (www.nononsense.com) identified the special relationship between girlfriends to be an important source of product information. This insight was translated into an advertising campaign.

differentiation—it must offer something unique and different—to survive. Second, it must be perceived by the target market as relevant to their needs and wants. Finally, it needs to build stature through esteem and knowledge. Once all these steps are accomplished, a brand achieves leadership status.

Following Y&R's lead, other agencies have developed their own brand equity studies. In 1998, WPP Group introduced a research tool titled "BRANDZ." Then, in 2000, DDB Worldwide introduced "Brand Capital," and Leo Burnett unveiled its brand of research dubbed "Brand Stock." All of these are aimed at understanding how consumers connect with brands before spending millions on advertising.[14]

Target Audience Selection We pointed out in Chapter 4 that no market includes everybody. Therefore, one of the major purposes of research is to develop a rich profile of the brand's target markets and audiences. The marketer will want to know which customers are the primary users of the product category and will study them carefully to understand their demographics, geographics, psychographics, and purchase behavior. If the target audience is accurately defined, the advertising will be delivered to the most prospects with the least waste.

In the case of Holiday Inn Express, Fallon believed it was important to find a target audience who would be heavy users of hotels but who would be unlikely to stay at its sister brand, Holiday Inn. Road warriors, consisting of independent-minded male businesspeople, typically working in small companies or for themselves, fit the bill perfectly. As heavy users of hotels, they represented a highly profitable market segment. And because road warriors believed that no hotel brand was particularly interested in them, Fallon could design ads that targeted their needs and concerns.

advertising strategy research Used to help define the product concept or to assist in the selection of target markets, advertising messages, or media vehicles.

media research The systematic gathering and analysis of information on the reach and effectiveness of media vehicles.

Media Selection To develop media strategies, select media vehicles, and evaluate their results, advertisers use a subset of advertising research called **media research**. Agencies subscribe to syndicated research services (such as Nielsen, Arbitron, Experian Simmons, or Standard Rate & Data Service) that monitor and publish information on the reach and effectiveness of media vehicles—radio, TV, newspapers, and so on—in every major geographic market in the United States and Canada. (We'll discuss these further in Chapter 8 and in Part 5.)

For Holiday Inn Express, Fallon researched the media habits of road warriors and discovered that this group tended to watch cable fare focused on news and sports, including such networks as ESPN, CNN, and the Weather Channel. Research also suggested that the target audience formulated travel plans early in the week, so Fallon ran the ads only on Sunday and Monday nights. While the overall ad budget was comparatively small, the concentration of ads on two evenings using a small number of networks gave the campaign a larger presence on those occasions when road warriors would actually be watching TV and thinking about travel. In addition, because the campaign was so fresh and unusual, it got an additional boost from unpaid references to the "No, but I did stay at a Holiday Inn Express last night" slogan on ESPN, *Late Night with David Letterman,* NPR, and the *Washington Post.*

"If the target audience is accurately defined, the advertising will be delivered to the most prospects with the least waste."

pretesting Testing the effectiveness of an advertisement for gaps or flaws in message content before recommending it to clients, often conducted through focus groups.

posttesting Testing the effectiveness of an advertisement after it has been run.

Advertisers can avoid mistakes and save money on production by testing creative concepts in animatic form. Animatics are illustrated by hand and then computer animated. This animatic was created by the Hive (www.hivedoes.com).

Message Element Selection Companies hope to find promising advertising messages by studying consumers' likes and dislikes in relation to brands and products. Kraft Foods, for example, was looking for ways to dissuade moms from switching to less-expensive brands of processed cheese. While its Kraft Singles brand dominated the processed cheese slices category, it was concerned that the brand wasn't keeping up with overall growth in the market.

Working with several research companies and its ad agency, J. Walter Thompson, the company conducted a series of qualitative consumer attitude studies to figure out how women, particularly mothers, felt about Kraft Singles, with the hope of discovering possible advertising themes. The mothers said they felt good giving their kids Kraft Singles because of the brand's nutritional value. But there was a catch—they also said they'd switch to a competitive product if it were cheaper. Fortunately, a phone survey provided some clues for solving the problem. Among those polled, 78 percent considered the brand an extra source of calcium for their kids. And 84 percent of women with kids under 12 said they'd be motivated to buy the brand because of that added benefit.[15]

From this information, the agency used concept testing to determine which message elements might prove most successful.

Creative Concept Research

Once it develops an advertising strategy, the company (or its agency) will begin developing creative concepts for the advertising. Here again, research is helpful in determining which concepts to use.

From all their studies, Kraft researchers came up with two message elements that might keep mothers from defecting to competitive brands. First, show how much kids like Kraft Singles, and second, emphasize the fact that the brand provides the calcium kids need. J. Walter Thompson prepared two rough TV spots and then conducted focus groups with mothers to get their reaction. With a moderator leading

the discussion, each group viewed the commercials. The groups' reactions were measured, taped, and observed by JWT and Kraft staff behind a one-way mirror. Immediately, problems surfaced. The idea that kids love the taste of Kraft Singles just didn't come across strongly enough. And the statement that Kraft provides calcium wasn't persuasive. Moms said, "Of course it has calcium, it's cheese." The agency had to find a newsier way to communicate the information.

Tweaking the commercials, JWT came up with a new spot showing youngsters gobbling gooey grilled-cheese sandwiches while a voice-over announcer stated that two out of five kids don't get enough calcium. More focus groups ensued. Now the mothers agreed that the shots of kids devouring sandwiches communicated the great-taste theme, but some moms thought the two-out-of-five statement played too much on their guilt.

Crispin Porter + Bogusky used hidden cameras to capture the reactions of real Burger King customers who were told that the Whopper sandwich had been "discontinued." Research showed the ads were better recalled than any other ever tested.

To soften the message, the agency switched to a female announcer and then brought in the Dairy Fairy, a character from an earlier campaign, to lighten the whole tone of the spot. This seemed to work better, so the agency proceeded to copy test a finished ad.

Pretesting and Posttesting

Advertising is one of the largest costs in a company's marketing budget. No wonder its effectiveness is a major concern! Companies want to know what they are getting for their money—and whether their advertising is working. And they'd like some assurance before their ads run.

Kraft was no exception. Millward Brown Research performed a number of copy tests to see how the agency's latest spot would perform. The tests showed that the spot performed significantly better than the norm on key measures such as branding and persuasion. Following the copy tests, the company aired "The Calcium They Need" commercial in five test markets to see how it would affect sales. They quickly achieved a 10 percent increase in sales in those markets. Based on such a strong showing, Kraft rolled the campaign out nationally in 1999 and sales took off, growing 11.8 percent.[16]

The campaign was so successful that the Advertising Research Foundation named Kraft and J. Walter Thompson finalists for its prestigious David Ogilvy Research Award, given to the most effective ad campaign guided by research.

The Purpose of Testing Ads To increase the likelihood of preparing the most effective advertising messages, companies use **pretesting**. Some agencies, like DDB Needham, pretest all ad copy for communication gaps or flaws in message content before recommending it to clients.[17] When companies don't pretest their ads, they may encounter a surprising reaction from the marketplace. Schering Canada received a torrent of complaint letters from customers who said they didn't like its commercial introducing the antihistamine Claritin to the over-the-counter market in Canada. Most negative responses, though, are more subtle: Consumers simply turn the page or change the channel, and sales mysteriously suffer. This is why it's also important to evaluate the effectiveness of an ad or campaign *after* it runs. **Posttesting** (also called *ad tracking*) provides the advertiser with useful guidelines for future advertising. We'll discuss methods for testing ads later in this chapter.

check yourself ✓

1. What are some things that might be tested with creative concept research?
2. Why do companies pretest their advertising?

LO6-3 Explain the basic steps in the marketing research process.

STEPS IN THE RESEARCH PROCESS

Now that we understand the various types of decision-related information that marketers seek, let's explore how they gather this information by looking at the overall research process and some of the specific techniques they use.

marketing information system (MIS) A set of procedures for generating an orderly flow of pertinent information for use in making marketing decisions.

secondary research The second step in the research process, designed to explore a problem by reviewing secondary data and interviewing a few key people with the most information to share.

primary data Research information gained directly from the marketplace.

secondary data Information that has previously been collected or published.

▼EXHIBIT 6–2 The marketing research process begins with evaluation of the company's situation and definition of the problem.

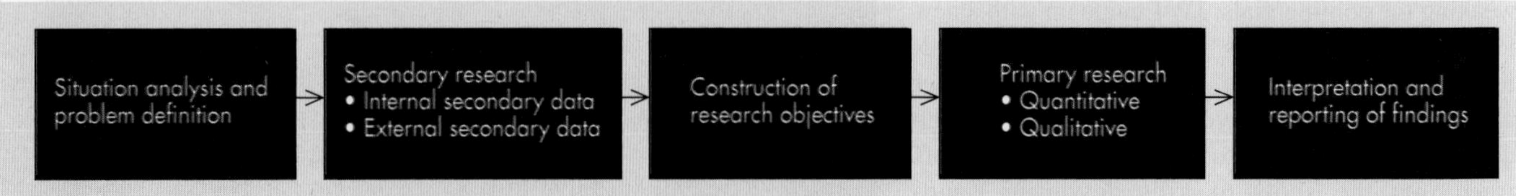

There are five basic steps in the research process (see Exhibit 6–2):

1. Situation analysis and problem definition.
2. Secondary research.
3. Construction of research objectives.
4. Primary research.
5. Interpretation and reporting of findings.

Step 1: Analyzing the Situation and Defining the Problem

The first step in the marketing research process is to *analyze the situation* and *define the problem.* Many large firms have in-house research departments. Often the marketing department also maintains a **marketing information system (MIS)**—a sophisticated set of procedures designed to generate a continuous, orderly flow of information for use in making marketing decisions. These systems ensure that managers get the information they need when they need it.[18]

Most smaller firms don't have dedicated research departments, and their methods for obtaining marketing information are frequently inadequate. These firms often find the problem-definition step difficult and time-consuming. Yet good research on the wrong problem is a waste of effort.

"Good research on the wrong problem is a waste of effort."

Step 2: Conducting Secondary Research

The second step in the process is to use **secondary research** to learn more about the market, the competition, and the business environment, and to better define the problem. Researchers may discuss the problem with wholesalers, distributors, or retailers outside the firm; with informed sources inside the firm; with customers; or even with competitors. They look for whoever has the most information to offer.

There are two types of research data: *primary* and *secondary.* Information collected from the marketplace about a specific problem is called **primary data**; acquiring it is typically expensive and time-consuming. So during the exploratory stage, researchers frequently use **secondary data**—information previously collected or published, usually for some other purpose, by the firm or by some other organization. This information is readily available, either internally or externally, and can be gathered more quickly and inexpensively than primary data.

Assembling Internal Secondary Data

Company records are often a valuable source of secondary information. Useful internal data include product shipment figures, billings, warranty-card records, advertising expenditures, sales expenses, customer correspondence, website tracking, and records of meetings with sales staffs.

A well-developed marketing information system can help researchers analyze sales data, review past tracking studies, and examine previous marketing research data. This information might point the way toward an interesting headline or positioning statement such as Motrin's "Medicine with Muscle."

Sources of External Secondary Data

Much information is available, sometimes at little or no cost, from the government, market research companies, trade associations, various trade publications, or computerized databases. Most large companies subscribe to any of a number of syndicated research reports about their particular industry. For

example, as the advertising manager for a large nutritional company introducing a new line of vitamins, you might need to know the current demand for vitamins and food supplements, the number of competitors in the marketplace, the amount of advertising each is doing, and the challenges and opportunities the industry faces.

In the United States, frequently used sources of secondary data include:

- Library reference materials (*Business Periodicals Index* for business magazines, *Reader's Guide to Periodical Literature* for consumer magazines, *Public Information Service Bulletin*, the *New York Times Index*, and the *World Almanac and Book of Facts*).
- Government publications *(Statistical Abstract of the United States)*.
- Trade association publications (annual fact books containing data gathered by various industry groups listed in the *Directory of National Trade Associations*).
- Research organizations and their publications or syndicated information (literature from university bureaus of business research, ACNielsen Store Audit, NPD Consumer Tracking, Experian Simmons's Multi-Media Engagement Study, IRI's Consumer Network, and Standard Rate & Data Service).
- Consumer/business publications (*Bloomberg Businessweek, Forbes, Fortune, American Demographics, Advertising Age, Prevention,* and thousands more).
- Computer database services (Dialog, ProQuest, Lexis-Nexis, and Dow Jones Newswires).
- Internet search engines (Bing, Ask, Google, Yahoo!, Dogpile, and others).

It's important to understand that secondary data carry some potential problems. Information may be out of date and therefore obsolete. Much of it is not relevant to the problem at hand. Some information from purported research is just wrong, so the findings are invalid. In other cases, the source may be unreliable. Finally, there is now so much information available (thanks to the Internet) that it's just overwhelming; it's extremely time-consuming to wade through it all.

Research [6–A]

Research is a complicated aspect of preparing a campaign, and without at least one course in advertising research you may find it tough going. However, without research you will find it difficult to make some of the tough creative and strategic decisions that lie ahead. Even without an extensive research background, you can do some secondary and qualitative research that can result in better choices for your campaign.

Secondary Research

Secondary research involves obtaining information from existing sources, including your client. Be sure to obtain all that you can, with the understanding that information shared by your client is valuable and that most clients will insist on strict confidentiality. Breaking a confidentiality agreement is a very serious transgression and should not happen under any circumstances, whether deliberately or through neglect.

For more information, access the secondary research tutorial, www.knowthis.com/principles-of-marketing-tutorials/finding-secondary-research.htm.

Qualitative Research

You can also plan some qualitative research studies. Two of the most common are focus groups and observational research. In a focus group, you bring together a collection of carefully chosen participants (users of your brand, users of competing brands, etc.) and lead a group discussion that has the potential to offer strategic insights. For more in-depth information about qualitative research, visit http://www.qrca.org.

Qualitative Research: Focus Groups

For a tutorial on using focus groups, see www.cse.lehigh.edu/~glennb/mm/FocusGroups.htm. Tips for using focus groups can be found at www.groupsplus.com/pages/mn091498.htm.

Observational Research

Observational research techniques involve monitoring the consumer in his or her native environment (the mall, a restaurant, a skateboard park, etc.). The goal is to see how the consumer behaves in a natural setting. Careful attention is ordinarily paid to language, dress, interactions, symbols, and style.

See the observational research tutorial at http://writing.colostate.edu/guides/research/observe/index.cfm. Tips for observational research can be found at www.quirks.com/articles/a1997/19971208.aspx?searchID=625728.

Quantitative Research

Your project may also involve administering a survey. Google Forms, introduced in the My Ad Campaign from Chapter 1, may be useful for creating an online survey that is easy and inexpensive to administer. The hard part is writing a good survey instrument and then choosing data analysis techniques that will provide you and your client with useful information. Some Web tutorials are listed below:

Surveys

Writing good questions: www.accesswave.ca/~infopoll/tips.htm.

Response options: http://dataguru.org/ref/survey/responseoptions.asp.

Data Analysis Using Excel

www.ncsu.edu/labwrite/res/gt/gt-menu.html.

Step 3: Establishing Research Objectives

Once the exploratory research phase is completed, the company may discover it needs additional information that it can get only from doing primary research. As was the case for Holiday Inn Express, it may want to identify exactly who its customers are and clarify their perceptions of the company and the competition. To do so, the company must first establish *specific research objectives.*

A concise written statement of the research problem and objectives should be formulated at the beginning of any research project. A company must be clear about what decisions it has to make that the research results will guide. Once it knows the application, it can set down clear, specific research objectives.[19] For example, a department store, noticing that it is losing market share, might write its problem statement and research objectives as follows:

> **Market Share**
>
> Our company's sales, while still increasing, seem to have lost momentum and are not producing the profit our shareholders expect. In the last year, our market share declined 3 percentage points. Our studies indicate we are losing sales to other department stores in the same malls and that customers are confused about our position in the market. We need to make decisions about how we position ourselves for the future.
>
> **Research Objectives**
>
> We must answer the following questions: (1) Who are our customers? (2) Who are the customers of other department stores? (3) What do these customers like and dislike about us and about our competitors? (4) How are we currently perceived? and (5) What do we have to do to clarify and improve that perception?

This statement of the problem is specific and measurable, the decision point is clear, and the questions are related and relevant. The research results should provide the information that management needs to decide on a new positioning strategy for the company. The positioning strategy facilitates the development of marketing and advertising plans that will set the company's course for years to come.

check yourself ✓

1. What is the difference between primary and secondary data?
2. What is the purpose of a "control group" when conducting research?

L06-4 Explain the common methods used in qualitative and quantitative research.

Step 4: Conducting Primary Research

When a company wants to collect data about a specific problem or issue, it uses **primary research**. Unlike secondary research, primary research is customized or tailored to the marketer's specific objectives. There are two types of primary research: qualitative and quantitative.

To get a general impression of the market, the consumer, or the product, advertisers typically start with **qualitative research**. This enables researchers to gain insight into both the population whose opinion will be sampled and the subject matter itself. Then, to get hard numbers about specific marketing situations, they may perform a survey or use some other form of **quantitative research**. Ideally, agencies use a balance of both qualitative and quantitative methods, understanding the limits of each and how they work together.[20] (See Exhibit 6–3.)

▼EXHIBIT 6–3 Differences between qualitative and quantitative research.

	Qualitative	Quantitative
Main techniques for gathering data	Focus groups and in-depth interviews.	Surveys and scientific samples.
Kinds of questions asked	Why? How so? In what way?	How many? How much?
Role of interviewer	Critical: interviewer must build rapport with research participants. She must think on feet and frame questions and probes in response to whatever respondents say. A highly trained professional is advisable.	Important, but interviewers need only be able to read scripts. They should not improvise. Minimally trained, responsible employees are suitable.
Questions asked	Questions vary in order and phrasing from group to group and interview to interview. New questions are added, old ones dropped.	Should be exactly the same for each interview. Order and phrasing of questions carefully controlled.
Number of interviews	Fewer interviews tending to last a longer time.	Many interviews in order to give a projectable scientific sample.
Kinds of findings	Develop hypotheses, gain insights, explore language options, refine concepts, help explain survey results, provide diagnostics on advertising copy.	Test hypotheses, prioritize factors, provide data for mathematical modeling and projections.

primary research Collecting data directly from the marketplace using qualitative or quantitative methods.

qualitative research Research that uses in-depth studies of small, non-random samples to explore the behavior, perceptions, needs, and motivations of a target audience.

quantitative research Research that uses larger, representative samples and surveys to quantify hypotheses and measure specific market variables.

projective techniques In marketing research, asking indirect questions or otherwise involving consumers in a situation where they can express feelings about the problem or product. The purpose is to get an understanding of people's underlying or subconscious feelings, attitudes, opinions, needs, and motives.

intensive techniques Qualitative research aimed at probing the deepest feelings, attitudes, and beliefs of respondents through direct questioning. Typical methods include in-depth interviews and focus groups.

in-depth interview (IDI) An intensive interview technique that uses carefully planned but loosely structured questions to probe respondents' deeper feelings.

focus group A qualitative method of research in which six or more people, typical of the target market, are invited to a group session to discuss the product, the service, or the marketing situation for an hour or more.

In this section we'll discuss the basic methods advertisers use for conducting qualitative and quantitative research and then we'll look at how they apply these techniques to testing ads.

Basic Methods of Qualitative Research To get people to share their thoughts and feelings, researchers use qualitative research that elicits in-depth, open-ended responses rather than yes or no answers. Some marketers refer to this as *motivation research.* Unfortunately, no matter how skillfully posed, some questions are uncomfortable for consumers to answer. When asked why they bought a particular status car, for instance, consumers might reply that it handles well or is economical or dependable, but they rarely admit that it makes them feel important. The methods used in qualitative research are usually either *projective* or *intensive techniques.*

Projective techniques. Advertisers use **projective techniques** to understand people's underlying or subconscious feelings, attitudes, interests, opinions, needs, and motives. By asking indirect questions (such as "What kind of people do you think shop here?"), the researcher tries to involve consumers in a situation where they can express feelings about the problem or product.

A focus group is an intensive research technique used to evaluate the effectiveness of the various elements of a sponsor's ad or advertising campaign. Focus groups are especially effective used in conjunction with quantitative research.

Projective techniques were adapted for marketing research after their use by psychologists in clinical diagnosis. But such techniques require the skill of highly experienced researchers.

Intensive techniques. **Intensive techniques**, such as in-depth interviews, also require great care to administer properly. In the **in-depth interview (IDI)**, carefully planned but loosely structured questions help the interviewer probe respondents' deeper feelings. The big pharmaceutical company Schering, for example, uses IDIs with physicians to find out what attributes doctors consider most important in the drugs they prescribe and to identify which brands the doctors associate with different attributes.[21] While IDIs help reveal individual motivations, they are also expensive and time-consuming.

One of the most common intensive research techniques is the **focus group**, in which the company invites six or more people typical of the target market to a group session to discuss the product, the service, or the marketing situation. The session may last an hour or more. A trained moderator guides the often freewheeling discussion, and the group interaction reveals the participants' true feelings or behavior toward the product. Focus-group meetings are usually recorded and often viewed or videotaped from behind a one-way mirror.

Online focus groups are gaining acceptance. A start-up company was preparing to launch a new "green" cleaning product to commercial markets. It had developed a website to support its marketing objectives and wanted reactions from purchase decision makers on the site content and features, as well as their preferred purchase method. During the 90-minute online focus groups, live Web pages of the client site were displayed to all participants and the moderator asked questions and probed responses. Each participant was able to navigate the site and report on desired features and content. The client team observed the group conversation remotely. After the groups, the client modified the sales strategy and plans to develop more specific content for the site

ethnographic research (ethnography) An intensive research technique that has been gaining in popularity among advertisers. It involves trying to understand behavior and culture by going out and talking to people wherever they are, while they're doing whatever it is they do.

observation method A method of research used when researchers actually monitor people's actions.

Universal Product Code (UPC) An identifying series of vertical bars with a 12-digit number that adorns every consumer packaged good.

experimental method A method of scientific investigation in which a researcher alters the stimulus received by a test group or groups and compares the results with those of a control group that did not receive the altered stimulus.

test market An isolated geographic area used to introduce and test the effectiveness of a product, ad campaign, or promotional campaign, prior to a national rollout.

based on concerns expressed by participants. Additional online focus groups are slated to occur after the product launches to obtain qualitative feedback from new users.[22]

Focus groups don't represent a valid sample of the population, but the participants' responses are useful for several purposes. They can provide input about the viability of prospective spokespeople, determine the effectiveness of visuals, concepts, and strategies, and identify elements in ads that are unclear or claims that don't seem plausible. As in the case of Kraft, focus groups can be particularly useful in gaining a deeper understanding of particular market segments. Focus groups are best used in conjunction with surveys. In fact, focus-group responses often help marketers design questions for a formal survey[23] or, following a survey, focus groups can put flesh on the skeleton of raw data.[24]

Ethnographic research (or ethnography) is an intensive research technique that tries to understand how people live their lives. Many high-tech companies use ethnography to uncover trends that will determine the direction of future technological development. Ethnographic information was collected by Fallon's planners on behalf of Holiday Inn Express when they accompanied the road warriors on their cross-country adventures. Ethnography involves trying to understand behavior and culture by going out and talking to people wherever they are, while they're doing whatever it is they do. It means entering someone's world for a while, be it a couple of hours or a couple of days.[25] This process can be very labor-intensive and therefore costly and may require long periods of time in the field. Ethnographers must be very skilled in their art and often have specialized training in social science fields such as anthropology.

Basic Methods of Quantitative Research Advertisers use quantitative research to gain reliable, hard statistics about specific market conditions or situations. There are three basic research methods used to collect quantitative data: *observation, experiment,* and *survey.*

This video frame from Envirosell shows how the company uses security-type cameras to observe in-store consumer shopping habits.

Observation. In the **observation method**, researchers monitor people's actions. They may count the traffic that passes by a billboard, measure a TV audience through instruments hooked to television sets, or study consumer reactions to products displayed in the supermarket. Most observation method research is performed by large, independent marketing research companies, such as ACNielsen and Information Resources, Inc. Healthtex, for example, subscribes to the services of National Panel Diary (NPD), which tracks the clothing purchases of 16,000 homes as a nationwide sample. From this, Healthtex can find out its market share and better understand statistical trends in the marketplace.

Technology has greatly facilitated the observation method. One example is the **Universal**

[There is no infallible way to predict advertising success or failure.]

survey A basic method of quantitative research. To get people's opinions, surveys may be conducted in person, by mail, on the telephone, or via the Internet.

Product Code (UPC) label, an identifying series of vertical bars with a 12-digit number that adorns every consumer packaged good. By reading the codes with optical scanners, researchers can tell which products are selling and how well. The UPC label not only increases speed and accuracy at the checkout counter; it also enables timely inventory control and gives stores and manufacturers accurate point-of-purchase data sensitive to the impact of price, in-store promotion, couponing, and advertising.

ACNielsen's ScanTrack provides data on packaged-goods sales, market shares, and retail prices from more than 4,800 stores representing 800 retailers in 52 markets. A companion service, National Consumer Panel, uses in-home bar-code scanners to collect data on consumer purchases and shopping patterns. As a result, marketers suddenly have reliable data on the effectiveness of the tools they use to influence consumers. With that information, they can develop empirical models to evaluate alternative marketing plans, media vehicles, and promotional campaigns.[26] In one case, for instance, data might indicate that a 40-cent coupon for toothpaste would create $150,000 in profits but a 50-cent coupon on the same item would create a $300,000 loss.

Video cameras have also affected observation techniques. Envirosell, a New York–based research company, uses security-type cameras to capture consumer in-store shopping habits. To determine the effectiveness of packaging and displays, the company analyzes how much time people spend with an item and how they read the label.[27]

Experiment. To measure actual cause-and-effect relationships, researchers use the **experimental method**. An experiment is a scientific investigation in which a researcher alters the stimulus received by a *test group* and compares the results with that of a *control group* that did not receive the altered stimulus. This type of research is used primarily for new product and new campaign introductions. As we saw in the Kraft story, marketers go to an isolated geographic area, called a **test market**, and introduce the product in that area alone or test a new ad campaign or promotion before a *national rollout.* For example, a new campaign might run in one geographic area but not another. Sales in the two areas are then compared to determine the campaign's effectiveness. However, researchers must use strict controls so the variable that causes the effect can be accurately determined. Because it's hard to control every marketing variable, this method is difficult to use and quite expensive.

Survey. The most common method of gathering primary quantitative research data is the **survey**, in which the researcher gains information on attitudes, opinions, or motivations by questioning current or prospective customers (political polls are a common type of survey). Surveys can be conducted by personal interview, telephone, mail, or on the Internet. Each has distinct advantages and disadvantages (see Exhibit 6–4).

check yourself ✓

1. What are some benefits of qualitative research?
2. Why would an advertiser use quantitative research?

LO6-5 Evaluate the challenges of pretesting and posttesting advertising.

Basic Methods for Testing Ads Although there is no infallible way to predict advertising success or failure, pretesting and posttesting can give an advertiser useful insights if properly applied.

Researchers often collect information on attitudes, opinions, or motivations by conducting surveys of current or prospective customers. A common technique is the mall intercept, in which an interviewer at a shopping mall intercepts a sample of those passing by to ask if they would be willing to participate in a brief research study.

▼EXHIBIT 6-4 Comparison of data collection methods.

	Data Collection Method			
	Personal Interview	Telephone	Mail	Internet
Data collection costs	High	Medium	Low	Low
Data collection time required	Medium	Low	High	Low
Sample size for a given budget	Small	Medium	Large	Large
Data quantity per respondent	High	Medium	Low	Low
Reaches widely dispersed sample	No	Maybe	Maybe	Yes
Interaction with respondents	High	High	None	Medium
Degree of interviewer bias	High	Medium	None	None
Severity of nonresponse bias	Low	Low	High	Medium
Presentation of visual stimuli	Yes	No	Maybe	Yes
Field worker training required	Yes	Yes	No	No

Pretesting methods. Advertisers often pretest ads for likability and comprehension by using a variety of qualitative and quantitative techniques.

For example, when pretesting print ads, advertisers often ask direct questions: What does the advertising say to you? Does the advertising tell you anything new or different about the company? If so, what? Does the advertising reflect activities you would like to participate in? Is the advertising believable? What effect does it have on your perception of the merchandise offered? Do you like the ads?

Through **direct questioning**, researchers can elicit a full range of responses from people and thereby infer how well advertising messages convey key copy points. Direct questioning is especially effective for testing alternative ads in the early stages of development, when respondents' reactions and input can best be acted on. There are numerous techniques for pretesting print ads, including *focus groups, order-of-merit tests, paired comparisons, portfolio tests, mock magazines, perceptual meaning studies,* and *direct-mail tests.* (See My Ad Campaign 6–B, "Methods for Pretesting Ads.")

Several methods are used specifically to pretest radio and TV commercials. In **central location tests**, respondents are shown test commercials, usually in shopping centers, and questions are asked before and after exposure. In **clutter tests**, test commercials are shown with noncompeting control commercials to determine their effectiveness, measure comprehension and attitude shifts, and detect weaknesses.

The challenge of pretesting. There is no best way to pretest advertising variables. Different methods test different aspects, and each has its own advantages and disadvantages—a formidable challenge for the advertiser.

Pretesting helps distinguish strong ads from weak ones. But since the test occurs in an artificial setting, respondents may

Starch Advertising Research (www.gfkmri.com) posttests magazine ad effectiveness by interviewing readers. They found that celebrity endorsers provide a significant lift to print advertising readership. Starch analyzed more than 81,000 print ads and discovered that ads with entertainment celebrities garnered 15.1% more readership than ads without a celebrity endorser. An Ellen DeGeneres print ad in this Cover Girl & Olay campaign generated a phenomenal 91% readership score.

Source: www.marketwired.com/press-release/-1400869.htm

assume the role of expert or critic and give answers that don't reflect their real buying behavior. They may invent opinions to satisfy the interviewer, or be reluctant to admit they are influenced, or vote for the ads they think they *should* like. This is why some creative people mistrust ad testing; they believe it stifles creativity.

direct questioning A method of pretesting designed to elicit a full range of responses to the advertising. It is especially effective for testing alternative advertisements in the early stages of development.

central location tests A type of pretest in which videotapes of test commercials are shown to respondents on a one-to-one basis, usually in shopping center locations.

clutter tests Method of pretesting in which commercials are grouped with noncompetitive control commercials and shown to prospective customers to measure their effectiveness in gaining attention, increasing brand awareness and comprehension, and causing attitude shifts.

Despite these challenges, the issue comes down to dollars. Small advertisers rarely pretest, but their risk isn't as great, either. When advertisers risk millions of dollars on a new campaign, they *must* pretest to be sure the ad or commercial is interesting, believable, likable, memorable, and persuasive—and reinforces the brand image.

Posttesting methods. Posttesting can be more costly and time-consuming than pretesting, but it can test finished ads under actual market conditions. As we saw with Kraft, some advertisers benefit from pretesting and posttesting by running ads in select test markets before launching a campaign nationwide.

As in pretesting, advertisers use both quantitative and qualitative methods in posttesting. Most posttesting techniques fall into five broad categories: *aided recall, unaided recall, attitude*

my ad campaign

Methods for Pretesting Ads [6–B]

Advertisers rarely trust intuition alone when evaluating their creative work. There is simply too much on the line. Pretesting is what occurs when advertisers test prototypes of their ads before they are run in the mass media. Below is a comprehensive list of ways that real agencies and advertisers test their work. You don't have the resources to do many of them. But you can use some of these methods to test your creative ideas with a small sample drawn from your target audience. Doing so will give you added ammunition for persuading your client that you've developed a strong strategy for his or her brand.

Print Advertising

- **Direct questioning.** Asks specific questions about ads. Often used to test alternative ads in early stages of development.
- **Focus group.** A moderated but freewheeling discussion and interview conducted with six or more people.
- **Order-of-merit test.** Respondents see two or more ads and arrange them in rank order.
- **Paired comparison method.** Respondents compare each ad in a group.
- **Portfolio test.** One group sees a portfolio of test ads interspersed among other ads and editorial matter. Another group sees the portfolio without the test ads.
- **Mock magazine.** Test ads are "stripped into" a magazine, which is left with respondents for a specified time. (Also used as a posttesting technique.)
- **Perceptual meaning study.** Respondents see ads in timed exposures.
- **Direct-mail test.** Two or more alternative ads are mailed to different prospects on a mailing list to test which ad generates the largest volume of orders.

Broadcast Advertising

- **Central location projection test.** Respondents see test commercial films in a central location such as a shopping center.
- **Trailer test.** Respondents see TV commercials in trailers at shopping centers and receive coupons for the advertised products; a matched sample of consumers just gets the coupons. Researchers measure the difference in coupon redemption.
- **Theater test.** Electronic equipment enables respondents to indicate what they like and dislike as they view TV commercials in a theater setting.
- **Live telecast test.** Test commercials are shown on closed-circuit or cable TV. Respondents are interviewed by phone, or sales audits are conducted at stores in the viewing areas.
- **Sales experiment.** Alternative commercials run in two or more market areas.

Physiological Testing

- **Pupilometric device.** Dilation of the subject's pupils is measured, presumably to indicate the subject's level of interest.
- **Eye movement camera.** The route the subject's eyes traveled is superimposed over an ad to show the areas that attracted and held attention.
- **Galvanometer.** Measures subject's sweat gland activity with a mild electrical current; presumably the more tension an ad creates, the more effective it is likely to be.
- **Voice pitch analysis.** A consumer's response is taped, and a computer is used to measure changes in voice pitch caused by emotional responses.
- **Brain pattern analysis.** A scanner monitors the reaction of the subject's brain.

attitude tests A type of posttest that usually seeks to measure the effectiveness of an advertising campaign in creating a favorable image for a company, its brand, or its products.

recall tests Posttesting methods used to determine the extent to which an advertisement and its message have been noticed, read, or watched.

inquiry tests A form of test in which consumer responses to an ad for information or free samples are tabulated.

sales tests A useful measure of advertising effectiveness when advertising is the dominant element, or the only variable, in the company's marketing plan. Sales tests are more suited for gauging the effectiveness of campaigns than of individual ads or components of ads.

tests, inquiry tests, and *sales tests.* (See My Ad Campaign 6–B, "Methods for Posttesting Ads.")

Some advertisers use **attitude tests** to measure a campaign's effectiveness in creating a favorable image for a company, its brand, or its products. Presumably, favorable changes in attitude predispose consumers to buy the company's product.

Nielsen IAG measures the effectiveness of television advertising, product placement, and the Internet for such clients as American Express, General Motors, and Procter & Gamble. Nielsen IAG collects key data about the ads that viewers watched the night before and generates a detailed performance analysis that includes brand recall, message understanding, likability, and purchase intent. This tool helps companies understand the actual effectiveness of their campaigns.[28]

Similarly, Nissan interviews 1,000 consumers every month to track brand awareness, familiarity with vehicle models, recall of commercials, and shifts in attitude or image perception. If a commercial fails, it can be pulled quickly.[29]

Children's clothing manufacturer Healthtex conducted some print-ad posttesting and discovered that, while new mothers appreciated the information in the long copy format, more experienced mothers didn't. For them, the headline and one line of copy were sufficient to get the point across. They already understood the rest. As a result, the company used the shorter format and redesigned the ads aimed at experienced parents.

The challenge of posttesting. Each posttesting method has limitations. **Recall tests** reveal the effectiveness of ad components, such as size, color, or themes. But they measure what respondents noticed and remembered, *not* whether they actually intend to buy the product.

For measuring sales effectiveness, attitude tests are often better than recall tests. An attitude change relates more closely to product purchase, and a measured change in attitude gives management more confidence to make informed decisions about advertising plans.

By using **inquiry tests**—in which consumers respond to an ad for information or free samples—researchers can test an ad's

Methods for Posttesting Ads [6–C]

Posttesting involves assessing the impact of a campaign after the ads have run. It is an important way that advertisers judge whether their messages have helped them to achieve their advertising objectives (see Chapter 8). You will most likely not do posttesting for your client. However, it is good practice for you to propose HOW the client might posttest your ads. This is material that you can incorporate in your campaigns book. Be sure to reference your advertising objectives when you propose a posttesting technique.

- **Aided recall (recognition–readership).** To jog their memories, respondents are shown certain ads and then asked whether their previous exposure was through reading, viewing, or listening.
- **Unaided recall.** Respondents are asked, without prompting, whether they saw or heard advertising messages.
- **Attitude tests.** Direct questions, semantic differential tests, or unstructured questions measure changes in respondents' attitudes after a campaign.
- **Inquiry tests.** Additional product information, product samples, or premiums are given to readers or viewers of an ad; ads generating the most responses are presumed to be the most effective.
- **Sales tests.** Measures of past sales compare advertising efforts with sales. Controlled experiments test different media in different markets. Consumer purchase tests measure retail sales from a given campaign. Store inventory audits measure retailers' stocks before and after a campaign.

attention-getting value, readability, and understandability. These tests also permit fairly good control of the variables that motivate reader action, particularly if a *split-run* test is used (split runs are covered in Chapter 10). Unfortunately, inquiries may not reflect a sincere interest in a product, and responses may take months to receive.

When advertising is the dominant element or the only variable in the company's marketing plan, **sales tests** are a useful measure of advertising effectiveness. However, many other variables can affect sales (competitors' activities, the season of the year, and even the weather). Sales response may not be immediate, and sales tests, particularly field studies, are often costly and time-consuming. For consumer packaged goods, though, the cost of sales tests has been greatly reduced thanks to grocery store scanners.

Learning that the wash mitt usually given to customers with the purchase of a new Beetle convertible wasn't earning them particularly high marks, Volkswagen (www.vw.com) contacted Arnold Worldwide to come up with a better idea. Arnold decided to create a guidebook to the many things that new owners could see and do in a convertible and included a star chart and wild birdseed with the book.

Step 5: Interpreting and Reporting the Findings

The final step in the research process involves interpreting and reporting the data. Research is very costly (see Exhibit 6–5), and its main purpose is to help solve problems. The final report must make the findings clear to the company's managers and relevant to their needs.

Tables and graphs are helpful, but they must be explained in words management can understand. Technical jargon (such as "multivariate analysis of variance model") should be avoided, and descriptions of the methodology, statistical analysis, and raw data should be confined to an appendix. The report should state the problem and research objective, summarize the findings, and draw conclusions. The researcher should make recommendations for management action, and the report should be discussed in a formal presentation to allow management feedback and questions and to highlight important points.

▼**EXHIBIT 6–5** The cost of professional research.

Type of Research	Features	Cost	Cost per Respondent	Factors That Can Affect Quality and Costs
Telephone and mail surveys	400 20-minute interviews, with report	$16,000 to $18,000	$40 to $45	Response rates Interview time Incidence of qualified respondents Level of analysis required in the report
E-mail surveys	400 surveys, with report	$ 3,000 to $ 5,000	$8 to $16	Extent population can be reached via e-mail Response rates Level of analysis required in the report
Focus group	2 groups with 10 respondents each, with report	$ 8,000 to $12,000	$400 to $600	Cost of focus group facilities Moderator costs Respondent costs

Sources: WestGroup Research, "Research Fundamentals: Estimating Telephone Survey Research Costs," www.westgroupresearch.com/research/phonecosts.html, accessed October 14, 2006; MC Squared Consulting, "Market Research," http://smallbusiness.yahoo.com/r-article-a-2188-m-6-sc-41-holding_a_focus_group_on_a_budget-i?aid=2188&mcid=6&scid=41&holding_a_focus_group_on_a_budget=i, accessed October 14, 2006; "Survey's Buyers Guide," http://Smallbusiness.yahoo.com/r-article-a-2040-m-6-sc-41-surveys_buyers_guide-i.

validity An important characteristic of a research test. For a test to be valid, it must reflect the true status of the market.

reliability An important characteristic of research test results. For a test to be reliable, it must be repeatable, producing the same result each time it is administered.

universe An entire target population.

sample A portion of the population selected by market researchers to represent the appropriate targeted population. Also, a free trial of a product.

check yourself ✓

1. What information might be collected when pretesting an advertisement?
2. What is the value in knowing if advertising changed a consumer's attitude?

LO6-6 Identify issues that can affect the accuracy and usability of quantitative research.

IMPORTANT ISSUES IN ADVERTISING RESEARCH

When marketers conduct primary research, there is always one legitimate concern—the accuracy of the findings. This is especially true when conducting quantitative research and when doing research in international markets.

Considerations in Conducting Primary Quantitative Research

Quantitative research requires formal design and rigorous standards for collecting and tabulating data to ensure its accuracy and usability. When conducting primary research, advertisers must consider certain issues carefully, especially whether the research is *valid* and *reliable.*

Validity and Reliability Assume you want to determine a market's attitude toward a proposed new toy. The market consists of 10 million individuals. You show a prototype of the toy to five people and four say they like it (an 80 percent favorable attitude). Is that test valid? Hardly. For a test to have **validity**, *results must be free of bias and reflect the true status of the market.*[30] Five people aren't enough for a minimum sample, and the fact that *you* showed a prototype of *your* toy to these people would probably bias their response.

Moreover, if you repeated the test with five more people, you might get an entirely different response. So your test also lacks **reliability**. For a test to be reliable, it must be *repeatable*—it must produce approximately the same result each time it is administered (see Exhibit 6–6).

▼**EXHIBIT 6–6** The reliability–validity diagram. Using the analogy of a dartboard, the bull's-eye is the actual value of some measure within a population. The top row shows high reliability (repeatability) because the darts are closely clustered. When reliability drops, the darts land more randomly and spread across a wider area, as in both examples in the bottom row. We got different results each time. The left column demonstrates high validity because in both examples the darts center around the bull's-eye. The right column represents low validity because bias in the testing process drew all the darts to one side; we were measuring the wrong thing. The upper-left quadrant reflects the truest picture of the data.

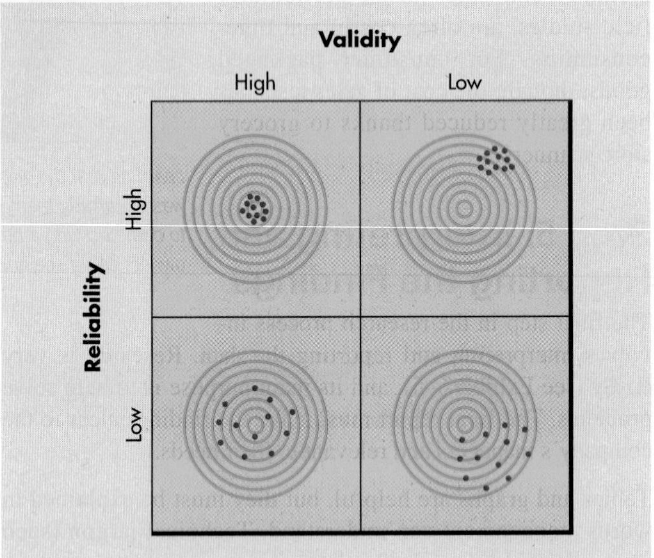

Validity and reliability depend on several key elements: the sampling methods, the survey questionnaire design, and the data tabulation and analysis methods.

Sampling Methods When a company wants to know what consumers think, it typically can't ask everybody. But its research should as nearly as possible reflect the **universe** (the entire target population) of prospective customers. Researchers therefore select from that population a **sample** that they expect will represent the population's characteristics. To accomplish this, they must decide whom to survey, how many to survey, and how to choose the respondents.

A sample must be large enough to achieve precision and stability. The larger the sample, the more reliable the results. However, reliability can be obtained with even very small samples, a fraction of 1 percent of the population, if the sample is drawn correctly. There are two types of samples: probability samples and nonprobability samples.

The greatest accuracy is gained from **probability samples** (sometimes referred to as *random samples*) because everyone in the universe has a quantifiable chance of being selected.[31] For example, a researcher who wants to know a community's opinion on an issue could select members of the community at random. But this method has its challenges. Every unit (person) must be known, listed, and numbered so each can be given an equal chance of being selected, an often prohibitively expensive and sometimes impossible task, especially with customers of nationally distributed products.

probability samples A research sample in which all members of the target population have an equal and independent chance of being selected for the study.

nonprobability samples Research samples that do not provide every unit in the population with an equal chance of being included. As a result, there is no guarantee that the sample will be representative.

[Constructing a good questionnaire requires considerable expertise.]

Instead, researchers often use **nonprobability samples** because they're easier, less expensive, and less time-consuming than probability samples. Sometimes referred to as *convenience samples*, respondents are selected on the basis of their availability (e.g., because they volunteered). Nonprobability samples don't give every unit in the universe an equal chance of being included, so there's no guarantee the sample is representative. As a result, researchers can't be as confident in the validity of the responses.[32] However, most marketing and advertising research needs only approximate measures of the data. For example, the nonprobability method of interviewing shoppers in malls may be sufficient to determine the shopping preferences, image perceptions, and attitudes of target customers.

How Questionnaires Are Designed Constructing a good questionnaire requires considerable expertise. Much bias in research is blamed on poorly designed questionnaires. Typical problems include asking the wrong types of questions, asking too many questions, using the wrong form of a question (which makes it difficult to answer or tabulate), and using a poor choice of words. Exhibit 6–7

▼ EXHIBIT 6–7 A personal questionnaire like this helps determine shoppers' feelings toward a chain of stores, its merchandise, and its advertising.

1. Do you intend to shop at _(Store name)_ between now and Sunday?
Yes 1 No 2 (If no, skip to question 5)

2. Do you intend to buy something in particular or just to browse?
Buy 1 Browse 2

3. Have you seen any of the items you intend to buy advertised by _(Store name)_?
Yes 1 (continue) No 2 (skip to question 5)

4. Where did you see these items advertised? Was it in a _(Store name)_ advertising insert included with your newspaper, a _(Store name)_ flyer you received in the mail, the pages of the newspaper itself, on TV, or somewhere else?

- ☐ Insert in newspaper
- ☐ Flyer in mail
- ☐ Pages of newspaper
- ☐ On TV
- ☐ Somewhere else (specify) ________
- ☐ Don't recall

5. Please rate the _(Store name)_ advertising insert on the attributes listed below. Place an X in the box at the position that best reflects your opinion of how the insert rates on each attribute. Placing an X in the middle box usually means you are neutral. The closer you place the X to the left or right phrase or word, the more you believe it describes the _(Store name)_ insert.

	1	2	3	4	5	6	7	
Looks cheap								Looks expensive
Unskillful								Cleverly done
Unappealing								Appealing
Does not show clothing in an attractive manner								Shows clothing in an attractive manner

6. Please indicate all of the different types of people listed below you feel this _(Store name)_ advertising insert is appealing to.

- ☐ Young people
- ☐ Bargain hunters
- ☐ Conservative dressers
- ☐ Fashion-conscious people
- ☐ Rich people
- ☐ Professionals
- ☐ High-income people
- ☐ Men
- ☐ Someone like me
- ☐ Career-oriented women
- ☐ Quality-conscious people
- ☐ Low-income people
- ☐ Budget watchers
- ☐ Older people
- ☐ Middle-income people
- ☐ Blue-collar people
- ☐ Women
- ☐ Office workers
- ☐ Smart dressers
- ☐ Other (specify) ________

EXHIBIT 6–8 Different ways to phrase research questions.

Type	Questions
Open-ended	How would you describe (*Store name*) advertising?
Dichotomous	Do you think (*Store name*) advertising is old-fashioned? ____ Yes ____ No
Multiple-choice	What description best fits your opinion of (*Store name*) advertising? ____ Modern ____ Unconvincing ____ Well done ____ Old-fashioned ____ Believable
Scale	Please indicate on the scale how you rate the quality of (*Store name*) advertising. 1 Poor ____ 2 ____ 3 ____ 4 ____ 5 Excellent

shows some typical questions that might be used in a survey for a retail store.

Consider the simple question: "What kind of soap do you use?" The respondent doesn't know what *soap* means. Hand soap, shampoo, laundry detergent, or dishwashing soap? Does *kind* mean brand, size, or type? Finally, what constitutes *use?* What a person buys (perhaps for someone else) or uses personally—or for what purpose? In fact, one person probably uses several different kinds of soap, depending on the occasion. It's impossible to answer this question accurately. Worse, if the consumer does answer it, the researcher doesn't know what the answer means and will likely draw an incorrect conclusion. For these reasons, questionnaires *must* be pretested. (See My Ad Campaign 6–D, "Developing an Effective Questionnaire.")

Effective survey questions have three important attributes: *focus, brevity,* and *clarity.* They focus on the topic of the survey. They are as brief as possible. And they are expressed simply and clearly.[33]

The four most common types of questions are *open-ended, dichotomous, multiple choice,* and *scale.* But there are many ways to ask questions within these four types. In Exhibit 6–8, for example, more choices could be added to the multiple-choice format. Neutral responses (the middle choice) could be removed from the scale question so the respondent must answer either positively or negatively. And there is obvious bias in the dichotomous question.

Developing an Effective Questionnaire [6–D]

In many years of teaching an advertising research class, I have always told students that the hardest thing they will do is write a good survey. When they hear this students are often skeptical, after all, many of them are good writers. But writing a survey is surprisingly tough if you've never done it before. The key is to write questions and statements that get to the heart of your objectives. Every survey item must be relevant, clear, and useful. Don't waste your respondents' time (or your own) with items that hold little potential for helping you better serve your client. Here are some tips for writing items that can help you make better decisions:

- **List specific research objectives.** Don't spend money collecting irrelevant data.
- **Write short questionnaires.** Don't tax the respondent's patience; you may get careless or flip answers.
- **State questions clearly** so there is no chance for misunderstanding. Avoid generalities and ambiguities.
- **Write a rough draft first,** then polish it.
- **Use a short opening statement.** Include the interviewer's name, the name of the organization, and the purpose of the questionnaire.
- **Put the respondent at ease** by opening with one or two inoffensive, easily answered questions.
- **Structure questions so they flow logically.** Ask general questions before more detailed ones.
- **Avoid questions that suggest an answer or could be considered leading.** They bias the results.
- **Include a few questions that cross-check earlier answers.** This helps ensure validity.
- **Put the demographic questions (age, income, education) and any other personal questions at the end of the questionnaire.**
- **Pretest the questionnaire** with 20 to 30 people to be sure they interpret the questions correctly and that it covers all the information sought.

Questions should elicit a response that is both accurate and useful. By testing questionnaires on a small subsample, researchers can detect any confusion, bias, or ambiguities and make revisions.

Data Tabulation and Analysis Collected data must be validated, edited, coded, and tabulated. Answers must be checked to eliminate errors or inconsistencies. For example, one person might answer two years, while another says 24 months; such responses must be changed to the same units for correct tabulation. Some questionnaires may be rejected because respondents' answers indicate they misunderstood the questions. Finally, the data must be tabulated and summarized, usually by computer.

Many researchers want *cross-tabulations* (for example, product use by age group or education). Software programs such as SAS®, SPSS®, and Minitab® make it possible for small advertisers as well as large corporations to tabulate data on a personal computer and apply advanced statistical techniques.[34] Many cross-tabulations are possible, but researchers must use skill and imagination to select only those that show meaningful and significant relationships.

Collecting Primary Data in International Markets

International marketers face a number of challenges when they collect primary data. For one thing, research overseas is often more expensive than domestic research. Many marketers are surprised to learn that research in five countries costs five times as much as research in one country; there are no economies of scale.[35]

But advertisers must determine whether their messages will work in foreign markets. (Maxwell House, for example, had to change its "great American coffee" campaign when it discovered that Germans have little respect for U.S. coffee.)

Advertisers need more than just facts about a country's culture. They need to understand and appreciate the nuances of its cultural traits and habits, a difficult task for people who don't live there or speak the language. Knowledgeable international advertisers such as Colgate-Palmolive work in partnership with their local offices and use local bilingual marketing people when conducting primary research abroad.[36]

For years, Mattel tried unsuccessfully to market the Barbie doll in Japan. It finally sold the manufacturing license to a Japanese company, Takara, which did its own research. Takara found that most Japanese girls and their parents thought Barbie's breasts were too big and her legs too long. It modified the doll accordingly, changed the blue eyes to brown, and sold 2 million dolls in two years.

Conducting original research abroad can be fraught with problems. First, the researcher must use the local language, and translating questionnaires can be tricky. Second, many cultures view strangers suspiciously and don't wish to talk about their personal lives. U.S. companies found that mail surveys and phone interviews don't work in Japan; they have to use expensive, time-consuming personal interviews.[37]

Marketers are often surprised by some of the differences they encounter when trying to conduct international research. Lead

This example from Procter & Gamble's Bonux detergent campaign in Lebanon illustrates some of the difficulties inherent in international advertising. Lebanese housewives take great pride in clean washing, so much so that they even brag about laundry secrets and hang their laundry on balconies to be seen by neighbors. Bonux created the "housewives moment of fame" campaign and bought advertising space on the roofs of buses so the ads could be seen from balconies. Radio spots featured interviews with housewives riding the buses. The campaign raised awareness 85 percent, and increased market share by 20 percent.

times to begin projects are typically longer, with the Far East being particularly troublesome. Groups can take twice as long to set up overseas. The structures differ too. Focus groups, for instance, rarely use more than 4 to 6 people rather than the 8 to 10 typical of the United States. Screening requirements for participants abroad are typically less rigid, and foreign moderators tend to be much less structured than their U.S. counterparts. Finally, the facilities don't usually have all the amenities of U.S. offices, but the costs are frequently twice as high in Europe and three times as high in Asia.[38]

Despite these problems—or perhaps because of them—it's important for global advertisers to perform research. Competent researchers are available in all developed countries, and major international research firms have local offices in most developing countries.

Today, nearly three-quarters of market research firms use the Internet to conduct some form of market research.[39] With the global adoption of the Internet, experts anticipate further cuts in costs and time for getting valuable customer input for marketing and advertising decision making. ■

check yourself ✓

1. Why do researchers "sample" the population?
2. Why must questionnaires be pretested?

learn about, practice, and apply account planning and research skills!

M: Advertising was developed for students who want information packaged in a concise, easy-to-read, yet interesting format.

Check out the book's website to:

- Learn why the agencies that have adopted account planning are the ones that are performing the best work. (Review Questions)
- Discover how pretesting advertising could yield misleading results. (Review Questions)
- Learn how to conduct research that will provide valuable marketing insights. (Exploring Advertising)

While you are there, check out the professional resource links, review the PowerPoint presentation, and test your knowledge with the Multiple Choice Quiz. Additionally, *Connect® Marketing* is available for M: Advertising.

www.mhhe.com/ArensM2e

chapter seven

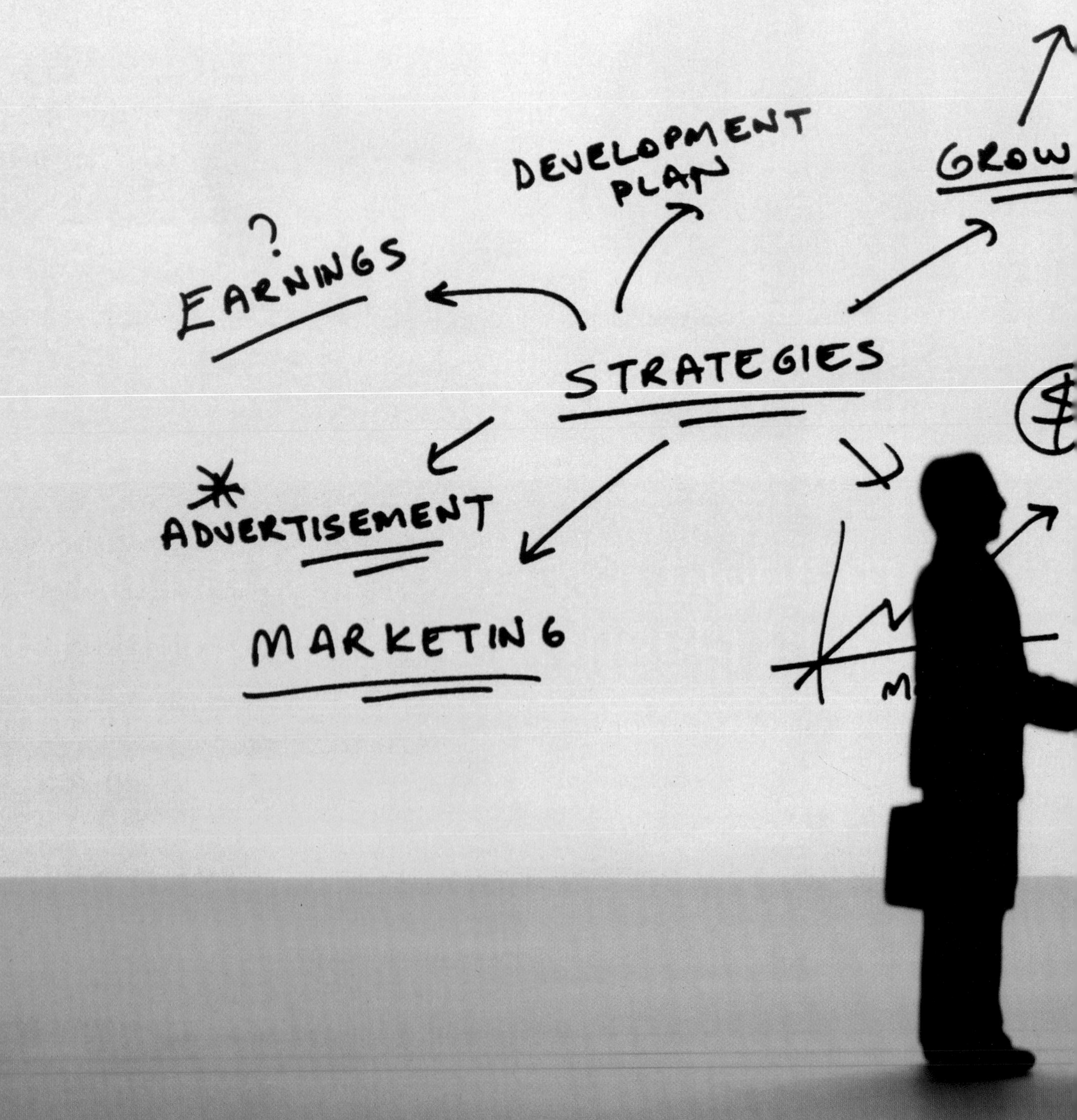

marketing, advertising, **and IMC planning**

This chapter describes the process of marketing and IMC planning. Marketers need to understand the various ways plans are created. They must also know how to analyze situations; set realistic, attainable objectives; develop strategies to achieve them; and establish budgets for marketing communications.

Nearly 70 years ago, Ally and Barney Hartman of Knoxville, Tennessee, cooked up a 7 Up–type brew and tested it on their families and friends. They seemed to like it, so the two started bottling the concoction and distributing it to the locals. In 1946, they designed a paper label for their beverage featuring a hillbilly toting a gun and a signature that read "By Barney and Ollie." In honor of the mountain moonshine famous in Tennessee, they named their drink "Mountain Dew."

Over the course of time, the brand grew. The gun-toting Willy the Hillbilly and the apt slogan, "Ya-hoo Mountain Dew," helped make it a regional player. In 1964, PepsiCo bought the brand and, for some years, continued using the old advertising approach.

continued on p. 174

LEARNING OBJECTIVES

After studying this chapter, you will be able to:

LO7-1 Describe the role and importance of a marketing plan.

LO7-2 Distinguish between objectives, strategies, and tactics in marketing and advertising plans.

LO7-3 Show what makes IMC planning different from traditional methods.

LO7-4 Explain how to establish specific, realistic, and measurable advertising objectives.

LO7-5 List the various approaches for determining advertising budgets.

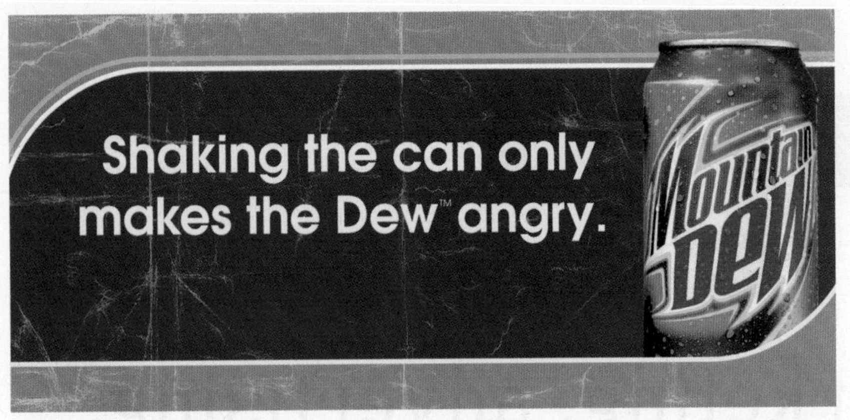

continued from p. 173

In 1973 Pepsi repositioned and re-launched Mountain Dew. No longer would it be a hillbilly mixer. Rather, the Dew would be cast as a high-energy, youth-oriented, flavored soft drink. New ads created by BBDO New York featured active young people enjoying outdoor activities to the theme "Hello Sunshine, Hello Mountain Dew." By 1978, the action-oriented approach sent Dew sales over the 100-million-case mark. The 1980s saw high-octane sports and adventure added to the advertising.[1]

Since that time, Mountain Dew has set a standard of how to remain true to its definition of exuberance across a variety of marketing platforms. "We have a great unity of message and purpose that has been consistent over time about what we are and what we aren't," says Scott Moffitt, director of marketing for Mountain Dew.[2] "The brand is all about exhilaration and energy, and you see that in all that we do, from advertising and community to grass-roots programs and our sports-minded focus. We have a very crystal clear, vivid positioning."

The positioning concept has allowed Mountain Dew to reach consumers in diverse venues—from skateboarding parks to mainstream extravaganzas such as the Super Bowl. Marketing across such a broad spectrum from grass-roots to grandiose advertising events is known within PepsiCo as "mass intimacy." One Pepsi-Cola executive puts it this way: "It's our way of saying we haven't sold out."[3]

Given the great success of BBDO's Dew campaign, the challenge became staying power throughout the 2000s. Young consumers are notoriously fickle and perpetually ready to try something new. One innovative tactic included developing a snowboarding documentary that made only brief references to the brand. The decision to finance a film, which carried a cost close to that of a traditional 30-second TV spot, may have resulted from recognition by the advertiser that its target audience watches less TV than other groups and often sees TV commercials as manipulative.[4]

In the mid-2000s, when some soda drinkers switched to noncarbonated alternatives, Mountain Dew experienced a volume increase of nearly 2 percent and the diet version surged nearly 8 percent. The same period saw volume sales of Coke Classic and Pepsi-Cola drop 2 percent and 3 percent, respectively.

For all its success, Mountain Dew is not sitting on its laurels. The brand has been a prominent advertiser on Xbox Live, used social media to encourage fans to design new flavors, and even shortened its name to "Mtn" Dew. In 2013 it may have gone a bit too far with an ad developed by hip-hop musician Tyler, the Creator, that drew heavy criticism and was pulled.[5] But the misstep is not likely to cause the brand to tone it down. Mtn Dew didn't grow from a small regional beverage to a national powerhouse by playing it safe. ■

L07-1 Describe the role and importance of a marketing plan.

THE MARKETING PLAN

The successful campaigns created by ad agency BBDO for Mountain Dew demonstrate that business success depends on marketing and advertising planning and advertising creativity.

The Importance of Marketing Planning

Since marketing drives a company's income, the marketing plan may well be its most important document.

The **marketing plan** assembles relevant facts about the organization, its markets, products, services, customers, competition,

marketing plan The plan that directs the company's marketing effort.

top-down marketing The traditional planning process with four main elements: situation analysis, marketing objectives, marketing strategy, and tactics or action programs.

situation analysis A factual statement of the organization's current situation and how it got there.

SWOT analysis After assessing a company's situation, the writer of a marketing plan prepares an analysis that identifies the brand's or product's strengths, weaknesses, opportunities, and threats.

and so on. It forces all departments to focus on the customer. Finally, it lists goals and objectives for specified periods of time and lays out the precise strategies and tactics to achieve them.

The written marketing plan must reflect the goals of top management and be consistent with the company's mission and capabilities. Depending on its scope, the plan may be long and complex or, in the case of a small firm, very brief. Formal marketing plans are reviewed and revised yearly, but planning is not a one-time event; it's an ongoing activity.

The Effect of the Marketing Plan on IMC

The marketing plan has a profound effect on an organization's marketing communications. It helps managers analyze and improve all company operations, including marketing and advertising programs. It defines the role of advertising in the marketing mix. It enables better implementation, control, and continuity of advertising programs, and it ensures the most efficient allocation of IMC dollars.

Companies have a choice in how they plan. Most still use the traditional top-down planning model; some use a bottom-up model; and many companies use an IMC model. Let's look at each.

check yourself ✓

1. What is a marketing plan and why is it a company's most important document?
2. How does the marketing plan affect IMC efforts?

L07-2 Distinguish between objectives, strategies, and tactics in marketing and advertising plans.

Top-Down Marketing Plans

The traditional **top-down marketing** plan is still quite common. As Exhibit 7–1 shows, the top-down plan has four main elements: *situation analysis, marketing objectives, marketing strategy,* and *marketing tactics* (or *action programs*). Large companies with extensive marketing plans sometimes include additional sections.

Situation Analysis

The **situation analysis** section is a *factual* statement of the organization's current situation and how it got there. It presents all the relevant facts about the company's history, growth, products and services, sales volume, share of market, competitive status, markets served, distribution systems, past advertising programs, marketing research studies, and other pertinent information. A situation analysis is more than a presentation of facts, however. Good marketing plans provide the context for factual information. For example, Diet Mountain Dew's sales growth of 8 percent in 2005 is put into a context when the marketing plan notes that overall sales of carbonated beverages declined that year.

Planners draw attention to the most important aspects of a brand's situation through a SWOT analysis. The **SWOT analysis** uses the facts contained in the situation analysis to point out strengths, weaknesses, opportunities, and threats for the brand. Strengths and weaknesses represent company capabilities, while opportunities and threats represent environmental factors. One obvious strength for Mountain Dew is its well-defined, attractive brand image as a high-energy, full-flavored, carbonated beverage. A possible weakness could be the brand's age. An opportunity for Mountain Dew might be the increased interest in energy drinks. Since Mountain Dew is a highly caffeinated beverage, it stands to profit from such a trend. Threats to Mountain Dew might include rising prices for commodities used to make the product (sugar, flavorings) or distribute the product (fuel) that would force Mountain Dew to raise prices to remain profitable. Another might be changes in the consumption behaviors of its target markets (some of the fastest growing soft-drinks today are vitamin-infused beverages such as Pepsi's Tava).[6]

▼EXHIBIT 7–1 Traditional top-down marketing plan.

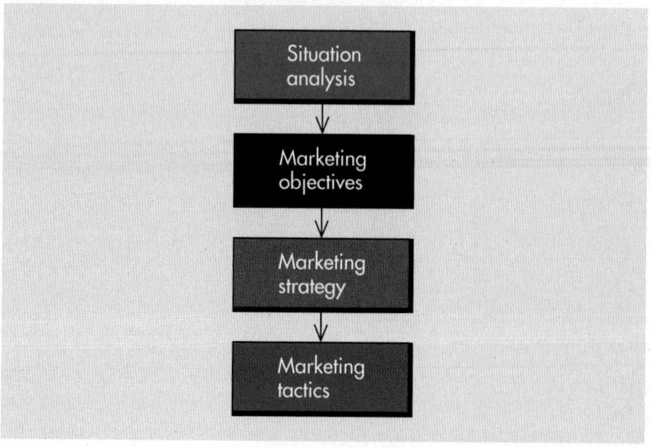

corporate objectives Goals of the company stated in terms of profit or return on investment.

marketing objectives Goals of the marketing effort that may be expressed in terms of the needs of specific target markets and specific sales objectives.

need-satisfying objectives A marketing objective that shifts management's view of the organization from a producer of products or services to a satisfier of target market needs.

sales-target objective Marketing objectives that relate to a company's sales. They may be expressed in terms of total sales volume; sales by product, market segment, or customer type; market share; growth rate of sales volume; or gross profit.

marketing strategy The statement of how the company is going to accomplish its marketing objectives.

> One of the best ways to define a market is to think about customer needs first and then identify the products that meet those needs.

Marketing Objectives The advertiser's next step is to determine specific marketing objectives. These must consider the amount of money the company has to invest in marketing and production, its knowledge of the marketplace, and the competitive environment.

For example, based on its knowledge about Mountain Dew drinkers, the company decided in 2009 to communicate directly with its user base on the Internet as a way of developing new flavors and brand extensions.[7]

Marketing objectives follow logically from a review of the company's current situation, management's prediction of future trends, and the hierarchy of company objectives. For example, **corporate objectives** are stated in terms of profit or return on investment, or net worth, earnings ratios, growth, or corporate reputation. **Marketing objectives**, which derive from corporate objectives, should relate to the needs of target markets as well as to specific sales goals. These may be referred to as general *need-satisfying objectives* and specific *sales-target objectives.*

To shift management's view of the organization from a producer of products to a satisfier of customers' needs, companies set **need-satisfying objectives**. These have a couple of important purposes. First, they enable the firm to view its business broadly. For example, Revlon founder Charles Revson once said a cosmetics company's product is hope, not lipstick. An insurance company sells financial security, not policies. Mountain Dew executive Cie Nicholson describes her brand as "a high energy drink for people with a zest for life." The beverage's unusual color and taste, its relatively high caffeine level, and its outstanding IMC appeals, all of which emphasize a nonconformist's view of life, mesh seamlessly with what Dew consumers want from a beverage.

Second, by setting need-satisfying objectives, managers must see through the customer's eyes. They have to ask "What are we planning to do for the customer?" and "What is the value of that to our customer?" One of the best ways to define a market is to think about customer needs first and then identify the products that meet those needs.[8]

Need-satisfying objectives address the real value that a product or service delivers to its customers. Virgin America distinguishes itself from competing airlines by promising better and friendlier service. This promise is attractive to customers unhappy with the frequently stressful experience of flying.

The second kind of marketing objective is the **sales-target objective**. This is a specific, quantitative, realistic marketing goal to be achieved within a specified period of time. A sales-target objective could be phrased as "What are we planning to do for ourselves?" They may be expressed in several ways: total sales volume; sales volume by product, market segment, customer type; market share in total or by product line; growth rate of sales volume in total or by product line; and gross profit in total or by product line. Mountain Dew, for example, uses a number of measures for its sales-target objectives: case volume, share of market, growth, and/or share of growth.

Marketing Strategy The **marketing strategy** describes how the company plans to meet its marketing objectives. "Developing and following a strategy is what keeps you and everybody else on the same course so that you can maximize the effectiveness of your marketing."[9]

Marketing strategy typically involves three steps: (1) defining the target markets; (2) determining the strategic positioning; and

Developing the Situation Analysis [7–A]

In previous chapters you've honed your understanding of the consumer, segmented the audience, and conducted research. It is time to pull all of this information together and create an assessment of your client's current situation. Marketers call such an assessment a situation analysis. Use the list below to organize your analysis.

The Industry

- **Companies in industry:** Dollar sales, strengths.
- **Growth patterns within industry:** Primary demand curve, per capita consumption, growth potential.
- **History of industry:** Technological advances, trends.
- **Characteristics of industry:** Distribution patterns, industry control, promotional activity, geographic characteristics, profit patterns.

The Company

- **The company story:** History, size, growth, profitability, scope of business, competence, reputation, strengths, weaknesses.

The Product or Service

- **The product story:** Development, quality, design, description, packaging, price structure, uses, reputation, strengths, weaknesses.
- **Product sales features:** Exclusive, nonexclusive differentiating qualities, competitive position.
- **Product research:** Technological breakthroughs, improvements planned.

Sale History

- **Sales and sales costs:** By product, model, sales districts.
- **Profit history.**

Share of Market

- **Sales history industrywide:** Share of market in dollars and units.
- **Market potential:** Industry trends, company trends, demand trends.

The Market

- **Who and where is the market:** How was market segmented, how can it be segmented, what are consumer needs, attitudes, and characteristics? How, why, when, where do consumers buy?
- **Past advertising appeals:** Successful or unsuccessful.
- **Who are our customers:** Past and future? What characteristics do they have in common? What do they like about our product? What don't they like?

Distribution

- **History and evaluation:** How and where product is distributed, current trend.
- **Company's relationship:** With the distribution channel and its attitudes toward product/company.
- **Past policies:** Trade advertising, deals, co-op programs.
- **Status:** Trade literature, dealer promotions, point-of-purchase displays.

Pricing Policies

- **Price history:** Trends, relationship to needs of buyers, competitive price situation.
- **Past price objectives:** Management attitudes, buyer attitudes, channel attitudes.

Competition

- **Who is the competition:** Primary, secondary, share of market, products, services, goals, attitudes. What is competition's growth history and size?
- **Strengths and competition:** Sales features, product quality, size. Weaknesses of competition.
- **Marketing activities of competition:** Advertising, promotion, distribution, sales force. Estimated budget.

Promotion

- **Successes and failures:** Past promotion policy, sales force, advertising, publicity.
- **Promotion expenditures:** History, budget emphasis, relation to competition, trend.
- **Advertising programs:** Review of strategies, themes, campaigns.
- **Sales force:** Size, scope, ability, cost/sale.

positioning The association of a brand's features and benefits with a particular set of customer needs, clearly differentiating it from the competition in the mind of the customer.

(3) developing an appropriate marketing mix for each target market. A company's marketing strategy has a dramatic impact on its advertising. It determines the role and amount of advertising in the marketing mix, its creative thrust, and the media to be employed.

Defining the target market. In top-down marketing, the first step in strategy development is to define and select the target market, using the processes of market segmentation and research discussed in Chapters 4 and 6.

When Joe Coulombe thought about how to design and stock his Trader Joe's stores, he considered his target market first. He wanted to attract well-educated, adventurous, highly particular shoppers. Because this group is more likely to travel and try new delicacies, he wanted to stock his store with unusual foods and wines. And he wanted the store experience to be a somewhat exotic one.

Mountain Dew defines its target market as active, young people in their teens as well as young adults 20 to 39 years old. In addition, the brand aims a significant portion of its marketing activities at urban youth, especially African Americans and Latinos.[10] To Mountain Dew, its prototypical consumer is an 18-year-old, street-smart, male teen.[11]

Positioning the product. Famed researcher and copywriter David Ogilvy said one of the first decisions in advertising is also the most important: how to position the product. **Positioning** refers to the place a brand occupies competitively in the minds of consumers. Every product has some position—whether intended or not—even if the position is "nowhere." Positions are based on consumer perceptions, which may or may not reflect reality. Strong brands have a clear, often unique position in the target market. Ogilvy & Mather, for example, differentiated Dove soap in 1957 by positioning it as a complexion bar for women with dry skin. Now, a half-century later, Dove is still the beauty bar with one-fourth moisturizing cream and is consistently the number one brand, with a 24 percent share of the multibillion-dollar bar soap market, nearly double the share of its closest competitor.

Positions are always available in a market. The big mistake many companies make is not staking out any position. They can't be everything; but they don't want to be nothing.[12] A company might pick a position similar to a competitor's and fight for the same customers. Or it might find a position not held by a competitor—a niche in the market—and fill it quickly, perhaps through product differentiation or market segmentation.

The photography and the copy in this print ad communicate that Chevrolet has a clear definition of the target market for its Chevy Spark.

Positioning helps differentiate products from the competition. In the crowded detergent category, Procter & Gamble has clearly positioned this Tide product as an alternative to using bleach. When a consumer wants to get clothes white without bleach, this is the product that should come to mind.

> EVERY PRODUCT HAS SOME POSITION—WHETHER INTENDED OR NOT.

One scholar proposes seven distinct approaches to developing a positioning strategy:

1. *Product attribute*—setting the brand apart by stressing a particular product feature important to consumers.
2. *Price/quality*—positioning on the basis of price or quality.
3. *Use/application*—positioning on the basis of how a product is used (e.g., Arm & Hammer).
4. *Product class*—positioning the brand against other products that, while not the same, offer the same class of benefits.
5. *Product user*—positioning against the particular group who uses the product.
6. *Product competitor*—positioning against competitors (e.g., Avis/Hertz), using the strength of the competitor's position to help define the subject brand.

Developing a Brand Strategy [7–B]

Jack Trout and Al Ries's *Marketing Warfare* is based on the classic book of military strategy, *On War*, written by Prussian general Carl von Clausewitz and published in 1832. The book outlines the principles behind all successful wars, and two simple ideas dominate: *force* and *the superiority of the defense.* Consider their strategic insights as you help develop your client's campaign.

The Strategic Square

How do the principles of warfare apply to marketing? It comes down to the "strategic square":

Out of every 100 companies:
One should play defense.
Two should play offense.
Three should flank.
And 94 should be guerrillas.

Defensive Warfare

Datril opened its war on Tylenol with a price attack. Johnson & Johnson immediately cut Tylenol's price, even before Datril started its price advertising. Result: It repelled the Datril attacks and inflicted heavy losses on the Bristol-Myers entry.

Here are the rules for defensive marketing warfare:

1. Participate only if you are a market leader.
2. Introduce new products and services before the competition does.
3. Block strong competitive moves by copying them rapidly.

Offensive Warfare

Colgate had a strong number one position in toothpaste. But rival Procter & Gamble knew a thing or two about Carl von Clausewitz.

P&G launched Crest toothpaste with not only a massive $20 million advertising budget, but also the American Dental Association "seal of approval." Crest went over the top to become the best-selling toothpaste in the country.

But overtaking the leader is not that common. Most companies are happy if they can establish a profitable number two position.

The rules for waging offensive marketing warfare are:

1. Consider the strength of the leader's position.
2. Launch the attack on as narrow a front as possible, preferably with single products.
3. Launch the attack at the leader's weakest position.

Flanking Warfare

The third type of marketing warfare is where the action is for many companies. In practice, it means launching products where there is no competition. Unilever introduced Mentadent, the first baking soda/peroxide toothpaste, which became a very successful brand.

Here are the principles of flanking marketing warfare:

1. Make good flanking moves into uncontested areas.
2. Use surprise. Too much research often wastes precious time.
3. Keep up the pursuit; too many companies quit after they're ahead.

Guerrilla Warfare

Most of America's companies should be waging guerrilla warfare. The key to success in guerrilla wars is flexibility. A guerrilla should abandon any product or market if the tide of battle changes.

Here are the principles of guerrilla marketing warfare:

1. Find a market segment small enough to defend.
2. No matter how successful you become, never act like the leader.
3. Be prepared to "bug out" at a moment's notice.

Bottom Up

Trout and Ries's later book, *Bottom-Up Marketing* (discussed later in this chapter), continues the military analogy.

"Deep penetration on a narrow front is the key to winning a marketing war," they say. By this they mean that smaller companies should keep their product narrowly focused on a single concept. Many companies spread their forces over too wide a front. In fact, most large corporations today expend significant resources fending off focused attacks by smaller companies.

product life cycle Progressive stages in the life of a product—including introduction, growth, maturity, and decline—that affect the way a product is marketed and advertised.

stakeholders In relationship marketing, customers, employees, centers of influence, stockholders, the financial community, and the press. Different stakeholders require different types of relationships.

tactics The specific short-term actions that will be used to achieve marketing objectives.

bottom-up marketing The opposite of standard, top-down marketing planning, bottom-up marketing focuses on one specific tactic and develops it into an overall strategy.

relationship marketing Creating, maintaining, and enhancing long-term relationships with customers and other stakeholders that result in exchanges of information and other things of mutual value.

value The ratio of perceived benefits to the price of the product.

7. *Cultural symbol*—positioning apart from competitors through the creation or use of some recognized symbol or icon.[13]

We add an eighth approach: *By category*—positioning by defining or redefining a business category. A simple way for a company to get the number one position is to invent a new product category.

Xerox, for example, was originally known as *the* copier company, but with increased competition, the copier market became glutted, so Xerox tried to reposition itself as a problem solver. Now calling itself "The Document Company," it offers to use technology to find ways for everyone in an organization to manage and share useful information. But what it has really done is create a new business category occupied by one company: Xerox.[14]

With all its high energy and exhilaration, "youth" is not only the positioning of Mountain Dew; it's the heartbeat of the brand.[15] PepsiCo positions Dew this way:

> To 18-year-old males who embrace excitement, adventure, and fun, Mountain Dew is the great-tasting soft drink that exhilarates like no other because it is energizing, thirst quenching, and has a unique citrus flavor.

Often, a product's positioning can be discerned from its advertising tagline—*BMW, the ultimate driving machine; Nobody doesn't like Sara Lee; You're in good hands with Allstate; Do the Dew.*

Determining the marketing mix. The next step in developing the marketing strategy is determining a cost-effective marketing mix for *each* target market. The mix blends the various marketing elements the company controls: *product, price, distribution,* and *communications.*

Mountain Dew is blessed with a broad marketing toolbox to draw upon. First, it offers consumers an energizing, thirst-quenching soft-drink *product* with a unique citrus flavor and an image of youthful exuberance, exhilaration, and adventure. To build *distribution,* it uses a variety of promotions to the trade that enable grocers and other resellers to increase both volume and profits. While its *price* is competitive with other soft drinks, Mountain Dew promotes itself aggressively with free samples, premiums, and prizes at various street and sporting events—which effectively lowers the price to consumers.

Strong brands have a clear and consistent positioning, often evident in their advertising taglines. BMW (www.bmw.com) has been advertised as "The Ultimate Driving Machine" since 1973.

Finally, Mountain Dew uses an integrated *communications* program that includes advertising on the Internet; sports and event sponsorships; appearances at grass-roots geographic events; plus a host of public relations activities—all designed to develop and promote the distinct Mountain Dew personality.

Companies have many marketing strategy options. They might increase distribution, initiate new uses for a product, change a product line, develop entirely new markets, or lower prices. Each option emphasizes one or more marketing mix elements. The choice depends on the product's target market, its position in the market, and its stage in the **product life cycle**, the progression of growth and decline through which a successful product typically moves.

Marketing Tactics (Action Programs)

A company's objectives indicate where it wants to go; the strategy indicates the intended route; and the **tactics** (or *action programs*) determine the specific short-term actions to be taken, internally and externally, by whom, and when. In 2009–2010, Mountain Dew blazed new trails with exciting tactics that included a "Dewmocracy" campaign in which consumers chose three new flavors to be distributed nationwide. Fans used the brand's Facebook site to vote online for their favorite, which became a permanent flavor of Dew. Advertising campaigns live in the world of marketing tactics. These tactics are the key to *bottom-up marketing.*

Bottom-Up Marketing: How Small Companies Plan

In small companies, everybody is both player and coach, and the day-to-day details seem to come first, leaving little or no time for formal planning. However, there is a solution to this dilemma: **bottom-up marketing** (see Exhibit 7–2).

EXHIBIT 7-2 Bottom-up marketing plan.

An excellent way for a company to develop a competitive advantage is to focus on an ingenious tactic first and then develop that tactic into a strategy. By reversing the normal process, advertisers sometimes make important discoveries.[16] Vicks developed an effective liquid cold remedy but discovered that it put people to sleep. Rather than throw out the research, Vicks positioned the formula as a nighttime cold remedy. NyQuil went on to become the most successful new product in Vicks's history.

The *tactic* is a singular, competitive technique. By planning from the bottom up, entrepreneurs can find unique tactics to exploit. But caution is required. Advertisers should find just *one* tactic, not two or three. The advertiser can then focus all elements of the marketing mix on this single-minded tactic. The tactic becomes the nail, and the strategy is the hammer that drives it home.

The artful combination of tactic and strategy creates a position in the consumer's mind. When Tom Monaghan thought of the tactic of delivering pizza to customers' homes, he focused his whole strategy on that singular idea. He ended up making a fortune and marketing history with Domino's Pizza.

Managers of small companies have an advantage here. Surrounded by the details of the business, they are more likely to discover a good tactic that can be developed into a powerful strategy. However, that's not to say that a large company cannot profit from bottom-up marketing. Many have, like 3M with its Post-it notes.

THE IMPORTANCE OF RELATIONSHIP MARKETING

Most marketers know that the key to building brand equity in the twenty-first century is to develop interdependent, mutually satisfying relationships with customers.

A market-driven firm's overriding purpose is to create happy, loyal customers. Customers, not products, are the lifeblood of the business.[17] This realization has moved firms away from simple *transactional marketing* to **relationship marketing**—creating, maintaining, and enhancing long-term relationships with customers and other stakeholders that result in exchanges of information and other things of mutual value.[18]

Today's affluent, sophisticated consumers can choose from a wide variety of products and services offered by producers located around the world. As a result, the customer relationship—in which the sale is only the beginning—is the key strategic resource of the successful twenty-first-century business.[19] As one commentator notes: "The new *market-driven conception* of marketing will focus on *managing strategic partnerships* and positioning the firm between vendors and customers in the value chain with the aim of delivering *superior value* to the customer."[20]

Value is the ratio of *perceived benefits* to the price of the product.[21]

The Importance of Relationships

To succeed, companies must focus on managing loyalty among customers and **stakeholders** (employees, centers of influence,

Some airlines run ads that talk to business travelers.
We're running an ad that says

WE LISTEN

to them.

1. INTRODUCING A WHOLE NEW, BETTER BOARDING PROCESS
It's a calmer, more relaxed way to board. There is no need to line up early because your boarding pass number holds your place in line. So you are free to work, relax, or do whatever.

2. INTRODUCING SOUTHWEST AIRLINES® BUSINESS SELECT
You deserve Southwest Airlines Business Select. For just a little extra, you can be part of the select group that's guaranteed to be one of the first to board and get a free drink and extra Rapid Rewards® credit. Plus, your fare is fully refundable.

3. INTRODUCING MORE NONSTOP FLIGHTS FOR YOUR NONSTOP BUSINESS
Fly long without the stops. Southwest offers over 3,400 daily nonstop flights, which lets you fly nonstop to more places you do business.

SOUTHWEST.COM®

Relationship marketing means companies don't just talk. They listen. Southwest uses this ad to let its customers know that their opinions matter.

A War of Comparisons

Which brand of cola tastes best, Coke or Pepsi? In the 1980s, each company advertised that its brand was preferred in blind taste tests. And which company, Pizza Hut or Papa John's, has the best ingredients? Not surprisingly, both thought their own brands did, and they said so in ads.

Comparative advertising, a technique where one company explicitly compares its brand to another in an effort to gain a competitive edge, was actually endorsed by the Federal Trade Commission in the 1970s "as a means of improving competition." Since its inception into the advertising world, comparative advertising has turned out to be a bit of a double-edged sword.

Ideally, comparative advertising should provide consumers with more information about competing products, thereby allowing them to make better-informed purchase decisions. However, research indicates that direct product comparisons often create greater awareness for the lesser-known brand, and that has been directly linked to a decline in sales for the more established brand, since at the point of purchase the consumer often confuses the two.

When taken too far, comparative advertising can be illegal. If an ad's comparisons are shown to be false, deceptive, or deliberately misleading, the campaign may result in litigation. Even ads that are literally correct can be found liable. According to one court, "innuendo, indirect intimations, and ambiguous suggestions" can unjustly injure a competitor. McNeil Consumer Products's Extra-Strength Tylenol, for example, successfully sued American Home Products's Maximum Strength Anacin even though Anacin's ad was literally true. Anacin had implied superiority over Tylenol when in fact both products contain the same amount of pain reliever.

A further complication arises when advertisers manipulate comparisons to cast a more favorable light on their products. In Australia, Duracell ran an ad showing a bunny powered by a Duracell battery outracing one powered by an Energizer battery. What Duracell neglected to mention in the ad was that it was comparing its top-of-the-line alkaline battery to one of Energizer's midrange carbon zinc batteries—apples and oranges in the world of batteries. Energizer took the unfair comparison to court, and Duracell had to add clarifying text to its ad before it could put it back on the air.

Papa John's attacks Pizza Hut, Visa attacks American Express, and Jack in the Box and Burger King taunt McDonald's. Name-calling, finger pointing, and insulting the competition are all contemporary weapons used in the marketing wars waged between virtually identical brands, which are desperate to stand apart from the competition.

Some researchers estimate that 40 percent of all advertising in the United States is now comparative, whereas in most of the world it is either illegal or strictly regulated.

To keep comparison battles from getting out of hand, numerous groups, including the American Association of Advertising Agencies, the National Association of Broadcasters, and the FTC, issued guidelines for comparative advertising that are often stricter than current laws. TV network NBC, for example, insists that "advertisers shall refrain from discrediting, disparaging, or unfairly attacking competitors, competing products, or other industries."

This is a good step, but the legal language governing comparisons is vague, allowing for a blurry line between healthy one-upmanship and illegal behavior. As competition continues to increase, and ethical and legal guidelines remain ambiguous, the public will no doubt continue to be bombarded by comparative ads. The responsibility, therefore, will continue to fall on consumers to sift through the ads and differentiate fact from fiction.

Questions

1. How do you feel about ads that compare the features and benefits of competitive products and services? Do you believe they are unethical even if the comparisons are honest? Should they be allowed? Why or why not?
2. Select a comparative ad and study the copy. What points of comparison does the ad make? Are the points made honestly and directly, or are they masked by innuendo and implication? Is the ad literally true but still potentially misleading? Do you feel the ad is ethical or not?

stockholders, the financial community, and the press).[22] This is important for a number of reasons:

1. *The cost of lost customers.* No amount of advertising is likely to win back a customer lost from shoddy products or poor service. The real profit lost is the **lifetime customer value (LCV)** of a customer to a firm. For example, the average customer of one major transportation firm represented a lifetime value of $40,000. The company had 64,000 accounts and lost 5 percent of them due to poor service. That amounted to an unnecessary loss of $128 million in revenue and $12 million in profits![23] Moreover, negative word of mouth can have a terrible snowballing effect. Imagine if one lost customer influences only one other customer to not patronize the business. That immediately doubles the LCV loss. Negative word of mouth is why bad movies disappear so quickly from theaters.
2. *The cost of acquiring new customers.* Defensive marketing typically costs less than offensive marketing because it is hard to lure satisfied customers away from competitors.[24] The fragmentation of media audiences and the resistance of sophisticated consumers to advertising messages make it increasingly difficult to succeed merely by stepping up the advertising volume.[25] In fact, it costs five to eight times as much in marketing, advertising, and promotion to acquire a new customer as it does to keep an existing one.[26]
3. *The value of loyal customers.* Direct-response expert Lester Wunderman says that 90 percent of a manufacturer's profit comes from repeat purchasers; only 10 percent comes from trial or sporadic purchasers.[27] Reducing customer defections by even 5 percent can improve profit potential by 25 to 85 percent.[28] And long-term customers are more willing to pay

lifetime customer value (LCV) The total sales or profit value of a customer to a marketer over the course of that customer's lifetime.

[No amount of advertising is likely to win back a customer lost from shoddy products.]

premium prices, make referrals, increase their annual buying, and demand less hand-holding.[29]

So a company's first market should always be its current customers. In the past, most marketing and advertising effort focused on *presale* activities aimed at acquiring new customers. Now sophisticated marketers shift more of their resources to *postsale* activities, making customer retention their first priority. They have discovered an important benefit of focusing on relationships: increasing retention and optimizing lifetime customer value.[30]

Levels of Relationships

Kotler and Armstrong distinguish five levels of relationships that can be formed between a company and its various stakeholders, depending on their mutual needs:

- *Basic transactional relationship.* The company sells the product but does not follow up in any way (Target).
- *Reactive relationship.* The company sells the product and encourages customers to call if they encounter any problems (Men's Wearhouse).
- *Accountable relationship.* The company phones customers shortly after the sale to check whether the product meets expectations and asks for product improvement suggestions and any specific disappointments. This information helps the company to continuously improve its offering (Acura dealers).
- *Proactive relationship.* The company contacts customers from time to time with suggestions about improved product use or helpful new products (Apple).
- *Partnership.* The company works continuously with customers (and other stakeholders) to discover ways to deliver better value (Nordstrom's Personal Shopper).[31]

Different stakeholders require different types of relationships. The relationship a company seeks with a customer will rarely be the same as it seeks with the press. However, there is often significant overlap in stakeholder roles. An employee may also be a customer and own stock in the company. Knowing intimately the customers and stakeholders is critical to the success of relationship marketing.

The number of stakeholders is also important. The more there are, the more difficult it can be to develop an extensive personal relationship with each. Moreover, some customers may not want anything more than a transactional relationship.[32] Most people wouldn't want a phone call from Oscar Mayer asking if the hot dogs tasted good or from Gillette asking about the smoothness of their last shave. However, when some Toyota models were accused of dangerous defects in 2010, the company contacted each existing car owner with a letter explaining the situation and telling the owner what, if anything, Toyota should do to ensure the car's safety. Toyota knew that some customers were likely to believe their relationship with the brand had been violated. Clearly, therefore, brand relationships can be psychological or symbolic as well as personal, and they can be created by brand promotion, publicity, and advertising as well as by people.

Mountain Dew considers that an important aspect of its brand relationship with its customers involves the "Dew-x-perience." Using guerrilla marketing tactics to reach out to urban youth, it employs a variety of hip-hop and Latin recording artists in various "street marketing" efforts to distribute bottles of Dew. It also sponsors extreme athletes and appears at sporting events

The SWOT Analysis [7–C]

Your situation analysis lays the factual groundwork. Now use this groundwork to recognize weaknesses and threats and to take advantage of strengths and opportunities. Use the grid below to organize your analysis.

	Facilitators of Success	Barriers to Success
Internal factors (brand or company attributes)	Strengths	Weaknesses
External factors (legal, competitive, societal, cultural factors)	Opportunities	Threats

Examples (using a fictitious American automobile company)

- Strengths: Made in the USA, classic heritage, improved reliability, new environmentally friendly models ready for production.
- Weaknesses: More expensive to manufacture than many imports in the same class, inefficient distribution network, smaller ad budget than the competition, high levels of unsold inventory.
- Opportunities: Cultural shift to more environmentally friendly products, weak dollar makes imports more expensive.
- Threats: Americans' concerns about U.S. auto industry, economic recession.

▼EXHIBIT 7–3 Relationship levels as a function of profit margin and number of customers.

Number of customers	Profit margins: High	Medium	Low
Many	Accountable	Reactive	Basic
Medium	Proactive	Accountable	Basic
Few	Partnership	Accountable	Reactive

such as the Gravity Games and ESPN's X Games with vans full of merchandise and giveaways.[33]

The final consideration is the profit margin. High-profit product or service categories make deeper, personal relationships more desirable (see Exhibit 7–3). Low profit margins per customer suggest that the marketer should pursue basic transactional relationships augmented by brand image advertising.[34]

check yourself ✓

1. What is the difference between an objective, a strategy, and a tactic?
2. What distinguishes a need-satisfying objective and sales-target objective?
3. How can small companies use bottom-up marketing to become big companies?

LO7-3 Show what makes IMC planning different from traditional methods.

USING IMC TO MAKE RELATIONSHIPS WORK

This interest in relationship marketing coincided with the interest in *integrated marketing communications (IMC)*. In fact, according to Northwestern professor Don Schultz, IMC is what makes relationship marketing possible.[35]

IMC: The Concept and the Process

Technology allows marketers to adopt flexible manufacturing, customizing products for different markets. Being "market driven" means bundling services together with products to create a "unique product experience." It means companies and customers working together to find solutions.[36]

The counterpart to flexible manufacturing is flexible marketing—and integrated marketing communications—to reach customers at different levels in new and better ways.

The *concept* of integration is *wholeness*. Achieving this wholeness in communications creates **synergy**—the principal benefit of IMC—because each product message reinforces the others for greater effect.[37]

For example, when a Mountain Dew grocer runs an **endcap promotion** (a special display at the end of an aisle) alone, it might generate a 10 percent increase in volume. If he runs an ad for Dew with a coupon, that might deliver a 15 percent increase. But running both together might grow volume by 35 percent. That's synergy—the whole is greater than the sum of its parts.

Tom Duncan, IMC expert, points out that IMC is also a *process* in which communication becomes the driving, integrating force in the marketing mix and throughout the organization.

The Evolution of the IMC Concept Glen Nowack and Joe Phelps, advertising professors from the Universities of Georgia and Alabama, argue that IMC has developed as a consequence of several important trends, including escalating media costs, splintering consumer markets, and skepticism about traditional mass media advertising. These have led marketers to question the wisdom of creating walls between disciplines such as public relations, direct-response advertising, and sales promotion.[38]

Many companies initially took a narrow, *inside-out* view of IMC. They saw it as a way to coordinate and manage their marketing communications (advertising, sales promotion, public relations, personal selling, and direct marketing) to give the audience a consistent message about the company.[39] The coordination of these communications elements is certainly important and we will examine them more closely in Chapters 15 and 16.

But a broader, more sophisticated, *outside-in* perspective of IMC sees customers as partners in an ongoing relationship, recognizes the terminology they use, acknowledges the importance of the whole communications system, and accepts the many ways they come into contact with the company or the brand. Companies committed to IMC realize their biggest asset

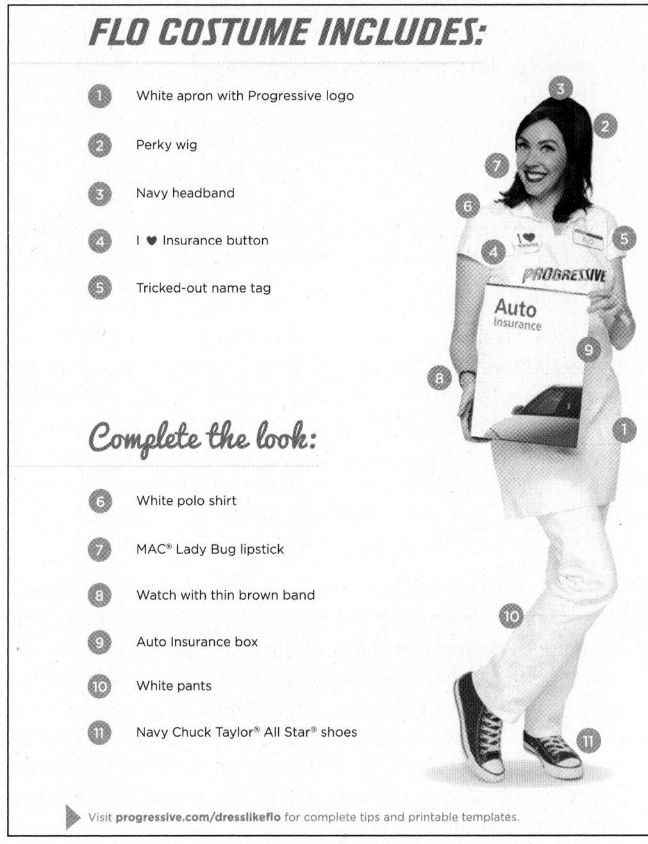

For many customers, having a relationship with an insurance company seems difficult at best. But Progressive makes it happen by personalizing the brand through the fictional character "Flo," The popularity of the character is reflected in this ad, running around Halloween, which encourages fans to dress like the spokeswoman.

> "The *concept* of integration is *wholeness*. Achieving this wholeness in communications creates synergy."

is not their products or their factories or even their employees, but their customers.[40] Defined broadly:

> **Integrated marketing communications (IMC)** is the process of building and reinforcing mutually profitable relationships with employees, customers, other stakeholders, and the general public by developing and coordinating a strategic communications program that enables them to have a constructive encounter with the company/brand through a variety of media or other contacts.

Whether a company employs the narrow view or the broad view depends to a great extent on its corporate culture. Some companies enjoyed rapid growth and strong customer relationships because they intuitively integrated and focused all corporate and marketing activities. Apple, Honda, Nike, and Banana Republic are just a few. Consider the success for Nike +, a social networking website where runners can meet and share observations with other runners.

How the Customer Sees Marketing Communications To truly understand IMC, we have to look through the customer's eyes. In one study, consumers identified 102 different media as "advertising"—everything from TV to shopping bags to sponsored community events.[41] Customers also develop perceptions of the company or brand through a variety of other sources: news reports, word of mouth, gossip, experts' opinions, financial reports, and even the CEO's personality.

All these communications or brand contacts, sponsored or not, create an *integrated product* in the consumer's mind.[42] In other words, customers automatically integrate all the brand-related messages that emanate from the company or some other source. The way they integrate those messages determines their perception of the company. IMC gives companies a better opportunity to manage or influence those perceptions and create a superior relationship with those stakeholders.

The Four Sources of Brand Messages The company that embraces IMC accepts the idea that *everything we do (and don't do) sends a message.* That is to say, every corporate activity has a message component. Duncan categorized four types of company/brand-related messages stakeholders receive: *planned, product, service,* and *unplanned.* Each of these influences a stakeholder's relationship decision, so marketers must know where these messages originate, what effect they have, and the costs to influence or control them.

synergy An effect achieved when the sum of the parts is greater than that expected from simply adding together the individual components.

endcap promotion A merchandising method that uses special displays on shelving at the end of aisles in a store.

Integrated marketing communications (IMC) The process of building and reinforcing mutually profitable relationships with employees, customers, other stakeholders, and the general public by developing and coordinating a strategic communications program that enables them to make consecutive contact with the company/brand through a variety of media.

> The company that embraces IMC accepts the premise that *everything we do . . . sends a message.*

1. **Planned messages**. These are the traditional marketing communication messages—advertising, sales promotions, personal selling, merchandising materials, publicity releases, event sponsorships. These often have the *least* impact because they are seen as self-serving. Planned messages should be coordinated to work toward a predetermined set of communications objectives. This is the most fundamental aspect of (inside-out) IMC.
2. **Product messages**. In IMC theory, every element of the marketing mix (not just promotion) sends a message. Messages from the product, price, or distribution elements are typically referred to as product messages. For example, customers and other stakeholders receive one product message from a $6,500 Rolex watch and a totally different one from a $30 Timex. Product messages also include packaging, which communicates a lot about the product through the use of color, type fonts, imagery, design, and layout.

   Product messages have great impact. When a product (or service) performs well, the customer infers a positive message that reinforces the purchase decision. However, a gap between the product's performance and advertised promises is likely to convey a negative message. Managers must realize that all marketing mix decisions are also communication decisions.
3. **Service messages**. Many messages result from employee interactions with customers. In many organizations, customer service people are supervised by operations, not marketing. Yet the service messages they send have greater marketing impact than the planned messages. Luxury brands like Nordstrom and Lexus believe great service is part of their brands' DNA. With IMC, marketing people work with operations to minimize negative messages and maximize positive ones.
4. **Unplanned messages**. Companies have little or no control over the unplanned messages that emanate from employee gossip, unsought news stories, comments by the trade or competitors, social media posts, or major disasters. When Walmart created a Facebook page, many of the initial fans criticized the company's policies. Unplanned messages may affect customers' attitudes dramatically, but they can sometimes be anticipated and influenced, especially by managers experienced in the online world.[43]

IMC is about more than communicating with customers, it is about engaging them and building relationships. Mountain Dew engages its users at its "Dewmocracy" website, where it allows them to vote on new products, colors, packaging, and even advertising campaigns.

planned messages Traditional marketing communications messages, including advertising, sales promotion, publicity, and personal selling. These messages have the least impact because they are seen as self-serving.

product messages Messages communicated by a product, its packaging, price, or distribution elements.

service messages Messages resulting from employee interactions with customers. These messages typically have greater impact than planned messages.

unplanned messages Messages that emanate from gossip, unsought news stories, rumors, or major disasters. Companies have little control over unplanned messages, but the messages can dramatically affect customers' attitudes.

EXHIBIT 7–4 The integration triangle.

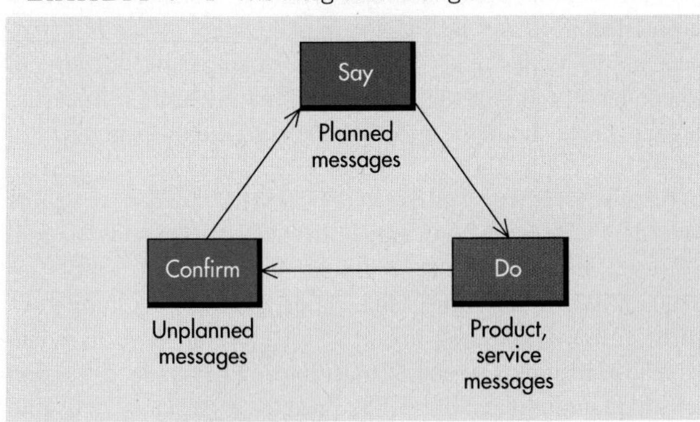

The Integration Triangle The integration triangle is a simple illustration of how perceptions are created from the various brand message sources (see Exhibit 7–4). Planned messages are *say* messages, what companies say about themselves. Product and service messages are *do* messages because they represent what a company does. Unplanned messages are *confirm* messages because that's what others say and confirm (or not) about what the company says and does. Constructive integration occurs when a brand does what its maker says it will do and then others confirm that it delivers on its promises.[44]

The Dimensions of IMC

To maximize the synergy benefits of IMC, Duncan suggests three dimensions to an organization's integration process. It should first ensure consistent positioning, then facilitate interactions between the company and its customers or other stakeholders, and finally actively incorporate a socially responsible mission into the organization's relationships with its stakeholders.

Duncan's IMC model shows that cross-functional planning and monitoring of IMC activities results in an enhanced relationship with customers and other stakeholders, which leads to stakeholder loyalty and ultimately to greater brand equity.[45]

The interest in IMC is global.[46] The $88 billion Swiss company Nestlé, for example, uses a variety of IMC strategies, such as building highway rest stops for feeding and changing babies, designed to establish deep, caring relationships between families and the Nestlé Baby Foods division in France.[47]

In short, IMC offers accountability by maximizing resources and linking communications activities directly to organizational goals and the resulting bottom line.[48]

The IMC Approach to Marketing and Advertising Planning

For many companies, IMC is now the standard approach to planning marketing and communications activities. Marketing and communications planning are done together. Using the outside-in process, the IMC approach starts with the customer. Marketers determine which media customers use, the relevance of their message to the customers, and when customers and prospects are most *receptive* to the message. They begin with the customer and work back to the brand.[49]

Marketers now have a wealth of information at their fingertips. With supermarket scanner data, for instance, packaged-goods marketers can (1) identify specific users of products and services; (2) measure their actual purchase behavior and relate it to specific brand and product categories; (3) measure the impact of various advertising and marketing communications activities and determine their value in influencing the actual purchase; and (4) capture and evaluate this information over time.[50] The Internet is another place that marketers can glean a wealth of information about their customers. In 2013 Mountain Dew replaced several different websites and a YouTube channel with a new content marketing site called Green-Label.com. The initiative is part of the broader emphasis on digital advertising for the brand.

A database of customer behavior can be the basis for planning future marketing and communications activities, especially if the database contains information on customer demographics, psychographics, purchase data, and attitudes.

Starting the planning process with a database forces the company to focus on the consumer, or prospect, not on sales or profit goals. Communications objectives and strategies are established for making contact with the consumer and influencing his or her attitudes, beliefs, and purchase behavior. The marketer then decides what other elements of the marketing mix (product, price, distribution) can be used to further encourage the desired behavior. Finally, the planner determines what communications tactics to use—media advertising, social media, publicity, sales promotion, special events. All forms of marketing are thus turned into communication, and all forms of communication into marketing.[51]

The Importance of IMC to Advertising

Because customers see all sponsored communications as advertising, advertising people (account managers, creatives, media planners) must grow beyond their traditional specialty to become enlightened generalists, familiar with and able to integrate all types of marketing communications. In a survey of 122 *Fortune* 500 marketing, advertising, and communications executives, most indicated a general understanding of IMC and agreed that synergy is the key benefit of integrated marketing.[52]

THE ADVERTISING PLAN

The **advertising plan** is a natural outgrowth of the marketing plan and is prepared in much the same way. It picks up where the marketing plan leaves off, building on the goals that have been established for the advertising program. Those goals are translated into specific advertising objectives, from which creative and media strategies are developed. The advertising plan typically also incorporates the rationale for a proposed budget and a plan for conducting research.

check yourself ✓

1. What is synergy and how is it created by IMC?
2. What factors do Phelps and Nowack suggest have led to the development of IMC?
3. What are the four types of brand messages identified by Duncan?

Reviewing the Marketing Plan

The advertising manager first reviews the marketing plan to understand where the company wants to go, how it intends to get there, and what role advertising plays in the marketing mix. The first section of the advertising plan should organize information from the marketing plan's situation analysis into a SWOT analysis.

For example, McDonald's restaurants' *strengths* include its strong name identity and thousands of retail locations. However, the company's *weaknesses* include a menu loaded with unhealthy food choices and an image to match. McDonald's is now taking advantage of an *opportunity* to capitalize on nutritious food trends by promoting healthier menu items and a fresh, new image. The company's upscale coffees distinguish it from its fast-food competitors and enable it to draw traffic from Starbucks. In doing so, it is combating *threats* from competitive restaurants and posting impressive sales gains.

LO7-4 Relate how to establish specific, realistic, and measurable advertising objectives.

Setting Advertising Objectives

Based on the marketing plan, the advertising manager determines what tasks advertising must take on. What strengths and opportunities can be leveraged? What weaknesses and threats need to be addressed? Unfortunately, some corporate executives (and advertising managers) state vague goals for advertising, like "increase sales and maximize profits by creating a favorable impression of the product in the marketplace." When this happens, no one understands what the advertising is intended to do, how much it will cost, or how to measure the results. Advertising objectives should be specific, realistic, and measurable.

Understanding What Advertising Can Do Most advertising programs encourage prospects to take some action. However, it is unrealistic to assign advertising the whole responsibility for achieving sales. Sales goals are marketing objectives, not advertising objectives. Before an advertiser can persuade customers to buy, it must inform, persuade, or remind its intended audience about the product or service. A simple adage to remember when setting objectives is "Marketing sells, advertising tells." In other words, advertising objectives should be related to communication outcomes.

The Advertising Pyramid: A Guide to Setting Objectives Suppose you're advertising a new brand in a new product category, but you're not sure what kind of results to expect. The pyramid in Exhibit 7–5 shows some of the tasks advertising can perform. Obviously, before your product is introduced, prospective customers are completely unaware of it. Your

▾**EXHIBIT 7-5** The advertising pyramid depicts the progression of advertising effects on mass audiences—especially for new products. The initial message promotes *awareness* of the product to a large audience (the base of the pyramid). But only a percentage of this large group will *comprehend* the product's benefits. Of that group, even fewer will go on to feel *conviction* about, then *desire* for the product. In the end, compared with the number of people aware of the product, the number of people who take *action* is usually quite small.

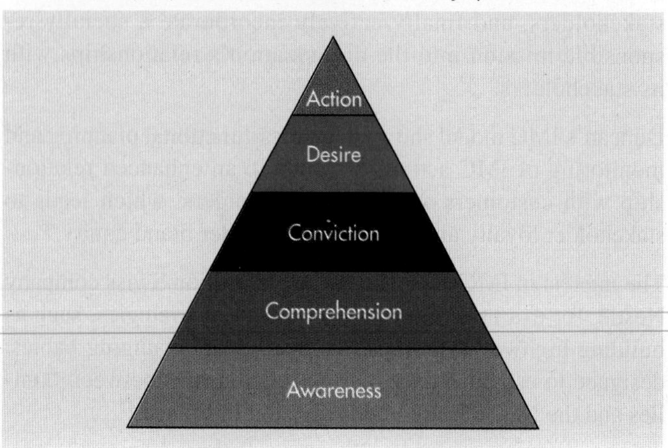

Advertising cannot be assigned full responsibility for a product's success or failure. In 2003, Heinz (www.heinz.com) launched a major ad campaign to introduce new varieties, like its hot ketchup. This campaign, from Leo Burnett's Lisbon office, attracted critical acclaim and earned a Cannes Bronze Lion, but could not sustain interest in specialty condiments.

advertising plan
The plan that directs the company's advertising effort. A natural outgrowth of the marketing plan, it analyzes the situation, sets advertising objectives, and lays out a specific strategy from which ads and campaigns are created.

first communication objective therefore is to create *awareness*—to acquaint people with the company, product, service, and/or brand.

The next task might be to develop *comprehension*—to communicate enough information about the product that some percentage of the aware group will understand the product's purpose, image, or position, and perhaps some of its features.

Next, you need to communicate enough information to develop *conviction*—to persuade a certain number of people to actually believe in the product's value. Once convinced, some people may be moved to *desire* the product. Finally, some percentage of those who desire the product will take *action.* They may request additional information, send in a coupon, visit a store, or actually buy the product.

The pyramid works in three dimensions: time, dollars, and people. Advertising results may take time, especially if the product is expensive or not purchased regularly. Over time, as a company continues advertising, the number of people who become aware of the product increases. As more people comprehend the benefits of the product, believe in it, and desire it, more will take the final action of buying it.

Let's apply these principles to a hypothetical case. Suppose you are in charge of advertising for the new "Lightning Bug," an electric car built by Volkswagen. Your initial advertising objectives for this fictional car might read as follows:

1. Within two years, communicate the existence of the Lightning Bug to half of the more than 500,000 people who annually buy imported economy cars.
2. Get two-thirds of this "aware" group to comprehend that the Lightning Bug is a superior economy car with many design, safety, and environmentally friendly features; that it is a brand-new nameplate backed with unmatched service, quality, and value; and that it is sold only through dedicated Volkswagen dealers.
3. Convince two-thirds of the "comprehending" group that the Lightning Bug is a high-quality car, reliable, economical, and fun to drive.
4. Stimulate desire within two-thirds of the "convinced" group for a test drive.
5. Motivate two-thirds of the "desire" group to take action and visit a retailer for a test drive.

These advertising objectives are specific as to time and degree and are quantified like marketing objectives. Theoretically, at the end of the first year, a consumer study could determine how many people are aware of the Lightning Bug, how many people understand the car's features, and so on, thus measuring the program's effectiveness.

Volkswagen's advertising may accomplish the objectives of creating awareness, comprehension, conviction, desire, and

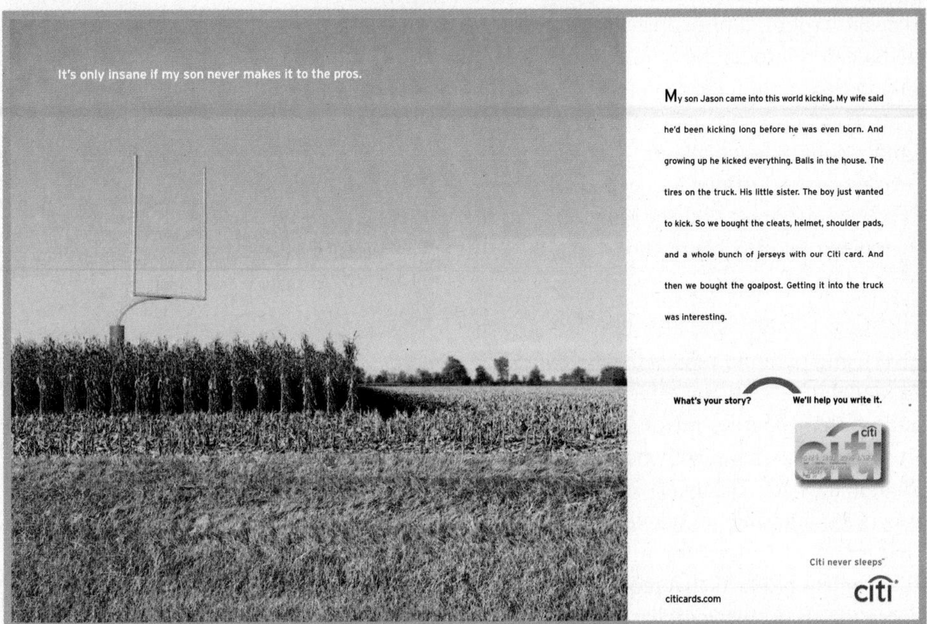

Not every ad follows the learn-feel-do approach. This ad for Citi invites readers to feel-learn-do with an evocative story about what Citi credit can provide.

advertising strategy The advertising objective declares what the advertiser wants to achieve with respect to consumer awareness, attitude, and preference. Advertising strategy describes how to get there. It consists of two substrategies: the creative strategy and the media strategy.

creative strategy A written statement that serves as the creative team's guide for writing and producing an ad.

media strategy A document that helps media planners determine how messages will be delivered to consumers. It defines the target audience, the communication objectives that must be achieved, and the characteristics of the media that will be used for delivery of the messages.

action. But once the customer is in the store, it's the retailer's responsibility to close the sale with effective selling and service.

From an IMC perspective, we can look at the pyramid in another way. By using a variety of marketing communication tools and a wide menu of traditional and nontraditional media, we can accomplish the communication objectives suggested by the pyramid in a more efficient manner. For instance, for creating sheer awareness for the new Lightning Bug as well as brand image for the car and the company, an intensive program of public relations activities supported by mass media advertising would be the communication tools of choice. Comprehension, interest, and credibility can be augmented by media advertising, press publicity, direct-mail brochures, and special events such as a sports car show. Desire can be enhanced by a combination of the buzz created by good reviews in car enthusiast magazines, plus media advertising, beautiful brochure photography, and the excitement generated by a sales promotion (such as a sweepstakes). Finally, action can be stimulated by direct-mail solicitation, sales promotion, a website where interested buyers can customize their cars, and the attentive service of a retail salesperson in an attractive showroom. Following the sale, social media can reinforce the purchase decision by linking drivers to their dealers and to one another. Facebook posts can help thank the customer, solicit feedback on that customer's experience, and offer any needed assistance. This acknowledges that the sale was just the beginning of a valuable relationship.

EXHIBIT 7–6 Messages go to the customer through advertising and other communication channels. Messages come back via direct response, surveys, social media, and purchase behavior data. The marketer's message evolves based on this feedback.

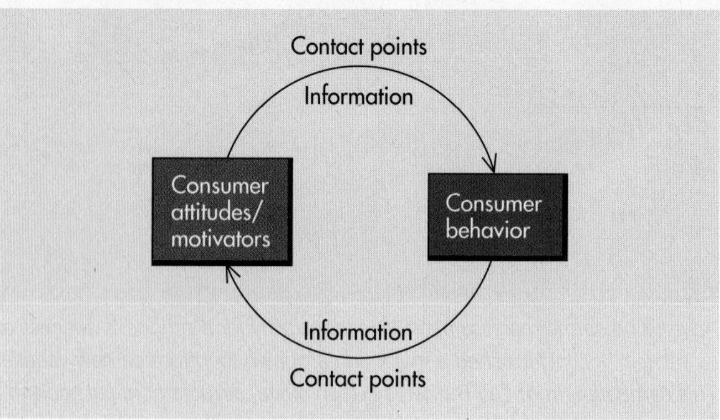

The Old Model versus the New

The advertising pyramid represents the *learn-feel-do* model of advertising effects. That is, it assumes that people rationally consider a prospective purchase, and once they feel good about it, they act. The theory is that advertising affects attitude, and attitude leads to behavior. That may be true for certain expensive, high-involvement products that require a lot of consideration. But other purchases may follow a different pattern. For example, impulse purchases at checkout may involve a *do-feel-learn* model, in which behavior leads to attitude which leads to knowledge. Other purchases may follow some other pattern. Thus, there are many marketing considerations when advertising objectives are being set, and they must be considered carefully.

The advertising pyramid also reflects the traditional mass-marketing monologue. The advertiser talks and the customer listens.[53] But today, as the IMC model shows, many marketers have databases of information on their customers—about where they live, what they buy, and what they like and dislike. When marketers can have a dialogue and establish a relationship, the model is no longer a pyramid but a circle (see Exhibit 7–6).

There are many ways to deliver a message besides using traditional media. In keeping with its theme of fun and adventure, Mountain Dew traveled around the country in a colorful subway car that was packed with all kinds of treats and memorabilia given away at key events.

> "WHEN MARKETERS ESTABLISH A RELATIONSHIP WITH CUSTOMERS, THE MODEL IS NO LONGER A PYRAMID BUT A CIRCLE. BY STARTING WITH THE CUSTOMER AND IMC, SMART, COMPANIES WORK TO ACHIEVE LASTING LOYALTY FROM GOOD PROSPECTS."

Consumers and business customers can send messages back to the marketer in the form of coupons, phone calls, surveys, and database information on purchases. With interactive media, the responses are in real time. This feedback can help the marketer's product, service, and messages evolve.[54] And reinforcement advertising, designed to build brand loyalty, will remind people of their successful experience with the product and suggest reuse.

By starting with the customer and then integrating all aspects of their marketing communications—package and store design, personal selling, advertising, public relations, special events, and sales promotions—companies can achieve lasting loyalty from *good* prospects, not just prospects.[55]

The creative strategy represents what a company wants to communicate about its product. The benefit communicated by Angie's List (www.angieslist.com) is that its reviews and ratings come from real people, not businesses. They accomplish this by saying, "Relentlessly authentic reviews from dentists to roofers to antique lamp repair written by people 'just like you.'"

check yourself ✓

1. What are the limits on what advertising can do and how do these affect setting ad objectives?
2. What is the advertising pyramid?
3. How does setting objectives under an IMC approach differ from that under the advertising pyramid?

Determining the Advertising Strategy

The advertising *objective* declares what the advertiser wants to achieve with respect to consumer awareness, attitude, and preference; the advertising *strategy* describes how to get there. **Advertising strategy** consists of two substrategies: the creative strategy and the media strategy.

The **creative strategy** is a guide for those developing the advertising. At a minimum, the creative strategy defines the *target audience,* restates the *objective* of the advertising, specifies the key *benefits* to be communicated, and offers *support* for those benefits. We discuss the development of the creative strategy in Chapter 8.

The **media strategy** provides direction to the media planners. It defines the communication objectives that must be achieved and then describes how these will be accomplished through the use of media vehicles. The media planning process is covered in Chapter 14.

LO7-5 List the various approaches for determining advertising budgets.

Allocating Funds for Advertising

The Internal Revenue Service considers advertising a current business expense. Consequently, many executives treat advertising as a budget item to be trimmed or eliminated like other expense items when sales are either very high or very low. This is understandable but extremely shortsighted.

The cost of a new factory or warehouse is an investment in the company's future ability to produce and distribute products. Similarly, advertising—as one element of the communication mix—is an investment in future sales. While advertising is often used to stimulate immediate sales, its greatest power is in its cumulative, long-range, reinforcement effect.[56]

Advertising builds consumer preference and promotes goodwill. This, in turn, enhances the reputation and value of the company name and brand. And it encourages customers to make repeat purchases.

So while advertising is a current expense for accounting purposes, it is also a long-term investment. For management to

Developing Advertising Objectives [7–D]

For the next big sets of decisions you will make, both media and creative, it will be essential that you specify what advertising and other promotions should *do*. Use the checklist below to focus your thinking on your advertising objectives.

Does the advertising aim at immediate sales? If so, objectives might be:

____ Perform the complete selling function.
____ Close sales to prospects already partly sold.
____ Announce a special reason for buying now (price, premium, and so forth).
____ Remind people to buy.
____ Tie in with special buying event.
____ Stimulate impulse sales.

Does the advertising aim at near-term sales? If so, objectives might be:

____ Create awareness.
____ Enhance brand image.
____ Implant information or attitude.
____ Combat or offset competitive claims.
____ Correct false impressions, misinformation.
____ Build familiarity and easy recognition.

Does the advertising aim at building a "long-range consumer franchise"? If so, objectives might be:

____ Build confidence in company and brand.
____ Build customer demand.
____ Select preferred distributors and dealers.
____ Secure universal distribution.
____ Establish a "reputation platform" for launching new brands or product lines.
____ Establish brand recognition and acceptance.

Does the advertising aim at helping to increase sales? If so, objectives would be:

____ Hold present customers.
____ Convert other users to advertiser's brand.
____ Cause people to specify advertiser's brand.
____ Convert nonusers to users.
____ Make steady customers out of occasional ones.
____ Advertise new uses.
____ Persuade customers to buy larger sizes or multiple units.
____ Remind users to buy.
____ Encourage greater frequency or quantity of use.

Does the advertising aim at some specific step that leads to a sale? If so, objectives might be:

____ Persuade prospect to write for descriptive literature, return a coupon, enter a contest.
____ Persuade prospect to visit a showroom, ask for a demonstration.
____ Induce prospect to sample the product (trial offer).

How important are supplementary benefits of advertising? Objectives would be:

____ Help salespeople open new accounts.
____ Help salespeople get larger orders from wholesalers and retailers.
____ Help salespeople get preferred display space.
____ Give salespeople an entrée.
____ Build morale of sales force.
____ Impress the trade.

Should the advertising impart information needed to consummate sales and build customer satisfaction? If so, objectives may be to use:

____ "Where to buy it" advertising.
____ "How to use it" advertising.
____ New models, features, package.
____ New prices.
____ Special terms, trade-in offers, and so forth.
____ New policies (such as guarantees).

Should advertising build confidence and goodwill for the corporation? Targets may include:

____ Customers and potential customers.
____ The trade (distributors, dealers, retail people).
____ Employees and potential employees.
____ The financial community.
____ The public at large.

What kind of images does the company wish to build?

____ Product quality, dependability.
____ Service.
____ Family resemblance of diversified products.
____ Corporate citizenship.
____ Growth, progressiveness, technical leadership.

treat advertising as an investment, however, it must understand how advertising relates to sales and profits.

The Relationship of Advertising to Sales and Profits Many variables, both internal and external, influence the effectiveness of a company's marketing and advertising efforts. Methods to measure the relationships between advertising expenditures and sales are far from perfect. However, substantial research does support the following principles:

- In consumer goods marketing, increases in market share are closely related to increases in the marketing budget. And market share is a prime indicator of profitability.[57]
- Sales normally increase with additional advertising. At some point, however, the rate of return flattens and then declines.
- Sales response to advertising may build over time, but the durability of advertising is brief, so a consistent investment is important.
- There are minimum levels below which advertising expenditures have no effect on sales.
- There will be some sales even if there is no advertising.
- There are saturation limits above which additional ad expenditures appear to do little to increase sales.

To management, these facts might mean: Spend more until it stops working. In reality, the issue isn't that simple. Advertising isn't the only marketing activity that affects sales. A change in market share may occur because of quality perceptions, word of mouth, the introduction of new products, competitive trade promotion, the opening of more attractive outlets, better personal selling, or seasonal changes in the business cycle.

Furthermore, most companies don't have a clear-cut way to determine the relationship between advertising and sales and profit. What if the company sells a variety of products? Which advertising contributes to which sales?

One thing remains clear. Like all expenditures, advertising should be evaluated for wastefulness. But historically, companies that make advertising the scapegoat during tough times end up losing substantial market share before the economy starts growing again.[58]

The corollary is also true. Sustained ad spending during difficult times protects, and in some cases even increases, market share and builds brands. The story that opened this chapter is an excellent example of the value of a sustained commitment to strong advertising by a distinctive brand. It is difficult to imagine how Mtn Dew, with its origins as a small regional beverage, could have achieved its current popularity and consumer loyalty without a consistent marketing investment by PepsiCo.

percentage-of-sales method
A method of advertising budget allocation based on a percentage of the previous year's sales, the anticipated sales for the next year, or a combination of the two.

Methods of Allocating Funds

Most business executives will spend more money on advertising as long as they are assured it will mean more profit. But how much is too much is hard to predict when advertising budgets are being developed.

> Advertising should be viewed as a long-term investment in future profits.

Companies use several methods to determine how much to spend on advertising, including the *percentage-of-sales, percentage-of-profit, unit-of-sale, competitive-parity, share-of-market,* and *objective/task methods.*

No technique is appropriate for all situations. The three methods discussed here are commonly used for setting national advertising budgets. However, local retailers can use them too.

Percentage-of-Sales Method The **percentage-of-sales method** is one of the most popular techniques for setting advertising budgets. It may be based on a percentage of last year's sales, anticipated sales for next year, or a combination of the two. Businesspeople like this method because it is the simplest, it doesn't cost them anything, it is related to revenue, and it is considered safe. The problem is knowing what percentage to use. Even leaders in the same industry use different percentages. Across industries, they range from just 1.5 percent to more than 22 percent.

Usually the percentage is based on an industry average or on company experience. Unfortunately, it is too often determined arbitrarily. An industry average assumes that every company in the industry has similar objectives and faces the same marketing challenges.

share-of-market/share-of-voice method A method of allocating advertising funds based on determining the firm's goals for a certain share of the market and then applying a slightly higher percentage of industry advertising dollars to the firm's budget.

objective/task method A method of determining advertising allocations, also referred to as the *budget-buildup method,* that defines objectives and how advertising is to be used to accomplish them. It has three steps: defining the objectives, determining strategy, and estimating the cost.

Using company experience assumes that the market is static, which is rarely the case.

However, when applied against a forecast of future sales, this method often works well. It assumes that a certain number of dollars is needed to sell a certain number of units. If the advertiser knows what that relationship is, the correlation between advertising and sales should remain reasonably constant, assuming the market is stable and competitors' advertising remains unchanged.

The greatest shortcoming of the percentage-of-sales method is that it violates a basic marketing principle. Marketing activities are supposed to *stimulate* demand and thus sales, not occur as a *result* of sales. If advertising only increases when sales increase and declines when sales decline, an opportunity is lost that might encourage an opposite move.

Share-of-Market/Share-of-Voice Method In markets with similar products, a high correlation usually exists between a company's share of the market and its share of industry advertising.

The **share-of-market/share-of-voice method** is a bold attempt to link advertising dollars with sales objectives.[59] It holds that a company's best chance of maintaining its share of market is to keep its share of advertising (voice) comparable to its market share. For example, if Mountain Dew has an 8 percent share of the soft-drink market it should spend roughly 8 percent of the soft-drink industry's advertising dollars.

The share-of-market/share-of-voice method is commonly used for new product introductions.[60] According to this formula, when a new brand is introduced, the advertising budget for the first two years should be about one and one-half times the brand's targeted share of the market in two years. This means that if the company's two-year sales goal is 10 percent of the market, it should spend about 15 percent of total industry advertising during the first two years.

One hazard of this method is the tendency to oversimplify. Maintaining the targeted percentage of media exposure usually isn't enough to accomplish the desired results. The top national packaged-goods marketers still spend 25 to 30 percent of their marketing budgets on consumer and trade promotion rather than consumer advertising.[61] Companies must be aware of *all* their competitors' marketing activities, not just advertising.

Objective/Task Method The **objective/task method**, also known as the *budget-buildup method,* is used by the majority of major national advertisers in the United States. It considers advertising to be a marketing tool to help generate sales.

my ad campaign

Ways to Set Advertising Budgets [7–E]

How much should you recommend that your client spend on advertising and promotions? Here is a list of ways companies set their marketing budgets.

- **Percentage of sales.** Advertising budget is determined by allocating a percentage of last year's sales, anticipated sales for next year, or a combination of the two. The percentage is usually based on an industry average, company experience, or an arbitrary figure.
- **Percentage of profit.** Percentage is applied to profit, either past years' or anticipated.
- **Unit of sale.** Also called the *case-rate method.* A specific dollar amount is set for each box, case, barrel, or carton produced. Used primarily in assessing members of horizontal co-ops or trade associations.
- **Competitive parity.** Also called the *self-defense method.* Allocates dollars according to the amounts spent by major competitors.
- **Share-of-market/share-of-voice.** Allocates dollars by maintaining a percentage share of total industry advertising comparable to or somewhat ahead of desired share of market. Often used for new product introductions.
- **Objective/task.** Also referred to as the *budget-buildup method,* this method has three steps: defining objectives, determining strategy, and estimating the cost to execute that strategy.
- **Empirical research.** Companies determine the most efficient level by running experimental tests in different markets with different budgets.
- **Quantitative mathematical models.** Computer-based programs developed by major advertisers and agencies rely on input of sophisticated data, history, and assumptions.
- **All available funds.** Go-for-broke technique generally used by small firms with limited capital, trying to introduce new products or services.

The task method has three steps: defining objectives, determining strategy, and estimating cost. After setting specific, quantitative marketing objectives, the advertiser develops programs to attain them. If the objective is to increase the sales of cases of coffee by 10 percent, the advertiser determines which advertising approach will work best, how often ads must run, and which media to use. The estimated cost of the program becomes the basis for the advertising budget. Of course, the company's financial position is always a consideration. If the cost is too high, objectives may have to be scaled back. If results are better or worse than anticipated after the campaign runs, the next budget may need revision.

The task method forces companies to think in terms of accomplishing goals. Its effectiveness is most apparent when the results of particular ads or campaigns can be readily measured. The task method is adaptable to changing market conditions and can be easily revised.

However, it is often difficult to determine in advance the amount of money needed to reach a specific goal. Techniques for measuring advertising effectiveness still have many weaknesses.

The Bottom Line The principal job of advertising is to influence perception by informing, persuading, and reminding. Advertising *affects* sales, but it is just one of many influences on consumer perception. Advertising managers must keep this in mind when preparing their plans and budgets. ■

check yourself ✓

1. What types of companies tend to use the percentage-of-sales method to set an ad budget? Why?
2. How might a packaged-foods manufacturer use the share-of-market/share-of-voice method to introduce a new product?

learn about, practice, and apply marketing, advertising and IMC planning!

M: Advertising was developed for students who want information packaged in a concise, easy-to-read, yet interesting format.
Check out the book's website to:

- Show you know the difference between objectives, strategies, and tactics in planning. (Review Questions)
- Understand how to develop a positioning strategy. (Review Questions)
- Conduct a SWOT analysis on a familiar brand. (Exploring Advertising)
- Develop a budget for a small advertiser. (Exploring Advertising)

While you are there, check out the professional resource links, review the PowerPoint presentation, and test your knowledge with the Multiple Choice Quiz. Additionally, *Connect® Marketing* is available for M: Advertising.

www.mhhe.com/ArensM2e

chapter eight

creating ads: strategy and process

This chapter demonstrates how advertising strategies are used to develop creative briefs and message strategies. It examines the characteristics of great campaigns, the nature of creativity, and the role of the agency creative team. We discuss how research operates as the foundation for creative development and planning, and point out common problems that can challenge the creative team.

Walmart has changed the retail world. The company's success, a result of its relentless focus on offering a broad selection of goods at low prices, has made it the largest public company in the world.

For its competitors (and in this day and age, that is most stores), finding the right strategy for success is an ongoing challenge.

Some do so by focusing on a single product category, like clothes, electronics, pet supplies, or toys, and offering a broader selection within that category.

An even riskier strategy is going head-to-head, as Kmart, Sears, Montgomery Ward, and others have learned the hard way. But standing tall among the scattered ruins of Walmart's direct competitors is one company that has found a way to prosper. And that is Target.

Target's origins date to 1962 when the Dayton Company opened the first store in a Minneapolis suburb.[1]

Today the company operates nearly 1,700 stores throughout the United States and is fifth in overall revenue among U.S. retailers. Not bad for an organization whose greatest expansion occurred during the same years that Walmart became a global leader.

continued on p. 198

LEARNING OBJECTIVES

After studying this chapter, you will be able to:

- LO8-1 Identify the members of the creative team and their primary responsibilities.
- LO8-2 Describe the characteristics of great advertising.
- LO8-3 Explain the role of the creative strategy and its principal elements.
- LO8-4 Show how advertising enhances creativity.
- LO8-5 Define the four roles people play at different stages of the creative process.

Then, there is the red. Lots of red. As Michael Francis, senior VP of marketing at the retailer, notes, "Trust us, red does go with everything." The strategy at Target is to "own red," that is, have the consumer associate the color with the brand.

One means for communicating that Target owns red is through its retail stores. But the color plays a prominent role in Target advertising as well and helps tie the many executions together.

Target spends nearly four times as much on its advertising as a percentage of sales than does Walmart. Its ads are fun and quirky, in direct contrast to Walmart's more conservative approach. Target's ads are softer, focusing on lifestyle themes that suggest ways that products sold at Target help the shopper have a better and more fun life.

continued from p. 197

Why has Target succeeded where other retail giants have not? In part by being one of the greatest practitioners of positioning, a concept we introduced in Chapter 7. Everyone knows that Walmart is synonymous with the concept of a "big box store." To the individual who is looking to save money but finds Walmart's offerings just a bit ordinary, Target proudly proclaims "Expect more, pay less."

The slogan says it all. You'll save money at Target (compared to many retailers) and you'll have more fun shopping (compared to Walmart). The promise of a better shopping experience (the "expect more" part of the equation) has been the key. As retailer trade journalist Jeff Arlen asks, "Without Andy Warhol, could Target Stores exist as it is today? Have CEO Bob Ulrich and his team of retailing alchemists learned the secret of turning the mundane into the sublime?"[2]

Start with the merchandise. Lots of the things you find at Target you can find at Walmart as well, but Target displays them with more style and space. And some things you can't get at Walmart, or anywhere else—in-house lines like Xhilaration and Cherokee, and specially produced products from Mossimo and Michael Graves.[3]

The recession of 2009 hit most retailers hard, including Target. But Target weathered the storm by sticking with its core advertising message. As the economy has slowly recovered, the chain has seen revenues increase from $67 billion in 2010 to $70 billion. It's not easy taking on Goliath. But Target has prospered by credibly offering consumers a real difference between it and Walmart. And by communicating that difference in beautiful and credible ads. ■

L08-1 Identify the members of the creative team and their primary responsibilities.

THE CREATIVE TEAM: ORIGINATORS OF ADVERTISING CREATIVITY

Every great ad campaign starts with human imagination. In most ad agencies, the people who first conceptualize the symbols, words, and images are the members of the creative team.

The team's **copywriter** develops the *verbal* message, the copy (words) within the ad. The copywriter typically works with an **art director** who is responsible for the *nonverbal*

Bright, colorful images, geometric shapes, and strong contrasts in both copy and graphics draw attention to Target messages and help brand the retailer as an "upscale" discount store.

copywriter Person who creates the words and concepts for ads and commercials.

art director Along with graphic designers and production artists, determines how the ad's verbal and visual symbols will fit together.

creative director Head of a creative team of agency copywriters and artists. He or she is ultimately responsible for the creative product—the form the final ad takes.

creatives The people who work in the creative department, regardless of the specialty.

aspect of the message, the design, which determines the look and feel of the ad. Together, they work under the supervision of a **creative director** (typically, a former copywriter or art director), who is ultimately responsible for the creative product—the form the final ad takes. As a group, the people who work in the creative department are generally referred to as **creatives**, regardless of their specialty.

This chapter focuses on the creative process: how it's developed and how it relates to a company's marketing and advertising strategy. But to get a proper perspective on creativity, we need to understand the characteristics of great advertising.

check yourself ✓

1. What does a copywriter do? What does an art director do?
2. Who is ultimately responsible for the creative product?

LO8-2 Describe the characteristics of great advertising.

CREATING GREAT ADVERTISING

What do we mean when we say an ad is great?

Some of the classic ads in history, offer a clue: Volkswagen's famous "Think small" ad; DeBeers's "A diamond is forever" line; Clairol's "Does she or doesn't she?"; Nike's "Just do it"; Apple's "Think different"; and Coca-Cola's "The real thing." What do these campaigns have in common that make them universally considered great?

This is a very important question, since a lot of research indicates that "ad liking" has a tremendous impact on "ad success." But is a likable ad the same as a great ad?

No matter the medium, great ads have certain things in common. We can lump most of these characteristics into two dimensions of greatness: *audience resonance* and *strategic relevance.*[4]

[Great ads have certain things in common: . . . *audience resonance* and *strategic relevance.*]

informational ads Promising benefits that will offer relief from an undesirable situation or condition. Informational ads tend to address *negatively originated purchase motives,* such as problem removal or avoidance, in an attempt to provide solutions to those problems.

transformational ads Promising benefits that will reward consumers. Transformational ads tend to address *positively originated purchase motives,* such as sensory gratification, intellectual stimulation, or social approval, in an attempt to make people feel happier.

One way that Target communicates about its extraordinary shopping experience is through the use of extraordinary ads.

The Resonance Dimension

To resonate means to echo, reverberate, or vibrate. It also means to boom, ring, or chime. And that's what a great ad does with the audience. It rings their chimes. It echoes in their ears. It reverberates. It *resonates.*

Why? Because of the boom factor.

When a cannon goes "boom," it gets your attention—right now! The same is true with an ad. It's the surprise element—the "aha," or the "wow." But in advertising, it not only gets your attention, it catches your imagination. In this sense it's like great art. It invites you to stop and think about the message.

Target counts on its ad campaigns to resonate with consumers. Because they do, the company can turn a simple set of stairs into a reminder about the popular retailer.

Look at the Target ad, juxtaposing the image of fashion with people suspended in air. The ad is unusual, even for Target, so we stop to examine it more closely. And as we do so, the colors and the familiar logo convey exactly where we can buy the fashions if they strike our fancy. The ad resonates.

Other ads may resonate for different reasons. In some of the classic campaigns we just mentioned, it's simply the headline that resonates—so much so that it becomes a part of our daily language. Other memorable classics include California Milk Processors's "Got Milk?", and iPhone's "There's an app for that."

Recall from Chapter 5 our discussion of consumer motives. *Negatively originated motives,* such as problem avoidance or problem removal, provide the foundation for many great ads. These resonate with the audience by being highly **informational**. Informational ads resonate because the consumer perceives that the brand offers a credible solution to a significant problem. (FedEx's "When it absolutely, positively has to be there overnight"). Other motives are *positively originated* as consumers seek pleasant experiences, intellectual stimulation, or social approval. Here, ads may achieve greatness by being **transformational**, using positive reinforcement to offer a reward (such as L'Oreal's tagline, "Because you're worth it").

Unfortunately, most ads, whether they're informational or transformational, fail to resonate with the audience. Why? Because they lack a "big idea" or they fall down in the *execution.* The copy may be uninspiring, the visual may be less than attractive, or the production techniques used may be low quality. From the consumer's point of view, these ads are just a waste of time, and from the client's point of view, a waste of money.

In fact, for them the greatness of the advertising is in the "bang per buck." Great ads give sponsors much more advertising effectiveness per dollar spent.

The Relevance Dimension

The second dimension of great advertising is strategic relevance. An ad may get you to think, but what does it get you to think about? In a column explaining why Apple's iPad succeeded so spectacularly while Microsoft's competing product, the Surface RT, failed, columnist Nick Bilton recently wrote, "the ads for the iPad and Surface RT are different. Apple simply shows the device, making the iPad the hero. Microsoft usually unveils snazzy ads that make the ads the hero, not the product."[5]

The famous ad agency Leo Burnett has its own take on resonance and relevance. It puts it this way:

> We don't make brands famous, we make brands popular. There's no greater goal for us than to take each of our clients' brands and put them in a position of popularity by making them a part of the fabric of real people's lives. We create work that is inclusive and bold and appeals to the mass market. We want to create work that a brand can grow into, that will appeal to more than just the immediate target audience. That's what we're about and that's what we always focus on.[6]

While the text and the visual carry the ad message, behind the creative team's choice of tone, words, and ideas lies an advertising strategy. When the ad is completed, it must be relevant to the sponsor's strategy, or it will fail—even if it resonates with the audience. In other words, it may be great *entertainment,* but not great *advertising.* Great advertising always has a strategic mission to fulfill. In fact, strategy is at the root of all great creative work.

check yourself ✓

1. What does it mean for advertising to resonate? What causes an ad to resonate?
2. In addition to resonance, what other dimension is important for advertising greatness?

LO8-3 Explain the role of the creative strategy and its principal elements.

FORMULATING CREATIVE STRATEGY: THE KEY TO GREAT ADVERTISING

Recall from Chapter 7 that the purpose of the advertising *objective* is to state what the advertiser wants to achieve with respect to consumer awareness, attitude, and preference. The advertising *strategy* then describes a means to achieve that objective through the development of advertising executions and media plans. The *creative strategy* is the component of the advertising strategy that guides those responsible for developing creative advertising.

To be sure that everyone has the same understanding of the task at hand, account managers (or, in larger agencies, account planners) develop a brief statement summarizing the agreed-upon objectives and strategies. Many individuals from both the client and agency—including representatives from creative, media, and research—should have input into this document. The agency and client team should sign off on the finished document before the creative process commences. This **creative strategy** serves as the creative team's guide for writing and producing the advertising. In some agencies this document may be referred to as a *creative brief,* a *work plan,* a *copy strategy,* or a *copy platform.*

creative strategy
A written statement that serves as the creative team's guide for writing and producing an ad. It decides the most important issues that should be considered in the development of the ad (the who, what, where, when, and why), including the objective of the advertising; a definition and description of the target audience; the key benefit to be promised; the product features that support that promise; the style, approach, or tone to be used; and generally, what the copy should communicate.

Writing the Creative Strategy

Regardless of the name, the creative strategy is a simple written statement of the most important issues to consider in the development of an ad or campaign. It usually includes the following elements:

- The basic problem the advertising must address.
- The objective of the advertising.
- A definition of the target audience.

Target ads are quirky and creative. But the nonverbal elements of color and the familiar logo make them instantly recognizable.

problem the advertising must solve What you want the advertising to do. The specific challenge that marketing communications must overcome to meet the marketing objectives.

advertising objective A specific communication task an advertising campaign should accomplish for a specific target audience.

target audience The specific group of individuals to whom the advertising message is directed.

- The key benefits to communicate.
- Support for those benefits.
- The brand's personality.
- Any special requirements.

Let's look at the creative strategy Target and its agencies developed. We'll then see how they translated that into a message strategy and a big idea and, finally, into effective ads.

- What is the **problem the advertising must solve**? Consumers may not be aware that they will save money AND enjoy shopping at Target. Consumers may also be unaware of the unique products that can be found only at Target. *This information often comes straight from the marketing plan's situation analysis.*
- What is the *objective of the advertising?* Target wants consumers to know that it has higher-quality offerings and a more attractive shopping environment than its competitors. The **advertising objective** is initially spelled out in the marketing plan.
- What is Target's **target audience**? Target focuses on value-conscious shoppers, usually adults ages 25–49 with families, who seek products that are nicer than those typically found at deep-discount stores. These shoppers are not poor, but they do look to save money (Target reports that the median household income of its shoppers, or "guests," as the company calls them, is $60,000). This group is Target's *primary market*—that's who the company sells to. So Target definitely wants them to see its advertising. Because Target offers both value and a sense of style, 18- to 25-year-olds are another important market. While this group as a whole may not spend as much as the primary market, they act as *centers of influence* (or *key influentials*). This group is a *secondary target audience* for the advertising.
- What is Target's *key benefit*? This is summarized nicely in the company's slogan, "Expect more, pay less." In other words, better quality, low prices. The **benefit statement** is the heart of the creative strategy. It is very important to make it as succinct and single-minded as possible. Complex benefit statements can lead to creative executions that promise everything and focus on nothing.
- How is that benefit *supported?* Target's ads provide price information, although not in the "hard sell" approach that Walmart favors. The "expect more" part of the equation is supported with beautiful, stylish, and unexpected ad executions, as many of the featured ads in this chapter demonstrate. The **support statement** should provide information about the product or service that will convince the target audience that the key benefit is true.
- What is the **brand personality**? Target wants its stores to be known for their quality, sophistication, beauty, and value. The

The Creative Brief [8]

Every agency has a slightly different twist on a creative brief. Common topics for the brief include:

- Who (the prospect).
- Why (specific wants or needs the ad should appeal to).
- What (are the product features that can satisfy consumer needs?).
- Where and when (will the messages be transmitted?).
- Style, approach, tone.

Leo Burnett keeps things even simpler for its largest client, P&G.

- An objective statement (what are you trying to do?).
- A support statement (the evidence that backs up the promised benefit).
- A tone or brand character statement (emotional descriptions of the advertising strategy).

Ogilvy includes these questions in the creative brief:

1. What are the communications objectives?
2. What should consumers do differently? Why?
3. How will messages affect consumer beliefs and actions?
4. How are our competitors advertising? How can we make our ads different?
5. Who is the target audience and what is their shared need that the brand can fulfill?
6. Demographics of the audience, but even more importantly, shared attitudes.
7. The brand
   - How does the brand address the shared need?
   - How should the brand experience (as defined by both planned and unplanned messages) be defined?
   - What is the proposition (or benefit)?
   - What evidence gives people a reason to believe the proposition?
   - What is the personality of the brand?
   - How can the mood or tone of the ads be matched to the personality of the brand?

benefit statement Describes what a product or service does to provide a benefit to the consumer. Whenever possible, benefit statements should focus on an important, single-minded process.

support statement Provides information about the product or service that will convince the target audience that the *key benefit* is true.

brand personality Describes a brand in terms of human characteristics. A significant component in effective branding is imparting personality to a brand, reflecting its reputation, attitudes, and behavior.

special requirements Unique characteristics of the advertiser, brand, target audience, media, competition, budget, etc. that should be considered during the creative development process.

creative process The step-by-step procedure used to discover original ideas and reorganize existing concepts in new ways.

creatives will consider this statement when they develop the message strategy.

- Are there any **special requirements**? Target allocates ad dollars to television ads, out-of-home magazines, and newspaper inserts. It has different audience objectives for each medium. But certain creative elements, such as the color red and the large "bull's-eye" logo, tie all of the ads together. It is important for the creatives to understand budget and media constraints before they begin.

The creative strategy identifies the benefits to be presented to consumers, but it doesn't cover execution. How the benefits will be presented is the creative team's job.

"The creative strategy identifies the benefits to be presented to consumers, but it doesn't cover execution. How the benefits will be presented is the creative team's job."

Procter & Gamble and Leo Burnett use a simple creative strategy with only three parts:

1. *An objective statement.* A specific, concise description of what the advertising is supposed to accomplish or what problem it is supposed to solve. The objective statement also includes the name of the brand and a brief, specific description of the target consumer. For example:

   > Advertising will convince value-conscious consumers that Target stores offer them a way to save money on their everyday purchases. In addition, Target offers a vast selection of products that are practical, attractive, and fun.

2. *A support statement.* A brief description of the evidence that backs up the product promise; the reason for the benefit. For example:

   > Support is found in two types of ads that Target regularly runs. Newspaper ads, including weekly inserts, demonstrate to consumers the low prices of the products sold at Target. Television ads emphasize the quality and value of the everyday products found at Target. Both TV and newspaper ads should do more than focus on the product alone, rather they should help to demonstrate that the products sold at Target make life easier and better.

3. *A tone or brand character statement.* A brief statement of either the advertising's tone or the long-term character of the brand. Tone statements are emotional descriptions of the advertising strategy. Brand character statements are descriptions of the enduring values of the brand. A tone statement might be phrased:

   > The tone of Target ads should convey a spirit of optimism and energy. The ads should suggest that Target understands the consumer and the challenges she faces in her life. They should suggest that shopping at Target is fun and that choosing Target as a retailer is a sign of both sensibility (low prices) and sophistication (better offerings).

   On the other hand, a brand character statement might be phrased:

   > Target offers consumers the selection and value typical of a mass merchandizer in a setting that has the elegance and flair of a department store.

The delivery of the creative strategy to the creative department concludes the process of developing an advertising strategy. It also marks the beginning of the next step: the **creative process**, in which the creative team develops a *message strategy* and begins the search for the *big idea.* After writing the first ad, the copywriter should review the creative strategy to confirm that the ad is "on strategy." If it isn't, the team must start again.

Elements of Message Strategy

From the information given by the account team (in the creative strategy) and any additional research it may perform, the creative team develops the message strategy. This may actually

Ads like this one communicate a great deal with little copy. How does Target use design to imply great selection with this out-of-home ad?

occur before, during, or after the creative process of searching for the big idea.

The **message strategy** is a simple description and explanation of an ad campaign's overall creative approach—the main idea, details about how the idea will be executed, and a rationale. The message strategy has three components:

- *Verbal.* Guidelines for what the advertising should say; considerations that affect the choice of words; and the relationship of the copy approach to the medium (or media) that will carry the message.
- *Nonverbal.* Overall nature of the ad's graphics; any visuals that must be used; and the relationship of the graphics to the media in which the ad will appear.
- *Technical.* Preferred execution approach and mechanical outcome, including budget and scheduling limitations (often governed by the media involved); also any **mandatories**—specific requirements for every ad, such as addresses, logos, and slogans.

The verbal elements are the starting point for many advertising campaigns. However, because all these elements of the message strategy intertwine, they typically evolve simultaneously. Language affects imagery, and vice versa.

The message strategy helps the creative team sell the ad or the campaign concept to the account managers and helps the managers explain and defend the creative work to the client. Of course, the message strategy must fit to the creative strategy or it will probably be rejected.

In the development of the message strategy, certain basic questions need to be answered: How is the market segmented? How will the product be positioned? Who are the best prospects for the product? Is the target audience different from the target market? What is the key consumer benefit? What is the product's (or company's) current image? What is the product's unique advantage? At this point, research data are important. Research helps the creative team answer these questions and support their proposed approach.

check yourself ✓

1. What are the important parts of the creative strategy (or creative brief)?
2. What is the message strategy? What are its important parts?

L08-4 Show how advertising enhances creativity.

HOW CREATIVITY ENHANCES ADVERTISING

The powerful use of imagery, copy, and even humor in Target campaigns demonstrates how creativity enhances advertising. But what exactly is creativity? What is the role of creativity in advertising? And where does creativity come from?

What Is Creativity?

To create means to originate, to conceive a thing or idea that did not exist before. Typically, though, **creativity** involves combining two or more previously unconnected objects or ideas into something new. As Voltaire said, "Originality is nothing but judicious imitation."

Many people think creativity springs directly from human intuition. But as we'll see in this chapter, the creative process is not a chaotic, unorganized means of thinking but a disciplined process that can be learned and used to generate original ideas. In the words of advertising legend Bill Bernbach, "Merely to let your imagination run riot, to dream unrelated dreams, to indulge in graphic acrobatics and verbal gymnastics is not being creative. The creative person has harnessed his imagination. He has disciplined it so that every thought, every idea, every word he puts down, every line he draws, every light and shadow in every photograph he takes make more vivid, more believable, more persuasive the original theme or product advantage he has decided he must convey."[7]

The Role of Creativity in Advertising

Advertisers often select an agency specifically for its creative style and its reputation for coming up with original concepts. While creativity is important to advertising's basic mission of informing, persuading, and reminding, it is vital to achieving the boom factor.

Creativity Helps Advertising Inform Advertising's responsibility to inform is greatly enhanced by creativity. Good creative work makes advertising more *vivid,* a quality that many researchers believe attracts attention, maintains interest, and stimulates consumers' thinking.[8] A common technique is to use plays on words and verbal or visual metaphors, such as "Put a tiger in your tank," "Fly the friendly skies," or "Solutions for a smart planet." The metaphor describes one concept in terms of another, helping the reader or viewer learn about the product.[9]

Other creative techniques can also improve an ad's ability to inform. For example, visual cues such as lighting, pose of the model, setting, and clothing style can instantly signal viewers nonverbally whether a fashion ad reflects a romantic adventure or a sporting event.

Creativity Helps Advertising Persuade The ancients created legends and myths about gods and heroes—symbols for humankind's hopes and fears—to affect human behavior and thought. To motivate people to some action or attitude, advertising copywriters have created new myths and heroes, like the Jolly Green Giant, the Geico gecko, and the Energizer Bunny. A creative story or persona can establish a unique identity for the product in the collective mindset, a key factor in helping a product beat the competition.[10]

To be persuasive, an ad's verbal message must be reinforced by the creative use of nonverbal message elements. Artists use these elements (color, layout, and illustration, for example) to increase vividness. Research suggests that, in print media, *information graphics* (colorful explanatory charts, tables, and the like) can raise readers' perception of quality.[11] Artwork can also stimulate emotions. Color, for example, often motivates consumers, depending on their cultural background and personal experiences.

Creativity Helps Advertising Remind Imagine using the same invitation to ask people to try your product again and again, year after year. Your invitation would become stale and tiresome. Only creativity can transform your boring reminders into interesting, entertaining advertisements. Nike is proof. Several commercials in a Nike campaign never mentioned the company name or even spelled it on the screen. The ads told stories. And the only on-screen cue identifying the sponsor was the single, elongated "swoosh" logo inscribed on the final scene. A Nike spokesperson said the ads weren't risky "given the context that the Nike logo is so well known." We are entertained daily by creative ads—for soft drinks, snacks, and cereals—whose primary mission is simply to remind us to indulge again.

Creativity Puts the "Boom" in Advertising Successful comedy also has a boom factor—the punchline. It's that precise moment when the joke culminates in a clever play on words or turn of meaning, when the audience suddenly gets it and laughs out loud.

Good punchlines come from taking an everyday situation, looking at it creatively, adding a bit of exaggeration, and then delivering it as a surprise. Great advertising often does the same thing.

When a group of friends greet each other with wagging tongues and an exaggerated "Whassup?" while "watching the game and having a Bud," the audience is completely caught off guard and roars with laughter. Boom!

In advertising, though, the boom doesn't always have to be funny. It may come from the sudden understanding of an

message strategy A document that helps media planners determine how messages will be delivered to consumers. It defines the target audience, the communication objectives that must be achieved, and the characteristics of the media that will be used for delivery of the messages.

mandatories The address, phone number, Web address, etc. that the advertiser usually insists be included within an ad to give the consumer adequate information.

creativity Involves combining two or more previously unconnected objects or ideas into something new.

Metaphors help readers understand the intended message. Leo Burnett, the ad legend who created the Jolly Green Giant, believed strongly in brand icons. Target does as well.

Fact-based thinking can also be creative. The UPS Store (www.theupsstore.com) printed this fact-based ad upside-down to attract the reader's attention and to play on the fear that this could happen in an important presentation. The UPS Store promises to get your presentations done right.

unexpected double-meaning, as in the case of Target ads. Or from the gentle emotional tug of a Hallmark Cards commercial. Or the breathtaking beauty of a magnificent nature photograph for Timberland shoes. In a business-to-business situation, it may come from the sudden recognition of how a new high-tech product can improve workplace productivity. In short, the boom factor may come from many sources. But it always requires creativity.

Understanding Creative Thinking

Creativity is "the generation, development, and transformation of ideas that are both novel and useful for solving problems," according to Glenn Griffin and Deborah Morrison, professors at the Universities of Alabama and Oregon, respectively. Their insightful book *The Creative Process Illustrated* suggests that many models of creative thought believe it is a process that generally follows four stages: preparation (thinking about the problem and what is needed to solve it), incubation (thought about the problem that occurs subconsciously), illumination (potential solutions that pop into awareness as a result of incubation), and verification (determining which solutions might work).[12]

Fact-Based versus Value-Based Thinking

Griffin and Morrison, like many creativity scholars, believe that all people have the potential to be creative. However, people often differ in their styles or preferred approaches to problem solving.

People whose preferred style of thinking is **fact-based** tend to fragment concepts into components and to analyze situations to discover the one best solution. Although fact-based people can be creative, they tend to be linear thinkers and prefer to have facts and figures—hard data—they can analyze and control. They are not comfortable with ambiguous situations. They like logic, structure, and efficiency.[13]

In contrast, **value-based** thinkers make decisions based on intuition, values, and moral codes. They are better able to embrace change, conflict, and paradox. This style fundamentally relies on melding concepts together. Value-based thinkers, for example, attempt to integrate the divergent ideas of a group into an arrangement that lets everyone win. They are good at using their imagination to produce a flow of new ideas and synthesizing existing concepts to create something new.[14]

How Styles of Thinking Affect Creativity

If the creative team prefers a value-based thinking style, it tends to

Value-based thinking guides the creation of many Target spots. The messages are emotional and avoid specific product facts.

fact-based thinking A style of thinking that tends to fragment concepts into components and to analyze situations to discover the one best solution.

value-based thinking A style of thinking where decisions are based on intuition, values, and ethical judgments.

advertising messages An element of the creative mix comprising what the company plans to say in its advertisements and how it plans to say it—verbally or nonverbally.

Explorer A role in the creative process that searches for new information, paying attention to unusual patterns.

produce ads such as those in The UPS Store and Target campaigns—soft, subtle, intuitive, metaphorical. That's fine if the client also prefers that style of thinking.

On the other hand, clients who prefer a fact-based style often seek agencies that produce practical, hard-edged work characterized by simple, straightforward layouts, rational appeals, and lots of data. A fact-based client may even find a value-based campaign to be unsettling.

The creative team needs to understand the campaign's target audience. In some market segments (high-tech, for example) customers may favor messages that result from one style of thinking over another. And that should dictate which approach to use.

As we shall see in the next section, the best art directors and copywriters use both styles to accomplish their task. In the creative process, they need to use their imagination (value-based thinking) to develop a variety of concepts. But to select the best alternative and get the job done, they often resort to the fact-based style.

check yourself ✓

1. What is creativity?
2. How does advertising help advertisers inform? Persuade? Remind?
3. How do different styles of thinking influence the creative process?

LO8-5 Define the four roles people play at different stages of the creative process.

THE CREATIVE PROCESS

The creative process is the step-by-step procedure used to discover original ideas and reorganize existing concepts in new ways. By following it, people can improve their ability to unearth possibilities, cross-associate concepts, and select winning ideas.

The advertising creative does not work in isolation, or create solutions just to please himself or herself. Rather, it is a collective activity. Advertising creatives must not only come up with good ideas, they must also help others see the value of the ideas.

Creativity consultant Roger von Oech developed a four-step creative model used today by many *Fortune* 100 companies. It is especially appropriate for creatives working as a team for a client who will ultimately judge the work. Von Oech describes four distinct, albeit imaginary, roles that every art director and copywriter has to personally take on at some point in the creative process:[15]

1. *The Explorer* searches for new information, paying attention to unusual patterns.
2. *The Artist* experiments and plays with a variety of approaches, looking for an original idea.
3. *The Judge* evaluates the results of experimentation and decides which approach is most practical.
4. *The Warrior* overcomes excuses, idea killers, setbacks, and obstacles to bring a creative concept to realization.

THE EXPLORER ROLE: GATHERING INFORMATION

Copywriters and art directors thrive on the challenge of creating **advertising messages**—the encoding process. But first they need the raw materials for ideas: facts, experiences, history, knowledge, feelings.

Taking on the role of the **Explorer**, creatives examine the information they have. They review the creative strategy and the marketing and advertising plan; they study the market, the product, and the competition. They may seek additional input from the agency's account managers and from people on the client side (sales, marketing, product, or research managers).

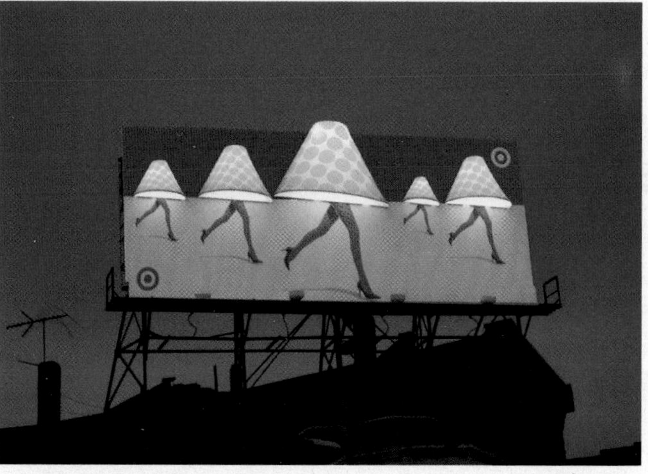

Creative juxtaposition is an essential ingredient for Target advertising.

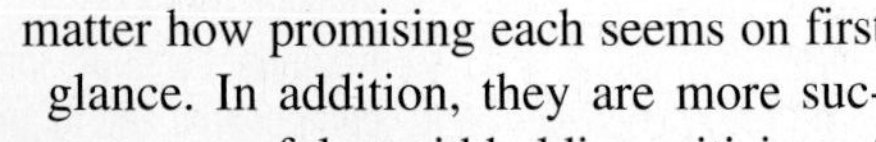

When the creative team developed ads for Target, they first assumed the Explorer role. They spoke with the company about its products, its marketing history, its competitors, and the competitors' advertising. They reviewed all appropriate sources of advertising for retail stores and studied the company's marketing environment. They carefully studied the creative brief prepared for them by the researchers, account planners, and account managers.

Develop an Insight Outlook

In advertising, it's important that when creatives play the Explorer role, they get off the beaten path to look in new and uncommon places for information—to discover new ideas and to identify unusual patterns. One important source of inspiration is the consumer herself. Target's agency creatives spent hours watching women shop at Target stores.

Von Oech suggests adopting an "insight outlook" (a conviction that good information is available and that you have the skills to find and use it). If you're curious and poke around in new areas, you'll improve your chances of discovering new ideas. Ideas are everywhere: a museum, an art gallery, a hardware store, an airport. The more diverse the sources, the greater your chance of uncovering an original concept.

> If you're curious and poke around in new areas, you'll improve your chances of discovering new ideas. Ideas are everywhere.

Know the Objective

Philosopher John Dewey said, "A problem well-stated is a problem half-solved." This is why the creative strategy is so important. It helps define what the creatives are looking for. The creatives typically start working on the message strategy during the Explorer stage because it, too, helps them define what they're looking for.

Brainstorm

As Explorers, the art director and copywriter look first for lots of ideas. One technique is **brainstorming**, a process in which two or more people team up to generate new ideas. A brainstorming session is often a source of sudden inspiration. To succeed, it must follow a couple of rules: All ideas are above criticism (no idea is "wrong"), and all ideas are written down for later review. Griffin and Morrison suggest that one of the critical differences between the approaches of novice advertising creative students and more seasoned ones is that the latter write down all ideas, no matter how promising each seems on first glance. In addition, they are more successful at withholding criticism of ideas that seem initially far-fetched. The goal is to record any inspiration that comes to mind, a process that psychologists call *free association*, allowing each new idea an opportunity to stimulate another.

Von Oech suggests other techniques for Explorers: Leave your own turf (look in outside fields and industries for ideas that could be transferred); shift your focus (pay attention to a variety of information); look at the big picture (stand back and see what it all means); don't overlook the obvious (the best ideas are right in front of your nose); don't be afraid to stray (you might find something you weren't looking for); and stake your claim to new territory (write down any new ideas or they will be lost).

To keep their creative juices flowing, most copywriters and art directors maintain an extensive library of advertising award books and trade magazines. Many also keep a file of ads that they like.

THE ARTIST ROLE: DEVELOPING AND IMPLEMENTING THE BIG IDEA

The next step, playing the Artist's role, is both tough and long, but it's also rewarding. The **Artist** must actually accomplish two major tasks: searching for the big idea and then implementing it.

Task 1: Develop the Big Idea

The first task for Artists is the long, sometimes tedious process of reviewing all the information they gathered when they played the Explorer role, analyzing the problem, and searching for a key verbal or visual concept to communicate what needs to be said.

It also means creating a mental picture of the ad or commercial before any copy is written or artwork begun. This step (also

brainstorming A process in which two or more people get together to generate new ideas; often a source of sudden inspiration.

Artist A role in the creative process that experiments and plays with a variety of approaches, looking for an original idea.

visualization The creative point in advertising where the search for the "big idea" takes place. It includes the task of analyzing the problem, assembling any and all pertinent information, and developing some verbal or visual concepts of how to communicate what needs to be said.

big idea The flash of creative insight—the bold advertising initiative—that captures the essence of the strategy in an imaginative, involving way and brings the subject to life to make the reader stop, look, and listen.

Some images make the point so well they require no words. This ad for Globetrotter outdoor gear connects the idea of giant seals snug in their skins with campers snug in their sleeping bags. It's amazing how much they look alike. There's a big idea here.

called **visualization** or *conceptualization*) is the most important in creating the advertisement. It's where the search for the **big idea**—that flash of insight—takes place. The big idea is a bold, creative initiative that builds on the strategy, joins the product benefit with consumer desire in a fresh, involving way, brings the subject to life, and makes the audience stop, look, and listen.[16]

What's the difference between a strategy and a big idea? A strategy describes the direction the message should take. A big idea gives it life. For example, the creative strategy proposed earlier for the Target campaign contained a strategic brand character statement:

> Target offers consumers the selection and value typical of a mass merchandizer in a setting that has the elegance and flair of a department store.

Target could have used that strategy statement as a headline. But it would have been dreadfully dull. It lacks what a big idea headline delivers: a set of multiple meanings that create interest, memorability, and, in some cases, drama. Note the short, punchy headline that Target chose to convey the same strategic concept: Expect more. Pay less.

John O'Toole said, "While strategy requires deduction, a big idea requires inspiration."[17] The big idea in advertising is almost invariably expressed through a combination of art and copy. Target's approach is to use short but witty copy, beautiful photography, and the immediately recognizable red "target" logo to visually communicate the essence of the brand. Target could save money and use much less creativity in its advertising. Rather than using striking, colorful graphics and layouts, Target's campaigns could emphasize facts and information. But this approach would reduce the boom factor and would end up ignored by the target audience (see Exhibit 8–1).

▼ **EXHIBIT 8–1** Advertising Big Ideas.

What brands use these big ideas?	
Quitting Sucks.[a]	Just do it.[j]
Mayhem.[b]	Eat fresh.[k]
It's finger lickin' good![c]	It's everywhere you want to be.[l]
American by birth. Rebel by choice.[d]	A diamond is forever.[m]
Innovation.[e]	Think small.[n]
The customer is always and completely right![f]	Think big.[o]
The greatest tragedy is indifference.[g]	The antidote for Civilization.[p]
Live in your world. Play in ours.[h]	Outwit. Outplay. Outlast.[q]
The happiest place on earth.[i]	We sell more cars than Ford, Chrysler, Chevrolet, and Buick combined.[r]

[a]Nicorette, [b]Allstate, [c]KFC, [d]Harley-Davidson, [e]3M, [f]Marks & Spencer, [g]Red Cross, [h]PS2, [i]Disneyland, [j]Nike, [k]Subway, [l]Visa, [m]DeBeers, [n]Volkswagen, [o]IMAX, [p]Club Med, [q]Survivor, [r]Matchbox.

Target's newspaper inserts focus more on price. But that doesn't mean they sacrifice creativity or beauty.

Transforming a Concept: Do Something to It Creative ideas come from manipulating and transforming resources. Von Oech points out that when we adopt the Artist role, we have to do something to the materials we collected as Explorers to give them value. That means asking lots of questions: What if I added this? Or took that away? Or looked at it backward? Or compared it with something else? The Artist has to change patterns and experiment with various approaches.

At this point in the creative process, a good Artist may employ a variety of strategies for transforming things. Von Oech suggests several techniques for manipulating ideas:[18]

1. *Adapt.* Change contexts. Think what else the product might be besides the obvious. A Campbell's Soup ad showed a steaming bowl of tomato soup with a bold headline underneath: "HEALTH INSURANCE."
2. *Imagine.* Ask what if. Let your imagination fly. What if people could do their chores in their sleep? What if animals drank in saloons? Clyde's Bar in Georgetown actually used that idea. The ad showed a beautifully illustrated elephant and donkey dressed in business suits and seated at a table toasting one another. The headline: "Clyde's. The People's Choice."
3. *Reverse.* Look at it backward. Sometimes the opposite of what you expect has great impact and memorability. A cosmetics company ran an ad for its moisturizing cream under the line: "Introduce your husband to a younger woman." A vintage Volkswagen ad used "Ugly is only skin deep."
4. *Connect.* Join two unrelated ideas together. Ask yourself: What ideas can I connect to my concept? A Target ad showed the rear view of a high-fashion-type model clad only with a backpack and a lampshade—the latter wrapped around her middle like a miniskirt. Next to the Target logo the ad said simply "fashion and housewares." To get people to send for its catalog, Royal Caribbean Cruises ran an ad that showed the catalog cover under the simple headline "Sail by Mail."
5. *Compare.* Take one idea and use it to describe another. Ever notice how bankers talk like plumbers? "Flood the market, laundered money, liquid assets, cash flow, take a bath, float a loan." The English language is awash in metaphors because they help people understand. Jack in the Box advertised its onion rings by picturing them on a billboard and inviting motorists to "Drive thru for a ring job." An elegant magazine ad for the Parker Premier fountain pen used this sterling metaphor: "It's wrought from pure silver and writes like pure silk."
6. *Eliminate.* Subtract something. Or break the rules. In advertising, there's little virtue in doing things the way they've always been done. 7 Up became famous by advertising what it wasn't ("the Uncola") and thereby positioned itself as a refreshing alternative. To introduce its new models one year, Volkswagen used a series of humorous teaser ads that didn't show any cars. In one, a shaggy dog sat patiently in front of a fan. He was presumably replicating what dogs do in cars,

Finding a creative way to deal with an unusual subject is the foundation of this ad's effectivness.

art direction The act or process of managing the visual presentation of an ad or commercial.

art The whole visual presentation of a commercial or advertisement—the body language of an ad. Art also refers to the style of photography or illustration employed, the way color is used, and the arrangement of elements in an ad so that they relate to one another in size and proportion.

sticking their heads out the window to catch the breeze. The only difference was he was doing it indoors.

7. *Parody.* Fool around. Have some fun. Tell some jokes—especially when you're under pressure. There is a close relationship between the ha-ha experience of humor and the aha! experience of creative discovery. Humor stretches our thinking and, used in good taste, makes for some great advertising. A classical radio station ran a newspaper ad: "Handel with care." And speaking of classics, Fila USA got a rave review from *Advertising Age* for its "bizarre, absolutely hilarious, and totally cool" spot of a praying mantis racing up a leaf stem in Fila sneakers to escape his murderous mate.[19]

Blocks to Creativity Everybody experiences times when the creative juices just won't flow. There are many causes: information overload, mental or physical fatigue, stress, fear, insecurity. Often, though, the problem is simply the style of thinking being used.

In the Explorer stage, when creatives study reams of marketing data, the facts and figures on sales and market share may put them in a fact-based frame of mind. But to create effectively, they need to shift gears to a value-based style of thinking.

Creative blocking may occur when people in the agency start "thinking like the client," especially if the client is a fact-based thinker. This can also be hazardous to the agency's creative reputation and is one reason agencies sometimes resign accounts over "creative differences."

Creative fatigue can also happen when an agency has served an account for a long time and all the fresh ideas have been worked and reworked. It can be difficult to avoid fatigue when a client has rejected a series of concepts; the inspiration is lost and the creatives start trying to force ideas. If this becomes chronic, the only solutions may be to appoint an entirely new creative team or resign the account.

Incubating a Concept: Do Nothing to It When the brain is overloaded with information about a problem, creatives sometimes find it's best to just walk away from it for a while, do something else, and let the unconscious mind mull it over. This approach yields several benefits. First, it puts the problem back into perspective. It also rests the brain, lets the problem incubate in the subconscious, and enables better ideas to percolate to the top. When they return to the task, the creatives frequently discover a whole new set of assumptions.

Task 2: Implement the Big Idea

Once the creatives latch onto the big idea, they must next focus on how to implement it. This is where the real art of advertising comes in—writing the exact words, designing the precise layout. To have a sense of how advertising creatives do that, we need to understand what art is in advertising, how artistic elements and tools are selected and used, and the difference between good art and bad art.

In advertising, art shapes the message into a complete communication that appeals to the senses as well as the mind. So while **art direction** refers to the act or process of managing the visual presentation of the commercial or ad, the term **art** actually refers to the whole presentation—visual and verbal. For example, the artful selection of words not only communicates information but also stimulates positive feelings for the product. An artfully designed typeface not only makes reading easier; it also evokes a mood. By creatively arranging format elements—surrounding the text with lines, boxes, and colors, and relating them to one another in proportion—the art director can further enhance the ad's message. Art also shapes the style and choice of photography and illustration. An intimate style uses soft focus and close views, a documentary style portrays the scene without pictorial enhancements, and a dramatic style features unusual angles or blurred action images.

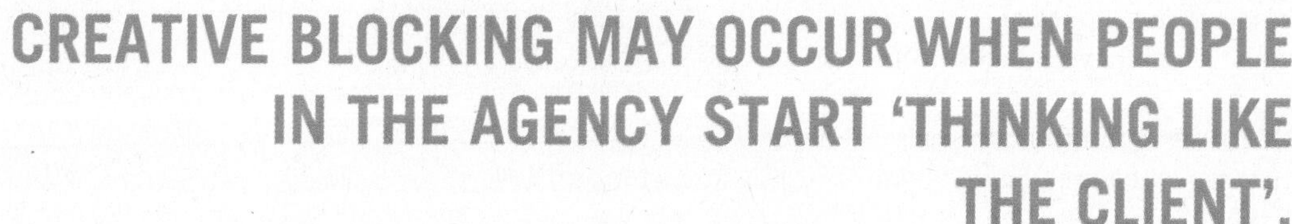

Target uses icons that appear to be reverse images of one another. This is similar to a suggestion by creativity guru Roger von Oech.

In short, if *copy* is the verbal language of an ad, *art* is the body language. TV uses both sight and sound to involve viewers. Radio commercials use sound to create mental *pictures.* The particular blend of writing, visuals, and sounds makes up an ad's expressive character. So while the quality may vary, every ad uses art.

In advertising, balance, proportion, and movement are guides for uniting words, images, type, sounds, and colors into a single communication so they relate to and enhance each other. We'll discuss more of these concepts in Chapter 9.

The Creative Pyramid: A Guide to Formulating Copy and Art

The **creative pyramid** is a model that can guide the creative team as it converts the advertising strategy and the big idea into the actual physical ad or commercial. The cognitive theory of how people learn new information uses a simple five-step structure (the first pyramid in Exhibit 8–2).

The purpose of much advertising copy and design is to either persuade prospective customers to take some action to satisfy a need or want or to remind them to take the action again. In a new-product situation, people may first need to be made aware of the problem or, if the problem is obvious, that a solution exists. For a frequently purchased product, the advertiser simply has to remind people of the solution close to the purchase occasion. In either case, the advertiser's first job is to get the prospect's *attention.* The second step is to stimulate the prospect's *interest*—in either the message or the product itself. Next, it's important, especially for new products, to build *credibility* for the product claims. Then the ad can focus on generating *desire* and finally on stimulating *action.* These five elements (the second pyramid in Exhibit 8–2) should be addressed in just about every ad or commercial. We'll deal with each step briefly.

Attention For an ad or commercial to be effective it must break through consumers' physiological screens to create the kind of attention that leads to perception. *Attention,* therefore, is the first objective of any ad and the foundation of the creative pyramid. The Artist may spend as much time and energy

> [(To keep the prospect involved,) the copywriter can answer a question asked in the attention step or add facts that relate to the headline.]

▼EXHIBIT 8–2 The advertising pyramid, discussed in Chapter 7, reflects how people learn new information. Each level of that pyramid can be related to a role that creativity must play. The creative pyramid thus translates advertising objectives into copywriting objectives.

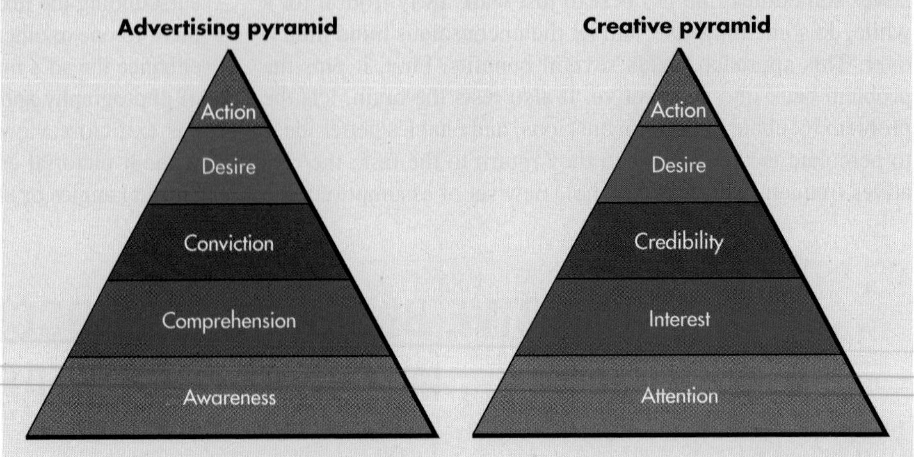

creative pyramid
A five-step model to help the creative team convert advertising strategy and the big idea into the actual physical ad or commercial. The five elements are: attention, interest, credibility, desire, and action.

This ad for a casino is likely to be very successful at the attention stage of the creative pyramid.

figuring out how to express the big idea in an interesting, attention-getting way as searching for the big idea itself.

The attention step is critically important to triggering the ad's boom factor. Print ads often use the headline as the major attention-getting device. Usually designed to appear in the largest and boldest type in the ad, the headline is often the strongest focal point. Many other devices also help gain attention. In print media, they may include dynamic visuals, unusual layouts, vibrant color, or dominant ad size. In electronic media, they may include sound effects, music, animation, or unusual visual techniques.

The attention-getting device should create drama, power, impact, and intensity. It must also be appropriate, relating to the product, the tone of the ad, and the needs or interests of the intended audience. This is especially true in business-to-business advertising, where rational appeals and fact-based thinking dominate.

Interest The second step in the creative pyramid, *interest,* is also extremely important. It carries the prospective customer—now paying attention—to the body of the ad. The ad must keep the prospect excited or involved as the information becomes more detailed. To do this, the copywriter may answer a question asked in the attention step or add facts that relate to the headline. To maintain audience interest, the tone and language should be compatible with the target market's attitude. As we discussed earlier, the successful ad resonates.

The writer and designer must lead prospects from one step to the next. Research shows that people read what interests them and ignore what doesn't, so the writer must maintain prospects' interest at all times.[20] One way to do so is to sneak through prospects' psychological screens by talking about their problems, their needs, and how the product or service will address them. Copywriters use the word *you* a lot.

There are many effective ways to stimulate interest: a dramatic situation, a story, cartoons, charts. In radio, copywriters use sound effects or catchy dialogue. Television frequently uses quick cuts to maintain interest. We discuss some of these techniques in Chapter 9.

Credibility The third step in the creative pyramid is to establish *credibility* for the product or service. Customers are sophisticated and skeptical. They want claims to be supported by facts. Comparison ads can build credibility, but they must be relevant to customers' needs—and fair.

Well-known presenters may lend credibility to commercials. For example, actor Justin Long effectively represented Macs with his personable, low-key, and slightly bemused style.

Advertisers often show independent test results to back up product claims. To work, such "proofs" must be valid, not just statistical manipulation. Advertisers and agencies must remember that many consumers have extensive product knowledge, even in specialized areas. And customers who believe, rightly or wrongly, that they have been misled rarely come back.

Desire In the *desire* step, the writer encourages prospects to imagine themselves enjoying the benefits of the product or service.

In print ads, copywriters use phrases like "Picture yourself" or "Imagine." In TV, the main character pulls a sparkling clean T-shirt from the washer, smiles, and says "Yeah!" In radio, the announcer says, "You'll look your best."

In print advertising, the desire step is one of the most difficult to write (which may be why some copywriters omit it). In TV, the desire step can simply show the implied consumer experiencing the benefit of the product. Ever notice how advertisers almost invariably show the happy life that awaits their product's user?

Does Sex Appeal?

It's one of the more blatant uses of sex in advertising in recent memory: a billboard features a young woman, holding a grease gun cartridge in each hand, and leaning over to exhibit an ample amount of cleavage. The headline reads "This is Debbie. She wants you to have this pair in your car." The ad is for auto parts, but the implication seems to be that if you buy this manufacturer's auto parts, you'll get Debbie in the bargain. Nothing in the ad says so explicitly, but the innuendo is all that's required to capture the viewer's attention.

Advertisers frequently use the power of suggestion to imply sex, encouraging viewers to come to their own conclusions. However, advertisers who run such risqué ads must contend with the critics and with the often tricky legal distinction between obscenity and indecency. Obscenity is illegal and carries criminal charges, whereas indecency does not. To be considered obscene, an ad must meet three conditions: it appeals to prurient interests, it is patently offensive, and it lacks any redeeming social value.

In general, most ads with sexual appeals don't meet the criteria for obscenity, but they may still be considered indecent, since indecency is in the eyes of the beholder. If enough people believe sexually oriented material is indecent, then "community standards" reflect this belief. In such cases, citizen pressure groups, along with media organizations and local courts, can enforce community standards by disallowing advertising that offends those standards.

Consider Abercrombie & Fitch. The clothing retailer sparked controversy at a mall in Omaha when its window posters featured a topless model covering her breasts with her hands. A Christian group, Family First, quickly objected, claiming that Abercrombie's posters created a "sexualized walkway." Family First began pressuring shoppers and other retailers in the mall to object to the photographs, and within nine days the window displays were changed.

Were the posters obscene or indecent? Advertisers like A&F, who continue to strive for the "sexy" appeal, are beginning to find it increasingly difficult to draw the line between simple sex appeal and unethical exploitation.

There is no easy solution to this dilemma, especially since research shows that sexual appeals can be very effective when sexuality relates to the product. However, when it doesn't, it can distract audiences from the main message and severely demean the advertiser in the consumer's eyes. Many argue that sexually oriented advertising is not only a distraction, but also a source of negative *externalities*—the social costs to consumers outside the target market, such as children who might be indirectly affected.

Advertisers must examine, on a case-by-case basis, at what point sexual appeals become unethical and therefore counterproductive. In one case, an executive on the Valvoline advertising account justified using "girlie calendars" for mechanics by noting that "the calendar may offend some groups—but they aren't our customers."

Miller Lite's "Catfight" campaign raised a few eyebrows. The campaign appeared to signal the company's return to "beer and babes" ads, depicting women as sexual objects. In the commercial, two women in a restaurant begin the classic "tastes great–less filling" debate over Miller Lite. The debate quickly turns into a full-fledged catfight, with the two women stripped down to their bras and panties, splashing around in an adjacent fountain. Moments later, we see the two buxom brawlers going at it in a soggy cement pit. The ad cuts to a bar. It turns out the fight was only the fantasy of two guys in a bar who were dreaming of the perfect beer commercial, much to the shock and disgust of their girlfriends, who were with them at the time.

So what does any of this have to do with selling beer? Hillary Chura, who covers the beer industry for *Advertising Age,* explains that ads such as the "Catfight" commercial are "aspirational." After watching these two beautiful women wrestle around for 30 seconds, Miller wants guys to say, "Hey, if I drink Miller Genuine Draft, I'll get those hot women." And Miller wants women to think "If I drink this beer, I'll look like those women."

But what is the social cost of these unrealistic "aspirations"? In a society rife with confidence-related disorders, should advertisers exploit consumer insecurities in an effort to sell more of their product? At what point do advertisers need to accept some ethical responsibility for the interests of the society to which they owe their existence?

Unfortunately, this debate over sex in advertising may actually be fueling advertisers' desire to continue using blatant sex appeals. The "Catfight" campaign sparked nationwide attention on talk radio, CNN's *Crossfire,* in *USA Today,* and in other media outlets. Similarly, Abercrombie & Fitch's quarterly catalog of scantily clad models makes national headlines with every issue. Controversy equals publicity. Publicity stimulates interest. And interest spawns sales.

Given the topic of this chapter, we can suggest another objection to sexualized appeals: laziness. By that we mean that while some brands have an obvious connection to sexual imagery (Victoria's Secret), others have no connection whatsoever. We suspect that the use of sex in these ads represents a creative team's unwillingness to do the hard work necessary to provide a client with a truly outstanding idea. And that, most industry professionals would agree, is truly obscene.

Questions

1. Explain why you believe that sexual appeals in advertising do or do not have "redeeming value."
2. Even if sexual appeals are considered okay by the audiences that are directly targeted, what responsibility does the advertiser have for any effect on indirect targets, such as adults who are offended or children? How can advertisers protect themselves from this problem?
3. Is it acceptable for advertisers to exploit consumer insecurities in an effort to sell more of their product? Should advertisers accept some ethical responsibility for creating unrealistic "aspirations" and intensifying confidence-related disorders?

Judge A role in the creative process that evaluates the results of experimentation and decides which approach is more practical.

Warrior A role in the creative process that overcomes excuses, idea killers, setbacks, and obstacles to bring a creative concept to realization.

Action The final step up the creative pyramid is *action.* The goal here is to motivate people to do something—send in a coupon, call the number on the screen, visit the store—or at least to agree with the advertiser.

The call to action may be explicit—"Order now"—or implicit—"Fly the friendly skies." Designers cue customers to take action by placing dotted lines around coupons to suggest cutting and by highlighting the company's telephone number or Web address with large type or a bright color.

This block of the pyramid reaches the smallest audience but those with the most to gain from the product's utility. So the last step is often the easiest. If the copy is clear about what readers need to do and asks or even nudges them to act, chances are they will.

With today's technology, it's important to not only ask people to act but to make it easy for them to do so, through either a toll-free phone number or an attractive website. In relationship marketing, the ad enables people to self-select being interested in a relationship. Then the marketer can use more efficient one-on-one media to deepen the relationship.

THE JUDGE ROLE: DECISION TIME

The next role in the creative process is the **Judge**. This is when the creatives evaluate the quality of their big ideas and decide whether to implement, modify, or discard them.[21]

The Judge's role is delicate. On the one hand, the creatives must be self-critical enough to ensure that when it's time to play the Warrior they will have an idea worth fighting for. On the other hand, they need to avoid stifling the imagination of their internal Artist. It's easier to be critical than to explore, conceptualize, or defend. But the Judge's purpose is to help produce good ideas, not to revel in criticism. Von Oech suggests focusing first on the positive, interesting aspects of a new idea. The negatives will come soon enough.

When playing the Judge, creatives need to ask certain questions: Is this idea an aha! or an uh-oh? (What was my initial reaction?) What's wrong with this idea? (And what's right with it?) What if it fails? (Is it worth the risk?) What is my cultural bias? (Does the audience have the same bias?) What's clouding my thinking? (Am I wearing blinders?)

Risk is an important consideration. When the advertising scores a hit, everybody's happy, sales go up, people get raises, and occasionally there's even positive publicity. But when a campaign flops, all hell breaks loose, especially on high-profile accounts. Sales may flatten or even decline, competitors gain a couple of points in market share, distributors and dealers complain, and the phone rings incessantly with calls from angry clients. Perhaps worst of all is the ridicule in the trade press. This is not good for either the agency's stock or the client's. And it's how agencies get replaced. So the Judge's role is vital.

If the Artist-as-Judge does a good job, the next role in the creative process, the Warrior, is easier to perform.

THE WARRIOR ROLE: OVERCOMING SETBACKS AND OBSTACLES

In the final step of the creative process, the **Warrior** wins territory for big new ideas in a world resistant to change. The Warrior carries the concept into action. This means getting the big idea approved, produced, and placed in the media.

"To get the big idea approved, the Warrior has to battle people within the agency and often the client, too."

To get the big idea approved, the Warrior has to battle people within the agency and often the client, too. So part of the Warrior's role is turning the agency account team into allies for the presentation to the client. At this point, it's imperative that the creatives have a completed message strategy document to support their rationale for the copy, art, and production elements in the concept they're presenting. And the message strategy had better mesh with the creative strategy, or the valiant Warrior will likely face a wide moat with no drawbridge.

Part of the Warrior's task may be to help the account managers present the campaign to the client. Bruce Bendinger says,

"How well you *sell* ideas is as important as how good those ideas are." To give a presentation maximum selling power, he suggests five key components:

1. *Strategic precision.* The selling idea must be *on strategy.* The presenting team must be able to prove it, and the strategy should be discussed first, before the big selling idea is presented.
2. *Savvy psychology.* The presentation, like the advertising, should be receiver-driven. The idea has to meet the client's needs, thinking style, and personality.
3. *Polished presentation.* The presentation must be prepared and rehearsed; it should use compelling visuals and emotional appeals.
4. *Structural persuasion.* The presentation should be well structured, since clients value organized thinking. The opening is crucial because it sets the tone.
5. *Solve the problem.* Clients have needs, and they frequently report to big shots who ask tough questions about the advertising. Solve the client's problem and you'll sell the big idea—and do it with style.

For clients, recognizing a big idea and evaluating it are almost as difficult as creating one. When the agency presents the concepts, the client is suddenly in the role of the Judge, without having gone through the other roles first. David Ogilvy recommended that clients ask themselves five questions: Did it make me gasp when I first saw it? Do I wish I had thought of it myself? Is it unique? Does it fit the strategy to perfection? Could it be used for 30 years?[22]

As Ogilvy pointed out, campaigns that run five years or more are the superstars: Dove soap (one-quarter cleansing cream), Ivory soap (99 and 44/100 percent pure), Perdue chickens ("It takes a tough man to make a tender chicken"), the U.S. Army ("Be all you can be"). Some of these campaigns are still running today, and some have run for as long as 30 years. Those are big ideas!

When the client approves the campaign, the creative's role as a Warrior is only half over. Now the campaign has to be executed. The Warrior will shepherd it through the intricate details of design and production to ensure that it is completed, faithful to the concept, on time, under budget, and of the highest quality possible. At the same time, the creatives revert to their Artist roles to finalize the design and copy and produce the ads.

The next step in the process, therefore, is to implement the big idea, to produce the ads for print and electronic media—the subject of our next chapter. ■

check yourself ✓

1. What is the role of the Explorer? The Artist?
2. What are blocks to creativity and how can the creative person deal with a block?
3. What are the steps of the creative pyramid and what role does creativity play in each?
4. What obstacles does the Warrior prepare to do battle with?

learn about, practice, and apply techniques for creating ad strategy!

M: Advertising was developed for students who want information packaged in a concise, easy-to-read, yet interesting format.

Check out the book's website to:

- Develop your own definition of creativity by summarizing the ideas of others. (Review Questions)
- Identify the boom factor in an ad. (Exploring Advertising)
- Conduct a brainstorming session. (Exploring Advertising)

While you are there, check out the professional resource links, review the PowerPoint presentation, and test your knowledge with the Multiple Choice Quiz. Additionally, *Connect® Marketing* is available for M: Advertising.

www.mhhe.com/ArensM2e

chapter nine

creative execution: art and copy

To present the role of art and copy—the nonverbal and verbal elements of message strategy—in print, radio, television, and on the Web, artists and copywriters include a variety of specialists who follow specific procedures for conceptualizing, designing, writing, and producing IMC messages. To be successful, creatives must be conversant with the copywriting and commercial art terms and formats used in the business. They must also develop an aesthetic sensitivity so they can recognize, create, evaluate, or recommend quality work .

The Sony name stands for quality technology, so when the company in 2005 introduced its BRAVIA line (BRAVIA stands for Best Resolution Audio Visual Integrated Architecture) of HDTVs, it wanted a campaign that would distinguish the brand from other sets. To do so, Sony retained the London office of Fallon Worldwide (you may remember Fallon from its American office's work for Holiday Inn Express, recounted in Chapter 6).

continued on p. 220

LEARNING OBJECTIVES

After studying this chapter, you will be able to:

- LO9-1 Describe the factors involved in creating print ads.
- LO9-2 Explain the types of copy and how great copy is created in print ads.
- LO9-3 Outline how great copy is created in electronic ads.
- LO9-4 Discuss the role of art in electronic ads.
- LO9-5 Review the unique requirements in writing for the Web.
- LO9-6 Differentiate the important print and broadcast production methods.

What kind of balls should they use? After testing a variety (tennis, ping-pong, etc.), the agency chose a staple of every kid's toy chest, the super ball. These high-bouncing spheres made from synthetic rubber compressed under extraordinarily high pressure seem, when dropped, to almost have minds of their own.

continued from p. 219

In the mid-2000s, high-definition TV was still very new. For most consumers, just replacing an old console with an HDTV would bring a huge jump in viewing quality. But because the technology was quite expensive at the time, many consumers looked for brands offering the lowest price.

Sony's challenge was to convince shoppers that spending a bit more on their new HDTV was well worth the viewing experience a BRAVIA could provide. Chris Willingham, a Fallon account executive, told Sony that research showed people wanted vibrant colors in an HDTV. Sony and Fallon agreed on a strategic focus summarized by the campaign's slogan, "Color like no other."

The creative team was led by long-time Fallon star Richard Flintham. His idea: a dreamlike ad in which two San Francisco streets (Filbert and Leavenworth) burst forth in an array of brilliant colors. He would use no special effects. Instead, the agency would release hundreds of thousands of bouncing colored balls. Careening down the steep inclines of the two roads, each ball would follow its own idiosyncratic path, bouncing past cars, homes, street lamps, and sidewalks. The ad would have no dialog, just haunting, simple music and superimposed text highlighting the brand.

Of course, no one had ever produced such an ad. The logistics of creating the spot began with a very simple question:

> "The nonverbal aspect of an ad carries at least half the burden of communication."

On the day of the shoot, the agency set up several mechanisms for launching the balls. For massive ball drops, it used three large skips capable of dropping tens of thousands of balls from 50 feet in the air (creating very big bounces!). These were supplemented with 12 air mortars for firing balls at different angles.

The agency did six takes over a four-day period. To protect the neighborhood, large nets were placed strategically on the streets and over drains. Large rubber hoses helped gather up the balls for reuse at the end of each take. Despite the precautions, a couple of neighborhood cars sustained some damage.

Over a dozen cameras captured the flight of the balls, many requiring shields to ensure camera men were not picked off by the ricocheting orbs. Balls were released from everywhere, the top of the street, side streets, even from gutters.

Agency interns (naturally) helped with the rather unglamorous task of collecting each of the balls. Assistant Director Chris Williams pointed out the advantages of working with high-bouncing, but low-maintenance, spheres. "They don't talk back to you," noted Williams, "and they never sit in makeup, they never make you wait on the set, and they throw no tantrums."

The shoot went well, and the crew sent film off for processing at a major London studio, The Mill. Flintham considered several musical scores before settling on a haunting

design Visual pattern or composition of artistic elements chosen and structured by the graphic artist.

layout An orderly formation of all the parts of an advertisement.

thumbnail A rough, rapidly produced pencil sketch that is used for trying out ideas.

song "Heartbeats," originally written by a Swedish group, The Knife. For the ad, a version recorded by José González, another Swedish artist, was used. The spot proved to be stunning, impressing the judges at Cannes enough to win a Gold Lion in 2006. You can see the ad, and how it was made, at: www.youtube.com/watch?v=2Bb8P7dfjVw. Like all great ads, this one started with an inspired idea. But spectacular production made it a spot like no other. ■

DELIVERING ON THE BIG IDEA: THE VISUAL AND THE VERBAL

As Sony's ad demonstrates, what's shown is just as important as what's said. The nonverbal aspect of an ad carries at least half the burden of communication. It helps position the product and create personality for the brand. It creates the mood of the ad, determining the way it *feels* to the audience. That mood flavors the verbal message, embodied in the *copy*.

In this chapter, we discuss how advertising concepts are executed from the standpoints of both art and copy. We examine the visual and the verbal details, first of print advertising and then of electronic and digital media.

THE ART OF CREATING PRINT ADVERTISING

LO9-1 Describe the factors involved in creating print ads.

Designing the Print Ad

The term **design** refers to how the art director, chooses and structures the artistic elements of an ad. A designer sets a style—the manner in which a thought or image is expressed—by choosing artistic elements and blending them in a unique way.

In general, clean lines, formally composed photographs, and sparse copy give an ad the breathing room needed to draw the reader's eye from one element to the next. Sufficient *white space* gives an ad unity and balance in spite of a diversity of elements.

A number of designers, working under the art director, may produce initial layouts of the ad concept. In collaboration with copywriters, these artists call on their expertise in graphic design (including photography, typography, and illustration) to create the most effective ad.

The Use of Layouts

A **layout** is an overall orderly arrangement of all the elements of an ad: visual(s), headline, subheads, body copy, slogan, seal, logo, and signature. The layout serves several purposes. First, it helps both the agency and the client anticipate how the ad will look and feel. It gives the client (usually not an artist) a tangible item to correct, change, and approve.

Second, the layout helps the creative team develop the ad's psychological elements: the nonverbal and symbolic components. Sophisticated advertisers want their advertising to do more than just bring in store traffic. They want their ads to create personality for the product and to build the brand's equity with the consumer. To do this, the "look" of the ad should elicit an image or mood that reflects and enhances both the advertiser and the product.

Third, once the best design is chosen, the layout serves as a blueprint. It shows the size and placement of each element. Once the production manager knows the dimensions of the ad, the number of photos, the amount of typesetting, and the use of art elements such as color and illustrations, he or she can determine production costs.

Advertising Design and Production: The Creative and Approval Process

The design process is both a creative and an approval process. In the creative phase, the designer uses thumbnails, roughs, dummies, and comprehensives (comps) to establish the ad's look and feel. Then in the *prepress* (or *production art*) phase, the artist prepares a mechanical: the final artwork with the actual type in place along with all the visuals the printer or the media will need to reproduce the ad. If you want to learn more about what happens after ads are sent for production, visit our special online only content called "Producing Ads," where you'll see how this design process works to produce a finished ad.

The approval process takes place at each step along the way. At any point in the design and production process, the ad—or the ad concept—may be altered or even canceled.

Thumbnail Sketches

The thumbnail sketch, or **thumbnail**, is a very small (about three-by-four inch), rough, rapidly produced drawing that the artist uses to visualize layout

The slogan for the popular video game Medal of Honor is "real as life." How do the ads use the nonverbal element to convey that benefit?

approaches without wasting time on details. Thumbnails are very basic. Blocks of straight or squiggly lines indicate text placement, and boxes show placement of visuals. The best sketches are then developed further.

Rough Layout In a **rough**, the artist draws to the actual size of the ad. Headlines and subheads suggest the final type style, illustrations and photos are sketched in, and body copy may be simulated with lines or random gibberish *(greek)*. The agency may present roughs to clients, particularly cost-conscious ones, for approval.

Dummy A **dummy** presents the handheld look and feel of brochures, multipage materials, or point-of-purchase displays. The artist assembles the dummy by hand, using color markers

my ad campaign

Product Facts for Creatives [9–A]

Art directors and copywriters must have a thorough understanding of the brand to create advertising that resonates. Make sure your creatives have the information that will help them write copy that sizzles and create layouts that stop consumers dead in their tracks.

- **Proprietary information**
  Product's trade name.
  Trademark.
  Product symbol.
  Other copyrighted or patented information.
- **History**
  When was the product created or invented?
  Who introduced it?
  Has it had other names?
  Have there been product changes?
  Is there any "romance" to it?
- **Research**
  Are research results available?
  What research about the product does the supplier have?
  Which research will be most useful for each medium?
- **Life cycle**
  What is the product's life or use span?
  What stage is it in now and what style of copy should be used for that stage?
  What stages are competitors in?
- **Market position**
  What is the product's share of the total market?
  Does its market share suggest a positioning strategy?
  What position does the company wish to occupy?
- **Competitive information**
  Who are the product's competitors?
  Does the product have any advantages over them?
  Does it have any disadvantages?
  Are they all about the same?
  Do rival products present problems that this one solves?
- **Product image**
  How do people view the product?
  What do they like about it?
  What do they dislike about it?
  Is it a luxury?
  Is it a necessity?
  Is it a habit?
  Is it self-indulgent?
  Do people have to have it but wish they didn't?
- **Customer use**
  How is the product used?
  Are there other possible uses?
  How frequently is it bought?
  What type of person uses the product?

poster-style format Layout that employs a single, dominant visual that occupies between 60 and 70 percent of an advertisement's total area. Also known as *picture-window layout* and *Ayer No. 1*.

picture-window layout Layout that employs a single, dominant visual that occupies between 60 and 70 percent of an advertisement's total area. Also known as *poster-style format* and *Ayer No. 1*.

Ayer No. 1 A single, dominant visual that occupies between 60 and 70 percent of an advertisement's total area.

illustrators The artists who paint, sketch, or draw the pictures we see in advertising.

photographers The artists who use cameras to create visuals for advertisements.

visuals All of the picture elements that are placed into an advertisement.

- Convince the reader of the truth of copy claims.
- Arouse the reader's interest in the headline.
- Emphasize the product's unique features.
- Create a favorable impression of the product or advertiser.
- Provide continuity for the campaign by using a unified visual technique in each ad.[9]

Selecting the Visual The kind of picture used is often determined during the conceptualization process. But frequently the visual is not determined until the art director or designer actually lays out the ad.

Selecting an appropriate photo or visual is a difficult creative task. Art directors deal with several basic issues. For example, not every ad needs a visual to communicate effectively. Some all-type ads are quite compelling. If the art director determines that a visual is required, how many should there be: one, two, or more? Should the visual be black-and-white or color? These may be budgetary decisions.

The marketing of luxury products such as DeScenza Diamonds is also guided by IMC principles. Consumers receive messages about such brands from many sources, including advertising, dealerships, and the popular press. Preserving the value of the DeScenza Diamonds brand thus requires careful attention to all consumer "touch points."

The art director must then decide the subject of the picture. Should it be one of the standard subjects listed earlier? Or something else altogether? And how relevant is that subject to the advertiser's creative strategy? The art director also has to decide how the visual should be created. Should it be a hand-rendered illustration? A photograph? What about a computer-generated illustration?

Finally, the art director has to know what technical and/or budgetary issues must be considered. With so many options, selecting visuals is obviously no simple task. Later in this chapter, we'll see how all these decisions come together in the process of producing the final ad.

Creating Great Headlines and Copy [9–B]

George Felton, in his book *Advertising Concept and Copy*, offers the following suggestions for aspiring copywriters:

Headlines

- "Achieve synergy, not redundancy." The headlines and artwork should work together to create an idea, but not be completely redundant.
- "Let the consumer do some of the work." Avoid ads that insult the audience's intelligence.
- "Combine overstatement and understatement." If the visual is BIG, make the headline small. And vice versa.
- "Emphasize one idea per ad." If you have several ideas, show how they are linked to make them one.

Copy

Freelance copywriter John Kuraoka offers some excellent advice for new copywriters at www.kuraoka.com/how-to-write-better-ads.html.

Here are summaries of his recommendations for your visuals:

- Capture the reader's attention.
- Clarify copy claims.
- Let the reader know the ad is directed at him or her.
- Show the product in use.
- Offer evidence for copy claims.
- Emphasize the product's unique features or benefits.
- Unify the different ads in the campaign.

> "HEADLINES SHOULD ENGAGE THE READER—FAST—AND GIVE A REASON TO READ THE REST OF THE AD. IF THE HEADLINE LACKS IMMEDIACY, PROSPECTS MOVE ON AND PASS THE AD'S MESSAGE BY."

check yourself ✓

1. What is a layout? What purposes does it serve in the process of print ad development, approval, and production?
2. How does an art director choose from among design formats?
3. What is the purpose of the visual in a print ad?

L09-2 Explain the types of copy and how great copy is created in print ads.

PRODUCING GREAT COPY IN PRINT ADVERTISING

Now that we understand the objectives and format elements of good design, let's examine some basic copywriting formats to see how art and copy are linked.

In print advertising, the key format elements are the *visual(s), headlines, subheads, body copy, slogans, logos,* and *signatures.* As Exhibit 9–2 shows, copywriters can correlate the visual and headline to the *attention* step of the creative pyramid (discussed in Chapter 8). The *interest* step typically corresponds to the subhead and the first paragraph of body copy. Body copy handles *credibility* and *desire,* and the *action* step takes place with the logo, slogan, and signature block. We'll discuss these elements first and then look at the formats for radio and television commercials.

Headlines

The **headline** contains the words in the leading position in the advertisement—the words that will be read first and are situated

Determining the Chief Focus for Visuals [9–C]

Selecting the focus for advertising visuals is a major step in the creative process. It often determines how well the big idea is executed. Print advertising uses many standard subjects for ad visuals, including

1. *The package containing the product.* Especially important for packaged goods, it helps the consumer identify the product on the grocery shelf.
2. *The product alone.* This usually does not work well for non-packaged goods.
3. *The product in use.* Automobile ads typically show a car in use while talking about its ride, luxury, handling, or economy. Cosmetics ads usually show the product in use with a close-up photo of a beautiful woman or a virile man.
4. *How to use the product.* Recipe ads featuring a new way to use food products have historically pulled very high readership scores.
5. *Product features.* Computer software ads frequently show the monitor screen so the prospect can see how the software features are displayed.
6. *Comparison of products.* The advertiser shows its product next to a competitor's and compares important features.
7. *User benefit.* It's often difficult to illustrate intangible user benefits. However, marketers know that the best way to get customers' attention is to show how the product will benefit them, so it's worth the extra creative effort.
8. *Humor.* If used well, a humorous visual can make an entertaining and lasting impression. But it can also destroy credibility if used inappropriately.
9. *Testimonial.* Before-and-after endorsements are very effective for weight-loss products, skin care lotions, and bodybuilding courses.
10. *Negative appeal.* Sometimes visuals point out what happens if you don't use the product. If done well, that can spark interest.

to draw the most attention. That's why headlines usually appear in larger type than other parts of the ad.

Role of Headlines Effective headlines attract attention, engage the audience, explain the visual, lead the audience into the body of the ad, and present the key benefit.

Headlines should engage the reader—fast—and give a reason to read the rest of the ad. If the headline lacks immediacy, prospects move on and pass the ad's message by.

headline The words in the leading position of an advertisement—the words that will be read first or that are positioned to draw the most attention.

Design Principles [9–D]

Make sure your layout follows these rules of thumb for creating attractive, informative ads.

Balance

The **optical center** is the reference point that determines the layout's balance. The optical center is about one-eighth of a page above the physical center of the page. Balance is achieved through the arrangement of elements on the page—the left side of the optical center versus the right, above the optical center versus below.

____ **Formal balance.** Perfect symmetry is the key to formal balance: matched elements on either side of a line dissecting the ad have equal optical weight. This technique strikes a dignified, stable, conservative image.

____ **Informal balance.** A visually balanced ad has elements of different size, shape, color intensity, or darkness at different distances from the optical center. Like a teeter-totter, an object of greater optical weight near the center can be balanced by an object of less weight farther from the center. Many ads use informal balance to make the ad more interesting, imaginative, and exciting.

Movement

Movement is the principle of design that causes the audience to read the material in the desired sequence. It can be achieved through a variety of techniques.

____ People or animals can be positioned so that their eyes direct the reader's eyes to the next important element.

____ Devices such as pointing fingers, boxes, lines, or arrows (or moving the actors or the camera or changing scenes) direct attention from element to element.

____ Design can take advantage of readers' natural tendency to start at the top left corner of the page and proceed in a Z motion to the lower right.

____ Comic-strip sequence and pictures with captions force the reader to start at the beginning and follow the sequence in order to grasp the message.

____ Use of white space and color emphasizes a body of type or an illustration. Eyes will go from a dark element to a light one, or from color to noncolor.

____ Size itself attracts attention because readers are drawn to the biggest and most dominant element on the page, then to smaller elements.

Proportion

____ Elements should be accorded space based on their importance to the entire ad. Attention-getting elements are usually given more space. Avoid the monotony of giving equal amounts of space to each element.

White Space (Isolation)

____ White space is the part of the ad not occupied by other elements (note that white space may be some color other than white). White space helps focus attention on an isolated element—it makes the copy appear to be in a spotlight. White space is an important contributor to the ad's overall image.

Contrast

____ An effective way of drawing attention to a particular element is to use contrast in color, size, or style; for example, a reverse ad (white letters against a dark background) or a black-and-white ad with a red border.

Clarity and Simplicity

____ Any elements that can be eliminated without damaging the overall effect should be cut. Too many type styles; type that is too small; too many reverses, illustrations, or boxed items; and unnecessary copy make for an overly complex layout and an ad that is hard to read.

Unity

____ Unity means that an ad's many different elements must relate to one another in such a way that the ad gives a singular, harmonious impression. Balance, movement, proportion, contrast, and color may all contribute to unity of design. Many other techniques can be used: type styles from the same family, borders around ads to hold elements together, overlapping one picture or element on another, judicious use of white space, and graphic tools such as boxes, arrows, or tints.

Continuity

____ Continuity is the relationship of one ad to the rest of the campaign. This is achieved by using the same design format, style, and tone; the same spokesperson; or the same graphic element, logo, cartoon character, or catchy slogan.

Imitation, Plagiarism, or Flattery?

When two companies run strikingly similar ads, is it imitation, plagiarism, or coincidence? Ads for Michelob Light beer and Colombian coffee were set in supermarkets and shared the same plot: grocery baggers manhandle products until the item being advertised comes down the conveyer belt. For both Michelob Light and Colombian, the bagger wraps the advertiser's package in bubble wrap and carefully gives it to the buyers.

Advertisers and the media commonly point to "coincidence." Bob Garfield, ad critic for *Advertising Age,* said, "It's seldom plagiarism, especially if the ads are appearing simultaneously." Both of the agencies representing Michelob Light beer and Colombian coffee agree. Peter le Comte, president of DDB Worldwide Marketing, said, "We have written it off as an incident of coincidence. Besides, I don't think we share the same consumers. They will run their commercial and we will run ours."

Unfortunately, plagiarism is difficult to prove, as long as you make a few changes. There is no set number of words that make up a plagiarized effort. And plagiarism covers not only words but ideas, plots, and characters. When Kendall-Jackson Winery filed a suit against E&J Gallo Winery, charging that Gallo's Turning Leaf Vineyards brand and labeling infringed on Kendall-Jackson's Colored Leaf trademark, a jury determined there was no infringement and that judgment was affirmed on appeal. It seems that grape-leaf designs have become generic emblems for wine.

The crux of the problem may be that imitation is an accepted part of the business, at least unofficially. Clients tend to avoid the debate, perhaps because they're more comfortable with well-worn ideas than with bold, original concepts. Many art directors and writers collect competitive ads for inspiration. And advertising is such a highly collaborative process that it's often difficult to determine each individual's creative contribution. With personal responsibility so unclear, ignoring professional ethics is relatively easy.

"There are very few original ideas," according to Philip Circus, an advertising law consultant to the Newspaper Society in London. "Plagiarism is the name of the game in advertising. It's about recycling ideas in a useful way."

That's why some industry leaders are passionate about the need for personal ethics. Jim Golden, executive producer of DMH MacGuffin, says, "All we have in this business are creativity and ideas. The moment someone infringes on that, they're reaching into the very core of the business and ripping it out." Ultimately, advertisers must stop "borrowing" ideas from each other and demand greater creativity from themselves.

Questions

1. Some art directors claim that "coincidental invention" explains why many ads look the same. Do you think that's really possible?
2. Who wins and who loses when advertising is imitated? Do you believe that it's actually an advantage to be copied?
3. What would you do if a client asked you to copy an ad that was already running? Is it acceptable to plagiarize advertising ideas, as long as they are recycled "in a useful way"?
4. Is plagiarism justified by the contention that "there are very few original ideas"?

Ideally, headlines communicate the complete selling idea. Research suggests that three to five times as many people read the headline as read the body copy. So if the ad doesn't sell in the headline, the advertiser is wasting money. Nike uses beautiful magazine and outdoor ads featuring just an athlete, the logo, and the memorable headline: "Just do it." Working off the visual, the headline creates the mood and tells the reader, through implication, to take action—buy Nike.

The traditional notion is that short headlines with one line are best but a second line is acceptable. Many experts believe that headlines with 10 words or less gain greater readership. In one study of more than 2,000 ads, most headlines averaged eight words in length.[10] Conversely, David Ogilvy said the best headline he ever wrote contained 18 words—and became a classic: "At 60 miles an hour, the loudest noise in the new Rolls-Royce comes from the electric clock."[11]

Headlines should offer a benefit that is apparent to the reader and easy to grasp. For example: "When it absolutely, positively has to be there overnight" (FedEx) or "Folds flat for easy storage" (Honda Civic Wagon).[12]

Finally, headlines should present *product news.* Consumers look for new products, new uses for old products, or improvements on old products. If they haven't been overused in a category, "power" words that suggest newness can increase readership and improve the boom factor of an ad. They should be employed whenever honestly applicable.[13] Examples include *free, now, amazing, suddenly, announcing, introducing, it's here, improved, at last, revolutionary, just arrived, new,* and *important development.*

Types of Headlines Copywriters use many variations of headlines depending on the advertising strategy. Typically, they use the headline that presents the big idea most successfully. Headlines may be classified by the type of information they carry: *benefit, news/information, provocative, question,* and *command.*

benefit headlines Type of headline that makes a direct promise to the reader.

news/information headline A type of headline that includes many of the "how-to" headlines as well as headlines that seek to gain identification for their sponsors by announcing some news or providing some promise of information.

provocative headlines A type of headline written to provoke the reader's curiosity so that, to learn more, the reader will read the body copy.

question headline A type of headline that asks the reader a question.

▼**EXHIBIT 9-2** An ad's success depends on the viewer's ability to absorb and learn its message. The creative pyramid helps the copywriter present the conceptual elements of the message. The format elements (headlines, subheads, body copy, slogan) segment the copy to help audiences decode the message. This is shown clearly in the ad below from Allstate, ca 1990s.

Advertisers use **benefit headlines** to promise the audience that experiencing the utility of the product or service will be rewarding. Benefit headlines shouldn't be too cute or clever, just simple statements of the product's most important benefit.[14] Two good examples are

Gore-Tex® Fabrics Keep you warm and dry. Regardless of what falls Out of the sky.	and	Speak a foreign language in 30 days or your money back.

Note that both of these headlines focus on the benefit of using the product, not the features of the product itself.[15]

The **news/information headline** announces news or promises information. Sea World began its TV announcement of a new baby whale with the headline "It's a girl." The information must be believable, though. A claim that a razor "shaves 200% smoother" probably isn't.[16]

Copywriters use **provocative headlines** to provoke the reader's curiosity—to stimulate questions and thoughts. For example: "Betcha can't eat just one" (Lay's Potato Chips). To learn more, the reader must read the body copy. The danger, of course, is that the reader won't read on. To avoid this, the creative team designs visuals to clarify the message or provide some story appeal.

A **question headline** asks a question, encouraging readers to search for the answer in the body of the ad. An ad for 4 Day Tire Stores asked: "What makes our tire customers smarter &

command headline A type of headline that orders the reader to do something.

subhead Secondary headline that may appear above or below the headline or in the text of the ad.

kicker A subhead that appears above the headline.

boldface Heavier type.

italic A style of printing type with letters that generally slant to the right.

body copy The text of an advertisement that tells the complete story and attempts to close the sale. It is a logical continuation of the headline and subheads and is usually set in a smaller type size than headlines or subheads.

Benefit headlines offer a reward to the reader. They should be straightforward and preferably include the name of the product that's providing the benefit.

A provocative headline provokes the reader's curiosity and stimulates questions.

richer than others?" A good question headline piques the reader's curiosity and imagination.

A **command headline** orders the reader to do something, so it might seem negative. But readers pay attention to such headlines. Sprite soft-drink ads target youth with the hip headline: "Obey your thirst." Some command headlines make a request: "Please don't squeeze the Charmin" (bathroom tissue).

Subheads

The **subhead** is an additional smaller headline that may appear above the headline or below it. Subheads above the headline are called **kickers** (or *overlines*), while those below the headline are called *underlines*. Subheads may also appear in body copy.

Subheads are usually set smaller than the headline but larger than the body copy or text. Subheads generally appear in **boldface** (heavier) or **italic** (slanted) type or a different color. Like a headline, the subhead transmits key sales points fast. But it usually carries less important information than the headline. Subheads are important for two reasons: Most people read only the headline and subheads, and subheads usually best support the interest step.

Subheads are longer and more like sentences than headlines. They serve as stepping-stones from the headline to the body copy, telegraphing what's to come.[17] And they help guide readers to get the information they are looking for in an ad.

Body Copy

The advertiser tells the complete sales story in the **body copy**, or **text**. The body copy comprises the interest, credibility, desire, and often even the action steps. It is a logical continuation of the headline and subheads, set in smaller type. Body copy covers the features, benefits, and utility of the product or service.

The body copy is typically read by only 1 out of 10 readers, so the writer must speak to the reader's self-interest, explaining how the product or service satisfies the customer's need.[18] The

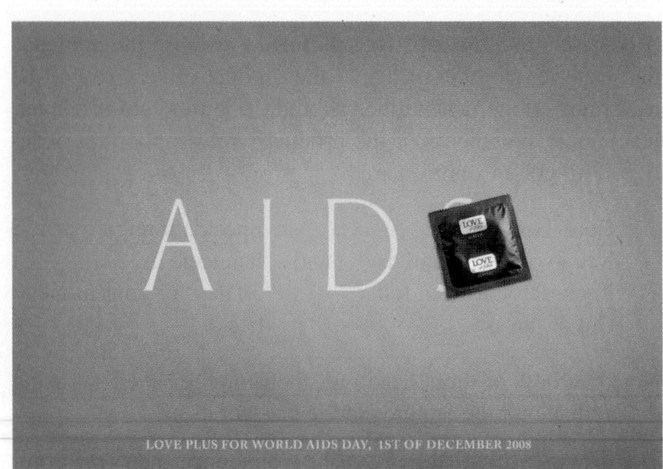

Ads are most effective when the parts work together. This PSA cleverly integrates art and copy.

text What tells the whole story and attempts to close the sale.

straight-sell copy A type of body copy in which the text immediately explains or develops the headline and visual in a straightforward attempt to sell the product.

institutional copy A type of body copy in which the advertiser tries to sell an idea or the merits of the organization or service rather than the sales features of a particular product.

narrative copy A type of body copy that tells a story. It sets up a problem and then creates a solution using the particular sales features of the product or service as the key to the solution.

dialogue/monologue copy A type of body copy in which the characters illustrated in the advertisement do the selling in their own words either through a quasi-testimonial technique or through a comic strip panel.

picture-caption copy A type of body copy in which the story is told through a series of illustrations and captions rather than through the use of a copy block alone.

best ads focus on one big idea or one clear benefit. Copywriters often read their copy aloud to hear how it sounds, even if it's intended for print media. The ear is a powerful copywriting tool.[19]

Body Copy Styles Experienced copywriters look for the technique and style with the greatest sales appeal for the idea being presented. Common copy styles include *straight sell, institutional, narrative, dialogue/monologue, picture caption,* and *device.*

In **straight-sell copy**, writers immediately explain or develop the headline and visual in a straightforward, factual presentation. The straight-sell approach appeals to the prospect's intelligence. Straight-sell copy is particularly good for high think-involvement products or products that are difficult to use. It's very effective for direct-mail advertising and for industrial or high-tech products.[20]

Advertisers use **institutional copy** to promote a philosophy or extol the merits of an organization rather than product features. Institutional copy is intended to lend warmth and credibility to the organization's image. Banks, insurance companies, public corporations, and large manufacturing firms use institutional copy in both print and electronic media.

Copywriters use **narrative copy** to tell a story. Ideal for the creative writer, narrative copy sets up a situation and then resolves it at the last minute by having the product or service come to the rescue. Narrative copy offers good opportunities for emotional appeals. Allstate uses this approach in its attention-getting "Mayhem" ads.[21]

By using **dialogue/monologue copy**, the advertiser can add the believability that narrative copy sometimes lacks. The characters portrayed in a print ad do the selling in their own words. A caution: Poorly written dialogue copy can come off as dull or, even worse, hokey and unreal.

Sometimes it's easier to tell a story with illustrations and captions. A photo with **picture-caption copy** is especially

Writing Effective Copy [9–E]

- **Get to the main point—fast.**
- **Emphasize one major idea simply and clearly.**
- **Be single-minded.** Don't try to do too much. If you chase more than one rabbit at a time, you'll catch none.
- **Position the product clearly.**
- **Keep the brand name up front and reinforce it.**
- **Write with the consumer's ultimate benefit in mind.**
- **Write short sentences.** Use easy, familiar words and themes people understand.
- **Don't waste words.** Say what you have to say—nothing more, nothing less. Don't pad, but don't skimp.
- **Avoid bragging and boasting.** Write from the reader's point of view, not your own. Avoid "we," "us," and "our."
- **Avoid clichés.** They're crutches; learn to get along without them. Bright, surprising words and phrases perk up readers and keep them reading.
- **Write with flair.** Drum up excitement. Make sure your own enthusiasm comes through in the copy.
- **Use vivid language.** Use lots of verbs and adverbs.
- **Stick to the present tense, active voice.** It's crisper. Avoid the past tense and passive voice. Exceptions should be deliberate, for special effect.
- **Use personal pronouns.** Remember, you're talking to just one person, so talk as you would to a friend. Use "you" and "your" whenever appropriate.
- **Use contractions.** They're fast, personal, natural. People talk in contractions (listen to yourself).
- **Don't overpunctuate.** It kills copy flow. Excessive commas are the chief culprits. Don't give readers any excuse to jump ship.
- **Read the copy aloud.** Hear how it sounds; catch errors. The written word is considerably different from the spoken word so listen to it.
- **Rewrite and write tight.** Edit mercilessly. Tell the whole story and no more. When you're finished, stop.

device copy Advertising copy that relies on wordplay, humor, poetry, rhymes, great exaggeration, gags, and other tricks or gimmicks.

lead-in paragraph In print ads, a bridge between the headlines, the subheads, and the sales ideas presented in the text. It transfers the reader interest to product interest.

interior paragraphs Text within the body copy of an ad where the credibility and desire steps of the message are presented.

trial close In ad copy, requests for the order that are made before the close in the ad.

close The part of an advertisement or commercial that asks customers to do something and tells them how to do it—the action step in the ad's copy.

useful for products that have a number of different uses or come in a variety of styles or designs.

With any copy style, the copywriter may use some device copy to enhance attention, interest, and memorability. **Device copy** uses figures of speech (such as puns, alliteration, and rhymes) as well as humor and exaggeration. Verbal devices help people remember the brand and tend to affect attitudes favorably.[22]

Humor can be effective when the advertiser needs high memorability in a short time, wants to dispel preconceived negative images, or needs to create a distinct personality for an undifferentiated product. However, humor should always be used carefully and never be in questionable taste. Humor also grows old very quickly; the same joke is not funny for long. Therefore, a variety of executions should be created to keep the idea fresh. Some researchers believe humor distracts from the selling message and can even be detrimental when used for serious services like finance, insurance, and crematoriums.[23]

Formatting Body Copy

The keys to good body copy are simplicity, order, credibility, and clarity. Or, as John O'Toole said, prose should be "written clearly, informatively, interestingly, powerfully, persuasively, dramatically, memorably, and with effortless grace. That's all."[24]

Four basic format elements are used to construct long copy ads: the *lead-in paragraph, interior paragraphs, trial close,* and *close.*

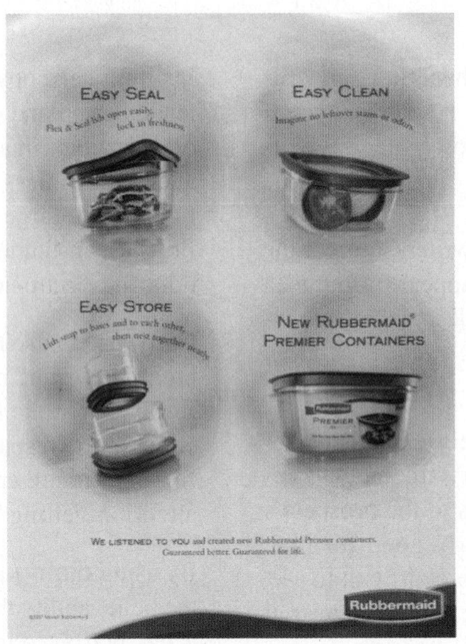

The selection of a body copy style can have a big impact on the effectiveness of an ad. The use of photos with picture-caption copy in this print ad from Rubbermaid (www.rubbermaid.com) does a good job communicating all of the benefits of its new premier containers.

As John O'Toole said, prose should be "written clearly, informatively, interestingly, powerfully, persuasively, dramatically, memorably, and with effortless grace. That's all."

Lead-in paragraph. The **lead-in paragraph** is a bridge between the headline and the sales ideas presented in the text. The lead-in paragraph is part of the *interest* step. It must engage and convert a prospect's reading interest to product interest.

Interior paragraphs. The **interior paragraphs** of the body copy should develop *credibility* by providing proof for claims and promises and they should build *desire* by using language that stirs the imagination. Advertisers should support their product promises with data, testimonials, and warranties. Such proofs convince customers of the validity of the product, improve goodwill toward the advertiser, and stimulate sales.

Trial close. Interspersed in the interior paragraphs should be suggestions to *act* now. Good copy asks for the order more than once; mail-order ads ask several times. Consumers often make the buying decision without reading all the body copy. The **trial close** gives them the opportunity to make the buying decision early.

Close. The **close** is the real *action* step. A good close asks consumers to do something and tells them how. The close can be indirect or direct (a subtle suggestion or a direct command). A direct close seeks immediate response in the form of a purchase, a store or website visit, or a request for further information.

Of course, not all ads sell products or services. Advertisers may want to change attitudes, explain their viewpoints, or ask for

slogans A standard company statement (also called a *tagline* or a *themeline*) for advertisements, salespeople, and company employees. Slogans have two basic purposes: to provide continuity for a campaign and to reduce a key theme or idea to a brief memorable positioning statement.

themelines A standard company statement for advertisements, salespeople, and company employees. Also called a *slogan* or *tagline*.

taglines A standard company statement for advertisements, salespeople, and company employees.

seal A type of certification mark offered by such organizations as the Good Housekeeping Institute and Underwriters' Laboratories when a product meets standards established by these institutions. Seals provide an independent, valued endorsement for the advertised product.

logotypes Special design of the advertiser's name (or product name) that appears in all advertisements. Also called a *signature cut*, it is like a trademark because it gives the advertiser individuality and provides quick recognition at the point of purchase.

signatures A product or company's primary graphic identity. A signature may be comprised of some combination of a graphic symbol, a logotype, and a slogan.

The slogan "M'm! M'm! Good!" is synonymous with Campbell's soup (www.campbells.com). It would be surprising to find a Campbell's soup print ad without the familiar red and white logo and the memorable phrase.

someone's vote. By giving a Web address, the advertiser can offer additional information to those readers who are interested in learning more.

Slogans

Many **slogans** (also called **themelines** or **taglines**) begin as successful headlines, like AT&T's "Reach out and touch someone." Through continuous use, they become standard statements, not just in advertising but for salespeople and company employees.

Slogans have two basic purposes: to provide continuity to a series of ads in a campaign and to reduce an advertising message strategy to a brief, repeatable, and memorable positioning statement. Wheaties cereal, for example, positions itself as the "Breakfast of Champions." And ads for DeBeers still use the famous "Diamonds are forever" slogan.

Seals, Logos, and Signatures

A **seal** is awarded only when a product meets standards established by a particular organization, such as the Good Housekeeping Institute or Underwriters Laboratories. Because these organizations are recognized authorities, their seals provide an independent, valued endorsement for the advertiser's product.

Logotypes (logos) and **signatures** are special designs of the advertiser's company or product name. They appear in all company ads and, like trademarks, give the product individuality and provide quick recognition at the point of purchase.

check yourself ✓

1. What are the key format elements in a print ad?
2. What are some important types of headlines?
3. When would an advertiser use straight-sell copy rather than device copy?

“RADIO WRITING HAS TO BE CLEARER THAN ANY OTHER KIND OF COPYWRITING.”

LO9-3 Outline how great copy is created in electronic ads.

CREATING GREAT COPY IN ELECTRONIC MEDIA

For electronic media, the fundamental elements—the five steps of the creative pyramid—remain the primary guides, but the copywriting formats differ. Radio and television writers prepare *scripts* and *storyboards*.

Writing Radio Copy

A **script** resembles a two-column list. On the left side, speakers' names are arranged vertically, along with descriptions of any **sound effects** (abbreviated **SFX**) and music. The right column contains the dialogue, called the **audio**.

Copywriters first need to understand radio's strengths and weaknesses. Radio provides entertainment or news to listeners who are busy doing something else—driving, washing dishes, reading the paper, or even studying. To get attention, an advertising message must be catchy, interesting, and unforgettable. Radio listeners usually decide within five to eight seconds if they're going to listen. To attract and hold attention, radio copy must be intrusive.

One of the greatest challenges for radio copywriters is making the script fit the time slot. The delivery changes for different types of commercials, so writers must read the script out loud for timing. With electronic compression, recorded radio ads can now include 10 to 30 percent more copy than text read live. Still, the following is a good rule of thumb:

10 seconds: 20–25 words
20 seconds: 40–45 words
30 seconds: 60–70 words
60 seconds: 130–150 words[25]

Radio writing has to be clearer than any other kind of copywriting. For example, the listener can't refer back, as in print, to find an antecedent for a pronoun. Likewise, the English language is so full of homonyms (words that sound like other words) that one can easily confuse the meaning of a sentence ("who's who is whose").[26]

Writing Television Copy

Radio's basic two-column script format also works for television. But in a TV script, the left side is titled "Video" and the right side "Audio." The video column describes the visuals and production: camera angles, action, scenery, and stage directions. The audio column lists the spoken copy, sound effects, and music.

Broadcast commercials must be believable and relevant. Even humorous commercials must exude quality in their creation and

Creating Effective Radio Commercials [9–F]

Writing for radio takes a sharp ear, empathy for the listener, and the ability to create pictures inside the consumer's head. These tips will help you create great radio spots.

- **Make the big idea crystal clear.** Concentrate on one main selling point. Radio is a good medium for building brand awareness, but not for making long lists of copy points or complex arguments.
- **Mention the advertiser's name early and often.** If the product or company name is tricky, consider spelling it out.
- **Take time to set the scene and establish the premise.** A 30-second commercial that nobody remembers is a waste of money. Fight for 60-second spots.
- **Use familiar sound effects.** Ice tinkling in a glass, birds chirping, or a door shutting can create a visual image. Music also works if its meaning is clear.
- **Paint pictures with your words.** Use descriptive language to make the ad more memorable.
- **Make every word count.** Use active voice and more verbs than adjectives. Be conversational. Use pronounceable words and short sentences.
- **Be outrageous.** The best comic commercials begin with a totally absurd premise from which all developments follow logically. But remember, if you can't write humor really well, go for drama.
- **Ask for the order.** Try to get listeners to take action.
- **Remember that radio is a local medium.** Adjust your commercials to the language of your listeners and the time of day they'll run.
- **Presentation counts a lot.** Even the best scripts look boring on paper. Acting, timing, vocal quirks, and sound effects bring them to life.

script Format for radio and television copywriting resembling a two-column list showing dialogue and/or visuals.

sound effects (SFX) Sounds other than music or dialogue used in radio and television.

audio The sound portion of a commercial. Also, the right side of a script for a television commercial, indicating spoken copy, sound effects, and music.

Healthier America
Lost Campaign
Radio: 60
"Neighbor"
Expiration date: 2/23/05

SFX: Phone ringing

Bill:	Hello...?
George:	Hi, Bill? This is George Dewey from up the street.
Bill:	Hey, George. How ya doin?
George:	Good, good. Say, I noticed you've been walking to work these days instead of driving...and I, uh, don't quite know how to say this, but...but...
Bill:	But what?
George: (*stammering*)	But...But...Your butt, your buttocks, your butt—I think I found your butt on my front lawn. Have you recently lost it?
Bill:	As a matter of fact, I have, George (*pleased*). It's about time someone noticed.
George: (*playful*)	Well, it was kinda hard to miss if you know what I mean... ...Anyways, would you like it back?
Bill:	Would I like it back? No, not really.
George:	So, it's okay if I throw it out?
Bill:	Sure, that's fine. Take it easy, George.

SFX: Phone ringing

Announcer:	Small step #8—Walk instead of driving whenever you can. It's just one of the many small steps you can take to help you become a healthier, well, you. Get started at www.smallstep.gov and take a small step to get healthy.
Legal:	A public service announcement brought to you by the U.S. Department of Health and Human Services and the Ad Council.

A radio script format resembles a two-column list, with speakers' names and sound effects on the left and the dialogue in a wider column on the right. This national public service announcement (PSA) was created by McCann Erickson and is one of many in a campaign designed to inspire Americans to take small steps toward a healthier lifestyle.

production to imply the product's quality. While the art director's work is very important, the copywriter typically sets the tone of the commercial, establishes the language that determines which visuals to use, and pinpoints when the visuals should appear.

To illustrate these principles, let's look at a particular commercial. Many people want smooth, soft skin and consider a patch of rough, flaky skin anywhere on their body a disappointment. If you were the copywriter for Lubriderm skin lotion, how would you approach this somewhat touchy, uncomfortable subject?

The creative staff of J. Walter Thompson crafted an artistic solution for Lubriderm. An alligator was the big idea. The gator's scaly sheath was a metaphor for rough, flaky skin. Its appearance ignited people's survival instincts; they paid attention, fast. A beautiful, sophisticated woman with smooth, feminine skin was seated in a lounge chair, completely unruffled by the passing gator. The swing of the animal's back and tail echoed the graceful curves of the two simple pieces of furniture on the set, and its slow stride kept the beat of a light jazz tune.

This ad follows the creative pyramid. The alligator captures attention visually while the announcer's first words serve as an attention-getting headline: "A quick reminder." The ad commands us to listen and sets up the interest step that offers this claim: "Lubriderm restores lost moisture to heal your dry skin and protect it." Now for the credibility step: "Remember, the one created for dermatologists is the one that heals and protects." And then the desire step recaps the primary product benefit and adds a touch of humor: "See you later, alligator."

check yourself ✓

1. From the writer's perspective, what are the important differences between a radio listener and a print ad reader?
2. What is the approximate word limit of a 30-second radio ad?
3. What are the two columns labeled in a TV script?

LO9-4 Discuss the role of art in electronic ads.

THE ROLE OF ART IN RADIO AND TV ADVERTISING

In the vignette that opened this chapter, Sony advertises its BRAVIA line of TVs with . . . bouncing colored balls. The unusual execution hints at the quality of the television and suggests the confidence of Sony in its product. Inspired. Cunning. Brilliant. A big idea.

Developing the Artistic Concept for Commercials

Creating the concept for a radio or TV commercial is similar to creating the concept for print ads. The first step is to determine the big idea. Then the art director and copywriter must decide what commercial format to use. Should a celebrity present the message? Or should the ad dramatize the product's benefits with a semifictional story? The next step is to write a script containing the necessary copy or dialogue plus a basic description of any music, sound effects, and/or camera views.

In both radio and TV, the art director assists the copywriter in script development. But in television, artistic development is much more extensive. Using the TV script, the art director creates a series of **storyboard roughs** to present the artistic approach, the action sequences, and the style of the commercial.

Formats for Radio and TV Commercials

Similar to print advertising, the format for a broadcast ad serves as a template for arranging message elements into a pattern. Once the art director and copywriter establish the big idea, they must determine the commercial's format.

Many radio and TV commercial styles have been successful. Here we consider eight common commercial formats that can be used in either radio or television: *straight announcement, presenter, testimonial, demonstration, musical, slice of life, lifestyle,* and *animation.*

Straight Announcement

The oldest and simplest type of radio or TV commercial and probably the easiest to write is the **straight announcement**. One person, usually a radio or TV announcer, delivers the sales message. Music may play in the background. Straight announcements are popular because they are adaptable to almost any product or situation. In radio, a straight announcement can also be designed as an **integrated commercial**—that is,

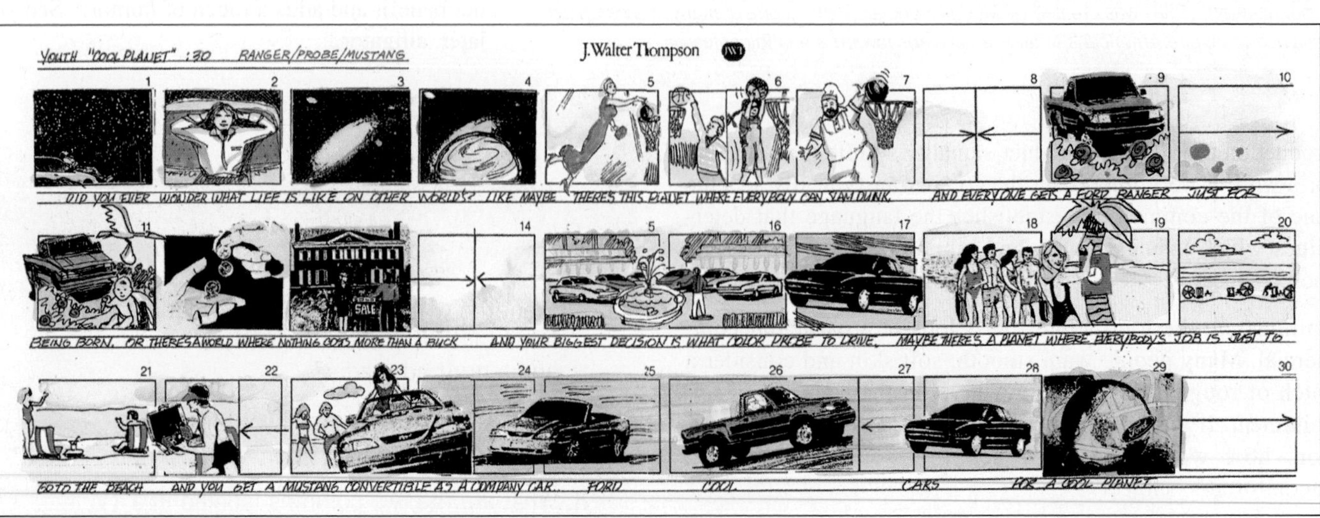

After the initial concepts for a television ad are finalized, creatives develop a storyboard rough composed of small sketches that depict the various scenes of the ad. The storyboard rough is used to present the creative concept to the account team and the client.

storyboard roughs A rough layout of a television commercial in storyboard form.

straight announcement The oldest type of radio or television commercial in which an announcer delivers a sales message directly into the microphone or on-camera or does so off-screen while a slide or film is shown on-screen.

integrated commercial A straight radio announcement, usually delivered by one person, woven into a show or tailored to a given program to avoid any perceptible interruption.

on camera Actually seen by the camera, as an announcer, a spokesperson, or actor playing out a scene.

voice-over In television advertising, the spoken copy or dialogue delivered by an announcer who is not seen but whose voice is heard.

presenter commercial A commercial format in which one person or character presents the product and sales message.

radio personality A radio host known to his or her listeners as a credible source.

testimonial The use of satisfied customers and celebrities to endorse a product in advertising.

it can be woven into a show or tailored to the style of a given program.

For TV, an announcer may deliver the sales message **on camera** or off screen, as a **voice-over**, while a demonstration, slide, or film shows on screen. If the script is well written and the announcer convincing, straight announcements can be very effective. Since they don't require elaborate production facilities, they save money, too.

Presenter The **presenter commercial** uses one person or character to present the product and carry the sales message. Some presenters are celebrities, such as Brad Pitt for Calvin Klein. Others may be experts, such as corporate officers (John Schnatter for Papa John's) or professionals (doctors), or they may be actors playing a role (Stephanie Courtney as "Flo" in ads for Progressive). A *man-on-the-street* may interview real people and get them to share their thoughts about a client's products or services. And, of course, a presenter doesn't have to be a real person. Remember Tony the Tiger?

A **radio personality**, such as Rush Limbaugh or Howard Stern, may *ad lib* an ad message live in his or her own style. Done well, such commercials can be very successful, as evidenced by the initial success of Snapple. However, the advertiser surrenders control to the personality.

Testimonial The true **testimonial**—where a satisfied user tells how effective the product is—can be highly credible in both TV and radio advertising. Celebrities may gain attention, but they must be believable and not distract from the product. Actually, people from all walks of life endorse products, from known personalities to unknowns and nonprofessionals. Which type of person to use depends on the product and the strategy. Satisfied customers are the best sources for testimonials because their sincerity is usually persuasive. Ogilvy suggested shooting candid testimonials when the subjects don't know they're being filmed.[27] Of course, advertisers must be sure to get their permission before using the piece.

Creating Effective TV Commercials [9–G]

- **Begin at the finish.** Concentrate on the final impression the commercial will make.
- **Create an attention-getting opening.** An opening that is visually surprising or full of action, drama, humor, or human interest sets the context and allows a smooth transition to the rest of the commercial.
- **Use a situation that grows naturally out of the sales story.** Avoid distracting gimmicks. Make it easy for viewers to identify with the characters.
- **Characters are the living symbol of the product.** They should be appealing, believable, nondistracting, and most of all, relevant.
- **Keep it simple.** The sequence of ideas should be easy to follow. Keep the number of elements in the commercial to a bare minimum.
- **Write concise audio copy.** The video should carry most of the weight. Fewer than 2 words per second is effective for demonstrations. For a 60-second commercial, 101 to 110 words is most effective; more than 170 words is too talky.
- **Make demonstrations dramatic but believable.** They should always be true to life and avoid the appearance of camera tricks.
- **Let the words interpret the picture and prepare viewers for the next scene.** Use conversational language; avoid "ad talk," hype, and puffery.
- **Run scenes five or six seconds on average.** Rarely should a scene run less than three seconds. Offer a variety of movement-filled scenes without "jumping."
- **Keep the look of the video fresh and new.**

demonstration A type of TV commercial in which the product is shown in use.

lifestyle technique Type of commercial in which the user is presented rather than the product. Typically used by clothing and soft drink advertisers to affiliate their brands with the trendy lifestyles of their consumers.

animation The use of cartoons, puppet characters, or demonstrations of inanimate characters that come to life in television commercials; often used for communicating difficult messages or for reaching specialized markets, such as children.

musical commercials A commercial that is sung with the sales message in the verse.

jingles Musical commercials usually sung with the sales message in the verse.

slice of life A type of commercial consisting of a dramatization of a real-life situation in which the product is tried and becomes the solution to a problem.

mnemonic device A gimmick used to dramatize the product benefit and make it memorable, such as the Imperial Margarine crown or the Avon doorbell.

Demonstration

Television is uniquely suited to visual demonstrations. And a **demonstration** convinces an audience better and faster than a spoken message. So don't say it, show it.[28] Naturally, it's easier to demonstrate the product on TV than on radio, but some advertisers have used the imaginative nature of radio to create humorous, tongue-in-cheek demonstrations.

Products may be demonstrated in use, in competition, or before and after. These techniques help viewers visualize how the product will perform for them.

Musical

The **musical commercials**, or **jingles**, we hear on radio and TV are among the best—and worst—ad messages produced. Done well, they can bring enormous success, well beyond the average nonmusical commercial. Done poorly, they can waste the advertising budget and annoy audiences beyond belief.

Slice of Life (Problem Solution)

A commercial that dramatizes a real-life situation is called **slice of life**. It usually starts with just plain folks, played by professional actors, discussing some problem or issue. Often the situation deals with a problem of a personal nature: bad breath, loose dentures, dandruff, body odor, or yellow laundry. A relative or a co-worker drops the hint, the product is tried, and the next scene shows the result—a happier, cleaner, more fragrant person off with a new date. The drama always concludes with a positive outcome. Such commercials can get attention and create interest, even though they are often irritating to viewers and hated by copywriters.

The key to effective slice-of-life commercials is simplicity. The ad should concentrate on one compelling product benefit and make it memorable. Often a **mnemonic device** (a technique that helps you remember something) can dramatize the benefit and trigger instant recall. The Aflac duck immediately reminds viewers that Aflac (www.aflac.com) is there to help pay your bills if you get hurt and can't work.

Lifestyle

To present the user rather than the product, advertisers may use the **lifestyle technique**. For example, Diesel pitches its denim to urbanites by showing characters working and playing while wearing its latest line. Likewise, beer and soft-drink advertisers frequently target their messages to active, outdoorsy young people, focusing on who drinks the brand rather than on specific product advantages.

Animation

Cartoons, puppet characters, and demonstrations with computer-generated graphics are **animation** techniques for communicating difficult messages and reaching specialized markets, such as children. The way aspirin or other medications affect the human system is difficult to explain. Animated pictures of headaches and stomachs can simplify the subject and make a benefit demonstration clear and understandable.

Ads that appeal to lifestyle present the type of user associated with the product, rather than the product itself. This ad for MasterCard is aimed at sports fans, and specifically Boston Red Sox fans, who are willing to do just about anything for their team.

VO: Red Sox World Series tickets

Baseball Enthusiast #1: Five hundred bucks.

Man Waiting in Line: I'd pay four grand.

Weightlifter: My car. My truck. My computer.

Girl #1: Two months' salary.

Weightlifter: . . . my entire savings account.

Man with Painted Face: Anything, anything.

Little Boy: My fish.

Young Woman: My dog.

Weightlifter: My girlfriend.

Fan at Ballpark: My first-born kid.

Girl #3: Really.

VO/Super: Seeing the Red Sox in the World Series: Priceless.

VO/Super: There are some things money can't buy.

VO/Super: For everything else there's MasterCard.

VO/Super: Devoted fan of the devoted fans.

storyboard A sheet preprinted with a series of 8 to 20 blank frames in the shape of TV screens, which includes text of the commercial, sound effects, and camera views.

animatic A rough television commercial produced by photographing storyboard sketches on a film strip or video with the audio portion synchronized on tape. It is used primarily for testing purposes.

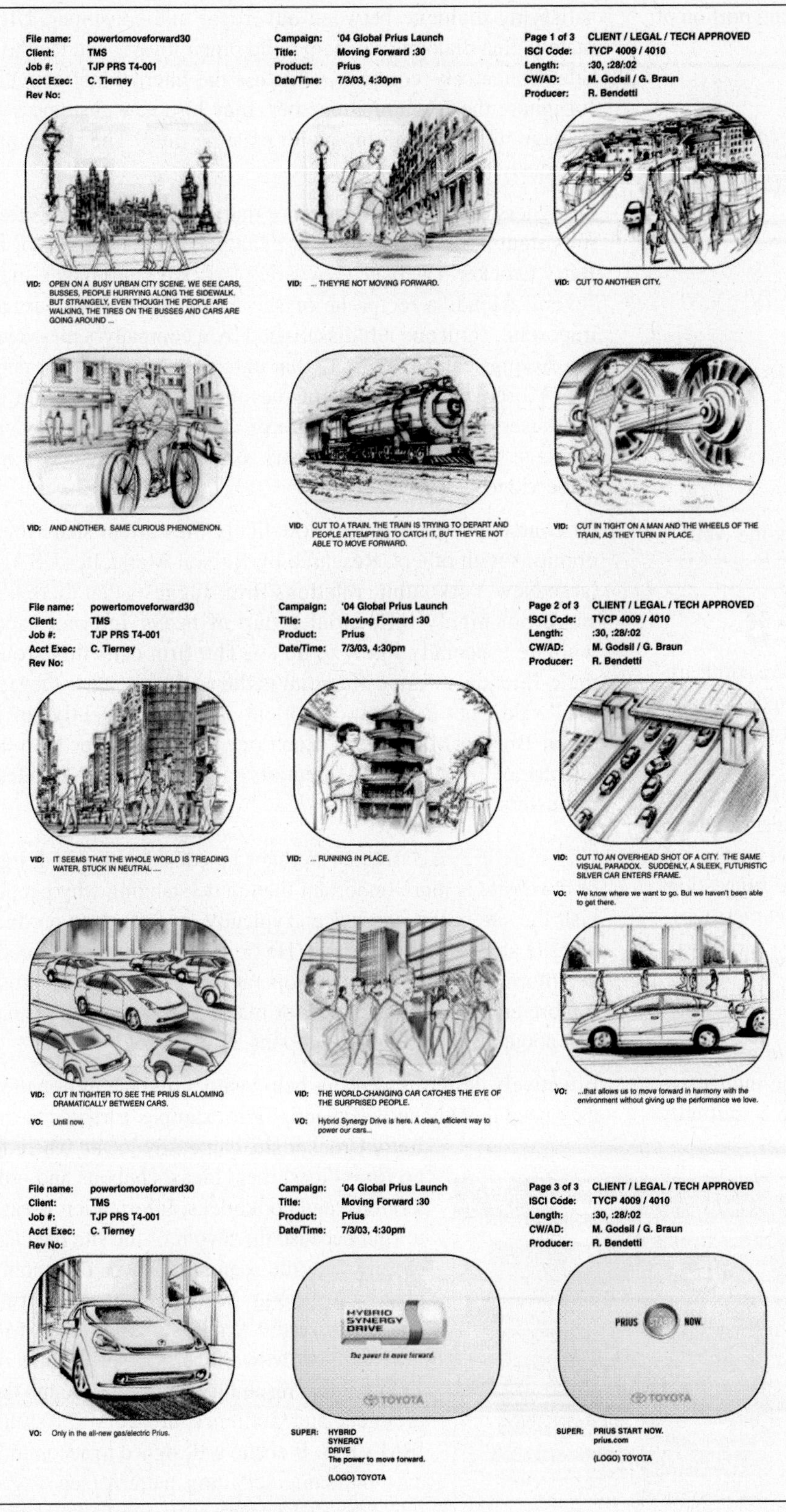

Storyboard of "Power to Move" TV commercial

The storyboard is a visual representation of the ad, made up of sketches that indicate the art director's concept of the various scenes, camera angles, sound effects, and special effects to be used in the final production.

Outlining a TV Commercial

After the creative team selects the big idea and the format for a TV commercial, the art director and the writer develop the script. Television is so visually powerful and expressive that the art director's role is particularly important. Art directors must be able to work with a variety of professionals—producers, directors, lighting technicians, and set designers—to develop and produce a commercial successfully. Ad production is discussed in our outline production chapter.

Storyboard Design Once the basic script is completed, the art director must turn the video portion of the script into real images. This is done with a **storyboard**, a sheet preprinted with a series of 8 to 20 blank windows (frames) in the shape of TV screens. Below each frame is room to place the text of the commercial, including the sound effects and camera views. The storyboard works much like a comic strip.

Through a process similar to laying out a print ad (thumbnail, rough, comp) the artist carefully designs how each scene should appear, arranging actors, scenery, props, lighting, and camera angles to maximize impact, beauty, and mood. The storyboard helps the creatives visualize the commercial's tone and sequence of action, discover any conceptual weaknesses, and make presentations for final management approval. It also serves as a guide for filming.

To supplement the storyboard or pretest a concept, a commercial may be taped in rough form using amateur talent as actors. Or an **animatic** may be shot—a film strip of the

sketches in the storyboard accompanied by the audio portion of the commercial synchronized on tape.

check yourself ✓

1. What is a storyboard?
2. What is the oldest and simplest radio or TV commercial format?
3. What TV format would help present the user rather than the product?

LO9-5 Review the unique requirements in writing for the Web.

WRITING FOR THE WEB

The Internet is young and advertisers and agencies are still learning how best to use the medium. This is to be expected. A similar learning period took place after the rapid spread of television in the 1950s. Agencies at first struggled to figure out how best to advertise in this new, thoroughly "modern" medium. For proof, watch some commercials from the 1950s and consider how simplistic and ineffective they seem compared to those of the present. Fortunately, research is beginning to offer concrete suggestions that can help a designer create more effective Internet messages.

A designer should understand that the Internet, while it contains elements of both print and broadcast media, is a completely new medium that engages its users in a fundamentally different way. At the core of this engagement is *interactivity*. Smart companies realize that used effectively, the interactive nature of the Internet creates opportunities for a mutually satisfying dialogue between advertiser and consumer. Ultimately, that dialogue can help build brand loyalty and lead to a sale. Conversely, companies that use the Internet ineffectively (or ignore the medium altogether) may lose new customers or damage their relationships with existing ones. The stakes are obviously high.

Designers should also remember that Internet users are often important opinion leaders. For example, a satisfied visitor to Betty Crocker's website (www.bettycrocker.com) may e-mail several friends a recipe he or she found there. And, just as important, someone left dissatisfied by a company's messages or offerings can easily share that unhappiness with other people. Moreover, e-mail is not the only channel available to Web users. They can also share product-related opinions via message boards, a social network site, blogs, or even a YouTube video.

Of course, people differ in how likely they are to share their opinions with others. Research by Burson-Marsteller USA, a large New York public relations firm, suggests that there is a small but highly influential group of heavy Internet users who are especially likely to do so. The firm calls this group the e-fluentials. "An e-fluential is the rock that starts the ripple," said Chet Burchett, president and chief executive officer at Burson-Marsteller. "Each one communicates with an average of 14 people." E-fluentials can be reputation builders or busters.[29]

Company Websites Perhaps no consideration in design of a website is more important than understanding why people visit the site in the first place. Typically, a visitor to a product website arrives with a purpose. He or she may be seeking product information, such as how to operate the product safely or use it more effectively. Or the visitor may be looking for information about accessories, tips, coupons, or user groups.

Effectively designed websites help visitors find the information they need quickly and efficiently. For example, a visitor to the Betty Crocker site can easily locate where to go for recipes, meal ideas, coupons and promotions, and cookbooks. Information is easy to find because the layout of the site matches closely with the scanning pattern commonly observed among Web page readers: two quick horizontal scans across the top followed by a downward vertical scan. Think of a pattern that resembles an "*F*." Although the products and audience are very different, IBM's U.S. Website is designed to accommodate the same scanning pattern (see www.ibm.com/us/) as are sites for Coke, Ford, Tide, and many other large advertisers. Each of these sites makes finding information simple and fast. Colors and photographs are carefully chosen to enhance the layout, attract Internet users, and guide their gaze through the page.

The most effective websites can be scanned quickly for useful information and are updated regularly with new content.

Banner Ads The purpose of a banner ad is to bring Internet users to a website other than the one they intended to visit. Once the dominant advertising approach, banner ads now compete with many other online forms, including video virals and paid search listings. Designers should keep in mind research findings that suggest effective banner ads are simple, focused, and clear about a product's benefit. Most effective banners make use of a striking image and emphasize a palette of rich, powerful colors.

Viral Ads The enormous popularity of video sites such as YouTube has inspired advertisers to place special video commercials on the Web. These are often called "viral" ads because they rely on Internet users to spread messages to others. The design process for viral videos can have much in common with that for traditional commercials. But viral creators have a somewhat heavier burden because they must consistently entertain while informing about a product. The challenge is that viewers can't just like a viral; they have to love it. Otherwise they won't bother sharing it with others.

According to creatives at Crispin Porter+Bogusky, the talented Miami agency that created the "Subservient Chicken" website, the key to effectiveness is intrigue. "Interruption or disruption as the fundamental premise of marketing" doesn't work, according to CPB partner Jeff Hicks. "You have to create content that is interesting, useful or entertaining enough to invite (the consumer). Viral is the ultimate invitation." How does a creative create intrigue? A big idea is important (like a chicken that will do anything it is asked to). The unexpected can also grab consumer interest. When Microsoft released its popular console game Halo 2, it used an online marketing scheme that suggested villains were taking over a completely innocuous website humorously named "ilovebees.com." ■

check yourself ✓

1. What should a Web ad designer understand about the medium?
2. In what ways are Internet users different from users of traditional media?

learn about, practice, and apply creative execution in advertising!

M: Advertising was developed for students who want information packaged in a concise, easy-to-read, yet interesting format.
Check out the book's website to:

- Explain the importance of a layout in ad development, approval, and production. (Review Questions)
- Distinguish the guidelines for Web writing from those for traditional media. (Review Questions)
- Show you know the key format elements and their purposes in print ads. (Exploring Advertising)

While you are there, check out the professional resource links, review the PowerPoint presentation, and test your knowledge with the Multiple Choice Quiz. Additionally, *Connect® Marketing* is available for M: Advertising.

www.mhhe.com/ArensM2e

print advertising

chapter ten

This chapter examines how print advertising enhances the advertiser's media mix. Newspapers and magazines, with their unique qualities, can complement broadcast, direct mail, and other media. By using print wisely, advertisers can significantly increase the reach and impact of their campaigns and still stay within their budgets.

In today's society of *on-demand* and *up-to-the-minute,* advertising has taken a blow to its classic form, the creation of "campaigns." A campaign is nothing more than a consistent, thematic approach to conveying a message across multiple media. Unfortunately, advertising for many of today's products and services focuses more on test, learn, and adjust, rather than employing a long-term strategy and sticking with it. However, there are dozens of examples that point to consistency and reliability as being cornerstones of brand building. Look at Coca-Cola, Starbucks, and McDonald's; for each brand you know exactly what to expect from each experience. So why then do so many brands focus their efforts on immediate returns rather than on long-term brand building?

continued on p. 248

LEARNING OBJECTIVES

After studying this chapter, you will be able to:

LO10-1 Explain the advantages and disadvantages of magazine advertising.

LO10-2 Discuss how magazine circulation is measured and rates are set.

LO10-3 Explain the advantages and disadvantages of newspaper advertising.

LO10-4 Describe the major types of newspapers and how they charge for advertising.

LO10-5 Explain the unique roles played by directory and Yellow Pages advertising.

heritage as the quintessential American jeans.[2] After years of Levi's bleeding market share and struggling with near obsolescence, Susan Hoffman, creative director at Wieden+Kennedy, felt it was time to pay homage to the brand's history.[3] The campaign focused on a pioneering spirit entrenched with self-made optimism of the "New Americans" and borrowed words and concepts from American poet Walt Whitman,[4] himself an optimist in a time when pessimism was much more prevalent.

The "Go Forth" campaign was inspired by research that showed that the youth of today believe it is up to them to make a positive difference in the world.[5] This campaign is a great example of what advertising is *supposed* to do: Find a truth that is relevant to your audience, hits at the very core of their being, and positions your brand as the only option to fulfill upon this underlying truth. The timing of the concept certainly couldn't have been better, as was evidenced by two other successful campaigns launched around the same time—the Obama "Hope" campaign and the Pepsi campaign of the same name. There are many variables that factor into the success of campaigns, but without an underlying theme, focused on the needs of the audience, that ties the promotional elements together, one might argue that advertising's sole purpose is merely to remind people that the brand still exists.

Nailing the theme is really just the start of effective advertising. The right message placed in front of the wrong people has the same effect as bad messaging. Levi's launched the highly targeted "Go Forth" print campaign in magazines including *The Fader, Filter, Vice, SOMA, BlackBook, Paper, Anthem, Spin, Interview, Bullett, ESPN,* and *Metropop.* The 2012 "Go Forth" campaign was accompanied by a series of TV, digital, and outdoor advertisements in key youth markets, including New York, Los Angeles, San Francisco, and Chicago. Woven throughout the creative platform was the caption, "This is a pair of Levi's." The caption was juxtaposed over unexpected pieces from the collection, such as dresses and tops, to emphasize that the

continued from p. 247

That is a long-standing debate in advertising. The greed of shareholders, the short tenure of CMOs, and the immediacy demanded by our fast-paced lifestyles have led to a greater focus on an immediate return from advertising. This drives advertising creatives absolutely mad. When executed properly, ad campaigns can have a life of their own. They have the power to create a brand image that is elicited by the mere recognition of the campaign theme. Famous campaigns like Nike's "Just Do It," McDonald's "You Deserve a Break Today," Coca-Cola's "The Pause That Refreshes," Miller Lite's "Tastes Great, Less Filling," and "The Marlboro Man" maintain a life outside the advertising and they enrich our culture. In 1999, Bob Garfield of *Advertising Age* proclaimed the just-mentioned campaigns as 5 of the top 10 of all time.[1]

The teachings of integrated marketing communications (IMC) are grounded in the principle of consistency throughout every brand touch point. So, how does a campaign become established? In 2009, the world was in the midst of the digital revolution and the United States found itself in one of the worst recessions since the Great Depression. The timing seemed ripe for Wieden+Kennedy, a global ad agency headquartered in Portland, Oregon, to unveil its new, optimistically focused campaign for Levi Strauss and Co.'s flagship brand—Levi's. The campaign was called "Go Forth" and drew on the brand's

craftsmanship, innovation, and style associated with the Levi's brand is embedded in every article of clothing.[6]

One way to identify a successful ad campaign is through longevity. At the time of this writing, the Levi's "Go Forth" campaign is 4 years old. To a 134-year-old brand this is just a blip; however, by today's standards it's an eternity. Much like the timeless campaigns that preceded it, "Go Forth" seems to be headed down the right path. ■

SELECTING MEDIA

Selecting the most appropriate media mix for an advertising campaign requires two distinct skills: understanding the unique characteristics of the various media alternatives and determining which medium will most efficiently and effectively reach the campaign's target audience.

These chapters in Part 5 will discuss the unique elements of the most common media classes. Then, in Chapter 14, we will examine how media planners and buyers decide which media to use, when to use them, and how to purchase them. In that chapter, we will also discuss audience measurements. For now, it will help if you have a basic understanding of two key terms: *reach*—the number of different people exposed, at least once, to a medium during a given period of time; and *frequency*—the average number of times those people are exposed to that medium during that period of time.

Understanding the characteristics of media options is important not only to media planners and buyers; account managers, planners, and creatives must also have an appreciation for the strengths and weaknesses of each medium so they can develop strategies and executions that will take full advantage of their alternatives.

PRINT MEDIA

Print advertising certainly includes magazines and newspapers, but it could include any message that is produced on printed surfaces, such as brochures, directories, mail, posters, and outdoor boards. The definition of print advertising must now be expanded to include online, digital publications, to be discussed later in this chapter. All print advertising has several unique elements in common. Compared to television or radio, print advertising has more permanence. Since it stays around for a while, it may be read more than once or passed along to other readers. People also tend to spend more time with print advertising, so it provides an opportunity to present more detailed information and longer explanations.

Obviously, print advertising can be an important ingredient in the **media mix**, the combination of media types that work together to most effectively deliver an advertiser's message. In this chapter, we'll examine the characteristics of magazines and newspapers. Other forms of print media will be discussed in Chapters 12 and 13.

media mix
The combination of media types that work together to most effectively deliver an advertiser's message.

LO10-1 Explain the advantages and disadvantages of magazine advertising.

USING MAGAZINES IN THE MEDIA MIX

Advertisers use magazines in their media mix for many reasons. First and foremost, magazines allow an advertiser to reach a particular target audience with a high-quality presentation. Levi Strauss is just one of the many leading advertisers that use magazines as an important element of their creative mix. (Exhibit 10–1 lists the top U.S. magazine advertisers.)

Magazines have, however, lost significant advertising revenue in recent years. Not long ago the second-largest medium, magazines have fallen behind not only television, but also the Internal and newspapers. Several well-known magazines, such as *Newsweek, U.S. News, Gourmet,* and *PC World,* no longer publish printed editions.

The Pros and Cons of Magazine Advertising

Magazines do continue to offer a wide variety of benefits to advertisers. The "Go Forth" campaign benefited greatly from the outstanding color reproduction available only from magazines. Further, by running in culture magazines such as *The Fader* and *Bullet,* read by youth of different lifestyles and ages,

▼**EXHIBIT 10-1** Top 10 Magazine Advertisers

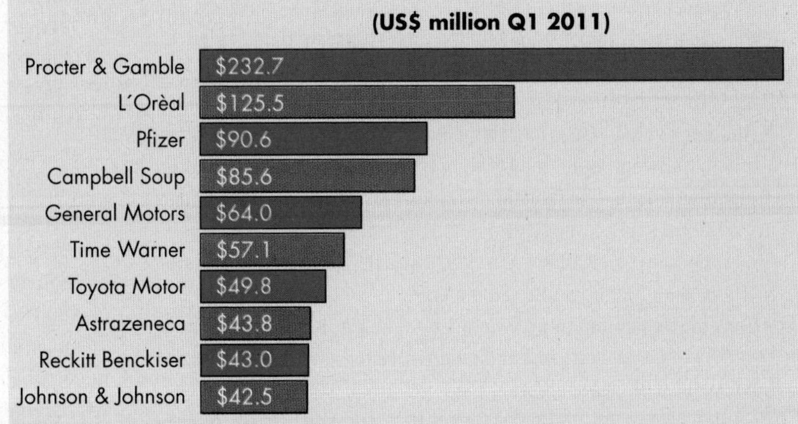

Source: Data as of August 3, 2013, ©2013 Magazine Publishers of America, Inc. PIB® is a registered trademark of Magazine Publishers of America, Inc., Kantar Media.

bleed Color, type, or visuals that run all the way to the edge of a printed page.

cover position Advertising space on the front inside, back inside, or back cover pages of a publication that is usually sold at a premium price.

junior unit A large magazine advertisement (60 percent of the page) placed in the middle of a page and surrounded by editorial matter.

island halves A half-page of magazine space that is surrounded on two or more sides by editorial matter. This type of ad is designed to dominate a page and is therefore sold at a premium price.

insert An ad or brochure that the advertiser prints and ships to the publisher for insertion into a magazine or newspaper.

Levi's was able to precisely target its audience. Magazines offer a host of other features too: flexible design options, prestige, authority, believability, and long shelf life. Magazines may sit on a coffee table for months and be reread many times. People can read a magazine ad at their leisure; they can pore over the details of a photograph; and they can study carefully the information presented in the copy. This makes it an ideal medium for high-involvement think and feel products.

However, like every medium, magazines also have a number of drawbacks (see My Ad Campaign 10–A, "The Pros and Cons of Magazine Advertising"). They are expensive (on a cost-per-reader basis), especially for color ads. And since they typically come out only monthly, or weekly at best, it's difficult to reach a large audience quickly or frequently. For these reasons, many advertisers use magazines in combination with other media—such as newspapers, which we'll discuss later in this chapter.

Special Possibilities with Magazines

Media planners and buyers need to be aware of the many creative possibilities magazines offer advertisers through various technical or mechanical features. These include bleed pages, cover positions, inserts and gatefolds, and special sizes, such as junior pages and island halves.

The Pros and Cons of Magazine Advertising [10–A]

The Pros

- **Flexibility** in readership and advertising. Magazines cover the full range of prospects; they have a wide choice of regional and national coverage and a variety of lengths, approaches, and editorial tones.
- **Color** gives readers visual pleasure, and color reproduction is best in slick magazines. Color enhances image and identifies the package. In short, it sells.
- **Authority and believability** enhance the commercial message. TV, radio, and newspapers offer lots of information but lack the depth needed for readers to gain knowledge or meaning; magazines often offer all three.
- **Permanence,** or long shelf life, gives the reader time to appraise ads in detail, allowing a more complete education/sales message and the opportunity to communicate the total corporate personality.
- **Prestige** for products advertised in upscale or specialty magazines such as *Architectural Digest, Connoisseur,* and *Town and Country.*
- **Audience selectivity** is more efficient in magazines than any other medium except direct mail. The predictable, specialized editorial environment selects the audience and enables advertisers to pinpoint their sales campaigns. Examples: golfers (*Golf Digest*), businesspeople (*Bloomberg Businessweek*), 20-something males (*Details*), or teenage girls (*Seventeen*).
- **Cost-efficiency** because wasted circulation is minimized. Print networks give advertisers reduced prices for advertising in two or more network publications.
- **Selling power** of magazines is proven, and results are usually measurable.
- **Reader loyalty** that sometimes borders on fanaticism.
- **Extensive pass-along readership.** Many people may read the magazine after the initial purchaser.
- **Merchandising assistance.** Advertisers can generate reprints and merchandising materials that help them get more mileage out of their ad campaigns.

The Cons

- **Lack of immediacy** that advertisers can get with newspapers or radio.
- **Shallow geographic coverage.** They don't offer the national reach of broadcast media.
- **Inability to deliver mass audiences at a low price.** Magazines are very costly for reaching broad masses of people.
- **Inability to deliver high frequency.** Since most magazines come out only monthly or weekly, the advertiser can build frequency faster than reach by adding numerous small-audience magazines to the schedule.
- **Long lead time** for ad insertion, sometimes two to three months.
- **Heavy advertising competition.** The largest-circulation magazines have 52 percent advertising to 48 percent editorial content.
- **High cost per thousand.** Average black-and-white cost per thousand (CPM) in national consumer magazines is high; some trade publications with highly selective audiences have a CPM over $50 for a black-and-white page.
- **Declining circulations,** especially in single-copy sales, is an industrywide trend that limits an advertiser's reach.

continued from page 200

The Producer

Possibly the most common late personality type there is, a producer doesn't see herself as late, but as someone who produces. "They tend to get an ego boost from how much they can get done in a day," DeLonzor says. But tardiness becomes a problem when a producer believes she can get a lot done in a little time, such as showering, dressing, applying makeup, washing dishes, and starting a load of laundry, all in the half hour set aside for getting ready in the morning.

TELLTALE SIGNS You write to-do lists during your coffee break. You feel the need to squeeze as much activity as humanly possible into each moment of each day.

GETTING BACK ON TRACK For at least a week, time everything you do—from the drive to work to that one last cleanup in the morning. "You'll start to see that what you thought you could do in 20 minutes actually takes 40," says DeLonzor. "You'll get a realistic idea of time."

Plan to be early and have something to do. "Take along the thank-you notes you're always meaning to get done," says Julie Morgenstern, author of *Time Management from the Inside Out*. "Organize your planner. Call a client or two. Or you could always carry along that novel you want to read."

More than 20 percent of people surveyed in the United States admit to being chronically late—no statistics on how many of the rest are lying.

PHOTO: JUPITER IMAGES

202 JUNE 2007 BETTER HOMES AND GARDENS

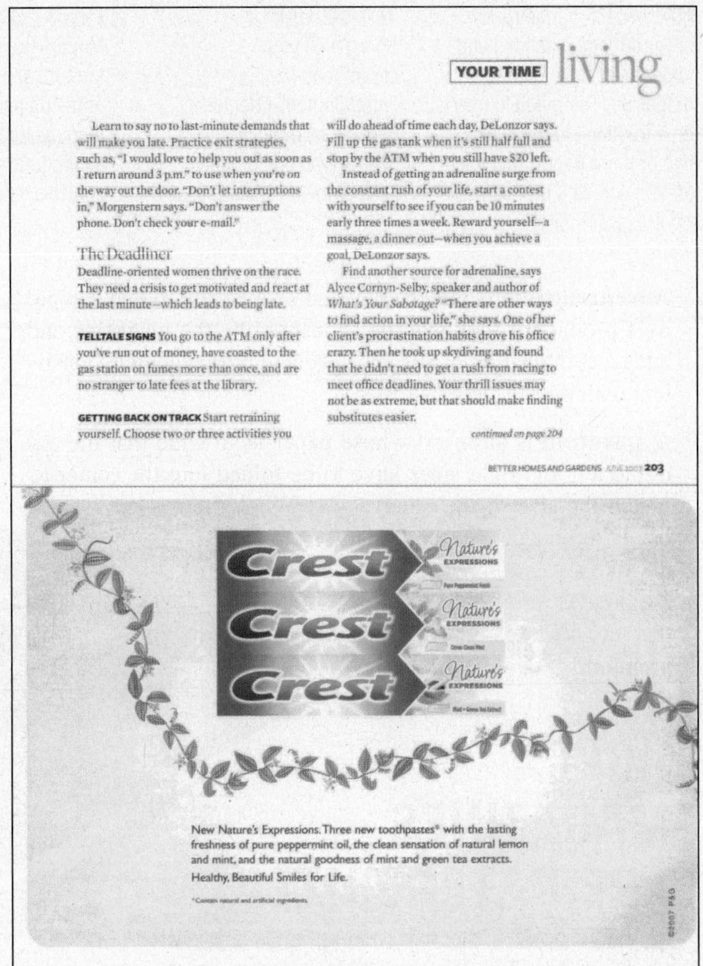

YOUR TIME living

Learn to say no to last-minute demands that will make you late. Practice exit strategies, such as, "I would love to help you out as soon as I return around 3 p.m." to use when you're on the way out the door. "Don't let interruptions in," Morgenstern says. "Don't answer the phone. Don't check your e-mail."

The Deadliner

Deadline-oriented women thrive on the race. They need a crisis to get motivated and react at the last minute—which leads to being late.

TELLTALE SIGNS You go to the ATM only after you've run out of money, have coasted to the gas station on fumes more than once, and are no stranger to late fees at the library.

GETTING BACK ON TRACK Start retraining yourself. Choose two or three activities you will do ahead of time each day, DeLonzor says. Fill up the gas tank when it's still half full and stop by the ATM when you still have $20 left.

Instead of getting an adrenaline surge from the constant rush of your life, start a contest with yourself to see if you can be 10 minutes early three times a week. Reward yourself—a massage, a dinner out—when you achieve a goal, DeLonzor says.

Find another source for adrenaline, says Alyce Cornyn-Selby, speaker and author of *What's Your Sabotage?* "There are other ways to find action in your life," she says. One of her client's procrastination habits drove his office crazy. Then he took up skydiving and found that he didn't need to get a rush from racing to meet office deadlines. Your thrill issues may not be as extreme, but that should make finding substitutes easier.

continued on page 204

BETTER HOMES AND GARDENS JUNE 2007 203

The opportunity to be creative is not limited to copywriters and art directors. Media planners and buyers can increase an ad's impact by exploring creative media buys. Crest toothpaste has made an impact greater than that which would be achieved by a full-page ad by purchasing staggered horizontal half-pages and developing an advertisement to effectively utilize that space.

> (Print advertising is) an ideal medium for high-involvement . . . products.

When the dark or colored background of the ad extends to the edge of the page (like the Levi's ad at the beginning of this chapter), it is said to **bleed** off the page. Most magazines offer bleed pages, but they charge 10 to 15 percent more for them. The advantages of bleeds include greater flexibility in expressing the advertising idea, a slightly larger printing area, and more dramatic impact.

If a company plans to advertise in a particular magazine consistently, it may seek a highly desirable **cover position**. Few publishers sell ads on the front cover, commonly called the *first cover.* They do however sell the inside front, inside back, and outside back covers (the *second, third,* and *fourth covers,* respectively), usually at a substantial premium.

A less expensive way to use magazine space is to place the ad in unusual places on the page or dramatically across spreads. A **junior unit** is a large ad (60 percent of the page) placed in the middle of a page and surrounded with editorial matter. Similar to junior units are **island halves**, surrounded by even more editorial matter. The island sometimes costs more than a regular half-page, but because it dominates the page, many advertisers consider it worth the extra charge. Exhibit 10–2 shows other space combinations that create impact.

Sometimes, rather than buying a standard page, an advertiser uses an **insert**. The advertiser prints the ad on high-quality paper stock to add weight and drama to the message, and then ships the finished ads to the publisher for insertion into the magazine at a special price. Another option is multiple-page inserts. Calvin Klein once promoted its jeans in a 116-page insert in *Vanity Fair.* The insert reportedly cost more than $1 million, but the news reports about it in major daily newspapers gave the campaign enormous publicity value.

gatefold A magazine cover or page extended and folded over to fit into the magazine. The gatefold may be a fraction of a page or two or more pages, and it is always sold at a premium.

consumer magazines Information- or entertainment-oriented periodicals directed toward people who buy products for their own consumption.

farm publications Magazines directed to farmers and their families or to companies that manufacture or sell agricultural equipment, supplies, and services.

business magazines The largest category of magazines, which target business readers and include *trade publications* for retailers, wholesalers, and other distributors; *industrial magazines* for businesspeople involved in manufacturing and services; and *professional journals* for lawyers, physicians, architects, and other professionals.

Advertising inserts may be devoted exclusively to one company's product or they may be sponsored by the magazine and have a combination of ads and special editorial content consistent with the magazine's focus.

A **gatefold** is an insert whose paper is so wide that the extreme left and right sides have to be folded into the center to match the size of the other pages. When the reader opens the magazine, the folded page swings out like a gate to present the ad. Not all magazines provide gatefolds, and they are always sold at a substantial premium.

HOW MAGAZINES ARE CATEGORIZED

In the jargon of the trade, magazines are called *books,* and media planners and buyers commonly categorize them by content, geography, and size.

Content One of the most dramatic developments in publishing is the emergence of magazines with special content, which has given many of them good prospects for long-term growth. The broadest classifications of content are *consumer magazines, farm magazines,* and *business magazines.* Each may be broken down into hundreds of categories.

- **Consumer magazines**, purchased for entertainment, information, or both, are edited for consumers who buy products for their own personal consumption: *Time, Sports Illustrated, Glamour, Good Housekeeping.* One would expect to see the Levi's "Go Forth" ads in consumer magazines.
- **Farm publications** are directed to farmers and their families or to companies that manufacture or sell agricultural equipment, supplies, and services: *Farm Journal, Progressive Farmer, Prairie Farmer, Successful Farming.*
- **Business magazines**, by far the largest category, target business readers. They include *trade publications* for retailers, wholesalers, and other distributors *(Progressive Grocer, Bakery News); business* and *industrial magazines* for businesspeople

▾**EXHIBIT 10-2** An ad's position on the page influences its effectiveness. The size and shape of the ad often determine where it will fall on the page. These eight two-page spreads show most of the positions a fractional ad can take.

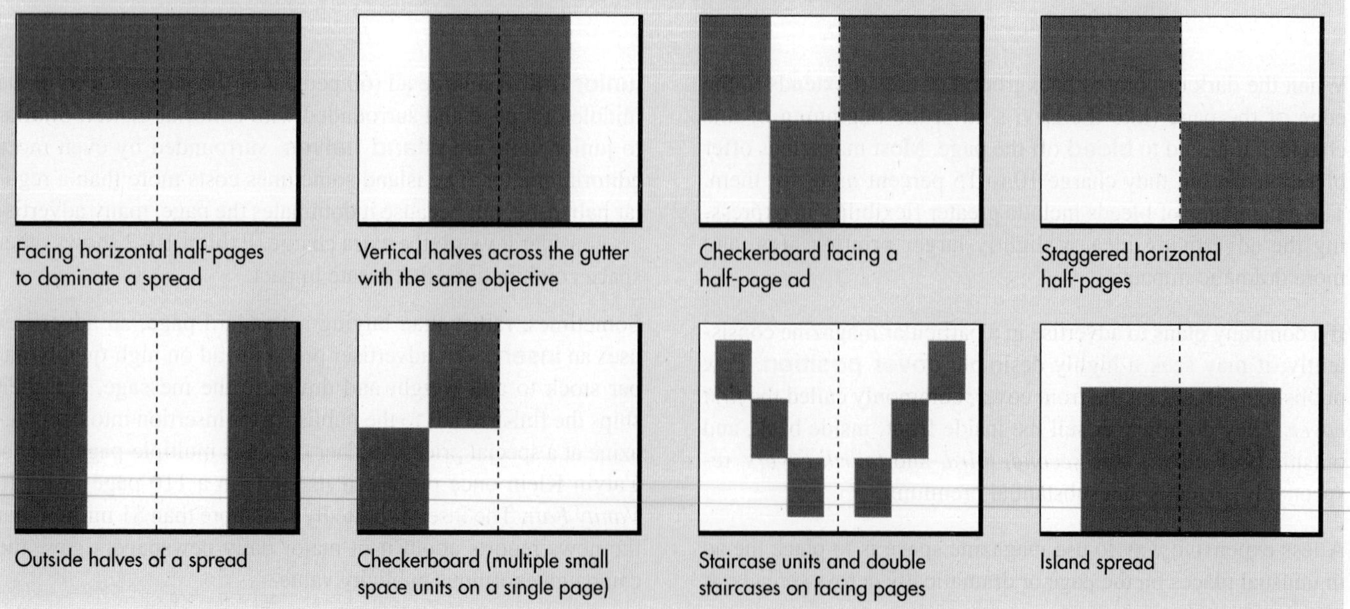

This print advertisement uses a technology called Augmented Reality to display a 3-D model of a MINI convertible simply by holding the ad up to your computer's webcam. The image of the model turns as you pivot the ad.

involved in manufacturing and services *(Electronic Design, American Banker);* and *professional journals* for lawyers, physicians, architects, and other professionals *(Archives of Ophthalmology).*

local city magazine
Most major U.S. cities have one of these publications. Typical readership is upscale, professional people interested in local arts, fashion, and business.

regional publications
Magazines targeted to a specific area of the country, such as the West or the South.

Geography A magazine may also be classified as *local, regional,* or *national.* Today, most major U.S. cities have a **local city magazine**: *San Diego Magazine, New York, Los Angeles, Chicago, Palm Springs Life.* Their readership is usually upscale business and professional people interested in local arts, fashion, and business.

Regional publications are targeted to a specific area of the country, such as the West or the South: *Sunset, Southern Living.* National magazines sometimes provide special market runs for specific geographic regions. *Time, Woman's Day,* and *Sports Illustrated* allow advertisers to buy a single major market. Exhibit 10–3 shows the 10 major geographic editions of *Reader's Digest.* This is important for local or regional advertisers who want the benefit of advertising in larger, more well-known publications while staying geographically relevant to the audience that may be reading the magazine.

EXHIBIT 10–3 Advertisers benefit from selecting regional editions similar to the 10 geographic editions of *Reader's Digest* shown on the map. With regional binding and mailing, advertisers can buy ad space for only the areas of distribution they need.

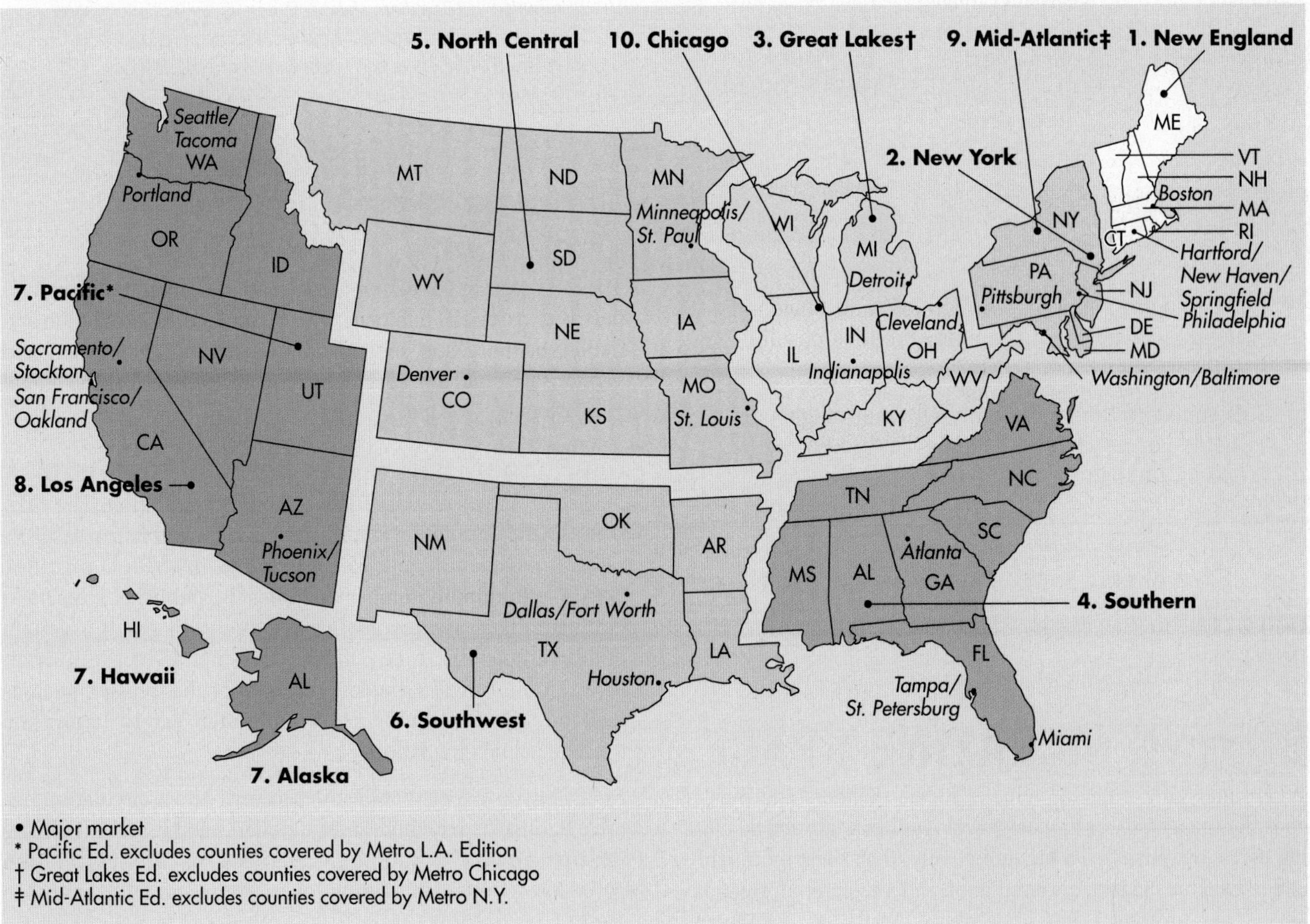

1. New England · **2. New York** · **3. Great Lakes†** · **4. Southern** · **5. North Central** · **6. Southwest** · **7. Pacific*** · **7. Hawaii** · **7. Alaska** · **8. Los Angeles** · **9. Mid-Atlantic‡** · **10. Chicago**

• Major market
* Pacific Ed. excludes counties covered by Metro L.A. Edition
† Great Lakes Ed. excludes counties covered by Metro Chicago
‡ Mid-Atlantic Ed. excludes counties covered by Metro N.Y.

national magazines Magazines that are distributed throughout a country.

rate base With magazines, the circulation figure on which the publisher bases its rates.

National magazines range from those with enormous circulations, such as *TV Guide,* to small, lesser-known national magazines, such as *Nature* and *Volleyball.* The largest circulation magazine in the United States today is *AARP The Magazine,* distributed to the 23 million–member households of the American Association of Retired Persons.

Size It doesn't take a genius to figure out that magazines come in different shapes and sizes, but it might take one to figure out how to get one ad to run in different size magazines and still look the same. Magazine sizes run the gamut, which can make production standardization a nightmare. The most common magazine sizes follow:

Size Classification	Magazine	Approximate Size of Full-Page Ad
Large	*Interview*	4 col. × 170 lines (9½ × 11⅓ inches)
Flat	*Time*	3 col. × 140 lines (7 × 10 inches)
Standard	*National Geographic*	2 col. × 119 lines (6 × 8½ inches)
Small or pocket	*Reader's Digest*	2 col. × 91 lines (4½ × 6½ inches)

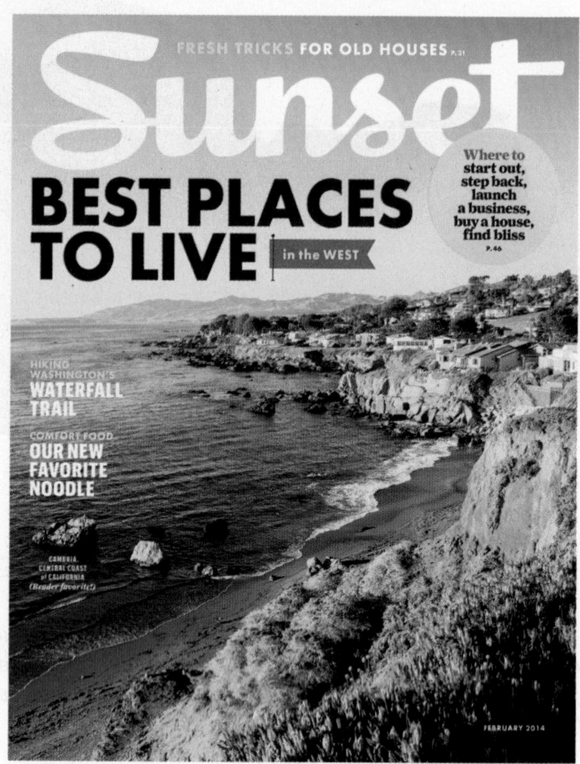

Magazines that cater to specific geographic areas are considered local or regional publications. Sunset *magazine focuses its distribution in 13 western states, offering its readers information relevant to western climates, lifestyles, architecture, and food preferences. Marketers can target even more precisely by advertising in* Sunset's *regional or metro editions.*

check yourself ✓

1. Why do you think media planners and buyers need to be aware of the many creative possibilities offered by magazines?
2. If you were the media planner, what magazines would you consider for the Levi's "Go Forth" print campaign?

LO10-2 Discuss how magazine circulation is measured and rates are set.

BUYING MAGAZINE SPACE

When analyzing a media vehicle, media planners and buyers consider readership, cost, mechanical requirements, and ad closing dates (deadlines). To buy effectively, they must thoroughly understand the magazine's circulation and rate-card information.

Understanding Magazine Circulation

The first step in analyzing a publication's potential effectiveness is to assess its audience. The buyer studies circulation statistics, primary and secondary readership, subscription and vendor sales, and any special merchandising services the magazine offers.

Guaranteed versus Delivered Circulation A magazine's rates are largely based on its circulation. The **rate base** is the circulation figure on which the publisher bases its rates. It is generally equivalent to the **guaranteed circulation**, the minimum number of copies the publisher expects to circulate. This assures advertisers they will reach a certain number of people. If the publisher does not deliver its guaranteed figure, it must provide a refund. For that reason, guaranteed circulation figures are often stated safely below the average actual circulation.

Media buyers expect publications to verify their circulation figures. Publishers pay thousands of dollars each year for a **circulation audit**—a thorough analysis of the circulation procedures, outlets of distribution, readers, and other factors—

guaranteed circulation The number of copies of a magazine that the publisher expects to sell. If this figure is not reached, the publisher must give a refund to advertisers.

circulation audit Thorough analysis of circulation procedures, distribution outlets, and other distribution factors by a company such as the Audit Bureau of Circulations (ABC).

Audit Bureau of Circulations (ABC) An organization supported by advertising agencies, advertisers, and publishers that verifies circulation and other marketing data on newspapers and magazines for the benefit of its members.

primary circulation The number of people who receive a publication, whether through direct purchase or subscription.

secondary (pass-along) readership The number of people who read a publication in addition to the primary purchasers.

vertical publication Business publications aimed at people in a specific industry; for example, *Nation's Restaurant News.*

horizontal publications Business publications targeted at people with particular job functions that cut across industry lines, such as *HR Magazine.*

paid circulation The total number of copies of an average issue of a newspaper or magazine that are distributed through subscriptions and newsstand sales.

by companies such as the **Audit Bureau of Circulations (ABC)**. Circulation actually gets overstated more often than people think. As many as 30 percent of consumer magazines audited by the ABC each year don't meet the circulation levels they guarantee to advertisers.[7]

Primary and Secondary Readership

Primary circulation represents the number of people who buy the publication, either by subscription or at the newsstand. **Secondary** (or **pass-along**) **readership**, which is an estimate determined by market research of how many people read a single issue of a publication, is very important to magazines. Some have more than six readers per copy. Multiplying the average pass-along readership by, say, a million subscribers can give a magazine a substantial audience beyond its primary readers.

Vertical and Horizontal Publications

There are two readership classifications of business publications: *vertical* and *horizontal.* A **vertical publication** covers a specific industry in all its aspects. For example, Penton publishes *Nation's Restaurant News* strictly for restaurateurs and food-service operators. The magazine's editorial content includes everything from news of the restaurant industry to the latest food and beverage trends.

Horizontal publications, in contrast, deal with a particular job function across a variety of industries. Readers of *HR Magazine* work in human resources in many different industries. Horizontal trade publications are very effective advertising vehicles because they usually offer excellent reach and they tend to be well read.[8]

Subscription and Vendor Sales

Media buyers also want to know a magazine's ratio of subscriptions to newsstand sales. Today, subscriptions account for the majority of magazine sales. Newsstands (which include bookstore chains) are still a major outlet for single-copy sales, but no outlet can handle more than a fraction of the many magazines available.

From the advertiser's point of view, newsstand sales are impressive because they indicate that the purchaser really wants the magazine and is not merely subscribing out of habit. However, according to the Audit Bureau of Circulations, single-copy sales accounted for only 9 percent of total magazine sales in 2012.[9] Newsstand sales have shown a steady decline in recent years, due not only to online editions of magazines, but also to social media options such as Twitter and Facebook.[10]

Paid and Controlled Circulation

Business publications may be distributed on either a *paid-circulation* or *controlled-circulation* basis. A paid basis means the recipient must pay the subscription price to receive the magazine. *Bloomberg Businessweek* is a **paid-circulation** business magazine.

Advertising Age *is a good example of a vertical publication. The magazine is geared toward a variety of issues specific to the advertising industry. Unlike horizontal publications, which focus on a single job function across various industries,* Ad Age *is read by people in a wide range of functions throughout the advertising industry.*

controlled circulation A free publication mailed to a select list of individuals the publisher feels are in a unique position to influence the purchase of advertised products.

cover date The date printed on the cover of a publication.

on-sale date The date a magazine is actually issued.

closing date A publication's final deadline for supplying printing material for an advertisement.

cost per thousand (CPM) A common term describing the cost of reaching 1,000 people in a medium's audience. It is used by media planners to compare the cost of various media vehicles.

In **controlled circulation**, the publisher mails the magazine free to individuals who the publisher thinks can influence the purchase of advertised products. For example, individuals responsible for packaging their company's products can receive a free subscription to *Packaging Digest* magazine. To qualify for the subscription list, people must indicate in writing a desire to receive it and must give their professional designation or occupation. Dues-paying members of organizations often get free subscriptions. For example, members of the Boat Owners Association of the United States receive free copies of *BoatU.S. Magazine*.

> Newsstand sales are impressive because they indicate that the purchaser really wants the magazine.

Publishers of paid-circulation magazines say subscribers who pay are more likely to read a publication than those who receive it free. But controlled-circulation magazines can reach good prospects for the goods and services they advertise.

Merchandising Services: Added Value

Magazines, and newspapers too, often provide liberal added-value services to their regular advertisers, such as:

- Special promotions at retail stores.
- Marketing services to help readers find local outlets.
- Response cards that allow readers to request brochures and catalogs.
- Help handling sales force, broker, wholesaler, and retailer meetings.
- Advance copies for the trade.
- Marketing research into brand preferences, consumer attitudes, and market conditions.

If a publication's basic characteristics—editorial, circulation, and readership—are strong, these additional services can increase the effectiveness of its ads.[11] Magazines offer great potential for relationship marketing since they already have a relationship with their subscribers.

Reading Rate Cards

Magazine rate cards follow a fairly standard format. This helps advertisers determine costs, discounts, mechanical requirements, closing dates, special editions, and additional costs for features like color, inserts, bleed pages, split runs, or preferred positions.

Three dates affect magazine purchases. The **cover date** is the date printed on the cover. The **on-sale date** is the date the magazine is actually issued. And the **closing date** is the date all ad material must be in the publisher's hands for a specific issue. Lead time may be as much as three months.

Rates

As we will discuss in Chapter 14, one way to compare magazines is to look at how much it costs to reach a thousand people based on the magazine's rates for a one-time, full-page ad. You compute the **cost per thousand (CPM)** by dividing the full-page rate by the number of thousands of subscribers:

$$\frac{\text{Page rate}}{(\text{Circulation} \div 1{,}000)} = \text{CPM}$$

For example, if the magazine's black-and-white page rate is \$10,000, and the publication has a circulation of 500,000, then:

$$\frac{\$10{,}000}{(500{,}000 \div 1{,}000)} = \frac{\$10{,}000}{500} = \$20 \text{ CPM}$$

Consider this comparison. In 2013, the page rate for a full-color, one-page ad in *Car & Driver* was \$206,464 on a total circulation of 1,206,360; *Road & Track* offered the same ad for \$113,734 on a total circulation of 603,990. Which was the better buy on a CPM basis?[12]

Many [businesses] would no longer be in business without [Yellow Pages advertising].

Over 400 million telephone directories are published each year and businesses pay nearly $7 billion for ads in them. Combining revenue from print and digital issues, directory companies took in 7.6 percent of all the money spent on advertising in the United States in 2011.[35]

In some markets, highly specialized directories aim at particular audiences, such as the Chinese-language Yellow Pages in San Francisco and the *Paginas Amarillas* in the border states.

Yellow Pages are often the sole advertising medium for local businesses, and nearly 85 percent of Yellow Pages revenue is derived from local advertisers.[36] But Yellow Pages directories can be an important medium for national advertisers, too. For example, U-Haul spends more than $20 million a year on Yellow Pages ads.

Nevertheless, the directory industry is transitioning from print publishers to providers of local search services. This became evident when the Yellow Pages Industry Association changed its name to the Local Search Association.[37] ■

check yourself ✓

1. What businesses likely rely on Yellow Pages advertising for survival?
2. What advantages do online Yellow Pages offer over the printed version?

learn about, practice, and apply the use of print advertising in the media mix!

M: Advertising was developed for students who want information packaged in a concise, easy-to-read, yet interesting format.

Check out the book's website to:

- **Learn when and why to use print advertising. (Review Questions)**
- **Discover the role of the Internet in the future of magazines and newspapers. (Review Questions)**
- **Understand why special print media formats are used by some advertisers. (Exploring Advertising)**

While you are there, check out the professional resource links, review the PowerPoint presentation, and test your knowledge with the Multiple Choice Quiz. Additionally, *Connect® Marketing* is available for M: Advertising.

www.mhhe.com/ArensM2e

directory Listings, often in booklet form, that serve as locators, buying guides, and mailing lists.

By now, virtually all metropolitan news organizations and national magazines have established an online presence. News organizations are information-rich, and much of the specialized information they don't run in the paper or the magazine fits perfectly with the online world's narrower interests. Hundreds of highly targeted, upstart publications are showing up on the Web, along with magazines created by users on sites such as Flipboard. They are all, however, still trying to figure out how best to incorporate advertising into their new ventures. Initially, most ads were simply banners or pop-ups, but now online publications are offering push-downs, floating ads, billboards, interstitials, videos, and more. It must be working, as spending on online ads passed that of combined newspaper and magazine advertising in 2012.[30] George Gilder, media expert and author, believes that the newspaper industry is in a particularly advantageous position to exploit this trend because "the convergence of text and video will cause a revolution in advertising, with targeted messages leading consumers step-by-step to a transaction."[31]

Time will tell whether digital advertising dollars will ever offset what newspapers and magazines are losing in print advertising. For now, publishers are looking to increase revenues generated by digital subscriptions. Several publications are experimenting by charging for access to certain content. In the third quarter of 2012, the *New York Times* earned more than 55 percent of its revenue from circulation, compared with only 29 percent in 2001.[32]

We will deal with these topics in greater depth in Chapter 12.

check yourself ✓

1. Why might an advertiser print an insert to be delivered with a newspaper rather than just buying a standard page in a newspaper? Why doesn't the advertiser just mail or deliver the insert separately?
2. Imagine you are reading a newspaper online. What advertising might appeal to you and possibly get you to purchase something on the spot?

LO10-5 Explain the unique roles played by directory and Yellow Pages advertising.

DIRECTORIES AND YELLOW PAGES

Directories represent a unique form of print advertising. A **directory** is an alphabetical or subject listing containing names, descriptions, and contact information for persons or organizations. Directories share print advertising's long shelf life and its ability to target a specific audience. They serve their consumers as a valuable reference, containing information that readers actually seek out when they need it. If you want to find out who does what in a particular product or service category, directories provide a listing for those companies that offer that product or service. For most businesses, there is little question whether they need to advertise in directories. Rather, they must decide in how many directories to advertise and how best to use them to serve their purposes.

Thousands of directories are published each year by phone companies, trade associations, industrial groups, and others. They mainly serve as locators, buying guides, and mailing lists, but they also carry advertising aimed at specialized fields. The Yellow Pages is by far the most frequently used directory. Approximately 84 percent of the U.S. population uses Yellow Pages online or in print to find a business.[33] Online directories provide photos, maps, and links to additional resources such as coupons or special promotions. Unlike the traditional Yellow Pages, the Internet versions can be routinely changed to provide updated information.

In Yellow Pages ads, content is most important. The ad should tell people how to make the purchase, not why. As with most advertising media, the larger the ad, the more attention it attracts.[34] Most businesses find that advertising in the Yellow Pages is very expensive, but many of them would no longer be in business without it.

Unlike other forms of print advertising, Yellow Pages advertising is typically sold on an annual basis. A basic one-line listing usually comes with business telephone service. A business can upgrade that listing and purchase a variety of ad sizes, ranging from setting a listing in boldface type to a large full-page advertisement. Some businesses add color to emphasize a logo, graphic, or line of type. The cost for advertising in the Yellow Pages, obviously, depends upon the amount of space, as well as the circulation size of the book. A large metropolitan Yellow Pages book commands a much higher rate per ad than does a small-town book, for instance.

ad appeared and sends it to the agency or advertiser. Today, most **tearsheets** for national advertisers are handled through a private central office, the Advertising Checking Bureau.

When a tearsheet arrives, the advertiser examines it to make sure the ad ran according to instructions: in the right section and page position, and with quality reproduction. If the ad did not run per instructions, the agency or advertiser is usually due an adjustment, a discount, or even a free rerun.

PRINT MEDIA AND NEW TECHNOLOGIES

With computers came revolutionary media options, such as the Internet and smartphones, challenging both traditional print media and advertisers to adapt. Newspapers and magazines are rushing to make alliances with cable, wireless telephone, and online companies to get a toehold in the interactive information market.

Planning and Evaluating Print Media [10–C]

At this point in your project you should have decided whether or not to use print (magazine and newspaper) as a communication vehicle. The next step is deciding which of the thousands of options makes the most sense for your client's brand.

The beauty of media planning and buying is that you have a blank slate from which to build your plan. As you start to build your plan, however, you need to consider what you are working toward. By answering a set of simple questions you can build the foundation of your recommendation. You should approach planning print media in the same way you would approach planning the brand strategy:

- Whom do you want to reach?
- Why use print?
- What are the brand objectives?
- Where do you want to place your advertising to best achieve your objectives?
- How should you execute your plan?

When you have answered these questions, it is time to analyze and evaluate your opportunities and develop your plan.

Selecting publications requires both critical thinking and hard and fast numbers. For instance, monthly magazines can take up to 12 weeks to gain full readership (called to "cume" their audience). This can obviously be an issue if your communication objectives are centered on building reach quickly. On the other hand, weekly magazines cume their audience in approximately one to two weeks, making them great to generate reach around key events. Last, the number of insertions by title also depends on your strategy. If you are telling a sequenced story through three ads, then you need to plan for three insertions in each publication (pub). This will obviously be expensive and likely will reduce the number of pubs on the plan, ultimately limiting your reach.

The great thing about print advertising is that it offers a large number of opportunities for brands to engage consumers in niche environments, thereby limiting brand wastage. However, not all brands want or need such niche vehicles, and lucky for those brands there are more mass-oriented publications too:

Targeted	**Mass Books**
Golf	*People*
Field and Stream	*TV Guide*
American Baby	*Parade*
Ski	*National Enquirer*
Martha Stewart Living	*Reader's Digest*

Some of you will be focusing on large national advertisers and can utilize nearly all types of print options. But what opportunities exist for the local advertiser? First, newspapers are typically a staple of any large local advertiser. Second, most of the print publications that we have discussed thus far will allow you to layer in demogeographical targeting to help fine-tune your plan. Take this into account as you build your plan. It doesn't make sense to advertise in a national pub if your client is only located in the southeastern United States.

See My Ad Campaigns 10–A and 10–B for checklists of the pros and cons of magazine and newspaper advertising.

As you can see, common sense plays a major role in planning print campaigns, especially for large advertisers. But for other brands, advertising in print is a bit more difficult because the names of the targeted publications don't just roll off the tongue like *Sports Illustrated* or *People.* To plan for those campaigns, most advertisers use syndicated research such as Media Mark's MRI product. This is a piece of planning software that indexes, through surveys, people's readership of tens of thousands of different publications. So when Microsoft wants to reach IT decision makers in the enterprise (in companies with over 100 employees), MRI tells the media planner that she can find a high composition (concentration of overall readership) of that target in publications like *eWeek, InformationWeek,* and *Baseline* magazine.

While we detail a number of tools in this chapter, for the large majority of projects access to these tools will be limited. Therefore, think about the medium in terms of the mindset of the readers when you place an ad in front of them. The closer you can get that mindset to match the category, industry, or association of your brand's product, the better off you are.

Newspaper Association of America (NAA) The promotional arm of the American Newspaper Publishers Association and the nation's newspaper industry.

insertion order A form submitted to a newspaper or magazine when an advertiser wants to run an advertisement. This form states the date(s) on which the ad is to run, its size, the requested position, and the rate.

proof copy A copy of the completed advertisement that is used to check for final errors and corrections.

tearsheets The printed ad cut out and sent by the publisher to the advertiser as a proof of the ad's print quality and that it was published.

ads. The advertiser runs two ads of identical size, but different content, for the same product on the same day in different press runs. The idea is to eliminate as many variables as possible. By measuring responses to the two ads, the advertiser is able to compare and contrast the effectiveness of each. For this service, newspapers typically charge extra and set a minimum space requirement.

Co-ops and Networks

As an aid to national advertisers, the NAB created the Newspaper Co-op Network (NCN). Salespeople from participating newspapers helped national advertisers line up retailers for dealer-listing ads. The advertiser would produce the ad and include a blank space for each paper to insert local retailers' names. The system also helped manufacturers manage local advertising tie-ins to national campaigns and themes. Before the development of NCN, national advertisers had to place ads and recruit local dealers individually.

In 1992, the Newspaper Advertising Bureau merged with the American Newspaper Publishers Association and five other marketing associations to form the **Newspaper Association of America (NAA)**, which continued to simplify national newspaper ad buys. In 1994, the NAA launched a *one-order, one-bill system* for national advertising, called the Newspaper National Network. Advertisers can make multimarket newspaper buys by placing one order and paying one bill, instead of having to contact—and pay—each paper individually.[26]

Chrysler was the first marketer to use the new network, placing ads for its national minivan sale in 75 newspapers in March 1994.[27] The Newspaper National Network offers advertisers competitive CPM pricing and guaranteed positioning, in addition to its one-order, one-bill appeal.[28] It also allows smaller papers to participate in national advertising.[29]

Insertion Orders and Tearsheets

When advertisers place an ad, they submit an **insertion order** to the newspaper stating the date(s) on which the ad is to run, its size, the desired position, the rate, and the type of artwork accompanying the order.

When a newspaper creates ad copy and art, it gives the advertiser a **proof copy** to check. In contrast, most national advertising arrives at the newspaper *camera ready,* either in the form of a photo print or an electronic file via e-mail. To verify that the ad ran, the newspaper tears out the page on which the

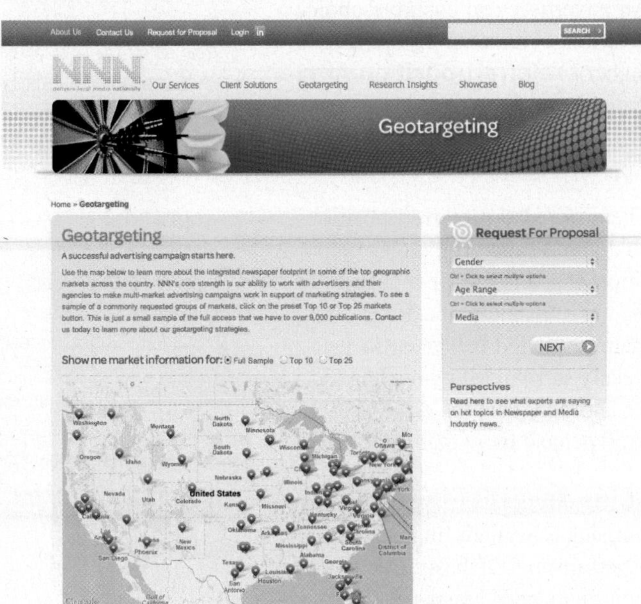

Co-ops and networks help simplify the ad buying process for advertisers by consolidating the purchasing paperwork and requirements for publications in a single location. This geotargeting page shows advertisers where they can buy ads to best fit their markets. Important information such as run date, size, and identifying captions is included.

Most newspapers and magazines have established websites that mirror their printed publications. Though traffic to these sites has increased dramatically, publishers have not yet succeeded in generating sufficient online ad revenue to offset the declines they have experienced in traditional media.

bulk discounts
Newspapers offer advertisers decreasing rates (calculated by multiplying the number of inches by the cost per inch) as they use more inches.

frequency discounts In newspapers, advertisers earn this discount by running an ad repeatedly in a specific time period.

earned rates
Discounts applied retroactively as the volume of advertising increases throughout the year.

short rate The rate charged to advertisers who, during the year, fail to fulfill the amount of space for which they have contracted. This is computed by determining the difference between the standard rate for the lines run and the discount rate contracted.

combination rates
Special newspaper advertising rates offered for placing a given ad in (1) morning and evening editions of the same newspaper; (2) two or more newspapers owned by the same publisher; or (3) two or more newspapers affiliated in a syndicate or newspaper group.

run-of-paper (ROP) advertising rates
A term referring to a newspaper's normal discretionary right to place a given ad on any page or in any position it desires—in other words, where space permits. Most newspapers make an effort to place an ad in the position requested by the advertiser.

preferred-position rate A choice position for a newspaper or magazine ad for which a higher rate is charged.

full position In newspaper advertising, the preferred position near the top of a page or on the top of a column next to reading matter. It is usually surrounded by editorial text and may cost the advertiser 25 to 50 percent more than ROP rates.

split runs A feature of many newspapers (and magazines) that allows advertisers to test the comparative effectiveness of two different advertising approaches by running two different ads of identical size, but different content, in the same or different press runs on the same day.

Rate Cards

Like the magazine rate card, the newspaper **rate card** lists advertising rates, mechanical and copy requirements, deadlines, and other information. Because rates vary greatly, advertisers should calculate which papers deliver the most readers and the best demographics for their money.

Local versus National Rates

Most newspapers charge local and national advertisers at different rates. The **national rate** averages 75 percent higher, but some papers charge as much as 254 percent more.[24] Newspapers attribute higher rates to the added costs of serving national advertisers. For instance, an ad agency usually places national advertising and receives a 15 percent commission from the paper.

But many national advertisers reject the high rates and take their business elsewhere. Only 6.1 percent of national ad money now goes to newspapers.[25] In response to declining national advertising revenue, newspapers are experimenting with simplified billing systems and discount rates for their national clients.

Flat Rates and Discount Rates

Many national papers charge **flat rates**, which means they allow no discounts; a few newspapers offer a single flat rate to both national and local advertisers.

Newspapers that offer volume discounts have an **open rate** (their highest rate for a one-time insertion) and **contract rates**, whereby local advertisers can obtain discounts of up to 70 percent by signing a contract for frequent or bulk space purchases. **Bulk discounts** offer advertisers decreasing rates as they use more inches. Advertisers earn **frequency discounts** by running a given ad repeatedly in a specific time period. Similarly, advertisers can sometimes get **earned rates**, a discount applied retroactively as the volume of advertising increases through the year.

Short Rate

An advertiser who contracts to buy a specific amount of space during a one-year period at a discount and then fails to fulfill the promise is charged a **short rate**, which is the difference between the contracted rate and the earned rate for the actual inches run. Conversely, an advertiser who buys more inches than contracted may be entitled to a rebate or credit.

Combination Rates

Combination rates are often available for placing a given ad in (1) morning and evening editions of the same newspaper; (2) two or more newspapers owned by the same publisher; and (3) in some cases, two or more newspapers affiliated in a syndicate or newspaper group.

Run of Paper versus Preferred Position

Run-of-paper (ROP) advertising rates entitle a newspaper to place a given ad on any newspaper page or in any position it desires. Although the advertiser has no control over where the ad appears in the paper, most newspapers try to place an ad in the position the advertiser requests.

An advertiser can ensure a choice position for an ad by paying a higher **preferred-position rate**. A tire manufacturer, for example, may pay the preferred rate to ensure a position in the sports section.

There are also preferred positions on a given page. The preferred position near the top of a page or at the top of a column next to reading matter is called **full position**. It's usually surrounded by reading matter and may cost the advertiser 25 to 50 percent more than ROP rates.

Color Advertising

Color advertising is available in many newspapers on an ROP basis. Because of their high-speed presses and porous paper stock, newspapers are not noted for high-quality color printing. The cost of a color ad is usually based on the black-and-white rate plus an extra charge for each additional color.

Split Runs

Many newspapers (and magazines) offer **split runs** so that advertisers can test the *pulling power* of different

rate card A printed information form listing a publication's advertising rates, mechanical and copy requirements, advertising deadlines, and other information the advertiser needs to know before placing an order.

national rate A newspaper advertising rate that is higher, attributed to the added costs of serving national advertisers.

flat rates A standard newspaper advertising rate with no discount allowance for large or repeated space buys.

open rate The highest rate for a one-time insertion into a newspaper.

contract rates Special rates for newspaper advertising usually offered to local advertisers who sign an annual contract for frequent or bulk-space purchases.

Understanding Readership and Circulation

Readership information is available from various sources, such as Experian Simmons and Scarborough Research Corp. Most large papers also provide extensive data on their readers.

In single-newspaper cities, reader demographics typically reflect a cross section of the general population. In cities with two or more newspapers, however, these characteristics may vary widely. The *Los Angeles Times* is directed to a broad cross section of the community while *La Opinion* targets Los Angeles's large Hispanic population.

What's at Stake with Sweepstakes?

Many of us have probably received an envelope in the mail with the phrase "You Are a Winner!" or something similar, plastered in large, bold type. And perhaps, for a split-second you believed that you had won the $100,000 prize. Then you discovered otherwise. Perhaps you were misled into believing that purchasing magazine subscriptions would increase your chances of winning.

Until recently, this is how many sweepstakes were pitched to consumers. According to the Direct Marketing Association, sweepstakes are by definition "an advertising or promotional device by which items of value (prizes) are awarded to participating consumers by chance, with no purchase or 'entry fee' required in order to win." However, by entering a sweepstakes you are volunteering your name and address to be put on lists for acquisition by other direct marketers. In turn you are offered a chance to win what seems like easy money. For years it was difficult for recipients to tell whether or not they had a winning entry. With statements claiming "You are a winner" and simulated checks, the line separating promotion and deception became very thin.

All of this changed in 2000. Following investigations of sweepstakes firms in more than 40 states, three of the biggest sweeps marketers—Publisher's Clearing House (PCH), Time Inc., and U.S. Sales Corp.—were each brought to court by numerous state regulators, alleging that the marketing giants conducted deceptive sweepstakes promotions. In California alone, state officials claimed that 5,000 consumers spent more than $2,500 each a year in unnecessary magazine subscriptions through PCH because they believed that it improved their odds of winning. Accusations were similar for all three companies, and each defended their marketing practices claiming they always believed their mailings were clear. One PCH spokesperson stated that 98 percent of the consumers who purchased magazines through their promotions were spending less than $300 a year. However, because litigation in so many states—47 in Time Inc.'s case—would have been too costly, each company decided to settle and agreed to reform its practices. Combined, the three marketers refunded more than $50 million in fines and restitution to state regulators and consumers who had purchased unnecessary magazines.

The reforms agreed to by these companies were in accord with the Deceptive Mail Prevention and Enforcement Act that became effective in April 2000. The act changed how direct-mail sweepstakes are presented and packaged. Some of the most significant changes included abandoning any "winner" proclamations unless the recipient had truly won a prize, and displaying a "fact box" that "clearly and conspicuously" explained all the terms and rules of the sweepstakes, including the odds of winning. Each mailing is also required to include the statements "No purchase is necessary to enter" and "A purchase does not improve your chances of winning" in boldfaced, capital letters in the mailing, in the rules, and on the order/entry form itself. In addition, each company is required to include a statement providing an address or toll-free number where recipients can either write or call to have their name and address removed from the mailing list.

Does this mean an end to sweepstakes? Probably not, since many people seem to jump at the chance to strike it rich for the cost of a stamp.

How much harm, if any, are sweepstakes really causing? Isn't part of promotion getting consumers to believe that they want what is being advertised? Without question, the ethical issues involved are complicated, but at least now you won't have to read the fine print to get the whole story.

Questions

1. Are sweepstakes companies really at fault for misleading their consumers? Why or why not?
2. Do you believe it is ethical for sweepstakes to "disguise" their promotions for the purpose of advertising?

The Times Record

3 Business Parkway • P.O. Box 10 • Brunswick, Maine 04011 • PHONE: (207) 729-3311 • FAX: (207) 725-8619 • E-MAIL: advertise@timesrecord.com

DISPLAY ADVERTISING / PREPRINTS

– 2014 –

DISPLAY RETAIL / CLASSIFIED RATES

ANNUAL MINIMUM*	DAILY – Mon.-Thurs.	WEEKEND – Friday
Open	$16.90	$17.80
$1,500–$2,499	$12.85	$13.55
$2,500–$4,999	$12.50	$13.30
$5,000–$7,499	$12.15	$12.90
$7,500–$9,999	$11.75	$12.55
$10,000–$14,999	$11.40	$12.20
$15,000–$24,999	$11.05	$11.80
$25,000–$34,999	$10.65	$11.45
$35,000–$49,999	$10.30	$11.10
$50,000–$74,999	$9.90	$10.70
$75,000+	$9.55	$10.35
Political	$21.00	$23.10
Non-Profit	$11.35	$11.90

REPEAT DISCOUNTS: We offer a 7x discount rate
Contact your ad rep for pricing details

TIMES RECORD ONLINE

Your in-paper ad will appear both in The Times Record and on our website timesrecord.com the day it's published for a $4.00 charge.

DEADLINES

PUBLICATION	DAY	TIME
Monday	Thurs.	4:00 P.M.
Tuesday	Fri.	4:00 P.M.
Wednesday	Mon.	4:00 P.M.
Thursday	Tues.	4:00 P.M.
Friday	Wed.	4:00 P.M.

COLOR RATES

AVAILABLE SPOT $150

FULL - CMYK $200

WWW.TIMESRECORD.COM

Leaderboard and Big Box:
$600 for 30-day run/ $300 15-day run

Skyscraper:
$480 for 30-day run/ $240 for 15-day run

Pencil (expandable) ads:
$149 for 24 hour period or
$112 for two or more days/ $99 for three or more
$57 per day for seven or more days

Marketplace Rotating Ad:
$199/mo.

MECHANICAL MEASUREMENTS

COLUMNS	RETAIL – 6 COLUMNS	CLASSIFIED – 8 COLUMNS
1 column	1.625"	1.167"
2 column	3.389"	2.5"
3 column	5.167"	3.833"
4 column	6.958"	5.167"
5 column	8.722"	6.5"
6 column	10.5"	7.833"
7 column	N/A	9.167"
8 column	N/A	10.5"
Column Depth	21.25"	21.25"
Full Page	127.5"	170"

PREPRINTED INSERTS

The Times Record is a cost-effective targeted choice for the distribution of your preprints. Whether you want delivery to every one of our readers or to a specific geographic zone only, your promotional piece can benefit from our position as a "welcomed friend" into our reader's homes.

If you would like quotes to print your insert, please contact your Account Executive.

***Please check for weight restrictions.**

FRIDAY
Full Run Distribution/Billing: 9,900
Full Run Needed: 10,200

MONDAY–THURSDAY
Full Run Distribution/Billing: 8,300
Full Run Needed: 8,500

ZONING CHARGE: additional $3 CPM
Minimum Run: 3,000

PRE-PRINT FREQUENCY

STD # PAGES	TAB # PAGES	FLEXI # PAGES	1-6 TIMES CPM	7-24 TIMES CPM	25-36 TIMES CPM	37-50 TIMES CPM	51-75 TIMES CPM	75+ TIMES CPM
NA	NA	single	50	46	42	40	38	36
2	4	8	54	50	46	44	42	40
6	12	24	60	54	50	48	46	44
10	20	40	64	58	54	52	50	48
14	28	56	68	62	58	56	54	52
20	40	80	72	66	62	60	58	56
26	52	104	76	70	66	64	62	60
30	60	120	80	74	70	68	66	64

The newspaper rate card for the Maine Times Record *is similar to that for magazines. It shows the variety of ad units available and lists their costs.*

cooperative (co-op) advertising The sharing of advertising costs by the manufacturer and the distributor or retailer. The manufacturer may repay 50 to 100 percent of the dealer's advertising costs or some other amount based on sales.

classified ads Newspaper, magazine, and now Internet advertisements usually arranged under subheads that describe the class of goods or the need the ads seek to satisfy. Rates are based on the number of lines the ad occupies. Most employment, housing, and automotive advertising is in the form of classified advertising.

classified display ads Ads that run in the classified section of the newspaper but have larger-size type, photos, art borders, abundant white space, and sometimes color.

public notices For a nominal fee, newspapers carry these legal changes in business, personal relationships, public governmental reports, notices by private citizens and organizations, and financial reports.

preprinted inserts Newspaper advertisements printed in advance by the advertiser and then delivered to the newspaper plant to be inserted into a specific edition. Preprints are inserted into the fold of the newspaper and look like a separate, smaller section of the paper.

from mistaking it for editorial matter, the word *advertisement* appears at the top.

As we discussed in Chapter 3, retailers often run newspaper ads through **cooperative** (or **co-op**) **advertising** programs sponsored by the manufacturers whose products they sell. The manufacturer pays fully or partially to create and run the ad, which features the manufacturer's product and logo along with the local retailer's name and address.

Classified Advertising

Classified ads provide a community marketplace for goods, services, and opportunities of every type, from real estate and new-car sales to employment and business opportunities. A newspaper's profitability often relies heavily on a large and healthy classified section. However, newspapers have been hit hard by the migration of classified ads to websites like Craigslist and Monster.com.

Preprinted inserts give advertisers control over the quality of their catalogs and brochures. Newspapers distribute these inserts at a lower cost than mailing or door-to-door delivery.

Classified rates are typically based on how many lines the ad occupies and how many times the ad runs. Some newspapers accept **classified display ads**, which run in the classified section of the newspaper but feature larger type and/or photos, art borders, and sometimes even color.

Public Notices

For a nominal fee, newspapers carry legal **public notices** of changes in business and personal relationships, public governmental reports, notices by private citizens and organizations, and financial reports. These ads follow a preset format.

Preprinted Inserts

Like magazines, newspapers carry **preprinted inserts**. The advertiser prints the inserts and delivers them to the newspaper plant for insertion into a specific edition. Insert sizes range from a typical newspaper page to a double postcard; formats include catalogs, brochures, mail-back devices, and perforated coupons.

Some large metropolitan dailies allow advertisers to limit their inserts to specific circulation zones. A retail advertiser that wants to reach only those shoppers in its immediate trading area can place an insert in the local-zone editions. Retail stores, car dealers, and large national advertisers are among those who find it less costly to distribute their circulars this way compared to mailing them or delivering them door to door.

An increasingly popular ad delivery method is a small sticker on the main section of the newspaper. It is removable and can double as a coupon. Guests at upscale Omni hotels found scented stickers on the front pages of their copies of *USA Today*. A blackberry aroma suggested that guests start the day with a cup of Starbucks "paired with a fresh muffin."[23]

HOW ADVERTISERS BUY NEWSPAPER SPACE

To get the most from the advertising budget, the media planner and buyer must know the characteristics of a newspaper's readership: the median age, sex, occupation, income, educational level, as well as buying habits of the typical reader.

column inch The basic unit by which publishers bill for advertising. It is one vertical inch of a column. Today, most newspapers—and virtually all dailies—have converted to the SAU system. An SAU column inch is 2¹⁄₁₆ inches wide by 1 inch deep.

Sunday supplement A newspaper-distributed Sunday magazine. Sunday supplements are distinct from other sections of the newspaper since they are printed by rotogravure on smoother paper stock.

shoppers Free publications, delivered by hand or direct mail or in supermarket racks, consisting almost entirely of local advertising. Consumers tend to use these publications to find dealers and to make price comparisons.

display advertising Type of newspaper advertising that includes copy, illustrations or photographs, headlines, coupons, and other visual components.

reading notice (advertorial) A variation of a display ad designed to look like editorial matter. It is sometimes charged at a higher space rate than normal display advertising, and the law requires that the word *advertisement* appears at the top.

Specialized newspapers also serve business and financial audiences. *The Wall Street Journal,* the leading national business and financial daily, enjoys a circulation of nearly 2.4 million readers and is now the largest weekday newspaper in the United States. *The New York Times* has the largest Sunday circulation. Other papers cater to fraternal, labor union, or professional organizations, religious groups, or hobbyists.

Other Types of Newspapers The United States has 900 Sunday newspapers, mostly Sunday editions of daily papers, with a combined circulation of nearly 49 million.[20] Sunday newspapers generally combine standard news coverage with special functions like these:

- Increased volume of classified ads.
- Greater advertising and news volume.
- In-depth coverage of business, sports, real estate, literature and the arts, entertainment, and travel.
- Review and analysis of the past week's events.
- Expanded editorial and opinion sections.

Most Sunday newspapers also feature a **Sunday supplement** magazine. Some publish their own supplements, such as the *Los Angeles Magazine* of the *Los Angeles Times.* Other papers subscribe to syndicated supplements; *Parade* magazine has a readership of more than 63 million readers every week.[21]

Printed on heavier, coated paper stock, Sunday supplements are more conducive to color printing than newsprint, making them attractive to national advertisers who want better reproduction quality.

Another type of newspaper, the independent shopping guide or free community newspaper, offers advertisers local saturation. Sometimes called *pennysavers,* these **shoppers** offer free distribution and extensive advertising pages targeted at essentially the same audience as weekly newspapers—urban and suburban community readers. Readership is often high, and the publishers use hand delivery or direct mail to achieve maximum saturation.

North Americans also read national newspapers, including the *Globe and Mail* in Canada, *USA Today,* and the *Christian Science Monitor.* With a circulation of 1.87 million, the *New York Times* recently passed *USA Today* (1.67 million) to become the second-largest U.S. newspaper. Both papers trail *The Wall Street Journal* with a circulation of 2.4 million.[22]

Types of Newspaper Advertising

The major classifications of newspaper advertising are display, classified, public notices, and preprinted inserts.

Display Advertising **Display advertising** includes copy, illustrations or photos, headlines, coupons, and other visual components—such as the ads for the *Village Voice* discussed earlier. Display ads vary in size and appear in all sections of the newspaper except the first page of major sections, the editorial page, the obituary page, and the classified advertising section.

One common variation of the display ad, the **reading notice** (or **advertorial**), looks like editorial matter and sometimes costs more than normal display advertising. To prevent readers

A creative solution to promote an everyday activity—going online—is a perfect concept for a full-color newspaper ad, as in this example by Yahoo! (www.yahoo.com).

frequency discounts Advertisers earn this discount by running advertising repeatedly in a specific time period.

volume discounts Discounts given to advertisers for purchasing print space or broadcast time in bulk quantities.

geographic editions Special editions of magazines that are distributed in specific geographic areas.

demographic editions Special editions of magazines that are distributed to readers who share a demographic trait, such as age, income level, or professional status.

EXHIBIT 10-4 Circulation and advertising costs for the five highest circulation U.S. consumer magazines (second half 2012).

Magazine	Total Paid Circulation	Page Cost for a Four-Color Ad	CPM (Cost per Thousand)
AARP The Magazine	22,721,661	$581,800	$25.61
AARP Bulletin	22,403,427	599,000	26.74
Game Informer Magazine	7,864,326	186,148	23.67
Better Homes and Gardens	7,621,456	526,640	69.10
Reader's Digest	5,527,183	159,200	28.80

Exhibit 10–4 lists the circulations, color page rates, and CPMs for the five highest circulation consumer magazines.

Discounts Magazines and newspapers often give discounts. **Frequency discounts** are based on the number of ad insertions, usually within a year; **volume discounts** are based on the total amount of space bought during a specific period. Most magazines also offer *cash discounts* (usually 2 percent) to advertisers who pay right away, and some offer discounts on the purchase of four or more consecutive pages in a single issue. In fact, many magazine publishers now negotiate their rates. According to Harold Shain, former Newsweek Inc. president, "Every piece of business is negotiated."[13]

Premium Rates Magazines charge extra for special features. Color printing normally costs 25 to 60 percent more than black and white. Bleed pages can add as much as 20 percent to regular rates, although the typical increase is about 15 percent.

Second and third cover rates (the inside covers) typically cost less than the fourth (back) cover. For example, in 2013, *People* magazine charged $324,400 for a normal color page and $405,500 and $356,800 for the second and third covers, respectively, but it charged $437,900 for the fourth cover.[14]

Newspapers are an important medium in the media mix, second only to television in advertising volume, but costing much less. This ad for the Village Voice *(www.villagevoice.com) shows how a niche business can use newspaper advertising to expand sales. Mimicking the freewheeling tone of the newspaper, the advertiser targeted those who already read the* Village Voice *but were not subscribers.*

Magazines charge different rates for ads in geographic or demographic issues. **Geographic editions** target geographic markets; **demographic editions** reach readers who share a demographic trait, such as age, income level, or professional status.

check yourself ✓

1. How does an advertiser know if a magazine doesn't deliver the circulation that it guarantees? What happens in such cases?
2. Why would an advertiser pay a premium to have an ad appear on the back cover of a magazine?

LO10-3 Explain the advantages and disadvantages of newspaper advertising.

USING NEWSPAPERS IN THE MEDIA MIX

When a small, alternative newspaper in Manhattan asked one of the newest and hottest creative shops in the city for help in promoting subscriptions, it had no idea what the little agency with the funny name, Mad Dogs & Englishmen, would do for it.[15]

The *Village Voice* newspaper had always knocked the Establishment with its radical coverage of social issues, politics, media, and culture. So perhaps it shouldn't have come as a surprise when the Mad Dogs took the newspaper's own prose style and turned it around in a series of impertinent, self-mocking ads.

"Hell, I wouldn't have my home contaminated with a subscription to your elitist rag if you were giving away five-speed blenders," rants one ad in the series. "You people think New York is the friggin' center of the world." But then a second paragraph offers a dramatic alternative: "YES, I

Advertising rates

Full run and regional editions

4-COLOR

CIRC. BASE	FULL PAGE	⅔ PAGE	½ PAGE	⅓ PAGE
Full run	$125,300	$100,200	$81,400	$56,400
Pacific Northwest	$48,031	$38,441	$31,212	$21,613
Northern California	$57,833	$46,286	$37,581	$26,025
Southern Californa	$53,544	$42,854	$34,795	$24,095

BLACK-AND-WHITE

CIRC. BASE	FULL PAGE	⅔ PAGE	½ PAGE	⅓ PAGE
Full run	$90,200	$72,200	$58,600	$40,600
Pacific Northwest	$34,689	$27,766	$22,540	$15,616
Northern California	$41,766	$33,430	$27,138	$18,802
Southern California	$38,670	$30,952	$25,126	$17,408

COVERS

4th cover	$163,000
3rd cover	$137,800
2nd cover	$150,300

These rates and all advertising transactions are subject to the 2013 Advertising Terms and Conditions of Sunset Publishing Corporation.

Effective January 2013 issue, circulation includes the print and digital editions of the Magazine. ⅓ page or greater qualified full-run advertisements will run in both editions. See ADVERTISING TERMS AND CONDITIONS for additional information including opt-out and upgrade options.

CPM table rates

4-COLOR

CIRC. BASE	FULL PAGE	⅔ PAGE	½ PAGE	⅓ PAGE
250,000	$45,580	$36,480	$29,620	$20,510
Add'l per M	122.53	98.06	79.61	55.15
500,000	$76,220	$61,000	$49,520	$34,310
Add'l per M	116.41	93.16	75.63	52.39
750,000	$105,320	$84,290	$68,430	$47,400
Add'l per M	114.68	91.78	74.51	51.61

BLACK & WHITE

CIRC. BASE	FULL PAGE	⅔ PAGE	½ PAGE	⅓ PAGE
250,000	$32,920	$26,350	$21,390	$14,820
Add'l per M	88.46	70.80	57.48	39.82
500,000	$55,040	$44,050	$35,760	$24,770
Add'l per M	83.87	67.12	54.49	37.75
750,000	$76,010	$60,830	$49,390	$34,210
Add'l per M	82.18	65.77	53.40	36.99

Ratebases

Full run	1,250,000
Pacific Northwest	270,000
Northern California	350,000
Southern California	315,000
Mountain	105,000
Southwest	110,000

Minimum circ: 250,000

Example: PNW and NC, 4-color page buy

Total Circulation.................... 620,000
First 500,000 Cost.................$76,220
120,000 at 116.41 per M........ $13,969
Total Cost..............................$90,189

Regional advertising coverage

PACIFIC NORTHWEST edition includes Alaska, British Columbia, Idaho, Oregon, and Washington.

NORTHERN CALIFORNIA edition extends from the Oregon border south to the counties of Fresno, Inyo, Kings, Mono, Monterey, and Tulare. Includes all of Nevada except Clark County.

SOUTHERN CALIFORNIA edition includes Imperial, Kern, Los Angeles, Orange, Riverside, San Bernardino, San Diego, San Luis Obispo, Santa Barbara, and Ventura counties, and Hawaii.

FULL RUN edition includes circulation in all 13 Western states, as well as national circulation.

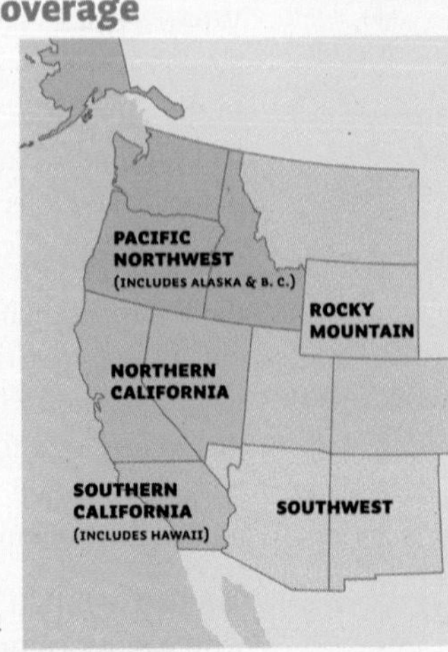

Sunset

This partial rate card for Sunset Magazine *(www.sunset.com) shows the advertising costs for common ad sizes. Notice the special pricing for black-and-white ads, cover positions, and regional editions. Other options, discounts, closing dates, and requirements are described on the complete rate card.*

chapter eleven

broadcast, cable, and satellite media: **television and radio**

This chapter presents the important factors advertisers need to evaluate when considering the use of broadcast, cable, and satellite media in the creative mix. Each medium has its own characteristics, advantages, and drawbacks. Advertisers must be able to compare their merits and understand the most cost-effective ways to buy advertising time.

Following the deep recession of the early 2010s, few companies were increasing spending on advertising. One car company, however, saw this as an opportunity, a chance to take on the historically aggressive-spending U.S. automakers and the highly popular Japanese automakers. Hyundai Motor America was ignored by the big automotive players, and by American car buyers, for many years. Because of durability and reliability issues, Hyundai sales plummeted in the United States in the mid- to late-nineties. Rather than abandoning the American market, Hyundai chose to invest heavily in new product designs and improvements in overall quality and reliability. However, just making the product better wasn't going to win over a now jaded consumer. Studies done at the time suggested that quality had in fact improved but that public perceptions had changed very little.

continued on p. 272

LEARNING OBJECTIVES

After studying this chapter, you will be able to:

LO11-1 Describe the advantages and disadvantages of broadcast television as an advertising medium.

LO11-2 Discuss the various options for advertising on television.

LO11-3 Explain how to measure television audiences and select the best programs to buy.

LO11-4 Describe the advantages and disadvantages of radio as an advertising medium.

LO11-5 Review the options for advertising on radio and how radio audiences are measured.

continued from p. 271

So in 1999 Hyundai shocked the automotive world by offering an unprecedented, 10-year, 100,000-mile warranty. Rightly dubbed "America's Best," the Hyundai Advantage covered all major components for the entire fleet. "We thought an improved warranty would make a statement about our quality and get us on more people's shopping lists," said Finbarr O'Neill, chief executive of Hyundai Motor America.

Fast-forward to late 2008 and another brilliant first for Hyundai Motor executives. Their launch pad was Super Bowl XLIII,

then the most-watched game of all time with 98.7 million viewers.[1] Teamed with Goodby, Silverstein and Partners, Hyundai planned a three-tier onslaught. First they unveiled the brand-new 2010 Hyundai Genesis Coupe. Next up was a brilliant ad showing fictitious executives from Lexus and BMW yelling angrily in their native tongues, with only one understandable word: "HYUNDAI," in response to the naming of the Genesis as North American Car of the Year by J.D. Power and Associates. Jeff Bridges reads the tagline: "Win one little award and suddenly everyone gets your name right. Hyundai, like Sunday."

But they didn't stop there. Hyundai realized that in troubling times the last thing that anyone wants, after losing a job, is facing creditors. So the Hyundai Assurance program was born. If you lose your income after you buy a Hyundai, the company will allow you to return the car and be released from all final payments.

The advertising clearly worked. Year over year sales for February 2009 were down 1.5 percent; however, when the industry as a whole was down 37 percent that number looked pretty good.[2]

For the second time in 10 years Hyundai had come through with a consumer-centered idea that changed the industry. For the second time in 10 years the little Korean car company that had been the brunt of many jokes was again turning heads. And for the first time it was seeing success in the midst of chaos.

Hyundai had big ideas, and to share them it chose television, the largest stage in the world. TV was a perfect choice because it introduced the brand to millions who might not ever have given Hyundai a thought. Fast-forward to the 2014 model year. Hyundai's biggest problem? It can't build cars fast enough to keep pace with demand. *The Wall Street Journal* quoted John Krafcik, CEO of Hyundai's U.S. operations, as saying, "Our plants are really taxed and really maxed out." We suspect there aren't many car companies that would mind that problem too much. ■

LO11-1 Describe the advantages and disadvantages of broadcast television as an advertising medium.

THE MEDIUM OF TELEVISION

Back in 1950, U.S. advertisers spent $171 million, or about 3 percent of total U.S. advertising volume, on the new medium of television. It didn't take long, though, for the nation's advertisers to discover the power of this new vehicle to reach mass audiences quickly and frequently. TV also offered unique creative opportunities to imbue their brands with personality and image like never before. In 2013, over $66 billion was spent on TV advertising, accounting for more than 45 percent of all U.S. ad spending.[3]

Television networks and stations are available to advertisers in two principal forms: broadcast and cable. Broadcast networks can reach audiences by transmitting electromagnetic waves through the air across some geographic territory. Cable networks reach audiences exclusively through cable or satellite systems.

Broadcast TV

Until the advent of the Internet, broadcast television grew faster than any other advertising medium in history. As both a news and entertainment medium, it caught people's fancy very quickly. From its beginnings after World War II, broadcast TV rapidly emerged as the only medium that offered sight, sound, and motion. People could stay home and still go to the movies. As TV's legions of viewers grew, the big national brand advertisers quickly discovered they could use the medium very efficiently to expand distribution across the country and sell

The growth in cable and satellite TV systems has dramatically increased the number of channels available to viewers. This has given consumers almost unlimited program alternatives, making it easier for advertisers to reach a more selective audience.

products like never before. Large advertisers found that medium was ideal for building an image for their brands—even better than magazines, which had previously been the image-building medium of choice. It didn't take long for marketers to switch their budgets from radio, newspapers, and magazines.

The United States now has 1,381 commercial TV stations.[4] Stations in the United States operate as independents unless they are affiliated with one of the national networks (ABC, NBC, CBS, Fox, CW). Both network affiliates and independent stations may subscribe to nationally syndicated programs as well as originate their own programming. However, increasing competition from cable TV is taking viewers from the national network programs. To compensate, some networks invested in cable TV systems or are starting their own. For example, NBC (which is owned by GE) started CNBC and MSNBC, and ABC (which is owned by Disney) owns a piece of ESPN, Lifetime, A&E, and other cable channels.

EXHIBIT 11–1 Prime-Time average viewers (live+SD) week ending August 11, 2013.

Network	Average Viewers (millions)
1 USA	2.6
2 Disney	2.6
3 History Channel	2.2
4 Discovery Channel	2.1
5 TNT	1.8
6 TBS	1.7
7 Fox News	1.5
8 A&E	1.4
9 AMC	1.3
10 ESPN	1.3

Source: Copyrighted Information of The Nielsen Company, licensed for use herein.

Cable TV

For more than 30 years, broadcast TV, especially network TV, was the dominant entertainment medium for most Americans. Today, other electronic media have dramatically changed that dominance. Chief among the challengers is cable television.

Cable TV has been around since the late 1940s. Initially, it carried television signals by wire to areas with poor reception such as mountainous regions. But in the 1970s, the advent of satellite TV signals, the proliferation of channels, and the introduction of uncut first-run movies via premium cable channels such as Home Box Office (HBO) and Showtime made cable TV more attractive to all viewers, even people in urban areas.

At first, many subscribers valued cable simply for the full array of regional channels and access to premium services such as HBO. But once this novelty wore off, subscribers wanted more. A variety of advertiser-supported cable networks soon appeared with specialized programming in arts, history, sports, news, cooking, and comedy, along with diversified pay services and many more local shows. All of this attracted more and more subscribers—and consequently drew viewers away from the big broadcast networks.

In the last three decades, cable's growth has been extraordinary. In 1975, only 13 percent of TV households in the United States had cable. By 2013 the Consumer Electronics Association estimates that 83 percent of American households get cable. However, that level of penetration is actually a decrease from 2010, perhaps reflecting the growing demand for on-demand services such as Netflix and Amazon Prime.[5] Other challenges to cable dominance come from satellite companies such as Dish Network and DirecTV.[6]

Most channels are privately owned and operated. These include local network affiliates and independents, cable networks, superstations, local cable system channels, and community access channels. The cable fees represent about one-third of cable TV revenues; advertising makes up the remainder. Networks such as CNN, USA, the Discovery Channel, Arts & Entertainment, Lifetime, Comedy Central, and Spike TV now compete for advertisers' dollars, each selling its own niche audience. For an additional price, subscribers can receive premium services such as HBO, Showtime, and Cinemax and see special events such as first-run films, championship boxing matches, and baseball and football games through pay-per-view subscriptions.

There are now over 100 ad-supported national cable networks in the United States and a growing number of regional networks.[7] Exhibit 11–1 lists the most highly rated. There are also a handful of *superstations* (such as TBS Atlanta) and local, over-the-air TV stations whose signals are delivered via satellite to cable systems across the country and that carry some national advertising. In the 2010s cable channels have found it increasingly profitable to develop unique content, including highly popular shows such as AMC's *Walking Dead* and A&E's *Duck Dynasty*. The latter premiered in 2013 to 11.8 million viewers, shattering previous cable ratings records.[8]

DTV

On June 12, 2009, as mandated by Congress, the United States made the switch to digital television (DTV). DTV sends and receives moving images and sound by digital signals ("0"s and "1"s) rather than the analog signals (waveforms).

Digital TV has many benefits. As stated on the website www.dtv.gov, consumers benefit because digital broadcasting allows stations to offer improved picture and sound quality, and digital is much more efficient than analog. For example, rather than being limited to providing one analog program, a broadcaster can offer a super sharp "high definition" (HD) digital program

or multiple "standard definition" (SD) digital programs simultaneously through a process called "multicasting." Multicasting allows broadcast stations to offer several channels of digital programming at the same time, using the same amount of spectrum required for one analog program. This means more programming choices for viewers. Further, DTV can provide interactive video and data services that are not possible with analog technology.

TV Audience Trends

As a way to reach a mass audience, no other medium today has the unique creative abilities of television: the combination

Planning and Buying TV and Radio [11–A]

Media planners use a variety of syndicated and proprietary research tools to plan and buy both TV and radio ads. Primarily these tools help identify the larger concentrations (composition) of a target audience in specific programming, and the cost associated with those audiences. The complexity of TV and radio arises from the need to build plans that cost-efficiently reach a target audience with an effective frequency. The currency for these two media is a ratings point, which represents 1 percent of the target audience a media buyer is trying to reach. Both TV and radio, therefore, are bought based on demographics. So when certain prime-time shows have a rating of 14 for A25–49, it means that a particular program reaches 14 percent of all adults between the ages of 25 and 49. A buyer's cost per point (CPP) is her way of determining a vehicle's (program's) efficiency in delivering her target audience. As this chapter will explain, ratings points are additive. Therefore two spots on shows with 14 targeted ratings points means that the advertiser has purchased 28 gross ratings points or GRPs.

Most of you will not have access to the types of tools that help you plan and optimize broadcast media plans, so your focus should be on the merits of each of these media in achieving your marketing and advertising objectives and how they match your overall media strategies. First we will discuss the advantages and nonmonetary value of TV and then of radio.

Television

TV is still the largest mass medium; 118 million homes in America have at least one TV set. However, it is becoming a fragmented marketplace. In fact, the average home receives over 118 different channels. While the average viewer only watches 15 channels on a regular basis, those channels may not be the same 15 channels as the ones his neighbor watches, making the media planner's job that much more difficult in building mass audiences.

Besides the large audiences, the other core benefit of TV is that it builds awareness relatively quickly. If you are launching a new product or trying to gain a high level of awareness in a relatively short period of time, TV is your medium. While TV will take up a large portion of your budget, its dynamic nature, the ability to include sight, sound, and motion in the advertisement, makes it a great storytelling medium.

Last, TV is still the best medium to generate excitement around a brand, whether that is with internal constituents (employees) or external audiences. As proclaimed by Marshall McLuhan in his book *Understanding Media: The Extensions of Man,* the medium is the message, and no medium, to date, gives people the same perception of legitimacy as a well-produced TV advertisement.

Radio

Like TV, radio is a broadcast medium, but its ability to generate mass awareness immediately is different. The radio formats appeal to more specific targets, giving it less spillover than TV, which can be both good and bad—good in that your audience is the only one that hears the message; bad in that an advertiser may not extend out of its target market and hit markets it wasn't aware would be receptive to its message.

So why do advertisers use radio? One reason is that radio is much more efficient than TV; CPPs are sometimes 1/10 that of TV. Radio also is much less expensive to produce; in fact typically all you need is copy and talent, making the lead time to go live with radio as short as one to two weeks. It also happens to be more promotional in nature—stations typically have a loyal audience following and advertisers can usually be a part of any local station events and get the station personalities to endorse the brand. Testimonials, and especially personality testimonials, can be very valuable to advertisers that are looking to build legitimacy in themselves or their product.

So while you think about what your TV and radio ads will do for your brand(s), it is important to reflect on what part of the objectives and strategies each will fulfill and how they might work in concert with each other. Think of starting a new advertising campaign with TV messages and the support of radio. The TV will generate awareness and legitimacy immediately, and the radio will allow you to get out of the higher cost media quickly while allowing for long-term continuity of messaging at a more efficient rate.

> As a way to reach a mass audience, no other medium today has the unique creative abilities of television.

of sight, sound, and motion; the opportunity to demonstrate the product; the potential to use special effects; the empathy of the viewer; and the believability for viewers of seeing it happen right before their eyes (see My Ad Campaign 11–B, "The Pros and Cons of Broadcast TV Advertising"). As Exhibit 11–2 shows, over half of adult viewers believe TV is the most authoritative advertising source, compared to only 21.7 percent for newspapers, 12.3 percent for magazines, 10.4 percent for radio, and 6.4 percent for the Internet. Television was also rated as the most influential, persuasive, and exciting medium.[9]

The heaviest viewers of broadcast TV are middle-income, high school–educated individuals and their families, so most programming is directed at this group. People with considerably higher incomes and more education typically make use of a more diverse range of media and entertainment options.

The Pros and Cons of Broadcast TV Advertising [11–B]

The Pros

Contemporary broadcast television offers advertisers many advantages over competing media.

- **Mass coverage.** A full 98 percent of all U.S. homes have a TV (most have more than one), and viewing time for the average household increased from about five hours a day in 1960 to over eight hours in 2009.
- **Relatively low cost.** Despite the often huge initial outlays for commercial production and advertising time, TV's equally huge audiences bring the cost per exposure down to $2 to $10 per thousand viewers.
- **Some selectivity.** Television audiences vary a great deal depending on the time of day, day of the week, and nature of the programming. Advertising messages can be presented when potential customers are watching, and advertisers can reach select geographic audiences by buying local and regional markets.
- **Impact.** Television offers a kind of immediacy that other forms of advertising cannot achieve, displaying and demonstrating the product with sound, motion, and full color right before the customer's eyes.
- **Creativity.** The various facets of the TV commercial—sight, sound, motion, and color—permit infinite original and imaginative appeals.
- **Prestige.** Because the public considers TV the most authoritative and influential medium, it offers advertisers a prestigious image. Hallmark, Xerox, Coca-Cola, and IBM increase their prestige by regularly sponsoring cultural programs on network TV.
- **Social dominance.** In North America, most people under age 35 grew up with TV as a window to their social environment. They continue to be stirred by TV screenings of the Olympics, space travel, assassinations, wars, and political scandals around the world.

The Cons

Sometimes broadcast TV just doesn't "fit" the creative mix because of cost, lack of audience selectivity, inherent brevity, or the clutter of competitive messages.

- **High production cost.** One of broadcast TV's greatest handicaps is the high cost of producing quality commercials. Depending on the creative approach, the cost of filming a national commercial today may run from $200,000 to more than $1 million.
- **High airtime cost.** The average cost of a prime-time network commercial ranges from $200,000 to $400,000. A single 30-second commercial for a top-rated show in prime time may cost over $500,000 and in special attractions like the Super Bowl cost over $2 million. The cost of wide coverage, even at low rates, prices small and medium-size advertisers out of the market.
- **Limited selectivity.** Broadcast TV is not cost-effective for advertisers seeking a very specific, small audience. And it is losing some of its selectivity because of changing audience trends. More women are working outside the home or watching cable TV, hurting advertisers on network soap operas.
- **Brevity.** Studies show that most TV viewers can't remember the product or company in the most recent TV ad they watched—even if it was within the last five minutes. Recall improves with the length of the commercial; people remember 60-second spots better than 30-second spots.
- **Clutter.** TV advertising is usually surrounded by station breaks, credits, and public service announcements, as well as six or seven other spots. All these messages compete for attention, so viewers become annoyed and confused and often misidentify the product.
- **Zipping and zapping.** DVR users who skip through commercials when replaying recorded programs are zipping; remote-control users who change channels at the beginning of a commercial break are zapping.

In the United States, nearly every home has a television set. The average adult viewer watches TV 3.9 hours per day. This compares with using the Internet (3.8 hours), listening to the radio (2.1 hours), and reading books (1.4 hours).[10]

Cable in North American homes has significantly altered TV viewing patterns and the use of other media. Households with cable spend less time watching broadcast TV. They also spend less time listening to the radio, reading, or going to the movies. Cable seems to reach an audience that is difficult to get to in any other way. As a result of this audience fragmentation, advertising on broadcast networks has become less cost-effective. Streaming TV content has also increased dramatically in the past few years, such that for the first time, cable TV penetration is down.[11]

National advertisers have been using cable since the late 1970s and cable advertising revenues have grown steadily, reaching over $25 billion in 2011.[12] One reason is that cable's upscale audience buys proportionately more goods and services than noncable subscribers (see Exhibit 11–3). Procter & Gamble traditionally spends the most on network cable. However, local retailers also find local cable a good place to advertise.

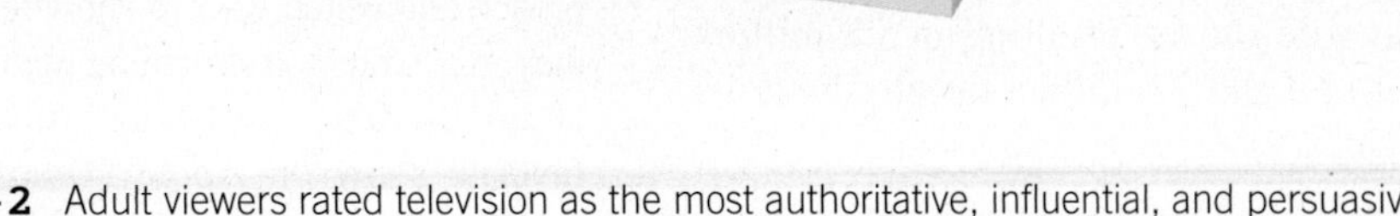

Nielsen studies indicate that the average U.S. household receives 118.6 TV channels. A larger number of channels, however, doesn't translate into more TV viewing. The Nielsen data indicate that the more channels a household has, the lower the percentage of channels watched. Households with the most channels (more than 150) tuned in to only 16.[13]

While there is no doubt that media play an ever-expanding role in our daily lives, there is a finite limit to the number of advertising exposures people can absorb. When that limit is reached, any new media will simply be fighting for market share. This is the reason for the increasing fragmentation of the audience and the precipitous decline in the huge share of audience once held by the broadcast networks. This is also why media buyers and planners are growing in importance as advertisers search for the elusive audience and fight for their share of that audience in an overcrowded media environment.

The Impact of Social Media and Streaming

The experience of television, and of the advertisements that appear in the medium, has been transformed by social media. People still gather the day after a favorite show airs to discuss what happened the night before to their favorite characters. But increasingly, they satisfy the need to share by "discussing" online as the show airs, connected through their favorite social media platform. These

EXHIBIT 11–2 Adult viewers rated television as the most authoritative, influential, and persuasive advertising medium.

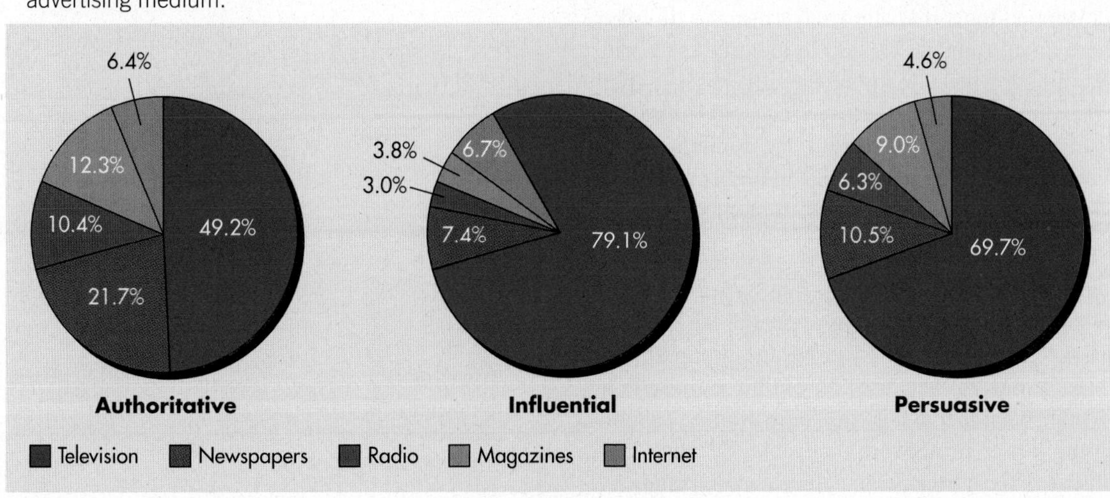

Source: From Television Bureau of Advertising and Nielsen Media Research. Reprinted with permission of Television Bureau of Advertising.

EXHIBIT 11–3 Cable households provide advertisers with attractive demographics (Index of 100 = U.S. average).

Cable versus Noncable Household Characteristics			
Upscale Profiles	**Cable HH vs. U.S. Average (Index)**	**Noncable HH vs. U.S. Average (Index)**	**% Advantage Cable HH**
Occupation: Professional	108	88	+23%
Education: Graduated college+	110	85	+29%
Occupation: Management/financial	105	93	+13%
Household income: $75,000+	112	80	+40%
Value of home: $500,000+	109	87	+25%
Downscale Profiles	**Cable HH vs. U.S. Average (Index)**	**Noncable HH vs. U.S. Average (Index)**	**% Advantage Cable HH**
Education: Did not graduate HS	86	122	−30%
Employment: Not working	99	101	−2%
Occupation: Construction/maintenance	87	120	−17%
Household Income: <$20,000	87	121	−28%
Value of Home: <$60,000	83	127	−35%

Source: Used by permission of Cable TV Advertising Bureau.

discussions, in turn, provide sponsors the chance to reach out to social media communities.

How prevalent is social media use during television? A 2012 survey conducted of respondents in the United States, United Kingdom, Germany, Spain, Sweden, China, and Taiwan suggested that 62 percent of global audiences use social networks while watching TV. In addition, 25 percent of viewers report that they discuss what they are watching in social media.[14] Twitter estimates that in 2012, 32 million people tweeted about their favorite shows, resulting in 5.8 million tweets about *American Idol* and 24 million tweets about the Super Bowl.[15]

Realizing the value of integrating the television and social media, Twitter developed tools that allow advertisers to discover when and where an ad runs on TV and to identify users who tweeted about the show that featured the advertiser's spot. Armed with this information, advertisers can buy promoted tweets to these users. Figure 11–4 shows, the combination of Promoted Tweets and TV exposure results in higher ratings of brand favorability and purchase intent when compared to TV ad exposure alone.[16]

Social media are also important in encouraging viewers to watch a program. As shown in Figure 11–5, 54 percent of the 18-to-34 age group and 48 percent of the 35-to-49 age group started watching a TV program because of online opinions in Facebook.[17] While social media hold immense promise as tools for increasing the power of network and cable TV, they may also prove a threat. This is because social media companies are exploring the value of running their own video ads. Facebook plans to sell its own TV-style ads to advertisers for $2.5 million a pop. The ads would allow marketers to purchase entry into a person's feed with 15-second spots, potentially reaching up to 100 million people.[18]

Streaming media are also transforming the TV viewing experience. Audiences have many options for how and when they view their favorite shows. They may choose the "appointment TV" approach and watch when a show airs on a network. Alternatively, they may watch on streaming platforms like the ones provided by Hulu+, Netflix, or Amazon Prime. Or they may download their favorite show on Apple iTunes or Amazon. These options

EXHIBIT 11–4 Impact of promoted tweets on brand metrics.

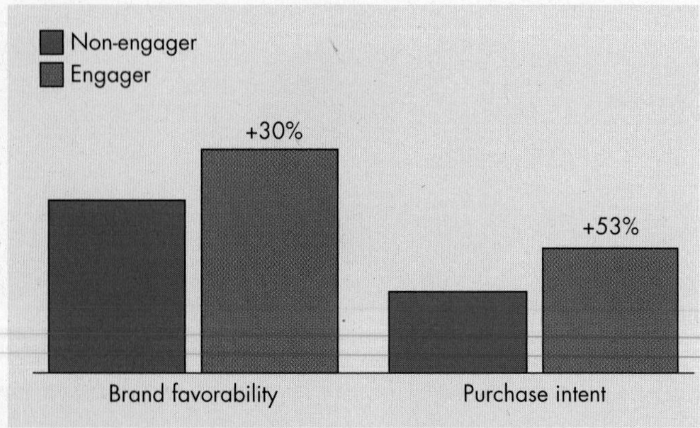

are available because of efforts by Google, Amazon, Microsoft, and Apple to make it easy to stream TV content.[19] Some of this content features commercials (like Hulu+). Some is commercial-free (like Netflix).

The Use of Television in IMC

Television today is very versatile. For many years it was strictly a mass medium, used to great advantage by the manufacturers of mass consumption goods: toiletries and cosmetics, food, appliances, and cars (see Exhibit 11–5). But today, thanks to the narrowcasting ability of cable TV, television can also be a highly selective niche medium. It's not unusual, for instance, to see ads for special feed for thoroughbreds and show horses on ESPN's *Grand Prix of Jumping.* And thanks to local cable, TV is now affordable for even small local advertisers. This makes it a very viable option for use in an IMC program.

While single programs don't deliver the mass audience they once did, television is still the most cost-effective way to deliver certain kinds of messages to large, well-defined audiences. When it comes to awareness and image advertising, for instance, television has no rival. The same is true for brand reinforcement messages.[20]

"When it comes to awareness and image advertising . . . , television has no rival."

Through its unique ability to deliver a creative big idea, television can impart *brand meaning* (the symbolism or personality of the brand) to either attract people to the brand or reinforce their current relationship with it. Television is also a good leverage tool. That is, an advertiser might take advantage of the relatively low CPM of television to reach out to many prospects. Prospects can identify themselves by responding to the commercial, and then the advertiser can follow up with less expensive, one-to-one or addressable media.

It's worth remembering that the high visibility of TV forces the sponsor to create ads that people find interesting and that consistently reinforce the brand's strategic position. The brands that succeed are the ones that are the most popular. And "ad liking" has a lot to do with brand popularity.

EXHIBIT 11–5 Influence of digital media on TV program trial.

US Internet Users Who Started Watching a TV Program Due to Opinions Online, by Site and Age, September 2012

% of respondents				
	18–34	35–49	50–64	Total
Facebook	54%	48%	30%	46%
Twitter	21	12	5	14
TV show websites	8	12	6	9
Forums of discussion boards	11	8	3	8
Entertainment sites	8	9	4	7
Pinterest	5	3	3	4
reddit	4	1	1	2
Viggle	3	2	1	2
foursquare	2	1	0	1
GetGlue	2	1	0	1
IntoNow	1%	1%	0%	1%

Note: $n = 828$

Source: Cable & Telecommunications Association for Marketing (CTAM), "How Chatter Matters in TV Viewing" conducted by Nielsen in collaboration with MBI TouchPoints and uSamp as cited by TVbytheNumbers, Dec 28, 2012.

check yourself ✓

1. What are some ways advertisers are innovating to adapt to the expanded use of digital video recorders?
2. Why has cable television been a good thing for local advertisers and those selling specialty products?

LO11-2 Discuss the various options for advertising on television.

Types of TV Advertising

Advertisers use different strategies to buy time on broadcast and cable television. The major broadcast networks offer a variety of *programs* that appeal to different audiences. So the advertiser buys ads based on the viewing audience of each program. A national advertiser that wants to reach a broad cross section of women ages 25 to 45, for example, might find *Glee* an efficient buy at a cost of $267,000 for a 30-second commercial.

▼ **EXHIBIT 11–6** Where does all the money go? Measured TV spending in billions of dollars (2008).

	2007 Ad Spending ($ billions)	2008 Ad Spending ($ billions)	Percentage Change
Network TV	$25.42	$26.71	+5.1%
Syndicated TV	4.17	4.44	+6.5
Spot TV	16.82	15.15	−9.9
Cable TV	18.02	18.83	+4.5
Total	**$64.43**	**$65.13**	**+1.1%**

Source: Reprinted with permission (June 23, 2008, *Advertising Age*). Copyright Crain Communications Inc.

When buying cable TV, an advertiser can buy ads over the full schedule of a channel because cable networks typically aim all of their programming to relatively specific *audiences.* The Lifetime and Family channels heavily weigh programs toward women; MTV targets viewers ages 16 to 25. Cable companies sell their network channels in bundles at a discount and offer discounts for *run-of-schedule* positioning—multiple ad purchases they can place throughout a channel's daily schedule (see My Ad Campaign 11–C, "The Pros and Cons of Cable TV Advertising").

There are various ways advertisers can buy time on TV. They include sponsoring an entire program, participating in a program, purchasing spot announcements between programs, and purchasing spots from syndicators. Exhibit 11–6 shows how much money is spent nationally on the various types of television advertising.

Network Advertising

Historically, major U.S. advertisers purchased airtime from one of the national broadcast **networks**. Cable has slowly eroded these audiences. At one time the big three (ABC, CBS, and NBC) had more than 90 percent of prime-time viewers. In the 2003–2004 season, ad-supported cable networks pulled ahead of the U.S. broadcast networks in prime time for the first time in the history of U.S. television, pulling in 44 percent of the audience, compared to 41 percent for the broadcast networks and 15 percent who were watching other television outlets, such as HBO and PBS. And the cable networks haven't looked back, more recently reporting a share in excess of 54 percent.

Networks offer large advertisers convenience and efficiency because they broadcast messages simultaneously across many affiliate stations throughout the country. Broadcast networks tend to reach masses of American consumers representing a cross section of the population, while cable networks tend to reach more selective niches.

An advertiser who underwrites the cost of a program is engaging in **sponsorship**. In a sole sponsorship, the advertiser is responsible for both the program content and the total cost of production. Sponsorship is so costly that single sponsorships are usually limited to specials. Companies that sponsor

networks Any of the national television or radio broadcasting chains or companies such as ABC, CBS, NBC, or Fox. Networks offer the large advertiser convenience and efficiency because the message can be broadcast simultaneously throughout the country.

sponsorship The presentation of a radio or TV program, or an event, or even a website by a sole advertiser. The advertiser is often responsible for the program content and the cost of production as well as the advertising. This is generally so costly that single sponsorships are usually limited to TV specials.

participation Several advertisers share the sponsorship of a television program. A "participating" advertiser has no control of the program content. Partnership commitment is usually limited to a relatively short period.

spot announcements An individual commercial message run between two programs but having no relationship to either. Spots may be sold nationally or locally. They must be purchased by contacting individual stations directly.

programs (AT&T, Xerox, and Hallmark, for example) gain two important advantages. First, the public more readily identifies with the product(s) due to the prestige of sponsoring first-rate entertainment. Second, the sponsor controls the placement and content of its commercials. The commercials can be fit to the program and run any length the sponsor desires so long as they remain within network or station regulations.

> "Local businesses are frequently seen on spot schedules."

To save money and reduce risks, many advertisers cosponsor programs, sponsoring on alternate weeks or dividing the program into segments. NFL games, for instance, are always sold as multiple sponsorships.

Most network TV advertising is sold on a **participation** basis, with several advertisers buying 30- or 60-second segments within a program. This enables them to spread their budgets and avoid long-term commitments to any one program. It also lets smaller advertisers buy a limited amount of time and still get the nationwide coverage they need.

Network advertising also has several disadvantages: lack of flexibility, long lead times, inconvenient restrictions, and forced adherence to network standards and practices, not to mention high prices. Costs can run high for a spot (see Exhibit 11–7). For this reason, most advertisers decide to buy *spot announcements.*

Spot Announcements

Spot announcements run in clusters between programs. They are less expensive and more flexible than network advertising because they can be concentrated in specific regions of the country. Therefore, local businesses are frequently seen on spot schedules. An advertiser with a small budget or limited

The Pros and Cons of Cable TV Advertising [11–C]

The Pros

- **Selectivity.** Cable offers specialized programming aimed at particular types of viewers. Narrowcasting allows advertisers to choose programming with the viewer demographics that best match their target customers.
- **Audience demographics.** Cable subscribers are younger, better educated, and more affluent, have higher-level jobs, live in larger households, and are more likely to try new products and buy more high-ticket items, such as cars, appliances, and high-tech equipment.
- **Low cost.** Many small companies get TV's immediacy and impact without the enormous expenditures of broadcast TV. Cable advertising can sometimes cost as little as radio. Many national advertisers find sponsorship attractive, since an entire cable series can cost less to produce than a single broadcast TV commercial.
- **Flexibility.** Broadcast TV commercials need to be short because of the high costs of production and airtime, but cable ads can run up to two minutes and, in the case of infomercials, much longer. They can also be tailored to fit the programming environment.
- **Testability.** Cable is a good place to experiment, testing both new products and various advertising approaches: ad frequency, copy impact, and different media mixes.

The Cons

Like every medium, cable TV has its drawbacks.

- **Limited reach.** Only about 10 percent of households don't have cable. This was cable's main weakness in the past, but it is less so today.
- **Fragmentation.** With more than 50 channels at their disposal, cable viewers do not watch any one channel in enormous numbers. To reach the majority of the cable audience in a particular market, ads must run on many stations.
- **Quality.** Cable, particularly local cable, sometimes has poorer production quality and less desirable programming than broadcast TV.
- **Zipping and zapping.** Cable TV has some of the same drawbacks as broadcast TV, such as zipping and zapping.

inventory Commercial time available to advertisers.

off-network syndication The availability of programs that originally appeared on networks to individual stations for rebroadcast.

first-run syndication Programs produced specifically for the syndication market.

barter syndication Marketing of first-run television programs to local stations free or for a reduced rate because some of the ad space has been presold to national advertisers.

program-length advertisement (PLA) A long-format television commercial that may run as long as an hour; also called an *infomercial.*

▼**EXHIBIT 11–7** Advertising cost per 30-second spot on 10 selected shows (2012 season).

Show and Network	30-Second Ad Cost
Sunday Night Football (NBC)	$545,000
American Idol (Fox)	340,000
Modern Family (ABC)	331,000
New Girl (Fox)	321,000
Family Guy (Fox)	277,000
The Voice (NBC)	225,000
Survivor (CBS)	149,500
Nashville (ABC)	143,000
Arrow (CW)	63,000
Nikita (CW)	23,000

Source: Reprinted with permission (October 21, 2012, *Advertising Age*). Crain Communications Inc.

distribution may use spots to introduce a new product into one area at a time. Or an advertiser can vary its message for different markets to suit promotional needs.

Spots may run 10, 15, 30, or 60 seconds and be sold nationally or locally. Spot advertising is more difficult to buy than network advertising because it involves contacting each station directly. The national rep system, in which individuals act as sales and service representatives for a number of stations, alleviates this problem.

Spot advertising is available only at network station breaks and when network advertisers have not purchased all of the available time, so spot ads may get lost in the clutter—which is why they tend to have less viewers and a smaller piece of the ad spending pie.

Syndication As audiences fragment, syndicated programs become an increasingly popular adjunct or alternative to network advertising. In a little over 10 years, the syndication industry has grown from almost nothing into a $5 billion advertising medium.

Syndication is the sale of programs on a station-by-station, market-by-market basis. In other words, a producer (for example, Warner Bros. or Disney) deals directly with stations, often through a distribution company, rather than going through the networks (see Exhibit 11–8). This efficient "direct-from-the-factory" approach gives local TV stations more programming control and greater profits. It also gives advertisers access to **inventory** (commercial time) that they might not get on network programs—often at better prices. Syndication has become the largest source of programming in the United States.

Television syndication comes in three forms: off-network, first-run, and barter. In **off-network syndication**, former popular network programs (reruns) are sold to individual stations for rebroadcast. Examples include *Seinfeld* and *Friends.* **First-run syndication** involves original shows, like *Oprah, Inside Edition,* and *Judge Judy,* which are produced specifically for the syndication market. One of the fastest-growing trends in television is **barter syndication** (also called *advertiser-supported syndication*). These are off-network or first-run programs offered by producers to local stations free or for a reduced rate, but with some of the ad space (usually more than half) pre-sold to national advertisers. *Wheel of Fortune, Jeopardy,* and *30 Rock* are some of the most popular examples.

Syndication is a popular tool for many national advertisers. It enables them to associate with popular programs and reach

▼**EXHIBIT 11–8** TV network and syndication distribution.
a. The networks are go-betweens.
b. Syndication is often a more efficient way of financing and distributing programs, as the networks are cut out of the transaction.

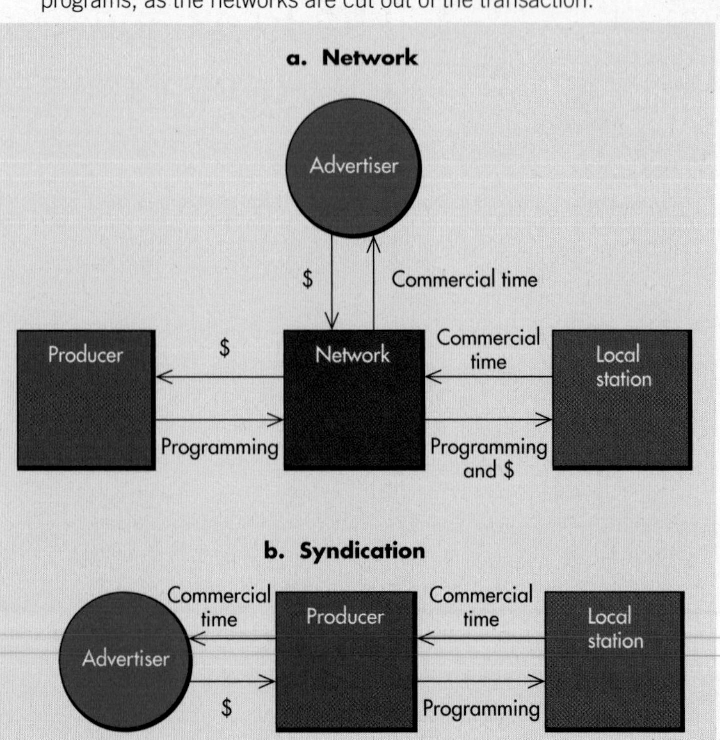

infomercial A long TV commercial that gives consumers detailed information about a product or service.

product placements Paying a fee to have a product prominently displayed in a movie or TV show.

Infomercials provide a unique opportunity for advertisers like Total Gym to demonstrate their products and generate immediate results.

some otherwise difficult to reach audiences at a lower cost per viewer than network shows. However, syndicated shows tend to be more cluttered with advertising and may not air in all markets or at consistent times.

Program-Length Ads (PLAs) Infomercials aren't new, but their respectability is. Ten years ago, most **program-length ad (PLA)** users were off–Madison Avenue marketers of hand mixers, juicers, and car waxes. Today, major marketers such as P&G, Microsoft, and Pfizer have ventured into the **infomercial** arena. And why not. Proactive, an acne medicine built largely on the basis of infomercial promotions, now has sales in excess of $1 billion. Total Gym and the Showtime Rotisserie have achieved similar levels of success.

Video Alternatives to TV Commercials

The 30-second commercial faces an ever-growing list of competitors for advertising dollars, not only from traditional rivals such as print and radio, but from video alternatives. Some of these, such as Web-based programming, we discuss more fully in Chapter 12. But here we present some non-Web-based advertising alternatives that either resemble or take the place of TV commercials.

TV Product Placements TV **product placements** occur when advertisers showcase their brands within television programming rather than commercials. Most people who've watched the popular show *American Idol* can't help but notice the prominent Coke cups placed in front of the judges. An entire episode of the ABC comedy *Modern Family* revolved around the Apple iPad. While these are some of the most obvious examples of product placements, advertisers such as Reynolds (Top Chef), Ford Fusion (New Girl), and Hyundai Tuscon (Walking Dead) have invested heavily in product placements. Viewers may not even be aware just how frequently product placements appear on television. Exhibit 11–9 demonstrates just how common the practice has become.

EXHIBIT 11–9 Top 10 best recalled product placements (2012–2013).

Rank	Brand	Program (Network/Air Date)
1	Subway	*Community* (NBC, 3/29)
2	Subway	*Community* (NBC, 3/15)
3	Porsche	*Two and a Half Men* (CBS, 1/2)
4	Chevrolet	*Hawaii Five-0* (CBS, 11/12)
5	Tootsie Roll	*Mike & Molly* (CBS, 5/7)
6	Louis Vuitton	*Person of Interest* (CBS, 4/26)
7	M&M's	*The Good Wife* (CBS, 11/25)
8	Charmin	*Revolution* (NBC, 9/17)
9	Chevrolet	*Hawaii Five-0* (CBS, 10/15)
10	Kit Kat	*The Middle* (ABC, 10/24)

Source: Copyrighted Information of The Nielsen Company, licensed for use herein.

The value of product placements can be difficult to quantify, at least in comparison to traditional advertising. Year-to-year growth in product placements was 39 percent in 2008 according

Product placement, where brands are woven into the content of shows, is turning up in more TV shows and movies as advertisers seek new ways to get their products noticed.

to Nielsen, a growth rate that is far higher than that for traditional commercials.[21]

Product placements offer advertisers several important benefits relative to traditional commercials. First, advertisers are increasingly concerned that many viewers avoid watching commercials. Research does suggest that in households with digital video recorders, many programs are recorded and watched after they are broadcast. People who watch a recorded show often skip through commercial messages. By placing a brand within the show, advertisers can minimize the impact of commercial avoidance. Second, having brands appear within programming offers advertisers the chance to link their products with popular characters. For example, *The Big Bang Theory* viewers got to watch their favorite characters play Twister, a Milton Bradley game, after Amy Farrah Fowler suggested they do so on the highly rated show.[22] Third, the use of product placements helps advertisers avoid the credibility issues that surround commercials. Viewers know that commercials, as sponsored messages, represent the biased viewpoint of the advertiser. But brand appearances in programming may help advertisers do an "end around" such credibility problems.

Film Product Placements Marketers can also take advantage of product placements in feature films. While product placements are often thought of as a television phenomenon, the practice has a long history in film. The James Bond movie *Goldfinger* created worldwide attention for Aston Martin cars (at a cost to Ford Motor of $35 million) and most people know that Reese's Pieces candy sales surged after an appearance in the film *ET*. The practice continues today. More recently, the 2012 animated *The Lorax* set a modern-day record with over 70 placement partners. But that record was quickly smashed after more than 100 brands partnered with the 2013 film *Man of Steel*.[23] Clearly, product placements are here to stay.

Commercials at Service Stations Prefilm commercials capitalize on an obvious reality: Filmgoers don't have much to do while they wait for the movie to start so perhaps they will find watching entertaining commercials preferable to doing nothing. This same logic lies behind the emerging practice of showing ads on service station gas pumps. The appeal for advertisers who purchase time on Gas Station TV(www.gstv.com) is that the audience is "basically tethered at the pump for an average of four to four-and-a-half minutes," according to GSTV CEO David Leider. His company offers national and local advertisers the chance to present standard-length commercials with ad costs that are comparable to spot cable. Early national sponsors include Chevrolet, Pepsi, Allstate, Goodyear, and Walmart.

Product placement is also common in films. The prominence of the Wonder bread logo in the movie Talladega Nights: The Ballad of Ricky Bobby *will ensure that viewers remember the brand even if they forget the movie.*

This gasoline pump from Austin, Texas–based Dresser Wayne offers Internet news headlines, traffic information, weather reports, and customized promotions on its 15-inch touchscreen. Consumers have the option to print coupons for special offers, such as a discount on a cup of coffee or an oil change. Local businesses can purchase advertising on the video screen, generating additional revenue for the fuel retailer. This WiFi- and Bluetooth-capable pump will also sell you music, which can be downloaded to your cell phone or automobile's entertainment system.

check yourself ✓

1. Why is syndication a popular tool for many national advertisers?
2. What are the possible benefits of product placement versus traditional commercials?

LO11-3 Explain how to measure television audiences and select the best programs to buy.

TV AUDIENCE MEASUREMENT

Efficient advertisers study the audiences of various programs and analyze their impact and cost-effectiveness against other media vehicles. To do this, they must

understand the techniques and terminology used in television audience measurement.

Rating Services

The companies that measure the program audiences of TV and radio stations for advertisers and broadcasters are called **rating services**. These firms pick a representative sample of the market and furnish data on the number and characteristics of the viewers or listeners. Companies subscribe to a service and use it as a basis for planning, buying, or selling media advertising.

In the United States, Nielsen Media Research is the major rating service for television. Its flagship service, the Nielsen Television Index (NTI), uses a national sample of households equipped with meters to develop audience estimates for all national TV programming. The meters are hooked up to TV sets in 25,000 homes across the country and continuously measure the channels to which each set is tuned. People meters go a step further in 25 major markets and gather information about who is watching in addition to the channel tuned.

At the local level, Nielsen surveys 1.6 million households. Household members record their viewing habits in diaries. Four times each year, during the **sweeps** month-long rating periods, Nielsen collects and processes the data. This information is used by networks and local stations to determine how much they can charge for advertising on their shows.

Some advertisers and broadcasters maintain that Nielsen's reports are unstable and inaccurate.[24] Nielsen faces an enormous challenge keeping up with changes in TV viewing habits. For example, many viewers watch shows on streaming platforms after they've been broadcast. Nielsen's existing measurement techniques are not well equipped to track such viewing habits. Popular platforms like Netflix and Amazon Plus are even delivering their own original programs. And the TV experience itself is changing, as people integrate social media use with TV viewing. Exhibit 11–10 provides insight to the methodology of collecting Nielsen ratings.

rating services These services measure the program audiences of TV and radio stations for advertisers and broadcasters by picking a representative sample of the market and furnishing data on the size and characteristics of the viewers or listeners.

sweeps The four, monthlong periods each year when rating services measure all TV markets for station viewing habits and demographic information for the purpose of setting advertising rates. Sweep months are February, May, July, and November.

▼EXHIBIT 11–10 Where do TV ratings come from?

For four decades, the life and death of network TV programs have been in the hands of the Nielsen families, households chosen with the aid of national census and other data to reflect the country's demographics. Originally there were two measuring types: those who kept diaries and those who had a black box attached to their TV sets. Someone in each of 2,400 diary homes kept a written record of which shows each person watched during the week. In the 1,700 black box households, an audiometer attached to the TV kept track of when the set was on and what channel it was tuned to. Nielsen Media Research paid these families for the permission to gather data from their viewing patterns. The information is used to compute its Nielsen Television Index (NTI), the sole source of national TV ratings.

But that method of determining national ratings has been replaced by the more accurate people meter (see illustration), an electronic device that automatically records a household's TV viewing. The people meter records the channels watched, the number of minutes of viewing, and who in the household is watching. Each person must punch in and punch out on a keypad. The microwave-based people meter keeps track of second-by-second viewing choices of up to eight household members and relays the data to a central computer, which tabulates the data overnight.

The original people meter was developed by AGB Research, a British company. AGB found clients in ad agencies, cable networks, and syndicators—all of whom believed NTI overreported broadcast network shows and underreported other types. However, Nielsen developed its own people meter, and AGB abandoned the U.S. market.

Nielsen conducts its survey sweeps four times a year in major market areas and publishes sweeps books that are the basis for network and local station ad rates. With the advent of the passive people meter, advertisers may once again believe in the ratings they're paying for.

A well-established technique in audience measurement is the single-source data made available by supermarket scanners. Once information on a family's viewing habits has been gathered, its packaged-goods purchases are measured. The implications are monumental for marketing and media planners. The leaders in single-source measurement today are Information Resources, Inc. (IRI), with its BehaviorScan service, and Nielsen, with its Home Scan service.

Today, Nielsen is introducing technologies to track the use of social media and television viewing. In an October 2013 press release, the company touted its new "Twitter TV Ratings." It describes the technology as "the first-ever measure of the total activity and reach of TV-related conversation on Twitter." Nielsen estimates that TV tweets reach an audience of almost 50 persons per tweet. It's clear that as TV technology changes, Nielsen will evolve to remain the best source of audience information.

designated market areas (DMAs) The geographic areas from which TV stations attract most of their viewers.

For demographic studies of TV audiences, advertisers also use the Simmons National Consumer Studies (www.experian.com/simmons-research/national-consumer-studies.html) and MRI+ (www.mriplus.com/). These companies perform extensive surveys of the U.S. marketplace and publish their findings on consumer lifestyles, product usage, and media habits. Advertisers use the results for strategic planning purposes.

Cable Ratings

Reliable information on the audiences for cable programs is even harder to gather. Traditional techniques often rely on too small a sample to be statistically significant, so major cable programming services provide their own reports of audience viewership by show. Interpreting cable ratings is a confusing process, since the media planner has to integrate so much information from so many different sources.

Defining Television Markets

Television rating services define unique geographic television markets to minimize the confusion of overlapping TV signals. The Nielsen station index uses the term **designated market areas (DMAs)** for geographic areas (cities, counties) in which the local TV stations attract the most viewing. For example, the DMA for Columbus, Georgia (see Exhibit 11–11), is the 17 counties in which the local area TV stations are the most watched.

Advertising to Children: Child's Play?

Kids make up a considerable consumer group whose number and purchasing power are growing. In 1999, children ages 4 to 12 took in $31.3 billion in income from allowances, jobs, and gifts, and spent 92 percent of it, says James MacNeal, a market researcher who specializes in the children's market. Today, children are influencing the family's buying behavior for everything from cars to orange juice—up to $500 billion a year. Whether they're spending their own money or asking their parents to spend theirs, marketing to kids is big business and it's only getting bigger.

The benefits of reaching children are great. If won over now, they tend to be loyal customers into adulthood. Besides selling to children, advertisers also sell through children. Some companies believe they can sell more by appealing to children's preferences than to those of adults. The minivan was created because children demanded more room, says MacNeal. When kids decided the vehicle was "uncool," their opinions helped develop the SUV. Saturday morning cartoons are the traditional vehicle for ads promoting cereals, candy, and toys. But parents are asked to buy particular brands of vacuum cleaners and other household goods because their kids saw them advertised on TV. Marketers rely on kids' "pester power" to get their products sold.

The dangers of marketing to kids from an ethical perspective are fairly clear: Children are the "vulnerable" market. They are less experienced. Their concepts of self, time, and money are immature. As a result, they know very little about their own desires, needs, and preferences—or how to use economic resources rationally to satisfy them. It is likely that child-oriented advertising can lead to false beliefs or highly improbable product expectations. Telling children about a product and accurately describing that product is probably ethical. Convincing them that they must have a toy to be popular with their friends is probably not. Nothing is likely to enrage parents and society-at-large more than the prospect of marketers manipulating and taking advantage of children.

Cereal is better if a fun character is selling it; so are beer and cigarettes as the Budweiser frogs and lizards and Joe Camel proved. In the United Kingdom, there was criticism over the use of TV characters such as the Simpsons and Teletubbies, as well as the Spice Girls, to sell snack foods high in fat, sugar, and salt. The junk food firms face a crackdown on the hard sell of products that can make children overweight and unhealthy.

Both critics and defenders agree that advertisers should not intentionally deceive children. Federal legislation has been introduced that would reimpose the 1974 guidelines limiting advertising on children's programs. These guidelines deal with truth and accuracy.

The mood in several European countries is to tighten up children-and-advertising guidelines. Sweden has some of the strictest controls in Europe on children and advertising, banning all television advertisements aimed at children under 12. This ban includes advertisements on toys, foods, sweets, drinks, and any products that might appeal to preteens.

In the United States, the Children's Advertising Review Unit (CARU) of the Council of Better Business Bureaus (BBB) promotes responsible children's advertising and responds to public concerns. The basic activity of CARU is the review and evaluation of child-directed advertising to help avoid deceptive messages. When children's advertising is found to be misleading, inaccurate, or inconsistent with its guidelines, CARU seeks changes through the voluntary cooperation of advertisers. The BBB website at http://epi.bbb.org/council/for-businesses/national-partnerships/bbbs-industry-self-regulation-solutions/childrens-advertising-review-unit-caru-/ discusses CARU's guidelines.

Questions

1. Do bans on marketing to children compromise a basic freedom of choice and speech? Whose responsibility is it to make sure children are not inappropriately influenced by advertising? Their parents? The government? Advertisers? How far should advertisers have to go to ensure that children are not misled by their ads?
2. Study the CARU guidelines and then watch the advertising on a children's network or Saturday morning television. How well do you feel the advertisers are adhering to those guidelines?

EXHIBIT 11-11 This map of the area surrounding Columbus, Georgia, shows media planners which counties are included in the designated market area (DMA) and will be reached by advertising placed on the local television stations. Columbus, Georgia, is the 125th largest DMA in the United States and contains over 200,000 TV households.

Columbus, GA, Audience Figures

- DMA Market Size: #125
- Total DMA TV Households: 207,820
- Total DMA Persons 18+: 388,000
- Total DMA Adults 25–54: 214,000
- Total DMA Working Women: 92,000
- % of Cable in DMA Households: 76%

Local TV Stations

WTVM ABC - Columbus (Muscogee) Georgia
WRBL CBS - Columbus (Muscogee) Georgia
WCGT Ind. - Columbus (Muscogee) Georgia
WMCF TBN - Opelika (Lee) Alabama
WJSP/WGTV PBS - Columbus (Muscogee) Georgia
WLGA UPN - Opelika (Lee) Alabama
WCAG UATV - Lagrange (Troupe) Georgia
WLTZ NBC - Columbus (Muscogee) Georgia
WGIQ/WBIQ PBS - Louisville (Barbour) Alabama
WXTX FOX - Columbus (Muscogee) Georgia
WLGA UPN - Opelika (Lee) Alabama

Dayparts

Advertisers must decide when to air commercials and on which programs. Programs continue to run or are canceled depending on their ratings (percentage of the population watching). Ratings also vary with the time of day a program runs. Television time is divided into dayparts roughly as follows:

Early morning:	6:00–9:00 a.m.	(Eastern and Pacific)
Daytime:	9:00 a.m.–4:30 p.m.	
Early fringe:	4:30–7:30 p.m.	
Prime access:	7:30–8:00 p.m.	
Prime time:	8:00–11:00 p.m.	
Late news:	11:00–11:30 p.m.	
Late night:	11:30 p.m.–2:00 a.m.	

Viewing is highest during **prime time** (8 to 11 p.m. Eastern and Pacific Time; 7 to 10 p.m. Central and Mountain Time). Late fringe ranks fairly high in most markets among adults, and daytime and early fringe tend to be viewed most heavily by women. To reach the greatest percentage of the advertiser's target audience with optimal frequency, the media planner determines a **daypart mix** based on TV usage levels reported by the rating services.

Audience Measurements

Rating services and media planners use many terms to define a station's audience, penetration, and efficiency. **TV households (TVHH)** refers to the number of households that own television sets. The number of TVHH in a particular market gives an advertiser a sense of the market's size. Likewise, the number of TVHH tuned in to a parti-cular program helps the advertiser estimate the program's popularity and how many people a commercial is likely to reach.

The percentage of homes in a given area that have one or more TV sets turned on at any particular time is expressed as **households using TV (HUT)**. If there are 1,000 TV sets in the survey area and 500 are turned on, HUT is 50 percent (500/1,000).

The **program rating** refers to the percentage of TV households in an area that are tuned in to a specific program. The rating is computed as follows:

$$\text{Rating} = \frac{\text{TVHH tuned to a specific program}}{\text{Total TVHH in area}}$$

prime time Highest level of TV viewing (8 p.m. to 11 p.m.)

daypart mix A media scheduling strategy based on a specific combination of broadcast time segments.

TV households (TVHH) The number of households in a market area that own television sets.

households using TV (HUT) The percentage of homes in a given area that have one or more TV sets turned on at any particular time. If 1,000 TV sets are in the survey and 500 are turned on, the HUT figure is 50 percent.

program rating The percentage of TV households in an area that are tuned into a specific program.

audience share The percentage of homes with TV sets in use (HUT) tuned to a specific program.

total audience The total number of homes reached by some portion of a TV program. This figure is normally broken down to determine the distribution of audience into demographic categories.

audience composition The distribution of an audience into demographic or other categories.

gross rating points (GRPs) The total audience delivery or weight of a specific media schedule. One rating point equals 1 percent of a particular market's population.

cost per rating point (CPP) A computation used by media buyers to determine which broadcast programs are the most efficient in relation to the target audience. The CPP is determined by dividing the cost of the show by the show's expected rating.

> POPULAR SHOWS CAN COMMAND HIGHER ADVERTISING RATES.

Networks want high ratings because they measure a show's popularity. More popular shows can command higher advertising rates.

The percentage of homes with sets in use (HUT) tuned to a specific program is called the **audience share**.

$$\text{Share} = \frac{\text{TVHH tuned to a specific program}}{\text{HH with a TV turned on}}$$

A program with only 500 viewers can have a 50 percent share if only 1,000 sets are turned on. *Ratings,* in contrast, measure the audience as a percentage of all TVHH in the area, whether the TV sets are on or off.

The actual number of homes reached by some portion of a program is called **total audience**. This figure is normally broken down into demographic categories to determine **audience composition**.

Gross Rating Points

In television, **gross rating points (GRPs)** are the total rating points achieved by a particular media schedule over a specific period. For example, a weekly schedule of five commercials on programs with an average household rating of 20 would yield 100 GRPs.

GRPs allow advertisers to draw conclusions about the different markets available for a client's ads by providing a comparable measure of advertising weight. However, GRPs do not reflect a market's size. For example, while campaigns in Knoxville and Charlotte might have the same GRPs, they would differ significantly in the number of homes reached.

	TV Homes (thousands)	Avg. Cost per Spot	Avg. Rating	Avg. Homes Reached (thousands)	Number of Spots	GRPs
Knoxville	1,002	$1,500	15	150	5	75
Charlotte	638	1,250	15	96	5	75

To better determine the relative value of television advertising markets, other measures are used, such as cost per rating point (CPP) and cost per thousand (CPM). These and other media terms will be described here and in Chapter 14.

BUYING TELEVISION TIME

The process of buying TV time can be lengthy and, depending on the number of stations in the buy, quite involved. The procedures are so complex that most large advertisers use ad agencies or media-buying services. Buying services have gained in popularity because they charge less and can save advertisers money by negotiating for desirable time slots at reduced rates. Local advertisers typically rely on station reps to help determine the best buys for their money.

Selecting Programs for Buys

Media buyers select the most efficient programs in relation to the target audience using the **cost per rating point (CPP)** and the **cost per thousand (CPM)** for each program:

$$\text{CPP} = \frac{\text{Cost}}{\text{Rating}}$$

$$\text{CPM} = \frac{\text{Cost}}{\text{Thousands of people}}$$

For example, assume *CSI* has a rating of 25, reaches 200,000 people in the primary target audience, and costs $2,000 for a 30-second spot on station WALB-TV in Albany, Georgia. Then,

$$\text{CPP} = \frac{\$2{,}000}{25} = \$80$$

$$\text{CPM} = \frac{\$2{,}000}{(200{,}000 \div 1{,}000)} = \$10$$

By calculating CPP, the media buyer can compare the cost of a rating point (reaching 1 percent of TVHH) from one

cost per thousand (CPM) A common term describing the cost of reaching 1,000 people in a medium's audience. It is used by media planners to compare the cost of various media vehicles.

preemption rate Lower TV advertising rates that stations charge when the advertiser agrees to allow the station to sell its time to another advertiser willing to pay a higher rate.

affidavit of performance A signed and notarized form sent by a television station to an advertiser or agency indicating what spots ran and when. It is the station's legal proof that the advertiser got what was paid for.

makegoods TV spots that are aired to compensate for spots that were missed or run incorrectly.

program or network to another. That's good information for beginning negotiations. But rating points relate to the whole market. The real important figure is the cost of reaching 1,000 prospects in your target market. That's why the CPM should be calculated against the size of your target audience, not the whole market. The lower the cost per 1,000 people in your target audience, the more efficient the show is at reaching your real prospects.

To get the best buys within the available budget, then, the media buyer substitutes stronger programs for less efficient ones.

Negotiating Prices

TV stations and cable companies publish rate cards to sell their airtime. However, since TV audiences are estimated at best, television reps will always negotiate prices.

The media buyer contacts the rep and explains what efficiency the advertiser needs in terms of CPM to make the buy. The buyer has numerous ways to negotiate lower rates: work out a package deal, accept *run-of-schedule positioning* (the station chooses when to run the commercials), or take advantage of preemption rates. A **preemption rate** is lower because the advertiser agrees to be "bumped" (preempted) if another advertiser pays the higher, nonpreemption rate.

After the advertising airs, the station returns a signed and notarized **affidavit of performance** to the advertiser or agency, specifying when the spots aired and what makegoods are available. **Makegoods** refer to free advertising time an advertiser receives to compensate for spots the station missed or ran incorrectly or because the program's ratings were substantially lower than guaranteed.

check yourself ✓

1. What are some of the criticisms of ratings services?
2. What is the difference between *program rating* and *audience share*?

LO11-4 Describe the advantages and disadvantages of radio as an advertising medium.

THE MEDIUM OF RADIO

Radio is a personal, one-on-one medium; people tend to listen alone. And radio is mobile. It can entertain people who are driving, walking, at home, or away from home. This makes it a particularly strong way to reach people who commute by car; almost half of radio listening takes place in a car.

Radio is also adaptable to moods. In the morning, people may want to hear the news, upbeat music, or interesting chatter; in the afternoon, they may want to unwind with classical or easy-listening music.

Who Uses Radio?

In an average week, 85 percent of the U.S. population listens to terrestrial radio. Almost 18 percent of Americans 18 years old or older listen at home to radio on a typical weekday, nearly 61 percent listen in their car, and over 10 percent listen at work.[25]

More national advertisers are discovering radio's audience potential (see Exhibit 11–12). Back when it was still a little company in Queens, New York, and strapped for money, Snapple Natural Beverages decided to use radio. It put its entire ad budget into a yearlong schedule with a young, relatively unknown

▼EXHIBIT 11–12

Company	2011 Radio Spending ($ millions)
1 Comcast Corp.	$118.2
2 Home Depot, Inc.	82.5
3 Chrysler Group LLC Dealer Association	72.3
4 Berkshire Hathaway, Inc. (GEICO, etc.)	62.7
5 Walmart Stores, Inc.	57.3
6 Verizon Communications, Inc.	52.6
7 Allstate Corp.	37.9
8 Safeway, Inc.	36.5
9 Sears Holdings Corp.	36
10 News Corp.	35.9

imagery transfer
The process by which visual elements of a TV commercial are transferred into the consumer's mind by using a similar audio track in its radio counterpart.

radio show host named Howard Stern. Snapple liked the way he delivered its spots as a live reader.

A few years later, Snapple began receiving letters and phone calls from people in the Midwest and West, where it didn't even have distribution. It seems that nationally syndicated talk show host Rush Limbaugh, on a restricted-calorie diet, had been giving enthusiastic on-air endorsements for Snapple Diet Iced Tea. The firm moved quickly to sign him as a paid endorser. What it learned was the power of radio, especially when combined with a popular radio personality.

> "While television tends to be a passive medium . . . , radio actively involves people."

As with other traditional media, radio has found it easier to collaborate with rather than fight new media. As an example, 31 percent of radio listeners report initiating an online search based on something they have heard on the radio.

Radio also helps to reach audiences underrepresented in other media. For example, it tends to have higher reach with audiences that are not watching television during a given daypart.[26]

The Use of Radio in IMC

While television tends to be a passive medium that people simply watch, radio actively involves people. They listen intently to their favorite personalities; they call in to make requests, participate during a contest, or contribute to a discussion; they use their ears and imaginations to fill in what they cannot see.

With radio, national companies can tie in to a local market and target the specific demographic group they want to reach. Most important, radio enables advertisers to maintain strategic consistency and stretch their media dollars through **imagery transfer**. Research shows that when advertisers run a schedule on TV and then convert the audio portion to radio commercials, fully 75 percent of consumers replay the TV spot in their minds when they hear the radio spot. That extends the life and builds the impact of a TV campaign at greatly reduced cost. In an IMC campaign, where message consistency is a primary objective, this is a very important feature of radio.

Local retailers like the medium for the same reasons. Also, they can tailor it to their needs. It offers defined audiences; its recall characteristics are similar to those of TV; and retailers can establish an identity by creating their own ads. Finally, since radio is so mobile, retailers can reach prospects just before they purchase. Hence, recent years have seen major spending increases by local grocery stores, car dealers, banks, and home-improvement, furniture, and apparel stores.

Radio is an important component of the media mix. It offers tremendous reach, attention, imagery, and selectivity, at a relatively low cost. In this ad, the Radio Advertising Bureau (www.rab.com) is publicizing the results of a research study that suggests advertisers can improve brand recall by replacing some of their TV and newspaper ads with radio spots (http://urlm.co/www.radioadlab.org).

Radio Programming and Audiences

Radio stations plan their programming carefully to reach specific audiences and to capture as many listeners as possible. The larger the audience, the more a station can charge for commercial time. Therefore, extensive planning and research go into radio programming and program changes. Stations can use tried-and-true formats, subscribe to network or syndicated programming, or devise unique approaches. Programming choices are greatly influenced by whether a station is on the AM or FM band. FM has much better sound fidelity, fewer commercial interruptions, and more varied programming.

To counteract FM's inroads, many AM stations switched to programs that don't rely on sound quality, such as news, talk, and sports. Some stations are experimenting with all comedy, midday game shows with audience participation, or formats geared to specific regions. AM stations are also trying to win back music listeners by improving their sound quality and offering stereo broadcasting.

When buying radio time, advertisers usually buy the station's *format,* not its programs. Most stations adopt one of the dozen or so standard **programming formats**: contemporary hit radio, adult contemporary, country, rock, easy listening, news/talk, and so on, as shown in Exhibit 11–13. Each format tends to appeal to specific demographic groups. The most common format is country music, which appeals to a broad cross section of Americans from 25 to 54 years old, but more adults listen to news/talk than any other format.

Contemporary hit radio (CHR) appeals to teenagers and women under 30. It provides a constant flow of top 40 hits, usually with minimal intrusion by disc jockeys. Another popular format, adult contemporary (or "easy oldies"), is often advertised as

heard the commercials three, four, or five times. By measuring the number of different people who listened to KKDA, rating services provide the *reach potential* of our radio schedule, which in this case was estimated to be 167,800.

The **cume rating** is the cume persons expressed as a percentage of the population being measured. For example,

$$\frac{167{,}800 \times 100}{3{,}072{,}727} = 5.5\%$$

This means that 5.5 percent of the Dallas/Fort Worth population listened to KKDA at least once during the afternoon drive. The average listener heard our commercial 4.8 times, but we'll learn how to calculate that in Chapter 14. ■

check yourself ✓

1. Why would a radio advertiser be willing to pay a premium for one specific daypart over another?
2. What is the difference between a radio advertisement schedule's *GRP* and *cume rating*?

learn about, practice, and apply principles for the use of print advertising!

M: Advertising was developed for students who want information packaged in a concise, easy-to-read, yet interesting format.
Check out the book's website to:

- **Show that you know the role of the Internet in the future of magazines and newspapers. (Review Questions)**
- **Defend the proposition that national advertisers should be charged a higher rate than local ones. (Review Questions)**
- **Confirm that you know how to effectively use a rate card. (Exploring Advertising)**

While you are there, check out the professional resource links, review the PowerPoint presentation, and test your knowledge with the Multiple Choice Quiz. Additionally, *Connect® Marketing* is available for M: Advertising.

www.mhhe.com/ArensM2e

chapter twelve

digital **interactive media**

This chapter explores the important factors advertisers weigh when considering digital interactive media. This medium has its own distinct characteristics, unique advantages, and drawbacks. Advertisers must be able to compare the merits of this medium and understand the most cost-effective ways to use them in their media mix.

The story of how one of the biggest companies on the planet began through a chance meeting of a couple of twenty-somethings contains important lessons about talent, genius, insight, and just plain luck. Larry Page, a Michigan alum was visiting Stanford in 1995 to get oriented to grad program in computer science. Sergey Brin, already in the program, was tasked with showing Page the campus. The two took a liking to one another, and began working on shared ideas.

The following year they partnered on a project to map the mathematical properties of the World Wide Web and, more specifically, examine the structure of the Web through an analysis of links (separate sites linking to one another). Using a Web crawler, software that explores links by systematically following them from page to page, the two were able to generate a map of the Web (which was still relatively easy to do in 1996).

Then, Page and Brin had an insight that would change the Internet forever. They realized that by applying an algorithm, eventually named "PageRank," to their analysis of links, they could create a superior measure of site relevance and credibility. PageRank was founded on the idea that credible sites receive many links from other websites, while those of little value do not. And because people who use search engines are looking for credible sites, the analysis of links could be the foundation of a superior search engine, one that returned relevant and useful results.

continued on p. 298

LEARNING OBJECTIVES

After studying this chapter, you will be able to:

LO12-1 Discuss the evolution of digital interactive media.

LO12-2 Explain how time and space on the Web are bought.

LO12-3 Discuss the types of digital interactive advertising.

LO12-4 Identify the opportunities and challenges of advertising in social media.

IKEA spends heavily on Web advertising, knowing it is popular with the young consumers who like their products.

continued from p. 297

Their search engine, named Google, received great coverage on introduction. Users found that they could count on Google to return rapid, accurate, relevant results. They also liked its hyper-spare layout and easy-to-use interface. Another benefit of Google was the absence of ads. Unlike some early (and now defunct) competitors, Google had no banner ads, and site rankings could not be purchased by companies. Soon Google was well on the way to becoming the top search engine in the world. As of July 2013, Google is the site for over two-thirds of all Internet searches in the U.S. and the site is even more powerful globally, with over 70 SOM.

So ends the story of the world's best search engine. But missing is the story of the world's best advertising machine. Page and Brin were coders, not marketers. In fact, they had little interest in putting ads on Google. And without some pressure from funders, they might never have. The venture capitalists that provided the monies to launch Google strongly encouraged the duo to appoint a CFO. Eric Schmidt joined the company in 2001 and began leading the process to figure out how to capitalize on searches for generating profits.

Page and Brin realized, perhaps reluctantly, that they would have to accept advertising on Google. They believed that the way to best do this, while remaining true to Google's core principles, was to allow advertisers to bid on key-words that audiences use in search. A Google search would then return two kinds of links: "organic" results, namely those generated by PageRank, and sponsored content. The founders insisted that these be kept distinct, so that Web searchers could always distinguish the two. They further stipulated that organic search be insulated from sponsorship, such that organic results would never be contaminated by advertising dollars. Finally, they advocated a "pay-per-click" model that charged advertisers only when users clicked on sponsored ads.

Would users accept such ads? Google's founders weren't sure. But eventually, it became clear that advertising did not bother users of the search engine. Indeed, users not only accepted sponsored links, they seemed to find value in them. Over the years, Google has determined that searches involving commercial keywords (in other words product or service related words) lead audiences to click sponsored links at a substantially higher rate than organic.

Google's sponsored links have transformed the Internet. Advertisers love the pay for performance model. They also love that sponsored links deliver people ready to buy. How ready? Google ad revenues for 2012 were an amazing $43 billion.[5] Compare that to NBC's total ad revenue of $2.41 billion. Search advertising doesn't just work; it is one of the most effective ways to reach a prospect.

Mick Jagger and Keith Richards happened upon one another at a train station, and eventually founded the Rolling Stones. Lennon and McCartney met under similar random circumstances. Page and Brin struck up a friendship during a seemingly insignificant campus tour. In life, many chance encounters lead to nothing at all. But sometimes, chance plus talent is a catalyst for outcomes that change the world. ■

Internet A worldwide network of computer systems that facilitates global electronic communications via e-mail, the Web, ftp, and other data protocols.

protocols Common rules for linking and sharing information.

LO12-1 Discuss the evolution of digital interactive media.

THE EVOLUTION OF DIGITAL INTERACTIVE MEDIA

Advertising-related technologies never stop evolving. They've already given us the personal computer, the mobile phone, the Internet, HDTV, 3D TV, digital media players, Blu-ray, IPTV, VOIP, and iPads—and the software to make it all simple enough for anybody to use.

Social networking site Facebook allows Web users to join networks organized by their school, city, or shared interest. Founded in 2004, the site has surged in popularity, attracting 700 million unique users worldwide in September 2013.

Evolving technologies present challenges to advertisers, who are often unsure how to best take advantage of the opportunities they afford. These opportunities may become clear only with time. When mobile phones were first introduced, advertisers thought only in terms of ads on the devices' screens. It turned out that such ads are the tip of the marketing iceberg. For example, a typical teen watching a high school basketball game won't just use his phone to place a call. He'll use it to snap a picture of the star player's Nike shoes, send the photo over Gmail to his dad (asking for his own pair), post it at Pinterest, and tweet his friends to seek their opinions about the shoes. All of this will be accomplished in a minute or two. Many of these interactions will take place outside of a Web browser via smartphone apps. While e-mailing and tweeting, the teen will be exposed to several marketing messages, some of which can easily identify his general location and interests. And he will leave a trail of activities for marketers to ponder.

Digital media are truly revolutionary in their effect on our daily lives, and it's a revolution for marketers, too. As the nation's biggest advertisers realized that digital media offer vast opportunities for engaging target audiences, they started increasing their spending dramatically. In light of this change, the Internet research company eMarketer reports that online ad spending reached nearly $40 billion in 2012. This is noteworthy because for the first time ever, money spent on digital advertising exceeded the combined totals for newspaper and magazines. And by 2016, spending on digital will exceed the combined totals of all print plus radio and outdoor combined.[1]

In addition to this phenomenal growth, by offering true interactivity, online media enable businesses and other organizations to develop and nurture relationships with their customers and other stakeholders on a global scale at very efficient cost.

The primary elements of digital interactive media are websites, mobile media, and social media. We deal with each of these in turn in this chapter. The Internet continues to surge in importance as a mass forum for advertising as well as other communications (see Exhibit 12–1). In recognition of this explosive growth, we need to understand what the medium is, how it is organized, how people get to it, and how advertisers buy it and use it in their marketing plans.

The Internet

The **Internet** is a global network of computers that communicate with one another through **protocols**, which are common rules for linking and sharing information. The Internet began in the early 1960s as a result of the Defense Department's Advanced Research Projects Agency (ARPA) plan to create a network that could survive a Cold War attack. ARPAnet had little commercial value; its primary users were governmental organizations and research universities, and the Internet of today is a far different medium. However, ARPAnet was important

EXHIBIT 12–1 Predicted digital interactive advertising expenditures ($ billions).

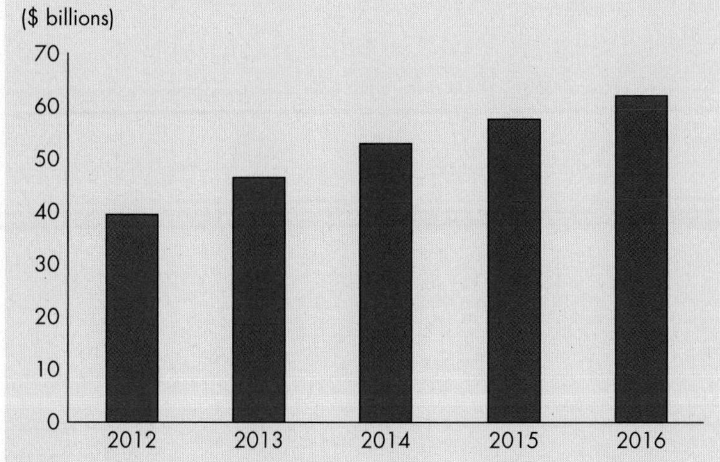

Source: eMarketer, "US Online Advertising Spending to Surpass Print in 2012," www.emarketer.com/Article/US-Online-Advertising-Spending-Surpass-Print-2012/1008783.

distributed network Characterized by many different hubs and links, which allows continuous communication even if some connections stop working.

centralized networks How media content was traditionally delivered. A hub, such as a TV station, a newspaper publisher, or a cable company distributes content to many receivers.

Web Information available on the Internet that can be easily accessed with software called a *browser*. It is named the *Web* because it is made up of many sites linked together; users can travel from one site to another by clicking on *hyperlinks*.

HTML HyperText Markup Language. This language allowed for the relatively easy creation of Web pages that can be easily linked to all kinds of content, including other Web pages or sites.

Web pages Documents or files, written in HTML, that are stored on a Web server and can be viewed over the Internet using a Web browser.

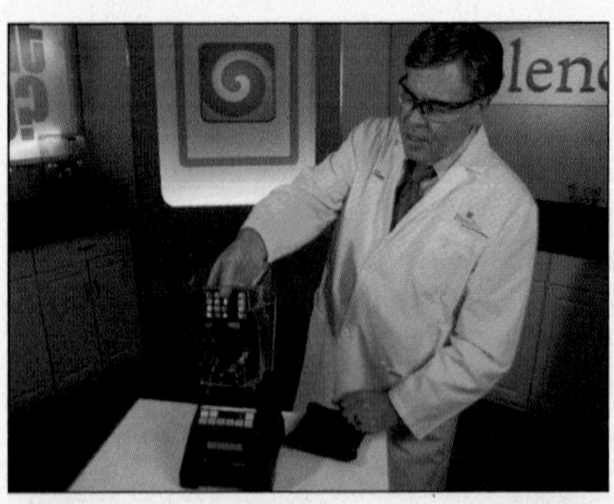

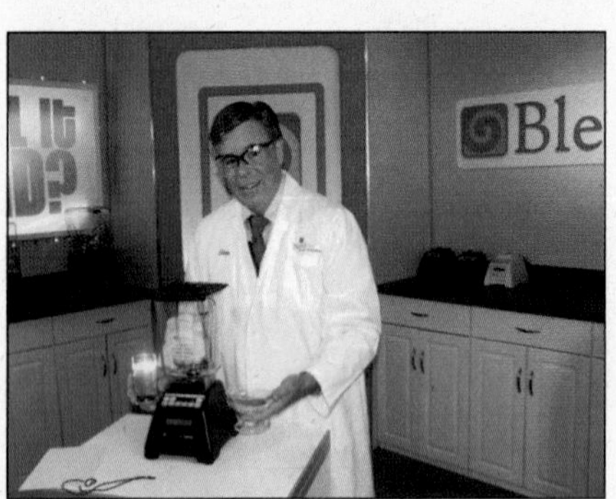

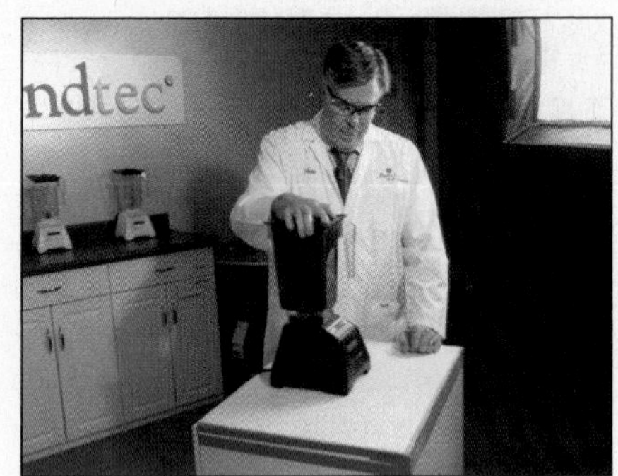

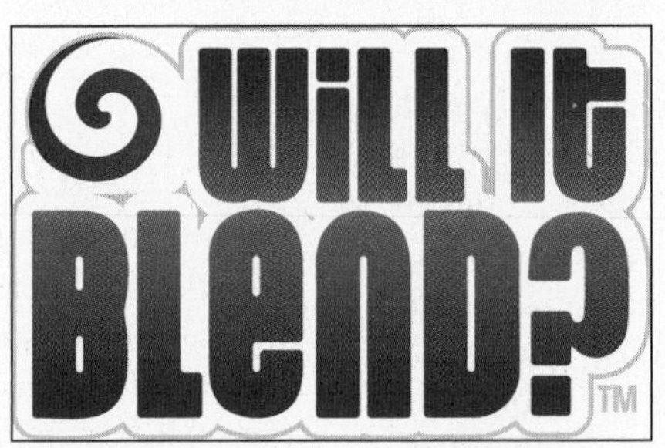

This ad from Blendtec is one of a series that you can find on the Blendtec channel on Youtube.com. The entire series is based on whether or not the Blendtec blender will be able to blend a particular object. To name a few, they have blended skis, magnets, an iPhone, glowsticks, and even batteries. The series was so successful that the company saw a 500 percent increase in consumer sales from its website.

because its structure, a **distributed network**, was revolutionary. Traditionally, media content has been delivered through **centralized networks**, in which a hub, such as a TV station, a newspaper publisher, or a cable company, distributes content to many receivers (see Exhibit 12–2). In a centralized system, if the hub is knocked out, receivers are left without information. But a distributed network is one characterized by many different hubs and links, which allows continuous communication even if some connections stop working. And, importantly, no single participant controls content.

▼ EXHIBIT 12–2 In a centralized network, a hub distributes content to many receivers. A distributed network has many different hubs and links.

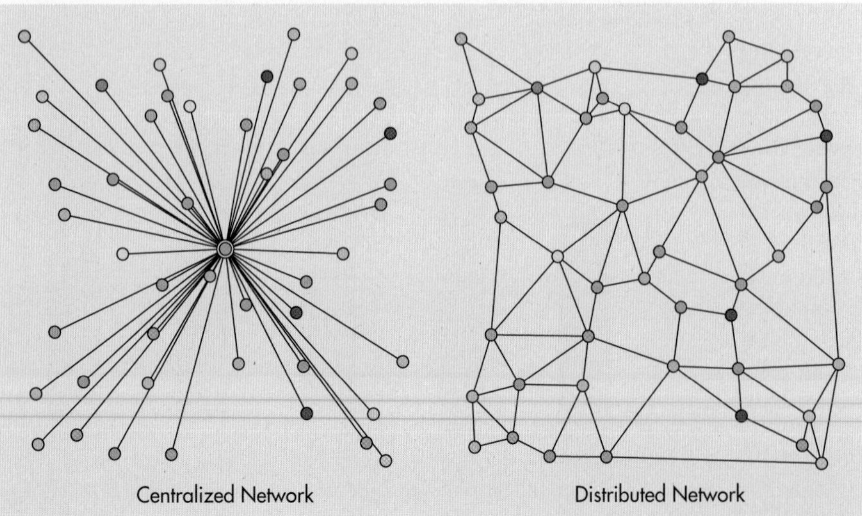

There are at least two other important distinctions between the digital interactive and traditional media. The first is the cost of time and/or space. In traditional media, time (on TV or radio) and space (in print) are precious and limited resources. Network TV commercials average 30 seconds, which is a very small window, and that window is expensive, sometimes costing advertisers hundreds of thousands of dollars. In contrast, space on the Internet is vast and inexpensive. Websites can store as much information as a company wishes. For consumers who require lots of facts before they make a decision to buy, this is

Web browsers Computer programs that provide computer users with a graphical interface to the Internet.

portals Web pages that provide starting points or gateways to other resources on the Internet.

search engines Websites that are devoted to finding and retrieving requested information from the Web. Because search engines are the gatekeepers to information on the Internet they are extremely popular with advertisers.

a real plus. And for small advertisers with limited budgets, the economics are very attractive.

The second distinction between traditional and digital interactive media concerns the relationship between those who create content and those who consume it. Traditional media companies are content creators while audiences are content consumers. As an example, NBC develops and schedules a show and, if you enjoy it, you sit down on at the same time and night each week to watch it. NBC is the creator and you are the consumer. But the Internet, from its beginnings, has been *interactive,* blurring the line between content providers and consumers. The Internet audience doesn't just consume online content; it interacts with it and helps create it.

The Web

In the early 1980s, the National Science Foundation expanded ARPAnet by supporting a fast data network that linked information centers across the United States. At the same time, online content providers such as AOL and CompuServe helped create an Internet audience by providing news, information, and e-mail services to subscribers.

During the 1990s, the number of people using the Internet doubled each year. Fueling the medium's growth were the increasing popularity and affordability of personal computers and modems, which allowed computers to tap into the Internet via an ordinary phone line. The 1990s was also the decade in which people began going online to access a particular part of the Internet known as the **Web**. The Web, as its name implies, was a distributed network of content providers and users, communicating through a protocol known as **HTML**, or HyperText Markup Language. HTML allowed for the relatively easy creation of Web pages that can be easily linked to all kinds of content, including other **Web pages** or sites (and, later, photographs, movies, databases, audio files, and such). Viewing Web pages was made easy by the development of **Web browsers**, software that interpreted HTML.

Today, the Internet is a global medium. People around the world use it to read news, research products, stay in touch with friends, and share information. They do so using high-speed broadband access, which makes it easy to watch videos, listen to audio programming, and download large files.

This new medium has proven highly popular. The Web has grown from about 50 sites in 1993 to over 206 billion by 2010.[2]

Web Portals and Popular Websites The first big Web success stories were known as portals. A **portal** is a site that provides an array of content and services so broad that (it is hoped) users spend a lot of time at the portal and very little time anywhere else. Portals, like Yahoo!, want to keep visitors for as long as possible to create many opportunities for exposing visitors to ads or fee-based content. Thus, making money at a portal involves attracting lots of people and keeping them around so they can see advertising. You may be thinking that this revenue model seems similar to that of traditional media and, in fact, it is. Yahoo! remains one of the most visited sites on the Web, reaching over a quarter of all Web users on a daily basis.

[Making money at a portal involves attracting lots of people and keeping them around so they can see advertising. . . . This revenue model seems similar to that of traditional media.]

Digital Interactive Today

Google and Internet Search Digital Interactive media have come a long way since the early days of the internet. From an advertising perspective, the most important trends include a) the importance of search advertising; b) the growth of social media, especially Facebook; c) the increased importance of mobile devices as technologies for accessing digital interactive media.

Most people looking to find information on the Web use a **search engine**. Search engines are sites that allow people to type a word or phrase into a text box and then quickly find information.

Brin and Page's company, Google, is at present, the most popular destination on the Web, reaching an astonishing 40 percent

social media Digital media that connect individuals.

of all Web users each day.[3] Search advertising revenues generate billions in revenue for Google, and in fact, represent the single largest category of ad expenditures in digital interactive media.

Social Media

Social media exist on the Web, so it may seem strange to consider them as a separate category. But for advertisers, social media represent a very different opportunity than traditional Web pages. First, social media, as compared with traditional, are uniquely created from audience content. Audiences go to social media not just to read or be entertained, but to post, blog, share, and create. This has the effect of changing the goal for many social media advertisers. They don't want consumers to only read or watch their messages, they want to engage them. They look for opportunities to get followers to blog, post, and share about their brands. And they look to interact with them in a free-wheeling, somewhat uncontrolled environment. The importance of social media can be seen by the fact that Facebook is beginning to challenge Google as the most popular destination on the Web. But what is **social media**? OnlineMatters defines social media as "any form of online publication or presence that allows end users to engage in multi-directional conversations in or around the content on the website."[4]

It's hard to believe that Facebook has existed for just under a decade as of the writing of this text. In October 2003 Harvard student Mark Zuckerberg launched Facemash, a program that allowed viewers to rate fellow students for their "hotness." Zuckerberg registered a domain for "thefacebook.com" in 2004 and shifted the focus to connecting people with friends, family, and acquaintances. Zuckerberg had clearly tapped an important social need, such that by 2009 Facebook was the second-most-visited site on the Web. In 2013 Facebook experienced two events that attracted a great deal of attention from advertisers. The first was the introduction of Graph Search, a program designed to help people find information about people, interests, hobbies, and activities of unique relevance to them. This was important because it clearly put Facebook in competition with Google for search activities. The second event was Facebook's success with mobile advertising on the site. In the summer of 2013 Facebook reported that nearly 40 percent of its advertising revenue was coming from ads served on mobile platforms. This surprised marketers and investors alike, as both groups had expressed doubts about Facebook's ability to be successful on mobile devices. While Facebook is not the only social media site on the Web (see Exhibit 12–3), it is clearly a dominant one at present.

▼EXHIBIT 12–3 Social media sites, 2012–2013.

		Percentage of online adults who use the following social media websites	
Rank	**Site**	**2012**	**2013**
1	Facebook	67	71
2	LinkedIn	20	22
3	Pinterest	15	21
4	Twitter	16	18
5	Instagram	13	17

Source: Maeve Duggan and Aaron Smith, "Social Media Update 2013," Pew Research Center, Washington, D.C., (December 30, 2013), www.pewinterest.org/2013/12/30/social-media-update-2013/, Retrieved February 23, 2014.

Pinterest, Snapchat, Facebook, and Twitter have revolutionized the way we communicate with each other, allowing one person to share anything that interests them, with his or her entire friends list, whether that be related to work, politics, leisure, family, shopping, product use, or other.

An attribute that attracts advertisers to social media is openness. When someone posts to Facebook, comments on another's blog, or posts a description of themselves on LinkedIn, that information may be open for anyone to see. A host of tools collects all of this information using keywords. Nielsen's Buzzmetrics or J.D. Power's Umbria Communications help marketers aggregate all the information being posted about their brands or products to understand the general consensus, negative or positive. Brands like Oreo, Coca-Cola, Virgin America, and Procter & Gamble all have a social media component for each brand or product they market.

Smart marketers understand that social media foster interactions that go beyond promotion or advertising. Social media go beyond promotion because companies must listen as much as they speak. But for all of the difficulties, marketers gain one enormous benefit: they are put back in touch with their customers. And that can be a very good thing.

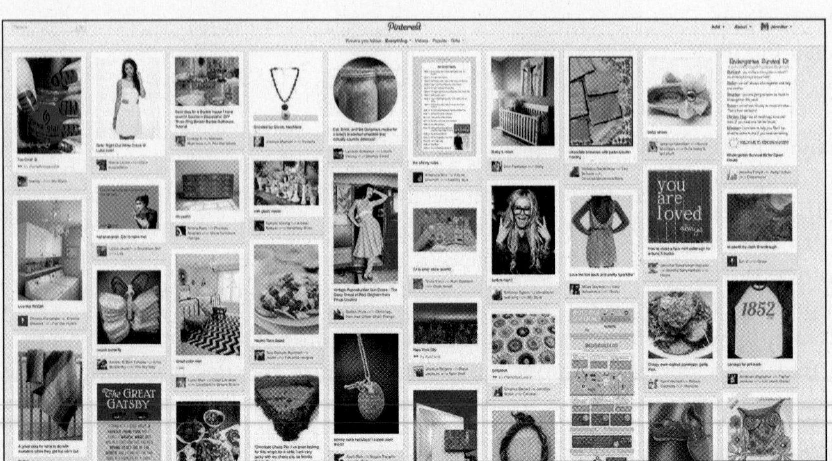

Pinterest is one of the fastest-growing social networks. It allows you to "pin" photos with a short caption and share them with your friends.

> **SOCIAL MEDIA GO BEYOND PROMOTION BECAUSE COMPANIES MUST LISTEN AS MUCH AS THEY SPEAK. BUT FOR ALL OF THE DIFFICULTIES, MARKETERS GAIN ONE ENORMOUS BENEFIT: THEY ARE PUT BACK IN TOUCH WITH THEIR CUSTOMERS.**

Mobile Advertising Apple's iPhone has revolutionized digital advertising in a way not seen since the introduction of the Web. As of May 2013, Apple had sold nearly 16 million iPhone 5 units.[5]

The iPhone has increased data plan usage, or non-voice-related consumption over the carriers' networks. iPhone users are heavy users of video and mobile TV.[6] People use their phones to download applications and games, surf the Web, and send multimedia messages. The appeal for advertisers is that the phone is the only truly portable and personally identifiable medium. And unlike most other media, when consumers view an ad on their phone that they like, they can buy right away. Large numbers of people already shop on the phone now.[7]

People access the Web from many sources besides computers. Smartphones like the iPhone are increasingly important to digital advertisers.

While it still constitutes less than 1 percent of all advertising globally, mobile ad spending increased 80 percent from 2008 to 2009.[8] The most common form of mobile advertising, banner advertising (also called WAP, Wireless Access Protocol, Banner), is very similar to online banner advertising. Banner advertising is standardized by the Mobile Marketing Association (MMA), which much like the Interactive Advertising Bureau (IAB) for online banner advertising, has guidelines and standards for mobile Web advertising (they can be found here: http://mmaglobal.com/policies/global-mobile-advertising-guidelines). Banner ads can also be placed into applications that have been downloaded to a user's phone and can be swapped as those applications reconnect with the network.

The other form of advertising and the one that represents the largest inventory is sponsored SMS (short message service). Mobile phone users usually refer to these as "text messages." One benefit to marketers who generate these ads is that the end user need not own a smartphone. Almost any mobile device can receive texts. Companies like 4INFO, in the United States, offer news, horoscopes, and sports scores, among other things, for free to users via SMS, and advertisers sponsor these messages. The carriers have set up very strict guidelines in the use of SMS and act as a gatekeeper for all messages that go over their networks in an effort to reduce SMS spam. A smartphone user can respond to an SMS ad, via a link, at a mobile Web page.

check yourself ✓

1. What are the major types of digital interactive media?
2. What are some of the opportunities marketers can take advantage of with digital interactive media?
3. What are some of the important marketing-related destinations on the Web?

MEASURING THE INTERNET AUDIENCE

When marketers and the media first began trumpeting the marvels of the Internet, they quickly noted the potentially vast size of its user population. Most Americans use the Internet. And around the world, the number of Internet users is approaching two billion.[9]

How People Access the Internet

While traditionally people think of accessing the Internet through a computer, the reality is that most people are accessing the Internet these days in a variety of ways with a variety of devices. The iPhone, and phones running Google's Android have increased consumer awareness and demand for access to the Internet. Millions of users also access the Web via gaming systems, such as the Xbox, the Sony PlayStation, and the Nintendo Wii.

This is all made possible through high-speed connections, both wired and wireless. According to one study, 91 percent of the 18-and-over online population has broadband Internet access, making it the main connection type to the Internet. **Broadband** connections are really just a description of the ability to transmit multiple signals simultaneously on one data line. For consumers it means faster Internet surfing and faster data uploads and downloads.

Why is this important to advertisers? There are many reasons, but primarily because as consumers get more comfortable interacting with and seeking out rich content such as videos, they will become more likely to supplement their other media usage with the Internet.

How People Use the Internet

Some people believe that the first era of the Web has already passed, and that a new philosophy drives the activities of some companies. This philosophy is characterized by the idea that the future of the Web is in companies that encourage user sharing and collaboration (see Exhibit 12–4). Wikipedia, the popular online encyclopedia, is often cited as a prime example of this new philosophy. Unlike most other encyclopedias, Wikipedia is not constructed from articles penned by authorities or experts. Instead, anyone can create an entry, which in turn can be edited by someone else. In this sense, the site represents the efforts of thousands of users, rather than hundreds of authorities. Other examples of this type of collaboration include Twitter, Flickr, Pinterest, and Craigslist.

One of the unique features of the Internet is the relative ease in finding and accumulating data based on advertising efforts. In this section we will discuss how the technology allows us to better understand users and refine our advertising efforts not only from campaign to campaign, but also while a campaign is in market. We will reflect on the two phases of online advertising that utilize and generate the most data: planning and tracking. Last, we will look at the issues surrounding all these data and how the industry approaches standardization.

▼**EXHIBIT 12–4** Contenders for Web 2.0 activities, according to 2008 Pew Internet & American Life Project surveys.

Internet Users Who Have Done This	Activity
37%	Upload photos to a website so you can share them with others online.
32	Rate a product, service, or person using an online rating system.
27	Share files from your own computer with others online.
21	Share something online that you created yourself, such as your own artwork, photos, stories, or videos.
11	Take material found online—such as songs, text or images—and remix it into your own artistic creation.
14	Create or work on your own Web page.
13	Create or work on Web pages or blogs for others, including for friends, groups you belong to, or work.
16	Use online social or professional networking sites such as Friendster or LinkedIn.
12	Create or work on your own online journal or blog.

Source: Pew Internet and American Life Project, www.pewinternet.org. Reprinted with permission.

broadband A type of digital transmission that enables a single wire to carry multiple signals simultaneously. Examples of broadband transmission include cable and DSL.

composition A facsimile of a finished ad with copy set in type and pasted into position along with proposed illustrations. The "comp" is prepared so the advertiser can gauge the effect of the final ad.

cookies Small pieces of information that get stored on your computer when you download certain websites. These cookies can keep track of whether a certain user has ever before visited a specific site. This allows the website to identify returning users and to customize the information based on past browsing or purchase behavior.

Media Planning Tools

Several companies specialize in delivering audited measurement of potential reach to help media planners choose the right vehicles based on their target audience. The two largest are Nielsen Online and comScore. Both have a suite of tools that help define target market size, behavior, and composition relative to each major website on the Internet. They also provide views into how other advertisers are using the Internet, thereby giving competitive insights into industry and category best practices.

These companies measure the activities of a set number of people or a panel of people and provide reports on their usage patterns across websites and Internet applications, such as iTunes. Nielsen randomly recruits individuals to download and utilize a *desktop meter* so all Internet activity on that computer is then tabulated, measured, and recorded. This process is very similar to one of the methods Nielsen utilizes to measure TV audiences. Using a limited sample size, Nielsen then projects these numbers to the rest of the Internet audience as averages. For instance, if a panel identifies that 50 percent of all men aged 18 to 34 go to ESPN.com daily, whereas on average most sites garner only 25 percent of the male panel audience, Nielsen will project those numbers to the rest of the Internet to arrive at an index of 200 for ESPN.com relative to the entire Internet traffic for men between the ages of 18 and 34. Media planners utilize these numbers to identify the highest concentration, or **composition**, of the target they are trying to reach. However, because of lack of standardization many companies report many different numbers, and it is a media planner's job to make heads or tails of the data.

The Promise of Enhanced Tracking

Companies now have some of the most precise tracking and targeting tools ever. In fact, every time you access the Internet, some computer may be tracking where you go. How? **Cookies** are small text files stored on your computer when you visit certain websites. These cookies can keep track of whether a certain user has ever visited a specific site. This allows the website to give users different information depending on whether they are repeat visitors. Cookies also indicate the users' frequency of visits, the time of last visit, and the domain from which they are surfing. Additionally, cookies give marketers

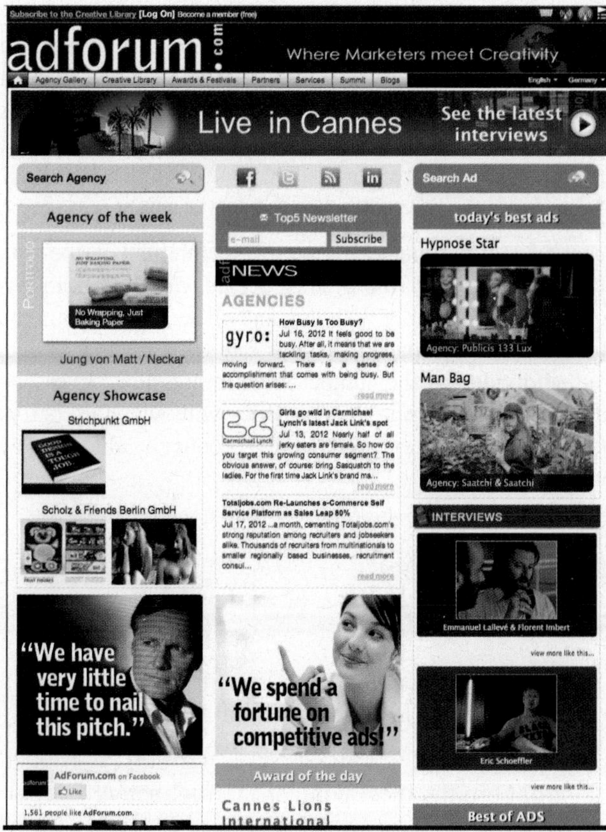

The Internet is a great repository and showcase for advertising that appears in many media. AdForum is a place where you can view thousands of ads from the present and the past.

One reason media budgets are shifting to the Internet is that the medium offers a variety of ways to track interactions of consumers with ads. One company that helps provide such metrics is comScore (www.comscore.com).

third-party ad servers A method of delivering ads from one central source, or server, across multiple Web domains, allowing advertisers the ability to manage the rotation and distribution of their advertisements.

behavioral tracking Ability to track people's behavior on the Internet.

ad impression A possible exposure of the advertising message to one audience member.

click rate In digital interactive advertising, the number of "clicks" on an advertisement divided by the number of ad requests. A method by which marketers can measure the frequency with which users try to obtain additional information about a product by clicking on an advertisement. Also called *click-through rate.*

great insights into their campaigns on a daily basis, such as the number of times users call for an ad, time of day, type of browsers they use, whether or not they click, and so on.

Typical online marketers employ the services of **third-party ad servers**. Third-party ad servers deliver ads from one central source, or server, across multiple Web domains, allowing advertisers the ability to manage the rotation and distribution of their advertisements. The best-known companies are DoubleClick, now owned by Google, and Atlas DMT, now owned by Microsoft. These companies allow advertisers to monitor the performance of their buys on a daily basis all the way down to conversion or sales. By placing a line of code on the last page of the sales process, DoubleClick and/or Atlas can match the user back to the last advertisement they saw, via the cookies placed on the user's computer, and credit that advertisement with the sale. This allows the agency to understand Internet metrics from advertising to sales in near real time. This hyper-accountability is what ultimately brought the online ad industry out of the dot-com crash of the early 2000s—marketers could justify their Web spending's impact on the company's bottom line.

More sophisticated technology provides marketers with additional details about the consumer. The computer first assigns each user an anonymous and encrypted identification number for tracking purposes. A user profile is then created with data on the content read, keywords used in search, time and day that a Web page was viewed, the frequency with which an ad is seen, the sequence of ads that are seen, the computer operating system of the user, the browser type, and the IP address. From these data, marketers can guess the user's ISP, telephone area code, and NAIC code. They might additionally match these data with demographic information gathered offline to create a clearer picture of consumer behavior than has ever been available.

However, **behavioral tracking**, this new ability to track people's behavior on the Internet, has stirred considerable debate. Although software developers claim that the users are tracked anonymously with encrypted identification numbers, privacy advocates believe the marketing method is too invasive.

Seeking Standardization

As much as Madison Avenue may want Web measurements to resemble traditional media measurements, the Internet cannot provide them. As we'll describe shortly, simply counting advertising impressions from a Web page is an impractical method of tabulation. However, the basic questions remain the same: Do people see our ads? Are they effective? Until fairly recently, when a task force of the Internet Advertising Bureau (IAB) provided some practical definitions, Internet audience measurement information lacked the standardization needed to be able to compare its advertising effectiveness to other media.

The simplest measurement, yet an area of great controversy, is the **ad impression**. The IAB originally defined an ad impression as "an opportunity to deliver an advertising element to a Web site visitor." When a user loads a Web page with ads on it, the browser will pull the advertisement from its host ad server and bring it up as a banner, button, or interstitial. The number of ad requests received can then be translated into the familiar cost form. The problem with this definition, from the point of view of advertisers and agencies, is that the advertiser is not guaranteed that a user will ever see an ad. People often click away to some other site before the requested ad ever comes up. Under the original definition, an advertiser would be charged for an ad that never had the opportunity to be seen. The AAAA prefers to define an ad request as an ad that is actually delivered to users' screens. Only then do they truly have an opportunity to see the ad. The controversy created reporting differences between what Web publishers count and what the agencies count and are willing to pay for. Eventually the IAB and other digital interactive advertising groups agreed that an impression has to be counted on the client side (the Web user's browser loads the ad) rather than the server side.[10]

A second measurement, unique to the Internet, is the **click rate** or *click-through rate*. A click occurs when a visitor moves the mouse's pointer to a Web link and clicks on the mouse button to get to another page. The click rate is the number of clicks on an ad divided by the number of ad impressions. In essence, marketers are measuring the frequency with which users try to obtain additional information about a product by clicking on an advertisement.

check yourself ✓

1. Roughly what percentage of all U.S. adults use the Internet? Is education level related to Internet use?
2. What are the most popular Internet activities?
3. What is behavioral targeting?

It's Not Always Nice to Share

Facebook has many users, nearly a billion worldwide. But it is especially popular on college campuses. This is due partially to its origins—while Facebook is now available to anyone over age 13, it was started with a focus on college students. In fact, when founder Mark Zuckerberg launched the site in 2004, it was open only to members of his school, Harvard.

What makes Facebook so irresistible? Certainly highly addictive features, where friends can post messages, likes, status updates, music, and videos, are part of the appeal. Users of Facebook can stay in touch with lots of people, almost in real time. The site is so addictive, in fact, that universities often find ways to limit access during class hours.

So Facebook is a site that is visited by young, influential, highly educated users who spend inordinate amounts of time there and are passionate about what they do. Can you think of anyone who might be interested in that group?

Of course the answer is advertisers, and in fact, advertising has, from the beginning, been a part of Facebook. Facebook revenues are almost exclusively from ads, which is why it is free for users.

But in social media, advertising and privacy don't always mix, as Facebook users found out in 2007 when the site launched "Beacon." Beacon was designed to let users share information about offsite activities, including purchases, with their friends. Here's how it worked, at least in theory. You join Facebook. Later you visit a different website, like that of movie ticket vendor Fandango. You buy a movie ticket. Just a short while later, your Facebook profile updates and tells your friends about the tickets you bought.

It was almost inevitable that Facebook would develop something like Beacon. That is because what excites advertisers about social networks like Facebook, even more than the desirable demographics, is the fact that people are busy influencing one another at the site. This is the real power of social networks, and the real draw for advertisers.

But from the start Beacon was flawed. For one thing, even though third-party sites were supposed to inform Facebook users about what would happen when they bought at the site, it appears that some did not. So a Facebook user who bought something at Overstock.com was supposedly never told that Overstock was a member of the Facebook advertising network and that his or her purchase would be shared with friends.

Second, users did not "opt in" to the program (sign up for it), they had to "opt out" (cancel it). That virtually guaranteed that a lot of people would be unaware of how much information they were sharing with others.

Even worse, a software engineer discovered that even if Facebook users explicitly indicated that they did not want to share information about purchases, Facebook collected the information anyway. This turned out to be a practice that directly contradicted its publicly stated policies.

In the end, Zuckerberg decided that Beacon had to be changed. This was prompted by the bad press the program had received, the cancellation of several large advertisers, including Vodafone, Virgin Media, and Prudential, and several user-based petitions, including one organized by Moveon.org.

The founder posted an apology to users at the Facebook blog on December 5, 2007. It read in part (go to http://blog.facebook.com/blog.php?post=7584397130 to read the entire apology):

> About a month ago, we released a new feature called Beacon to try to help people share information with their friends about things they do on the web. We've made a lot of mistakes building this feature, but we've made even more with how we've handled them. . . . When we first thought of Beacon, our goal was to build a simple product to let people share information across sites with their friends. . . . But we missed the right balance. At first we tried to make it very lightweight so people wouldn't have to touch it for it to work. The problem with our initial approach of making it an opt-out system instead of opt-in was that if someone forgot to decline to share something, Beacon still went ahead and shared it with their friends. It took us too long after people started contacting us to change the product so that users had to explicitly approve what they wanted to share. . . . I'm not proud of the way we've handled this situation and I know we can do better. Thanks for taking the time to read this.

So, for Zuckerberg and many Facebook users, the Beacon experience was a hard lesson learned. To Zuckerberg's credit, he acted fast and apologized for his mistakes when it became clear that users would not tolerate Beacon's privacy settings. Facebook continues to be one of the most popular (and valuable) locations on the Web. And there is little doubt that advertisers will continue to search for ways to leverage the unique attributes of social networks for promoting their brands.

Questions

1. Why was Beacon created? Was it ethical to ask users to "opt out" rather than "opt in" to the program?
2. Think of a purchase you have recently made that you would not want shared with your friends. How would you feel about a site that did so without your explicit permission?
3. Did Facebook's missteps with Beacon amount to a poor business decision, or do you think that it rose to the level of being unethical?

Sources: Brad Stone, "Facebook Executive Discusses Beacon Brouhaha," New York Times Bits, http://hits.blogs.nytin1es.cod2007/11/29/facebook-responds-to-beacon-brouha11a/; CA Security Advisor Research Blog, "Facebook's Misrepresentation of Beacon's Threat to Privacy; Tracking Users Who Opt Out or Are Not Logged In," http://community.ca.com/blogs/securityadvisor/archive/2007/II/29/facebook-s-misrepresentation-of-beacon-s-theat-to-privacy-tacking-users-who-opt-out-or-are-not-logged-in.aspx; Juan Carlos Perez, "Facebook's Beacon More Intrusive than Previously Thought," *PCWorld,* www.pcworld.codarticle/id, 140182-c,onlineprivacy/article.html; "Facebook Beacon," www.facebook.com/business/?beacon; "Leading Websites Offer Facebook Beacon for Social Distribution," www.facebook.com./press/releases.php?p=9166.

keyword A single word that a user inputs into an Internet search engine to request information that is similar in subject matter to that word.

click-throughs A term used in reference to a Web user clicking on an ad banner to visit the advertiser's site. Some Web publishers charge advertisers according to the number of click-throughs on a given ad banner.

affiliate marketing program A contractual advertising program, often used in e-commerce, under which a seller pays a manufacturer, marketer, or other business a percentage of the sale price of an item sold.

LO12-2 Explain how time and space on the Web are bought.

BUYING TIME AND SPACE IN DIGITAL INTERACTIVE

Media planners cannot think of the Internet in mass media terms. Interactive media are *personal audience venues*. That means one on one. So cost per thousand, ratings points, and share of audience don't really mean the same things in the interactive world. With interactive media, advertisers aren't always building sales volume. They're building relationships, one customer at a time. And the care companies exercise in buying and developing their interactive programs and integrating them with their mass media programs will determine their overall success.

Currently, the leading national advertisers spend a small piece of their marketing communications pie on interactive media—less than 7 percent of their budgets. However, it still is the fastest-growing segment. Exhibit 12–5 lists the top 10 Internet advertisers ranked by spending. The best marketers are testing extensively. That means being willing to lose money for a while, which is, of course, not exciting to most advertisers or agencies. Many direct marketers are investing heavily in online catalogs. The effort is clearly worth it. Amazon.com averages over $65 million in sales a day.[11]

EXHIBIT 12–5 Top Internet advertisers 2013.

Company	Estimated Spending
E*TRADE FINANCIAL Corp.	$97,780,000
Capital One Financial Corporation	96,286,800
TD Ameritrade Inc.	89,265,100
Ybrant Digital Ltd.	77,386,600
Netflix, Inc.	75,157,900
AT&T Corp.	61,471,900
Comcast Corporation	61,155,500
Progressive Casualty Company	58,080,200
The Charles Schwab Corporation	53,118,000
Apple Computer, Inc.	52,125,100

Source: AdAge DataCenter, 2012. Copyrighted Information of The Nielsen Company, licensed for use herein.

Pricing Methods

Advertising space on the Internet can be purchased in several different ways, as we will discuss later in the chapter. The most common means is the banner ad, typically billed on a cost-per-thousand basis determined by the number of ads displayed. On most Web pages, the base banner rate pays for exposure on a rotating display that randomly selects which ads to show.

The real marketing power of the Internet, however, is the ability to specifically target an audience in a way that is virtually impossible in traditional media. In addition to general banners, media buyers may opt to purchase more selective space. For example, ads may be purchased in a portal's information categories and subcategories, such as finance, news, travel, or games. Prices vary according to category and increase as the buyer targets a more selective audience. Costs are tiered according to thousands, hundreds of thousands, or even millions of page requests per month.

Another augmentation to the general banner purchase is the **keyword** purchase, available on major search engines. Advertisers may buy specific keywords that bring up their ads when a user's search request contains these words. Keywords may be purchased individually or in packages that factor in the information categories and subcategories of a search engine site. In the early days of the Internet, some "keyword entrepreneurs" purchased large numbers of keywords from the search engines. They were later able to license these words to third parties at a substantial profit. This model has since changed to a bidding model, effectively killing keyword "entrepreneurs." We will go into more depth on these issues later when we discuss Google's AdSense and AdWords programs.

Some publishers will charge their clients according to **click-throughs**—that is, when a user actually clicks on a banner ad to visit the advertiser's landing page. Although the CPM cost for simple impressions is considerably lower, this method is still unpopular with publishers. When an advertiser buys on a per-click basis, the publisher may expose many users to an advertiser's banner message without being able to charge for the service.

For advertisers involved in e-commerce, some publishers offer an **affiliate marketing program** whereby they charge a percentage of the transaction cost. For example, a site devoted to music reviews may have a banner link to an online music retailer. When consumers buy music from the retailer, the site publisher receives a percentage of the sale.

The Cost of Targeting

The very selective nature of the Internet can, for additional cost, be combined with tracking technology to be discussed later. This makes for a very focused campaign. Companies such as Tacoda work behind the scenes to meet the advertiser's CPM guarantees by using software that directs specific ads to a highly selective audience. Because Tacoda technology "tags" users, it can build a consumer profile and show those ads that are likely to be of the greatest interest to that specific Web user.

But contrary to popular belief, consumer targeting on the Internet is very cost intensive. While it is true that millions of people do indeed scour the Internet each day, it is still difficult to find and reach specific consumers. Thus, prices for precise Internet business-to-business targeting can eclipse even those of direct mail.

Stretching Out the Dollars

One of the problems facing most Internet marketers is how to get enough reach from their advertising. The enormous numbers of users who utilize the major search engines make these sites attractive for advertisers. However, Internet users surf millions of other Web pages each day, many of which are potential sites for effective ads. Contacting all of these sites and negotiating advertising contracts on each is impossible.

For this reason, most advertisers work through **ad networks**, which act as brokers for advertisers and websites. Ad networks pool hundreds or thousands of Web pages together and facilitate advertising across these pages. The advantage is that this allows advertisers to gain maximum exposure by covering even the smaller sites. The drawback is that such advertising is more difficult to monitor. Each site must be watched for traffic and content, which creates problems when trying to calculate costs. Exhibit 12–6 lists the largest ad networks in the United States.

ad networks The Internet equivalent of a media rep firm, *ad networks* act as brokers for advertisers and websites. They pool hundreds or even thousands of Web pages together and facilitate advertising across these pages, thereby allowing advertisers to gain maximum exposure by covering even the small sites.

EXHIBIT 12–6 Companies can now take advantage of ad networks that reach a majority of Internet users over the course of a month. The 10 largest networks are listed here.

Rank	Property	Unique Visitors (000)	% Reach
1	Google Ad Network	193,806	92.30%
2	AOL Advertising	177,628	84.60
3	Yahoo! Sites	177,538	84.60
4	Yahoo! Network Plus	176,517	84.10
5	Turn Media Platform	168,186	80.10
6	Google	167,063	79.60
7	ValueClick Networks	164,860	78.50
8	24/7 Real Media	162,595	77.50
9	AdBrite	151,364	72.10
10	Facebook.com	150,670	71.80

check yourself ✓

1. Why are some of the best advertisers losing money with digital interactive advertising?
2. What are some important ways to purchase digital interactive ads?

LO12-4 Know the types of digital interactive advertising.

TYPES OF DIGITAL INTERACTIVE ADVERTISING

The nature of the Internet is a constant state of evolution. Therefore advertisers have new and interesting ways to reach target audiences that extend beyond the more standard ad placements. We will discuss the less fluid advertising elements first and then look at the ways in which the medium is continuing to grow. In approaching this topic we will work our way back up the generic online "sales funnel." The Internet is truly

website A collection of Web pages on the Web that are linked together and maintained by a company, organization, or individual.

microsite A supplement to a Web site that is typically singular in focus and delivers on the current advertising message.

landing page The Web page that a person reaches when clicking on a search engine listing or ad.

search engines Web sites that are devoted to finding and retrieving requested information from the Web.

search-results page A listing of sites produced by using a search engine.

unique as a medium in its ability to lead directly to sales so we will approach the section in that way, but beware of pigeonholing the Internet as a direct marketing medium. It has often been said that the accountability factor is not only the Internet's saving grace, it is also the bane of its existence.

The technical definition of a **website** is a collection of Web pages, images, videos, or data assets that is hosted on one or more Web servers, usually accessible via the Internet. A corporate site is used to give background information about an organization, product, or service. A commerce site is used primarily to sell a product or service. Of course there is a fine line between these definitions; for companies like Amazon.com the corporate site is the commerce site and vice versa. Good marketers look at their Web site broadly. They understand that the Web site is an extension of the brand and that the Web site experience is synonymous with a brand experience. Knowing that not all corporate sites are quite up to snuff to deliver on this brand extension, many marketers use microsites and landing pages to deliver the desired experience.

A **microsite** is used as a supplement to a Web site. For advertisers it is typically singular in focus and delivers on the current advertising message. For instance, when Electronic Arts (EA) launched the *Return of the King* video game after the very popular movie trilogy *The Lord of the Rings,* it had Freestyle Interactive build a robust microsite that gave users cheats, codes, game screens, and exclusive videos and also gave users a chance to win a replica sword from the movie. The kicker was that to unlock the content, users actually had to go on an Internet-based scavenger hunt to find four pieces, or shards, of the sword. Each piece unlocked more content until the sword was "reforged" and the user could open the cheats and enter to win the replica sword. The microsite was able to identify how many pieces each user had found.

Any Web page can be a **landing page**—the term used to describe direct links to deeper areas of the Web site that advertising drives consumers to beyond the homepage. Typically advertisers use landing pages to give consumers a more relevant experience as it relates to the message from the advertising. For instance, if someone searches for "men's dress pants" on Google, Dockers wants to send them directly to the *men's apparel* section, and more specifically all the way to the pants page, rather than making the user click two or three more times just to find the relevant products.

Search Engine Ads

Most people looking to find information on the Web use a **search engine**. Search engines are websites that allow people to type a word or phrase into a text box and quickly receive a listing of information on a **search-results page**.

▼EXHIBIT 12-7 Ad formats—full year 2012.

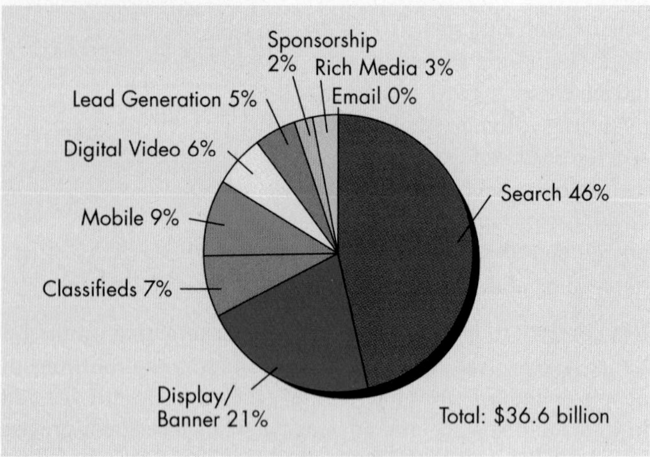

Source: IAB Internet Advertising Revenue Report, retrieved September 9, 2013 at www.iab.net/insights_research/industry_data_and_landscape/adrevenvuereport.

Revenue from search engine ads accounts for almost half of all digital interactive ad revenue (see Exhibit 12-7). Search is dominated by one company, Google (see Exhibit 12-8). But such ads didn't even exist in the early days of the Web, and the story of how Google developed search advertising is worth telling.

When Google's creators, Sergey Brin and Larry Page, first met at Stanford, they did not know how search could be profitable. But at the time, profits were not their main interest. Brin and

▼EXHIBIT 12-8 Search engine market share (July 2013).

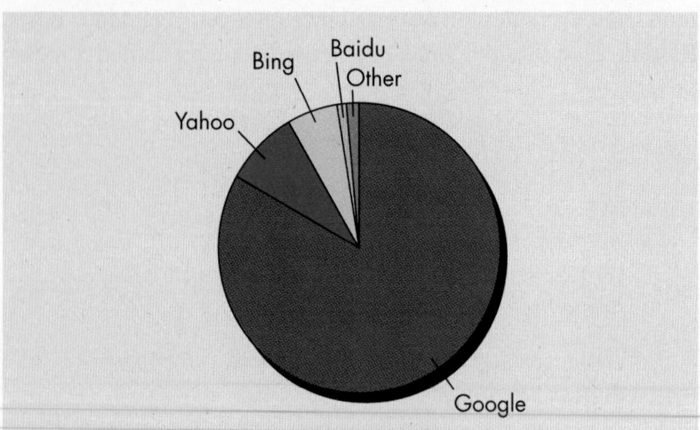

Source: Techwyse Internet Marketing: www.techwyse.com/blog/internet-marketing/search-engine-market-share-july-2013/.

sponsored links
Links that are sponsored by the search engine used.

pay-per-click
A type of advertising price structure where the advertiser pays based on the number of times a published ad is clicked on.

Page were focused on helping users find information and believed they had a better system for doing so.

The two created an algorithm, named *PageRank,* that analyzed the links and relationships of Internet sites to come up with rankings. When a keyword is entered in a search, Google looks for sites that mention the word. But in addition, Google analyzes links to determine what sites are considered credible. Consider two sites that each use the term *marketing* five times. If a Web user used *marketing* as a search term, Google's search engine would locate both sites. But which site should be listed relatively high in the search-results listings, where it will be viewed quickly, and which should be listed lower? This is where PageRank comes in. Sites that other sites link to are assigned higher PageRanks and end up with prominent listings in search results. The algorithm also analyzes the *quality* of the links. Specifically, sites with especially popular or authoritative Web sites linking to them get higher PageRanks. The net result of this is a fast search engine that returns remarkably relevant search results.

attire, where do you spend your money? On a magazine ad that may or may not get in the hands of someone thinking about clothes or on an AdWords placement for the phrase *dress pants?*

Google's search results page is composed of two distinct areas: search results based on PageRank, which are organic (unaffected by sponsorship), and **sponsored links**. Sponsored links have three important characteristics. First, advertisers do not pay for impressions, a common practice with banner ads. Instead, advertisers pay only when a user clicks on the link and visits the sponsor's site. This performance-based **pay-per-click** model has proven very attractive to advertisers.

> "For advertisers . . . there is really no better place to put a message [than search]. There is no other environment that allows advertisers to gain such insight into what consumers are thinking."

Because the company created a better search engine, Google was able to attract growing numbers of Web users. However, throughout the 1990s it lacked a clear way to make money from search. Like many companies at the time, Google sustained itself on venture capital. After the dot-com bust of the early 2000s, Google investors encouraged Brin and Page to develop a revenue model. Their response was two advertising programs, AdWords and AdSense. It is difficult to overstate how successful these programs have been, because in a few short years Google has used them to create an annual revenue stream in excess of $31 billion.[12]

AdWords

Do a search on Google and you will notice that search results are not the first thing you encounter on the results page. The first listings are in a light-blue shaded area that is described as "Sponsored Links." These sponsored links are not search results, but paid listings. For advertisers there is really no better place to put a message. There is no other environment that allows advertisers to gain such insight into what consumers are thinking while at the same time presenting an immediate opportunity to buy. For instance, if you are working for Dockers and you are targeting men seeking business

Second, the amount that an advertiser owes for each click is determined in an auction, where companies bid for keywords. Higher bids generally lead to better listings, but don't guarantee them, because the ranking of sponsored listings is also

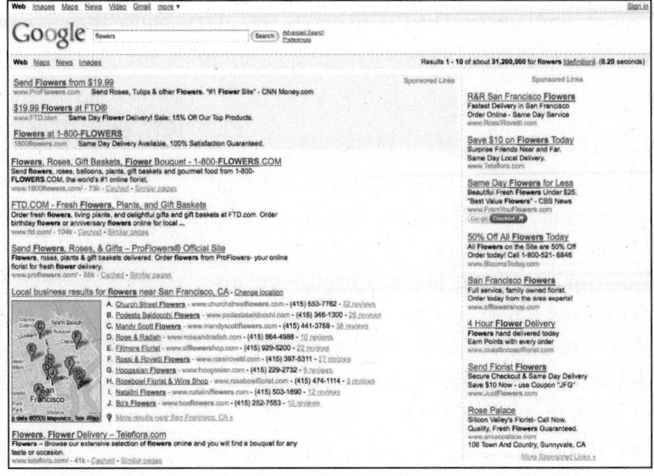

Searching for marketing on Google produces a page that displays both sponsored links (which are created by AdWords) and search results (created by PageRank).

determined by an ad's performance. Text ads that attract lots of clicks rise in the rankings, while links that are ignored fall. Third, Google benefits from the targeted nature of search. When people are hunting for a term like *marketing,* they often find that the sponsored links are as useful as the search results. Google estimates that almost 15 percent of searches result in click-throughs to sponsors, an astonishingly high *conversion rate* in comparison with other media, interactive or traditional. Google's model clearly emphasizes performance.

AdSense

Google's other major ad program is AdSense. Websites that use AdSense set aside a portion of pages for Google text ads. The ads themselves are selected by Google software and inserted automatically, without any input from the sponsoring site.

The revenue model for the AdSense program is very similar to AdWords. Advertisers pay Google only when Web users click the link and visit the sponsor sites. In this case, the owner of the site also gets revenue. For popular websites this can generate a great deal of revenue, and it is thus a powerful incentive for site owners to participate in the Google program.

Large websites, such as Microsoft or Yahoo!, generally don't use programs such as AdSense, preferring to sell ad space themselves. But AdSense has helped thousands of small to midsized sites and blogs develop steady revenue streams. Tiny, targeted, and text-based ads have revolutionized the Web.

Nothing demonstrates the Web's power better than sites that offer the helping professions ways to improve their efforts. The site teAchnology is one such Web destination. Teachers can find thousands of lesson plans and worksheets, as well as teaching tips and themes. Revenue from advertising helps keep the site fresh and easy to use.

From an advertiser's perspective, search-based ad programs are beneficial only if the company has a website that converts visitors into customers. Businesses ranging from your local florist to global manufacturers are using the Internet to present multimedia content that includes catalogs, videos, games, and music. The key is making a sale, because the advertiser pays Google for every customer sent to its site.

Display Advertising

Display ads on the Web are ads that appear on content sites. The most common kinds of display ads are banners and buttons. A **banner** is a little billboard that spreads across the top or bottom of the Web page. When users click their mouse pointer on the banner, it sends them to the advertiser's site or a buffer page.

While banners are a common unit of Web advertising, the cost of a banner can range wildly—anywhere from free to thousands of dollars per month. Some standardization is taking place in the business, with most sites now charging, on a cost-per-thousand basis, anywhere from $0.25 to $100.00 CPM, depending on the number and type of visitors the site regularly receives.

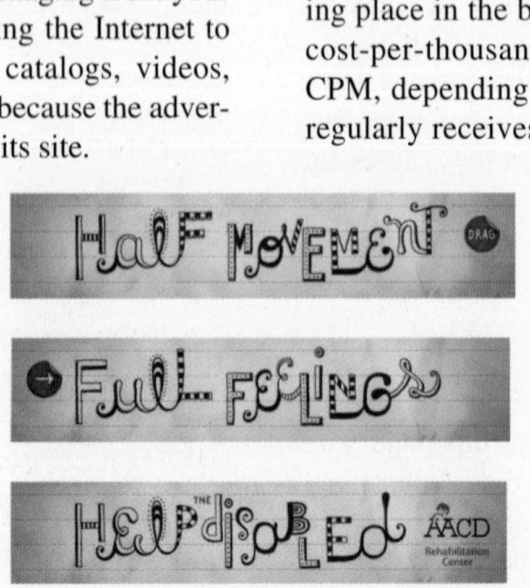

In the banner ad above, the user drags the top half of the text across the bottom, eventually revealing the message "Help the disabled." The ad won a Cannes Bronze Lion.

In response to many agency requests to simplify the ad-buying process, the Interactive Advertising Bureau (IAB) introduced the Universal Ad Package, a suite of 16 standard ad sizes (including skyscrapers, rectangles, pop-ups, banners, and buttons) designed to improve the efficiency and ease of planning, buying, and creating online media.

Similar to banners are **buttons**, small versions of the banner that often look like an icon and usually provide a link to an advertiser's landing page, a marketing tool that leads people into the purchasing or

banners Little billboards of various sizes that appear when a visitor lands on a particular website.

buttons Small versions of a banner that sometimes look like an icon, and they usually provide a link to an advertiser's home page.

sponsorship The presentation of a radio or TV program, or an event, or even a website by a sole advertiser.

e-mail advertising One of the fastest growing and most effective ways to provide direct mail.

spam Unsolicited, mass e-mail advertising for a product or service that is sent by an unknown entity to a purchased mailing list or newsgroup.

relationship-building process. Because buttons take up less space than banners, they also cost less.

After disappointing effectiveness in the early years of the Internet, display ads have improved as a result of the growth of ad networks. Ad networks bring together large numbers of different advertisers and content producers under a single roof. When an Internet user visits an ad from a company that belongs to a network, a cookie is left on the user's computer that begins a sequence of events known as behavioral tracking. Behavioral tracking involves determining the interests of an Internet user by following that user's visits to different sites in the network and ensuring that display ads match those interests. As an example, imagine someone visits a Web catalog and looks at lamps. The user ultimately decides none of the catalog offerings meet her needs, so she leaves the catalog to visit a news site. If the catalog company and the news site are members of the same ad network, the user will likely see display ads at the news site that feature lamps or related products. Although this activity raises privacy concerns among many, the user herself is never identified by the advertiser. Rather, behavior patterns are analyzed to ensure the right ad is put in front of the right person.

Sponsorships and Added-Value Packages

A form of advertising on the Internet that is growing in popularity is the **sponsorship** of Web pages. Corporations sponsor entire sections of a publisher's Web page or sponsor single events for a limited period of time, usually calculated in months. In exchange for sponsorship support, companies are given extensive recognition on the site. Sometimes an added-value package is created by integrating the sponsor's brand with the publisher's content, as a sort of advertorial, or with banners and buttons on the page.

IBM has exclusively sponsored the Super Bowl Web page, at an estimated cost of $1 million for each event. Other forms of sponsorships have included Web serials, sites devoted to women's issues, contests, and giveaways.

E-Mail Advertising

According to *Forbes*'s "2009 Ad Effectivness Study," 74 percent of marketers send **e-mail advertising** to customers who have asked for it. Marketers have always known that direct-mail advertising is the most effective medium for generating inquiries and leads and for closing a sale. It's also been the most expensive medium on a cost-per-exposure basis. Now, thanks to the Internet, the power of direct mail is increased even more, and the cost is reduced dramatically.[13]

A word of caution, though: It's important to differentiate responsible e-mail advertising from **spam**, which is really just electronic junk mail. Spam generally refers to unsolicited, mass e-mail advertising for a product or service that is sent by an unknown entity to a purchased mailing list or newsgroup.

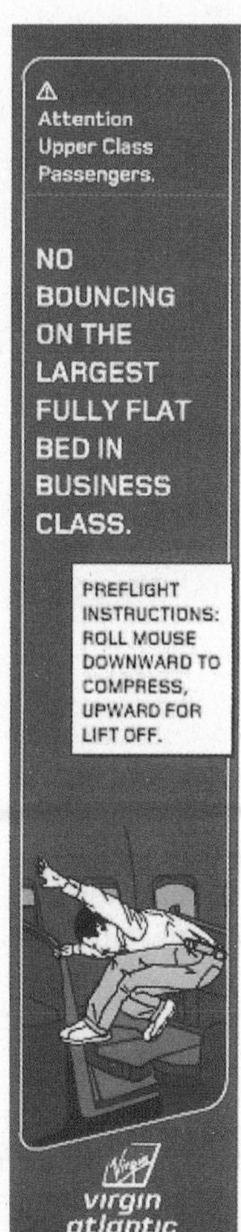

Crispin Porter + Bogusky struck gold with its Web campaign for Virgin Atlantic Airways (www.virgin-atlantic.com), which won a Pencil (a prestigious ad award) at the One Show Awards. The lighthearted banners deliver the benefits of Virgin's services and keep to the brand's playful, cheeky tone.

ONE OF THE KEYS TO VIRAL MARKETING SUCCESS IS TO PRESENT AN OFFER WITH REAL PERCEIVED VALUE—ONE THAT PEOPLE WILL WANT TO SHARE WITH ONE ANOTHER.

Spammers face the wrath of frustrated customers, tired of having their inboxes filled with unwanted e-mails. Since January 2004, spammers also face litigation under the CAN-SPAM Act (Controlling the Assault of Non-Solicited Pornography and Marketing). Legitimate e-mail advertisers are required to (1) clearly mark the e-mail as advertising, (2) provide a valid reply-to e-mail address, and (3) allow recipients to opt out of future mailings. The first lawsuits under the act were filed in April 2004, against two companies that had sent nearly a million e-mails advertising bogus diet patches and growth hormones. Lawsuits have also been filed against companies that sent e-mails that falsely appeared to come from recipients' friends[14] or with misleading subject lines.[15] With this in mind, wary marketers are focusing their e-mail efforts on **customer retention and relationship management (CRM)** rather than on prospecting.

Viral marketing is the Internet version of word-of-mouth advertising. The term was coined by Steven Jurvetson and his partners at the venture capital firm Draper Fisher Jurvetson. They were describing free e-mail provider Hotmail's incredible growth to 12 million users in just 18 months through the use of a little message at the bottom of every e-mail. The message invited recipients to sign up for their own free Hotmail account.

Since that time, many other marketers have come up with ways to induce their satisfied customers to recommend their product or service to friends and family members. One of the keys to viral marketing success is to present an offer with real perceived value—one that people will want to share with one another. Audible, a website featuring digital audiobooks, for example, uses a referral program whereby members are rewarded with free books each time someone they refer to the site signs up and becomes a member. Since members enjoy the site so much, it's natural that they would want to share the pleasure with their friends and families. Another example is Blendtec's "Will it blend" series, which was started on YouTube.com (it can now be found at www.willitblend.com) and has brought a new consumer market to a blender company that formerly served industry.

Local Listings A number of firms, including Google, Yahoo!, and Yelp, provide free business listings. In many cases local firms need do nothing, as information is provided by third parties such as InfoUSA. However, local firms should constantly monitor their listings to ensure they are up-to-date, complete, and accurate.

Group Buying Sites such as Groupon and other "deal-a-day" sites grab consumer attention by enticing consumers with great savings, especially on local products.

Affiliate Marketing Companies such as Amazon drive traffic to their sites through the use of affiliate marketing programs. Affiliate marketing involves sales referrals from ordinary people who encourage sales by placing links to products or brands at their websites, social media sites, or blogs. Affiliates earn a commission on each sale and can be a relatively inexpensive way for companies to create inbound traffic.

check yourself ✓

1. What are the major types of digital interactive advertising?
2. What is Google's AdWords program and how is it different from nonsearch digital advertising?

customer retention and relationship management (CRM) A promotional program that focuses on existing clients rather than prospecting for new clients.

viral marketing The Internet version of word-of-mouth advertising e-mail.

LO12-4 Identify the opportunities and challenges of advertising in social media.

PROBLEMS WITH DIGITAL INTERACTIVE AS AN ADVERTISING MEDIUM

Digital interactive, like any medium, has its drawbacks. It is not a mass medium in the traditional sense, and it may never offer mass-media effectiveness. Some marketers may decide it's too complex, too cumbersome, too cluttered, or not worth the time and effort.

It is not controlled by any single entity, so there may be no one to hold accountable. Security (for example, for credit card purchases) has improved, but it's still a problem for some. One potential problem with digital interactive advertising was summed up by Nielsen this way: "Ask a friend a simple question: 'What's your favorite online ad?'" The company's point was your friend probably couldn't think of ANY online ads.[16]

As this chapter has shown, the Internet now addresses consumers in so many forms that it is not possible to identify a constant set of strengths and weaknesses. Smart advertisers are availing themselves of multiple forms—websites, search advertising, mobile, and social media—to balance out weaknesses.

But whatever the form, any advertiser who commits to digital interactive should be prepared to stay engaged with his or her target audiences. That engagement requires constant attention and time. While relationships can be automated at some websites, it is not possible, or desirable, in social media. The bottom line: the online marketer must be prepared to engage consumers on a daily basis.

USING THE DIGITAL INTERACTIVE IN IMC

As we discussed in Chapter 7, one of the keys to successfully developing an integrated marketing communications program is to promote purposeful dialogue between the company and its stakeholders. That is what interactivity really means. And that is where digital interactive offers its greatest potential.

For the first time, customers and other stakeholders can truly respond to a company's media communications in real time, using the same channel for feedback that the company used for promotion. This means that even if a customer finds herself accidentally at the company's website and, if something there strikes her fancy, she can commence a dialogue (relationship) with the company immediately. Of course, this also means that, if the website triggers memories a less-than-satisfactory experience, she can use the same mechanism for complaining. But that's actually good, because a customer that complains usually cares. And a complaint gives the company the opportunity to correct the situation and set things right. It also gives the company information on how to do better. Sophisticated marketers cherish feedback.

> [Today's consumer doesn't want to talk to the retailer . . . . If she's got a complaint . . . she wants to talk to [the company].]

In the good old days of simple mass-media advertising, manufacturers placed their ads on network TV and went on about their business. The retailers took care of customers, so the manufacturers didn't really have to be concerned about them. In the new age of integrated marketing communications, that is no longer the case. Yes, the retailer is still there. But today's consumer doesn't want to talk to the retailer. She's a pretty sophisticated person. She knows who makes the product and if she's got a complaint that's who she wants to talk to. So it's not good enough for companies to put up a pretty website and then walk away from it. It has to be staffed—daily—and it must be kept up to date—daily. But this is expensive—often requiring companies to double or triple their Internet budget with no increase in advertising exposure. So the decision to use the Internet for integration is a big one and cannot be taken lightly.

To refresh yourself about the savvy use of digital media in IMC, reread the Obama campaign opener from Chapter 1.

Recall that the campaign spent the vast majority of its money on traditional (intrusive) media like television, not on digital interactive.

But it would be a mistake to confuse dollars spent with impact, because Obama used digital interactive and traditional media for different purposes. Traditional media were used to reach low-involvement voters who were relatively unengaged with the election, especially new voters who would prove crucial to his eventual success.

Digital interactive media were used to connect with fans and supporters. The result was that many in these groups were transformed into volunteers and donors, two vital resources for any campaign. Obama's fans wanted information about the candidate. Lots of information. And guided by the campaign's digital presence, they responded with time, effort, and cash. Political campaigns are not the same as brand campaigns. But the lessons from Obama's campaign about the value of digital interactive media have not been lost on the world's best marketers. ■

check yourself ✓

1. What are the potential problems facing advertisers who use digital media?
2. How can digital advertisements be used in IMC?

Using Facebook and Google [12]

It is amazingly easy to help your client begin advertising on two of the most popular sites on the Internet: Facebook and Google.

With Facebook visit: www.facebook.com/advertising. You or the client will need a Facebook account, of course. Once you are at the site, you can read some case studies about how Facebook advertising helped advertisers achieve their IMC objectives.

Facebook makes it fairly simple to begin a campaign. You begin by inputting a destination URL, which is where the Facebook ad will send a potential customer that clicks on your message. You will also give your ad a title (limited to 25 characters), body text, (135 characters), and an image.

Next you choose a target. In the United States, you can indicate whether your ad should be seen everywhere, or limited by state or city. You can also limit the ad to different age categories and just men or just women. You can even target people based on likes and interests, people who have different connections, or marital status and education.

You then give your campaign a name and set a budget. Your budget will limit how much the client will pay on a daily basis for click-throughs. Once the budget has been reached, the ad will not be shown to Facebook users.

The last bit of information you provide is the maximum you are willing to bid per click. Higher bids will be viewed more often, but can quickly eat up a daily budget.

Once the campaign starts, you have many tools available to track your results. Facebook reports the CTR (click-through rate, a measure of how often people exposed to your ad click on it), your CPM, the amount you've spent, the impressions you've generated, and even provides a helpful graph that can show clicks, CTR, or Impressions over a period of time.

Google AdWords has a similar, easy-to-use series of steps for placing ads that will appear during searches on the popular site (https://adwords.google.com). The company provides a wealth of helpful instructions about how to reach customers, understand costs, and benefit from AdWords success stories. As with Facebook, AdWords campaigns are based on a pay-for-performance model and it is easy to set daily budgets.

Google stresses the importance of the keywords that you choose for the campaign, because it is these words or phrases that determine which searches will present your ad to your target audience. Google suggests the following tips for choosing keywords:

1. **Choose your keywords carefully.** Make sure they're specific and directly relate to the theme of your ad and the page you are directing your customers to. Keywords of two or three words tend to work most effectively.
2. **Include relevant variations** of your best keywords, including singular and plural versions. If applicable, consider using colloquial terms, synonyms, and product or serial numbers.
3. **Be specific.** Keywords that are too broad or general will not reach users as effectively as keywords that are highly targeted.

Whether you choose to run a Facebook or Google campaign, or both, you'll be amazed how quick and easy it is to be up and running, and how many tools each company provides to help you track your success. If your website does its part by converting visitors into customers, you are on the way to using the Web as a profitable medium.

learn about, practice, and apply principles for using electronic media!

M: Advertising was developed for students who want information packaged in a concise, easy-to-read, yet interesting format.

Check out the book's website to:

- Suggest the advantages to Hyundai Motor America for advertising in the Super Bowl. (Review Questions)
- Describe the demographics of your favorite radio station. (Review Questions)
- Find out why there is a trend away from push strategies and toward pull strategies. (Review Questions)
- Predict the products you expect to see advertised on various cable networks. (Exploring Advertising)

While you are there, check out the professional resource links, review the PowerPoint presentation, and test your knowledge with the Multiple Choice Quiz. Additionally, *Connect® Marketing* is available for M: Advertising.

www.mhhe.com/ArensM2e

out-of-home, direct-mail, and promotional products

chapter thirteen

This chapter presents the factors advertisers consider when evaluating various out-of-home, direct-mail, and promotional product options. Many advertisers use these vehicles to either complement or replace print and electronic media, so it's important to understand how advertisers buy these media and the advantages and disadvantages of each.

So what do you do if you are a local company and want to gain some visibility without spending hundreds of thousands of dollars on advertising? What about billboards? They communicate your message quickly, at a low cost per thousand, and they "hang" around for a long time. That was the conclusion reached by James Ready and Leo Burnett Toronto.

For those of you who don't know James Ready, here is a quick lesson. James Ready is an Ontario microbrewery and not a person. This brand of beer has been brewed since 1875 by the James Ready Brewing Company of Niagara Falls, Ontario, Canada.[1] It features jokes on the undersides of the bottle caps and prides itself on selling for "a buck" ($1). So when the Ontario province decided to raise taxes on alcoholic beverages, James Ready and Leo Burnett Toronto devised the "Share Our Billboard" campaign to help keep James Ready at a buck.[2]

James Ready fans were already accustomed to helping the brand maintain its low price by routinely sending back bottle caps and labels for reuse. So taking it a step further only helped aid the cult-like status the beer was achieving with its loyal audience. The idea was simple, but truly effective. The message was "Help Keep James Ready a Buck" by making an offer to share their billboard space. To enlist the community, Leo Burnett Toronto used a multimedia approach—out-of-home, newspaper, e-mails, Web banner ads, and newsletters. The campaign began with a series of classified ads that appeared in local newspapers directing people to www.jamesready.com where they could post their best offer (no money was actually accepted) and upload messages and photos to be included on the billboards. Within a week, the website was flooded with requests to share the billboards, from band posters, to wedding announcements, to photos demonstrating

continued on p. 320

LEARNING OBJECTIVES

After studying this chapter, you will be able to:

- **LO13-1** Discuss the various types of outdoor advertising and its pros and cons.
- **LO13-2** Describe how outdoor advertising is purchased.
- **LO13-3** Discuss the various types of transit advertising and its pros and cons.
- **LO13-4** Discuss the various types of direct-mail advertising and its pros and cons.
- **LO13-5** Describe the basic components of direct-mail advertising.
- **LO13-6** Explain the value of promotional products.

continued from p. 319

the people's love for the brand. And, as is true with any social endeavor, there was content that could never be put on a billboard. But most importantly, the 106 billboards around southern Ontario showcased people in their hometowns, making them instant celebrities and spokespeople for the beer. To see details of the campaign and more examples of the billboards, go to vimeo.com/4175824. Under each customer photo, the copy read: "THANKS (your name here) FOR KEEPING J.R. A BUCK."[3]

The unspoken goal of advertising is to get people to talk about your brand. Pick up any study about what influences people to purchase and by and large word of mouth is always the first answer. So advertising's main goal is to involve people in such a manner that they "pass it on." The James Ready campaign stayed true to the brand. You didn't see high-gloss photography or expensive TV commercials. And what's most remarkable is the amount of consumer participation from a social media campaign. This just goes to show that good campaigns leverage the medium of choice, and great campaigns have no media boundaries. Leo Burnett's Canadian president and CEO David Moore summarized it well: "I'm particularly proud of the simplicity of the

idea—no high tech, no special effects, just pure creativity in one of the world's oldest mediums."[4]

The James Ready case study is an excellent example of how brands can engage with their consumers and establish lifelong loyalists, promote pass-along, and generally build a buzz around the brand with a single campaign. The work claimed victory and entered its second year, but not without taking home a few awards—a Gold Lion from Cannes, a Gold ANDY, and a Gold CLIO.

But how to maintain that buzz? James Ready and Leo Burnett Toronto did it in 2010 with another outdoor campaign. Recognizing the impact of the recession, James Ready invited consumers to "save money on necessities and spend it on James Ready Beer instead." The company partnered with local businesses to offer "JR-type deals for things JR drinkers need," like "two holes pierced for the price of one." By taking pictures of billboard coupons and showing them to the corresponding establishments, consumers "helped local establishments in tough times" and "saved money so they could spend it on more James Ready Beer."[5] Now James Ready is trying to figure out online beer tasting. Again, true to the brand. ■

OUT-OF-HOME MEDIA

Media that reach prospects outside their homes—like outdoor advertising, bus and taxicab advertising, subway posters, and terminal advertising—are part of the broad category of **out-of-home media** (see Exhibits 13–1 and 13–2). Today, there are more than 40 different types of out-of-home media, generating $6.7 billion in revenues in 2012.[6] The most common is *on-premise signage,* which promotes goods and services or identifies a place of business, on the property where the sign is located.[7] The golden arches at McDonald's franchises are a good example. On-premise signage is important for helping us find a place of business, but it doesn't provide any kind of market coverage, and it isn't an organized medium like, for instance, the standardized outdoor advertising business.

In the past three chapters, we've looked at the traditional mass media forms as well as some of the interesting new media vehicles that have burst upon the advertising scene in recent years. Now, to round out our discussion of advertising media, we'll present in this chapter some of the other vehicles that advertisers use today.

out-of-home media
Media such as outdoor advertising (billboards) and transit advertising (bus and car cards) that reach prospects outside their homes.

We'll start with the last major media category: the organized out-of-home media. These include standardized outdoor and transit advertising. We'll also briefly discuss some other out-of-home vehicles that are gaining in popularity: cinema advertising, ATMs, mobile billboards, in-store and mall advertising, and digital signs and displays. Then

▼**EXHIBIT 13–1** Spending in the four major out-of-home product categories (2012) ($ millions).

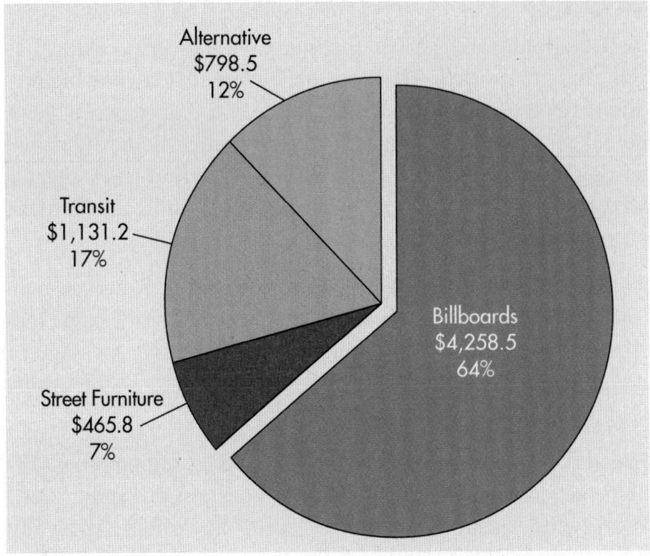

Source: Reprinted with permission of Outdoor Advertising Association of America, Inc.

▼**EXHIBIT 13–2** Types of displays in each of the out-of-home product categories.

Number of Out-of-Home Displays (2013)			
Billboards	**Street Furniture**	**Transit**	**Alternative**
Bulletins 158,868	**Bus Shelters** 49,082	**Buses** 205,426	**Cinema** 17,800
Digital Billboards 4,400	**Urban Furniture, i.e.** Phone Kiosks, Newsracks	**Airports** 68,560	**Digital Place-Based** 300 networks
Posters 165,606 faces	**Shopping Malls** 30,532	**Subway & Rail** 184,078 faces	**Arena & Stadiums** 1,352
Junior Posters 33,336 faces		**Truckside/Mobile** 10,593 vehicles	**Interior Place-Based, i.e.** Convenience Stores, Health Clubs, Restaurants/Bars
Walls/Spectaculars 4,029		**Taxis/ Wrapped Vehicles** 46,194	**Exterior Place-Based, i.e.** Airborne, Marine, Resorts & Leisure

Source: © 2013 The Outdoor Advertising Association of America http://www.oaaa.org/Portals/0/Images/No.%20of%20OOH%20Displays%20chart.png.

outdoor advertising
An out-of-home medium in the form of billboards.

bulletin structures
Large, outdoor billboards meant for long-term use that work best where traffic is heavy and visibility is good. They carry printed or painted messages, are created in sections, and are brought to the site where they are assembled and hung on the billboard structure.

we'll discuss direct-mail advertising, one of the most efficient, effective, economical and most widely used media today. And finally, we'll touch on promotional products, an important component of the very large promotional products industry.

LO13-1 Discuss the various types of outdoor advertising and its pros and cons.

OUTDOOR ADVERTISING

As a national and global medium, outdoor advertising has achieved great success. It was probably the first advertising medium ever used, dating back more than 5,000 years to when hieroglyphics on obelisks directed travelers. In the Middle Ages, bill posting was an accepted form of advertising in Europe. And in the nineteenth century, it evolved into a serious art form, thanks to the poster paintings of both Manet and Toulouse-Lautrec.[8]

Today, from Africa to Asia to Europe to South America, both local and global marketers use outdoor media for the same reasons as James Ready: to communicate a succinct message or image to a mass audience quickly and frequently at the lowest cost per thousand of any major medium.

In 2012, U.S. advertisers spent a total of $4.2 billion on out-of-home advertising, an increase of 5.1 percent over the prior year.[9] Worldwide spending on out-of-home advertising grew by 8.3 percent in 2011, faster growth than that seen for any other non-Internet form of advertising.[10] Outdoor's popularity is expected to continue as advertisers seek alternatives to the declining audiences and ad clutter of other mass media forms. Now that TV viewers can choose from hundreds of channels, it has become increasingly difficult for national advertisers to tell their story to mass audiences. But there's still one medium that can carry their message 24 hours a day, seven days a week, without interruption. It's never turned off, zipped, zapped, put aside, or left unopened. And it's big. That's outdoor. For that reason, some experts refer to billboards as the last mass medium.[11]

One of the most common forms of out-of-home advertising is the billboard. Compared to other major media, billboards offer the lowest cost per thousand. Chevy made clever use of this medium to demonstrate that its Volt runs on electricity.

A 2009 Arbitron study[12] showed that 71 percent of us "often look at the messages on roadside billboards (traditional and digital combined) and more than one-third (37%) report looking at an outdoor ad each or most of the time they pass one." According to the study, billboard viewers aged 18 or older

- Learned about an event they were interested in attending (58 percent).
- Learned about a restaurant they later visited (50 percent).
- Were reminded to tune in to a TV program (33 percent) or a radio station (44 percent).
- Noted a phone number (26 percent) or website address (28 percent) written on an outdoor billboard.
- Were motivated to visit a particular store that day because of an outdoor ad message (24 percent).
- Visited a retailer they saw on a billboard later that week (32 percent).
- Received directional information from a billboard (50 percent).
- Have immediately visited a business because of an outdoor ad message (24 percent).

Outdoor advertising may be used for a variety of purposes. For example, nothing beats outdoor as a directional medium for motorists. It can reach a large percentage of a market, with high frequency, at a very reasonable cost. Of course, outdoor cannot communicate with the same depth as other media, but in an integrated marketing program, outdoor greatly enhances awareness of or reinforces the advertiser's core message.

Standardization of the Outdoor Advertising Business

Standardized **outdoor advertising** uses scientifically located structures to deliver an advertiser's message to markets around the world.

In the United States, there are approximately 400,000 outdoor ad structures owned and maintained by some 2,100 outdoor advertising companies, known as *plants*.[13] Plant operators find suitable locations (usually concentrated in commercial and business areas), lease or buy the property, acquire the necessary legal permits, erect the structures in conformance with local building codes, contract with advertisers for poster rentals, and post the panels or paint the bulletins. Plant operators also maintain the structures and keep the surrounding areas clean and attractive.

The plant operator may have its own art staff to supply creative services for local advertisers; ad agencies usually do the creative

work for national advertisers. The biggest outdoor advertisers are services, amusements, media and advertising, retailers, restaurants, hotels, financial services, and communications companies (see Exhibit 13–3). Typically, the smaller the market, the larger the percentage of local advertisers. On average, 77 percent of billboard advertisers are locally owned businesses.[14]

Types of Outdoor Advertising

To buy outdoor advertising effectively, the media planner must understand its advantages and disadvantages and the types of structures available (see My Ad Campaign 13–A, "The Pros and Cons of Outdoor Advertising"). Standardized structures come in three basic forms: *bulletins, 30-sheet poster panels,* and *eight-sheet posters.* For extra impact, some companies may use the nonstandard *spectacular.*

Bulletins Where traffic is heavy and visibility is good, advertisers find that the largest **bulletin structures** work best, especially for long-term use. Bulletins measure 14 by 48 feet,

EXHIBIT 13–3 Top 10 outdoor advertisers (2012).

Rank	Advertiser	Outdoor Spending ($ millions)
1	Comcast Corp.	$87.0
2	McDonald's Corp.	76.3
3	Time Warner	63.2
4	Verizon Communications	60.7
5	Samsung Electronics Co.	52.4
6	JPMorgan Chase & Co.	48.3
7	Apple	42.9
8	Walt Disney Co.	42.6
9	SABMiller (MillerCoors)	40.0
10	T-Mobile US	39.9

Source: "Spenders by Medium," Ad Age DataCenter, *Advertising Age,* June 24, 2013, p. 20. Reprinted with permission. Copyright Crain Communications Inc.

The Pros and Cons of Outdoor Advertising [13–A]

The Pros

- **Accessibility.** Outdoor carries the message 24 hours per day and cannot be fast-forwarded, put aside, zapped, or turned off.
- **Reach.** For the same dollars, outdoor reaches over 86 percent compared with spot TV (76 percent), radio (72 percent), and newspaper (72 percent) of the same target audience in the same city. The audience is mostly young, educated, affluent, and mobile—an attractive target to many national advertisers.
- **Frequency.** Most people reached with outdoor advertising see it daily.
- **Geographic flexibility.** Outdoor advertisers can place their advertising where they want it nationally, regionally, or locally in more than 9,000 markets across North America.
- **Demographic flexibility.** Messages can be concentrated in areas frequented or traversed by young people, upper-income people, or people of specific ethnic backgrounds. With computerization, it's possible to characterize outdoor audiences by age, sex, income, and lifestyle down to the block level.
- **Cost.** Outdoor offers the lowest cost per exposure of any major advertising medium. Rates vary depending on market size and concentration, but the GRP system makes cost comparisons possible from market to market.
- **Impact.** Because advertisers can build up GRPs very fast, outdoor is the ideal medium for those with a short, simple message.
- **Creative flexibility.** Outdoor offers a large display and the spectacular features of lights, animation, and brilliant color. New fiber optics, giant video screens, and backlit display technologies offer even more creative options.
- **Location.** Outdoor can target consumers by activity, reaching shoppers on their way to the store, businesspeople on their way to work, or travelers on their way to the airport, thereby influencing consumers just before they make a purchase decision.

The Cons

- **Fleeting message.** Customers pass quickly, so outdoor advertising must be intrusive to be effective. The design and copy must tell a story briefly and crisply, and the words must sell.
- **Environmental influence.** Outdoor messages are influenced by their environment. Placement in a rundown area can detract from a product's image.
- **Audience measurement.** Audience demographics are difficult to measure. Not every passerby sees or reads the ad, so some media buyers distrust audience estimates.
- **Control.** Unlike print and broadcast ads, it's difficult to physically inspect each outdoor poster panel.
- **Planning and costs.** Outdoor messages usually require six to eight weeks of lead time for printing and posting. High initial preparation cost may discourage local use. And for national advertisers, buying outdoor is complex. As many as 30 companies may sell ad space in a single market.
- **Availability of locations.** Outdoor is so popular that demand for good locations now exceeds the supply.
- **Visual pollution.** Some people object to outdoor advertising as visual pollution. They may have a negative reaction to advertisers who use it.

30-sheet poster panel The basic outdoor advertising structure; it consists of blank panels with a standardized size and border. Its message is first printed on large sheets of paper and then mounted by hand on the panel.

stock posters A type of outdoor advertising consisting of ready-made 30-sheet posters, available in any quantity and often featuring the work of first-class artists and lithographers.

eight-sheet posters A smaller type of outdoor advertising, often used in urban areas, close to the point of purchase.

spectaculars Giant electronic signs that usually incorporate movement, color, and flashy graphics to grab the attention of viewers in high-traffic areas.

EXHIBIT 13–4 Most and least readable typefaces on outdoor advertising.

Most Readable	Least Readable
Upper- and Lowercase	ALL UPPERCASE
Regular Kerning	Tight Kerning
Boldface	Lightface
Uniform Thicknesses	**Too Thick or** Thin

McDonald's not only uses out-of-home advertising, it does so in a creative way.

plus any extensions, and may carry either painted or printed messages. They are created in sections in the plant's shop and then brought to the site, where they are assembled and hung on the billboard structure.

Outdoor advertising is generally viewed from 100 to 500 feet away by people in motion. So it must be simple, brief, and easy to discern. Large illustrations, bold colors, simple backgrounds, clear product identification, and easy-to-read lettering are essential for consumer comprehension. The recommended maximum for outdoor copy is seven words. Very bold typefaces appear blurred and thin ones seem faded. Ornate typefaces are too complicated. Simple type is the most effective. Spacing between letters and words (kerning) should be increased to improve readability (see Exhibit 13–4).

Painted displays are normally lighted and are repainted several times each year. Some bulletins are three-dimensional or embellished by extensions (or cutouts) that stretch beyond the frames of the structure. Variations include cutout letters, backlighting, moving messages, and electronic time and temperature units called *jump clocks.*

Painted bulletins are very costly, but some advertisers overcome this expense by rotating them to different choice locations in the market every 60 or 90 days. Over time, this gives the impression of wider coverage than the advertiser is actually paying for. The dominating effect of bulletins frequently makes them well worth the extra cost—especially in small markets.

Poster Panels A poster consists of blank panels with a standardized size and border. Its message is printed on large sheets of paper or vinyl and then mounted by hand on the panel. Poster sizes are referred to in terms of *sheets.* This term originated in the days when printing presses were much smaller and it required many sheets to cover a poster panel.

The **30-sheet poster panel** *(standard billboard)* is the most widely used form of outdoor advertising. It is far less costly per unit than the bulletin. The poster sheets are mounted on a board with a total surface of 12 by 25 feet and are usually changed every 30 days. The majority of them are illuminated.

Some local advertisers get high-quality outdoor advertising at reduced cost by using **stock posters**. These ready-made, 30-sheet posters are available in any quantity and often feature the work of first-class artists and lithographers. Local florists, dairies, banks, or bakeries simply place their name in the appropriate spot.

Eight-Sheet Posters Manufacturers of grocery products, as well as many local advertisers, use smaller poster sizes. Called **eight-sheet posters** (or *junior panels*), these offer a 5- by 11-foot printing area on a panel surface 6 feet high by 12 feet wide. They are typically concentrated in urban areas, where they can reach pedestrian as well as vehicular traffic. Space costs roughly half that of a 30-sheet poster and production costs are significantly lower. They are an excellent medium for advertising close to the point of purchase.

Spectaculars Times Square in New York is well known for its **spectaculars**—giant electronic signs that usually incorporate movement, color, and flashy graphics to grab attention in high-traffic areas. Spectaculars are very expensive to produce

Spectaculars are expensive, elaborate animated signs found primarily in the hearts of large cities. They incorporate movement, color, and flashy graphics to grab attention in high-traffic areas.

and are found primarily in the world's largest cities, such as Tokyo, London, New York, Los Angeles, and, of course, Las Vegas. A variation on the spectacular is the *wall mural,* a painted or vinyl mural that might cover an entire building.

check yourself ✓

1. Why can't outdoor advertising communicate with the same depth as other media?
2. Which form of outdoor advertising is the most widely used?

LO13-2 Describe how outdoor advertising is purchased.

Buying Outdoor Advertising

Advertisers use outdoor advertising for a variety of purposes. For example, to introduce a new product or announce a change in package design, an advertiser might want to saturate the market rapidly. When eBay wanted to communicate its new line of mobile apps, the online firm used bulletins, wallscapes, transit shelters, phone and street kiosks, and subway station dioramas next to high-traffic shopping districts in key markets. The executions included QR codes and bar codes, allowing consumers to shop for products on the spot. As a result, eBay experienced a record 2011 holiday shopping season, with some eBay merchants reporting a 15 percent increase in sales on Black Friday and a record Cyber Monday, with PayPal seeing a 514 percent increase in payments made from mobile devices.[15]

100 showing The basic unit of sale for billboards or posters is 100 gross rating points daily. One rating point equals 1 percent of a particular market's population.

The basic unit of sale for billboards, or posters, is *100 gross rating points daily,* or a **100 showing**. One rating point equals 1 percent of a particular market's population. Buying 100 gross rating points does not mean the message will appear on 100 posters or on 100 percent of the posters; it means the message will appear as many places as needed to provide a daily exposure *theoretically* equal to 100 percent of the market's total population.

For less saturation, a company can purchase 75, 50, or 25 gross rating points (GRPs), equivalent to 75 percent, 50 percent, or 25 percent of the market's population. For example, if a showing provides 750,000 total impression opportunities daily in a market with a population of 1 million, it delivers 75 GRPs (75 percent of the population) daily. Over a period of 30 days, the showing would earn 2,250 GRPs (30 days × 75 GRPs per day).

A showing, as indicated above, has historically been measured by a rudimentary equation that takes the number of people who pass by an out-of-home display as its measure of reach. This measurement is called Daily Effective Circulation, or DEC. However, in 2009 the Outdoor Advertising Association of America (OAAA) and the Traffic Audit Bureau developed a new method of measuring out-of-home's true reach and frequency. Their new rating system was initially called Eyes On Impressions (EOI), but has since been renamed TAB Out of Home Ratings. It actually takes into account many factors other than the number of people that pass a display, such as size of the display, angle to the road, format, street type, distance from the road, roadside position, and illumination. This new rating system then calculates those factors into a formula that

Outdoor advertising doesn't consist of billboards only. Customers entering the parking lot to fetch their cars are met with this inventive ad for Matchbox, which employs photographic adhesives to create a lifelike image.

global positioning systems (GPSs)
New satellite-based system whereby outdoor advertising companies give their customers the exact latitude and longitude of particular boards. Media buyers, equipped with sophisticated new software on their desktop computers, can then integrate this information with demographic market characteristics and traffic counts to determine the best locations for their boards without ever leaving the office.

[Location is everything in outdoor advertising.]

estimates the number of people that *actually* see the ad in a week. The main factor that differentiates DECs from TAB Out of Home Ratings is estimating how many *pass by* the ad on a daily basis versus estimating how many *see* the ad on a weekly basis. The net effect is twofold: (1) out-of-home is now the only ad medium that tracks viewers of ads, rather than just the potential to see ads, and (2) the frequency of out-of-home has been drastically reduced over a monthly period where the difference in reach is negligible.[16]

▼ EXHIBIT 13–5 Typical billboard locations in Baton Rouge that would achieve at least 100 GRPs daily when posted for 30 days. The red semicircles indicate which way the boards face.

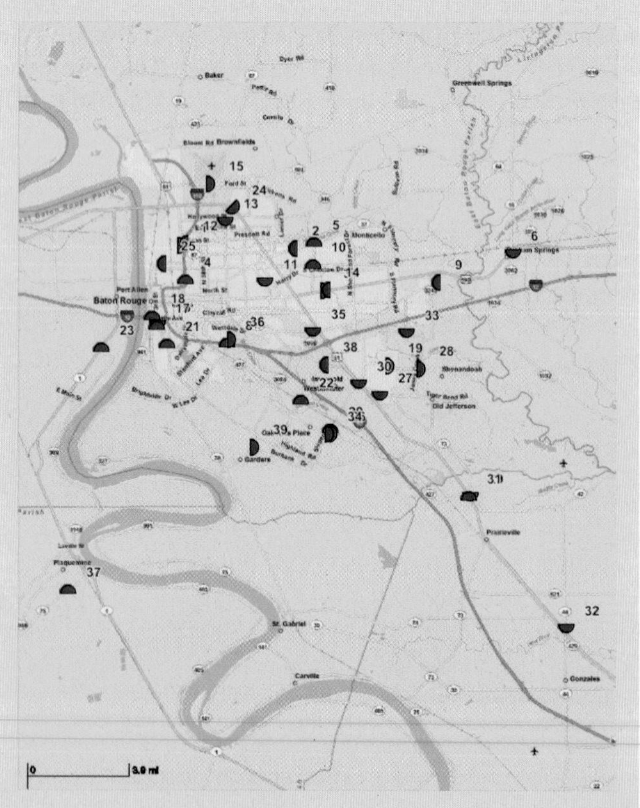

Location, Location, Location As in real estate, location is everything in outdoor advertising. Advertisers that want more saturation can increase the number of posters or purchase better locations to achieve 200 or 300 GRPs per day. The map in Exhibit 13–5 shows the billboard locations in Baton Rouge, Louisiana, that together would total 100 or more GRPs per day. To achieve a 100 showing in Baton Rouge, Lamar Outdoor Advertising would place 30-sheet posters along all major traffic arteries, facing in both directions. Rates vary considerably from market to market due to variations in property prices, labor costs, and market size. As you would expect, Exhibit 13–6 shows that locations in larger markets with high traffic volume have higher rates. A standard billboard costs between $500 and $1,500 per month. At that rate, billboards still offer the lowest cost per thousand impressions (an average of about $5.00 a 30-sheet poster) of any major mass medium.[17] The only other medium that comes close is radio.

Technology in Outdoor Advertising In the past it was always a problem for a media buyer in New York to adequately supervise the selection of outdoor boards in Peoria, Illinois. A buyer can't just jump on a plane and travel to all the cities where the client's boards are posted to verify the value of the locations. Fortunately, though, technology has helped solve this dilemma and has thus made outdoor an even more attractive medium to national advertisers. Today, outdoor companies can use sophisticated **global positioning systems (GPSs)** to give the exact latitude and longitude of particular boards using satellite technology. Media buyers, equipped with sophisticated new software on their desktop computers, can then integrate this information with demographic market characteristics and traffic counts to determine the best locations for their boards.[18]

Many outdoor companies provide digitized videos of their locations so the buyer can see the actual boards and the environment in which they are located. Other developments include bar coding of materials so they can be tracked, posted, and authenticated, all by computer. Computerized painting on flexible vinyl guarantees a high-quality, high-resolution, faithful reproduction of the advertiser's message regardless of the market.[19]

Perhaps the most exciting development in outdoor advertising is the availability of digital (or electronic) billboards. Ads can be implemented the same day and updated quickly and easily, from

▼ EXHIBIT 13-6 Four-week rates for standard 30-sheet posters in selected markets (2012).

Market (DMA)	18+ Population	100 Weekly GRPs		4-Week GRP	4-Week Impressions	CPP	CPM	4-Week Reach	4-Week Frequency
		Number	Cost						
Bakersfield	598,107	11	$12,463	400	2,409,484	$ 31.16	$5.17	63.3%	8.5
Baton Rouge	685,684	15	12,900	400	2,817,120	32.25	4.58	48.1	6.9
Boise	538,655	12	11,880	400	2,181,024	29.70	5.45	58.8	7.8
Buffalo–Niagra, NY	1,251,647	40	38,800	400	5,128,000	97.00	7.57	59.9	8.6
Cincinnati	1,759,545	39	25,350	400	7,046,832	63.68	3.60	51.5	7.6
Chicago	7,309,947	131	78,600	400	29,221,384	196.50	2.69	40.7	9.3
Lima, OH	114,528	6	4,830	400	516,816	12.08	9.36	71.0	9.5
Omaha	820,901	14	8,750	400	3,290,448	21.88	2.66	51.0	8.7
Pittsburgh	2,260,433	55	79,750	400	9,081,600	199.38	8.78	60.1	8.5
Tallahassee	558,740	16	9,888	400	2,261,632	24.72	4.37	43.9	8.3

Note: Costs are for space only, based on a 4-week posting period; they do not include production. Rates are effective as of the date of publication and are subject to change.

Source: http://www.lamar.com/.

hundreds of miles away, over the Internet. Digital billboards can rotate ads among various advertisers or move ads around town, changing them once every 4 to 10 seconds. A restaurant can feature breakfast specials in the morning and dinner specials in the evening. Law enforcement can display the image of a missing person or update emergency information in minutes. Production costs are reduced dramatically. Some digital billboards will even interact with passersby, responding to a friendly wave or communicating with consumers' cell phones. Presently, there are about 4,000 digital billboards in the United States, with several hundred being added each year at a cost of about $250,000 each, versus less than $50,000 for a traditional billboard. Due to safety concerns, more than a dozen cities have banned digital billboards. Los Angeles sign operators were ordered to turn off nearly 100 digital billboards in early 2013. Other cities have placed strict limitations on them while government agencies evaluate their possibly distracting effect on drivers. So far, some studies indicate that there is no relationship between traffic accidents and digital billboards,[20] while other studies suggest that electronic signs are distracting.[21]

Among the most important users of digital billboards are law enforcement agencies. The FBI uses digital billboards to track down wanted fugitives and crack difficult cases. To date, the FBI credits digital billboards with directly leading to more than 50 arrests. (Source: http://nvate.com/10933/fbi-billboard-ads/)

Exciting new technologies may change the future of how we "see" outdoor and other out-of-home ads. TeamOne launched a revolutionary campaign for Lexus that included a full-size hologram of the IS sedan. Using interactive kiosks located in Times Square and other prime U.S. locations, the display featured a hologram of the Lexus in motion and touch pads that allowed visitors to change the car's color and other features.[22] This opens up many thrilling possibilities for advertisers: Imagine a bulletin-size structure on the highway promoting the latest Batman film, with a larger-than-life superhero coming at you in 3-D.

Regulation of Outdoor Advertising

The Highway Beautification Act of 1965 controls outdoor advertising on U.S. interstate highways and other federally subsidized highways. It was enacted partly in response to consumer complaints that outdoor advertising was spoiling the environment. Over 700,000 billboards were removed by 1991, the year Congress banned the construction of new billboards on all scenic portions of interstate highways.[23] Since that time, the image of outdoor advertising has improved dramatically. Today, most people polled say they like billboards, believe they promote business, and find they provide useful travel information for drivers.[24]

Each state also regulates, administers, and enforces outdoor advertising permit programs through its department of transportation. Some states (Maine, Vermont, Hawaii, and Alaska) prohibit outdoor advertising altogether. Ironically, though, some of these states use outdoor advertising themselves in other states to promote tourism.

The Ethical Issue, "Does Spillover Need Mopping Up?", discusses some of the problems inherent in the very public nature

Does Spillover Need Mopping Up?

While numerous laws and self-regulatory efforts have banished products like tobacco and hard liquor from the airwaves, it is virtually impossible to keep minors from being exposed to such advertising due to the spillover nature of some media. The ethical issues involved with spillover media are complex, including the kind of advertising appeals used to target audiences.

Take outdoor advertising, for example. It is the most public mass medium. It cannot be turned off like television, radio, or the Internet, and it's displayed 24 hours a day for all to see—even children.

The trend in outdoor advertising today is toward eye-catching, sexually explicit ads, seen especially in densely populated urban areas. Most outdoor advertising regulations have focused on the location of billboards, not the content. The Outdoor Advertising Association of America's (OAAA) Code of Principles says that they "support the right to reject advertising that is misleading, offensive, or otherwise incompatible with community standards." But it is unknown how often this clause is invoked. Communities, therefore, have taken it upon themselves to regulate the placement and content of outdoor advertising, rather than relying on self-regulation by the advertising industry. In 1998, for example, the Los Angeles City Council passed an ordinance that prohibited alcoholic beverage advertising on virtually all publicly visible sites, even store windows. The OAAA and other local Los Angeles trade association members filed a federal civil rights action, claiming that the ordinance violates the right to free speech.

As technology advances, so do the venues for advertising. Advertisers have found ways to work around billboard restrictions. Taxicabs and buses have carried ads for years; however, now appearing on Boston cabs are electronic billboards that have the ability to change their message minute by minute—depending on a few desired variables. The full-color ads change depending on the time of day and location of the cab. Different neighborhoods will see different ads and, if appropriate, in different languages. The taxi's location is monitored by a GPS tracking system. This new technology is inexpensive for advertisers and may become a common feature on taxicabs across America. However, this raises legal and ethical questions. Should mobile billboards be subjected to the same restrictions as stationary billboards? Neighborhoods and schools may be protected from unwanted billboard advertising, but can concerned parents protect their children from advertising that travels on taxis?

Spillover also reaches children in other media vehicles besides out-of-home. The movies, for example, consistently show people smoking. And if the smoker is a celebrity, an impressionable child might interpret that as an endorsement. In a study conducted by Dartmouth Medical School, researchers concluded that actor endorsements of tobacco brands jumped 10-fold in the 1990s. The study also found that 87 percent of popular movies contain tobacco use and about one-third display identifiable brand-name logos. Minors make up a large percentage of moviegoers and through movies they may be getting more exposure to smoking endorsements than in real life. Young people who look up to sport stars and movie celebrities may be vulnerable to intentional and unintentional endorsements. Benedict Carey of the *Los Angeles Times* calls today's movies "almost as smoke-laden as the stock car racing circuit."

Many people feel that ads are not to blame for the rise of teen sexual activity and tobacco and alcohol use. Others feel that advertisers have a greater responsibility to separate youth from the adult world of unhealthy and explicit activity. Regardless of who is right, advertisers, agencies, and media companies must be sensitive to public opinion and seek creative solutions to protect impressionable children. Otherwise, the industry will risk severe restriction and regulation for having failed to responsibly and conscientiously assert firm ethical standards itself.

Questions

1. Do you believe the goal of protecting children justifies banning the advertising of legal products or their glorification in movies? Which products specifically?
2. Should ads in spillover media be censored for sexually explicit content? If so, who should the censors be and what specifically should they prohibit?
3. What alternatives might be available to fight teenage smoking, drinking, and sexual promiscuity besides banning advertising for legal adult products?

of outdoor advertising and whether regulation will be needed here too.

check yourself ✓

1. What is unique about the TAB Out of Home Ratings system?
2. What are the advantages of digital billboards?

LO13-3 Discuss the various types of transit advertising and its pros and cons.

TRANSIT ADVERTISING

When Campbell Soup started advertising in 1910, the company spent its first $5,000 placing ads on one-third of the buses in New York City for one year. The ads were so successful that after only six months, Campbell enlarged the contract to include all surface vehicles in the city. People started buying more Campbell's soup and soon sales were up 100 percent. For

This clever transit ad makes it appear that the passenger is receiving an injection. The headline reads, "Doesn't hurt at all." It's promoting a competitively priced health insurance plan in Hong Kong.

the next 12 years, transit advertising was the only medium Campbell employed. Today, Campbell is still a major user of transit advertising.

transit advertising An out-of-home medium that includes three separate media forms: inside cards; outside posters; and station, platform, and terminal posters.

Transit advertising is a category of out-of-home media that includes bus and taxicab advertising as well as posters on transit shelters, terminals, and subways. Although transit is not considered a major medium by most advertising practitioners, standardization, better research, more statistical data, and measured circulation have made transit advertising more attractive to national advertisers. National marketers of designer apparel and movies, for example, are two of the many categories of advertisers spending dramatically more in this medium, replacing the traditional transit advertising leaders such as petroleum products, financial services, and proprietary medicines.[25]

Transit advertising is a cost-effective way for marketers to reach a large audience of people. Buses and taxis provide high ad exposure by traversing the busiest streets of a city many times a day. A 1-800-Flowers.com campaign promoting the company's specialty bouquets featured ads on buses, on subway stations, and in other urban locations. The company's sales were seven times higher in markets where the outdoor campaign ran.[26]

Transit advertising is equally popular with local advertisers. Retailers can expand their reach inexpensively and often receive co-op support from national marketers, which thrive on the local exposure[27] (see My Ad Campaign 13–B, "The Pros and Cons of Transit Advertising").

The Pros and Cons of Transit Advertising [13–B]

The Pros

- **Long exposure.** The average transit ride is 25 minutes.
- **Repetitive value.** Many people take the same routes day after day.
- **Eagerly read messages.** Riders get bored, so readership is high and ad recall averages 55 percent.
- **Low cost.** Transit ads cost less than any other medium.
- **Creative flexibility.** Special constructions and color effects are available at relatively low cost.
- **Need satisfying.** Transit can target the needs of riders—with ads for cool drinks in summer, for example. Food ads do well as evening riders contemplate dinner.
- **Environmentally sensitive.** As social pressure to use public transportation increases, transit is well positioned as a medium of the future.

The Cons

- **Status.** Transit lacks the status of the major advertising media, like print and broadcast.
- **Crowded environment.** Rush-hour crowding limits the opportunity and ease of reading. The vehicle itself, if dirty, may tarnish the product's image.
- **Limited selectivity.** Transit reaches a nonselective audience, which may not meet the needs of some advertisers.
- **Clutter.** Cards are so numerous and look so similar they may be confusing or hard to remember.
- **Location.** With outlying shopping malls, fewer suburbanites make trips downtown.
- **Creative restrictions.** Although transit cards may carry longer messages than billboards, copy is still limited.

transit shelter advertising A form of out-of-home media, where advertisers can buy space on bus shelters and on the backs of bus-stop seats.

taxicab exteriors In transit advertising, internally illuminated two-sided posters positioned on the roofs of taxis. Some advertising also appears on the doors or rear.

terminal posters One-sheet, two-sheet, and three-sheet posters in many bus, subway, and commuter train stations as well as in major train and airline terminals. They are usually custom designed and include such attention getters as floor displays, island showcases, illuminated signs, dioramas (three-dimensional scenes), and clocks with special lighting and moving messages.

inside card A transit advertisement, normally 11 by 28 inches, placed in a wall rack above the windows of a bus.

car-end posters Transit advertisements of varying sizes, positioned in the bulkhead.

outside posters The variety of transit advertisements appearing on the outside of buses, including king size, queen size, traveling display, rear of bus, and front of bus.

Types of Transit Advertising

Transit advertising targets the millions of people who use commercial transportation (buses, subways, elevated trains, commuter trains, trolleys, and airlines), plus pedestrians and car passengers, with a variety of formats: transit shelters; station, platform, and terminal posters; inside cards and outside posters on buses; and taxi exteriors.

Transit Shelters

In cities with mass-transit systems, advertisers can buy space on bus shelters and on the backs of bus-stop benches. **Transit shelter advertising** is a relatively new out-of-home form enjoying great success. It reaches virtually everyone who is outdoors: auto passengers, pedestrians, bus riders, motorcyclists, bicyclists, and more. It is extremely inexpensive and available in many communities that restrict billboard advertising in business or residential areas. In fact, shelter advertising is sometimes the only form of outdoor advertising permitted. It's also an excellent complement to outdoor posters and bulletins, enabling total market coverage in a comprehensive outdoor program.

> [Transit shelter advertising] reaches virtually everyone who is outdoors.

Terminal Posters

In many bus, subway, and commuter train stations, space is sold for one-, two-, and three-sheet **terminal posters**. Major train and airline terminals offer such special advertising forms as floor displays, island showcases, illuminated cards, dioramas (3-D scenes), and clocks with special lighting and moving messages.

In Paris, Nike made a splash at the French Open tennis tournament even though a competitor had locked up advertising rights within the stadium. Nike covered the city by buying space on some 2,500 buses during the tournament. As the coup de grace, it bought up every bit of signage space at the Porte d'Auteuil metro (subway) station close to the stadium and turned it into a Nike gallery of terminal posters featuring famous tennis players from around the world.[28]

Inside and Outside Cards and Posters

The **inside card** is placed in a wall rack above the vehicle windows. Cost-conscious advertisers print both sides of the card so it can periodically be reversed to change the message, saving on paper and shipping charges. Inside **car-end posters** (in bulkhead positions) are usually larger than inside cards, but sizes vary. **Outside posters** are printed on high-grade cardboard and often varnished for weather resistance. The most widely used outside posters are on the side, rear, and front of a bus.

Advertisers may also buy space on **taxicab exteriors**, generally for periods of 30 days, to display internally illuminated, two-sided posters positioned on the roofs. Some advertising also appears on the doors or rear of taxicabs. In Southern California, advertisers can rent cards mounted on the tops of cabs that travel throughout Los Angeles, Orange, and San Diego counties, serving major airports and traveling the busiest freeways in the country. Costing an average of $100 to $200 per month per cab ($400 in New York City!), this is a very cost-effective way to reach the mobile public.

Buying Transit Advertising

The unit of purchase for transit advertising is a **showing**, also known as a *run* or *service*. A **full showing** (or *100 showing*) means that one card will appear in each vehicle in the system. Space may also be purchased as a *half* (50) or *quarter* (25) *showing*.

Rates are usually quoted for 30-day showings, with discounts for 3-, 6-, 9-, and 12-month contracts. Advertisers supply the

showing A traditional term referring to the relative number of outdoor posters used during a contract period, indicating the intensity of market coverage.

full showing A unit of purchase in transit advertising where one card will appear in each vehicle in the system.

basic bus In transit advertising, all the inside space on a group of buses, giving the advertiser complete domination.

take-ones In transit advertising, pads of business reply cards or coupons, affixed to interior advertisements for an extra charge, that allow passengers to request more detailed information, send in application blanks, or receive some other product benefit.

bus-o-rama signs A bus roof sign, which is actually a full-color transparency backlighted by fluorescent tubes, running the length of the bus.

total bus A special transit advertising buy that covers the entire exterior of a bus, including the front, rear, sides, and top.

brand trains An advertising program under which all the advertising in and on a train is from a single advertiser. This advertising concept was first used in subway trains in New York City and is being used on the Las Vegas monorail.

immersive advertising The integration of advertising into the message delivery mechanism so effectively that the product is being promoted while the audience is being entertained.

Unique and resourceful use of transit advertising is on display in this bus design from the National Geographic Channel. The clever illusion created by the opening and closing of the bus doors is a concept that was sure to get people talking.

cards at their own expense, but the transit company can help with design and production.

Cost depends on the length and saturation of the showing and the size of the space. Rates vary extensively, depending primarily on the size of the transit system. Advertisers get rates for specific markets from local transit companies.

Special Inside Buys In some cities, advertisers gain complete domination by buying the **basic bus**—all the inside space on a group of buses. For an extra charge, pads of business reply cards or coupons (called **take-ones**) can be affixed to interior ads for passengers to request more detailed information, send in application blanks, or receive some other benefit.

Special Outside Buys Some transit companies offer **bus-o-rama signs**, jumbo full-color transparencies backlighted by fluorescent tubes and running the length of the bus. A bus has two bus-o-rama positions, one on each side. A single advertiser may also buy a **total bus**—all the exterior space, including the front, rear, sides, and top.

Any visitor riding on the Las Vegas monorail can't help but become totally immersed in the BankWest of Nevada brand. In addition to a full exterior train wrap, BankWest of Nevada has branded the floor, the roof, the train entry doors, and the lightbox graphics.

For years, New York subways have been running **brand trains**, which include all the subway cars in a particular corridor. However, with the July 2004 opening of its monorail system, the city of Las Vegas took the concept further. The glitz of the city's strip extends to its public transportation: Each of the nine monorail trains and seven stations has a corporate sponsor, and many feature elaborate immersive advertising themes. **Immersive advertising** describes the integration of advertising into the message delivery mechanism so effectively that the product is being promoted while the audience is being entertained. The result is that the prospect becomes totally immersed in the message and the brand.

Las Vegas city officials banked on the monorail system (www.lvmonorail.com), which is entirely funded by passenger fares instead of tax dollars, to generate at least $6.5 million annually in advertising

cinema advertising
Advertising in movie theaters.

mobile billboard
A cross between traditional billboards and transit advertising; some specially designed flatbed trucks carry long billboards up and down busy thoroughfares.

revenue. However, with the help of ad agency Promethean Partners, ad revenues are now expected to be at least three times that amount. Consider the deal that the city struck with Nextel, estimated at $50 million. The company signed on for a 12-year sponsorship of one train and the system's "crown jewel," the main station at the Las Vegas Convention Center, which more than 1 million annual visitors are expected to pass through each year.[29] A complete train wrap costs $15,000 per week, plus $45,000 to produce, install, and remove the wrap.

OTHER OUT-OF-HOME MEDIA

As mentioned earlier, there are many forms of out-of-home media. Some are so new that they are still unproven. However, several seem to be gaining in popularity, and they demonstrate how far advertisers will go to get their messages seen by the consuming public.

Cinema Advertising

There was a time not long ago when the only thing cinema audiences could watch before a feature film was a couple of coming attractions. In recent years marketers have leapt to fill in the empty time before a movie starts with advertisements. Advertising in movie theaters is a growing but controversial practice. **Cinema advertising** includes on-screen advertising, such as commercials airing in advance of movie previews and the feature presentation, as well as lobby-based videos, sampling, special events and concession-based promotions. Although some moviegoing audiences resent watching ads, cinema advertising is becoming more and more attractive to marketers. "Unlike traditional media, we don't have to fight for our audience's attention; they don't flip channels," says Bob Martin, president and chair of the Cinema Advertising Council.[30] Cinema advertising grew to a $644 million industry in 2011, up an average of 15.7 percent per year since 2002, an impressive gain compared to the steep drops in print and broadcast.

Cinema advertising offers some compelling advantages to marketers. Arbitron estimates that 81 percent of teens and 67 percent of young adults see a movie at least once a month. A full 25 percent of teens see 20 or more movies each year. Arbitron also reports that while those who go to movies, in comparison to non-moviegoers, are more likely to skip ads on TV, most don't mind ads in movies. Moviegoers also tend to be young, affluent, tech-savvy peer leaders. Nonetheless, some movie theater chains prohibit on-screen advertising for fear of offending their audience.

ATMs

With so many thousands of money devices in service, it's only natural that the captive audience of automated teller machines (ATMs) be targeted for creative promotional tactics. Fleet Financial Group has capitalized on ATM technology by printing retailer coupons on the backs of receipts, the other piece of paper that customers receive from the machines. The coupons, which were initially redeemable at Bruegger's Bagels, Firestone, Great Cuts, Oil Doctor, and Pizza Hut, originated in Massachusetts and provided advertising that customers were likely to carry around in their wallets or cars.

One ATM innovation, developed by Electronic Data Systems Corp., puts full motion video ads on the machine's screen as customers wait for their transactions to be processed. The 15-second ads, which debuted in 7-Eleven stores in San Diego, replace the "Transaction being processed" or "Please wait" messages that appeared on the screen. The original ads promoted Fox Searchlight Pictures's films *The Ice Storm* and *The Full Monty*.

[Any blank space is an invitation to advertise.]

Free ATMs NYC (thefreeatm.com) is testing a program that allows customers to forgo any ATM transaction fees by agreeing to view a short commercial. The transactions don't take any longer than they would without the advertising.[31]

Mobile Billboards

The **mobile billboard**, a cross between traditional billboards and transit advertising, was conceived as advertising on the sides of tractor-trailer trucks. Today in some large cities, specially designed trucks carry long billboards up and down busy thoroughfares. Local routes for mobile ads are available on delivery trucks in several cities. And, of course, many of these mobile billboards are going digital. Speaking of digital, a San Francisco company called Smart Plate has developed a license plate that can display custom advertising messages if your car is halted for more than four seconds in traffic or at a red light. California is evaluating

digital signs Signs that display text and graphic messages similar to the big screens in sports stadiums. The signs can transmit commercial messages to retail stores, where shoppers see them. The stores pay nothing for the signs and receive a percentage of the advertising revenue.

guerrilla marketing Using unconventional, low-cost techniques to promote products and services.

this idea as a way to generate revenue for the state. The plates could also be used to update vehicle registration, pay tolls, and broadcast Amber Alerts or traffic information.[32]

Digital Signage

Digital signs display text and graphic messages much like the big screens in sports stadiums. The signs can transmit commercial messages to retail stores, where shoppers see them. The stores pay nothing for the signs and receive a percentage of the advertising revenue. In Montreal, Alstom (www.telecite.com) used its visual communication network (VCN) technology to install digital display panels on subway cars. Advertisers got a powerful, inexpensive, and flexible medium with a large, captive audience; the transit authority got a modern, self-financed emergency and public information system; and passengers got something to watch while they ride.[33]

Digital signs can be updated easily or even automatically, based on store traffic, weather conditions, and so on. Some digital signs allow shoppers to interact directly with the information on the screen.

In the 2002 film *Minority Report,* billboards scan passing consumers' eyeballs, compute their purchasing history, and address them by name. Tom Cruise walks into a clothing store and a holographic sales representative greets him: "Hello Mr. Yakamoto, welcome back to the Gap. How'd those assorted tank tops work out for you?" In the real world, shoppers will probably not be identified by iris scans, but by the smartphones in our pockets.[34] Bank of America already has an interactive billboard in Times Square that allows passersby to participate in a poll via their smartphones. It updates poll results throughout the day.[35]

Mall Advertising

Retail advertising doesn't have to be high tech to be effective. Over 90 percent of the population visits a shopping mall each month and the average shopper visits 3.3 times per month. This results in over 1 million shoppers visiting the average mall in the United States each month. Mall advertising thus offers advertisers an opportunity to place their message in front of millions of consumers in the mood to make purchases.

Mall advertising can include posters on mall directories, door- and window-mounted signage, advertising on escalators and elevators, banners hanging from ceilings, tabletop ads in food courts, and any other location that might be seen by shoppers.

StoreBoard Media (www.storeboards.net) has been placing ads on the entryway security panels of major retail chains since 2006. The company touts an average 20 percent product sales lift over the four-week period in which its ads appear. While the security system may be high tech, the ads themselves are "no tech," says Rick Sirvaitis, president of StoreBoard, New York, which has placed ads in some 14,000 U.S. stores for brands including Coca-Cola, Crest, Halls, and Garnier. "If you pass your peripheral vision test on your driver's license, you can't miss these ads. They have a much greater assurance of being viewed by 100 percent of customers than anywhere else in the store."[36]

Guerrilla Marketing

It seems that any blank space is an invitation to advertise. The term **guerrilla marketing** was coined in 1984 by Jay Conrad Levinson in his book by the same name. He defines the concept as "achieving conventional goals, such as profits and joy, with unconventional methods, such as investing energy instead of money."[37] In recent years, guerrilla marketing tactics have also come to be referred to as stealth, buzz, ambush, street, or viral marketing. Some examples of guerrilla advertising include Folgers converting a steaming New York manhole cover into an advertisement for a hot cup of coffee, Casinò di Venezia decorating a luggage carousel in the Venice airport to resemble a roulette wheel, the Salvation Army printing advertisements to promote donations on blankets distributed to the homeless, Burger King dressing Ronald McDonald statues in Asia with Burger King t-shirts, and streakers running onto a rugby field in Australia with Vodafone logos painted on their bodies. The ultimate goal is to attract attention in an increasingly advertising-cluttered environment.

Creativity is as the heart of every great media placement. Here the World Wildlife Foundation uses the depletion of paper towels to convey their conservation message.

direct-mail advertising All forms of advertising sent directly to prospective customers without using one of the commercial media forms.

dimensional direct mail Direct-mail advertising that utilizes three-dimensional shapes and unusual materials.

e-mail Electronic mail messages transmitted electronically between computers.

sales letters The most common form of direct mail. Sales letters may be typeset and printed, or computer generated.

postcards Cards sent by advertisers to announce sales, offer discounts, or otherwise generate consumer traffic.

check yourself ✓

1. How does the meaning of "100 showing" differ between outdoor advertising and transit advertising?
2. What creative application of digital signage would be effective on your college campus?

LO13-4 Discuss the various types of direct-mail advertising and its pros and cons.

DIRECT-MAIL ADVERTISING: THE ADDRESSABLE MEDIUM

All forms of advertising sent directly to prospects through a government, private, or electronic mail delivery service are called **direct-mail advertising**. As we will discuss in Chapter 15, direct-mail advertising is one form of direct marketing since it allows advertisers to communicate directly with the customer. Measured on advertising dollars spent, direct mail is second only to television. This is not all spent by large national direct-mail marketers. Local retail businesses are expected to spend over $11 billion on direct mail in 2013, nearly four times as much as on online advertising.[38]

Both large and small companies use direct mail. New firms often use direct mail as their first advertising medium. The reason is clear: Of all media, direct-mail advertising offers the most direct path to the desired customer. And businesses don't need big budgets to advertise with direct mail. With a computer and desktop publishing software, a business can create a professional-looking mailer. And some websites provide companies with tools to design a mailer, import a mailing list, and have the campaign printed and sent, all online.

Direct mail is used by for-profit businesses, charities, and political campaigns. Mailings are typically targeted to the advertiser's best prospects, selected based on where they live, demographic characteristics, past purchasing behavior, or interest they have expressed in certain product categories. Direct mail may also be targeted to businesses rather than individuals, in an effort to generate orders or leads for a sales force. Since direct-mail marketers don't want to waste money sending advertising to disinterested prospects, consumers can opt out by contacting the Direct Marketing Association's Mail Preference Service (www.dmachoice.org).

Many experts predicted that the combination of the recession, rising postage rates, and a growing preference among marketers for low-cost, digital communications would lead to a steep decline in the dollars spent on direct-mail advertising. But contrary to those predictions, spending on direct mail was projected to grow by 3 percent in 2012 to $50 billion, still ahead of ad spending on the Internet.[39]

Today's leading mailers include the financial services and catalog companies shown in Exhibit 13-7. Direct mail (not including catalogs) can also boast an impressive ROI, returning over $15 for every dollar spent.

▼EXHIBIT 13–7 2013's Top 50 mailers as measured by mail volume.

Name	Industry
1. American Express Co.	Financial Services
2. L.L. Bean	Catalog
3. Chase Manhattan Bank	Financial Services
4. Citibank	Financial Services
5. AAA	Clubs/Associations
6. Lands' End	Catalog
7. Capital One	Financial Services
8. Verizon Communications	Telecom
9. GEICO Direct	Insurance
10. Omaha Steaks	Foods

Source: *Target Marketing* http://www.targetmarketingmag.com/article/spotlight-top-10-direct-mailers-2013/1.

business reply mail A type of return mail that enables the recipient of direct-mail advertising to respond without paying postage.

folders Large, heavy-stock fliers, often folded and sent out as self-mailers.

brochures Sales materials printed on heavier paper and featuring color photographs, illustrations, and typography.

Types of Direct-Mail Advertising

Direct-mail advertising comes in a variety of formats, from handwritten postcards to **dimensional direct mail**, utilizing three-dimensional shapes and unusual materials. The message can be one sentence or dozens of pages. And within each format—from tiny coupon to thick catalog or box—the creative options are infinite. In 2003, the United States Postal Service approved Customized Market-Mail (CMM), a new class of mail that gives direct-mail advertisers the opportunity to truly innovate. The new regulations allow for pieces of mail of almost any shape, within certain dimensions, to be sent without an envelope. No longer limited to rectangles, direct mail can now take more novel, eye-catching forms. From simple geometric shapes, like circles, to more curious and bizarre shapes, like Zambonis (used by First Tennessee Bank to promote a checking account associated with a local hockey team), CMM stands out in a sea of mail that might otherwise go directly into the trash.[40] In addition to the dimensional direct-mail category are the following:

E-mail, as mentioned in Chapter 12, is an important tool in direct marketing and is best used for customer retention and relationship management. It is most effective when the marketer first seeks *permission* to mail. In other words, advertisers should always give people the opportunity to opt in and to opt out of their e-mail programs. For new business acquisition, the best use is in a viral marketing campaign—otherwise it will probably be perceived as spam.

Sales letters, the most common direct-mail format, are often mailed with brochures, price lists, or reply cards and envelopes.

Mail-order catalogs are big business. They also help support retailers' stores and websites. Hammacher Schlemmer is America's longest running catalog. More than 30 million copies are mailed each year, generating an estimated 70 percent of the company's revenues, with the remainder coming from online sales and the retail location in New York City.

Direct-mail advertising can be very targeted and personal. Universities attempt to attract the smartest applicants by sending highly personalized postcards to top-performing high school students across the country.

Postcards are used to announce sales, offer discounts, or generate customer traffic. National postal services regulate formats and dimensions. Some advertisers use a double postcard, enabling them to send both an advertising message and a perforated reply card. To encourage response, some advertisers use **business reply mail** so the recipient can respond without paying postage. On receiving a response, the advertiser pays postage plus a handling fee of a few cents.

Folders and **brochures** are usually printed in multiple colors with photos or other illustrations on good paper stock.

broadsides A form of direct-mail advertisement, larger than a folder and sometimes used as a window display or wall poster in stores. It can be folded to a compact size and inserted into a mailer.

self-mailers Any type of direct-mail piece that can travel by mail without an envelope. Usually folded and secured by a staple or a seal, self-mailers have a special blank space for the prospect's name and address.

statement stuffers Advertisements enclosed in the monthly customer statements mailed by department stores, banks, utilities, or oil companies.

house organs Internal and external publications produced by business organizations, including stockholder reports, newsletters, consumer magazines, and dealer publications. Most are produced by a company's advertising or public relations department or by its agency.

catalogs Reference books mailed to prospective customers that list, describe, and often picture the products sold by a manufacturer, wholesaler, jobber, or retailer.

> "THE MAILING LIST IS RESPONSIBLE FOR UP TO 60 PERCENT OF THE SUCCESS OF A MAILING."

Broadsides are larger than folders and are sometimes used as window displays or wall posters in stores. They fold to a compact size to fit in a mailbag.

Self-mailers are any form of direct mail that can travel without an envelope. Usually folded and secured by a staple or seal, they have special blank spaces for the prospect's name and address.

Statement stuffers are ads enclosed in monthly customer statements from department stores, banks, oil companies, and the like. To order, customers write in their credit card number and sign the reply card.

House organs are publications produced by associations or business organizations—for example, shareholder reports, newsletters, and dealer publications.

Catalogs are reference books that list, describe, and often picture the products sold by a manufacturer, wholesaler, or retailer. With more high-income families shopping at home, specialized catalogs have become very popular.

Some catalog retailers prosper with specialized approaches like lifestyle clothing (L.L.Bean, Anthropologie, Lands' End), electronic gadgets (Sharper Image), and gourmet foods (Dean & Deluca).

Despite the growth of online catalogs on e-commerce, printed catalogs remain a big business. More than 12 billion catalogs were mailed in 2012. However, due largely to rising postage costs, that figure is down from 18 billion only four years earlier. Over 8,000 catalog companies have disappeared in recent years. But catalogs remain popular. Printed catalogs are tactile; unlike electronic catalogs, you can hold them in your hands, mark them up, fold over their page corners, and put them down and pick them up later.

Not too long ago, most catalog orders were transacted by mail or telephone. Some customers would visit a store (such as Sears) or order from a local representative (like the Avon lady). Now, a great many catalog orders are placed on Internet websites. People read a catalog, decide what they want, and then go online to place the order. Most catalogs are mailed monthly, more frequently around the holidays, and there's usually a spike on the website right after print catalogs are delivered.[41]

It doesn't appear that printed catalogs are going to disappear soon. The best marketers use catalogs, the Internet, and retail stores synergistically, to complement one another and maximize sales.

Using Direct Mail in the Media Mix

Direct mail is an efficient, effective, and economical medium for sales and business promotion (see My Ad Campaign 13–C, "The Pros and Cons of Direct-Mail Advertising"). That's why it's used by a wide variety of companies, charity and service organizations, and individuals. Direct mail can increase the effectiveness of ads in other media. For example, Publishers Clearinghouse typically uses TV spots to alert viewers to the impending arrival of its direct-mail sweepstakes promotions.

Direct mail has two main drawbacks: cost and the "junk mail" image, both of which are almost inescapable. No other medium (except personal selling and consumer targeting on the Internet) has such a high cost per thousand. For this reason, many small advertisers participate in cooperative (rather than solo) mailings with companies such as ADVO, which serves most major U.S. cities. ADVO mails an envelope containing a coupon for each participating company to targeted zip codes.

Some large advertisers don't send unsolicited mail. To locate prospects, they use other direct-response media such as advertising with toll-free "800" numbers or soliciting inquiries on the Internet. Then they use direct mail to respond to those inquiries. They save money by mailing only to qualified prospects, and by sending higher-quality materials, they build their image and improve their chances of establishing a worthwhile relationship.

check yourself ✓

1. Why is Customized Market-Mail (CMM) a benefit to direct-mail advertisers?
2. What are some ways that direct mail could be effectively used in conjunction with other elements of the media mix?

LO13-5 Describe the basic components of direct-mail advertising.

Components of Direct-Mail Advertising

The three basic components of direct-mail advertising are the mailing list, the offer, and the creative package. Direct-mail experts say the mailing list is responsible for up to 60 percent of the success of a mailing. The offer is good for 25 percent of a mailing's success and the creative package is worth 15 percent. Many advertisers focus too much time and money developing the creative side of a mailing but give insufficient attention to the actual lists.

house list A company's most important and valuable direct-mail list, which may contain current, recent, and long-past customers or future prospects.

Acquiring Direct-Mail Lists

The heart of any direct-mail program is the mailing list. Each list actually defines a market segment. Direct-mail advertisers use three types of lists: *house, mail-response,* and *compiled.*

House lists. The company's database of current, recent, and long-past customers as well as identified prospects comprises the **house list** for direct-mail programs. Because customers are its most important asset, every company should focus sufficient resources on developing a rich database of customer and prospect information and profiles. There are several ways a company can build its own house list.

Consumer product companies like General Electric gather customer data by enclosing an owner registration form with their

The Pros and Cons of Direct-Mail Advertising [13–C]

The Pros

- **Selectivity.** Direct mail helps advertisers communicate directly with the people most likely to buy. Computerized mailing lists group people by occupation, region or state, income, and other characteristics.
- **Intensive coverage and extensive reach.** Everyone has a mailbox. With direct mail, an advertiser can reach 100 percent of the homes in a given area.
- **Flexibility.** Direct-mail advertising can be uniquely creative, limited only by the advertiser's ingenuity and budget and postal regulations. Advertisers can produce direct-mail pieces fast and distribute them quickly.
- **Control.** Preprinted direct-mail pieces enable an advertiser to precisely control circulation and reproduction quality.
- **Personal impact.** Advertisers can personalize direct mail to the needs, wants, and whims of specific audiences without offending other prospects or customers.
- **Exclusivity.** There are no distractions from competitive ads (in solo mailings).
- **Response.** Direct mail achieves the highest response of any advertising medium. About 15 percent of the responses arrive within the first week, so the advertiser can quickly judge a campaign's success.
- **Testability.** Direct mail is good for testing prospect reactions to products, pricing, promotions, copy approaches, sales literature, and so on.

The Cons

- **High cost per exposure.** Direct mail has the highest cost per exposure of any major medium, about 14 times as much as most magazine and newspaper advertising.
- **Delivery problems.** The mass media offer precise delivery times, but the postal service makes no delivery commitments on third-class mail. And up to 10 percent of mailings may be undeliverable because people move.
- **Lack of content support.** Direct mail must capture and hold the reader's attention without the support of editorial or entertainment content.
- **Selectivity problems.** Effective direct mail depends on correctly identifying the target audience and obtaining a good list. Some groups of prospects, such as physicians, are so saturated with direct mail they ignore it.
- **Negative attitudes.** Many consumers think of direct mail as junk mail and automatically throw it away. This may also negatively impact the product's image.
- **Environmental concerns.** Some consumers see direct mail as landfill fodder. Some direct marketers (Eddie Bauer, L.L.Bean) print parts of their catalogs on recycled paper, and now new de-inking facilities will make more catalogs recyclable.
- **Antispam laws.** The CAN-SPAM Act and similar laws impose many requirements, making it more difficult for marketers to electronically send prospective clients unsolicited marketing materials.

mail-response lists A type of direct-mail list, composed of people who have responded to the direct-mail solicitations of other companies, especially those whose efforts are complementary to the advertiser's.

compiled lists A type of direct-mail list that has been compiled by another source, such as lists of automobile owners, new home purchasers, business owners, union members, and so forth. It is the most readily available type of list but offers the lowest response rate.

list broker An intermediary who handles rental of mailing lists for list owners on a commission basis.

products. On the mail-in form, purchasers give their name, address, phone number, birth date, occupation, income range, home ownership status, and number of children. They also indicate their hobbies and interests (such as golf, foreign travel, photography, or bowling). Companies use this information for their own mailings and sell it to other direct-mail advertisers.

Mail-response lists. The advertiser's second most important prospects are people who respond to direct-mail pieces from other companies—especially those with complementary products or services. **Mail-response lists** are the house lists of other direct-mail advertisers, and they can be rented with a wide variety of demographic breakdowns.

Compiled lists. The most readily available lists are those that some entity compiles for a different reason and then rents or sells—for example, lists of car owners, new-home purchasers, business owners, and so on. **Compiled lists** typically offer the lowest response rate, so experts suggest using numerous sources, merging them on computer with mail-response and house lists, and then purging them of duplicate names.[42]

Kantar Media SRDS, the direct marketing database of SRDS.com, published by Kantar Media, is the leading provider of media rates for advertisers. The SRDS Direct Marketing List Source® provides sources, costs and other valuable information to help find and evaluate lists for direct marketing campaigns.

Direct-mail lists can be bought or rented. Purchased lists can be used without limit; rented lists may be used for a single mailing only. List owners plant decoy names in the list to be sure renters don't use it more than once.

Some list owners pay a **list broker** a commission (usually 20 percent) to handle the rental details. The advertiser, in turn, benefits from the broker's knowledge of list quality without having to pay more than the rental cost.

Lists can be tailored to reflect customer location (zip code); demographics such as age, income, and home ownership; or psychographic characteristics such as personality and lifestyle. The SRDS *Direct Marketing List Source* contains more than 70,000 list selections in 230 consumer and business classifications.

Mailing list prices vary according to the accuracy and currency of the data. Consumer list rental rates average $74 per thousand names but can be as little as $35 per thousand or as much as $400 per thousand. The more stringent the advertiser's selection criteria, the more expensive the list. An extra $10 per thousand is often well worth the savings in mailers and postage that would otherwise be wasted.

letter shop A firm that stuffs envelopes, affixes labels, calculates postage, sorts pieces into stacks or bundles, and otherwise prepares items for mailing.

promotional products Useful or decorative articles of merchandise, usually imprinted with a company's name, logo, or message, that are utilized in marketing communications programs.

advertising specialties Promotional products that are distributed free.

The average mailing list changes more than 40 percent a year as people relocate, change jobs, get married, or die. So mailing lists must be continually updated *(cleaned)* to be sure they're current and correct. Advertisers can also test the validity and accuracy of a given list. They rent or buy every *n*th name and send a mailer to that person. If the results are favorable, they purchase additional names, usually in lots of 1,000.

[The direct mail offer] should give the prospect a reason to act NOW.

Developing the Offer Every direct-mail package should contain an offer. The offer is the incentive or reward that motivates prospects to respond to a mailing, either with an order or with a request for more information. To be effective, an offer must be clear and specific, it must offer value to the potential customer, it must be believable, and it must be easy to acquire. The more difficult it is for prospects to respond to an offer, the lower the response rate will be. The direct-mail package should provide clear instructions, a conspicuous address (mailing and Internet), and a toll-free phone number.

The offer should promote a benefit that will address a prospect's needs. It should clearly explain why this mail is being sent to this prospect at this time. In other words, there should be a *call to action:* What does the advertiser want the recipient to do when he or she receives the mail? And finally, it should give the prospect a reason to act NOW.

Creating, Producing, and Distributing the Package To create a direct-mail package, the advertiser may use in-house staff, an ad agency, or a freelance designer and writer. Some agencies specialize in direct mail.

The direct-mail piece normally goes through the same production process as any other print piece. The size and shape of the mailing package, as well as the type, illustrations, and colors, all affect printing costs. Special features such as simulated blue-ink signatures, cardboard pop-ups, and die-cutting (the cutting of paper stock into an unusual shape) add to the cost. But the larger the printing volume, or run, the lower the printing cost per unit.

Remaining production and handling tasks can be done by a local **letter shop** (or *mailing house*), or the advertiser can do them internally. On a cost-per-thousand basis, letter shops stuff and seal envelopes, affix labels, calculate postage, and sort, tie, and stack the mailers. Some shops also offer creative services. If the advertiser is using third-class bulk mail, the letter shop separates mailers by zip code and ties them into bundles to qualify for low bulk rates. Then the letter shop delivers the mailers to the post office.

Distribution costs are based chiefly on the weight of the mailer and the delivery method. U.S. advertisers can use the U.S. Postal Service, air freight, or private delivery services like UPS and FedEx. The most common, the U.S. Postal Service, offers several types of delivery.

check yourself ✓

1. Why is the house list typically the most effective direct-mail list?
2. What is meant by a "call to action" in every direct-mail package?

LO13-6 Explain the value of promotional products.

PROMOTIONAL PRODUCTS

The Promotional Products Association International (PPAI) says that **promotional products**—usually imprinted with a company's name, logo, or message—include useful or decorative articles of merchandise that are utilized in marketing communications programs. Imprinted products that are distributed free are called **advertising specialties**.[43] Today, nearly

premiums Imprinted promotional items that are given as an incentive for a specific action.

every business uses promotional products of some sort. As many as 15,000 different items, ranging from coffee mugs to ballpoint pens, key chains, and T-shirts, represent an annual volume of nearly $18.5 billion. The largest product category for promotional items is *wearables,* which include T-shirts, golf shirts, aprons, uniforms, jackets, caps, footwear, and the like, which make up nearly 30 percent of the total. Other popular categories include writing instruments (9.0 percent), bags (7.2 percent), calendars (6.9 percent), drinkware (6.7 percent), and desk and office accessories (6.0 percent).[44]

Promotional products are effective tools for improving people's perception and recollection of a business. They are often distributed in association with trade shows, public relations programs, employee events, new product introductions, or brand-building programs. Some promotional items may be kept for years and serve as continuous, friendly reminders of the advertiser's business. In fact, 58 percent of the recipients keep these gifts for at least a year. Companies often spend substantial sums for goodwill items to promote their businesses, and studies indicate that this investment pays off. Nearly 90 percent of recipients could recall the name of the advertiser on a promotional item they received in the past 24 months.[45]

Almost every business uses promotional products, and almost any item can be imprinted with a company's advertising message and logo.

Premiums are also promotional products; they are typically more valuable and usually bear no advertising message. However, to get a premium, recipients must buy a product, send in a coupon, witness a demonstration, or perform some other action advantageous to the advertiser.

Business-to-Business Specialties In the business-to-business arena, companies use more structured specialty promotions to improve their goodwill standing over competitors. In one case, including an ad specialty with a thank-you letter improved customer attitude by 34 percent compared to sending a thank-you letter alone. At the same time, customers' general feelings about the company and its sales reps improved 52 percent.[46]

In one test, a group of realtors received a $1.49 ballpoint pen imprinted with a mortgage company's name, a second group received a $10 sports bag (also imprinted), and a third group got nothing. In a follow-up questionnaire, realtors who received nothing were least inclined to recommend the product, but both the sports bag and ballpoint groups responded equally positively. Evidently, gift recipients felt obliged to reciprocate, but the value of the gift was not crucial. So the $1.49 pen offered the better return on investment.

Inappropriate specialty items can backfire no matter what the cost. A recipient may perceive an overly expensive gift as a form of bribery, yet a cheap trinket could make a quality-conscious business look cheap. Finally, marketers should realize that the value and nature of gifts may raise ethical issues. ■

check yourself ✓

1. What is the difference between a promotional product and a premium?
2. How might a business-to-business gift raise ethical issues?

learn about, practice, and apply the use of out-of-home, direct mail, and specialty advertising!

M: Advertising was developed for students who want information packaged in a concise, easy-to-read, yet interesting format.

Check out the book's website to:

- Learn why outdoor advertising is referred to as the last mass medium. (Review Questions)
- Discover what factors can make a direct-mail campaign successful. (Review Questions)
- Learn how direct-mail advertisers got your name on their mailing lists. (Exploring Advertising)

While you are there, check out the professional resource links, review the PowerPoint presentation, and test your knowledge with the Multiple Choice Quiz. Additionally, *Connect® Marketing* is available for M: Advertising.

www.mhhe.com/ArensM2e

media planning and buying

chapter fourteen

This chapter shows how communications media help advertisers achieve marketing and advertising objectives. To get their messages to the right people in the right place at the right time, media planners follow the same procedures as marketing and advertising planners: setting objectives, formulating strategies, and devising tactics. To make sound decisions, media planners must possess marketing savvy, analytical skill, and creativity.

People love smartphones, or at least that is what the long lines and sold-out inventory of new iPhones at Apple stores in November of 2013 would suggest.

continued on p. 344

LEARNING OBJECTIVES

After studying this chapter, you will be able to:

- **LO14-1** Describe how media planning has changed and what has caused these changes.
- **LO14-2** Discuss the types of media objectives and identify the strategies for achieving these objectives.
- **LO14-3** Identify the factors that influence media strategy and tactics.
- **LO14-4** Articulate what is meant by "the art of media planning."
- **LO14-5** Describe different types of advertising schedules and the purpose for each.
- **LO14-6** Explain the role of the media buyer.

EMAIL

NEWSGROUP

OPTIMIZATION

ADVERTISING

H ENGINE

L MEDIA

ATE MARKETING

continued from p. 343

It was not always so. When MIT asked people in 2004 to name the invention that you hate the most but can't live without, standing at the top of the list was the mobile phone, easily outscoring the alarm clock. Users doubtless liked that mobile phones helped for staying in touch with family, friends, customers, and coworkers. But back then the phones were not always easy to use. And they often weren't much fun either.

So back in 2007, when then CEO Steve Jobs announced that Apple had reinvented the phone, people took notice. For many, the marriage of mobile phone utility and Apple's skill at designing products with both beautiful form and function seemed irresistible. When it finally arrived, critics and consumers alike agreed that the iPhone lived up to the hype.

Consumers weren't the only ones excited about the iPhone. Advertisers were too. But for them, it wasn't the hardware that was so exciting. It was software.

To see why this is so, do a thought experiment. Ask yourself, from an advertiser's perspective, what would the ideal medium look like? Several criteria come to mind. Lots of people should use the medium and they should spend a lot of time with it. And people should interact with the medium throughout the day, not just in the morning (as they do with newspapers) or evening (as they do with television). The ideal medium would allow people to use coupons (like newspapers) but also view video (like TV) and hear sound (like radio). The medium should be responsive and interactive, allowing consumers to find out more about an advertiser's product if they wish (like the Web). The medium should allow advertisers to track what people are doing with their ads (like direct response advertising). Since we are just dreaming, why not add that the medium should be able to draw people a map so they can find the product. And when they find it, the medium should let the consumer post a picture of it in Instagram and send tweets to all of his or her friends about how much they like it.

Sound like any medium you know? Actually, the only medium that can accomplish all of these things, at least for now, is the smart phone.

Many people bring (and use) their phones in places they would never think to bring other media. For example, one survey suggests that most Americans consider it acceptable to use mobile phones in the supermarket and just under half think it is fine to use them while riding on public transportation. One out of five believes it is OK to use mobile phones in a restaurant. And nearly 4 out of 10 say it is acceptable to use the phone in the bathroom. The bottom line: Many people spend more time with their phones than with any other thing, person, or place.

So how do advertisers take advantage of the greatest medium ever created? As a device that serves web content, the iPhone offers advertisers every channel available on desktops: search ads in Google, social ads in Facebook, promoted tweets in Twitter, display ads in magazines, and so forth. And because people are spending more time accessing the web on their phones, and less on computers, mobile advertising is growing at an astounding rate. To give just one example, nearly half of Facebook's advertising in 2013 comes from mobile ads. And while not all mobile ads use Apple's iOS, Apple does have an impressive 44.0 share of market in impressions and 50% share of ad revenue.

Apple also offers an easy way for advertisers to use behavioral tracking. You may recall from Chapter 12 that a consumer's Internet activities can be (anonymously) tracked as he or she goes from site to site, leaving a trail of rich data behind. Apple's iPhone 5s uses a system called IDFA to track page visits and serve relevant ads. IFDA, not coincidentally, stands for "Identifier For Advertisers."

Finally, there are the apps. For hundreds of thousands of developers, the phone offers a new and exciting opportunity for revenue via applications sold (or available free) through Apple's store. In 2012, Apple's iOS and Android generated revenue, via both app sales and advertising, of nearly $9 billion. The portion of that number from ad revenue is much smaller than that from app purchases, but the trend is moving strongly in the direction of advertising. Why? Consumers like their apps free, and seem more willing than ever to "put up with" in-app ads.

As we've noted elsewhere, Jobs was a game-changer in many areas; computers, music, tablets, software, and movie animation come to mind. But for marketers, it may be that no Jobs innovation is more profound than the iPhone.

Of course sometimes being first out of the gate doesn't mean success will last forever. Apple may one day soon lose its market share lead to Android, just as Ford, America's first car company, eventually fell to second place in U.S. market share to G.M. But Henry Ford is man we remember as the inventor of the automobile industry. In similar fashion, we should remember Steve Jobs as the man who created the perfect advertising medium. ■

LO14-1 Describe how media planning has changed and what has caused these changes.

MEDIA PLANNING: INTEGRATING SCIENCE WITH CREATIVITY IN ADVERTISING

The purpose of **media planning** is to conceive, analyze, and creatively select channels of communication that will direct advertising messages to the right people in the right place at the right time. The Media Edge believes that "anything you put your message on is media." That includes shopping bags, book covers, and parking meters. As a result, media planning today involves many decisions. For example,

- Where should we advertise? (In what countries, states, or parts of town?)
- Which media vehicles reach and engage our target markets?
- When during the year should we concentrate our advertising?
- How often should we run the advertising?
- What opportunities exist for integrating our advertising with other communication tools?

media planning
The process that directs advertising messages to the right people in the right place at the right time.

Some of these decisions require research and detailed mathematical analysis, aided by sophisticated computer software programs.

The Challenge

Historically, the people who plan and buy media have enjoyed relative anonymity compared to the "stars" in the creative departments. Today the media planner's assignment is just as critical as the creative director's: One media planner can be responsible for millions of client dollars. The planner's work attests to an agency's strategic ability to negotiate the best prices and use effectively the incredible array of media choices.

Jack Klues, when he was the director of U.S. media services for Leo Burnett USA, said, "Our mission is to buy and plan media so effectively that our clients obtain an unfair advantage versus their competitors."[1]

The media department gained new prominence in the 1990s when clients started taking an à la carte approach to agency services, and agencies began competing for media planning assignments.[2] By the early 2000s, media wins were big news: Universal McCann won the $150 million Nestlé account; Gillette awarded its $600 million media account to Mindshare; and Kraft consolidated its $800 million media business at Starcom MediaVest Group.[3]

With greater complexity, media decisions become more critical and clients more demanding. Advertisers want agencies to be more than efficient. They want accountability and information, particularly about media options. And they want creative buys.

What makes media planning today so much more complicated and challenging than it was just a few years ago?

Increasing Media Options There are many more media to choose from today, and each offers more choices. It wasn't long ago that major advertisers could ensure a big audience by simply advertising on TV. Not anymore. Today it's much more difficult to reach a big audience. Consider that in 1960, the top-rated TV show (*Gunsmoke*) was viewed in over 40 percent of U.S. households. By comparison, the top show in the fall of 2012 (*Sunday Night Football*) was watched in under 8 percent of U.S. households.[4]

The reason for this decline is that TV is now fragmented into network, syndicated, spot, and local television, as well as network and local cable. Specialized magazines now aim at every population and business segment. Even national magazines publish editions for particular regions or demographic groups. Finally, the incredible growth of the Web and social media has brought a host of new options. But it has also added to the complexity of media work as planners face the challenge of staying current with the constantly expanding technology and mastering a whole new vocabulary.

Nontraditional media—which can include mobile media, apps, cinema advertising, and product placement—also expand the

Effective media professionals don't just rely on traditional ad space to communicate a message. In this execution, HBO media planners negotiated for space on the side of a building.

menu of choices. In addition, many companies spend a considerable portion of their marketing budgets on specialized communications like direct marketing, sales promotion, public relations activities, and personal selling, topics we'll discuss in the next two chapters (see Exhibit 14–1). In fact, these "below-the-line" (noncommissionable) activities are the fastest-growing segments at some of the large agency holding companies, like WPP and Interpublic.

job. Readers and viewers have scattered across the new media options, selectively reading only parts of magazines or newspapers, watching only segments of programs, and listening to many different radio stations. This makes it very difficult to find the prospect. Consumers spend an average of 12 hours per day with media—but an increasing proportion of that time is spent with less traditional media vehicles.[5]

For companies practicing IMC, the "media menu" needs to include everything that carries a message to and/or from customers and other stakeholders. The proliferation of toll-free phone numbers, e-mail, and websites makes it easy and cost-effective to facilitate customer feedback. The result is that advertisers can be very creative in designing systems for both sending and receiving messages. That means that companies and agencies need to think in terms of message handling, being as responsible for receiving messages as for sending them.

Increasing Fragmentation of the Audience Further evidence of the maturing marketplace is the fragmentation of the media audience. This also complicates the media planner's

▼**EXHIBIT 14–1** 2013 U.S. advertising (blue) and marketing and communications (red) spending by channel ($ millions).

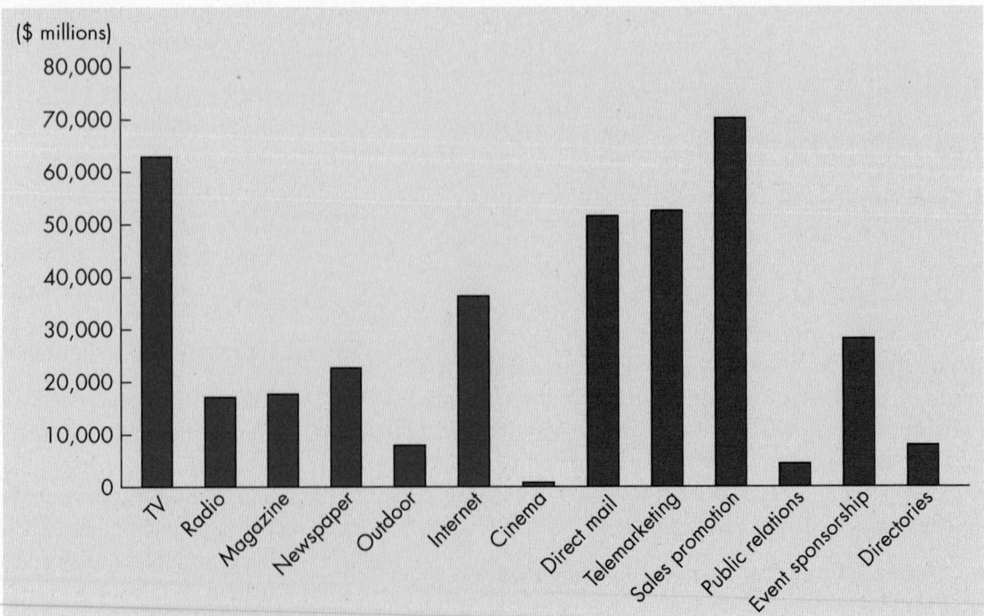

Source: AdAge.com DataCenter. Measured-media spending by medium from WPP's Kantar Media. More info: kantarmediana.com. Network TV includes Spanish-language networks. Local newspaper includes Spanish-language newspapers. Consumer magazine includes Spanish-language magazines. Unmeasured spending is estimated by *Ad Age*.

Increasing Costs While there are more media choices, the number of messages that need to be communicated has also grown—so much so, in fact, that they have outstripped the ability of consumers to process them. People can cope with only so many messages, so media restrict the number of ads they sell. As a result, the costs are increasing for almost all media. In the last decade, the cost of exposing 1,000 people to each of the major media (cost per thousand) rose faster than inflation. Shows that can deliver a big audience are sold at a premium. To take one example, consider Exhibit 14–2, which tracks statistics for the "average" network TV show from 1965 through 2013. The number of households watching the average show has been in steady decline since the early 1980s. But the cost of a 30-second ad for that show has held steady, resulting in a much higher cost per household. The cost of an average TV ad? Well over $100,000.[6] Rising costs make media planning more challenging than ever, especially for advertisers with small budgets. Clients want proof that planners are squeezing the most they can out of every media dollar.

▼**EXHIBIT 14–2** Metrics for the "average network TV primetime show," 1965 through 2013.

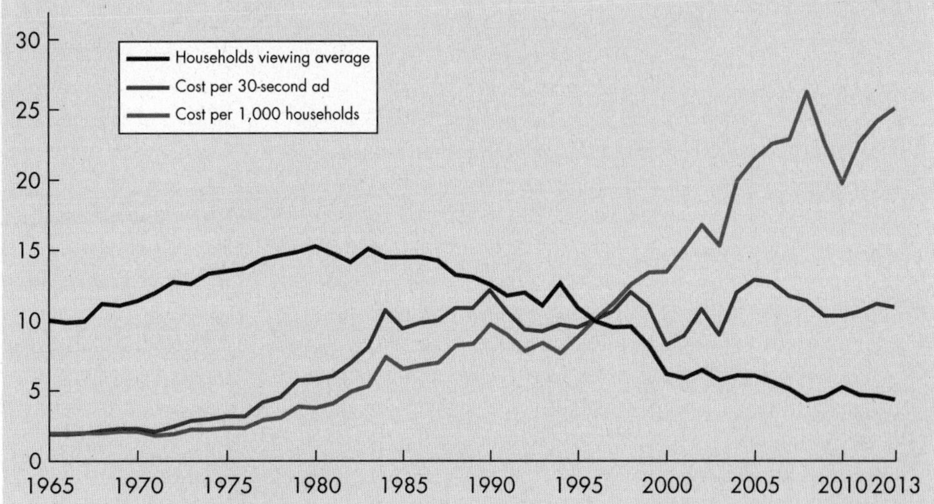

Blue line indicates average number of households (millions) viewing "typical" show. Red line indicates absolute cost (ten thousands) of a 30-second ad. Green line shows cost per 1,000 homes of an ad in a "typical" show.

Source: www.tvb.org/trends/4718/4709.

Increasing Complexity in Media Buying and Selling As the process of buying media has become more complex, so has the process of selling media. In the battle for additional sales, many print and broadcast media companies developed "value-added" programs to provide extra benefits. Besides selling space or time, these companies now offer reprints, merchandising services, special sections, event sponsorships, and mailing lists. To get a bigger share of the advertiser's budget, larger media companies bundle the various stations, publications, or properties they own and offer them in integrated combinations as further incentives.

The Discovery Network, for example, which includes the Travel Channel, TLC, Animal Planet, Discovery, Discovery Health, and the Science Channel, offers its advertisers "multiplatform convergence content sponsorships." This means that each advertiser gets a major Internet/TV sponsorship with four or five commercials in a special-event Discovery show and webcast. Specially created TV spots promote the program and the webcast, as well as Discovery's website and the advertiser's website. Moreover, advertisers get additional off-air exposure in hundreds of Discovery Network retail stores nationwide, which also run in-store videos promoting the shows and the sponsors.[7]

The sports fan's perennial heckle, "Come on, ref, do you need glasses?" has finally been answered. Specsavers, a Scottish optical care provider and retailer, has begun to sponsor soccer referees. In addition to providing eye exams and optical eyewear for referees, the company outfits them and advertises in stadiums. The media mix for the campaign combined the clever sponsorship with point-of-sale advertising and newspaper-friendly press releases. As the 22 percent increase in sales shows, Specsavers has positioned itself squarely in Scottish men's field of vision.

IMC and relationship marketing are creating a new breed of media planner: younger, computer-savvy, and schooled in new media. The good media specialist today is actually a real advertising generalist. Media professionals have finally come into their own.

Increasing Competition The final element making media planning more challenging is the competitive environment, which in just a few years has completely changed the structure of the advertising business. In the 1990s, as clients sought greater efficiency with their media dollars, independent media buying services came into the fore, attracting some of the best and brightest talent in the business to compete with agencies for what was once their private domain. Initially, the independents bought advertising at lower bulk rates and then sold it for a commission to advertisers or agencies lacking a fully staffed media department. As the media specialists grew, though, clients came to realize the virtues of scale,

Meet Social Media and the Web

What happens when unregulated meets anonymous?

Welcome to public relations in the Internet age.

PR practitioner Todd DeFren raises several real-world digital public relations ethical issues in his blog "PRsquared." In one, Defren asked "What would you do if a client contact—who had a pretty solid Twitter following—asked you to tweet from his account as if you were him? Crazy? Wrong? Unethical?"

Defren raises the same issue about a corporate blog. He refers to the practice of a PR agency writing unattributed posts for a client as "ghostblogging." "You can rail against it as a black mark against authenticity," notes Defren, "but, it is happening and it is a trend that will only grow. Not enough people see this as a bright line separating 'good' from 'bad' . . ."

And speaking of blogs, how ethical is it to pay people to give a brand or company favorable coverage? The site "payperpost.com" en-courages visitors to "Make money blogging! PayPerPost lets you pick your advertisers, name your own price and negotiate your own deals. You can get paid to blog on virtually any subject. Sign up below!" How credible would you find such posts if you knew they were sponsored?

Even big brands are getting in on the game. Coach collaborates with bloggers, even asking them to appear in its ad campaigns. WWD.com quotes David Duplantis, executive VP of global and digital media as saying "We see bloggers as editors, influencers and entrepreneurs who reach a very specific and unique audience. We find great value in working with those who are relevant to our brand, and are willing to pay fairly for projects." Duplantis believes that while Coach benefits from bloggers, the bloggers in turn benefit from working with a brand as important as Coach. But how do consumers benefit if they are unaware of a brand-blogger relationship?

The analyst firm Forrester thinks it's smart for companies to pay bloggers to engage in "sponsored conversations." Marshall Kirkpatrick at ReadWriteWeb.com disagrees, noting "We respectfully disagree with Forrester's recommendations on this topic. In fact, we think that paying bloggers to write about your company is a dangerous and unsavory path for new media and advertisers to go down."

Maybe all of this has convinced you that if you are looking for advice, you might want to skip blogs. Better to use a search engine, like Google, that can deliver search results that reflect the wisdom of millions of consumers. But what if a company tried to take advantage of Google's search engine? JC Penney decided it would try. Thousands of fake pages were created featuring key words valuable to the store. The initiative was designed to take advantage of Google's PageRank system and send shoppers to Penney's website. Not illegal, certainly. But ethical? Google eventually intervened and made it less likely Penney's results would show up in "organic" search.

But if Google polices Penney's, who polices Google? The company admitted that it paid bloggers to promote its Chrome browser. Dailytech.com reported that Google indicated it had "investigated" and that it would be "taking manual action to demote https://www.google.com/intl/en/chrome/browser/ and lower the site's PageRank for a period of at least 60 days." Maybe all of this seems so frustrating to you that you've resolved to stick to Twitter, where at least you can judge a source's credibility by observing the number of followers that the individual or group has. After all, millions of followers can't be wrong. Unfortunately, the number of "followers" of a Twitter source may be very misleading, because sources can actually buy followers. The New York Times and USA Today reported recently that up to 70 percent of Barack Obama's followers, and 71 percent of Lady Gaga's, are "fake" or "inactive."

The Web is an evolving medium, and companies are searching for ways to profit from it. The history of advertising suggests that consumers will reject companies that try to take advantage of them unfairly, unethically, or dishonestly. That is something every brand manager might want to keep in mind.

Questions

1. Do any of the activities described above strike you as unethical? Why?
2. Do you agree that consumers will not long stand for deceptive or underhanded practices? That actions, both corporate and governmental, will evolve if consumers lose faith in social media and the Web as sources of marketing information?

Source: For more information visit Todd Defren's blog at: http://www.pr-squared.com/index.php/2010/02/guess-whos-talking-social-media-ethical-dilemmas, and Marshall Kirkpatrick at http://www.readwriteweb.com/archives/forrester_is_wrong_about_payin.php. Austin Considine, "Buying their way to Twitter fame," http://www.nytimes.com/2012/08/23/fashion/twitter-followers-for-sale.html.

and financial clout emerged as a potent weapon in negotiating media buys.[8]

In response, ad agencies unbundled their media departments, setting them up as subsidiaries like Starcom USA, the largest U.S. media agency. These companies compete with the independents as well as with other agencies for media-only accounts. Their expertise and buying clout has led to a surge in billings, which in turn has funded the development of new research tools, critical given the continued fragmentation of the mass media into smaller and smaller niches.

The Role of Media in the Marketing Framework

As we've discussed, the key to successful advertising is proper planning. Thus, before media planning begins companies must first establish their overall marketing and advertising plans.

The top-down marketing plan defines the market need and the company's sales objectives and details strategies for attaining those objectives. Exhibit 14–3 shows how objectives and strategies of a marketing plan result from the marketing situation

EXHIBIT 14-3 This diagram shows how media objectives, strategies, and plans result from the marketing and advertising plans.

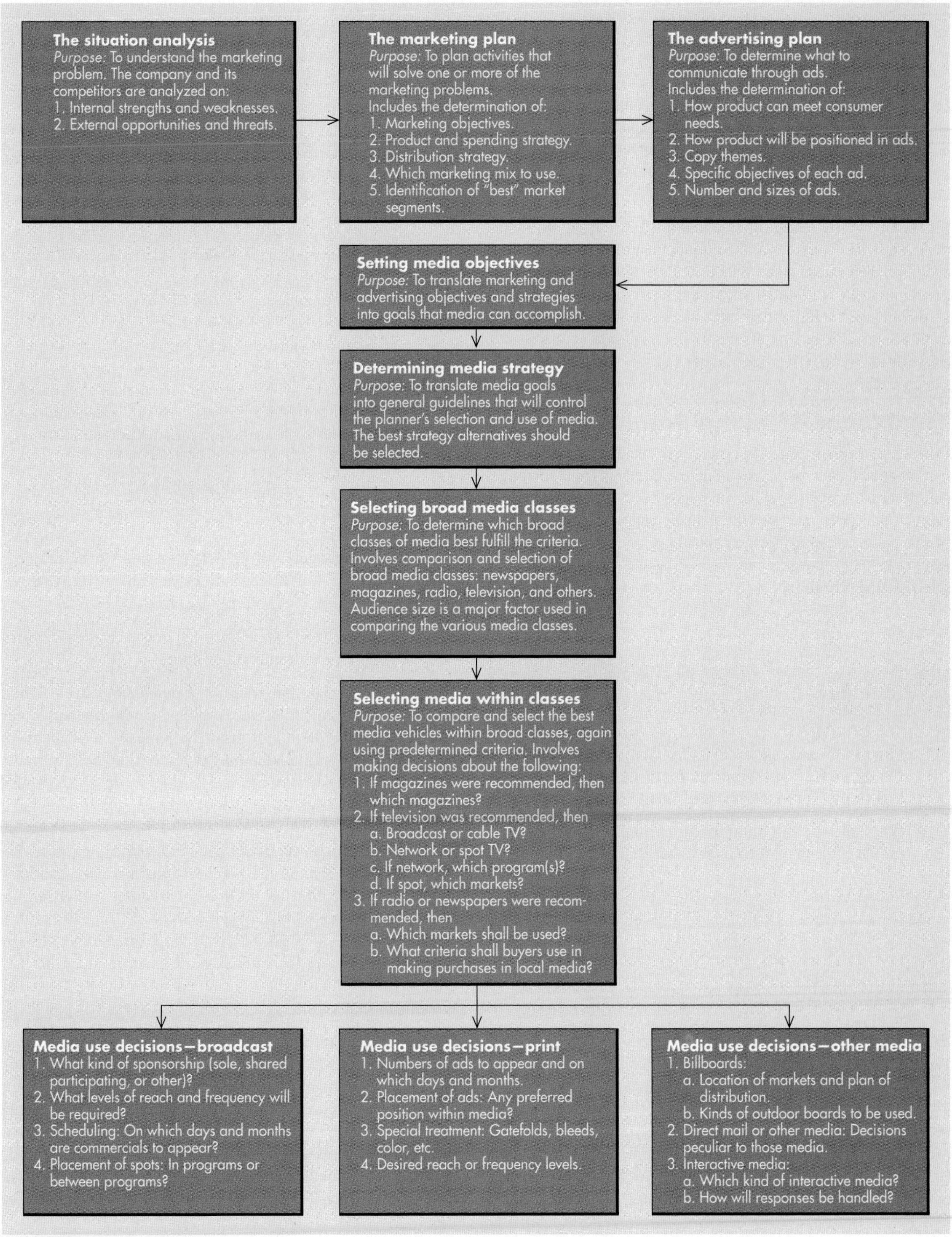

The situation analysis
Purpose: To understand the marketing problem. The company and its competitors are analyzed on:
1. Internal strengths and weaknesses.
2. External opportunities and threats.

→

The marketing plan
Purpose: To plan activities that will solve one or more of the marketing problems.
Includes the determination of:
1. Marketing objectives.
2. Product and spending strategy.
3. Distribution strategy.
4. Which marketing mix to use.
5. Identification of "best" market segments.

→

The advertising plan
Purpose: To determine what to communicate through ads.
Includes the determination of:
1. How product can meet consumer needs.
2. How product will be positioned in ads.
3. Copy themes.
4. Specific objectives of each ad.
5. Number and sizes of ads.

↓

Setting media objectives
Purpose: To translate marketing and advertising objectives and strategies into goals that media can accomplish.

↓

Determining media strategy
Purpose: To translate media goals into general guidelines that will control the planner's selection and use of media. The best strategy alternatives should be selected.

↓

Selecting broad media classes
Purpose: To determine which broad classes of media best fulfill the criteria. Involves comparison and selection of broad media classes: newspapers, magazines, radio, television, and others. Audience size is a major factor used in comparing the various media classes.

↓

Selecting media within classes
Purpose: To compare and select the best media vehicles within broad classes, again using predetermined criteria. Involves making decisions about the following:
1. If magazines were recommended, then which magazines?
2. If television was recommended, then
   a. Broadcast or cable TV?
   b. Network or spot TV?
   c. If network, which program(s)?
   d. If spot, which markets?
3. If radio or newspapers were recommended, then
   a. Which markets shall be used?
   b. What criteria shall buyers use in making purchases in local media?

↓

Media use decisions—broadcast
1. What kind of sponsorship (sole, shared participating, or other)?
2. What levels of reach and frequency will be required?
3. Scheduling: On which days and months are commercials to appear?
4. Placement of spots: In programs or between programs?

Media use decisions—print
1. Numbers of ads to appear and on which days and months.
2. Placement of ads: Any preferred position within media?
3. Special treatment: Gatefolds, bleeds, color, etc.
4. Desired reach or frequency levels.

Media use decisions—other media
1. Billboards:
   a. Location of markets and plan of distribution.
   b. Kinds of outdoor boards to be used.
2. Direct mail or other media: Decisions peculiar to those media.
3. Interactive media:
   a. Which kind of interactive media?
   b. How will responses be handled?

audience objectives Definitions of the specific types of people the advertiser wants to reach.

media vehicles Particular media programs or publications.

(or SWOT) analysis, which defines the company's strengths and weaknesses and uncovers any marketplace opportunities and threats. The objectives and strategies of an advertising plan unfold from the marketing plan. But advertising objectives focus on communication goals.

Media objectives and strategies flow from the advertising plan. They determine how the communications goals will be accomplished through the selection of media. The media department's job is to make sure the advertising message (developed by the creative department) gets to the correct target audience (established by the marketing managers and account executives) in an effective manner (as measured by the research department).

The Media Planning Framework

Development of a media plan proceeds in much the same way as marketing and advertising planning. First, review the marketing and advertising objectives and strategies and set relevant, measurable objectives that are both realistic and achievable by the media. Next, devise an ingenious strategy for achieving these objectives. Finally, develop the specific tactical details of media selection and scheduling.

check yourself ✓

1. What is meant by "increasing fragmentation of the audience" and why has that trend made a media planner's job more difficult?
2. What caused the unbundling of media departments? Did it benefit advertisers?

LO14-2 Discuss the types of media objectives and identify the strategies for achieving these objectives.

DEFINING MEDIA OBJECTIVES

Media objectives translate the advertising strategy into goals. Exhibit 14–4 shows general media objectives for a hypothetical new food product. They explain who the target audience is and why, where messages will be delivered and when, and how much advertising weight needs to be delivered over what period of time.

EXHIBIT 14–4 How media objectives are expressed.

***ACME* Advertising**

Client: Econo Foods

Product/Brand: Chirpee's Cheap Chips

Project: Media plan, first year introduction

Media Objectives

1. To target large families with emphasis on the family's food purchaser.
2. To concentrate the greatest weight of advertising in urban areas where prepared foods traditionally have greater sales and where new ideas normally gain quicker acceptance.
3. To provide extra weight during the introductory period and then continuity throughout the year with a fairly consistent level of advertising impressions.
4. To deliver advertising impressions to every region in relation to regional food store sales.
5. To use media that will reinforce the copy strategy's emphasis on convenience, ease of preparation, taste, and economy.
6. To attain the highest advertising frequency possible once the need for broad coverage and the demands of the copy platform have been met.

Media objectives have two major components: audience objectives and message-distribution objectives.

In this section we outline traditional media objectives, which still apply today to broadcast, print, and outdoor media. Later in this section we highlight ways that objectives on the web, particularly in social media, may diverge from those of traditional media.

Audience Objectives

Audience objectives define the types of people the advertiser wants to reach. Media planners typically use geodemographic classifications to define their target audiences. In Exhibit 14–4, for example, objectives 1 and 2 suggest that the target audience is food purchasers for large families who live in urban areas. This group might even be narrowed further according to specific income, educational, occupational, or social groupings—any of the segments we discussed in Chapter 4.

Media planners rely heavily on secondary research sources, such as Nielsen Media Research, which provide basic demographic characteristics of media audiences. Other sources, such as Mediamark Research, Inc. (MRI), describe media audiences based on purchase tendencies. These syndicated reports give demographic profiles of heavy and light users of various products and help planners define the target audience. The reports also specify which TV programs or magazines heavy and light

distribution objectives Where, when, and how advertising should appear.

circulation A statistical measure of a print medium's audience; includes subscription and vendor sales and primary and secondary readership.

readers per copy (RPC) Variable used to determine the total reach of a given print medium. RPC is multiplied by the number of vendor and subscription sales to determine the total audience size.

pass-along rate The number of people who read a magazine without actually buying it.

message weight The total size of the audience for a set of ads or an entire campaign.

advertising impression A possible exposure of the advertising message to one audience member.

opportunity to see (OTS) A possible exposure of an advertising message to one audience member.

gross impressions The total of all the audiences delivered by a media plan.

Media planners must be more creative than ever. Sometimes that means purchasing a product placement rather than a traditional ad.

users watch and read, which helps planners select media with large audiences of heavy users. Planners can then select **media vehicles**—particular magazines or shows—according to how well they offer an audience that most closely resembles the desired target consumer.

Unfortunately, due to cost restraints, some media research is not as specific as marketers would really like. Most radio, TV, newspaper, and outdoor audience reports, for example, are limited to age and gender. So media planners often have to rely on judgment and experience to select the right vehicles.[9]

Message-Distribution Objectives

Distribution objectives define where, when, and how often advertising should appear. Objectives 3 through 6 from Exhibit 14–4 represent this type. To answer distribution objectives, a media planner must understand a number of terms, including *message weight, reach, frequency,* and *continuity.*

Audience Size and Message Weight

Marketers are naturally interested in having their messages exposed to as many customers and prospects as they can afford. So they are also logically most interested in those vehicles that offer the largest audiences.[10] The basic way to express audience size is simply to count the number of people in a vehicle's audience. This is what media research firms like Nielsen do for broadcast media, typically using a statistical sample to project the total audience size. For print media, firms like the Audit Bureau of Circulations verify a vehicle's subscribers and newstand sales (the **circulation**) and then multiply by the estimated number of **readers per copy (RPC)** to determine the total audience. RPC takes into account the **pass-along rate**, the number of people who read a magazine or newspaper without actually buying it. For example, most households subscribe to a single issue of a newspaper, even though multiple family members read it.

Media planners often define media objectives by the schedule's **message weight**, the total size of the audience for a set of ads or an entire campaign, because it gives some indication of the exposure of the campaign in a given market. There are two ways to express message weight: *gross impressions* and *gross rating points.*

If planners know the audience size, they can easily calculate the number of advertising impressions in a media schedule. An **advertising impression** is a *possible* exposure of the advertising message to one audience member. It is sometimes referred to as an **opportunity to see (OTS)**. Why? Because when a newspaper or magazine is delivered or bought, that counts as an impression. It cannot be determined whether the individuals who received those vehicles actually saw any particular ad. By multiplying a vehicle's total audience size by the number of times an advertising message is delivered during the period, planners arrive at the **gross impressions**, or potential exposures, possible in that vehicle. Then, by summing the gross impressions for each medium used, they know the total gross impressions for the schedule (see Exhibit 14–5).

EXHIBIT 14-5 Gross impressions analysis for Alpha brand in the second quarter.

Media Vehicle	Target Audience*	Messages Used	Gross Impressions
TV–Ch. 6 News	140,000	15	2,100,000
Daily newspaper	250,000	7	1,750,000
Spot radio	10,000	55	550,000
Total gross impressions			4,400,000

*Average.

rating The percentage of homes or individuals exposed to an advertising medium.

continuity The duration of an advertising message or campaign over a given period of time.

television households or **TVHH** Households with TV sets.

gross rating points (GRPs) The total audience delivery or weight of a specific media schedule. One rating point equals 1 percent of a particular market's population.

reach The total number of *different* people or households exposed to an advertising schedule during a given time, usually four weeks. Reach measures the *unduplicated* extent of audience exposure to a media vehicle and may be expressed either as a percentage of the total market or as a raw number.

frequency The number of times the same person or household is exposed to a vehicle in a specified time span. Across a total audience, frequency is calculated as the average number of times individuals or homes are exposed to the vehicle.

With large media schedules, though, gross impressions can run into the millions and become difficult to comprehend, so that's where the concept of ratings comes in. The **rating** is simply the percentage of homes exposed to an advertising medium. Percentages are not only simpler numbers to deal with; they are also more useful in making comparisons. One rating point is equal to 1 percent of a given population group. When we hear that a particular TV show garnered a 20 rating, it means 20 percent of the households with TV sets (expressed as **television households** or **TVHH**) were tuned in to that show. The higher a program's rating, the more people are watching.[11] This definition applies to many media forms, but it is most commonly used for radio and TV.

By adding the ratings of several media vehicles (as we did for gross impressions) we can determine the message weight of a given advertising schedule, only now it's expressed as **gross rating points (GRPs)** (see Exhibit 14–6). When we say a schedule delivered 440 GRPs, that means the impressions generated by our schedule equaled 440 percent of the target market population. For broadcast media, GRPs are often calculated for a week or a four-week period. In print media, they're calculated for the number of ads in a campaign. For outdoor advertising, they're calculated on the basis of daily exposure.

In the calculation of message weight, advertisers ignore the fact that there is overlap or duplication. As a result, certain individuals within the audience may see the message several times while others don't see it at all. So, while message weight gives an indication of audience size, it does not reveal much about who is in the audience or how often they are reached. This fact led to the development of other media objectives, including reach, frequency, and continuity.

▼EXHIBIT 14–6 Gross rating points analysis for Alpha brand in the second quarter.

Media Vehicle	Adult Rating*	Messages Used	Gross Rating Points
TV–Ch. 6 News	10	15	150
Daily newspaper	25	10	250
Spot radio	1	35	35
Total gross rating points			435

*Assumes market size of 1 million people.

Audience Accumulation and Reach

The term **reach** refers to the total number of *different* people exposed, at least once, to a medium during a given period of time, usually four weeks.[12] For example, if 40 percent of 100,000 people in a target market tune in to radio station WKKO at least once during a four-week period, the reach is 40,000 people. Reach should not be confused with the number of people who will actually be exposed to and consume the *advertising,* though. It is just the number of people who are exposed to the *vehicle* and therefore have an *opportunity* to see or hear the ad or commercial.

An advertiser may accumulate reach in two ways: by using the same media vehicle repeatedly or by combining two or more media vehicles.[13] Naturally, as more media are used, some duplication occurs. Exhibit 14–7 is a statistical table that estimates how reach builds as additional media are added. To see how it works, locate the column for the first vehicle showing a reach of 60. Then locate the row for vehicle 2 showing a reach of 35. The number at their intersection is 74. But 35 added to 60 is 95. Why has reach increased to only 74? The answer is the two vehicles share some of their users. The greater the overlap of the audiences for two vehicles, the less using those vehicles in a campaign will grow reach. And if the audience for two vehicles is identical, reach cannot grow at all.

Exposure Frequency

To express the number of times the same person or household has an opportunity to see a message—a radio spot, for example—in a specified time span, media people use the term *frequency.* Whereas reach measures the *breadth,* **frequency** measures the *intensity* of a media schedule, based on repeated exposures to the vehicle or the program. Frequency is important because repetition is the key to learning and memory.

Frequency is calculated as the *average* number of times individuals or homes are exposed to the vehicle during a specific period of time. For instance, suppose in our hypothetical 100,000-person market that 20,000 people tune in to WKKO and have three OTSs during a four-week period, and another

▼**EXHIBIT 14–7** Find the reach of the first vehicle on the horizontal axis. Find the reach of the second vehicle on the vertical axis. The point of intersection shows the combined reach of the two. The difference between the sums of the reach of each vehicle and the numbers in the table are due to audience duplication between the vehicles.

Reach of Second Vehicle	Reach of First Vehicle														
	25	30	35	40	45	50	55	60	65	70	75	80	85	90	95
25	46	47	51	55	59	62	66	70	74	77	81	85	89	92	95
30	—	51	54	58	61	65	68	72	75	79	82	86	90	93	95
35	—	—	58	61	64	67	71	74	77	80	84	87	90	93	95
40	—	—	—	64	67	70	73	76	79	82	85	88	91	94	95
45	—	—	—	—	70	72	75	78	81	83	86	89	92	94	95
50	—	—	—	—	—	75	77	80	82	85	87	90	92	95	95
55	—	—	—	—	—	—	80	82	84	86	89	91	93	95	95
60	—	—	—	—	—	—	—	84	86	88	90	92	94	95	95
65	—	—	—	—	—	—	—	—	88	89	91	93	95	95	95
70	—	—	—	—	—	—	—	—	—	91	92	94	95	95	95
75	—	—	—	—	—	—	—	—	—	—	94	95	95	95	95
80	—	—	—	—	—	—	—	—	—	—	—	95	95	95	95
85	—	—	—	—	—	—	—	—	—	—	—	—	95	95	95
90	—	—	—	—	—	—	—	—	—	—	—	—	—	95	95
95	—	—	—	—	—	—	—	—	—	—	—	—	—	—	95

20,000 have five OTSs. To calculate the average frequency, divide the total number of exposures by the total reach:

$$\begin{aligned}\text{Average frequency} &= \text{Total exposures} \div \text{Audience reach}\\ &= [(20{,}000 \times 3) + (20{,}000 \times 5)] \div 40{,}000\\ &= 160{,}000 \div 40{,}000\\ &= 4.0\end{aligned}$$

For the 40,000 listeners reached, the average frequency, or number of exposures, was four.

Once we understand reach and frequency, we have another, simple way to determine the message weight. To calculate gross rating points, just multiply a show's reach (expressed as a rating percentage) by the average frequency. In our radio example, 40 percent of the radio households (a 40 rating) had the opportunity to hear the commercial an average of four times during the four-week period:

$$\begin{aligned}\text{Reach} \times \text{Frequency} &= \text{GRPs}\\ 40 \times 4 &= 160 \text{ GRPs}\end{aligned}$$

Thus, the message weight of this radio campaign would be equal to 160 percent of the total market—or 160,000 gross impressions.

Continuity Media planners refer to the duration of an advertising message or campaign over a given period of time as **continuity**. Few companies spread their marketing efforts evenly throughout the year. They typically *heavy up* before prime selling seasons and slow down during the off-season. Likewise, to save money, a media planner for a new product might decide that after a heavy introductory period of, say, four weeks, a radio campaign needs to maintain *continuity* for an additional 16 weeks but on fewer stations. We'll discuss some common scheduling patterns in the section on media tactics.

While frequency is important to create memory, continuity is important to *sustain* it. Moreover, as people come into and out of the market for goods and services every day, continuity provides a means of having the message there when it's most needed. Ads that can be scheduled to hit targets when they are ready to make a purchase are more effective and require less frequency.[14]

OPTIMIZING REACH, FREQUENCY, AND CONTINUITY: THE ART OF MEDIA PLANNING

Good media planning is both an art and a science. The media planner must get the most effective exposure on a limited budget. As Exhibit 14–8 shows, the objectives of reach,

effective reach A term used to describe the quality of exposure. It measures the number or percentage of the audience who receive enough exposures for the message to truly be received.

effective frequency The average number of times a person must see or hear a message before it becomes effective.

wearout The point at which an advertising message has been seen or heard so often that it starts to irritate consumers and therefore loses its effectiveness.

advertising response curve A graphical representation of the relationship between advertising levels and sales results.

EXHIBIT 14-8 Reach, frequency, and continuity have an inverse relationship to one another. For instance, in the example below, an advertiser can reach 6,000 people once, 3,000 people approximately 5.5 times, or 1,000 people 9 times for the same budget. However, to achieve continuity over time, the advertiser might have to sacrifice some reach and/or frequency.

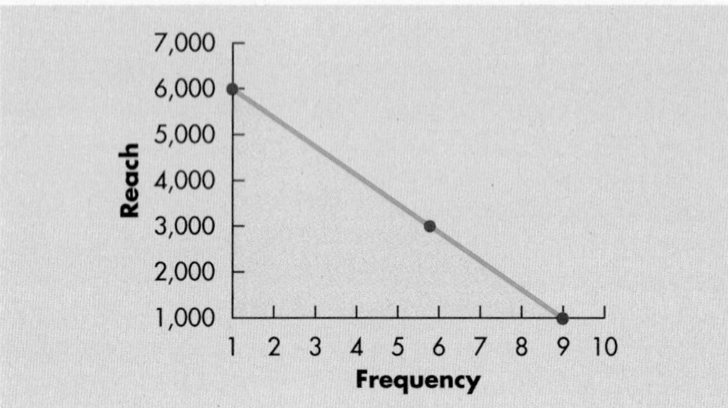

EXHIBIT 14-9 The S-shaped response curve suggests that a minimum threshold (A) of advertising frequency must be crossed before a meaningful response is achieved. At some level of frequency, another threshold (B) is crossed and the response begins to level off or even decline due to overexposure.

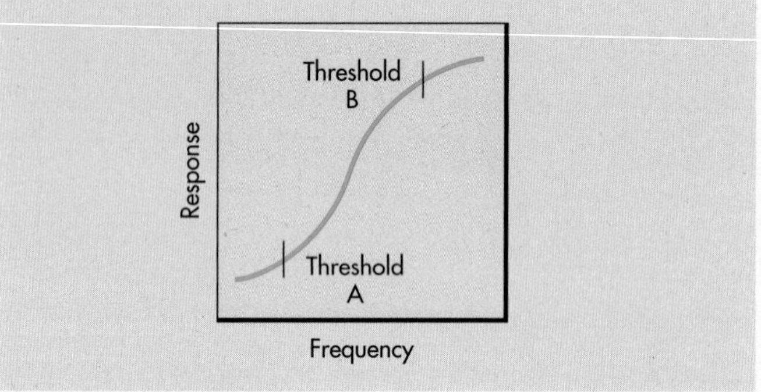

frequency, and continuity have inverse relationships to each other.

To achieve greater reach on a limited budget, some frequency and/or continuity has to be sacrificed, and so on. Research shows that all three are critical. But since all budgets are limited, which is most critical? This has always been the subject of hot debate in advertising circles.

Effective Reach One of the problems with reach is that, by itself, the measurement doesn't take into account the *effectiveness* of the exposures. Some people exposed to the vehicle still won't be aware of the message. So, on the surface, reach doesn't seem to be the best measure of media success. Media people use the term **effective reach** to describe the *quality* of exposure. It measures the percentage of the audience who receive enough exposures to truly notice the message. That brings us to effective frequency.

Effective Frequency Similar to the concept of effective reach is **effective frequency**, defined as the average number of times a person must see or hear a message before it becomes effective. In theory, effective frequency falls somewhere between a minimum level that achieves message awareness and a maximum level that becomes overexposure, which leads to **wearout** (starts to irritate consumers).

The S-shaped **advertising response curve** in Exhibit 14–9 suggests that at a low frequency there is little response. This is because the intensity of advertising is below a threshold where most of the target audience would notice it. Once that threshold is crossed, there is a dramatic response to increasing levels of advertising. Eventually though, the target market becomes saturated and, while advertising frequency continues to increase, the market response levels off or may even decline. The challenge to media planners is to determine the frequency of advertising that will exceed threshold A but remain below threshold B. To complicate matters further, different products or different advertising campaigns may generate different advertising response curves.

Following the publication of Michael Naples's classic book *Effective Frequency,* the industry fell in love with his claim that, in most cases, effective frequency could be achieved by an average frequency of three over a four-week period. Here was a nice, simple conclusion that all media planners could use.

However, this assumes that all exposures are equal. If that's the case, then where does advertising creativity come in? And what about the environment in which the advertising appears? Doesn't that have some effect on the quality of exposure? There is no simple solution to this problem.

Once the media objectives have been determined—that is, the optimum levels of message weight, reach, frequency, and continuity—the media planner can develop the strategy for achieving them.

five Ms The elements of the media mix that include markets, money, media, mechanics, and methodology.

markets Groups of potential customers who share a common interest, need, or desire; who can use the offered good or service to some advantage; and who can afford or are willing to pay the purchase price.

money In media planning, one of the five elements in the media mix.

media A plural form of *medium,* referring to communications vehicles paid to present an advertisement to their target audience.

mechanics One of the five Ms of the media mix; dealing creatively with the available advertising media options.

check yourself ✓

1. What are the two types of media objectives? Give examples of each.
2. What is message weight?
3. How does the media planner optimize reach, frequency, and continuity?
4. How are GRPs and CPMs calculated?

LO14-3 Identify the factors that influence media strategy and tactics.

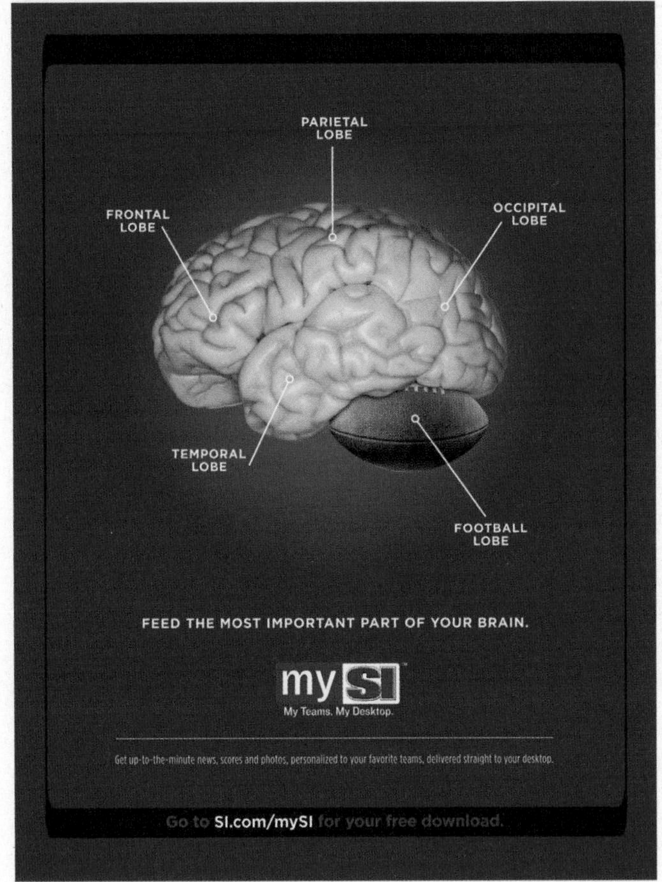

Market research helps advertisers understand their target audiences. The interactive nature of the Web allows Sports Illustrated *to provide its users with personalized content. In turn, the magazine and its advertisers gain a richer understanding of* SI's *audience.*

DEVELOPING A MEDIA STRATEGY: THE MEDIA MIX

The media strategy describes how the advertiser will achieve the stated media objectives: which media will be used, where, how often, and when. Just as marketers determine marketing strategy by blending elements of the marketing mix, media planners can develop media strategies by blending the elements of the media mix.

Factors in the Media Strategy: The Five Ms

Many factors go into developing an effective media strategy. For simplicity and ease of memory, we have sorted them into five categories and given them the alliterative moniker of the **five Ms:** *markets, money, media, mechanics,* and *methodology.*

Markets refers to the various targets of a media plan: trade and consumer audiences; global, national, or regional audiences; ethnic and socioeconomic groups; or other stakeholders. In an integrated marketing communications plan, the media planner wants to understand the reasons and motivations for the prospect's purchase and usage patterns and then create a media plan based on those findings.[15]

Using intuition, experience, marketing savvy, and analytical skill, the media planner determines the second element, **money**—how much to budget and where to allocate it. How much for print media, how much in TV, how much to nontraditional or supplemental media, how much to each geographic area?

Media includes *all* communications vehicles available to a marketer—anything you can put your name on. This includes radio, TV, newspapers, magazines, outdoor, the Internet, and direct mail, plus sales promotion, direct marketing, public relations activities and publicity, special events, brochures, and even shopping bags. Good media planners champion the integration of all marketing communications to help achieve their companies' marketing and advertising objectives. They look at the media element both analytically and creatively.

The media planner also has to deal with the complex **mechanics** of advertising media and messages. Radio and TV commercials

methodology The overall strategy of selecting and scheduling media vehicles to achieve the desired reach, frequency, and continuity objectives.

brand development index (BDI) The percentage of a brand's total sales in an area divided by the total population in the area; it indicates the sales potential of a particular brand in a specific market area.

category development index (CDI) The percentage of a product category's total U.S. sales in an area divided by the percentage of total U.S. population in the area.

come in a variety of time units, and print ads are created in a variety of sizes and styles. The myriad media options now available offer exciting, creative ways to enhance consumer acceptance of the advertiser's message and offer the consumer a relevant purchase incentive.

The **methodology** element refers to the overall strategy of selecting and scheduling media vehicles to achieve the desired message weight, reach, frequency, and continuity objectives. It offers the opportunity for creativity in planning, negotiating, and buying.

Factors That Influence Media Strategy Decisions

Media decisions are greatly influenced by some factors over which the media planner has little or no control. These include the scope of the media plan, sales potential of different markets, competitive strategies and budget considerations, availability of different media vehicles, nature of the medium, mood of the message, message size and length, and buyer purchase patterns.

Scope of the Media Plan

The location and makeup of the target audience strongly influence the scope of the media plan, thereby affecting decisions regarding the market, the money, and the media elements.

Domestic markets. A media planner normally limits advertising to areas where the product is available. If a store serves only one town, or if a city has been chosen to test-market a new product, then the advertiser will use a *local* plan.

A *regional* plan may cover several adjoining metropolitan areas, an entire state or province, or several neighboring states. Regional plans typically employ a combination of local media, regional editions of national magazines, spot TV and radio, and the Internet.

Advertisers who want to reach several regions or an entire country use a *national* plan. This may call for network TV and radio, full-circulation national magazines and newspapers, nationally syndicated Sunday newspaper supplements, and the Web.

Sales Potential of Different Markets

The market and money elements of the media mix also depend on the sales potential of each area. National advertisers use this factor to determine where to allocate their advertising dollars. Planners can determine an area's sales potential in several ways.

The brand development index. The **brand development index (BDI)** indicates the sales strength of a particular brand in a specific market area. It compares the percentage of the brand's total U.S. sales in an area to the percentage of the total U.S. population in that area. The larger the brand's sales relative to the area's percentage of U.S. population, the higher the BDI and the greater the brand's sales development. BDI is calculated as

$$\text{BDI} = \frac{\text{Percentage of the brand's total U.S. sales in the area}}{\text{Percentage of total U.S. population in the area}} \times 100$$

Suppose sales of a brand in Los Angeles are 1.58 percent of the brand's total U.S. sales and the population of Los Angeles is 2 percent of the U.S. total. The BDI for Los Angeles is

$$\text{BDI} = \frac{1.58}{2} \times 100 = 79$$

An index number of 100 means the brand's performance is in balance with the size of the area's population. A BDI index number below 100 indicates poor development of the brand in that market. Conversely, a BDI greater than 100 indicates better than average development.

The category development index. To determine the strength of the whole product category, media planners use the **category development index (CDI)**, which works on the same principle as the BDI and is calculated in much the same way:

$$\text{CDI} = \frac{\text{Percentage of the product category's total U.S. sales in the area}}{\text{Percentage of total U.S. population in the area}} \times 100$$

If category sales in Los Angeles are 4.92 percent of total U.S. category sales, the CDI in Los Angeles is

$$\text{CDI} = \frac{4.92}{2} \times 100 = 246$$

The combination of BDI and CDI can help the planner determine a media strategy for the market (see Exhibit 14–10). In our example, a low BDI (under 100) and a high CDI (over 100) in Los Angeles indicate that the product category offers great potential but the brand is not selling well (low market share). This may represent a problem or an opportunity. If the brand has been on the market for some time, the low BDI raises a red flag; some problem is standing in the way of brand sales. But if the brand is new, the low BDI may be a positive sign. The high

EXHIBIT 14–10 Media buyers compare the brand development index with the category development index for their products to better understand which markets will respond best to advertising. Advertising can be expected to work well when BDI and CDI are both high, but probably not when both are low.

	Low BDI	High BDI
High CDI	Low market share *but* Good market potential	High market share *and* Good market potential
Low CDI	Low market share *and* Poor market potential	High market share *but* Poor market potential

CDI may indicate the brand can grow substantially, given more time and greater media and marketing support. At this point, the media planner should assess the company's share of voice (discussed in Chapter 7) and budget accordingly.

Competitive Strategies and Budget Considerations

Advertisers always consider what competitors are doing, particularly those that have larger advertising budgets. This affects the *media, mechanics,* and *methodology* elements of the media mix. Several services, like TNS Media Intelligence Adspender, detail competitive advertising expenditures in the different media. By knowing the size of competitors' budgets, the media they're using, the regionality or seasonality of their sales, and any new-product tests and introductions, advertisers can better plan a counterstrategy.

Again, the media planner should analyze the company's share of voice in the marketplace. If an advertiser's budget is much smaller than the competition's, the brand could get lost in the shuffle. While it sometimes makes sense to use media similar to the competition's if the target audiences are the same or if the competitors are not using their media effectively, advertisers should generally bypass media that competitors dominate and choose other media in which they can achieve a strong position.

When Anne Myers, media director of Palmer Jarvis DDB, Toronto, had to develop a media plan for Panasonic Canada's Power Activator batteries, she didn't have the budget of Energizer or Duracell to work with. So she didn't want to place her ads where theirs were. Myers and her team creatively fashioned a guerrilla media plan that targeted a cynical, hard-to-reach audience, 15- to 22-year-olds, right where they lived—in the clubs, on the street, and on the Internet. The campaign included posters in the dance clubs; sponsorship of popular DJs and VJs; free Power Activator T-shirts, hats, posters, and stickers; an eight-week run of television spots on popular music shows tied to a monthlong cross-promotion with a new CD release; and a special contest run on a micro website that was linked to Panasonic's home page. The response was excellent: Sales were up 136 percent over the previous year, and the contest promotion generated more than 16,300 entries on the website with a click-through rate of 35 percent.[16]

Nature of the Medium and Mood of the Message

An important influence on the *media* element of the mix is how well a medium works with the style or mood of the particular message.

Advertising messages differ in many ways. Some are simple messages: "Just do it" (Nike). Others make emotional or sensual appeals to people's needs and wants: "The great taste of fruit squared" (Jolly Rancher candies). Many advertisers use a reason-why approach to explain their product's advantages: "Twice the room. Twice the comfort. Twice the value. Embassy Suites. Twice the hotel."

Complex messages, such as ads announcing a new product or concept, require more space or time for explanation. Each circumstance affects the media selection as well as the *methodology* of the media mix.

A new or highly complex message may require greater frequency and exposure to be understood and remembered. A

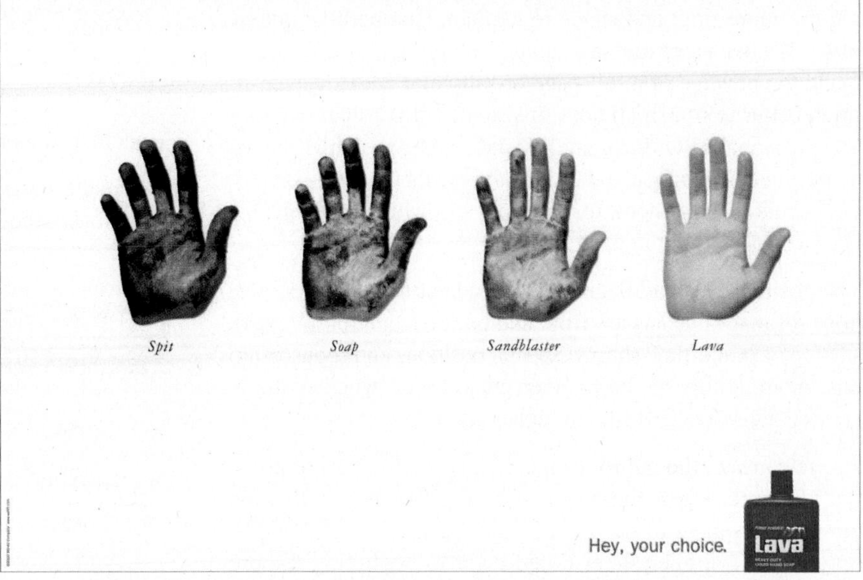

This ad for Lava Soap is executed simply and to the point. Unexpected imagery helps the ad to get noticed. Reach and frequency are of little value if nobody pays attention to the ad.

EXHIBIT 14–11 Effect of size and color on ad readership (total ads studied = 107,506).

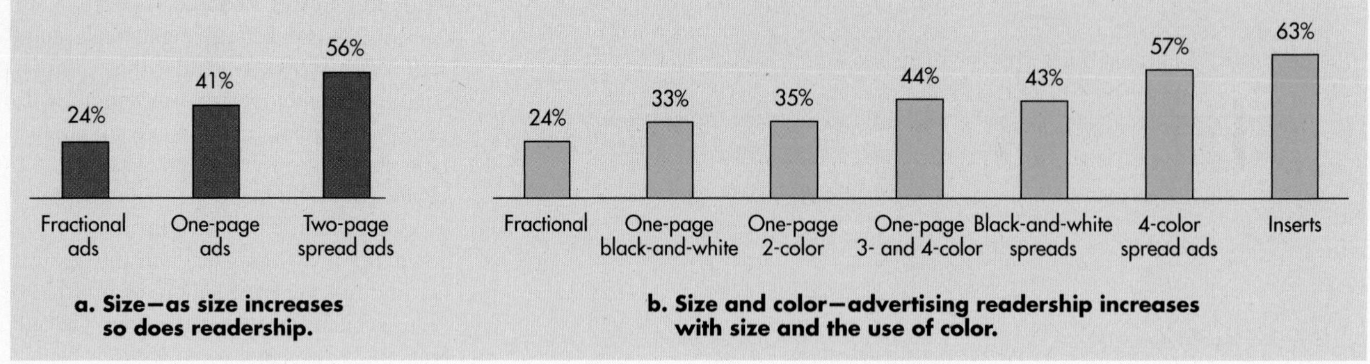

dogmatic message like Nike's may require a surge at the beginning, then low frequency and greater reach, plus continuity.

Once consumers understand reason-why messages, pulsing advertising exposures at irregular intervals is often sufficient. Emotionally oriented messages are usually more effective when spaced at regular intervals to create enduring feelings about the product. We discuss these scheduling methods further in the next section on media tactics.

Message Size, Length, and Position Considerations The particular characteristics of different media affect the mechanics element of the media mix. For example, in print, a full-page ad attracts more attention than a quarter-page ad and a full-color ad more than a black-and-white one (see Exhibit 14–11).

Should a small advertiser run a full-page ad once a month or a quarter-page ad once a week? Is it better to use a few 60-second commercials or many 15- and 30-second ones? The planner has to consider the nature of the advertising message; some simply require more time and space to explain. Competitive activity often dictates more message units. The product itself may demand the prestige of a full-page or full-color ad. However, it's often better to run small ads consistently rather than one large ad occasionally. Unfortunately, space and time units may be determined by someone other than the media planner—creative or account management, for example—in which case the planner's options are limited.

The position of an ad is another consideration. Preferred positions for magazine ads are front and back covers; for TV, sponsorship of prime-time shows. Special positions and sponsorships cost more, so the media planner must decide whether the increased audience is worth the higher costs.

As we can see, the nature of the creative work has the potential to greatly affect the media strategy. This means that media planners have to be flexible, since the initial media plan may well have been determined prior to beginning the creative work.

Buyer Purchase Patterns Finally, the customer's product purchasing behavior affects every element of the media mix. The media planner must consider how, when, and where the product is typically purchased and repurchased. Products with short purchase cycles (convenience foods and paper towels) require more constant levels of advertising than products purchased infrequently (refrigerators and notebook computers).

Stating the Media Strategy

A written rationale for the media strategy is an integral part of any media plan. Without one, it's difficult for client and agency management to analyze the logic and consistency of the recommended media schedule.

Generally, the strategy statement begins with a brief definition of target audiences (the market element) and the priorities for weighting them. It explains the nature of the message and indicates which media types will be used and why (the media element). It outlines specific reach, frequency, and continuity goals and how they are to be achieved (the methodology element). It provides a budget for each medium (the money element), including the cost of production and any collateral materials. Finally, it states the intended size of message units, and any position or timing considerations (the mechanics element).

Once the strategy is delineated, the plan details the tactics to be employed, the subject of the next section.

check yourself ✓

1. What is BDI? What is CDI?
2. What is the "sweet spot" of the BDI/CDI index?
3. What factors influence media strategy decisions?

LO14-4 Describe different types of advertising schedules and the purpose for each.

MEDIA TACTICS: SELECTING AND SCHEDULING MEDIA VEHICLES

Once the general media strategy is determined, the media planner can select and schedule particular media vehicles. The planner usually considers each medium's value on a set of specific criteria. Exhibit 14–12 summarizes many of the media advantages discussed in Chapters 10–13.

Criteria for Selecting Individual Media Vehicles

In evaluating specific media vehicles, the planner considers several factors: overall campaign objectives and strategy; size and characteristics of each vehicle's audience; exposure, attention, and motivation value of each vehicle; and cost-efficiency.

Overall Campaign Objectives and Strategy The media planner's first job is to review the nature of the product or service, the objectives and strategies, and the primary and secondary target markets and audiences. The characteristics of the product often suggest a suitable media choice. A product with a distinct personality or image, such as a fine perfume, might be advertised in media that reinforce this image. The media planner considers how consumers regard various magazines and TV programs—feminine or masculine, highbrow or lowbrow, serious or frivolous—and determines whether they're appropriate for the brand.

EXHIBIT 14–12 Media selection: Quick list of advantages.

Medium	Advantages
Newspapers	Quick placement. Local targeting. Audience interest. Current.
Magazines	High-quality graphics/reproduction. Prestige factor. Color. Selective targeting.
TV	Combines sight, sound, movement. A single message. Demonstration. Social dominance.
Radio	Intimacy. Loyal following. Ability to change message quickly. Repetition and frequency.
Internet	Immediate response. Interactive. Highly selective targeting. Global. Fastest-growing medium. Relevance of ads.
Direct mail	Measurable. Graphics, color. 3-D. Highly personal. Adaptable message length.
Outdoor/Transit	Local targeting. Graphics, color. Simple message. Larger than life. Repetition.

Applying the Breaks

What creative advantages can you add to the list? What are some drawbacks of the media listed here?

The content and editorial policy of the media vehicle and its compatibility with the product are important considerations. *Tennis* magazine is a poor vehicle for cigarette or alcohol ads even though its demographic profile and image might match the desired target audience.

Consumers choose a particular vehicle because they gain some "reward": self-improvement, financial advice, career guidance, or simply news and entertainment. Advertising is most effective when it positions a product as part of the solution that consumers seek. Otherwise, consumers may see it as an intrusion.[17]

If the marketing objective is to gain greater product distribution, the planner should select media that might also influence resellers. If the goal is to stimulate sales of a nationally distributed product in isolated markets, ads should be placed in local and regional media that penetrate those markets. Pricing

The language and imagery of this Godiva chocolate (www.godiva.com) ad exudes a sense of elegance that suits the audience of the medium selected. Godiva placed the ad in magazines such as Architectural Digest *to reach a target audience of affluent, well-educated individuals. The photo, type, and layout elements reflect the nature of the magazine, the advertiser, and even the audience.*

audience The total number of people exposed to a particular medium.

exposure value The value of a medium determined by how well it exposes an ad to the target audience.

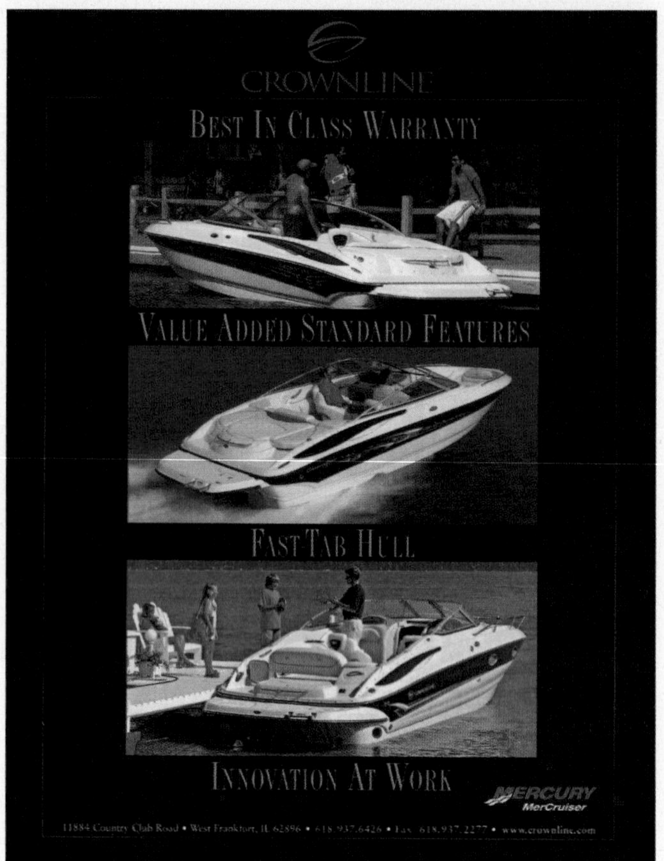

This ad for Crownline boats will get more exposure and receive more attention in Lakeland Boating magazine than in a general-interest publication. Readers will have nautical activities on their minds and may be very motivated if they are actively seeking product information.

strategy influences media choices too. A premium-priced product should use prestigious media to support its market image.

Characteristics of Media Audiences

An **audience** is the total number of people or households exposed to a vehicle. The planner needs to know how closely the vehicle's audience matches the profile of the target market and how interested prospective customers are in the publication or program. A product intended for a Latino audience, for example, would likely appear in specific media directed toward Hispanics. Simmons Market Research Bureau (SMRB) provides research data on age, income, occupational status, and other characteristics of magazine readers. Simmons also publishes demographic and psychographic data on product usage of consumers. Likewise, Nielsen provides audience statistics for television programs and Arbitron for radio stations.

The *content* of the vehicle usually determines the type of people in the audience. Some radio stations emphasize in-depth news or sports; others feature jazz, rock, or classical music. Each type of programming attracts a different audience.

Exposure, Attention, and Motivation Value of Media Vehicles

The media planner has to select media that will not only achieve the desired *exposure* to the target audience, but also attract *attention* and *motivate* people to act.

Exposure. As we discussed earlier, just because someone reads a particular magazine or watches a certain program doesn't mean he or she sees the ads. Some people read only one article, set aside the magazine, and never pick it up again. Many people change channels during commercial breaks or leave to get a snack. Comparing the **exposure value** of different vehicles, therefore, is very difficult. Without statistics, media planners have to use their best judgment based on experience.

Five factors affect the probability of ad exposure:

1. The senses used to perceive messages (for example, scratch-and-sniff ads really improve the exposure value of magazines).
2. How much and what kind of attention the vehicle requires (higher involvement suggests greater ad exposure).
3. Whether the vehicle is an information source or a diversion (for example, radio news programs offer greater ad exposure than elevator music).
4. Whether the vehicle or program aims at a general or a specialized audience (exposure value will be higher with specialized audiences).
5. The intrusiveness of the ad in the vehicle (placement within broadcast programs gives greater exposure than placement between programs; ads placed next to editorial material get greater exposure than ads placed next to other print ads, larger ads attract more attention).

Attention. Degree of attention is another consideration. As we discussed in Chapter 5, consumers with no interest in motorcycles or cosmetics won't remember ads for those products. For a variety of reasons, they fail to penetrate the viewer's perceptual screens. But someone in the market for a new car tends to notice every car ad.

Exposure value relates only to the vehicle; **attention value** concerns the advertising message and copy, as well as the vehicle. Special-interest media, such as boating magazines, can offer good attention value to a marine product. But what kind of attention value can the daily newspaper offer such a product? Do sailors think about boats while reading the newspaper? Much research still needs

to be done, but six factors are known to increase attention value:[18]

1. Audience involvement with editorial content or program material.
2. Specialization of audience interest or identification.
3. Number of competitive advertisers (the fewer, the better).
4. Audience familiarity with the advertiser's campaign.
5. Quality of advertising reproduction.
6. Timeliness of advertising exposure.

Motivation. These same factors affect a vehicle's **motivation value**, but in different ways. Familiarity with the advertiser's campaign may affect attention significantly but motivation very little. The attention factors of quality reproduction and timeliness can motivate someone, however.

attention value
A consideration in selecting media based on the degree of attention paid to ads in particular media by those exposed to them.

motivation value
A consideration in selecting media based on the medium's ability to motivate people to act. Positive factors include prestige, good-quality reproduction, timeliness, and editorial relevance.

Media planners analyze these values by assigning numerical ratings to their judgments of a vehicle's strengths and weaknesses. Then, using a weighting formula, they add them up. Planners use similar weighting methods to evaluate other factors, such as the relative importance of age versus income.

Cost-Efficiency of Media Vehicles Finally, media planners analyze the cost-efficiency of each vehicle. A common

Developing Media Objectives and Strategies [14]

In your lifetime, the media landscape has changed dramatically, becoming much more fragmented and full of choice. This has elevated the complexity of the media planning role. In this part of your assignment you are nonetheless considering all types of media to help distribute your message. You will most likely be given a media budget and asked to formulate a plan of attack. To better support your choices it is imperative that you develop sound objectives and strategies.

In some cases, your professor may have given you a set of marketing objectives or your research on clients may have indicated their main goals for advertising. It is important to note here that marketing objectives do not equal media objectives. They do, however, help us shape our media objectives, which in turn help us develop sound media strategy.

Developing Media Objectives

The first place to start in developing media objectives is with the marketing objectives themselves. You should view media objectives as the goals that become the building blocks of the media plan and that ultimately help clients meet their marketing goals.

Here are some examples of marketing objectives, translated into media objectives:

Marketing Objectives	Media Objectives
• Increase awareness among target audience by 23 percent.	• Generate mass awareness among target audience.
• Steal 2 percent share of sales from competitors.	• Differentiate brand from competitors.
• Build customer database of 5,000 individuals.	• Generate leads/requests for more information.

While the media objectives seem very similar to marketing objectives, they are actually quite different. Media objectives should focus on only what the media can achieve. Remember that the media plan is one of many components that go into building a successful promotional or communications plan and it has a distinct role, which is what you are trying to highlight in the objectives.

Developing Media Strategies

Media strategies are born out of the media objectives and describe a specific plan of action for achieving stated objectives. The strategy seeks to accomplish two things: setting the foundation for media ideas that help you meet the objective or goal and providing a position of advantage over your client's competitors.

The media strategy itself is built on key plan parameters on which the entire communications team has had input:

- Target audience
- Seasonality
- Geography
- Overall communication goals
- Budget
- Creative
- Competitive analysis

So how do media objectives translate into strategies? Let's look at the three we detailed earlier:

Media Objectives	Media Strategies
• Generate mass awareness among target audience.	• Use mass media (broadcast) to build reach against M18–34.
• Differentiate brand from competitors.	• Secure high-profile sponsorship with category exclusivity.
• Generate leads/requests for more information.	• Use interactive media to elicit registration.

cost per thousand or **CPM** A common term describing the cost of reaching 1,000 people in a medium's audience.

synergy An effect achieved when the sum of the parts is greater than that expected from simply adding together the individual components.

cost-efficiency The cost of reaching the target audience through a particular medium as opposed to the cost of reaching the medium's total circulation.

target CPM (TCPM) The *cost per thousand* to expose a message to the *target audience* rather than to the total circulation.

cost per point (CPP) A simple computation used by media buyers to determine which broadcast programs are the most efficient in relation to the target audience.

mixed-media approach Using a combination of advertising media vehicles in a single advertising campaign.

term used in media planning and buying is **cost per thousand,** or **CPM** (M is the Roman numeral for 1,000). If a daily newspaper has 300,000 subscribers and charges $5,000 for a full-page ad, the cost per thousand is the cost divided by the number of thousands of people in the audience. Since there are 300 *thousand* subscribers, you divide $5,000 by 300:

$$\text{CPM} = \frac{\$5{,}000}{300{,}000 \div 1{,}000} = \frac{\$5{,}000}{300}$$
$$= \$16.67 \text{ per thousand}$$

However, media planners are more interested in **cost-efficiency**—the cost of exposing the message to the *target audience* rather than to the total circulation. Let's say the target audience is males ages 18 to 49, and 40 percent of a magazine's subscriber base of 250,000 fits this category. If the magazine charges $3,000 for a full-page ad, the **target CPM (TCPM)** is computed as follows:

$$\text{Target audience} = 0.40 \times 250{,}000 = 100{,}000$$
$$\text{TCPM} = \frac{\$3{,}000}{100{,}000 \div 1{,}000} = \$30 \text{ per thousand}$$

Buyer Purchase Patterns

Finally, the customer's product purchasing behavior affects every element of the media mix. The media planner must consider how, when, and where the product is typically purchased and repurchased. Products with short purchase cycles (convenience foods and paper towels) require more constant levels of advertising than products purchased infrequently (refrigerators and furniture).

Stating the Media Strategy

A written rationale for the media strategy is an integral part of any media plan. Without one, it's difficult for client and agency management to analyze the logic and consistency of the recommended media schedule.

The more costly (on an absolute basis) daily newspaper might turn out to be more cost-efficient than the magazine if 60 percent of its readers (180,000) belong to the target audience:

$$\text{TCPM} = \frac{\$5{,}000}{180{,}000 \div 1{,}000}$$
$$= \$27.78 \text{ per thousand}$$

The media planner may also want to compare the **cost per point (CPP)** of different broadcast programs. This is done the same way as cost per thousand, except you divide the cost by the rating points instead of the gross impressions.

Comparing different vehicles by CPM or CPP is important but does not take into account each vehicle's other advantages and disadvantages. The media planner must evaluate all the criteria to determine

1. How much of each vehicle's audience matches the product's target audience.
2. How each vehicle satisfies the campaign's objectives and strategy.
3. How well each vehicle offers attention, exposure, and motivation.

The Synergy of Mixed Media

A combination of media is called a **mixed-media approach**. There are numerous reasons for using mixed media:

- To reach people who are unavailable through only one medium.
- To provide repeat exposure in a less expensive secondary medium after attaining optimum reach in the first.
- To use the intrinsic value of an additional medium to extend the creative effectiveness of the ad campaign (such as music on radio along with long copy in print media).
- To deliver coupons in print media when the primary vehicle is broadcast.
- To produce **synergy**, where the total effect is greater than the sum of its parts.

Television, for example, can be used to introduce a new product and give importance to the message. Magazine ads can then follow up for greater detail, image enhancement, longevity, and memory improvement.

A mixed-media campaign was effective for General Electric's lighting products. The promotion used a combination of network TV spots, print advertising, Sunday supplement inserts, in-store displays in more than 150,000 stores, and a highly creative publicity program. By using an integrated, mixed-media approach, the campaign produced "unprecedented" consumer awareness and dealer support. It achieved synergy.[19]

Methods for Scheduling Media

After selecting the appropriate media vehicles, the media planner decides how many space or time units to buy of each vehicle and schedules them for release over a period of time when consumers are most apt to be in the market for the product.

continuous schedule A method of scheduling media in which advertising runs steadily with little variation.

flighting An intermittent media scheduling pattern in which periods of advertising are alternated with periods of no advertising at all.

pulsing Mixing continuity and flighting strategies in media scheduling.

bursting A media scheduling method for promoting high-ticket items that require careful consideration, such as running the same commercial every half-hour on the same network in prime time.

roadblocking Buying simultaneous airtime on all three television networks.

blinking A scheduling technique in which the advertiser floods the airwaves for one day on both cable and network channels to make it virtually impossible to miss the ads.

EXHIBIT 14–13 Three ways to schedule the same number of total gross rating points: continuous, flighting, and pulsing.

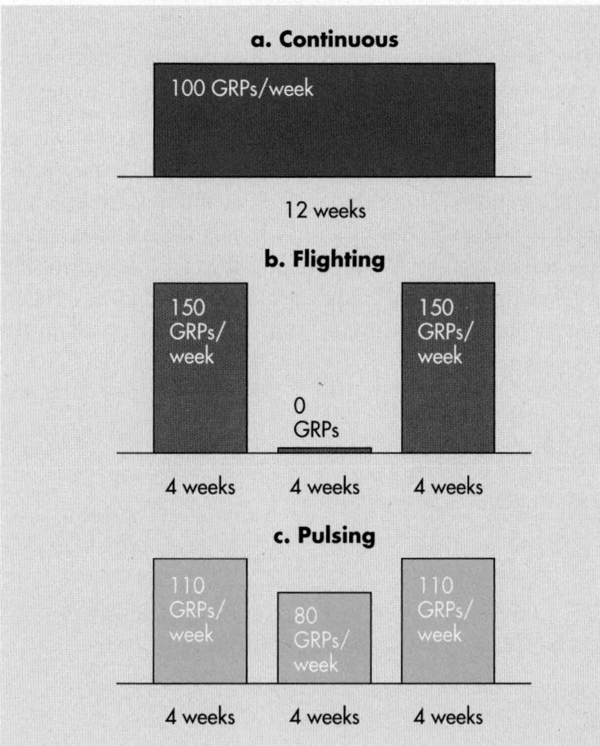

Continuous, Flighting, and Pulsing Schedules

To build continuity in a campaign, planners use three principal scheduling tactics: *continuous, flighting,* and *pulsing* (see Exhibit 14–13).

In a **continuous schedule**, advertising runs steadily and varies little over the campaign period. It's the best way to build continuity. Advertisers use this scheduling pattern for products consumers purchase regularly.

Flighting alternates periods of advertising with periods of no advertising. This intermittent schedule makes sense for products and services that experience large fluctuations in demand throughout the year (tax services, lawn-care products, cold remedies). The advertiser might introduce the product with a four-week flight and then schedule three additional four-week flights to run during seasonal periods later in the year. Flighting is also often used by products and services to stretch limited budgets.

The third alternative, **pulsing**, mixes continuous and flighting strategies. The advertiser maintains a low level of advertising all year but uses periodic pulses to heavy up during peak selling periods. This strategy is appropriate for products like soft drinks, which are consumed all year but more heavily in the summer.

Additional Scheduling Patterns

For high-ticket items that require careful consideration, **bursting**—running the same commercial every half-hour on the same network during prime time—can be effective. A variation is **roadblocking**, buying airtime on all three networks simultaneously. Chrysler used this technique to give viewers the impression that the advertiser was everywhere, even if the ad showed for only a few nights. Digital Equipment used a scheduling tactic called **blinking** to stretch its slim ad budget. To reach business executives, it flooded the airwaves on Sundays (on both cable and network TV channels) to make it virtually impossible to miss the ads.[20]

Once the scheduling criteria are determined, the media planner creates a flowchart of the plan. The flowchart is a graphic presentation of the total campaign to let the creative department, media department, account services, and the client see the pattern of media events that will occur throughout the campaign, usually one year (see Exhibit 14–14).

EXHIBIT 14–14 A media plan flowchart like this computerized printout of Telmar's FlowMaster gives a bird's-eye view of the major media purchases and where and when they will appear over a specified period of time.

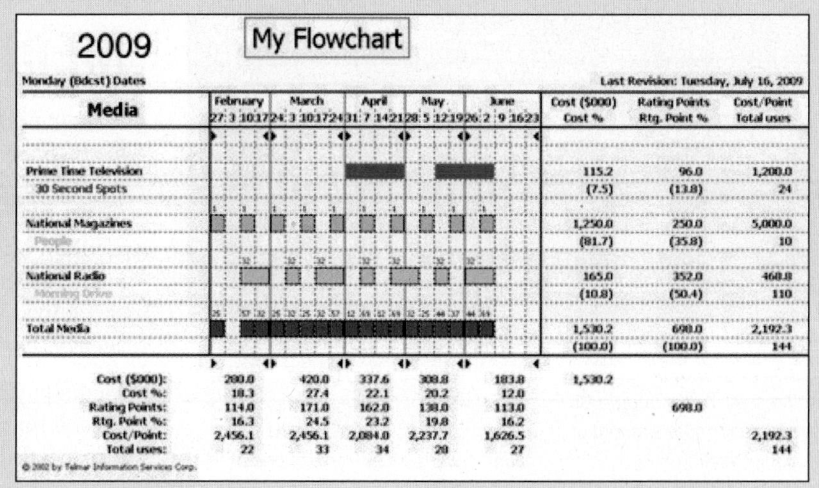

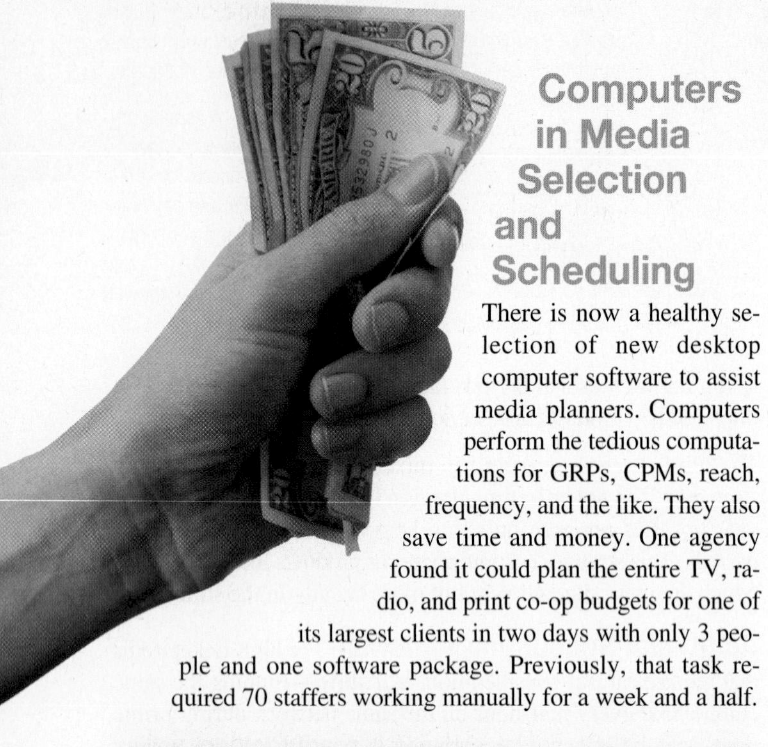

Computers in Media Selection and Scheduling

There is now a healthy selection of new desktop computer software to assist media planners. Computers perform the tedious computations for GRPs, CPMs, reach, frequency, and the like. They also save time and money. One agency found it could plan the entire TV, radio, and print co-op budgets for one of its largest clients in two days with only 3 people and one software package. Previously, that task required 70 staffers working manually for a week and a half.

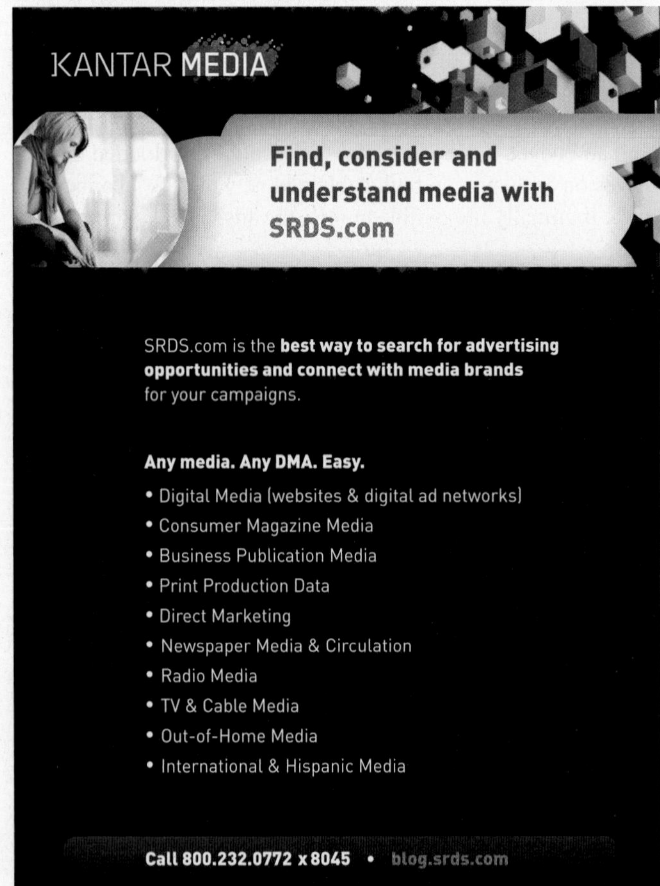

The advent of computer software has taken some of the more grueling, laborious work out of media planning. Planners can now crunch numbers, track results, and compute GRPs and CPMs right at their desktops. This saves an enormous amount of time and money. The SRDS Media Planning System (www.srds.com) shown here is an example of one of the many programs available.

Established in 1968, Telmar (www.telmar.com) was the first independent supplier of computerized media planning systems. Today, it is the world's leading supplier of media planning software and support services. More than 5,000 users in 85 countries use Telmar systems for media and marketing decision making.[21]

Telmar's software suite is designed to help media planners, buyers, research analysts, and sellers work more efficiently and to help them make better judgments in the evaluation or sales process. The software allows advertising executives to estimate the effectiveness of multifaceted marketing plans that use various combinations of media including print, broadcast, in-store, special promotions, special events, PR, and other "new media." Its flexibility permits the user to analyze the potential effectiveness of any and every marketing tool used to reach the consumer.

Even with technology, though, it's still up to the media planner to know the product, the market, and the media, and to then make the call. Computers can't decide which medium or environment is best for the message. They can't evaluate the content of a magazine or the image of a TV program. They can't judge whether the numbers they're fed are valid or reliable, and they can't interpret the meaning of the results. What they can do is help the process along.

check yourself ✓

1. What is meant by "continuity"?
2. How does an advertiser choose a media schedule? What options are available to him or her?

LO14-5 Explain the role of the media buyer.

THE ROLE OF THE MEDIA BUYER

Planning is only the first stage in the media process. Once the media plans are developed, they must be executed. The person in charge of negotiating and contracting with the media is called a **media buyer**. Media buyers often specialize in one medium or another, so there are print media buyers, spot TV media buyers, network media buyers, and so on. The degree of specialization depends on the size of the advertiser or the agency. In small agencies, for example, media buyers do it all.

Media buying is a complicated process. Buyers must perform several functions in the process of converting a media plan into a successful buy. Placing an ad is not as easy as it may seem, especially when there are hundreds of television and radio

stations, newspapers, and magazines around the country with different deadlines, different requirements, and different rates. The job can be very tedious and time-consuming.

Fortunately, media buyers now have a variety of software programs available to assist them. STRATA Marketing, Inc. (www.stratag.com), for example, has developed media buying software for each form of media. It offers media buyers various ways to keep track of orders, clients, and rate information, while providing a large variety of formats for generating reports.

These programs, and others similar in function, save media buyers a lot of time, thereby increasing productivity and efficiency. More time can be spent analyzing information, evaluating various vehicles, and exercising creativity.

The most successful media buyers have developed key skills in the following areas:

Knowing the marketplace. Media buyers have frequent contact with media representatives. As a result, they often gain insights about trends or opportunities. Some of the best media buys are the result of an alert buyer taking advantage of an opportunity or anticipating a problem.

Negotiating the buy. Media vehicles have published rate cards, but everything is negotiable. Media buyers can often bargain for special rates on volume buys, uncover last-minute deals, negotiate preferred positions, or garner promotional support.

Monitoring performance. The media buyer is responsible for ensuring that what was purchased was delivered. Did the advertising appear where and when it was scheduled? Was the size of the audience what was promised? If not, payments must be adjusted or *makegoods* must be negotiated. Whatever the outcome, the client expects to see a *post-buy report* on what audience was actually delivered. ■

media buyer Person responsible for negotiating and contracting the purchase of advertisement space and time in various media.

check yourself ✓

1. How is a media buyer different from a media planner?
2. What are the important skills for a media buyer?

learn about, practice, and apply techniques for media planning and buying!

M: Advertising was developed for students who want information packaged in a concise, easy-to-read, yet interesting format.
Check out the book's website to:

- Share your knowledge of the two key objectives for media planners. (Review Questions)
- Suggest how planners can determine the right reach and frequency for a message. (Review Questions)
- Create a list of client questions for developing a great media plan. (Exploring Advertising)
- Develop a flow chart for a hot new toy. (Exploring Advertising)

While you are there, check out the professional resource links, review the PowerPoint presentation, and test your knowledge with the Multiple Choice Quiz. Additionally, *Connect® Marketing* is available for M: Advertising.

www.mhhe.com/ArensM2e

chapter fifteen

Our goal in this chapter is to reinforce the importance of relationships in today's high-tech, overcommunicated world and to demonstrate how a variety of marketing tools can be integrated with advertising to enhance an organization's relationships with its stakeholders. Direct marketing, personal selling, packaging, and sales promotion play different but often overlapping roles in IMC programs. Each offers many opportunities, but also has limitations.

The rules of using direct-response advertising are straightforward: use a simple pitch, keep the campaign unified, and don't worry too much about the creative, since it's the offer that closes the sale. For several years now, insurer GEICO has done quite well despite ignoring two of those three rules.

The pitch is certainly simple—"15 minutes can save you 15 percent or more on car insurance." Ads encourage consumers to make a toll-free call or visit a website to get a quote and compare rates with their existing carrier.

continued on p. 368

LEARNING OBJECTIVES

After studying this chapter, you will be able to:

- **LO15-1** Explain the importance of relationship marketing and IMC.
- **LO15-2** Discuss the benefits and challenges of direct marketing.
- **LO15-3** Explain the various types of direct marketing activities.
- **LO15-4** Describe the advantages and drawbacks of personal selling.
- **LO15-5** Identify the elements that must be considered in establishing a trade-show program.
- **LO15-6** Explain the factors that must be considered in designing packaging.
- **LO15-7** Describe the roles that sales promotion can play in a marketing strategy.

IMC: direct marketing, personal selling, packaging, and sales promotion

continued from p. 366

But GEICO's campaigns are anything but unified. One, accompanied by the tag line "So easy a caveman could do it," humorously portrayed the disgust of cavemen at the slogan's insensitivity. In another, a gentle, British-accented, computer-generated gecko whimsically proclaims the benefits of GEICO to anyone who will listen. A not-so-wise owl challenges the belief that "everybody knows" GEICO can save you money on car insurance. In another ad, we're told that people who spend hundreds of dollars switching to GEICO are happier than a camel on hump day, than Dracula volunteering at a blood drive, than the Pillsbury Doughboy on his way to a baking convention. And when he's not crying "wee, wee, wee" all the way home, GEICO's latest spokesperson, Maxwell the Pig, demonstrates the GEICO smartphone app to a couple of skeptical flight attendants. And in yet another campaign, a man made of money dramatizes the claim that you shouldn't overpay for insurance.

Why so many different executions? Doesn't that just confuse consumers?

GEICO's approach is guided by a clear "share of voice" strategy (see Chapter 7). In 1996, when it became a subsidiary of Warren Buffett's company Berkshire Hathaway, GEICO controlled less than 3 percent of the car insurance market, behind giants like State Farm and Allstate. In 2012, after spending $921 million on advertising, GEICO's market share had grown to 9 percent. That year, GEICO ranked as the fifth most advertised brand across all industries.[1] The investment has paid off—91 percent of shoppers recall being exposed to a GEICO message over the past year versus 80 percent and 78 percent for the brand's top competitors, respectively. GEICO is the fastest growing major auto insurer and assumed the number two position from Allstate in the first quarter of 2013.[2]

So consumers are apparently not confused by all of the executions. In fact, the reason GEICO runs so many different campaigns simultaneously is that each is intended for a different audience.[3] As a large insurance company, GEICO sells policies to customers from many demographic and psychographic backgrounds. Knowing that one campaign will not be equally effective with everyone, the company uses some of the spots, like the caveman, to appeal to younger audiences. Others, like the gecko, resonate more with older audiences.[4]

Committing a relatively large amount to advertising is also part of the company's overall IMC strategy, since GEICO relies on a much smaller sales force than its competitors. As we will see later in this chapter, personal selling is an effective but expensive way to market a product. Using a smaller sales force means lower costs, which GEICO passes along to customers. But it also means advertising must do much of the heavy lifting when it comes to reaching new customers. That can be a smart move, but only if the ads are effective.

Ted Ward is the chief marketing officer at GEICO. When he started with the company in 1984 the ad division relied exclusively on direct-mail campaigns. He notes that "We have essentially a direct-to-consumer business model. We try to strip out costs to deliver the lowest price—it includes having very few agents in a process by having a superior technology model, which back in the '70s was direct mail; in the '80s and '90s, a telephone; and in the last 10 years, the online delivery of rates."[5]

GEICO's partner in creating the ads is the Martin Agency, headquartered in Richmond,

IMC: direct marketing, personal selling, packaging, and sales promotion

continued from p. 366

But GEICO's campaigns are anything but unified. One, accompanied by the tag line "So easy a caveman could do it," humorously portrayed the disgust of cavemen at the slogan's insensitivity. In another, a gentle, British-accented, computer-generated gecko whimsically proclaims the benefits of GEICO to anyone who will listen. A not-so-wise owl challenges the belief that "everybody knows" GEICO can save you money on car insurance. In another ad, we're told that people who spend hundreds of dollars switching to GEICO are happier than a camel on hump day, than Dracula volunteering at a blood drive, than the Pillsbury Doughboy on his way to a baking convention. And when he's not crying "wee, wee, wee" all the way home, GEICO's latest spokesperson, Maxwell the Pig, demonstrates the GEICO smartphone app to a couple of skeptical flight attendants. And in yet another campaign, a man made of money dramatizes the claim that you shouldn't overpay for insurance.

Why so many different executions? Doesn't that just confuse consumers?

GEICO's approach is guided by a clear "share of voice" strategy (see Chapter 7). In 1996, when it became a subsidiary of Warren Buffett's company Berkshire Hathaway, GEICO controlled less than 3 percent of the car insurance market, behind giants like State Farm and Allstate. In 2012, after spending $921 million on advertising, GEICO's market share had grown to 9 percent. That year, GEICO ranked as the fifth most advertised brand across all industries.[1] The investment has paid off—91 percent of shoppers recall being exposed to a GEICO message over the past year versus 80 percent and 78 percent for the brand's top competitors, respectively. GEICO is the fastest growing major auto insurer and assumed the number two position from Allstate in the first quarter of 2013.[2]

So consumers are apparently not confused by all of the executions. In fact, the reason GEICO runs so many different campaigns simultaneously is that each is intended for a different audience.[3] As a large insurance company, GEICO sells policies to customers from many demographic and psychographic backgrounds. Knowing that one campaign will not be equally effective with everyone, the company uses some of the spots, like the caveman, to appeal to younger audiences. Others, like the gecko, resonate more with older audiences.[4]

Committing a relatively large amount to advertising is also part of the company's overall IMC strategy, since GEICO relies on a much smaller sales force than its competitors. As we will see later in this chapter, personal selling is an effective but expensive way to market a product. Using a smaller sales force means lower costs, which GEICO passes along to customers. But it also means advertising must do much of the heavy lifting when it comes to reaching new customers. That can be a smart move, but only if the ads are effective.

Ted Ward is the chief marketing officer at GEICO. When he started with the company in 1984 the ad division relied exclusively on direct-mail campaigns. He notes that "We have essentially a direct-to-consumer business model. We try to strip out costs to deliver the lowest price—it includes having very few agents in a process by having a superior technology model, which back in the '70s was direct mail; in the '80s and '90s, a telephone; and in the last 10 years, the online delivery of rates."[5]

GEICO's partner in creating the ads is the Martin Agency, headquartered in Richmond,

> **Seamless, consistent communication—from every corner of the company—is how a firm earns a good reputation.**

Virginia. The agency and advertiser have an unusually long working relationship, more than 15 years. The value of a close and comfortable fit between advertiser and agency is reinforced in Ward's recall of how the gecko was born. "I was sitting around with . . . [an] art director at Martin, shooting the breeze after some focus groups and literally it was on a napkin and the rest just played out."[6]

Not that Ward was completely sold. "It was not my favorite campaign, personally" he recalls. "I quickly became much more fond of him as we sold more policies. I'm a big fan of anything that makes our phone ring or website click. He really has helped us brand-wise."[7]

The GEICO story suggests some important lessons. Direct-response advertising should be focused, but it doesn't have to be boring. And GEICO's success reveals that an advertiser does not have to choose between generating an immediate response versus building brand equity. Great ads can do both. ■

LO15-1 Explain the importance of relationship marketing and IMC.

THE IMPORTANCE OF RELATIONSHIP MARKETING AND IMC

In Chapter 7, we pointed out that the key to building brand equity in the twenty-first century is the development of interdependent, mutually satisfying relationships with customers and other stakeholders. Further, to manage these relationships, companies need to consciously (and conscientiously) integrate their marketing communications activities with all their other company functions so that all the messages the marketplace receives about the company are consistent.

However, this is a lot easier said than done, since everything a company does (and doesn't do) sends a message. Seamless, consistent communication—from every corner of the company—is how a firm earns a good reputation. And that is the principal objective of IMC—integrated marketing communications—the process of building and reinforcing relationships by developing and coordinating a strategic communications program through a variety of media or other contacts.

In the past, a large company could often muscle its way into significant market share. But with tighter budgets and more competitive markets, companies realize that even the most ordinary contact with the customer is a prime opportunity to build and maintain relationships. Companies like Dell (www.dell.com) that adopt such integrated strategies are much more likely to succeed in the long run.

GEICO is a good example of how IMC works. To attract prospects and initiate the relationship-building process, GEICO integrates its advertising efforts with a host of other marketing communications tools—direct marketing, sales promotion, personal selling, and public relations activities. While the forms and styles of these messages may vary, all reinforce a consistent proposal—that GEICO can save you money on insurance.

A simple adage: Advertising can create an image, but a reputation must be earned. For GEICO, this means delivering on its low-rate promise.

While the integration of marketing with other company functions is beyond the scope of an advertising textbook, it is important for advertising people to understand how to integrate the various tools of marketing communications. As they plan a campaign, advertising practitioners need a basic understanding of what other communications tools are available to them and how they can best be used in the overall marketing communications mix. In this chapter, we will discuss the interactive, one-to-one communication tools of direct marketing and personal selling. We'll also look at packaging and sales promotion, which might be called "value-added" tools. In the next chapter, we'll address the "credibility" tools companies use to enhance their reputations. These include various public relations activities, sponsorships, and corporate advertising.

direct marketing A system of marketing in which companies build their own database of customers and use a variety of media to communicate with them directly such as through ads and catalogs.

database marketing Tracking and analyzing the purchasing patterns of specific customers in a computer database and then targeting advertising to their needs.

database The corporate memory of all important customer information: name and address, telephone number, NAIC code (if a business firm), source of inquiry, cost of inquiry, history of purchases, and so on.

Direct marketing is an interactive system in which buyers and sellers participate in a dialogue. Its intent is to stimulate a response in the form of a request for information, an actual purchase, or a visit. This poster by Britain's National Society for the Prevention of Cruelty to Children (NSPCC) prompted calls from abused teenagers to jump 124 percent in just six weeks. The number of website visitors also increased, from 4,000 to more than 32,000.

check yourself ✓

1. Make a list of the "tools" of marketing communications.
2. Why can't advertising create a reputation?

LO15-2 Discuss the benefits and challenges of direct marketing.

UNDERSTANDING DIRECT MARKETING

There is a lot of confusion surrounding the term *direct marketing,* even among the experts.

Direct marketing is defined by the Direct Marketing Association (DMA) as "an interactive process of addressable communication that uses one or more advertising media to effect, at any location, a measurable sale, lead, retail purchase, or charitable donation, with this activity analyzed on a database for the development of ongoing mutually beneficial relationships between marketers and customers, prospects, or donors."[8] Along with mass advertising, direct marketing allows organizations to inform potential customers, create brand awareness, or spur immediate purchase behavior. In addition, direct marketing enjoys certain advantages over mass advertising such as measurability, accountability, efficiency, and higher return on investment.

There are several key characteristics of direct marketing within this definition. First and foremost, direct marketing is *interactive,* meaning buyers and sellers can exchange information with each other directly. GEICO can direct its message to prospective customers and those prospects can interact with GEICO by requesting rate quotes. Interactivity is so important that Joan Throckmorton, a prominent direct marketing consultant and writer, urged that the term direct marketing be dropped completely and replaced with *interactive marketing.*[9] Of course, this interaction can take place *at any location.* Customers may respond by telephone, via mail-in coupons, over the Internet, at a retail store, or even at a kiosk. GEICO processes the vast majority of its quote requests by phone and via the Web.

This DMA definition also refers to *addressable* communication, suggesting that marketers can identify those prospects, customers, or donors most likely to be interested in their product or service. Addressability is the goal of **database marketing**. Database marketers build and maintain a pool of data on current and prospective customers (and other stakeholders) and communicate with them using a variety of media (from personal contact to direct mail to mass media). Database marketing is a widely adopted marketing method because it has

direct-response advertising An advertising message that asks the reader, listener, or viewer to provide feedback straight to the sender. It can take the form of direct mail, or it can use a wide range of other media, from matchbook covers or magazines, to radio, TV, Internet links or billboards.

proven to be a cost-efficient way to increase sales. A good **database** enables marketers to target, segment, and grade customers. It helps them to know who their customers and prospects are, what and when they buy, and how to contact them. That, of course, leads to the possibility of the *ongoing mutually beneficial relationships* described above. So today, database marketing is a major component of many IMC programs.

The famous gecko uses a softer, less edgy style to describe the benefits of saving on insurance by calling GEICO. That may explain the appeal of this campaign with older audiences.

Note that the definition of direct marketing refers to the use of *one or more advertising media.* Part of the confusion with the direct marketing name is its similarity to direct mail. But direct mail is just one of the many media that direct marketers use. In the GEICO story, for instance, we saw how the company used a mass media form—television—to elicit responses from people who might be interested in saving on insurance. GEICO uses other media as well, including radio and direct mail, to reach its target audience. In fact, experienced direct marketers have known for years that using more than one medium can be far more productive than using a single medium.[10] As noted, direct marketing works effectively "with mass advertising" to *inform, create awareness, and spur immediate purchase behavior.*

The final point is that direct marketing can be distinguished from mass advertising in the areas of measurability, accountability, efficiency, and return on investment. The kind of advertising direct marketers use is called **direct-response advertising**. This is because direct marketing efforts are always aimed at stimulating some action or response on the part of the customer or prospect. It may be in the form of a request for information, a store visit, or an actual purchase. Because these responses can be *measured,* direct marketing is *accountable*. And that, more than any other reason, accounts for the tremendous growth of direct marketing in recent years. Managers like it because they can measure its *efficiency* and *return on investment*—what they got for their money.

Because millions of consumers are comfortable shopping on the Web, direct-response messages only need to provide a compelling benefit and a memorable Web address. Priceline.com is successful at both of these objectives.

THE ROLE OF DIRECT MARKETING IN IMC

Today, sophisticated companies use the skills developed by direct marketers to establish, nourish, and maintain relationships, not just with customers, but with all stakeholders.

GEICO, for instance, uses TV advertising as one of its linkage media—media that help prospects and customers link up with a company—to inform prospects how to inquire about its products. Next, it uses these responses to build its database of names, addresses, and e-mail addresses. Then it uses the database to communicate with prospects, open a dialogue, and establish a relationship. It may send a mail piece with ordering information or direct people to its Web site to enable prospects to connect with GEICO directly.

The Evolution of Direct Marketing

Direct marketing is the oldest marketing method, and today it is growing incredibly fast, propelled by the major social and technological changes of recent decades. Sixty percent of American women now work outside the home.[11] So while families have more income, they have less time to spend shopping, thus making the convenience of telephones and the Internet an important factor in direct marketing.

Likewise, the expanding use of credit cards has revolutionized the way consumers buy goods and services. Electronic, cashless transactions make products easier and faster to purchase. And now, with advances in payment security, more and more people are shopping right from their computers.

THE COMPANY THAT UNDERSTANDS ITS CUSTOMERS' NEEDS AND WANTS . . . WILL CREATE A SUSTAINABLE COMPETITIVE ADVANTAGE.

EXHIBIT 15–1 Largest direct-response agencies in the United States (2011).

2011 Rank	Agency	Headquarters	2011 U.S. Revenue ($ millions)	Percentage Change vs. 2010
1	Epsilon (Alliance Data Systems)	Irving, TX	$898	+9.4%
2	Acxiom Corp.	Little Rock, AR	656	+5.3
3	Wunderman (WPP)	New York	441	+6.6
4	Rapp (Omnicom)	New York	438	+10.6
5	Digitas (Publicis)	Boston	400	+20.6
6	Merkle	Columbia, MD	303	+19.3
7	DraftFCB (Interpublic)	Chicago/New York	299	−7.9
8	OgilvyOne Worldwide (WPP)	New York	263	+4.6
9	Rosetta (Publicis)	Hamilton, NJ	250	+20.8
10	The Agency Inside Harte-Hanks	Yardley, PA	145	+4.3

Companies spent an estimated $163 billion on direct marketing in the United States in 2011 (Exhibit 15–1 shows the largest direct-response agencies in the United States.). This accounts for over 52 percent of total advertising spending in this country. This share is expected to increase steadily through 2016. This is not surprising, given that the return on investment for direct marketing is estimated to be $12.03 of sales per dollar spent, compared to $5.24 for general advertising. Much of the growth is driven by online media. Those expenditures generated $1.96 trillion in sales in 2011, or 8.7 percent of the total U.S. gross domestic product.[12]

The boom in telecommunications and computer technology is spurring the growth of direct marketing worldwide. In the mid-1990s, for instance, European spending on direct marketing jumped by more than 23 percent to $46 billion. Today, Germany is by far the largest national market in Europe, spending more than $25 billion on direct marketing efforts annually. Britain comes in second at more than $17 billion, followed closely by France. Interestingly, outside the United States, Japan is by far the number one market for direct marketing, with estimated annual spending close to $70 billion.[13]

Telephone companies worldwide provide toll-free numbers for customers to place orders or request information. Toll-free numbers give companies immediate, direct responses and help them collect information to create and refine their databases. GEICO relies heavily on a toll-free number to sell insurance.

Certain challenges in foreign markets have limited the growth of direct marketing efforts. There are, of course, a wide variety of legal and regulatory environments to contend with. Likewise, payment and postal systems in different countries vary considerably, as do conventions for addressing mail. And finally, cultural nuances and language can get in the way.

The Impact of Databases on Direct Marketing

Modern computer technology enables marketers to compile and analyze important customer information in unprecedented ways. Pitney Bowes, for instance, was the dominant company in the postal meter business. However, its growth rate and profitability were flattening. So the company used its database to identify its best customers, their value to the organization, and their needs and buying behavior. From this, Pitney Bowes created a **customer lifetime value (CLTV)** model based on the customer's historical and potential worth. Computing and ranking the lifetime value of all of its 1.2 million customers showed that more than two-thirds of the customer base value resided in fewer than

customer lifetime value (CLTV) The total sales or profit value of a customer to a marketer over the course of that customer's lifetime.

loyalty (continuity) programs Programs that reward customers with discounts and free products in return for frequent and continuous patronage. Consumer purchases are tracked on a company's database.

10 percent of the customers. The company also found it had a major retention problem within its low-volume, low-cost accounts. Cancellation rates were running as high as 40 percent per year in some segments. This analysis led Pitney Bowes to develop a distinct direct marketing strategy for both its best and its worst customers. It began a sophisticated *loyalty program* for its best customers and a *retention program* for its problem accounts. By the end of the first year, the program had reduced attrition by 20 percent, and the reduction in cost of sales alone paid back the entire direct marketing investment.[14] In another situation, a company might determine from its CLTV analysis that its best course of action is simply to drop the most unprofitable customers.

Loyalty (or **continuity**) **programs** are designed to reward customers for their continued business. Most loyalty programs compensate consumers for frequent and continuous patronage. The frequent flyer club, introduced by American Airlines in 1981, is the model for today's continuity programs. Consumer purchases are tabulated on a company's database and discounts, free products, or services are awarded when specific levels are reached. The database can also provide the company with a demographic profile and purchase history for each customer.

The database is the key to direct marketing success, especially in an IMC program. It enables marketers to target, segment, and grade customers. It is the corporate memory of all important customer information: name and address, telephone number, e-mail address, source of inquiry, history of purchases, and so on. It should record every transaction across all points of contact with both channel members and customers. The company that understands its customers' needs and wants better than any of its competitors will create a sustainable competitive advantage.

The database also lets the company measure the efficiency of its direct-response advertising efforts to determine, for instance, which radio or TV commercials, or which mailing lists, perform the best.

The Importance of Direct Marketing to IMC

Perhaps the greatest reason for direct marketing's current growth is that marketers and agencies realize they can't do the job with just one medium anymore. As the mass audience fragmented and companies began to integrate their marketing communications, customer databases became key to retaining and growing customers.

Direct marketing is the best way to develop a good database. The database enables the marketer to build a relationship by

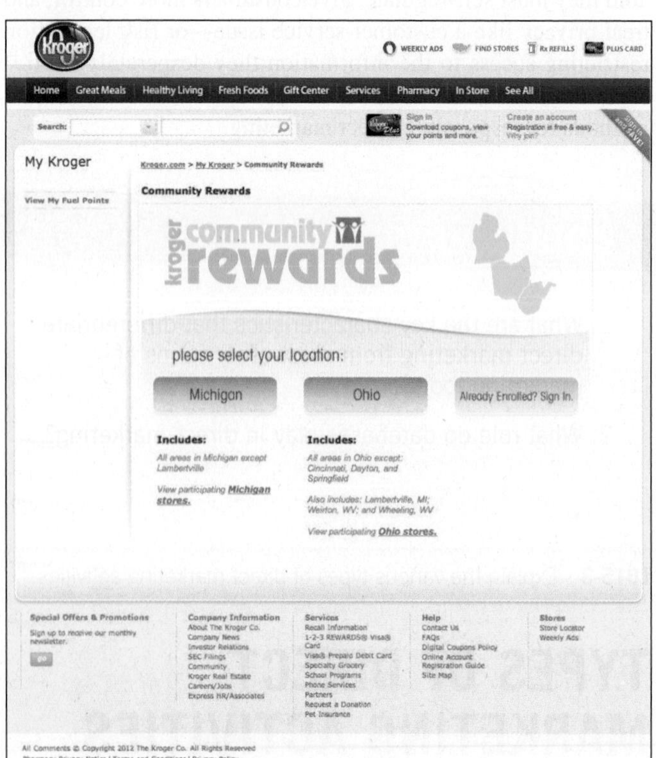

Most business is conducted with repeat customers. This places a premium on customer retention. Retention can be achieved by offering special benefits to loyal customers, effectively rewarding and thanking them for business, and providing an incentive for a continued relationship in the future.

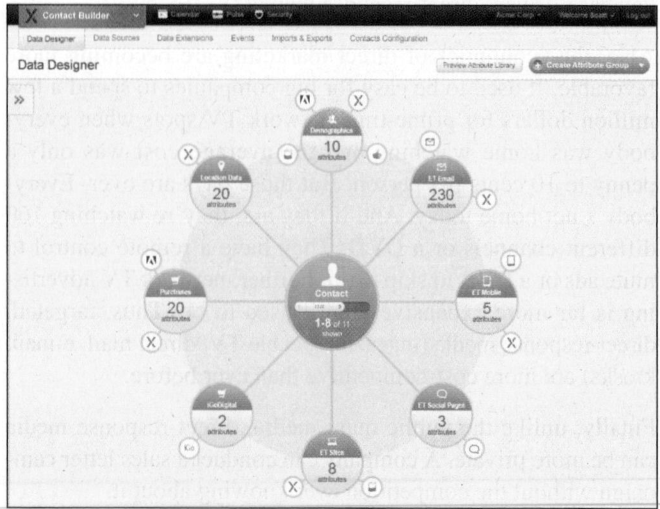

Database marketing was much more difficult before the development of personal computers because of the intense data management requirements. Today, with the low cost of personal computers, even the smallest companies can engage in complex database building and marketing strategies.

learning about customers in-depth: their nuances, what and where they buy, what they're interested in, and what they need. With a database, companies can choose the prospects they can serve most effectively and profitably—the purpose of all marketing. "You don't want a relationship with every customer," says Philip Kotler. "In fact, there are some bad customers out there."[15] Retailer Best Buy uses direct mail to send sales promotions materials, but only to its best customers.[16]

People like to see themselves as unique, not part of some 100-million-member mass market. Through direct marketing, especially addressable electronic media, companies can send discrete messages to individual customers and prospects. With different types of sales promotion (discussed in the last part of this chapter), a company can encourage individuals, not masses, to respond and can develop a relationship with each person. By responding, the prospect self-selects, in effect giving the marketer permission to begin a relationship.[17] The direct marketing database, then, becomes the company's primary tool to initiate, build, cultivate, and measure the effectiveness of its loyalty efforts.[18]

By providing a tangible response, direct marketing offers accountability. Marketers can count the responses and determine the cost per response. They can also judge the effectiveness of the medium they're using and test different creative executions.

Direct marketing offers convenience to time-sensitive consumers, and it offers precision and flexibility to cost-sensitive marketers. For example, to reach small B2B markets, there is no more cost-effective method than the database-driven, direct-response media.

Also, the economics of direct marketing are becoming more favorable. It used to be easy for big companies to spend a few million dollars for prime-time network TV spots when everybody was home watching and the average cost was only a penny to 10 cents per person. But those days are over. Everybody's not home today. And if they are, they're watching 160 different channels or a DVD. They have a remote control to mute ads or a DVR to skip them. Further, network TV advertising is far more expensive than it used to be. Thus, targeted, direct-response media (magazines, cable TV, direct mail, e-mail, kiosks) are more cost-competitive than ever before.

Finally, unlike the public mass media, direct-response media can be more private. A company can conduct a sales letter campaign without the competition ever knowing about it.

Drawbacks to Direct Marketing

At the same time, direct marketing still faces some challenges. In the past, direct marketers were sales oriented, not relationship oriented. This gave direct marketing a bad reputation in the minds of many consumers. Some people also enjoy the experience of visiting retail stores and shopping. They like to see and feel the goods personally, and they are hesitant to buy goods sight unseen. This is why the objective of many direct marketing campaigns is now to help drive traffic to retail locations.

Direct marketing efforts often have to stand on their own without the content support of the media that advertising enjoys. They don't always get the prestigious affiliation offered by some media. This makes it more difficult (and costly) to build an image for the product, something mass media advertising is particularly good at.

Direct marketing also suffers from clutter. People are deluged with mail from commercial sponsors and drum-beating politicians. Cable channels are filled with infomercials for food processors. Telemarketing pitches intrude on consumers at home and at work. Internet ads and e-mails permeate our daily lives.

Many consumers are also concerned with privacy. They don't like having their names sold by list vendors. At one national forum of direct marketers, attendees were told they must self-regulate, give consumers more control, and treat privacy like a customer service issue—or risk legislation restricting access to the information they desperately need.[19] Wise marketers have heeded these warnings and developed methods for responsible direct marketing.

check yourself ✓

1. What are the key characteristics that differentiate direct marketing from most other forms of marketing tools?
2. What role do databases play in direct marketing?

L015-3 Explain the various types of direct marketing activities.

TYPES OF DIRECT MARKETING ACTIVITIES

All direct marketers face two basic strategy decisions: the extent to which they will use *direct sales* and the extent to which they will use *direct-response advertising*. They can use either or both.

direct sales Selling to customers directly, at home or at work, rather than through a retail establishment or other intermediary.

direct selling Face-to-face selling away from a fixed retail location. Usually refers to a method of marketing consumer goods—everything from encyclopedias and insurance to cosmetics and nutritional products.

telemarketing Selling products and services by using the telephone to contact prospective customers.

Direct Sales

In a **direct-sales** strategy, marketers' representatives sell to customers directly, either at home or at work, rather than through a retail establishment or some other intermediary. Direct sales feature *personal* (face-to-face) *direct selling* or *telemarketing*.

Personal Direct Selling Professors Robert Peterson and Thomas Wotruba define **direct selling** as face-to-face selling away from a fixed retail location. In this sense, direct selling usually refers to a method of marketing consumer goods—everything from encyclopedias and insurance to cosmetics and nutritional products.[20] Companies such as Avon, Amway, Herbalife, Mary Kay Cosmetics, World Book, and Tupperware achieved very high levels of success in direct sales. In personal direct selling, the representative introduces the product to the customer, convinces the customer of the product's value, and, if successful, completes the sale. There are two main forms of personal selling: person-to-person and group sales. In some *network marketing* (or multilevel marketing—MLM) organizations such as Amway, Nikken, and Shaklee, the direct salespeople are both distributors (sellers) and end users. They often do very little actual retailing of the products. Their primary effort is usually to recruit new distributors who will buy the products at wholesale and consume them personally. We will discuss personal selling more completely in the next section of this chapter.

Each year telemarketing generates an estimated $538 billion in sales in the United States. It is cited as the direct marketing medium of choice, providing elements of direct personal sales yet at a substantially lower cost. Telemarketing also integrates easily into database management campaigns for gathering new data and for utilizing the collected data.

> Good telemarketers can develop strong, lasting relationships with customers they have never met.

Telemarketing As a method of direct sales, telemarketing has been used for decades, but the term is relatively new. **Telemarketing** includes selling and prospecting by telephone, answering phone inquiries, and providing sales-related services to callers. The information collected is also used to update the company's customer database. Telemarketing is the major source of income for some companies and organizations, such as nonprofit and charitable causes, political candidates, and home-study courses. In 2013, marketers are expected to spend $52.4 billion on telemarketing to consumers and businesses, making it the third largest spending category behind television and sales promotion.[21]

The reasons for this are economics and consumers' acceptance of teleculture. First, telemarketing costs a lot less money than personal selling. In the insurance business, for example, the expense ratio for car and home insurance is currently running at 27 percent for all insurers. The most efficient insurers, like GEICO, employ high-tech database marketing techniques from phone centers and operate at around a 20 percent expense ratio.[22] That difference goes straight to the bottom line.

Second, people have come to accept the idea of shopping by phone. It's convenient, hassle-free, and inexpensive. In the United States, the toll-free telephone business is booming. In any given week, 30,000 to 50,000 toll-free numbers are added across North America. Heavy demand caused the pool of 800 numbers to run dry in 1996. Soon thereafter, concern grew that even the 888 numbers faced depletion, leading to limits on their allocation. Then 877, 866, 855, and 844 numbers were introduced, with other numbers to be added for toll-free use as needed.[23]

Telemarketing is the next best thing to a face-to-face, personal sales call. In the business-to-business arena, for example, good telemarketers can develop strong, lasting relationships with customers they have never met but with whom they speak every week. Stand Out Designs in San Diego employs highly skilled telemarketers who call on zoos, museums, and boutique retailers all across the country to get them to order and stock

direct-response advertising An advertising message that asks the reader, listener, or viewer to provide a response (ideally in the form of a purchase) straight to the sender. It can take the form of direct mail, or it can use a wide range of other media, from matchbook covers or magazines to radio, TV, or billboards.

catalogs Reference books mailed to prospective customers that list, describe, and often picture the products sold by a manufacturer, wholesaler, jobber, or retailer.

the company's unique line of silk-screened T-shirts. The telemarketers don't just take orders; they counsel the dealers with display and promotion suggestions, offer advertising tips, and arrange for special imprints on the shirts when appropriate.

Of course, not everybody likes receiving uninvited telephone solicitations at inconvenient times of the day. The National Do Not Call Registry, created by Congress and launched by the Federal Trade Commission in 2003, is intended to give U.S. consumers an opportunity to limit the telemarketing calls they receive. As one might expect, there are many exceptions and loopholes. The registry applies to only residential lines, not business lines, and you may still receive calls from political and nonprofit organizations, research firms, bill collectors, and companies with which you have recently conducted business.

Nevertheless, telemarketing continues to be a very effective marketing tool. When combined with other direct-response media, telemarketing becomes even more effective. For example, experience shows that when telemarketing is combined with direct mail, there is usually at least a 10 percent increase in responses—often a lot more.

Direct-Response Advertising

Advertising that asks the reader, viewer, or listener to provide a response (ideally in the form of a purchase) straight to the sender is called **direct-response advertising**. Any medium can be used for direct response, but the most common are direct mail, catalogs, magazines, television, and digital interactive media (e-mails and search engines). In all cases, a prospective customer is urged to respond immediately and directly to the advertiser, through the use of a direct-response mechanism provided in the advertisement. The mechanism might be a coupon or reply card, a toll-free telephone number, an e-mail address, or an Internet link.

Direct Mail Next to personal selling and telemarketing, direct mail is the most effective method for closing a sale or generating inquiries. It's very useful to direct marketers seeking an immediate response.

Only direct mail that is intended to elicit a direct response is considered direct-response advertising. Some direct mail is used like other traditional advertising media, simply to communicate information about products and services. The trend in direct mail is away from printed materials and toward digital media, like e-mail and mobile marketing. Even though direct mail elicits far higher response rates than digital media, the high cost of printing and mailing results in a better return on investment for electronic advertising.[24]

Catalog Sales The largest direct marketers are catalog companies and catalogs are still the most popular medium for multichannel marketers. **Catalogs** are expensive to produce and mail, but consumers like to hold them in their hands. They like to circle the products they like and tear out the pages. Print catalogs have advantages over other marketing tools in creating product awareness, acquiring customers, and building brand loyalty. Consumers commonly then turn to their computers or telephones to order, but they start by shopping the catalogs. We discussed the use of direct mail and catalogs in greater detail in Chapter 13.

Direct-Response Print Advertising Newspaper ads and inserts featuring coupons or listing toll-free phone numbers can be very effective at stimulating customer responses. Today, the same is true with magazines. Moreover, in magazines, advertisers can devote most of the space to image-building, thus maximizing the medium's power. We discussed the use of print media in Chapter 10.

Catalog sales make up the largest portion of direct marketing. Catalogs, such as this one from J. Crew (www.jcrew.com), display a company's products and enable customers to order at their convenience via mail, phone, fax, or Internet. Victoria's Secret, L. L. Bean, and Lands' End are just a few of the multitude of consumer catalogs available today.

Television is a powerful instrument for direct marketers like Home Shopping Network (www.hsn.com) because of its mass coverage and the ability to display and demostrate the product with sound and full color right before the customers' eyes. Bobbi Ray Carter, shown here, has been one of HSN's most popular hosts for more than 30 years.

Direct-Response Broadcast Advertising Direct marketers' use of TV and radio has increased dramatically in recent years. Total Gym, whose products are normally sold through health care and physical fitness professionals, worked with American Telecast to develop a 30-minute infomercial featuring TV star Chuck Norris and supermodel Christie Brinkley. The campaign exceeded their wildest expectations, producing more than $100 million in sales the first year and continuing to generate similar returns for the next four years.[25] As Exhibit 15-2 shows, relatively young and affluent people are watching infomercials and buying the advertised products.

EXHIBIT 15-2 Who watches (and buys from) infomercials.

	Total Viewers	Total Buyers
Primary gender	Female, 53.2%	Female, 51.7%
Mean age	41.2	45.9
Primary ethnicity	Caucasian	Caucasian
Primary employment	Full-time	Full-time
Marital status	Married, 49.3%	Married, 60.3%
Children present	Yes, 40.1%	Yes, 43.1%
Residence	Suburban	Suburban
Mean household income	$56,000	$55,000

For many years, radio commentator Paul Harvey was very successful pitching a wide variety of products to his loyal audience. Likewise, talk jocks Howard Stern and Rush Limbaugh made Snapple an overnight success by drinking the product and touting its good taste on the air. Still, until fairly recently, radio has rarely been the medium of choice for direct-response advertising. In 2011, GEICO spent nearly 20 percent of its advertising budget on radio, referring interested listeners to the GEICO website. Radio industry executives now expect to see a dramatic increase in the number of direct-response ads on radio. We discussed radio, TV, and infomercials in Chapter 11.

Direct-Response Digital Interactive Media Direct-response advertising represents the vast majority of online advertising efforts. These are discussed more thoroughly in Chapter 12. Using e-mail to distribute marketing messages remains popular because of its low cost and effectiveness. Online direct response includes display ads and search ads. Social media sites are increasingly featuring ads that allow an immediate response. Mobile is another popular direct-response medium. Mobile includes SMS (short message service, or text ads), MMS (multimedia message service, or text plus images, audio, or video), mobile applications (better known as apps), QR (quick response) bar codes, and mobile banner ads. Although still in the development stage, interactive TV may allow viewers to respond to questions during a commercial, or even order products. Now let's take a brief look at the ultimate interactive communication tool, personal selling.

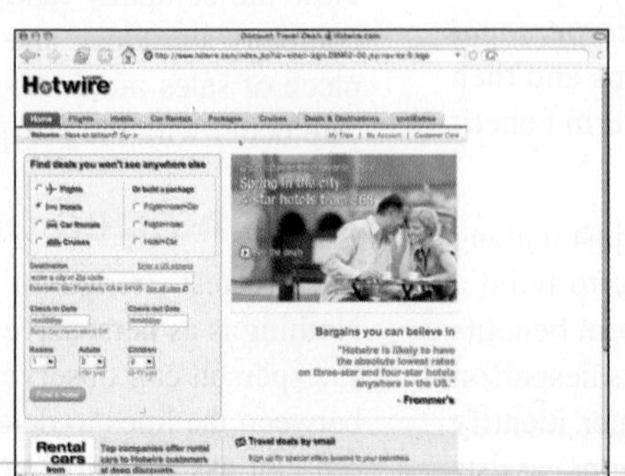

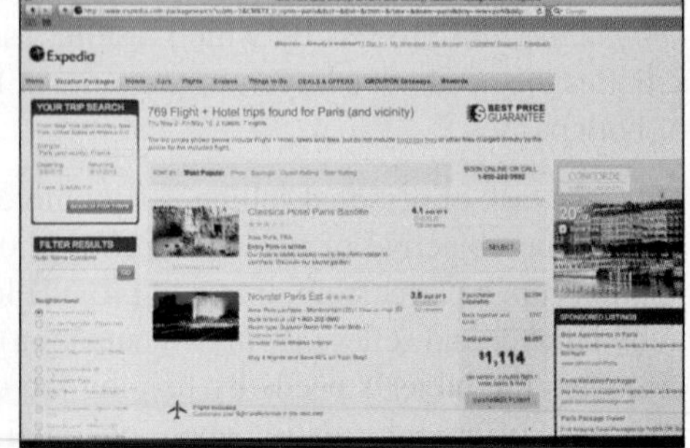

The Internet's impact has been extraordinary. Consumers are free to make inquiries, book flights, find hotels, and access a vast amount of information at their leisure, often eliminating the need for person-to-person communication. Shown here are three competing companies that offer just those services: Orbitz (www.orbitz.com), Hotwire (www.hotwire.com), and Expedia (www.expedia.com).

personal selling
A sales method based on person-to-person contact, such as by a salesperson at a retail establishment or by a telephone solicitor.

[The objective of personal selling should be to build a relationship.]

check yourself ✓

1. What is the key difference between direct sales and direct-response advertising?
2. Which of those strategies is more effective for closing a sale or generating inquiries and why do you think that's the case?

LO15-4 Describe the advantages and drawbacks of personal selling.

PERSONAL SELLING: THE HUMAN MEDIUM

Personal selling is the best marketing communications tool for relationship building because the sales rep and the customer are face to face. It's the ultimate one-to-one medium. It's also the most expensive medium. For most companies, personal selling expenditures far exceed expenditures for advertising. And in many companies, the primary role of advertising is to lend support to the sales force either directly by producing leads or indirectly by creating a positive atmosphere for the sales call. That is certainly true for all of the GEICO ads that direct audiences to the company's toll-free number.

Personal selling can be defined in a number of ways, depending on the orientation of the company using it. For our purposes we define **personal selling** as the *interpersonal communication* process by which a seller ascertains and then satisfies the needs of a buyer, to the mutual, long-term benefit of both parties.[26]

Thus, the task of personal selling is a lot more than just making a sale. The objective of personal selling should be to build a relationship, a partnership, that will provide long-term benefits to both buyer and seller (a win–win situation). The salesperson discovers the buyer's needs by helping the customer identify problems, offers information about potential solutions, assists the buyer in making decisions, and provides after-sale service to ensure long-term satisfaction. Influence and persuasion are only one part of selling. The major part is problem solving.

Types of Personal Selling

Everyone sells, at one time or another. Children sell lemonade, magazine subscriptions, and Girl Scout cookies. Students sell prom tickets, yearbook ads, and term papers. Doctors sell diets to unwilling patients. Lawyers sell pleas to skeptical juries. And cops sell traffic safety to nervous motorists.

The fact is that everything has to be sold, by someone to somebody. A retail clerk may sell you a cell phone. Behind that clerk is a virtual army of other salespeople who sold raw materials to the manufacturer, capital equipment for use in the manufacturing process, business services such as human resources and accounting, plant and office furniture, vehicles, advertising services, media space and time, and insurance. Then the manufacturer's salespeople sold the cell phone to a wholesaler who, of course, had to buy transportation services and warehousing from other salespeople. And then the wholesaler's sales reps sold the phone to the retail outlet where you bought it.

As this scenario shows, people in sales work for a wide variety of organizations and call on an equally wide variety of customers. They may call on other businesses to sell products or services used in the manufacture of other products. They may call on resellers—people who buy the product, add value, and resell it. Or they may sell to consumers, either in a retail store or, as we discussed earlier, in a direct selling situation away from a fixed retail location.

Because advertising is basically designed to support and reinforce a company's sales efforts, advertising people (whether in the company or at an agency) have to understand the selling environment their companies or clients deal in. Many companies have their advertising people make calls with the sales force for this very reason. The advertising person can experience firsthand what questions prospects ask, how customers view the company (and its competitors), how people use the company's product, and what information (in either an ad or a piece of sales material) might help the salesperson communicate better with the prospect.

Advantages of Personal Selling

The greatest strength of personal selling is its personal nature. Nothing is as persuasive as personal communication. A skilled salesperson can observe a prospect's body language and read between the lines to detect what's troubling the customer. The rep can ask questions and answer queries as they arise. The face-to-face situation facilitates instant feedback. And the rep has the flexibility to adjust the presentation, tailoring it specifically to the needs and interests of the particular prospect. Not

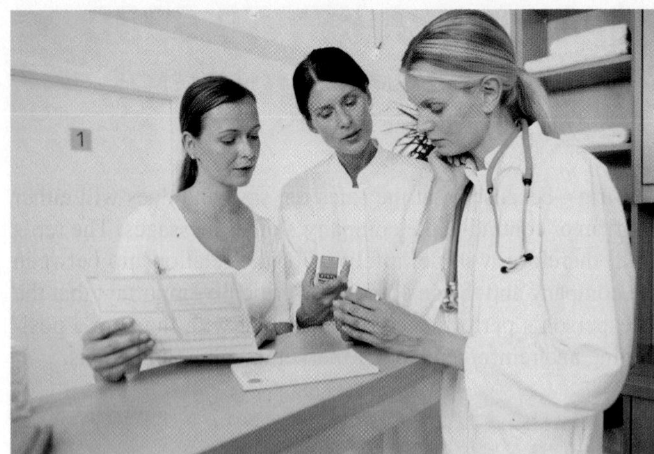

This pharmaceutical sales representative is engaging in missionary selling when she presents the benefits of her products to a doctor. The representative understands that the doctor will not place an order, but she is attempting to get the doctor to prescribe the pharmaceutical for her patients so the sale representative's company will get an order from the patient's drugstore.

only that, the salesperson can demonstrate the product live. And the rep can negotiate, finding those terms that best suit the buyer's needs.

Time is on the rep's side, too. The sale doesn't have to be made today. The relationship has to be established, though, and a human being is better at doing that than any nonpersonal medium.

One of the major jobs of personal selling is to gain distribution for new products—a task no other communications tool can do as well. In fact, in many trade and industrial situations, personal contact may be vital to closing the sale. This is also true for certain high-ticket or technical consumer products such as computers, health care, and estate planning. In these cases, personal selling is well worth its high cost—because it gets the job done.

Drawbacks of Personal Selling

Personal selling is very labor-intensive. That's why it's the most costly way to communicate with prospects. This is its single biggest weakness. The average business-to-business sales call today costs in nearly $600.[27] Not only that, it's very time-consuming. Because it is basically a one-on-one medium, there are few economies of scale.

This is why one important role of advertising is to reduce the cost of sales by communicating as much relevant information as possible about the company and its products to prospects and customers before the salesperson even calls. That information may be functional (specifically about the product) or symbolic (building image and credibility for the company).

Another drawback is the poor reputation of personal selling with many people. Decades of "suede shoe" salesmen employing high-pressure tactics have dishonored the profession. Thus the common jibe: "Would you buy a used car from that man?" Salespeople are frequently given fancier titles such as marketing associate, marketing representative, or account manager in an attempt to reduce guilt or the rejection associated with personal selling.[28]

There's an old saw about one bad apple ruining a barrel. Imagine spending millions of dollars on a nationwide advertising campaign to communicate your expertise and good customer service and then sending an unprofessional sales force out that is improperly groomed or, worse, ignorant of product features and benefits and lacking empathy for customer needs. Unfortunately, it happens all the time. The salesperson has incredible power to either make or break a delicate relationship. As a result, sophisticated firms go to great lengths to screen sales applicants to find the right personality attributes and then invest heavily in training. Of course, this goes both ways. A tasteless advertising campaign can hurt a company's national reputation more than one bad salesperson. As always, it's the responsibility of marketing management to ensure consistency among what the advertising presents, what the sales force promises, and what the company actually delivers.

The Role of Personal Selling in IMC

Salespeople are the company's communicators. In fact, to the customer who doesn't know anybody else at the company, the salesperson doesn't just represent the firm. He or she *is* the firm. The customer's impression of the salesperson, therefore, will frequently govern his or her perception of the company. Again, this makes the sales rep a very important person.

In an integrated marketing communications program, personal selling can play a very important role. Salespeople provide four distinct communications functions: information gathering, information providing, order fulfillment, and relationship building. We'll discuss each of these briefly.

Personal selling is especially important in the high-end cosmetics industry. Two factors account for this. First, consumers expect and enjoy the assistance of a well-trained cosmetics salesperson. Second, the profit margins for cosmetics are high enough to support an expensive sales staff. But even here advertising still has an important role to play by providing consumers with information about cosmetics and creating strong brand images.

> **"GOOD INTERNAL COMMUNICATION IS A KEY TO GOOD EXTERNAL RELATIONSHIPS."**

Gathering Information

Sales reps often serve as the eyes and ears of the company. Because they are out in the field talking to customers or attending trade shows, they have access to information and they can see trends. For example, salespeople provide information on who's new in the business, how customers are reacting to new products or styles, what the competition is doing, and where new sales opportunities might exist. Generally, information gathering by the sales force relates to three areas: prospecting; determining customer wants, needs, and abilities; and monitoring the competition.

Providing Information

Salespeople not only gather information; they deliver it. The stereotype (both negative and positive) of a good salesperson is someone who is a good talker, articulate and persuasive. In truth, a superior salesperson is a good listener first and a good talker second. Salespeople impart information both upstream and downstream within their organization. They deliver information to customers about the company and its products, they recommend solutions to problems, and they use information to communicate value and to build relationships and trust.

Personal selling incorporates all three legs of the IMC integration triangle we learned about in Chapter 7—say → do → confirm—because what the sales rep says and does will either confirm or contradict the company's other messages. The rep's skill, therefore, will definitely color the relationship between the company and the customer. It's critically important that the salesperson's performance be consistent with the firm's positioning and reinforce its other marketing communications.

Nordstrom strives to provide exceptional service to its customers. An engaging and helpful website is part of that effort. So is the company's lenient returns policy and justifiably famous focus on consumer satisfaction.

Fulfilling Orders

There comes a time in every relationship when someone has to make a commitment. Asking for that commitment can be very difficult if the preceding steps have not been handled well. The inevitable tasks of personal selling are to motivate the customer to action, close the sale, and then make sure the goods and services are delivered correctly.

An important part of personal selling is following up after the sale, making sure the goods or services are delivered in a timely fashion, and seeing to it that the customer is completely satisfied. This is a combination of the "do" and "confirm" steps, and it's critical to continued relationship building.

This is also where cross-functional management and open communication come back into play. If there is any kind of manufacturing glitch or delay in shipping, the salesperson needs to notify the customer immediately. But to do that, the salesperson must be informed. Similarly, goods need to be protected and shipped with care. Salespeople hate to receive calls from new customers saying their first shipment arrived with damaged goods. All employees, including those in the warehouse, need to understand the impact of their actions.

Likewise, if the company is advertising a certain model of a product and the salesperson closes the sale on the product, that model had better be in stock. Again, good internal communication is a key to good external relationships.

Building Relationships

A company's sales staff should be the ultimate relationship marketers. People naturally want to buy from the salesperson they like and trust. Salespeople build relationships by paying attention to three simple things: keeping commitments, servicing their accounts, and solving problems. Interestingly, those are also probably the three basic requirements for any company's success.

Here again, advertising people can help. When a company advertises, it is making a commitment to its customers and prospects. It is very difficult for a salesperson to keep those commitments if the advertising has overpromised. So puffery should be avoided wherever possible, since by its very nature, it tends to overpromise.

Likewise, it's difficult for salespeople to adequately service their accounts if every time people call customer service they get a busy signal or they never get replies to their e-mails. This happened to the giant telephone utility U.S. West when it downsized and reengineered the company. It continued running ads touting its great service, but nobody could get through to them. Not smart. Advertising people have to know what's going on in the company, and sometimes they need to recommend that advertising be stopped.

Finally, advertising as well as salespeople should be concerned with solving problems. If the sales staff uncovers a problem that customers frequently encounter, and the company's product can help solve that problem, then that should become the focus of some planned communications—advertising, publicity, or company-sponsored events.

Developing a Plans Book [15–A]

A plans book, quite simply, is the representation of all the hard work you have put in to develop the ideas for your project. For some of you this is an actual deliverable for the project; for the rest of you, it is good practice and good process management to develop a plans book to ensure that all of your thinking exists in one place.

Don't let the word *book* fool you—what we are talking about here is a binder or a set of binders that houses information relevant to your client's problem. Whether it is competitive news and information, industry news, research on target audiences, and/or SWOT analysis, this binder should comprise all of that organized information. The plans book is the foundation you will use to build the final presentation (we talk about the final presentation in Chapter 16), a concise explanation of how you will utilize the information in the plans book to put your campaign ideas into action.

Here is the information that should be represented in your plans book:

- Objectives
- Challenges
- SWOT analysis
- Target audience analysis
- Creative strategy
- Creative brief
- Creative concepts
- Media strategy and plan
- Evaluation or success metrics

Objectives

This is a statement or a set of statements that describes what you hope to achieve from advertising for your client's product. Some common goals are lifting awareness within a new audience, stealing share from competitors, or changing perceptions of consumers. It is better to stay focused and not try to do too much.

Challenges

Think about what you are trying to achieve and what barriers exist that make your work that much harder. If you are trying to lift sales for your client's products, one challenge may be that there is little to no awareness.

SWOT or Situation Analysis

Understanding the strengths, weaknesses, opportunities, and threats for your client's product(s) helps you focus on the appropriate strategy to market the brand. Along with target analysis the SWOT analysis should lead right into your strategy for marketing the product/brand.

Target Audience Analysis

Hopefully you have done a combination of primary research (interviews) and secondary research (syndicated or already done by a third party) to help understand what motivates your consumers to take action. Once you understand this, advertising becomes much easier; this section should highlight the research done and the insights from that work.

Creative Strategy

Your creative strategy is an overarching guide to how you will approach reaching your target with your client's message. All of your tactics should easily fall out of your strategy statement.

Creative Brief

This can be a single document or a set of documents, but either way it should be the parameters for all of your creative work. Look back to Chapter 8 for how to develop a brief.

Creative Concepts

The creative concept is a visual representation of your idea or set of ideas, complete with messaging and layouts.

Media Strategy and Plan

The media strategy should act as a framework for all of your tactical media ideas. The media plan itself is just a representation of the tactical ideas with timing included. (See Chapter 14 for an example of a media plan.)

Evaluation or Success Metrics

Of course all of your ideas will work, mainly due to the fact that you have done all of your homework, but what if one of them didn't . . . how would you know? This is where you detail how you plan to track and measure your campaign's effectiveness. This could be as simple as sales growth or more complex, like a pre/post attitudinal study.

trade shows Exhibitions where manufacturers, dealers, and buyers of an industry's products can get together for demonstrations and discussion; expose new products, literature, and samples to customers; and meet potential new dealers for their products.

booths At trade shows, a major factor in sales promotion plans. To stop traffic, it must be simple and attractive and have good lighting and a large visual.

exhibits A marketing or public relations approach that involves preparing displays that tell about an organization or its products; exhibits may be used at fairs, colleges and universities, or trade shows.

check yourself ✓

1. What should be the objective of personal selling? What is the major part of the task?
2. Describe the four distinct communications functions provided by salespeople.
3. Why do companies have their advertising people make calls with the sales force?

LO15-5 Identify the elements that must be considered in establishing a trade show program.

TRADE SHOWS

Trade shows provide an extraordinary opportunity for personal selling. A unique aspect of trade-show selling is that prospective clients and customers come to you; they already have a desire to learn about you and your product and the services you provide. Approximately one of every two trade-show attendees is planning to buy one or more products exhibited as a result of attending trade shows.[29]

Every major industry sponsors annual **trade shows**—exhibitions where manufacturers, dealers, and buyers get together for demonstrations and discussions. More than 14,000 industrial, scientific, and medical shows are held in the United States each year, and many companies exhibit at more than one show. Exhibit 15–3 lists the 10 largest U.S. trade shows, ranked by the size of the exhibit space (4 of the top 10 are held in Las Vegas). Trade shows are also very important for global marketers, because they may be the only place where an advertiser can meet the company's major international prospects at one time. Moreover, some of the world's largest trade shows are held overseas.

The construction of trade-show **booths** and **exhibits** has become a major factor in sales promotion plans. To stop traffic, a booth must be impactful and attractive and have good lighting and a large visual. It should also provide a comfortable atmosphere to promote conversation between salespeople and prospects. Many trade-show exhibitors use state-of-the-art technology, such as holograms, fiber optics, and interactive computer systems, to attract and hold the attention of visitors.

When establishing an exhibit booth program, managers must consider planning, budgeting, promotion, people, and productivity.[30]

Planning Planning pivots on four major areas: the budget, the image of the company or brand, the frequency of the shows, and the flexibility of the booth configuration.[31] In planning the actual exhibits or trade-show booths, advertisers need to consider numerous factors: size and location of the space; desired image or impression of the exhibit; complexities of shipping, installing, and dismantling; number of products to be displayed; need for storage and distribution of literature; use of preshow advertising and promotion; and the cost of all these factors.

▼**EXHIBIT 15–3** Top 10 U.S. trade shows based on floor space (2012).

Event	Industry	# of Exhibitors	# of Attendees
International Consumer Electronics Show	Consumer electronics	3,239	104,316
International Manufacturing Technology	Manufacturing technology	1,909	100,200
January International Gift & Home Furnishings Market	Gifts and home furnishing	2,517	95,000
PACK EXPO International	Packaging machinery and materials	1,965	45,338
July International Gift & Home Furnishings Market	Gifts and home furnishings	2,375	91,267
NBAA Annual Meeting & Convention	Business aircraft, services, and products	1,073	25,150
Specialty Equipment Market Assoc.	Automotive specialty products	2,250	135,000
MAGIC Marketplace	Apparel, accessories, and footwear	4,312	66,103
NPE 2012	Plastics	1,933	40,385
RECon 2012	Shopping centers	989	31,000

Source: The Trade Show News Network.

Trade shows are an important component in the marketing mix. They provide a unique opportunity for advertisers to meet with a large number of prospects. Over half of trade-show visitors make buying plans as a result of visiting a show.

Budgeting Trade shows are expensive, and costs have increased substantially in the last decade. A large company may spend $1 million or more on a booth for one trade show. With staffers' travel, living, and salary expenses and preshow promotion added to booth costs, the cost per visitor engaged averages $274.[32] Despite the expense, trade shows can still be a cost-effective way to reach sales prospects, less expensive than a sales call.

Promotion To build traffic for a trade-show booth or exhibit, marketers send out personal invitations, conduct direct-mail campaigns, place ads in trade publications, issue news releases, and perform telemarketing. The pie chart in Exhibit 15–4 portrays how customers typically learn about the trade shows they attend.[33]

At the show itself, activities at the booth and promotional materials (handouts, brochures, giveaway items, raffles) can stimulate customer interest and improve product exposure. 3M's Telcomm Products Division mailed 6,000 potential show attendees a Pony Express theme folder that invited them to pick up a trail map at the booth. The map guided the visitors (Pony Express riders) through a series of stations shared by seven product groups within the huge booth. Once the visitors' maps had been stamped at each station, they were given a "pay envelope" containing replicas of 1850 coins and vouchers redeemable for merchandise awards.[34]

▼EXHIBIT 15–4 How do customers learn about trade shows?

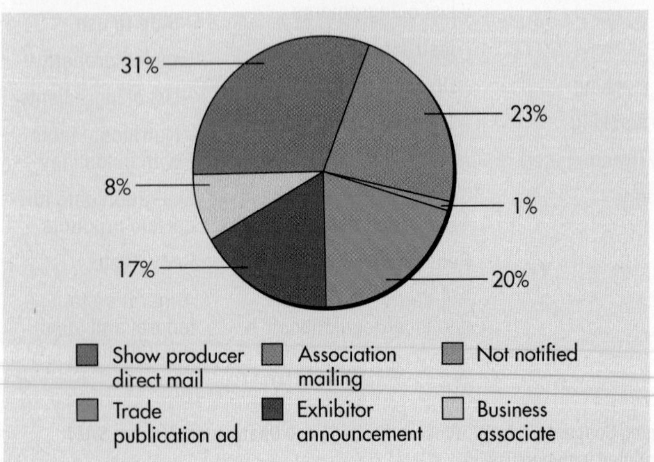

People The company representatives staffing the booth personify the kind of service the customer can expect to receive. They should be articulate, people-oriented, enthusiastic, knowledgeable about the product, and empathetic listeners.[35]

The primary goal of a trade-show booth is to meet with qualified prospects face to face. Ideally, 80 percent of the salesperson's time should be spent listening and 20 percent talking.[36]

Productivity A company's trade-show effort may be wasted if prospects' names are not collected and organized properly. Each lead should be evaluated as to the prospect's readiness to receive another contact (A = now; B = 2 weeks; C = 6 months; D = never).[37] The resulting lead list is the link to future sales and augments the company's prospect database. Follow-up contacts are key to extracting the maximum value from trade shows.

check yourself ✓

1. What makes a trade show a unique personal selling opportunity?
2. What trade-show activity is critical to augmenting the company's prospect database?

LO15-6 Explain the factors that must be considered in designing packaging.

PRODUCT PACKAGING

In 2011, North American companies spent $169 billion on packaging.[38] Since upward of 70 percent of all buying decisions are made at the point of purchase, packages play a major role in both advertising and selling. The package is not only the last "ad" a consumer sees before purchasing the product, it is the only "ad" the consumer sees when using the product. So it is more than just another *planned message*. Packaging influences the *product message* as well, since (as we discussed in Chapter 7) it is often an intrinsic aspect of the basic product concept.

packaging
The container for a product—encompassing the physical appearance of the container and including the design, color, shape, labeling, and materials used.

Packaging encompasses the physical appearance of the container and includes design, color, shape, labeling, and materials. Packaging serves marketers in four major ways: protection, preservation, information, and promotion.[39] Although the protection and preservation aspects reduce the costly effects of damage, pilferage, and spoilage, the importance of packaging as an informational and promotional tool cannot be underestimated. An attractive package can create an immediate relationship with the customer, influence in-store shopping decisions, help set the product apart from competitors, and inform customers of the product's features and benefits.

Designers consider three factors: the package's stand-out appeal, how it communicates verbally and nonverbally, and the prestige or image desired.

Packaging design can be as important as advertising in building a product's brand image. Packaging establishes or reinforces the brand's personality at the point of sale. So if status is the goal, the package designer must consider what consumers regard as prestigious. This is especially important for so-called nonrational products—cosmetics and perfumes, sports accessories, confection gifts, and certain luxury products—in which fantasy, impulsiveness, or mystique may overrule rational choice.

"The package is . . . the last 'ad' a consumer sees before purchasing the product."

To sell products off the shelf, packages may use shape, color, size, interesting visuals, or even texture to deliver a marketing message, give product information, and indicate application. After they are purchased, packages continue promoting the product in the home, reinforcing the brand's image, so they should open and close with minimal effort and be easy to handle.

Buying packaging includes two major phases: *concept* and *production*. The *conceptual process* involves input from five major stakeholders: consumers, manufacturers, marketing intermediaries, consumer advocacy groups, and government agencies.[40] The conflicting concerns of these groups strongly influence the nature and the cost of packaging (see Exhibit 15–5).

Environmental Issues in Packaging

As manufacturers continue to produce environmentally safe packaging, the marketer's cost of materials rises. And what some consumers expect from *green packaging* is not

▼EXHIBIT 15–5 Expectations and concerns about packaging among major stakeholders.

Consumers	Manufactures	Marketing Intermediaries (Retailers/Wholesalers)	Consumer Advocacy Groups	Government Agencies
Ease (to handle and store)	Sturdiness	Sturdiness (of case and packages)	Package safe to:	Free of deception
Convenience	Suppleness	Convenience (of removal)	–handle	Free of harmful effects to ecology
List of ingredients	Attractiveness	Tamperproof	–use	Biodegradable
Instructions	Safety (to users and for the product)	Identifiable	Environmentally safe (biodegradability, etc.)	Free of health hazards
Life of product	Cost of:	Safety (to users and for the product)	Package free of health hazards	All-around safety
Disposal method	–materials	Ease of:	Self-informative	–Safe to handle
Toll-free phone number for emergencies	–fabrication	–storage	–List of ingredients	–Safe to use
Performance guarantees	–labor	–shelving stocking	–Instructions	Labeled properly
Safety guarantees	–inventory	–package stacking	–Disposal method	–List of ingredients
Environmental safety (biodegradability)	–shipping	–inventory (by computer)	–Toll-free phone number for emergencies	–Nutritional facts with guidelines
Reusable	–storage	Room for price	–Warranties	Expiration date for certain products
Recyclable	Need to change	Stickers	–Expiration date	Recyclable
	Lighter weight (with safety)		Recyclable	Adherence to federal and local regulations
	Tamperproof		Adherence to federal and local regulations	
	Package size (promotion space versus materials cost and environmental safety)			
	Availability of materials			

Source: From "Balancing Traditional Packaging Functions with the New 'Green Packaging Concerns,'" by W. Wossen Kassage and Dharmendra Verma, *SAM Advanced Management Journal*, pp. 15–23, 29, Volume 57, Number 4, Autumn 1992. Reprinted with permission.

necessarily what manufacturers traditionally offer or what marketing intermediaries prefer to use.[41]

With the public's growing concern for the environment, especially in international markets, recyclable tin-coated steel and aluminum packages are enjoying a resurgence in popularity. Because European countries are so densely populated, their regulations requiring environmentally friendly packaging are far more stringent than in North America. Marketers need to take this into consideration since such regulations add to the cost of doing business overseas.

Packaging is an extremely important medium since it typically serves as the last advertising a consumer sees before taking the product home. Plus, package design plays a major role in how the quality of the product is perceived. Good packaging can often make or break the deal for a consumer. How does the packaging for Gleukos Performance Punch help the product better appeal to consumers interested in fitness?

Government Impact on Packaging

Government agencies also influence package design. The Food and Drug Administration (FDA), for example, and the Nutrition Labeling and Education Act of 1990 (which went into effect in 1994) imposed stricter labeling requirements for nutrition and health products. Additional legislation is pending that would require the labeling of all genetically engineered foods. Sometimes a state's packaging requirements differ from the federal government's, adding even more complexity for manufacturers.

Package Manufacturing

Packages may come in many forms: wrappers, cartons, boxes, crates, cans, bottles, jars, tubes, barrels, drums, and pallets. And they may be constructed of many materials, from paper and steel ("tin" cans) to wood, glass, and burlap. Newer packaging materials include plastic-coated papers, ceramics, metal foils, and even straw. Thinner plastic beverage bottles and smaller labels eliminate millions of pounds of waste each year and save companies money. The plastic film pouch for food products has become a substitute for tin cans and is more flexible, light, and compact. For pharmaceutical products, consumers prefer plastic containers.[42]

The second phase of packaging, the *production process,* may require the use of many packaging specialists: experts in package engineering (box designers, packaging materials consultants, and specialists in equipment configuration); graphic artists (designers, production/computer artists, illustrators, and photographers); label producers (printers and label manufacturers); die-cutters for custom packages; and package warehousing companies (wholesalers of prefabricated packages and package manufacturers).

Ad agencies are not usually involved in packaging decisions. This is typically the realm of specialists. However, it's not uncommon for an agency to be consulted on the design of labels and packages, and some may even prepare the copy that goes on them. In an IMC program, the agency can be very helpful in coordinating this work with the overall theme of the ad campaign.

When Should a Package Be Changed?

There are many reasons to change a package: product alteration or improvement, substitution in packaging materials, competitive pressure, environmental concerns, changes in legislation, or the need to increase brand recognition.[43]

Advertisers spend millions researching and promoting new images. And packages have to reflect a contemporary brand image consistent with constantly changing consumer perceptions and desires. However, marketers must always exercise caution. Designers should change packaging very gradually to avoid confusing consumers.

check yourself ✓

1. What are the four functions of packaging?
2. What role might advertising agencies play in packaging decisions?

LO15-7 Describe the roles that sales promotion can play in a marketing strategy.

THE ROLE OF SALES PROMOTION IN IMC

Imagine walking into the fresh-fruit section of your local grocery store, picking up a big, juicy mango, and discovering a sticker on it stating: "Now available in Snapple. Mango Madness." You turn around and suddenly notice that there, right next to the fresh-fruit bin, stands a big display of, you guessed it, Snapple Mango Madness.

It actually happened. New York agency Kirshenbaum, Bond & Partners launched Snapple's new Mango Madness drink nationally with stickers on 30 million pieces of fruit.[44] Talk

sales promotion
A direct inducement offering extra incentives all along the marketing route—from manufacturers through distribution channels to customers—to accelerate the movement of the product from the producer to the consumer.

about out-of-the-box thinking and creative media planning! Moreover, it was an outstanding example of how sales promotion can be perfectly integrated with a company's positioning, in this case Snapple's "100% natural" message strategy.

The term *sales promotion* is often misunderstood or confused with advertising or publicity. This may be because sales promotion activities often occur simultaneously and use both advertising and publicity as part of the process. In truth, though, it is a very specific marketing communications activity.

Sales promotion is a direct inducement that offers extra incentives anywhere along the marketing route to enhance or accelerate the product's movement from producer to consumer. Within this definition, there are three important elements to consider. Sales promotion

- May be used anywhere in the marketing channel: from manufacturer to wholesaler, wholesaler to dealer, dealer to customer, or manufacturer to customer.
- Normally involves a direct inducement (such as money, prizes, extra products, gifts, or specialized information) that provides extra incentives to buy now or buy more, visit a store, request literature, display a product, or take some other action.
- Is designed to change the timing of a purchase or to shift inventory to others in the channel.

Let's see how this definition applies to Snapple. In an interesting combination of both consumer advertising and *trade promotion* (sales promotion aimed at members of the distribution channel), Snapple used the fresh mangoes as an unusual new advertising medium to introduce its Mango Madness to consumers and to stimulate initial demand for the drink. The magnitude of that media effort (30 million pieces of fruit) served as a huge incentive to retailers to grant Snapple extra floor space (very expensive real estate, by the way) to display Mango Madness right next to the fresh-fruit stand. The result: Snapple sold a lot more Mango Madness a lot faster, and for a lot less money, than it would have if it had just placed some expensive ads in consumer magazines or on TV. Moreover, by creatively integrating different forms of marketing communications, Snapple simultaneously bolstered its positioning strategy and enhanced its relationship with the retail trade—its primary customer.

Snapple's clever promotion of its Mango Madness flavor demonstrates an ingenious integration of sales promotion and product positioning. By placing a sticker ad on actual mangoes in the fresh-fruit section, Snapple reinforced its slogan of "100% natural"and grabbed the attention of customers not necessarily looking to buy the beverage. The marketing strategy was supported by placing bottles of Mango Madness in close proximity to the fruit.

Some marketers consider sales promotion supplementary to advertising and personal selling because it binds the two together, making both more effective. In reality, however, sales promotion is far more than supplementary. One study showed marketers spend 54 percent of their advertising/promotion budget on sales promotion compared to only 46 percent for advertising.[45] We'll see why shortly.

Sales promotion is expensive. But it's also effective. Unfortunately, it has serious drawbacks, which lead to furious battles in marketing circles between proponents of sales promotion and proponents of advertising. Each approach has an important role to play, but advertisers must consider the positives and negatives and get the balance right.

The Positive Effect of Sales Promotion on Brand Volume

Effective sales promotion accomplishes a number of things. First of all, it adds tangible, immediate, extra value to the brand. Snapple's creative media buy suddenly made Mango Madness more valuable to the retail trade. This induced retailers to stock up on the new product and display it prominently. Similarly, when McDonald's runs its Monopoly game, it's adding instant value to the products it sells. This is why we refer to sales promotion as the *value-added tool.*

Second, by adding immediate value, sales promotion *maximizes* sales volume. A short-term price cut or rebate, for instance, may be very effective at boosting sales. While advertising helps develop and reinforce a quality, differentiated brand reputation and build long-term market value, sales promotion helps build short-term *market volume.* To become a market leader, therefore, a brand needs both advertising and sales promotion.

Finally, when all brands appear to be equal, sales promotion can be more effective than advertising in motivating customers to try a new brand or to select one brand over another. It can also motivate some customers who might be unmoved by advertising efforts. And sales promotions often generate a more immediate, measurable payoff than traditional advertising campaigns. This is why we might also refer to sales promotion as the "sales accelerator."

To succeed, sales promotions should be creative and hard to imitate. Kirshenbaum,

Bond & Partners certainly demonstrated that with its Snapple labels. My Ad Campaign 15–B, "Creating Effective Sales Promotions," outlines some basic ideas to consider in designing promotions.

The Negative Effect of Sales Promotion on Brand Value

Advertisers need to understand the negative effects of sales promotion, too. For instance, excessive sales promotion at the expense of advertising can reduce profitability. Some marketers believe a proper expenditure balance for consumer packaged-goods products is approximately 60 percent for trade and consumer promotion, 40 percent for advertising.

A high level of trade sales promotion relative to advertising and consumer sales promotion has a positive effect on short-term market share but may have a negative effect on brand attitudes and long-term market share. Without an effective advertising effort to emphasize brand image and quality, customers become deal-prone rather than brand loyal. And overemphasis on price (whether in advertising or sales promotion) eventually destroys brand equity.[46]

Another drawback of sales promotion is its high cost. One analysis showed that only 16 percent of sales promotions were profitable. In other words, many manufacturers spend more than $1 to generate an extra $1 of profits.[47]

Finally, overly aggressive sales promotion or advertising can draw competitors into a price war, which leads to reduced sales and profits for everyone.

Thus, if too much of the marketing mix is allocated to advertising, the brand may gain a high-quality, differentiated image but not enough volume to be a market leader. On the other hand, as Larry Light, McDonald's chief global marketing officer, says, "Too much [sales] promotion, and the brand will have high volume but low profitability. Market leadership can be bought through bribes, but enduring profitable market leadership must be earned through building both brand value as well as volume."[48]

> **To become a market leader, . . . a brand needs both advertising and sales promotion.**

Creating Effective Sales Promotions [15–B]

- **Set specific objectives.** Undisciplined, undirected creative work is a waste of time and resources.
- **Set a theme that is relevant.** Start with a strategy, preferably from a unified marketing or advertising plan. Stay on track.
- **Involve the trade.** Build relationships. Carrier Air Conditioning sponsored the Junior Olympics in key markets, sharing sponsorship with its dealer in each city.
- **Coordinate promotional efforts with other marketing plans.** Be sure to coordinate schedules and plans. A consumer promotion should occur simultaneously with a trade promotion; a free sample promotion should be timed to the introduction of a new line.
- **Know how basic promotion techniques work.** A price-off deal can't reverse a brand's downward sales trend.
- **Use simple, attention-getting copy.** Most promotions are built around a simple idea: "Save 75 cents." Emphasize the idea and don't try to be cute.
- **Use contemporary, easy-to-read graphics.** Don't expect to fit 500 words and 20 illustrations into a quarter-page freestanding insert.
- **Clearly communicate the concept.** Words and graphics must work together to get the message across.
- **Add advertising when you need measurable responses.** When part of a promotion, advertising directed at too broad an audience is usually wasted. However, trial-building promotions designed to attract new users, for example, can be helped by targeted advertising.
- **Reinforce the brand's advertising message.** Tie promotions to the brand's ad campaign.
- **Support the brand's positioning and image.** This is especially important for image-sensitive brands and categories, like family-oriented Kraft.
- **Know the media you work through.** Determine which media will work best. Should samples be distributed in stores, door to door, or through direct mail? Does the promotion need newspaper or magazine or Internet support?
- **Pretest promotions.** Pretesting doesn't have to be expensive. For packaged goods, small samplings in a few stores can reveal how to maximize coupon redemption rates by testing various values, creative approaches, and delivery methods.

push strategies Marketing, advertising, and sales promotion activities aimed at getting products into the dealer pipeline and accelerating sales by offering inducements to dealers, retailers, and salespeople.

trade promotions Promotion activities aimed at wholesalers and retailers to induce product purchase, display, and consumer sales promotion.

trade advertising The advertising of goods and services to intermediaries to stimulate wholesalers and retailers to buy goods for resale to their customers or for use in their own businesses.

pull strategies Marketing, advertising, and sales promotion activities aimed at inducing trial purchase and repurchase by consumers.

consumer sales promotions Promotions aimed at consumers to stimulate product interest, trial, or repurchase.

SALES PROMOTION STRATEGIES AND TACTICS

To move their products through the distribution channel from the point of manufacture to the point of consumption, marketers employ two types of strategies: push and pull. **Push strategies** are primarily designed to secure the cooperation of retailers. **Trade promotions**—sales promotions aimed at members of the distribution channel—are one of the principal tactics marketers use to push products through the distribution pipeline and gain shelf space. We'll discuss some of these tactics in the next section. Marketers may also use **trade advertising** (advertising in publications read by members of the trade) as a push tactic.

Pull strategies, on the other hand, are designed to attract customers and increase demand for the product (see Exhibit 15–6). Consumer advertising and **consumer sales promotions** are examples of pull strategies because they are designed to induce consumers to seek out or ask for the product, in effect pulling the product through the pipeline. Today, some national advertisers spend more dollars on trade sales promotions than on either consumer sales promotions or media advertising. But that is often the price they have to pay to gain and maintain distribution, without which they cannot make any sales.

▼EXHIBIT 15–6 Two marketing communications approaches.

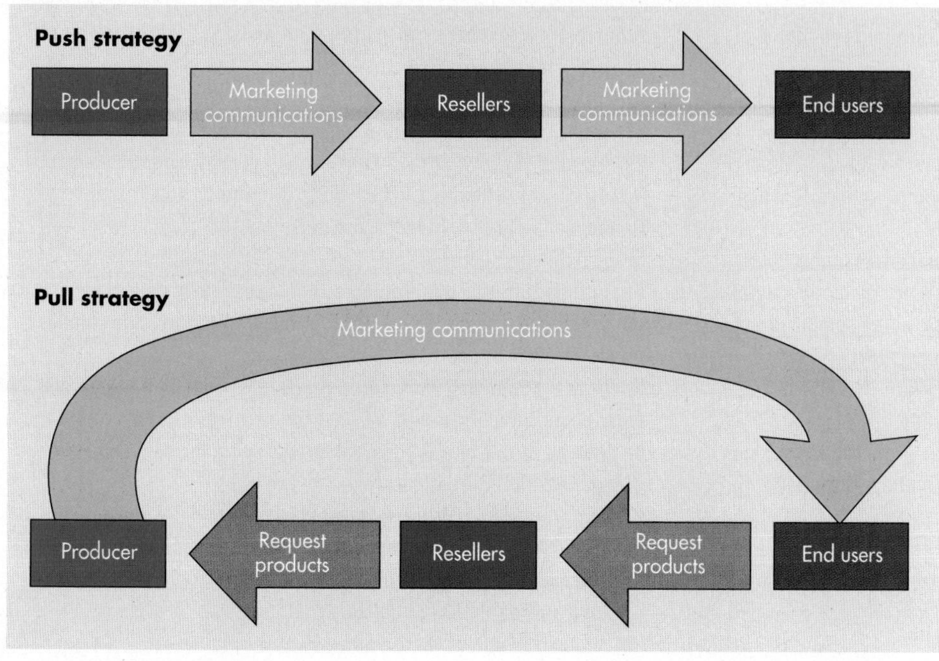

Giving Brands a Push with Trade Promotions

In supermarkets today, shelf space and floor space are hard to come by. To maintain their own images, department stores set standards for manufacturers' displays (planograms). This means that retailers often won't use the special racks, sales aids, and promotional literature supplied by manufacturers.

These are minor problems; major ones have to do with control of the marketplace. **Trade concentration**—more products going through fewer retailers—gives greater control to the retailers and less to the manufacturers. Increased competition for shelf space gives retailers even more power, enabling them to exact hefty deals and allowances. As a result, manufacturers of national brands often don't have enough money left to integrate consumer advertising or sales promotions.[49]

Despite these problems, many manufacturers still implement effective push strategies. And the smart ones safeguard enough money for consumer advertising. Trade tactics include slotting allowances, trade deals, display allowances, buyback allowances, advertising allowances, cooperative advertising and advertising materials, dealer premiums and contests, push money, and company conventions and dealer meetings.

Slotting Allowances In response to the glut of new products, some retailers charge manufacturers **slotting allowances**—fees ranging from $15,000 to $40,000 or more for the privilege of obtaining shelf or floor space for a new product. The practice is controversial because some manufacturers think they're being forced to subsidize the retailer's cost of doing business. Smaller manufacturers complain that the allowances shut out all but the largest suppliers. The Federal Trade Commission (FTC) considered taking steps to limit the use of slotting allowances because they reduce competition. But a 2003 FTC report

trade concentration More products being sold by fewer retailers.

slotting allowances Fees that manufacturers pay to retailers for the privilege of obtaining shelf or floor space for a new product.

trade deals Short-term dealer discounts on the cost of a product or other dollar inducements to promote a product.

forward buying A retailer's stocking up on a product when it is discounted and buying smaller amounts when it is at list price.

diverting Purchasing large quantities of an item at a regional promotional discount and shipping portions to areas of the country where the discount isn't being offered.

display allowances Fees paid to retailers to make room for and set up manufacturers' displays.

buyback allowance A manufacturer's offer to pay for an old product so that it will be taken off the shelf to make room for a new product.

advertising allowances Either a percentage of gross purchases or a flat fee paid to the retailer for advertising the manufacturer's product.

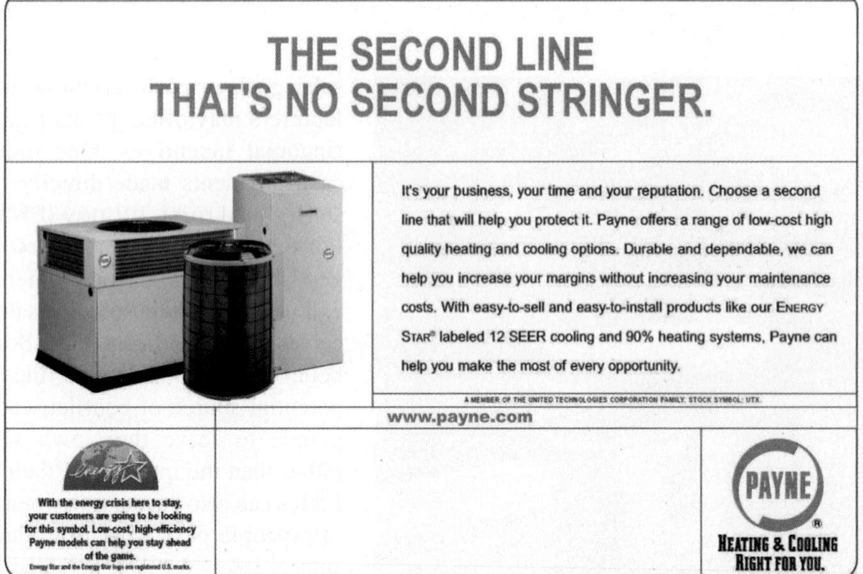

Trade promotions are business-to-business programs that are strategically aimed at increasing distribution. This ad for Payne Heating and Cooling (www.payne.com) aims to persuade buyers for HVAC companies to purchase and install Payne units for their customers.

concluded that slotting allowances encourage the stocking of new products by defraying the retailers' costs associated with new product introductions.[50]

Trade Deals Manufacturers make **trade deals** with retailers by offering short-term discounts or other dollar inducements. To comply with the Robinson-Patman Act, trade deals must be offered proportionally to all dealers. Dealers usually pass the savings on to customers through short-term sale prices, or "specials."

Excessive trade deals threaten brand loyalty because they encourage customers to buy whatever brand is on sale. Furthermore, marketers who use trade discounts extensively find themselves in a vicious circle: If they cut back on the promotions, they may lose shelf space and then market share.

In addition, some retailers capitalize on trade discounts by engaging in forward buying and diverting. With **forward buying**, a retailer stocks up on a product when it is on discount and buys smaller amounts when it sells at regular price. **Diverting** means using the promotional discount to purchase large quantities of an item in one region, then shipping portions of the buy to areas where the discount isn't offered.

Display Allowances More and more stores charge manufacturers **display allowances**—fees to make room for and set up displays. In-store displays include counter stands, floor stands, shelf signs, and special racks that give the retailer ready-made, professionally designed vehicles for selling more of the featured products.

Buyback Allowances When introducing a new product, manufacturers sometimes offer retailers a **buyback allowance** for the old product that hasn't sold. To persuade retailers to take on their product line, some manufacturers even offer a buyback allowance for a competitor's leftover stock.

Advertising Allowances Manufacturers often offer **advertising allowances** as either a percentage of purchases or a flat fee paid to the retailer. Advertising allowances are more common for consumer than industrial products. They are offered primarily by large companies, but some smaller firms give them to high-volume customers. The purpose of these allowances is to encourage retailers to advertise the manufacturer's products, but compliance is not always enforced.

cooperative (co-op) advertising The sharing of advertising costs by the manufacturer and the distributor or retailer.

push money (PM) Monetary inducements for salespeople to push the sale of particular products. Also called *spiffs.*

spiffs Also called *push money.* Monetary inducement for retail salespeople to push the sale of particular products.

company conventions Meetings held by companies with their employees, sales representatives, and/or customers to announce new products, policies, and marketing programs.

dealer meetings Meetings held by companies with their authorized brokers, distributors, and/or retailers to announce new products, policies, and marketing programs.

Manufacturers like DeWalt often pay a display allowance for their in-store exhibits, banners, and shelf signs. These fees benefit retailers like Home Depot by compensating them for the space occupied by the displays. And the manufacturer benefits from the increased exposure.

Co-op Advertising and Advertising Materials

With **cooperative (co-op) advertising**, national manufacturers reimburse their dealers for advertising the manufacturer's products or logos in their trading area. The manufacturer usually pays 50 to 100 percent of the dealer's advertising costs based on a percentage of the dealer's sales. Special co-op deals are used to introduce new products, advertise certain lines, or combat competitors.

Unlike advertising allowances, co-op programs typically require the dealer to submit invoices and proof of the advertising (*tearsheets* from the newspaper or affidavits of performance from radio or TV stations). Many manufacturers also give their dealers prepared advertising materials: ads, glossy photos, sample radio commercials, and so on. To control the image of their products, some advertisers insist that dealers use these materials to qualify for the co-op advertising money.

Dealer Premiums, Contests, and Push Money

To encourage retail dealers and salespeople to reach specific sales goals or push certain products, manufacturers may offer special prizes, gifts, or financial incentives. One inducement is cash payments made directly to the sales staff, called **push money (PM)**, or **spiffs**. For example, a shoe salesperson may suggest shoe polish or some other high-profit extra; for each item sold, the salesperson receives a 25- to 50-cent spiff. Some retailers believe that manufacturers' incentives are a potential source of conflict, causing salespeople to serve their own self-interests rather than the interests of their employers. Ethics can also be an issue when dealers and salespeople push certain products on consumers solely for their personal gain.

Company Conventions and Dealer Meetings

Most major manufacturers hold **company conventions** and **dealer meetings** to introduce new products, announce sales promotion programs, or show new advertising campaigns. They may also conduct sales and service training sessions. Meetings can be a dynamic sales promotion tool for the manufacturer.

Push strategies are virtually invisible to consumers. Yet successful inducements mean the product gets more shelf space, a special display, or extra interest and enthusiasm from salespeople. And extra sales interest can spell the difference between failure and success.

Using Consumer Promotions to Pull Brands Through

One reason for today's increased focus on consumer sales promotions is the change in TV viewing habits. With cable TV, DVRs, and DVDs, fewer people watch any one program. Advertising audiences are more fragmented, and major manufacturers must turn to new methods to reach these moving targets.

Common consumer sales promotions include point-of-purchase materials, coupons, electronic coupons and convenience cards,

point-of-purchase (P-O-P) materials Materials set up at a retail location to build traffic, advertise the product, and promote impulse buying.

coupon A certificate with a stated value that is presented to a retail store for a price reduction on a specified item.

freestanding inserts (FSIs) Coupons distributed through inserts in newspapers.

cents-off promotions, refunds, rebates, premiums, sampling, combination offers, contests, and sweepstakes. A successful IMC campaign may integrate several of these techniques along with media advertising, product publicity, and direct marketing.

Point-of-Purchase (P-O-P) Materials Walk into any store and notice the number of display materials and advertising-like devices that are designed to build traffic, exhibit and advertise the product, and promote impulse buying. Collectively, these are all referred to as **point-of-purchase (P-O-P) materials**.

P-O-P works best when used with other forms of advertising. For example, by advertising its gum and candy, one marketer increased sales by about 150 percent. But when P-O-P was added to the same program, the purchase rate jumped 550 percent.[51]

In one poll, 56 percent of mass-merchandise shoppers and 62 percent of grocery shoppers said they noticed point-of-purchase materials. More than half reported noticing signs and displays, 18 percent remembered coupon dispensers, and 14 percent could recall samplings and demonstrations.[52]

Today's consumers make their decisions in the store 66 percent of the time and make unplanned (impulse) purchases 53 percent of the time, so P-O-P can often be the major factor in stimulating purchases.[53]

P-O-P materials may also include window displays, counter displays, floor and wall racks to hold the merchandise, streamers, and posters. Often, the product's shipping cartons are designed to double as display units. A complete information center may even provide literature, samples, product photos, or an interactive computer in a kiosk.

The trend toward self-service retailing has increased the importance of P-O-P materials. With fewer and less knowledgeable salespeople available to help them, customers are forced to make purchasing decisions on their own. Eye-catching, informative displays can give them the nudge they need. Even in well-staffed stores, display materials can offer extra selling information and make the product stand out from the competition.

The proliferation of P-O-P displays has led retailers to be more discriminating in what they actually use. Most are beginning to insist on well-designed, attractive materials that will blend harmoniously with their store atmosphere.

The emphasis on P-O-P has led to a variety of new approaches, including ads on shopping carts and grocery aisle floors, on-shelf coupon dispensers, advertising jingles activated when in-store refrigerator doors are opened, and interactive computers for selecting everything from shoe styles to floor coverings. Digital technology has led to Hallmark Cards's Touch-Screen Greetings interactive kiosks, which print a customer's personal message onto any card.[54] To send it, look for one of the Automated Postal Centers rolled out by the U.S. Postal Service. The kiosks allow customers to weigh materials to be mailed, buy postage, and look up zip codes.[55]

Consumer sales promotions expose potential customers to a product and induce them to seek it out. While trade promotions push products through distribution channels, consumer sales promotions are intended to pull the product through due to customer demand. This STK (www.stkusallc.com) point-of-purchase display serves to incite interest in its durable truck bedliners.

Coupons A **coupon** is a certificate with a stated value presented to the retail store for a price reduction on a specified item. Marketers in the United States distributed more than 300 billion coupons in 2012, but only about 2.9 billion were ever redeemed. Nearly 80 percent of consumers surveyed say they use coupons at least sometimes while shopping.[56]

Coupons may be distributed in newspapers or magazines, door to door, on packages, in stores, by direct mail or online. Over 91 percent reach consumers through colorful preprinted newspaper ads called **freestanding inserts (FSIs)**.[57] FSIs have a higher redemption rate than regular newspaper and magazine coupons; coupons in or on packages have the highest redemption levels of all.[58] Online coupons now represent 5.6 percent of all coupons redeemed.[59]

Manufacturers lose hundreds of millions of dollars annually on fraudulent coupon submissions. Some coupons are counterfeited; others are submitted for products that were never purchased. To fight this problem, some companies have developed computerized systems to detect fraudulent submissions and charge them back to the retailers who made them.

electronic coupons Offer benefits similar to paper coupons, but they are distributed at the point of purchase, based on customer information stored in an electronic database.

premium An item offered free or at a bargain price to encourage the consumer to buy an advertised product.

convenience cards Cards issued by retailers that allow them to track their customers' purchasing habits and demographic profiles.

cents-off promotions A short-term reduction in the price of a product designed to induce trial and usage.

rebates Cash refunds on items from groceries to household appliances to cars, offered as incentives to purchase the products.

slippage Rebate offers that are never redeemed and coupons that are never submitted because people forget, find them inconvenient, or don't follow the instructions.

Most coupons reach consumers through newspaper freestanding inserts (FSIs), which have a higher redemption rate than regular newspaper or magazine coupons.

Electronic Coupons and Convenience Cards High-tech **electronic coupons** work like paper coupons in that they entitle the shopper to a discount, but their method of distribution is entirely different. Interactive touch-screen videos at the point of purchase and coupon printers at checkout counters generate instant discounts, rebates, and offers to try new brands. Electronic coupons are spreading quickly in the nation's supermarkets, though they still represent only a small percentage of the total coupons distributed annually.

Nonetheless, most of the nation's top brand marketers are involved with the Catalina Marketing Network. Catalina's system is installed in more than 30,000 stores across the country and influences more than 230 million shoppers.[60]

Electronic couponing targets consumers with specific offers in ways that would not be possible with paper coupons. Many supermarket chains now issue customers **convenience cards** entitling them to discounts at the checkout counter. Consumers often provide detailed information about themselves when they apply for these cards. When customers use a card, a record of their purchases is sent to a database. The card saves customers the hassle of clipping paper coupons, it allows retailers to better understand their customers' purchasing behaviors, and it provides consumers with targeted offers.

Coupon-to-card (C2C) coupons can be downloaded by customers to their grocery store convenience cards from retailers' websites or smartphone apps. Measured for the first time in 2012, C2C and mobile coupons represented 1.3 percent of coupons redeemed.[61] Catalina's newest offering, BuyerVision Mobile, delivers personalized mobile advertising to 70 million households on their smartphones. Catalina utilizes the buying history of millions of U.S. households to target mobile advertising to a brand's most valuable consumers and then measures the impact based on in-store sales.

Cents-Off Promotions, Refunds, and Rebates **Cents-off promotions** are short-term reductions in the price of a product in the form of cents-off packages, one-cent sales, free offers, and box top refunds. Some packages bear a special cents-off sticker, which the clerk removes and credits at the checkout counter.

Some companies offer *refunds* in the form of cash or coupons that can be applied to future purchases of the product. To obtain the refund, the consumer must mail in a proof of purchase, such as three box tops.

Rebates are larger cash refunds on items from cars to household appliances. Large rebates (like those given on cars) are handled by the seller. For small rebates (like those given for coffeemakers), the consumer sends in a certificate.

Research indicates that many people purchase a product because of an advertised rebate but never collect the rebate because of the inconvenience.[62] This is a phenomenon called **slippage**. Consumers Union estimates that 60 percent of all rebates go unfilled.[63]

Premiums A **premium** is an item offered free or at a bargain price to encourage the consumer to buy an advertised product. Premiums affect purchase behavior the same way as rebates but tend to be more effective at getting consumers to buy a product they didn't really need (see Exhibit 15–7). Premiums are intended to improve the product's image, gain goodwill, broaden the customer base, and produce quick sales.

A premium should have strong appeal and value and should be useful or unusual. It may be included in the product's package *(in-pack premium)*, on the package *(on-pack premium)*, mailed

sampling Offering consumers a free trial of a product, hoping to convert them to habitual use.

polybagging Samples that are delivered in plastic bags with the daily newspaper or a monthly magazine.

In-store sampling The handing out of free product samples to passing shoppers.

combination offers A sales promotion device in which two related products are packaged together at a special price, such as a razor and a package of blades.

▼EXHIBIT 15-7 Next to coupons, premiums are one of the most effective sales promotion techniques for changing consumer behavior.

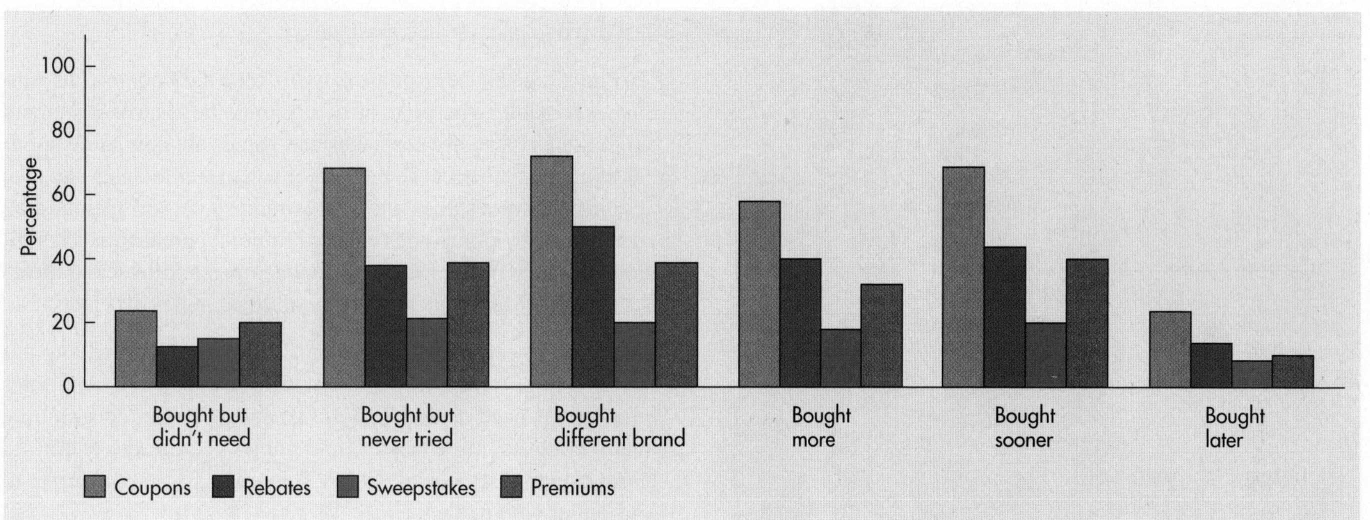

free or for a nominal sum on receipt of proof of purchase (box top or label), or given with the product at the time of purchase. Cosmetics companies often hold department store promotions in which scarves, purses, and cosmetics samplers are given free or for a low price with a purchase. The purchased cosmetics sampler is an example of a *self-liquidating* premium: The consumer pays enough so that the seller breaks even but doesn't make a profit.

Sampling

Sampling is the most costly of all sales promotions. It is also one of the most effective for new products, because it offers consumers a free trial in hopes of converting them to habitual use. Sampling should be supported by advertising and must involve a product available in small sizes and purchased frequently. Successful sampling depends heavily on the product's merits. It offers the greatest credibility and can turn a nonuser into a loyal customer instantly—if the product lives up to its promise.

Samples may be distributed by mail, door to door, via coupon advertising, or by a person in the store. They may be given free or for a small charge. Sometimes samples are distributed with related items, but this limits their distribution to those who buy the other product. In **polybagging**, samples are delivered in plastic bags with the daily newspaper or a monthly magazine. This enables distribution to targeted readers and lets publications give their subscribers added value at no cost.[64]

Catalina Mobile combines personalized promotions delivered in the aisle and mobile self-checkout on a customer's smartphone. It delivers relevant offers and messages to the consumer based on her purchase history, brand preferences, location in the store, and basket contents.

In-store sampling is very popular. Most in-store sampling programs are tied to a coupon campaign. Depending on the nature of the product, samples can be used as either a push strategy or a pull strategy.

Combination Offers

Food and drug marketers use **combination offers**, such as a razor and a package of blades or a toothbrush with a tube of toothpaste, at a reduced price for the two. For best results, the items should be related. Sometimes a combination offer introduces a new product by tying its purchase to an established product at a special price.

Contests, Sweepstakes, and Games

Many people use the terms *contests* and *sweepstakes* interchangeably.

contest A sales promotion device for creating consumer involvement in which prizes are offered based on the skill of the entrants.

sweepstakes A sales promotion activity in which prizes are offered based on a chance drawing of entrants' names.

game A sales promotion activity in which prizes are offered based on chance. A game is conducted over a longer period of time than a sweepstakes.

In-store sampling displays allow consumers to test products in an environment where they may be readily purchased.

Technically, however, a **contest** offers prizes based on an entrant's skill. For example, an entrant needs to answer a question correctly or submit an original recipe. A **sweepstakes** offers prizes based solely on a chance drawing of entrants' names. A **game** has the chance element of a sweepstakes but is conducted over a longer time (like McDonald's Monopoly game). A game's big marketing advantage is that customers must make repeat visits to the dealer to continue playing.

Contests, sweepstakes, and games all encourage consumption of the product by creating consumer involvement. These devices pull millions of entries. Usually contest entrants must send in some proof of purchase, such as a box top or label. For more expensive products, consumers may only have to visit the dealer or take a test drive to pick up an entry blank.

To encourage entries, sponsors try to keep their contests as simple as possible. The prize structure must be clearly stated and all the rules listed. Sweepstakes and games are now more popular than contests because they are much easier to enter and take less time. Sweepstakes and games require careful planning by the advertiser. Companies cannot require a purchase as a condition for entry or the sweepstakes becomes a lottery and therefore illegal. Marketers must obey all local and postal laws.

Contests, sweepstakes, and games must be promoted and advertised to be successful, and this can be expensive. And sales promotions need dealer support. To ensure dealer cooperation, many contests, sweepstakes, and games require the entrant to name the product's local dealer. They may also award prizes to the dealer who made the sale. ■

check yourself ✓

1. What are the possible negative effects of sales promotion?
2. What is the difference between a push strategy and a pull strategy? Which one is directed toward the consumer and which one toward the trade?

learn about, practice, and apply the use of direct marketing, personal selling, packaging, and sales promotion!

M: Advertising was developed for students who want information packaged in a concise, easy-to-read, yet interesting format.

Check out the book's website to:

- Discover which company representatives are most effective at staffing a trade show booth. (Review Questions)
- Learn the three things salespeople must do to build relationships. (Review Questions)
- Find out why there is a trend away from push strategies and toward pull strategies. (Review Questions)
- Learn how to evaluate the effectiveness of a product's packaging. (Exploring Advertising)

While you are there, check out the professional resource links, review the PowerPoint presentation, and test your knowledge with the Multiple Choice Quiz. Additionally, *Connect® Marketing* is available for M: Advertising.

www.mhhe.com/ArensM2e

DIAMOND
Culinary Walnuts
SAFEWAY
Ingredients for life
salesforce
PSVITA
Tim
Lincecum
TOYOTA
Budweiser
382
YAHOO!
McAfee
399

chapter sixteen

IMC: public relations, sponsorship, and corporate advertising

This chapter explains the role of public relations, sponsorship, and corporate advertising in relationship marketing and integrated marketing communications. By integrating public relations, event sponsorship, and institutional advertising with its general advertising activities, a company can improve the overall effectiveness of its marketing efforts.

Netflix, a provider of on-demand Internet video streaming and DVD rentals by mail, is one of the most successful companies of the 2000s. Legend has it that founder and CEO Reed Hastings launched his company after balking at fees he owed for a late DVD rental. His great idea was to deliver DVD rentals without the annoyances consumers faced when renting from Blockbuster and Hollywood Video: late fees, return dates, and the drive to the store.

Launched in 1998, Netflix allowed consumers to get their movie in the mail, keep it as long as they wanted, and drop it in the mailbox to return when they were done. All for one low monthly fee.

The company grew from 1 million subscribers in 2002 to nearly 14 million just eight years later. And while it was not profitable until 2003, once Netflix's model took hold, the writing was on the wall for brick-and-mortar companies like Blockbuster.

Netflix benefited from a number of technologies in its surge to the top, not least of which was the Internet. Customers could go to the company's website and order or plan for their next selection. But by 2010, the Internet also ensured that Netflix would face a new, nimbler, faster-growing, and more convenient challenger: Netflix. Netflix began competing with itself when it allowed a small portion of its catalog to be streamed to computers or TVs. The streaming service was offered for no additional charge to individuals on the mail plan.

continued on p. 398

LEARNING OBJECTIVES

After studying this chapter, you will be able to:

- **LO16-1** Distinguish between advertising and public relations.
- **LO16-2** Describe the key tasks of public relations practitioners.
- **LO16-3** Explain the potential benefits and drawbacks of sponsorships in an IMC plan.
- **LO16-4** Discuss the functions of corporate advertising.

continued from p. 397

While most customers still ordered their DVDs by mail, streaming was clearly the future. But now Netflix had two distinct delivery models, and the company was therefore, in a sense, competing with itself. Supporting two models was expensive. Netflix soon saw its profit margins eroding as the streaming service grew.

So Hastings made a decision: Customers who wanted to continue receiving DVDs by mail and enjoy unlimited streaming would see their monthly rate jump from $9.99 to $15.98. When the company introduced the price increase to its customers, it called the change "a terrific value." True or not, customers did not respond to this public relations message favorably. In fact many, shocked at the price jump, were outraged. Austin Carr, writing for Fastcompany.com, wrote, "Subscribers saw right through this corporate boilerplate, leaving nearly 13,000 comments on Netflix's blog, creating a social media nightmare for the company on Twitter and Facebook, and overwhelming Netflix's call center with complaints."

But there was more to come. Hastings decided to split mail delivery and streaming into two different companies. Netflix would be the company focused on streaming delivery, and a new independent subsidiary, Qwikster, would deliver DVDs by mail. The companies would be completely separate and require separate subscriptions. The public response? More outrage.

Hastings understood that his company had done a poor job explaining its decisions. In his company's blog he wrote:

> When Netflix is evolving rapidly . . . I need to be extra-communicative. This is the key thing I got wrong. . . . In hindsight, I slid into arrogance based upon past success. We have done very well for a long time by steadily improving our service, without doing much CEO communication. Inside Netflix I say, "Actions speak louder than words," and we should just keep improving our service. But now I see that, given the huge changes we have been recently making, I should have personally given a full justification to our members of why we are separating DVD and streaming, and charging for both.

The CEO also dove into the comments section of his blog to deal with consumers directly. Fastcompany.com recounts the following exchange between Hastings and a customer:

> "Seriously, you thought a good idea to make up for miscommunications was to separate the websites and make it more complicated for us to manage our queues? Really?" reads one of the most popular comments on the site.
>
> Responds Hastings, "We think the separate websites (a link away from each other) will enable us to improve both faster than if they were single websites."

Consumers were unhappy, and Netflix estimated that it lost nearly a million subscribers in the third quarter of 2011. But while it was easy for consumers to dislike the company's decisions, in truth Hastings had little choice. Offering both services for under $10 was unsustainable. Netflix needed to alter its pricing model, or face the harsh realities dictated by the marketplace. Could it have done so in a better way, one that would have allowed its customers to clearly understand the need for the company's actions?

Perhaps. But Netflix has survived this bump in the road. By the fourth quarter of 2011, it was adding subscribers again, nearly replacing all it had lost. In mid-2013, Netflix reached a record 28.6 million video streaming subscribers in the United States and its stock was up 185 percent for the year.[1] Hastings, by showing a willingness to engage with his consumers, listen to their complaints, and respond proactively, is still at the helm of one of the fastest-growing companies in the world. ■

public relations (PR) The management function that focuses on the relationships and communications that individuals and organizations have with other groups (called *publics*) for the purpose of creating mutual goodwill.

publics In PR terminology, employees, customers, stockholders, competitors, suppliers, or the general population of customers are all considered among an organization's publics.

LO16-1 Distinguish between advertising and public relations.

THE ROLE OF PUBLIC RELATIONS

The primary role of public relations is to manage a company's reputation and help build public support for its activities. Today's business environment has become so competitive that public approval can no longer be assumed; it must be earned continuously.[2]

The term *public relations* is widely misunderstood and misused. Part of the confusion is due to the fact that public relations covers a very broad range of activities. Depending on the context and one's point of view, it can be a concept, a profession, a management function, or a practice. For our purposes, we define **public relations (PR)** as the strategic management of the relationships and communications that individuals and organizations have with other groups for the purpose of creating mutual goodwill.

As we've already discussed, every company, organization, or government body has relationships with groups of people who are affected by what it does or says. They may be employees, customers, stockholders, competitors, suppliers, legislators, or the community in which the organization resides. Marketing professionals refer to these people as *stakeholders* because they all have some vested interest in the company's actions. In PR terminology, each of these groups is considered one of the organization's **publics**, and the goal of PR is to develop and maintain goodwill with most, if not all, of its publics. Failure to do so may mean loss of customers and revenues, time lost dealing with complaints or lawsuits, and loss of respect (which weakens the organization's brand equity as well as its ability to secure financing, make sales, and expand business).

A company's publics change constantly. After being acquired by Unilever, Ben & Jerry's Homemade Ice Cream encountered previously silent publics. Criticism of the company appears to have increased after the acquisition. The Center for Science in the Public Interest (CSPI) accused Ben & Jerry's of misleading the public by claiming that some of its products were "all-natural" when they in fact contained hydrogenated oils and artificial flavors. CSPI called upon the FDA to take action against the company.[3] Ben & Jerry's hedged response was that the term "all-natural" had various definitions in the food industry, but that it would work with natural food organizations on the issue.[4] After receiving one illness complaint, the company voluntarily recalled pints of Karamel Sutra ice cream that contained peanuts not mentioned on the label. Subsequently, CEO Yves Couette stated that "Our primary concern is always for the health and safety of our consumers."[5]

Rachael Ray has enormous influence with millions of consumers who enjoy her shows. So when Ray suggests she has a strong brand preference, the impact on sales can be substantial.

Because of the powerful effect of public opinion, companies and organizations must consider the breadth of the impact of their actions. This is especially true in times of crisis, emergency, or disaster. But it also holds true for major policy decisions: changes in management or pricing, labor negotiations, the introduction of new products, or changes in distribution methods. Each decision affects different groups in different ways. Effective public relations can channel groups' opinions toward mutual understanding and positive outcomes.

In short, the goals of public relations are to improve public opinion, build goodwill, and establish and maintain a satisfactory reputation for the organization. PR efforts may rally public support, obtain public understanding, or simply respond to inquiries. Well-executed public relations is an ongoing process that molds good long-term relationships and plays an important role in relationship marketing and integrated communications.[6]

The Difference between Advertising and Public Relations

Since they both use the media to create awareness or to influence markets or publics, advertising and public relations are similar—but they're not the same. Advertising reaches its audience through media the advertiser pays for. It appears just as the advertiser designed it, with the advertiser's bias built in. Knowing this, the public views ads with some skepticism or ignores them outright. So, in an integrated marketing communications program, advertising is rarely the best vehicle for building credibility.

Many public relations communications, like publicity, are not openly sponsored or paid for. People receive these communications in the form of news articles, editorial

interviews, or feature stories after the messages have been reviewed and edited—filtered—by the media. Since the public thinks such messages are coming from the media rather than a company, it trusts them more readily. For building credibility, therefore, public relations is usually the better approach. Netflix, for example, benefited heavily from favorable press reviews during its heady growth years.

However, while advertising is carefully placed to gain particular reach and frequency objectives, PR is less precise. Public relations objectives are not as easy to quantify. In fact, the results gained from public relations activities depend greatly on the experience and skill of the people executing them and the relationship they have with the press. But PR can go only so far. Editors won't run the same story over and over. An ad's memorability, however, comes from repetition. While PR activities may offer greater credibility, advertising offers precision and control.

Advertising and PR in the Eyes of Practitioners

Another major difference between public relations and advertising is the orientation of professional practitioners. Advertising professionals see *marketing* as the umbrella process companies use to determine what products and services the market needs and how to distribute and sell them. To advertising professionals, advertising and public relations are marketing tools used to promote sales.

Public relations professionals take a different view. With their background often in journalism rather than marketing, they believe *public relations* should be the umbrella process. They think companies should use PR to maintain relationships with all publics, including consumers. As *Inside PR* magazine says, "Public relations is a management discipline that encompasses a wide range of activities, from *marketing and advertising* to investor relations and government affairs."[7]

A recent news event draws attention to the value that public relations plays, both in IMC and as part of a broader concern with managing relationships. Like many companies, Apple uses Chinese factories to produce iPads and other technologies at relatively low costs. This in turn helps Apple market iPads for a price that is difficult for competitors to beat in the marketplace. Offering a strong value proposition is, of course, an important marketing goal. But when rumors of terrible factory conditions at the Chinese plant began circulating, Apple faced a problem that went beyond marketing. Acting on the advice of its public relations counsel, Apple invited ABC news to tour its Chinese partner's factory. ABC found that the rumors were false and that employees were well treated. Crisis averted. That is the value of public relations.

To date, though, few companies are structured with a public relations orientation; most are still marketing oriented, perhaps due to marketing's bottom-line focus. But today's marketing people would be well advised to adopt the multiple-stakeholder approach and relationship consciousness that PR people bring to the table. Moreover, in times of crisis, the candid, open-information orientation of PR is invariably the better perspective to adopt. Fortunately, with the growing interest in relationship marketing, two-way interactivity, and IMC, companies are finally beginning to embrace a public relations philosophy.

When PR activities are used for marketing purposes, the term **marketing public relations (MPR)** is often used. In support of marketing, public relations activities can raise awareness, inform and educate, improve understanding, build trust, make friends, give people reasons or permission to buy, and create a climate of consumer acceptance—usually better than advertising.[8] Marketing strategists Al and Laura Ries believe the best way to build a brand is through publicity—a PR activity. They cite numerous examples of leading companies that achieved their cachet with relatively little advertising but extensive publicity: Starbucks, The Body Shop, and Walmart, to name a few.[9]

In an integrated marketing communications program, advertising and MPR need to be closely coordinated. Many ad agencies now have PR departments or affiliate with public relations firms. Exhibit 16–1 shows some of the PR industry's largest firms and the conglomerates that own them. And many companies now have communications departments that manage both advertising and PR.

[While PR activities offer greater credibility, advertising offers precision and control.]

check yourself ✓

1. Why is it important for a company to develop and maintain goodwill with its stakeholders?
2. Why does the public tend to trust news stories more readily than advertising?

marketing public relations (MPR) The use of public relations activities as a marketing tool.

opinion sampling A form of public relations research in which consumers provide feedback via interviews, toll-free phone lines, focus groups, and similar methods.

reputation management In public relations, the name of the long-term strategic process to manage the standing of the firm with various publics.

publicity The generation of news about a person, product, or service that appears in broadcast or print media.

EXHIBIT 16–1 Largest public relations agencies in the United States (2011).

2011 Rank	Agency	Headquarters	2011 U.S. Revenue ($ millions)	Percentage Change vs. 2010
1	Edelman	Chicago	$383	+9.8%
2	Weber Shandwick (Interpublic)	New York	354	+10.6
3	Fleishman-Hillard (Omnicom)	St. Louis	352	+4.9
4	Ketchum (Omnicom)	New York	218	+17.8
5	Burson-Marsteller (WPP)	New York	212	0.0
6	MSL Group (Publicis)	Paris	182	NA
7	Ogilvy Public Relations (WPP)	New York	154	+18.6
8	Hill & Knowlton Strategies (WPP)	New York	125	NA
9	Waggener Edstrom Worldwide	Bellevue, WA	101	+0.8
10	GolinHarris (Interpublic)	Chicago	98	+9.0

Source: Reprinted with permission (Advertising Age Agency Report 2012, April 30, 2012). Copyright Crain Communications Inc.

LO16-2 Describe the key tasks of public relations practitioners.

THE PUBLIC RELATIONS JOB

The public relations job comprises a variety of activities, from crisis communications to fundraising. And PR practitioners use many tools besides press conferences and news releases.

PR Planning and Research

The first function of a PR practitioner is to plan and execute the public relations program. Part of this task may be integrated with the company's marketing efforts (for instance, product publicity), but the PR person typically takes a broader view. He or she must prepare an overall public relations program for the whole organization.

Because public opinion is so important, the PR person must constantly monitor, measure, and analyze changes in attitudes among a variety of publics. A common form of public relations research is **opinion sampling** using techniques discussed in Chapter 6: shopping center or phone interviews, focus groups, analysis of incoming mail, and field reports. Some advertisers set up toll-free phone lines and invite consumer feedback.

The PR practitioner analyzes the organization's relationships with its publics; evaluates people's attitudes and opinions toward the organization; assesses how company policies and actions relate to different publics; determines PR objectives and strategies; develops and implements a mix of PR activities, integrating them whenever possible with the firm's other communications; and solicits feedback to evaluate effectiveness.

Social media provides PR experts a window into the minds of consumers, especially "influentials," the individuals whose opinions matter a great deal to others (we referred to these individuals as "centers of influence" in earlier chapters). Influentials are easy to spot online—they have large numbers monitoring their tweets, blog postings, or comments. It is no surprise then that the arrival of social media has transformed public relations so dramatically that some now refer to it as "public relations 2.0."[10]

Reputation Management

One of the principal tasks of public relations is to manage the standing of the firm with various publics. **Reputation management** is the name of this long-term strategic process.[11] PR practitioners employ a number of strategies and tactics to help them manage their firm's or client's reputation, including publicity and press agentry, crisis communications management, and community involvement.

Publicity and Press Agentry

Many public relations professionals focus primarily on generating news and placing it in the media for their companies or clients. A major activity of public relations, **publicity** is the generation of news about a person, product, or service that appears in print or electronic media. Companies employ this activity either for marketing purposes or to enhance the firm's reputation.

Some people think of publicity as "free" because the media don't charge to run it (they also don't guarantee they'll use it).

"TO ATTRACT MEDIA ATTENTION, PUBLICITY MUST BE *NEWSWORTHY*."

SACRAMENTO BUSINESS JOURNAL | JANUARY 4, 2008

sacramento.bizjournals.com

Coffee roaster gets buzz with cash infusion

Woodland company has a patented method to make lower-acid coffee

MARK ANDERSON | STAFF WRITER

A Woodland coffee company with a low-acid product got a jolt of $700,000 from a Bay Area investment group.

Puroast Coffee Co. Inc. closed a second-stage seed round of funding from Keiretsu Forum, an angel investment group.

The money will be used to expand production and marketing of Puroast, an organic coffee with half the acid of regular coffee, Puroast spokeswoman Jessica Rea said. The coffee purchased with "fair trade" practices, which guarantee a living wage to the small farmers who grow it.

The company raised equity and debt financing, and it has options for additional financing in the first quarter of the year.

Kerry Sachs, Puroast's founder and chief executive, is an agricultural engineer. He used South American methods to roast coffee beans that produce a coffee with half the acid of regular roasts. The method is patented and considered by the company to be proprietary, Rea said.

Roasters take acute care in regulating the temperature during the roasting process, which uses wood chips. The roasting is done in Woodland, and the coffee is distributed across the country. So far, the West Coast is its largest market, but East Coast states are also catching on, Rea said.

Puroast's claims of low acid were corroborated by research done at the University of California Davis, she said.

Puroast's investors think there is a bright future for the beverage company. In 2006, Americans spent almost $1 billion for over-the-counter antacids, and they paid more than $13 billion on prescribed medications for digestive acid problems.

"Puroast had all the attributes of a great investment opportunity for Keiretsu Forum members with its well-defined market, solid management team and sales in a number of supermarket chains," said Barry Hotchkies, Keiretsu due-diligence team leader. He and another forum member took seats on Puroast's advisory board.

Puroast is selling its coffee at locations including Ralph's, Kroger's, Albertson's, Sweet Bay and Save Mart stores.

Keiretsu is a structured group of investors who work together to perform due diligence on investment decisions and then decide individually whether to invest.

In the Puroast deal, four West Coast chapters decided to make the investment. The accredited private-equity investors include individual angel investors, venture capital companies and corporate and institutional investors.

The forum was founded in the East Bay, and it has a worldwide network of people looking at deals, doing due diligence and making investments.

There are Northern California chapters in San Francisco, East Bay, Silicon Valley and North Bay. There are also four chapters in Southern California, two chapters in Washington state, and one each in Idaho, Colorado, Beijing, London and Barcelona.

manderson@bizjournals.com | 916-558-7874

Puroast Coffee Co. Inc. received $700,000 in funding from investors for its low-acid coffee.

PHOTO COURTESY OF PUROAST COFFEE CO. INC.

A company will often use publicity to enhance or defend the firm's reputation. Here, the Puroast Coffee Company (www.puroast.com) used the press to announce its receipt of $700,000 in venture funding from Keiretsu Forum (www.keiretsuforum.com), an investment group. This publicity will help promote Puroast to grocery retailers and the general public and Keiretsu to other companies that might need venture funding.

This is a misconception, though. Someone still gets paid to write the release and coordinate with the press. However, as a marketing communications vehicle, publicity often offers a considerably greater return on money invested than other communications activities. A large ad campaign might require an investment of 5 to 20 percent of sales; a major publicity program, only 1 to 2 percent.

To attract media attention, publicity must be *newsworthy*. Typical publicity opportunities include new-product introductions, awards, company sales and earnings, major new contracts, mergers, retirements, and speeches by company executives. Sometimes publicity is unfavorable and accrues unintentionally, such as when Netflix instituted its price increases. And since publicity can originate from any source, it may be difficult—or impossible—to control. In IMC terms, unintentional publicity is an *unplanned message.*

The planning and staging of events to generate publicity is called **press agentry**. Press agentry helps to bring attention to new products or services or to portray their organizations favorably. For print media, the publicity person deals with editors and feature writers. For broadcast media, he or she deals with program directors, assignment editors, or news editors. Successful PR practitioners develop and maintain close, cordial relations with their editorial contacts. An MPR professional practicing IMC sees the press as an important *public,* and writers and editors as important *stakeholders.*

Crisis Communications Management One of the most important public relations tasks for any corporation is **crisis management**. Brand value can be quickly destroyed if "damage control" is not swift and thorough. For example, Martha Stewart's profitable marketing persona quickly became a liability in 2002, when her involvement in an insider-trading scheme surfaced. (She was later tried and sentenced to a prison term.) Even though her company, Martha Stewart Living Omnimedia, immediately took steps to distance itself from its founder's legal troubles by removing her name from some products and publications, its stock value and revenues both dropped by more than 30 percent between 2003 and 2004.[12]

But the classic case of exemplary crisis communications management was Johnson & Johnson's handling of a product-tampering episode in 1982. Several people died when a criminal laced bottles of J&J's Extra-Strength Tylenol with cyanide on retail shelves. The moment they received the news, management strategists at J&J and McNeil Products (the J&J subsidiary that markets Tylenol) formulated three stages of action:

1. Identify the problem and take immediate corrective action. J&J strategists got information from the police, FBI, FDA, and press; identified the geographic area affected; corrected rumors; and immediately withdrew the product from the marketplace.

2. Actively cooperate with authorities in the investigation. Johnson & Johnson was proactive. It helped the FBI and other law enforcement agencies generate leads and investigate security at its plants, and it offered a $100,000 reward.
3. Quickly rebuild the Tylenol name and capsule line, including Regular Strength capsules, which were recalled, too. Although J&J believed the poisoning had taken place at the retail end of the chain, it first made sure that the tampering hadn't occurred at McNeil. The company's two capsule production lines were shut down, and dog teams were brought in to search for cyanide.

press agentry The planning of activities and the staging of events to attract attention to new products or services and to generate publicity about the company or organization that will be of interest to the media.

crisis management A company's plan for handling news and public relations during crises.

community involvement A local public relations activity in which companies sponsor or participate in a local activity or supply a location for an event.

The insatiable appetite of the news media plus a flood of inquiries from anxious consumers put J&J's PR people under enormous pressure. All communications between the media and the company were channeled through the corporate communications department. All customer, trade, and government communications were coordinated within the company. This way, J&J maintained open, clear, consistent, legal, and credible communications and avoided rumors, political backbiting, and corporate defensiveness.

In the first 48 hours after the news broke, phone calls to Johnson & Johnson and McNeil were nonstop. In the basement at McNeil, a bank of phones usually used for sales was staffed by employees who were briefed on what to say, what not to say, and where to refer tough questions.

At the same time, management and employees had to be informed, authorities contacted, and many others notified. J&J and McNeil public relations managers and staff had to plan, coordinate, and supervise this enormous task.

As infrequent as disasters are, there is no more important activity for PR professionals and public information officers than crisis communications management—especially those in highly sensitive fields such as airlines, government agencies, the military, law enforcement, chemical and oil companies, and public utilities.

Since the Tylenol incident, many companies in normally nonsensitive industries have prepared crisis management plans. The manner in which a company handles communications during emergencies or catastrophes will determine to a great extent how the public responds to the news. When corporations have no plans for coping with a crisis, the resulting press coverage can be disastrous. Experts on crisis management encourage all companies to follow J&J's example by being open and candid. Withholding information or evading questions inevitably backfires, as many politicians have learned.

Attitudes toward a former crisis can soften over time. Netflix, after losing subscribers over its botched growth plans, eventually resumed growth. And Martha Stewart, Michael Vick, Tiger Woods, and many others have had "second chances" after bad publicity.

Community Involvement The goal of **community involvement** is to develop a dialogue between the company and the community.[13] This is best done by having company officers, management, and employees contribute to the community's social and economic development. Every community offers opportunities for corporate involvement: civic and youth groups, charitable fundraising drives, cultural or recreational activities, and so on. A company should ideally adopt one program relevant to its expertise and focus its *mission marketing* activities. The PR department may help set up such programs and publicize them to the community.

The social mission of Ben & Jerry's website reflects global and local initiatives. This site shows Ben & Jerry's use of social media and their support for raising awareness of the Fair Trade initiative by encouraging users of Twitter to donate their Tweets for a good cause.

public affairs All activities related to the community citizenship of an organization, including dealing with community officials and working with regulatory bodies and legislative groups.

lobbying Informing government officials and persuading them to support or thwart administrative action or legislation in the interests of some client.

speechwriting Function of a public relations practitioner to write speeches for stockholder meetings, conferences, conventions, etc.

online newsroom (or pressroom) A website that provides PR and investor information about corporations and organizations.

corporate blog A Web-based source of information about a company, its policies, products, or activities. Corporate blogs are one way companies can facilitate relationships with their consumers or other publics.

Other Public Relations Activities

In addition to planning and reputation management, public relations professionals are often involved in activities such as public affairs and lobbying, speechwriting, fundraising and membership drives, creation of publications, and special-events management.

Public Affairs and Lobbying Organizations often need to deal with elected officials, regulatory and legislative bodies, and various community groups—the realm of **public affairs**. Public affairs usually requires a specialist. Many experts think PR and public affairs should become more integrated to combine the skills and policy expertise of the specialist with the PR person's media and community relations savvy.

Lobbying refers to informing government officials and persuading them to support or thwart administrative action or legislation in the interests of some client. Every organization is affected by the government, so lobbying is big business.

Speechwriting Because company officials often have to speak at stockholder meetings, conferences, or conventions, PR practitioners often engage in **speechwriting**. They are also frequently responsible for making all the arrangements for speaking opportunities and developing answers for questions company representatives are likely to be asked. Since public relations people may sometimes represent their employers at special events, press conferences, and interviews, they too should be articulate public speakers.

To meet demanding operating budgets, nonprofit organizations often devote a significant portion of their advertising to raising funds. The Rainforest Action Network (www.ran.org) ran this ad to create awareness of the destruction of virgin old-growth forests.

Fundraising and Membership Drives A public relations person may be responsible for soliciting money for a nonprofit organization or for a cause the company deems worthwhile, such as the United Way or a political action committee (PAC).

Charitable organizations, labor unions, professional societies, trade associations, and other groups rely on membership fees or contributions. The PR specialist must communicate to potential contributors or members the goals of the organization and may integrate promotional tie-ins to publicize the drive or encourage participation. In the process, the company PR people may work closely with the advertising department or agency to create ads promoting the particular cause or to publicize the company's involvement with the cause in product ads.

Publications Public relations people prepare many of a company's communications materials: news releases and media kits; booklets, leaflets, pamphlets, brochures, manuals, and books; letters, inserts, and enclosures; annual reports; posters, bulletin boards, and exhibits; audiovisual materials; and position papers. It's important that these materials are also accessible in an **online newsroom**. Here again, PR people may work with the advertising department or the agency to produce these materials. The advertising people need to keep the company's overall positioning strategy in mind while trying to help accomplish the particular PR objectives.

Social Media As with all areas of advertising, the Internet has transformed the way we approach business and our communication to consumers. However, for PR the world seems to be flipped upside down. With the advent of social media and the rise in popularity of blogging and tweeting, staying on top of who is

> With the advent of social media . . . staying on top of who is writing about what is a full-time job.

writing about what is a full-time job. It used to be that a PR professional would have to know a score of people from each industry; nowadays that number is exponentially bigger. However, with the bad comes the good, and the clarity that comes from social media allows PR professionals to stay on top of any trends and deal with them before they become brand epidemics. With a good social media strategy, PR professionals can help get influential people to showcase their client's products as they launch, keeping early adopters and loyalists abreast of new developments before the advertising hits.

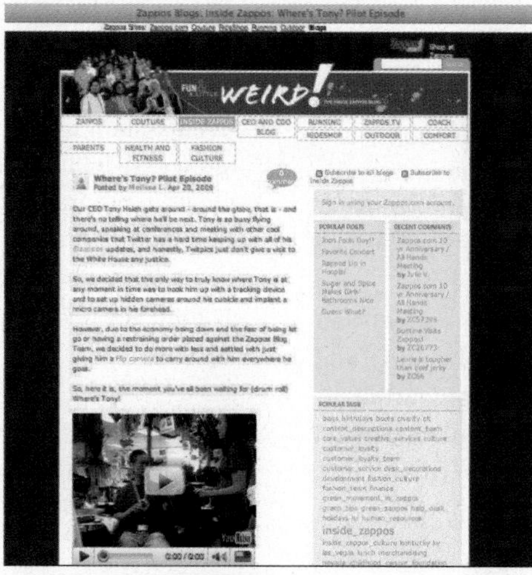
Zappos has built its company using social media. Employees are encouraged to use Twitter, Facebook, and YouTube. Here is its company blog written by a large collection of employees.

Corporate Blogs Maintaining and managing a **corporate blog** can help address important concerns, introduce new products or services, and maintain a dialogue between a company and its publics. My Ad Campaign 16–A, "Corporate Blogging," provides some guidelines for using this public relations activity.

Special-Events Management

The sponsorship and management of special events is a rapidly growing field. In fact, it has become such an important topic that we devote the next major section of this chapter to it, following our discussion of PR tools.

Public Relations Tools

The communications tools at the PR person's disposal vary widely, from news releases and photos to audiovisual materials and even advertising. We'll discuss some of the more common ones briefly.

Corporate Blogging [16–A]

Most corporations have guidelines for blogging. Here is a set of marketing-related guidelines that every corporation should think about if it intends on using blogging for a marketing tool.

- **Know the environment.** What are people saying about you and your products? Venture out into the Web and see what happens when you type your company name into Google or visit popular blogs that deal with your company's product category.
- **Determine what you hope to accomplish.** What is your purpose? Why have you started the blog? To address rumors? Share company news? Inform customers about new products? Develop a corporate personality? Having clear objectives will make decisions about what and when to blog much easier.
- **Practice, practice, practice.** Do a trial run. Blogging is time-consuming, sometimes difficult, and a different kind of activity for many organizations. Smart companies generate initial blog posts internally until it is clear that the tactic will be useful and rewarding.
- **Remember that it's a two-way street.** Learn to share control. Blogs without comments have minimal value, but with comments comes criticism. Smart companies value input from critics at their blogs because it offers them an opportunity to respond and educate.
- **Live up to the commitment.** Attention to blogs withers if postings aren't regular.
- **Offer value.** Providing information that publics can't find elsewhere gives people a reason to visit your blog or subscribe to feeds.
- **Ask if you have readers.** Is your public suitable for blogging? Not every market contains people who read blogs. If yours doesn't, you're wasting time and resources. Search for other blogs related to your industry or product and locate secondary information on your target market's use of the Web to find out whether your blog might make a difference.
- **Avoid hype and puffery.** The online community has a different personality than that of people who rely on traditional media. Web users are suspicious of hype and can be critical when they sense they are being preached to or misled.
- **Monitor the one place everyone visits**—its name is Wikipedia. If your company or product is mentioned there it is important to monitor, and occasionally correct, what is posted.
- **Use blogging as one piece of the puzzle.** Blogging can be an effective way to reach and respond to your publics. But it is rarely a stand-alone tactic. Smart companies make it a part of their overall IMC and public relations plans.

news (press) release A printed or electronic sheet of information (usually 8½ by 11 inches) issued to print and broadcast outlets to generate publicity or shed light on a subject of interest. Also called a *press release*.

press (media) kit A package of publicity materials used to give information to the press at staged events such as press conferences or open houses.

feature articles Soft news about companies, products, or services that may be written by a PR person, the publication's staff, or a third party.

house organ Internal and external publications produced by business organizations, including stockholder reports, newsletters, consumer magazines, and dealer publications.

e-zine A magazine published online or sent by e-mail.

News Releases and Press Kits A **news release** (or **press release**), the most widely used PR tool, consists of one or more printed or electronic pages of information issued to generate publicity or shed light on a subject of interest. News releases cover time-sensitive hard news. Topics may include the announcement of a new product, promotion of an executive, an unusual contest, landing of a major contract, or establishment of a scholarship fund.

For pointers in preparing releases, see My Ad Campaign 16–B, "How to Write a News Release."

A **press kit** (or **media kit**) supports the publicity of special events such as press conferences, grand openings, and trade shows. It includes a basic fact sheet of information about the event, a program or schedule of activities, and a list of the participants and their biographical data. The kit also contains a news story about the event for the broadcast media, news and feature stories for the print media, and any pertinent photos and brochures.

Photos Photos of events, products in use, new equipment, or newly promoted executives can lend credence or interest to a dull news story. In fact, a photo tells the story faster. Photos

How to Write a News Release [16–B]

The Role of the News Release

The news release is an effective tool for publicizing information for several reasons. It helps protect the publicist and the client from being misquoted. It permanently records the preferred word usage, specific terms, key phrasing, and unique details.

Its standardized format also speeds up the process. It eliminates debate over how to format the information, highlights the data most needed by the recipient (contact person's name and telephone, date, etc.), and spells out the source and topic of the story.

The news release also simplifies dissemination by providing a form that is easily reproduced and transferred (e-mail, fax, postal mail, etc.) and by ensuring that all recipients receive the same message.

Preparing the News Release

The news release follows a format generally accepted throughout the news industry.

- **Double-space the text and use wide margins.**
- **At the top of the page (left or right side) place the name and phone number of your contact person.** If your page is not preprinted with your company's name and address, add it below the contact person. Finally, write FOR IMMEDIATE RELEASE or TO BE RELEASED AFTER [date].
- **Write a headline that signals the key fact or issue of the story.** For example, TECHCO PRESIDENT SPEAKS TO BAY CITY LIONS CLUB THURSDAY.
- **Place the most important information first.** The editors may shorten your news release by cutting from the bottom.
- **Lead sentence.** The lead sentence is the most important. Keep it focused strictly on who, what, where, when, why, and how. For example, "Techco President Ralph J. Talk will address the Bay City Lions Club at 8 p.m., Monday, September 16, 2013."
- **Body text.** Add directly related support information. "Mr. Talk's speech will be 'Technology in Albania.' Mr. Talk served five years as assistant to the president of the Albania Travel Association."
- **Final text.** Fill in background details. "Mr. Talk was born on April 30, 1956, and is married to Alice Johnson of Bay City. They have two children. Mr. Talk is a board member of the Bay City Little League."
- **Keep the text as factual, direct, and short as possible.**
- **Carefully proof your copy.**

Etiquette

- **Don't call to see whether the editor received your release.** Editors don't like to be pressured. Don't ask for tearsheets. An editor has little time to send you a copy. Don't promise you'll advertise if the item is published; the editor will be offended at the suggestion that news can be bought. If the article is run, send a thank-you letter to the editor.

Mailing List

- **Prepare a list of local publications.** You may want to group them so that you mail out appropriate news releases to publications that are likely to use that type of information. Refrain from sending mass mailings. Update your list regularly because editors change and offices move.
- **Ascertain in advance if the editors on your list prefer to have news releases sent by e-mail or postal mail.**

Special Olympics

For Programs | Sports & Games | Communications | Fundraising | For Volunteers | Youth & Schools

Main » North America

Toys"R"Us Named Founding Partner of 2014 Special Olympics USA Games

Wednesday, March 14, 2012

Building on a Company-wide Commitment to Supporting Children with Special Needs, Toys"R"Us® will Serve as the Presenting Sponsor of the 2014 Games First-ever Young Athletes™ Festival

SPECIAL OLYMPICS
2014 USA GAMES
NEW JERSEY

2014 Special Olympics USA Games to be hosted by New Jersey. 3,500 athletes to compete in 17 sports 2014 Special Olympics USA Games

(PRINCETON, NJ) -- March 15, 2012 -- The Organizing Committee of the 2014 Special Olympics USA Games and Toys"R"Us® today announced a $1 million commitment from the Toys"R"Us Children's Fund, making Toys"R"Us the first Founding Partner of the 2014 Special Olympics USA Games. In addition to its Founding Partner status, Toys"R"Us will be the Presenting Sponsor of the Young AthletesTM Festival, a first-of-its-kind feature at a Special Olympics USA Games even

The Toys"R"Us Young Athletes Festival will provide opportunities for children, ages 2-7, and their families to take part in the Special Olympics Young Athletes program, Healthy Athletes® activities and family seminars geared toward the future stars of Special Olympics.

"Toys"R"Us signing as the first Founding Partner of the 2014 Special Olympics USA Games continues their on-going support of our movement," said Timothy Shriver, Chairman and CEO of Special Olympics. "Their vision and leadership in the area of inclusive play will only add to the unity that these National Games will create throughout New Jersey and the nation."

Follow Us

Spirit E-Newsletter

Stay in touch! See inspiring stories, photos and videos in our Special Olympics newsletter.

Sign Up Now

SOI Calendar

"Events" is a top search term for SO.org. Add your own events.

Events »

Find events near you and learn about volunteer opportunities at one of our 220 worldwide locations.

This electronic press release announced the role Toys "R" Us® will play as a Founding Sponsor of the 2014 Special Olympics USA Games. Toys "R" Us® hopes to receive favorable publicity for its role in this event.

should be high quality and need little or no explanation. Typed captions should describe the photo and accurately identify the people shown.

Feature Articles Many publications, especially trade journals, run **feature articles** (soft news) about companies, products, or services. They may be written by a PR person, the publication's staff, or a third party (such as a freelance business writer). As an MPR tool, feature articles can give the company or product great credibility. Editors like them because they have no immediate deadline and can be published at the editor's convenience or when space is available.

Features may be case histories, how-to's (such as how to use the company's product), problem-solving scenarios (how one customer uses the company's product to increase production), or state-of-the-art technology updates. Other formats include roundups of what's happening in a specific industry and editorials (such as a speech or essay by a company executive on a current issue).

Printed Materials Printed materials are the most popular tools used by public relations professionals.[14] They may be brochures or pamphlets about the company or its products, letters to customers, inserts or enclosures that accompany monthly

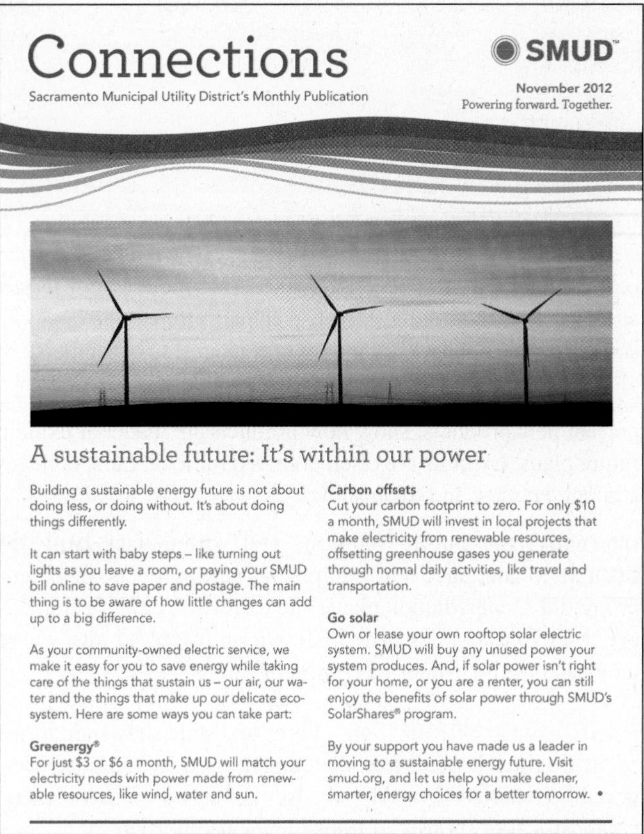

Connections

Sacramento Municipal Utility District's Monthly Publication

SMUD

November 2012
Powering forward. Together.

A sustainable future: It's within our power

Building a sustainable energy future is not about doing less, or doing without. It's about doing things differently.

It can start with baby steps – like turning out lights as you leave a room, or paying your SMUD bill online to save paper and postage. The main thing is to be aware of how little changes can add up to a big difference.

As your community-owned electric service, we make it easy for you to save energy while taking care of the things that sustain us – our air, our water and the things that make up our delicate ecosystem. Here are some ways you can take part:

Greenergy®
For just $3 or $6 a month, SMUD will match your electricity needs with power made from renewable resources, like wind, water and sun.

Carbon offsets
Cut your carbon footprint to zero. For only $10 a month, SMUD will invest in local projects that make electricity from renewable resources, offsetting greenhouse gases you generate through normal daily activities, like travel and transportation.

Go solar
Own or lease your own rooftop solar electric system. SMUD will buy any unused power your system produces. And, if solar power isn't right for your home, or you are a renter, you can still enjoy the benefits of solar power through SMUD's SolarShares® program.

By your support you have made us a leader in moving to a sustainable energy future. Visit smud.org, and let us help you make cleaner, smarter, energy choices for a better tomorrow. •

House organs may be sent to customers to promote goodwill, increase sales, or influence public opinion. SMUD, a Sacramento, California, energy provider, encloses this two-page newsletter in its monthly mailings. It provides public interest stories, important news, and energy-saving ideas in an appealing and easy-to-read format.

statements, the annual report to stockholders, other reports, or house organs.

A **house organ** is a publication about happenings and policies at the company. An internal house organ is for employees only. External house publications go to company-connected people (customers, stockholders, suppliers, and dealers) or to the general public. They may take the form of a newsletter, tabloid-size newspaper, magazine, or even a periodic **e-zine** (a magazine published online or sent by e-mail). Their purpose is to promote goodwill, increase sales, or influence public opinion. A well-produced house organ can do a great deal to motivate employees and appeal to customers. However, writing, printing, and distributing can be expensive—and very time-consuming.

A well-produced house organ can do a great deal to motivate employees and appeal to customers.

posters For public relations purposes, signs that impart product information or other news of interest to consumers, or that are aimed at employee behavior, such as safety, courtesy, or waste reduction.

exhibits A marketing or public relations approach that involves preparing displays that tell about an organization or its products.

bulletin boards An internal public relations means for announcing new equipment, meetings, promotions, new products, construction plans, and recreation news.

intranet A restricted-access computer network, based on Internet technology, that is designed to meet the internal needs for sharing information within a single organization or company.

audiovisual materials Slides and videos that may be used for training, sales, or public relations activities.

Posters, Exhibits, and Bulletin Boards

Posters can be used internally to stress safety, security, reduction of waste, and courtesy. Externally, they can impart product information, corporate philosophy, or other news of interest to consumers.

Companies use **exhibits** to describe the organization's history, present new products, show how products are made, or explain future plans. Exhibits are often prepared for local fairs, colleges and universities, and trade shows.

Internally, the public relations staff often uses **bulletin boards** to announce new equipment, new products, meetings, promotions, construction plans, and recreation news to employees. Many companies now maintain an **intranet** site where they can post their internal communications.

Audiovisual Materials

Films and slide shows are forms of **audiovisual materials** that may be used for training, sales, or public relations. Considered a form of *corporate advertising,* nontheatrical or sponsored films (developed for public relations reasons) are often furnished without charge to movie theaters, organizations, and special groups, particularly schools and colleges. Classic examples include *Why Man Creates,* produced for Kaiser Aluminum, and Mobil Oil's *A Fable,* starring the famous French mime Marcel Marceau.

Many PR departments provide **video news releases (VNRs)**—news or feature stories prepared by a company and offered free to TV stations, which may use the whole video or just segments. Video news releases are somewhat controversial. Critics see them as subtle commercials or even propaganda and object when stations run the stories without disclosing that they came from a public relations firm, not the station's news staff.

check yourself ✓

1. What tools does an organization have to determine how it is viewed by its publics?
2. In what ways have social media affected the PR professional's job?

LO16-3 Explain the potential benefits and drawbacks of sponsorships in an IMC plan.

SPONSORSHIPS AND EVENTS

In 1984, the owner of a large bicycle shop in the upper Midwest sent some of his mechanics to a local bicycle race sponsored by a national charity. At the time, his store was doing about $200,000 per year in retail sales, and he wanted to help out the charity while finding out what the racers thought of his and his competitors' businesses.

An unexpected benefit of the company's presence at the race was that participants started showing up in his store. Encouraged by these results, the company now supports more than 100 bicycle events each year and sends staff members to dozens of such events. It has hired a full-time representative to coordinate company involvement in special bicycle events that have the potential of increasing its exposure and business revenue.

In 20 years, the company went from a low-key presence at bicycling events, donating a few water bottles embossed with the company's name, to large-scale sponsorship, participating in event registration, providing event participants with workshops on bicycle maintenance, and offering in-store discounts to event participants. Within a week of one event, 30 participants had visited his store. Even better news for the company was that nearly half of the more than 5,000 riders reported purchasing goods from it.

By 1996, the company had revenues of $3 million. The owner attributes much of his success to his sponsorship of bicycle events. In his words, "I support them, and they support us."[15]

The Growth of Sponsorship

Advertising and public relations people get involved in sponsoring many kinds of special events. In fact, sponsorship may be the fastest-growing form of marketing today. It actually embraces two disciplines: sales promotion and public relations. Some sponsorships are designed to create publicity, others to improve public relations through personal contact and

video news releases (VNRs) A news or feature story prepared in video form and offered free to TV stations.

sponsorship A cash or in-kind fee paid to an event or organization in return for access to the exploitable commercial potential associated with that event or organization.

in kind The donation of goods and services as payment for some service such as a sponsorship.

cause marketing A promotion in which a portion of the proceeds from certain for-profit products are donated to a nonprofit cause. The goal is usually to increase sales for the products while raising money and visibility for the cause.

philanthropy Support for a cause without any commercial incentive.

> "SPONSORSHIP MAY BE THE FASTEST-GROWING FORM OF MARKETING TODAY."

affiliation with a worthy cause, and others to immediately improve the sales and bottom line. Companies appear to be recognizing that, in an IMC program, sponsorship is an effective way to gain attention and establish brand loyalty.

A **sponsorship** is a cash or in-kind fee paid to a property (which may be a sports, entertainment, or nonprofit event or organization) in return for access to the exploitable commercial potential associated with that property.[16] In other words, just as advertisers pay a fee to sponsor a program on radio or TV, they may also sign on to sponsor a bike race, an art show or chamber music festival, a fair or exhibition, or the Olympics. The sponsorship fee may be paid in cash or **in kind** (that is, through a donation of goods and services). For instance, if a local TV station signs on as a sponsor of a 10K run, it will typically pay for some part of its sponsorship by providing advertising time for the event.

Cause marketing, a related strategy, is a partnership between a for-profit company and a nonprofit organization, which increases the company's sales while raising money and visibility for the organization's cause. Typically, a portion of the proceeds from the sale of certain products is donated to the cause. For example, Yoplait yogurt's *Save Lids to Save Lives* campaign urges consumers to buy pink-lidded cups of yogurt and mail the lids back. For each lid mailed in, Yoplait donates ten cents to Susan G. Komen's Race for the Cure, more than $34 million since 1997.

While the sponsored event or organization may be nonprofit, sponsorship is not the same as philanthropy. **Philanthropy** is support of a cause without any commercial incentive. Sponsorship is used to achieve commercial objectives. According to the *IEG Sponsorship Report*, spending on partnerships in North America grew 4.4 percent to $18.9 billion in 2012. For 2013, a 5.5 percent growth to $19.9 billion is expected in sponsorship spending by North American companies. As we discuss later in this chapter, by far the largest and fastest-growing category in North America continues to be sports sponsorships. Worldwide, spending increased 5.1 percent in 2012 to $51.1 billion. The forecast growth in 2013 is 4.2 percent to $53.3. Significant increases in sponsorships can be expected in South America in 2014 in support of the FIFA World Cup (soccer) and the 2016 Summer Olympics, both hosted by Brazil.[17]

The reasons for the historical pattern of sponsorship growth relate to the economics of marketing we discussed earlier: the escalating costs of traditional advertising media, the fragmentation of media audiences, the growing diversity in leisure activities, and the desire to reach targeted groups of people economically. Initial growth probably came from the tobacco and alcohol companies, which many governments banned from broadcast advertising. Legislation in the United Kingdom, Canada, and the United States threatens to end tobacco sponsorships altogether, but their success at sponsoring sports and other events has shown the way for mainstream advertisers, who are rapidly picking up the slack.

Today, there is greater media coverage of sponsored events—everything from beach volleyball to Texas hold 'em poker to

Companies sponsor events or organizations by providing money or other resources that are of value to the sponsored event. This is usually in return for advertising space at the event or as part of the publicity of the event. DATEV (www.datev.com), one of Europe's largest software companies, is the title sponsor of the annual DATEV Challenge Roth Triathlon in Roth, Germany (www.challenge-roth.com/en). The event attracts 5,000 participants and approximately 200,000 spectators.

Xtreme games to cultural events. This provides a highly desirable venue for advertisers seeking young, upwardly mobile, educated consumers. Likewise, for transnational marketers, there is growing interest in global events such as World Cup soccer, the Olympics, and the America's Cup yacht race. The international soccer tournament generated $1.6 billion in sponsorship revenue during the 2007–2010 period, up from $584 million between 1999 and 2002. adidas, Coca-Cola, Emirates Airlines, Hyundai/Kia, Sony, and Visa each paid an estimated annual fee of between $24 million and $44 million for global rights to a broad array of FIFA activities, including World Cup.[18]

Benefits of Sponsorship

In the past, for marketers with limited media alternatives (such as tobacco and alcohol companies), sponsorship simply offered a means of communicating with customers and prospects. Today, the many benefits of sponsorship are well documented and more far-reaching.

Certainly one benefit of sponsorship is that the public approves of it. One study by Roper Starch Worldwide reported that 80 percent of Americans believe corporate sponsorship is an important source of money for professional sports. This is a far higher approval rating than most companies would get for their advertising programs.

More than almost any other marketing communications tool, sponsorships and events have the ability to involve customers, prospects, and other stakeholders. Events are also highly self-selective of their target audience. So marketers that define their audiences tightly can select just those sponsorships that offer the closest fit. A significant benefit is the opportunity to enhance the company's public image or merchandise its positioning through affiliation with an appropriate event. Marketers that sponsor an event simply because it has a large audience are misusing this tool.[19]

Unlike advertising, sponsorships and events can provide face-to-face access to current and potential customers. Depending on the venue, this access can be relatively clean and

The Client Presentation [16–C]

For most of you, the culmination of your project will be a presentation to the class or client that will be judged by the teacher, a group of peers, or local marketing and advertising executives. This presentation is by far the most important aspect of selling your ideas to the "client." It is not always the best idea that wins, and a great presentation can make a bad idea look great.

By now you have spent hours belaboring the who, what, when, and where of your advertising campaign, and now you need to explain why. You should think of your presentation as a Cliff Notes version of your thinking. While going through the process of developing a campaign, it is likely that you did not work sequentially—in fact most advertising processes are done in parallel—but your presentation should illustrate the linear path of thinking that netted your results.

Most advertising presentations utilize PowerPoint, but if you have the resources and the gumption, think about different ways to illustrate your thinking and your ideas. Remember that the more creative your approach, the more (virtual) points you'll receive, assuming of course that the creativity doesn't get in the way of coherent thoughts.

Follow this basic outline and focus on how each section transitions from one to the other:

- Goals and/or objectives of the campaign—What is the campaign trying to achieve?
- Target audience analysis—Whom are we planning on speaking to and why?
- SWOT analysis—What are the strengths of the brand, the weaknesses, the opportunities, and the impending threats that factor into our decision-making process?
- Strategic insight(s)—Based on all of these factors, how are you going to solve the business challenge at hand?
- Creative presentation—Ideas, ideas, ideas. And don't forget to explain why these ideas will help achieve the goals/objectives.
- Media presentation—Where will these ads be placed, and what target and strategy insights led you to choose those vehicles?

The main objective of the presentation is to communicate, in a concise and succinct manner, your ideas, both strategic and tactical. One of the biggest misconceptions is that the strategy should be an ah-ha moment. In truth the strategy should feel more like a statement of the obvious because all of your research has led you down a certain path. If you explain the path appropriately you will receive the proverbial head-nods on the strategy slides. Where the whiz-bang should come in is how you tactically execute the strategy in its creative and placement (media) form.

Be sure to include everyone on your team in the presentation. This will be difficult as some people are better presenters than others, but that's okay because if the ideas and thinking are good they will break through.

Last, if you are doing a PowerPoint, hand out copies of the presentation (in color) so the "clients" can follow along and take notes. Props and gadgets are great to use too, so long as they don't distract from the presentation. When Foote, Cone and Belding was pitching kibu.com (a teen girl site) in 2000, it turned one of its conference rooms into a girl's bedroom, setting the mood and ambience for the presentation. It helped the firm win the pitch, because elements of the room were used to highlight the insights into the mindset of the site's main user, a teen girl.

EXHIBIT 16–2 Top U.S. sponsors.

Company	Amount ($ millions)	2012 Rank	2011 Rank
PepsiCo, Inc.	$330–$335	1	1
The Coca-Cola Co.	$275–$280	2	2
Anheuser-Busch InBev	$235–$240	3	3
Nike, Inc.	$230–$235	4	4
AT&T, Inc.	$175–$180	5	5
General Motors Co.	$170–$175	6	6
Toyota Motor Sales U.S.A., Inc.	$145–$150	7	7
Ford Motor Co.	$135–$140	8	9
MillerCoors LLC	$115–$120	9	8
adidas North America, Inc.	$110–$115	10	10

Source: From Who Spent WHAT IN 09: IEG's Top Sponsors List, IEG Sponsorship Report, 4/26/10. Reprinted with permission.

uncluttered by competition. Sponsoring a seminar, for instance, creates an opportunity for both customer education and brand involvement. In some cases, it even enables product demonstrations and the opportunity to give a personal sales pitch to multiple prospects at a time when they are open to new information.[20] This is especially good for business-to-business marketers.

Also important, but often overlooked, is the effect sponsorship can have on employees. Affiliating with a dynamic event can really boost the morale and pride of the troops in the trenches. And many companies offer attendance at the event (Super Bowl, Olympics, etc.) as an incentive to their sales staff.[21]

Some marketers have discovered that sponsorships can rapidly convert fan loyalty into sales. For example, 74 percent of stock-car racing fans report that they often buy products they see promoted at the racetrack. This is also true for other sports: 58 percent for baseball, 52 percent for tennis, and 47 percent for golf. Finally, sponsorships can be very cost-efficient, providing significant media exposure at a comparatively low cost. Volvo International believes the media exposure it gets from its $3 million sponsorship of local tennis tournaments is equivalent to $25 million worth of advertising time and space.[22] PepsiCo has been the top U.S. sponsorship spender for several years. Other top sponsors are listed in Exhibit 16–2.[23]

Drawbacks of Sponsorship

Like all marketing communications tools, sponsorship has some drawbacks. First, it can be very costly, especially when the event is solely sponsored. For this reason, most companies participate in co-sponsored events, which spreads the cost among several participants.

The problem with co-sponsored events is clutter. Some events have so many sponsors that getting one marketer's message through is extremely difficult. Look again at stock-car racing. How many logos do those cars sport?

Finally, evaluating the effectiveness of a particular sponsorship can be tricky at best—especially since it rarely happens in a vacuum. The problem is in separating the effects of a sponsorship from the effects of other concurrent marketing activities. We'll deal with these issues shortly.

Types of Sponsorship

While there are many, many avenues and events available for sponsorship, IEG Inc. groups most of them into six categories: sports; entertainment, tours, and attractions; causes; the arts; festivals, fairs, and annual events; and associations and membership organizations (see Exhibit 16–3).[24]

Sports Marketing North American corporations spent an estimated $13 billion in 2012 on sports marketing sponsorships, as reported by the *IEG Sponsorship Report*.[25] The most popular of these are motorsports and golf.[26] In fact, the vast

EXHIBIT 16–3 Annual sponsorship spending in North America (2012) ($ millions).

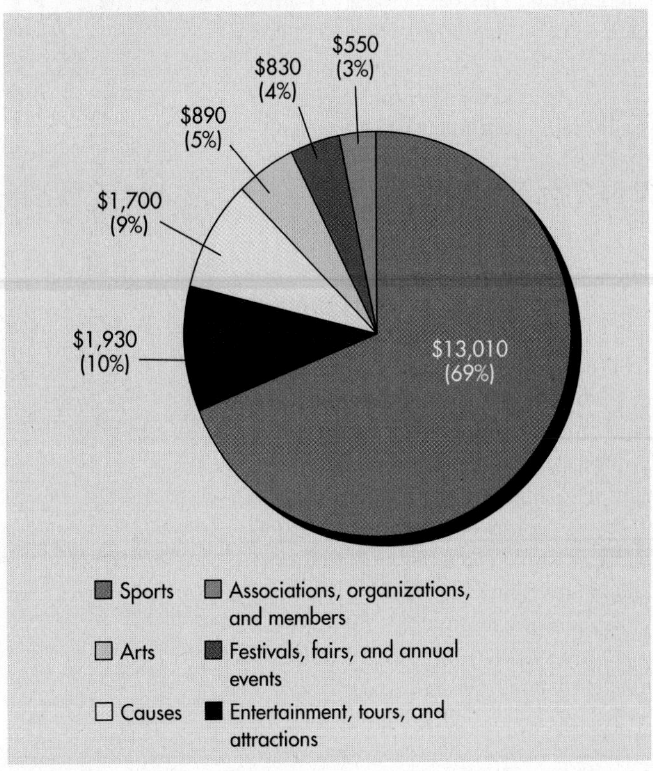

Source: Annual Sponsorship Forecast, IEG, LLC. Reprinted with permission.

"COMPANIES DON'T HAVE TO BE BIG MULTINATIONALS TO REAP RICH REWARDS FROM SPONSORSHIPS."

majority of sponsorship money, approximately 69 percent, is spent on sports events. This includes everything from the Olympics to NASCAR racing to professional athletic leagues. And as we saw from the bicycle shop story, companies don't have to be big multinationals to reap rich rewards from sponsorships—if they do it properly.

By buying the rights to serve Gatorade on the sidelines of professional basketball and football games, that brand has received more credibility than any television ad could provide, at a fraction of the cost. During every game, TV cameras show pros drinking the product in big Gatorade cups. And it's clear they're doing it because they want to, not because their agent told them to.[27]

In hotly contested markets, the giants in their fields fight over sponsorship rights. Nike battles adidas, Coke spars with Pepsi, and Visa struggles against American Express. This has certainly contributed to the rising cost of sponsorships. General Motors, for instance, signed an unprecedented $1 billion, eight-year sponsorship deal to ensure its exclusivity as the automotive sponsor for the U.S. Olympic Committee.[28]

In addition to spending more than $1 million for each 30-second television spot during the 2012 London Olympics, Nike and adidas outfitted a combined 6,000 Olympic athletes. Although adidas's traditional stronghold is in soccer gear, it still supplied an estimated 1.5 million pieces of clothing, equipment, and other logo-emblazoned articles for the two-week event. Nike is not an official Olympic sponsor, but it traditionally attempts to blanket the host city with its Swoosh anyway (see ambush marketing below). Since adidas is estimated to have paid in excess of $61 million to be an official sponsor of the games, it is not surprising that event hosts do everything they can to stop unauthorized associations.[29]

Cause marketing is a partnership between a for-profit company and a nonprofit organization. Campbell Soup Company (www.campbellsoup.com) joins forces with the National Association of Letter Carriers (www.nalc.org) annual food drive. Campbell is supporting this initiative by donating more than 800,000 meals to Feeding America member food banks. The company also sponsors, along with the U.S. Postal Service, a reminder postcard being mailed to more than 75 million homes the week of the drive. Now in its 21st year, Stamp Out Hunger (www.stampouthunger.info) has collected more than 1 billion pounds of food, including more than 70 million pounds in 2012.

Many sports events are strictly local and therefore cost much less while giving the sponsor closer access to attendees and participants. Firms with modest event-marketing budgets, for example, use options ranging from local golf tournaments and tennis matches to surfing contests. An increasingly popular promotion is the company-sponsored sports event. The event can serve as an effective focal point for an IMC campaign if it ties the company to the local community hosting the event as well as to the event's regional or national audience. But without a concerted effort to tie an event to other marketing communications activities like a currently running ad campaign, the money spent on sponsorships is generally wasted.[30]

Some companies associate their names with existing events. Mountain Dew, Taco Bell, Sony, and T-Mobile, for instance, are the "gold" sponsors of ESPN's Winter X Games and regularly renew their sponsorships.[31]

But controversy often swirls around big sports sponsorships. The most controversial practice is **ambush marketing**, which is a promotional strategy nonsponsors use to capitalize on the popularity or prestige of an event or property by giving the false impression that they are sponsors. Ambush marketing techniques, like buying up all the billboard space around an athletic stadium, are often employed by the competitors of the property's official sponsor. Budweiser was the official beer of the 2010 FIFA World Cup South Africa and the only beer company permitted to advertise within the stadium grounds. However, 36 women attended the Denmark versus Netherlands match wearing orange minidresses that were provided by Dutch beer brewer, Bavaria. They were ejected from the game. Ironically, the women received a lot of media coverage, informing the world that beautiful girls like Dutch soccer and

ambush marketing
A promotional strategy utilized by nonsponsors to capitalize on the popularity or prestige of an event or property by giving the false impression that they are sponsors, such as by buying up all the billboard space around an athletic stadium. Often employed by the competitors of the property's official sponsor.

Venue marketing has surged in poplularity. By selling the naming rights to stadiums, arenas, and centers, cities get help paying for public venues. Advertisers get a high-profile way to see their brands mentioned thousands of times each year in sports stories.

Dutch beer. Bavaria's UK marketing manager Sean Durkan said, "Brand awareness has definitely increased. There's a lot more activity on Twitter and social media."[32]

One of the reasons this works is because people are often confused about who the official sponsors actually are—again, the problem is clutter. Just because a company advertises on the Olympic broadcast, for instance, does not mean it is an official sponsor. Ambush marketers take advantage of this.[33]

Entertainment After sports marketing, the largest area of sponsorship is entertainment, which includes things like concert tours, attractions, and theme parks. For instance, numerous attractions at Disneyland and Disney World are sponsored by major corporations such as GE, AT&T, ARCO, Kodak, and Carnation. In 2012, U.S. companies spent an estimated $1.9 billion on this category.

Brands even sponsor entire tours. The Vans Warped Tour (vanswarpedtour.com) has a rotating lineup of nearly 150 bands, with multiple stages sponsored by other companies, like Kia, Monster Energy, and dozens more. The tour visits more than 50 cities in eight countries.

Causes Sponsorship of charity events and educational institutions is a tried-and-true PR activity that often fits with the IMC strategy of mission marketing. A number of large corporations (including Chevrolet, AT&T, American Airlines, Pepsi, and Kodak) co-sponsored the Live Aid concerts, for instance. In 2012, marketers spent an estimated $1.7 billion in cause-related sponsorships.

Health care marketers such as hospitals, health maintenance organizations (HMOs), and managed-care companies are increasing their sponsorship activities. Oxford Health Plans, for example, signed up with the Franklin Institute Science Museum to host Cyber Seniors, a free seminar at the Philadelphia museum that teaches older people how to use the Internet.[34]

A vice president for corporate relations refers to mission marketing activities as "enlightened self-interest." People appreciate the fact that businesses do not really get anything tangible out of them to put in the bank.[35]

Arts Symphony orchestras, chamber music groups, art museums, and theater companies are always in desperate need of funding. In 2012, sponsors spent an estimated $890 million to support the arts—one of the least funded of the major sponsorship categories. What this means is that this is still a relatively untapped area, and it provides outstanding sponsorship and underwriting opportunities for both national and local firms interested in audiences on the highest end of the income scale.

Festivals, Fairs, and Annual Events Over 3,200 fairs are held in North America each year. When IEG surveyed 1,000 members of the International Association of Fairs and Expositions, the findings revealed a very healthy, growing environment. The average yearly sponsorship increased a whopping 20 percent over the previous four years. Moreover, renewal rates averaged 88 percent! By 2012, sponsorship revenue increased to an estimated $825 million.

One of the largest annual events in the state of Michigan is the National Cherry Festival in Traverse City. Held every year around the Fourth of July, it boasts an impressive lineup of events and promotional activities that drive both attendance and sponsor visibility. Events include band parades, races, concerts, tournaments, an antiques show, an air show, Native American exhibits, and much more. Among the official sponsors are Pepsi, MillerCoors, Best Buy, Mountain Dew, Subway, Verizon, Toyota, and many other national and local companies.

Associations and Membership Organizations This sponsorship category was added by IEG in 2004. These sponsorships were previously considered a part of festivals, fairs, and annual events because most associations sponsored annual conventions. But that is no longer the case, as sponsors

venue marketing
A form of sponsorship that links a sponsor to a physical site such as a stadium, arena, auditorium, or racetrack.

are now more likely to sign year-round partnerships with trade groups, professional membership organizations, and other associations. Those sponsors spent an estimated $550 million in this category in 2012.

Venue Marketing Finally, an area not covered by IEG's report is **venue marketing**, a form of sponsorship that links a sponsor to a physical site such as a stadium, arena, auditorium, or racetrack. In 2013, Levi Strauss agreed to pay $220 million for the right to name the San Francisco 49ers' new Santa Clara stadium "Levi's Stadium." The deal is good for 20 years and Levi Strauss has the right to extend their naming rights for an additional 5 years for $75 million. The stadium owner will receive 70% of the revenue and the 49ers will receive the balance. Levi Strauss is also expected to be the 49ers' exclusive, non-sportswear apparel partner.[36]

Likewise, Denver has Coors Field, and Charlotte, North Carolina, has Bank of America Stadium. And AT&T has put its name on San Francisco's baseball park. But what happens when sponsors with naming rights become a liability? When Enron filed for bankruptcy in 2001, the Houston Astros shelled out $2.1 million to buy back the naming rights to Enron Field. The story had a happy ending however, when the Minute Maid Company, a locally based subsidiary of the Coca-Cola Company since 1960, paid an estimated $170 million for a 28-year naming rights deal in 2002.

Venue marketing is changing the economics of professional sports. Sponsorships help pay for stadium renovations and upgrades and may assist the home team in defraying high operational costs. Many teams keep the money from their stadium luxury suites, stadium advertising, naming rights, and food and beverage concessions. Under the new economic rules, big stadium revenues are essential to signing big-name players and staying competitive.[37]

Methods of Sponsorship

Companies interested in sponsorship have two choices: buy into an existing event or create their own. Event marketing specialist Paul Stanley predicts that many corporate event sponsorships will become "sponsownerships," where the sponsor owns and controls the entire event. This would allow more control and would likely be more cost-effective. It would also help the company achieve its marketing objectives.[38]

For most companies, though, it's easier to buy into an existing event, either as the sole sponsor (the Buick Invitational) or as one of many co-sponsors. What's most important is to get a good fit between the sponsor and the event. Nabisco's Cornnuts brand, for instance, teamed up with the Aggressive Skaters Association (ASA) to sponsor the ASA Pro Tour and Amateur Circuits and to use the ASA World Champion female skater Fabiola da Silva as the product's spokesperson. According to Rich Bratman, president of the ASA, he chose Cornnuts because "the brand management and promotions team at Cornnuts really understands how important it is to reach teens in a credible way and is committed to supporting the skating lifestyle."

In his book *Aftermarketing,* Terry Vavra suggests several guidelines for selecting the right sponsorship opportunity or event. See My Ad Campaign 16–D, "How to Select Events for Sponsorship."

Measuring Sponsorship Results

One of the problems with event sponsorship (as with public relations activities in general) has historically been how to

How to Select Events for Sponsorship [16–D]

- Can the sponsorship be an exclusive one?
- The demographics of the mass media audience and event participants should match, as closely as possible, the demographics of the target consumer.
- The event should in some way demonstrate, evoke, or represent a key attribute of the product or service (for example, a luxury product sponsoring a thoroughbred racing event—"the sport of kings").
- The value to the sponsored event of the company's association should be no greater than the benefit to the company from the additional mass media exposure from the sponsorship. (This has to do with who is leveraging whom.)
- The participation should promise sufficient (and appropriate) mass media exposure to offset any costs associated with the sponsorship.
- The association of the product with the event should ideally offer or suggest a meaningful sales campaign or theme to be run concurrently with sponsorship.
- Did the company initiate the negotiation or was the company solicited by the event promoters?
- How much financial support is required?

evaluate results. Experts suggest there are really only three ways to do this:

1. Measure changes in awareness or image through pre- and postsponsorship research surveys.
2. Measure spending equivalencies between free media exposure and comparable advertising space or time.
3. Measure changes in sales revenue with a tracking device such as coupons.

Unfortunately, none of these methods covers all the reasons for sponsoring. For example, how do you measure the effect on employee morale? What if the sponsorship is aimed at rewarding current customers or enhancing relationships within the trade? These are important possible objectives, but they are very difficult to measure.

Still, most companies are very concerned about the bottom line and look for a substantial return on investment for their sponsorship dollars. Delta Airlines, for example, is said to require $12 in new revenue for every dollar it spends on sponsorship—a ratio the airline claims to have achieved during its Olympic sponsorship.[39]

IEG suggests the following pointers for measuring the value of event sponsorships:[40]

- Have clear goals and narrowly defined objectives.
- Set a measurable goal.
- Measure against a benchmark.
- Do not change other marketing variables during the sponsorship.
- Incorporate an evaluation program into the overall sponsorship and associated marketing program.
- At the outset establish a budget for measuring results.

check yourself ✓

1. Why is sponsorship such a popular and growing strategy for marketers?
2. How can a company determine if a sponsorship has been effective?

LO16-4 Discuss the functions of corporate advertising.

CORPORATE ADVERTISING

When a company wants to communicate a PR message and control its content, it may use a form of *corporate advertising.* In an integrated marketing communications program, corporate advertising can set the tone for all of a company's public communications. **Corporate advertising** covers the broad area of nonproduct advertising, including public relations advertising, institutional advertising, corporate identity advertising, and recruitment advertising.

corporate advertising The broad area of nonproduct advertising aimed specifically at enhancing a company's image and increasing lagging awareness.

public relations advertising Advertising that attempts to improve a company's relationship with its publics.

institutional advertising A type of advertising that attempts to obtain favorable attention for the business as a whole, not for a specific product or service the store or business sells. The effects are intended to be long term.

Public Relations Advertising

To direct a controlled public relations message to one of its important publics, a company uses **public relations advertising.** PR ads may be used to improve the company's relations with labor, government, customers, suppliers, and even voters.

When companies sponsor art events, programs on public television, or charitable activities, they frequently place public relations ads in other media to promote the programs and their sponsorship, enhance their community citizenship, and create public goodwill. If the public relations people don't have advertising experience, they will typically turn to the firm's advertising department or agency for help.

Corporate/Institutional Advertising

In recent years, the term *corporate advertising* has come to denote a particular type of nonproduct advertising aimed at increasing awareness of the company and enhancing its image. The traditional term for this is **institutional advertising.** These ad campaigns may serve a variety of purposes: to report company accomplishments, position the company competitively in the market, reflect a change in corporate personality, shore up stock prices, improve employee morale, or avoid communications problems with agents, dealers, suppliers, or customers.

Historically, companies and even professional ad people have questioned, or misunderstood, the effectiveness of corporate advertising. Retailers, in particular, cling to the idea that institutional advertising, although attractive and nice, "doesn't make the cash register ring." A series of marketing research studies, however, offered dramatic evidence to the contrary. Companies using corporate advertising registered significantly better awareness, familiarity, and an overall better impression than those using only product advertising. Five corporate advertisers in the study drew higher ratings in every one of 16 characteristics measured, including being known for quality products, having competent management, and paying higher dividends.[41] Ironically, the companies in the study that did no corporate advertising spent far more in total advertising

advocacy advertising Advertising used to communicate an organization's views on issues that affect society or business.

advertorials Ads that are half advertising, half editorial, and aimed at swaying public opinion rather than selling products.

umbrella advertising Advertising campaigns intended to simultaneously communicate messages about a company and its products.

corporate identity advertising Advertising a corporation creates to familiarize the public with its name, logos, trademarks, or corporate signatures, especially after any of these elements are changed.

recruitment advertising A special type of advertising, most frequently found in the classified sections of daily newspapers or in online job boards, aimed at attracting employment applications.

for their products than the corporate advertisers did. Yet, despite the higher expenditures, they scored significantly lower across the board.

David Ogilvy, the late founder and creative head of Ogilvy & Mather, was an outspoken advocate of corporate advertising, but not of all corporate ads: "I am appalled by the humbug in corporate advertising. The pomposity. The vague generalities and the fatuous platitudes. Corporate advertising should not insult the intelligence of the public."

Unlike product advertising, Ogilvy said, a corporate campaign is the voice of the chief executive and his or her board of directors. It should not be delegated. "It takes years for corporate advertising to do a job. It doesn't work overnight. Only a few companies have kept it going long enough to achieve measurable results," Ogilvy concluded.

What can good corporate advertising hope to achieve? Ogilvy thought at least one of four objectives:

1. **It can build awareness of the company.** Opinion Research Corp. states, "The invisibility and remoteness of most companies is the main handicap. People who feel they know a company well are five times more likely to have a highly favorable opinion of the company than those who have little familiarity."
2. **Corporate advertising can make a good impression on the financial community,** enabling you to raise capital at lower cost—and make more acquisitions.
3. **It can motivate your present employees and attract better recruits.** "Good public relations begins at home," Ogilvy said. "If your employees understand your policies and feel proud of your company, they will be your best ambassadors."
4. **Corporate advertising can influence public opinion on specific issues.** Abraham Lincoln said, "With public opinion against it, nothing can succeed. With public opinion on its side, nothing can fail."

Responding to such criticisms and to marketplace forces, corporations now design their corporate advertising to achieve specific objectives: develop awareness of the company and its activities, attract investors, improve a tarnished image, attract quality employees, tie together a diverse product line, or take a stand on important public issues. The primary media used for corporate advertising are consumer business magazines and network TV.

A variation on corporate advertising is **advocacy advertising**. Companies use it to communicate their views on issues that affect their business, to promote their philosophy, or to make a political or social statement. Such ads are frequently referred to as **advertorials** since they are basically editorials paid for by an advertiser.

Corporate advertising can also build a foundation for future sales, traditionally the realm of product advertising. Many

OUR MISSION
TO ENSURE EVERY VETERAN HAS A SAFE PLACE TO CALL HOME

OUR COMMITMENT
$80 MILLION OVER 5 YEARS & THE SWEAT EQUITY OF THOUSANDS OF ASSOCIATE VOLUNTEERS

FOUNDATION

Between 9/11 and Veterans Day, we'll complete 350+ projects to improve the homes of veterans and their families.

Follow along at homedepotfoundation.org and facebook.com/homedepotfoundation.

Through Team Depot, The Home Depot Foundation (www.homedepotfoundation.org) provides opportunities for employees and suppliers to contribute their home improvement know-how to make a meaningful impact in the community. In 2013, Team Depot completed more than 1,470 projects across the country; 868 of those were focused specifically on veterans, from building wheelchair ramps and renovating the homes of wounded warriors to repairing and remodeling transitional housing for homeless veterans. This public relations advertising serves to acknowledge the efforts of Home Depot employees, as well as to let the public know that The Home Depot is a good corporate citizen.

CHAPTER 7

1. Updated promo sheet and letter from BBDO-NY (1995).
2. Theresa Howard, "Brand Builders: Being True to Dew," *Brandweek,* April 24, 2000, p. 28.
3. Ibid., p. 30.
4. Christopher Lawton, "PepsiCo's Mountain Dew Backs Film," *The Wall Street Journal,* September 12, 2005, p. B4.
5. "Mountain Dew, Hyundai and others take major ad missteps," USA Today, (retrieved at http://www.usatoday.com/story/money/business/2013/05/01/pepsico-pulls-mountain-dew-ad-after-criticism/2126453/), June 11, 2013.
6. William O. Bearden, Thomas N. Ingram, and Raymond W. LaForge, *Marketing Principles & Perspectives,* 2nd ed. (Burr Ridge, IL: Richard D. Irwin, 1998), pp. 75–76.
7. Natalie Zmuda, "Why Mountain Dew Let Skater Dudes Take Control of Its Marketing," *Advertising Age,* February 22, 2010 (retrieved at http://adage.com/digitalalist10/article?article_id=142201).
8. "Market Analysis—Defining the Market," Tutor2u, (retrieved from www.tutor2u.net/business/marketing, February 26, 2003).
9. Sergio Zyman, *The End of Marketing As We Know It* (New York: HarperBusiness, 1999).
10. Kate MacArthur and Hillary Chura, "Urban Youth," *Advertising Age,* September 4, 2000, pp. 16–17.
11. Private interview with Scott Moffitt, Director of Marketing, Pepsi-Cola Company, December 2000.
12. Automation Marketing Strategies, "The Art of Market Positioning," Strategic Advantage Newsletter, January 2000 (retrieved from www.automationmarketing.com, February 2003).
13. Ernest Martin, "Target Marketing: Summary and Unit Learning Outcomes," Course Syllabus CADV 213 (retrieved from www.campbell.edu/faculty/martine/index.htm, February 26, 2003).
14. Raju Narisetti, "Xerox Aims to Imprint High-Tech Image," *The Wall Street Journal,* October 6, 1998, p. B8.
15. Farrell, "Dew Poses Real Pepsi Challenge to Coke," *USA Today,* 2000, p. B2.
16. Adapted from Al Ries and Jack Trout, *Bottom-Up Marketing* (New York: McGraw-Hill, 1989), p. 8.
17. Frederick E. Webster, Jr., "Executing the New Marketing Concept," *Marketing Management* 3, no. 1 (1994), pp. 8–16.
18. Philip Kotler and Gary Armstrong, *Principles of Marketing* (Englewood Cliffs, NJ: Prentice Hall, 1994), p. 560; Don E. Schultz, Stanley I. Tannenbaum, and Robert F. Lauterborn, *Integrated Marketing Communications: Putting It Together & Making It Work* (Lincolnwood, IL: NTC Business Books, 1993), p. 52.
19. Frederick E. Webster, Jr., "Defining the New Marketing Concept (Part I)," *Marketing Management* 2, no. 4 (1994), pp. 22–31.
20. Frederick E. Webster, Jr., "The Changing Role of Marketing in the Corporation," *Journal of Marketing,* October 1992, pp. 1–17, 22–31.
21. Ibid.
22. Ibid.
23. Kotler and Armstrong, *Principles of Marketing,* p. 559.
24. Ibid., p. 560.
25. Stan Rapp and Thomas L. Collins, "Nestlè Banks on Databases," *Advertising Age,* October 25, 1993, pp. 16, S–7.
26. Denison Hatch, "The Media Mix: How to Reach the Right Person with the Right Message in the Right Environment," *Target Marketing,* July 1994, pp. 8–10; and Kenneth Wylie, "Direct Response: Database Development Shows Strong Growth as Shops Gain 16.9% in U.S.," *Advertising Age,* July 12, 1993, p. S8.
27. Gary Levin, "Wunderman: 'Personalized' Marketing Will Gain Dominance," *Advertising Age,* October 25, 1993, p. S1.
28. Kotler and Armstrong, *Principles of Marketing,* p. 560.
29. Glen Nowak and Joseph Phelps, "Conceptualizing the Integrated Marketing Communications Phenomenon: An Examination of Its Impact on Advertising Practices and Its Implications for Advertising Research," *Journal of Current Issues and Research in Advertising,* Spring 1994, pp. 49–66.
30. Thomas R. Duncan and Sandra E. Moriarty, *Driving Brand Value: Using Integrated Marketing to Manage Stakeholder Relationships* (New York: McGraw-Hill, 1997), p. 42.
31. Adapted from Kotler and Armstrong, *Principles of Marketing,* pp. 560–61.
32. Arthur M. Hughes, "Can This Relationship Work?" *Marketing Tools,* July/August 1994, p. 4.
33. Hillary Chura and Kate MacArthur, "Flat Colas Anxiously Watch Gen Yers Switch," *Advertising Age,* September 25, 2000; and Howard, "Brand Builders," p. 30.
34. Kotler and Armstrong, *Principles of Marketing,* p. 561.
35. Schultz, Tannenbaum, and Lauterborn, *Integrated Marketing Communications,* p. 52.
36. Regis McKenna, "Marketing Is Everything," *Harvard Business Review,* January/February 1991, p. 65.
37. Tom Duncan, "Integrated Marketing? It's Synergy," *Advertising Age,* March 8, 1993, p. 22.
38. Glen J. Nowak and Joseph Phelps, "Conceptualizing the Integrated Marketing Communications' Phenomenon: An Examination of Its Impact on Advertising Practices and Its Implications for Advertising Research," *Journal of Current Issues & Research in Advertising,* vol. 26(1), 1994, pp. 49–66.
39. Karlene Lukovitz, "Get Ready for One-on-One Marketing," *Folio: The Magazine for Magazine Management,* October 1, 1991, pp. 64–70.
40. Don E. Schultz, "Four Basic Rules Lay Groundwork for Integration," *Marketing News,* August 16, 1993, p. 5.
41. William F. Arens and Jack J. Whidden, "La Publicité aux Etats-Unis, 1992; Les Symptomes et les Stratégies d'une Industrie Surpeuplée," *L'industrie de la Publicité au Québec 1991–1992* (Montreal: Le Publicité-Club de Montréal, October 1992), pp. 365–99.
42. Regis McKenna, "Marketing in an Age of Diversity," *Harvard Business Review,* September/October 1988, p. 88; Schultz, Tannenbaum, and Lauterborn, *Integrated Marketing Communications,* p. 21.
43. Duncan and Moriarty, *Driving Brand Value,* pp. 78–90.
44. Ibid., p. 90.
45. Adapted from Tom Duncan, "A Macro Model of Integrated Marketing Communication," paper presented to the annual conference of the American Academy of Advertising, Norfolk, VA, March 23–24, 1995, pp. 7–10.
46. Don E. Schultz, "The Next Step in IMC?" *Marketing News,* August 15, 1994, pp. 8–9.
47. Rapp and Collins, "Nestlé Banks on Databases," pp. 16, S7.
48. Don E. Schultz, "Trying to Determine ROI for IMC," *Marketing News,* January 3, 1994, p. 18; Don E. Schultz, "Spreadsheet Approach to Measuring ROI for IMC," *Marketing News,*

February 28, 1994, p. 12; and Matthew P. Gonring, "Putting Integrated Marketing Communications to Work Today," *Public Relations Quarterly,* Fall 1994, p. 45.

49. Don E. Schultz, "Integration Helps You Plan Communications from Outside-In," *Marketing News,* March 15, 1993, p. 12.
50. McKenna, "Marketing Is Everything."
51. Schultz, Tannenbaum, and Lauterborn, *Integrated Marketing Communications,* pp. 55–58.
52. Wayne Henderson, "The IMC Scale: A Tool for Evaluating IMC Usage," *Integrated Marketing Communications Research Journal,* vol. 3, no. 1 (Spring 1997), pp. 11–17.
53. Don E. Schultz and Paul Wang, "Real World Results," *Marketing Tools,* premier issue, May 1994, pp. 40–47.
54. Ibid.
55. Don E. Schultz, "Integrated Marketing Communications: A Competitive Weapon in Today's Marketplace," *Marketing Review,* July 1993, pp. 10–11, 29.
56. Gregg Ambach and Mike Hess, "Measuring Long-Term Effects in Marketing," *Marketing Research: A Magazine of Management and Applications,* American Marketing Association, Summer 2000, pp. 23–30.
57. Robert D. Buzzell and Frederick D. Wiersema, "Successful Share-Building Strategies," *Harvard Business Review,* January/February 1981, p. 135; Siva K. Balasubramanian and V. Kumar, "Analyzing Variations in Advertising and Promotional Expenditures: Key Correlated in Consumer, Industrial, and Service Markets," *Journal of Marketing,* April 1990, pp. 57–68.
58. Bernard Ryan Jr., *Advertising in a Recession: The Best Defense Is a Good Offense* (New York: American Association of Advertising Agencies, 1991), pp. 13–29; Priscilla C. Brown, "Surviving with a Splash," *Business Marketing,* January 1991, p. 14; Edmund O. Lawler, "A Window of Opportunity," *Business Marketing,* January 1991, p. 16; Rebecca Colwell Quarles, "Marketing Research Turns Recession into Business Opportunity," *Marketing News,* January 7, 1991, pp. 27, 29.
59. Leo Bogart, *Strategy in Advertising,* 2nd ed. (Chicago: Crain Books, 1984), pp. 45–47.
60. John Philip Jones, "Ad Spending: Maintaining Market Share," *Harvard Business Review,* January/February 1990, pp. 38–42; James C. Schroer, "Ad Spending: Growing Market Share," *Harvard Business Review,* January/February 1990, pp. 44–49.
61. Peter Breen, "Seeds of Change," Promo Sourcebook Supplement, Copyright 2000, INTERTEC, p. 18 (retrieved from www.lexisnexis.com).

CHAPTER 8

1. "Target through the Years," (retrieved at http://sites.target.com/site/en/company/page.jsp?contentId=WCMP04-031697).
2. Jeffrey Arlen, "Why Is Target So Cool?" DSN Retailing Today, April 2, 2001 (retrieved at http://findarticles.com/p/articles/mi_m0FNP/is_7_40/ai_73181652/).
3. Deborah Belgum, "Mossimo and Cherokee in Battle over Finder's Fees," Los Angeles Business Journal, Monday, July 15, 2002 (retrieved at http://www.allbusiness.com/north-america/united-states-california-metro-areas/252558-1.html).
4. Adapted from Bruce Bendinger, *The Copy Workshop Workbook* (Chicago: The Copy Workshop, 2002), pp. 128–47.
5. Nick Bilton, "Why the Surface RT failed and the iPad did not," *New York Times,* July 19, 2013, retrieved at http://bits.blogs.nytimes.com/2013/07/19/why-the-surface-rt-failed-and-the-ipad-did-not/.
6. Leo Burnett Advertising Agency, retrieved at http://creativebrief.com/agency/info/21141/leo-burnett.
7. Bernbach quote in William M. O'Barr, Creativity in Advertising, *Advertising & Society Review* (2011). Retrieved at http://muse.jhu.edu/journals/advertising_and_society_review/summary/v011/11.4.o-barr01.html.
8. Hank Seiden, *Advertising Pure and Simple* (New York: AMACOM, 1990), pp. 23–240.
9. Nancy A. Mitchell, Diane M. Badzinski, and Donna R. Pawlowski, "The Use of Metaphors as Vivid Stimuli to Enhance Comprehension and Recall of Print Advertisements," in Karen Whitehill King, ed., *Proceedings of the 1994 Conference of the American Academy of Advertising* (Athens, GA: Henry W. Grady College of Journalism and Mass Communication, the University of Georgia, 1994), p. 199.
10. Sal Randazzo, *The Mythmakers: How Advertisers Apply the Power of Classic Myths and Symbols to Create Modern Day Legends* (Chicago: Probus Publishing, 1995), pp. 28–51.
11. Barry A. Hollander, "Infomation Graphics and the Bandwagon Effect: Does the Visual Display of Opinion Aid in Persuasion?" paper presented to the annual convention of the Association for Education in Journalism and Mass Communication, Montreal, August 1992, p. 21.
12. Glenn Griffin and Deborah Morrison, "The creative process illustrated," (HOW, 2010),
13. Allen F. Harrison and Robert M. Bramson, *The Art of Thinking* (New York: Berkley Books, 1984), pp. 26, 34, 181.
14. Ibid.
15. Roger von Oech, *A Kick in the Seat of the Pants* (New York: HarperPerennial, 1986), p. 12.
16. John O'Toole, *The Trouble with Advertising,* 2nd ed. (New York: Random House, 1985), p. 132; Fred Danzig, "The Big Idea," *Advertising Age,* November 9, 1988, pp. 16, 138–40.
17. O'Toole, *The Trouble with Advertising,* pp. 132–33.
18. Adapted with permission from von Oech, *A Kick in the Seat of the Pants,* pp. 55–87.
19. Bob Garfield, "Lovestruck Praying Mantis Is Hooked on Fila," *Advertising Age,* February 13, 1995, p. 3.
20. William D. Perreault Jr. and E. Jerome McCarthy, *Basic Marketing,* 17th ed. (Burr Ridge, IL: Richard D. Irwin, 2008).
21. Adapted with permission from von Oech, *A Kick in the Seat of the Pants,* pp. 89–111.
22. David Ogilvy, *Ogilvy on Advertising* (New York: Random House, 1985), pp. 17–18.

CHAPTER 9

1. "What Types of Ads Are Most Helpful," Search Engine Land (retrieved at http://searchengineland.com/what-ads-types-are-most-helpful-search-ads-follow-newspapers-tv-21913).
2. Bonnie Drewniany and A. Jerome Jewler, "Creative Strategy in Advertising," (Cengage 2010).
3. Roy Paul Nelson, *The Design of Advertising* (Dubuque, IA: Brown & Benchmark, 1994), p. 107; J. Douglas Johnson, *Advertising Today* (Chicago: Science Research Associates, 1978).
4. John O'Toole, *The Trouble with Advertising,* 2nd ed. (New York: Random House, 1985), p. 149.
5. Axel Andersson and Denison Hatch, "How to Create Headlines That Get Results," *Target Marketing,* March 1994, pp. 28–35.

6. Murray Raphel and Neil Raphel, "A New Look at Newspaper Ads," *Progressive Grocer,* November 1993, pp. 13–14; David Ogilvy, *Ogilvy on Advertising* (New York: Random House, 1985), pp. 88–89.
7. Philip Ward Burton, *Advertising Copywriting,* 6th ed. (Lincolnwood, IL: NTC Business Books, 1999), pp. 65–66, 70.
8. Nelson, *The Design of Advertising,* p. 91.
9. Drewniany & Jewler, *Creative Strategy in Advertising,* p. 115; Burton, *Advertising Copywriting,* p. 188; Julia M. Collins, "Image and Advertising," *Harvard Business Review,* January/February 1989, pp. 93–97.
10. Neil Raphel and Murray Raphel, "Rules to Advertise By," *Progressive Grocer,* December 1993, pp. 13–14; Murray Raphel, "How to Get Ahead in Direct Mail," *Direct Marketing,* January 1990, pp. 30–32, 52.
11. Ogilvy, *Ogilvy on Advertising,* p. 71.
12. Raphel and Raphel, "A New Look at Newspaper Ads," pp. 13–14.
13. James H. Leigh, "The Use of Figures of Speech in Print Ad Headlines," *Journal of Advertising Research,* June 1994, pp. 17–33.
14. Ogilvy, *Ogilvy on Advertising,* pp. 10–11.
15. Andersson and Hatch, "How to Create Headlines That Get Results," pp. 28–35.
16. Burton, *Advertising Copywriting,* p. 54; Arthur J. Kover and William J. James, "When Do Advertising 'Power Words' Work? An Examination of Congruence and Satiation," *Journal of Advertising Research,* July/August 1993, pp. 32–38.
17. Burton, *Advertising Copywriting,* p. 58.
18. Raphel and Raphel, "A New Look at Newspaper Ads," pp. 13–14.
19. Burton, *Advertising Copywriting,* p. 54.
20. Burton, *Advertising Copywriting,* p. 12.
21. Raphel and Raphel, "Rules to Advertise By," pp. 13–14.
22. Bendinger, *The Copy Workshop Workbook,* p. 192.
23. Burton, *Advertising Copywriting,* p. 74.
24. Ogilvy, *Ogilvy on Advertising,* p. 119.
25. Burton, *Advertising Copywriting,* p. 79.
26. Leigh, "The Use of Figures of Speech in Print Ad Headlines," pp. 17–33.
27. Ogilvy, *Ogilvy on Advertising,* p. 109.
28. Bendinger, *The Copy Workshop Workbook,* p. 284.
29. "Corporate Advertising Study," Burson-Marsteller, October 13, 2003, www.efluentials.com/documents/pr_101303.pdf.

CHAPTER 10

1. Bob Garfield, "Ad Age Advertising Century: Top 100 Campaigns," AdAge.com, March 29, 1999, http://adage.com.
2. HaggBridge.com Blog, www.haggbridge.com/2009/06/30/levis-go-forth/.
3. Ibid.
4. The Inspiration Room Blog, posted by Duncan July 7, 2009, http://theinspirationroom.com/daily/2009/levis-go-forth-inamerica/.
5. "The Levi's Brand Debuts 2012 Go Forth™ Global Marketing Campaign," Levi Strauss & Co. press release, July 26, 2012, www.levistrauss.com/news/press-releases/levi-s-brand-debuts-2012-go-forth-global-marketing-campaign.
6. Ibid.
7. Patrick M. Reilly and Ernest Beck, "Publishers Often Pad Circulation Figures," *The Wall Street Journal,* September 30, 1997, p. B12.
8. Shu-Fen Li, John C. Schweitzer, and Benjamin J. Bates, "Effectiveness of Trade Magazine Advertising," paper presented to the annual conference of the Association for Education in Journalism and Mass Communication, Montreal, Quebec, August 1992.
9. Emma Bazilian, "Magazine Circulation Flat, Despite Soft Newsstand Sales. Digital Sales Are Small but Growing Part of the Industry," *Adweek*, February 7, 2013, www.adweek.com/news/press/magazine-circulation-flat-despite-soft-newsstand-sales-147118.
10. Tanzina Vega, "Magazine Newsstand Sales Suffered Sharp Falloff in Second Half of 2011," *The New York Times*, February 7, 2012, http://mediadecoder.blogs.nytimes.com/2012/02/07/magazine-newsstand-sales-suffered-sharp-falloff-in-second-half-of-2011/.
11. Gene Willhoft, "Is 'Added Value' Valuable?" *Advertising Age,* March 1, 1993, p. 18.
12. "Car and Driver Media Kit," www.caranddrivermediakit.com; "Road & Track Media Kit," www.roadandtrackmediakit.com.
13. Lisa I. Fried, "New Rules Liven Up the Rate-Card Game," *Advertising Age,* October 24, 1994, p. S8.
14. "People Magazine 2013 Rate Card," effective January 1, 2013, www.people.com/people/static/mediakit/media/pdf/ratecard.pdf.
15. "Not America's Favorite Paper Campaign," *Encyclopedia.com,* www.encyclopedia.com/article-1G2-3446600299/village-voice-llc.html.
16. Joyce Rutter Kaye, *Print Casebooks 10/The Best in Advertising,* 1994–95 ed. (Rockville, MD: RC Publications, 1994), pp. 63–65; Tony Case, "Getting Personal," *Editor & Publisher,* February 1, 1992, pp. 16, 31; Ann Cooper, "Creatives: Magazines—Believers in the Power of Print," *Adweek* (Eastern ed.), April 12, 1993, pp. 34–39.
17. TNS Media Intelligence, June 22, 2009, http://adage.com/images/random/datacenter/2009/spendtrends09.pdf.
18. Ronald Redfern, "What Readers Want from Newspapers," *Advertising Age,* January 23, 1995, p. 25.
19. www.naa.org.
20. Ibid.
21. "Parade Media Solutions," *Parade* website, http://mediakit.parade.com/parade/mediasolutions.html.
22. "U.S. newspaper circulation drops 8.7%," *USA Today*, April 26, 2010, http://content.usatoday.com/communities/ondeadline/post/2010/04/us-newspaper-circulation-drops-87/1.
23. "Joint Promotion Adds Stickers to Sweet Smell of Marketing," Stuart Elliott, *The New York Times,* April 2, 2007, www.nytimes.com/2007/04/02/business/media/02adcol.html?_r=1&ref=media.
24. *Newspaper Rate Differentials* (New York: American Association of Advertising Agencies, 1990); Christy Fisher, "NAA Readies National Ad-Buy Plan," *Advertising Age,* March 1, 1993, p. 12.
25. *The Source: Newspapers by the Numbers,* Newspaper Association of America, www.naa.org/thesource.
26. John Flinn, "State of the National Buy," *Adweek,* June 26, 1995, p. 56.
27. Christy Fisher, "Chrysler's One-Stop Ad Buys Boost Ailing Newspapers," *Advertising Age,* March 7, 1994, p. 49.

28. Dorothy Giobbe, "One Order/One Bill System Gets a Dress Rehearsal," *Editor & Publisher,* March 12, 1994, pp. 26, 46.

29. Fisher, "Chrysler's One-Stop Ad Buys Boost Ailing Newspapers," p. 49; ibid.

30. Edmund Lee, "New York Times Tops USA Today to Become No. 2 U.S. Paper," *Bloomberg.com,* April 30, 2013, www.forbes.com/sites/roberthof/2012/01/19/online-ad-revenues-to-pass-print-in-2012/.

31. Stephen Barr, "Moving Ahead," *Adweek,* January 31, 1994, p. 26.

32. "After years of bad headlines the industry finally has some good news," *The Economist*, December 8, 2012, www.economist.com/news/business/21567934-after-years-bad-headlines-industry-finally-has-some-good-news-news-adventures.

33. samh, "Survey says Yellow Pages drive as much business as search engines," *Adworz,* June 20, 2011, www.adworkz.com/blog/yellow-pages-search-engines/.

34. *Yellow Pages Industry Facts Booklet,* 1994–95 edition (Troy, MI: Yellow Pages Publishers Association, 1994), p. 32.

35. www.businessweek.com/articles/2012-03-22/the-golden-allure-of-the-yellow-pages.

36. Bradley Johnson, "Yellow-Pages Deals Red Hot as Telecom Industry Regroups," *Advertising Age,* January 6, 2003, www.proquest.com.

37. Karen Weise, "The Golden Allure of the Yellow Pages," *BloombergBusinessweek,* March 22, 2012, www.prnewswire.com/news-releases/yellow-turns-page-on-new-chapter-yellow-pages-association-rebrands-as-local-search-association-120055859.html.

CHAPTER 11

1. Associated Press, "Updated Ratings Make Super Bowl XLIII the Most-Watched Ever," *USA Today,* February 4, 2009 (retrieved June 1, 2009, from http://www.usatoday.com/sports/football/nfl/2009-02-04-ratings_N.htm).

2. Hyundai Motor America Reports February 2009 Sales, Press Release, March 3, 2009 (retrieved from http://www.marketwatch.com/story/hyundai-motor-america-reportsfebruary-2009?distmsr_2).

3. Lauren Indvik, "Television Advertising Still Dominant, Still Growing" Mashable, April, 2013, retrieved at: http://mashable.com/2013/04/03/tv-advertising-study/.

4. TVB, "A Report on the Growth and Scope of Television," June, 2012, retrieved at: http://www.tvb.org/media/file/TV_Basics.pdf.

5. Ibid.

6. Ibid.

7. Cable Advertising Bureau, "Cable Network Schedules, retrieved at: http://www.thecab.tv/main/resources/cableNetSchedules/index.shtml.

8. Anthony Crupi, "Duck Dynasty Smashes Cable Ratings Records," Adweek, August 15, 2013, retrieved at http://www.adweek.com/news/television/duck-dynasty-smashes-cable-ratings-records-151862.

9. TVB, "A Report on the Growth and Scope of Television."

10. Markting Charts, "Daily Media Usage," April 3, 2013, retrieved at http://www.marketingcharts.com/wp/television/daily-media-usage-mobile-internet-consumption-grows-y-o-y-tv-stable-28342/.

11. Jason Knott, "Cable TV Penetration Continues to Drop, July 30, 2013, retrieved at http://www.cepro.com/article/cable_tv_penetration_continues_to_drop/.

12. NCTA, "Industry Data," retrieved at http://www.ncta.com/industry-data/item/310.

13. Nielsen, "Average U.S. Home Now Receives a Record 118.6 TV Channels," retrieved at http://www.nielsen.com/us/en/press-room/2008/average_u_s_home.html.

14. The Rise of Social TV: How Social Media Is Amplifying TV Advertising. Business Insider, June 11, 2013, retrieved at: http://www.businessinsider.com/social-media-amplifying-tv-advertising-2013-6.

15. Ibid.

16. Michael Fleischman, "Extend TV Commercials on Twitter: Premiering TV ad targeting." Twitter Blogs, May 23, 2013, retrieved at: https://blog.twitter.com/2013/amplify-tv-commercials-twitter-premiering-tv-ad-targeting.

17. Robin Wauters, "As the Social TV Industry Comes of Age, Stay Tuned for What Facebook Has in Store," TNW, Feb. 9, 2013, retrieved at http://thenextweb.com/facebook/2013/02/09/facebook-social-tv-checkin-feature/.

18. Edmund Lee, "Facebook Said to Plan to Sell TV-Style Ads for $2.5 Million Each," Bloomberg.com, July 31, 2013, retrieved at: http://www.bloomberg.com/news/2013-07-30/facebook-said-to-plan-to-sell-tv-style-ads-for-2-5m-each.html.

19. Brian Stelter, "Devices Lead the Way to a Smarter TV," New York Times, August 21, 2013, retrieved at: http://www.nytimes.com/2013/08/22/technology/personaltech/streaming-devices-lead-the-way-to-smart-tv.html?emc=rss.

20. "Television, Internet and Mobile Usage in the U.S., A2/M2 Three Screen Report," The Nielsen Company, retrieved from http://i.cdn.turner.com/cnn/2009/images/02/24/screen.press.b.pdf.

21. "Nielsen: Product Placement on the Rise on Broadcast TV," John Eggerton, *Broadcasting & Cable*, 5/5/2008 (retrieved from http://www.broadcastingcable.com/article/113587-Nielsen_Product_Placement_On_The_Rise_On_Broadcast_TV.php, June 22, 2010).

22. Laura Stampler, "How 'Big Bang Theory' Dominated the 10 Best Product Placements of 2011," Business Insider, Dec. 23, 2011, retrieved at: http://www.businessinsider.com/product-placement-nielsen-top-ten-2011-12?op=1.

23. Brad Tuttle, "Superman the Sellout? Man of Steel Has Over 100 Promotional Partners," June 4, 2013, retrieved at http://business.time.com/2013/06/04/superman-the-sell-out-man-of-steel-has-over-100-promotional-partners/.

24. John C. Abell, "Nielsen: the past, the present, but not the future of TV," February 22, 2013, retrieved at: http://blogs.reuters.com/mediafile/2013/02/22/nielsen-the-past-the-present-but-not-the-future-of-tv/; George Winslow, "New 'Frankenmetrics' leave monster of a task for Nielsen, TV networks and other stakeholders," July 22, 2013, retrieved at http://www.broadcastingcable.com/article/494609-The_Measurement_Mess.php.

25. "Media Comparisons," *1997 Radio Marketing Guide and Fact Book for Advertisers*; Imagery Transfer Study (New York: Network Radio Association, 1993).

26. Ibid.; *Media Facts: The Complete Guide to Maximizing Your Advertising* (New York: Radio Advertising Bureau, 1994), pp. 8–9.

CHAPTER 12

1. eMarketer, "U.S. Online Advertising Spending to Surpass Print in 2012," retrieved at www.emarketer.com/Article/US-Online-Advertising-Spending-Surpass-Print-2012/1008783.

2. Netcraft, "June 2010 Web Server Survey," retrieved at http://news.netcraft.com/archives/2010/06/16/june-2010-web-server-survey.html.

3. Alexa, "Google.com," retrieved June 27, 2010, at http://www.alexa.com/siteinfo/google.com.
4. OnlineMatters.com, "Glossary of Online Marketing Terms," retrieved at http://www.onlinematters.com/glossary.htm.
5. Fortune, "Rumor: 40-45 million iPhones in 2010," December 23, 2009, retrieved at http://tech.fortune.cnn.com/2009/12/23/rumor-40-45-million-iphones-in-2010/.
6. Steve Miller and Mike Beirne, "The iPhone Effect," Brandweek, April 28, 2008 (retrieved from http://www.adweek.com/aw/content_display/news/agency/e3ibef1ad200773laba65le-6216ba3b6267).
7. eMarketer Digital Intelligence, "Mobile Shopping Doubles in 2010," June 3, 2010, retrieved at http://www2.emarketer.com/Article.aspx?R=1007734.
8. Buzzcity, "Mobile Advertising Continues Strong Growth," Buzzcity, July 22, 2009 (retrieved from http://www.mobile-tech-today.com/story.xhtml?story_id=67945&full_skip=1).
9. Miniwatts Marketing Group, "Internet Usage Statistics," retrieved at http://www.internetworldstats.com/stats.htm.
10. IAB, "Ad Impression Measurement Guidelines," retrieved June 27, 2010, at http://www.iab.net/iab_products_and_industry_services/1421/1443/1455.
11. IAB, "Leading Global Advertising Industry Organizations Endorse Interactive Advertising Campaign Measurement Guidelines," retrieved June 27, 2010, at http://www.iab.net/about_the_iab/recent_press_releases/press_release_archive/press_release/4682.
12. http://investor.google.com/financial/tables.html.
13. Samantha Yaffe, "Are Marketers Undervaluing the Internet?" *Strategy,* March 8, 2004, p. 1, retrieved September 3, 2004, at www.global.lexisnexis.com/us.
14. Wendy Davis, "Judge Brings Reunion.com and Spam Suit Together Again," Online Media Daily, April 12, 2010, retrieved at http://www.mediapost.com/publications/?fa=Articles.showArticle&art_aid=125938.
15. Matt Hines, "ISP Hammers Bob Vila Site with Spam Suit," CNET News, March 5, 2004, retrieved at http://news.cnet.com/2100-1024-5170631.html.
16. Amanda Beeler, "Word-of-Mouth Pitches Mutate into New Forms on the Internet," *Advertising Age,* April 2000 (retrieved January 2001 from www.adage.com).

CHAPTER 13

1. "James Ready Beer—Share Our Billboard Campaign," March 4, 2010, *AdDude's Insights* http://lifson.com/?tag=james-ready-beer.
2. James Ready (Beer), Wikipedia.org, http://en.wikipedia.org/wiki/James_Ready_(beer).
3. "James Ready—Share Our Billboard Campaign," Case Study, Adforum.com, http://www.adforum.com/adfolio/reel_detail.asp?page=1&ID=34444670&TDI=Vdnpg80Qj8.
4. "Leo Burnett, James Ready Win Top International Outdoor Honour," Jeromy Lloyd, April 21, 2009, *Marketing,* www.marketingmag.ca/english/news/agency/article.jsp?content=20090421_145348_6236.
5. "James Ready: Billboard Coupon," *Creativity,* http://creativityonline.com/work/james-ready-billboard-coupon/19864.
6. "OOH Revenue by Format," Outdoor Advertising Association of America, www.oaaa.org/ResourceCenter/MarketingSales/Factsamp;Figures/Revenue/OOHRevenuebyFormat.aspx.
7. "Introduce Yourself to Outdoor Advertising," Outdoor Advertising Association of America, Inc., www.oaaa.org.
8. *Billboard Basics* (New York: Outdoor Advertising Association of America, 1994), p. 5.
9. "Spenders by Medium," Ad Age Data Center, *Advertising Age,* June 24, 2013, p 20.
10. "Billboard boom," *The Economist,* April 20, 2011, www.economist.com/node/18587305.
11. Mary Jo Haskey, "The Last Mass Medium," *Mediaweek,* December 6, 1993, p. 17.
12. Diane Williams, "The Arbitron National In-Car Study, 2009 Edition," Arbitron Inc., www.arbitron.com/downloads/InCarStudy2009.pdf.
13. "Key Messages, Outdoor Advertising Association of America, www.oaaa.org/DesktopModules/SearchBoost/DownloadDoc.ashx?filepid=0&file=2336.
14. www.lamar.com.
15. "Business & Technology Case Studies: eBay," Outdoor Advertising Association of America, August 1, 2012, www.oaaa.org/ResourceCenter/MarketingSales/CaseStudies/BusinessTechnology/tabid/309/id/3890/Default.aspx.
16. TAB Eyes On—Out-Of-Home Media Measurement The Basics 2009. www.eyesonrating.com.
17. "CPM Comparisons for Major Media," Outdoor Advertising Association of America.
18. "Technology Standards," Outdoor Advertising Association of America, 1997 www.oaaa.org/Tech.
19. Ibid.
20. "Digital Billboard Safety Confirmed," Watchfire Digital Outdoor, March 8, 2011, www.watchfiredigitaloutdoor.com/press/digital-billboard-safety-confirmed.
21. "New Study Finds Digital Billboards Distract Drivers," *Automotive Fleet,* January 3, 2013, www.automotive-fleet.com/channel/safety-accident-management/news/story/2013/01/new-study-finds-digital-billboards-distract-drivers.aspx.
22. Karl Greenberg, "Lexus Accelerates into All Venues in Push for Revamped IS Sedan," *Brandweek,* August 31, 2005 www.brandweek.com/bw/news/autos/article_display.jsp?vnu_content_id=1001052022.
23. Cyndee Miller, "Outdoor Advertising Weathers Repeated Attempts to Kill It," *Marketing News,* March 16, 1992, pp. 1, 9; *Billboard Basics,* pp. 15–16.
24. "Surveys Show Americans Like Their Billboards," Outdoor Advertising Association of America, 1997 www.oaaa.org.
25. Riccardo A. Davis, "Apparel, Movies Orchestrate an Outdoor Rebirth," *Advertising Age,* November 22, 1993, p. S1.
26. Riccardo A. Davis, "Retailers Open Doors Wide for Co-op," *Advertising Age,* August 1, 1994, p. 30. Melissa Korn, "Bricks Rivaling Clicks in Ad Spending," *Financial Times,* July 21, 2006 http://search.ft.com/searchArticle?queryText=1-800-flowers&y=4&javascriptEnabled=true&id=060721008312&x=8, "Outdoor Grows Online Sales: 1-800-Flowers.com Sales 7 Times Greater in Outdoor Markets," CBS Outdoor, www.cbsoutdoor.com/news.php.
27. "Advertising That Imitates Art," *Adweek,* June 20, 1994, p. 18.
28. Larry Dobrow, "If the Cap Fits . . .," Mediapost.com, April 2006 http://publications.mediapost.com/index.cfm?fuseaction=Articles.showArticle&art_aid=40183.
29. Shahna Mahmud, "Cinema Ad Revenue up 15 Percent," *Adweek,* October 15, 2007.

30. "Why Digital License Plates Are a Great Idea," Chris Matyszczyk, cnet news, June 21, 2010 http://news.cnet.com/8301-17852_3-20008394-71.html.

31. Susanna Kim, "ATM Surcharges Could Be Waived With Commercials," ABC News, December 5, 2011, http://abcnews.go.com/Business/advertisements-atms-replace-surcharges/story?id=15077078.

32. "California May Issue Digital License Plates, Privacy Groups Concerned," CBS Local Media, July 18, 2013, http://sanfrancisco.cbslocal.com/2013/07/18/california-may-issue-digital-license-plates-privacy-groups-concerned/.

33. James Ferrier, "Spotlight on Technology—Telecite," *Advertising Age,* November 22, 1993, p. SS10.

34. www.theguardian.com/business/2013/apr/28/mobile-phone-networks-electronic-wallet.

35. www.adweek.com/sa-article/out-home-130643.

36. ibid.

37. www.gmarketing.com/.

38. "Direct Mail Spending Continues to Surge," Associates International Inc., September 14, 2012, http://associatesinternational.com/direct-mail-spending-continues-to-surge/.

39. Ryan Joe, "North American advertising spend to increase in 2012," *Direct Marketing News,* March 14, 2013, www.dmnews.com/north-american-advertising-spend-to-increase-in-2012/article/232016/.

40. "Lost in the Mail," Matthew Philips, *Newsweek,* March 30, 2010, www.newsweek.com/2010/03/29/lost-in-the-mail.html.

41. www.forbes.com/sites/loisgeller/2012/10/16/why-are-printed-catalogs-still-around.

42. "Promotional Products Fact Sheet," Promotional Products Association International, Irving, TX, 1995.

43. Promotional Products Association International, www.ppai.org.

44. 2013 Promotional Products Fact Sheet, PPAI, www.PromotionalProductsWork.org.

45. "How Specialty Advertising Affects Goodwill," (Irving, TX: Specialty Advertising Association International, 1993).

46. Avraham Shama and Jack K. Thompson, "Promotion Gifts: Help or Hindrance?" *Mortgage Banking,* February 1989, pp. 49–51.

CHAPTER 14

1. Julie Liesse, "Inside Burnett's Vaunted Buying Machine," *Advertising Age,* July 25, 1994, p. S6.

2. Yumiko Ono, "Cordiant Puts Hamilton in Key U.S. Post," *Advertising Age,* July 18, 1997, p. B2.

3. Stephanie Thompson, "Universal McCann Gets $150 Million Nestlé Account," AdAge.com, April 12, 2002; Richard Linnett and Jack Neff, "Mindshare Wins $600 Million Gillette Media Account," AdAge.com, September 26, 2002, www.adage.com.

4. Lynette Rice, "Fall 2012: Most Popular Shows So Far," October 24, 2013, www.cnn.com/2012/10/24/showbiz/tv/fall-tv-popular-ew/index.html; Bill Gorman, "We Look Back at the Top TV Shows of 1960," June 7, 2008, http://tvbythenumbers.zap2it.com/2008/06/07/we-look-back-at-the-top-tv-shows-of-1960/4053/. Randy Stone, "Let's Stand Up to the Attack on Marketing Mix Models," *Advertising Age,* June 19, 2013, http://adage.com/article/media/stand-attack-marketing-mix-models/242173/.

5. "Digital Set to Surpass TV in Time Spent with US Media," *eMarketer,* August 1, 2013, www.emarketer.com/Article/Digital-Set-Surpass-TV-Time-Spent-with-US-Media/1010096.

6. Anthony Crupi, "In Their Prime: Broadcast Spot Costs Soar," *Adweek,* June 22, 2011, www.adweek.com/news/television/their-prime-broadcast-spot-costs-soar-132805.

7. Wayne Friedman, "Discovery Pitches Ad Convergence," *Advertising Age,* March 2000, www.adage.com.

8. Christina Merrill, "Media Rising," *Adweek,* November 9, 1998, http://members.adweek.com/archive.

9. Larry D. Kelley, Donald W. Jugenheimer, and Kim Bartel Sheehan, *Advertising Media Workbook and Sourcebook* (Armonk, NY: M. E. Sharpe, 2012).

10. Ibid., pp. 131–33.

11. Ronald D. Geskey, *Media Planning and Buying in the 21st Century* (Auburn Hills, MI: 2020: Marketing Communications LLC, 2013).

12. Ibid.

13. Kelley et al., *Advertising Media Workbook and Sourcebook.*

14. Joe Mandese, "Revisiting Ad Reach, Frequency," *Advertising Age,* November 27, 1995, p. 46.

15. Robyn Blakeman, *Integrated Marketing Communication* (Lanham, MD: Rowman & Littlefield, 2007).

16. Special Report: Best Media Plan Competition, "Guerrilla Tactics Get Panasonic Noticed," *Strategy* (Canada), March 27, 2000, p. BMP10.

17. Neil Kelliher, "Magazine Media Planning for 'Effectiveness': Getting the People Back into the Process," *Journal of Consumer Marketing,* Summer 1990, pp. 47–55.

18. Kenneth Longman, *Advertising* (New York: Harcourt Brace Jovanovich, 1971), pp. 211–12.

19. Henry Assael, "From Silos to Synergy: A Fifty-Year Review of Cross-Media Research Shows Synergy Has Yet to Achieve Its Full Potential," *Journal of Advertising Research* 51, no. 1 (2011), pp. 42–58.

20. Kevin Goldman, "Digital Warms Couch Potatoes with Only-on-Sunday TV Ads," *The Wall Street Journal,* November 22, 1994, p. B8.

21. Telmar website, September 2013, www.telmar.com.

CHAPTER 15

1. E.J. Schultz, "Muscling past Mayhem: Why Geico's Marketing Works," *Advertising Age,* July 8, 2013, p. 6.

2. E.J. Schultz, "Geico Poised to Drive Past Allstate," *Advertising Age,* June 28, 2013, http://adage.com/article/news/geico-poised-drive-past-allstate/242895/.

3. Maya Frazier, "GEICO's $500 M Outlay Pays off, "*Advertising Age,* July 9, 2007.

4. "Little Lizard Says Ello to a New Inflection," *Hartford Courant,* February 22, 2006.

5. Mya Frazier, "GEICO Ad Chief Builds Insurer into Master of Marketing," *Advertising Age,* June 19, 2006.

6. Ibid.

7. Theresa Howard, "Gecko Wasn't First Choice for GEICO," *USA Today,* July 16, 2006, www.usatoday.com/money/advertising/adtrack 2006-07-16-geico_x.htm.

8. Direct Marketing Association (DMA), www.the-dma.org/press/dmasnapshot.shtml.

9. Joan Throckmorton, "We Are Interactive—Repeat—We Are Interactive," *Direct,* November 1997.
10. Bob Stone, *Successful Direct Marketing Methods,* 4th ed. (Chicago: NTC Business Books, 1988), p. 3.
11. www.dol.gov.
12. DMA Releases New 'Power of Direct' Report; DM-Driven Sales Growth Outpace Overall Economic Growth October 2, 2011, www.the-dma.org/cgi/dispannouncements?article=1590.
13. "Facts & Stats–Direct Marketing," CMO Council, http://www.cmocouncil.org/facts-stats-categories.php?category=direct-marketing.
14. Peppers and Rogers Group, Marketing 1 to 1, www.m1to1.com/success_stories.
15. Thomas E. Caruso, "Kotler: Future Marketers Will Focus on Customer Data Base to Compete Globally," *Marketing News,* June 8, 1992, pp. 21–22.
16. Tom Van Riper, "The Why of Best Buy," www.forbes.com/business/2008/04/02/retail-best-buy-bizcommerce-cx_tvr_0402 retail.html.
17. Seth Godin, "GUEST COLUMNIST: Permission Key to Successful Marketing," *Advertising Age,* November 1997 http://adage.com.
18. Poulos, "Customer Loyalty and the Marketing Database," pp. 32–35.
19. Mollie Neal, "Marketers Looking Ahead in Chicago," *Direct Marketing,* March 1993, pp. 9–11.
20. Robert A. Peterson and Thomas R. Wotruba, "What Is Direct Selling?—Definition, Perspectives, and Research Agenda," *Journal of Personal Selling and Sales Management,* 16, no. 4 (Fall 1996), pp. 1–16.
21. Zenithoptimedia U.S. Ad Spending Forecast, *Ad Age Datacenter,* June 24, 2013.
22. Cyndee Miller, "Telemarketing Cited as Chief Form of Direct Marketing," *Marketing News,* p. 6.
23. "Brief History of Toll-Free Numbers," www.tollfreenumbers.com.
24. Larry Riggs, "Direct Mail Gets Most Response, But Email Has Highest ROI: DMA," *Chief Marketer,* June 22, 2012, www.chiefmarketer.com/direct-marketing/direct-mail-gets-most-response-but-email-has-highest-roi-dma-22062012.
25. Personal Interview with Tom Campanaro, President, Total Gym Inc., December 2000.
26. Adapted from Barton A. Weitz, Stephen B. Castleberry, and John F. Tanner Jr., *Selling: Building Partnerships* (Burr Ridge, IL: Richard D. Irwin, Inc., 1992), p. 5.
27. Mike Ishmael, "The Cost of a Sales Call," 4DSales, October 22, 2012, http://4dsales.com/the-cost-of-a-sales-call/.
28. Edwin Klewer, Robert Shaffer, and Bonnie Binnig, "Sales Is an Investment, Attrition an Expense," *Journal of Health Care Marketing,* September 1995, p. 12.
29. "All-Show Averages," Exhibit Surveys, www.exhibitsurveys.com/trends.
30. Susan A. Friedmann, *Exhibiting at Trade Shows* (Menlo Park, CA: Crisp Publications, 1992), p. V.
31. Ibid., p. 16.
32. "All-Show Averages," Exhibit Surveys, www.exhibitsurveys.com/trends.
33. Friedmann, *Exhibiting at Trade Shows,* p. 24.
34. Ibid., pp. 34–39.
35. Ibid., p. 44.
36. Ibid., pp. 70–71.
37. Ibid., p. 90.
38. Lisa McTigue Pierce, "North American packaging market remains wary about the future," *Packaging Digest,* 11/12/2012, www.packagingdigest.com/article/522689-North_American_packaging_market_remains_wary_about_the_future.php.
39. W. Wossen Kassaye and Dharmendra Verma, "Balancing Traditional Packaging Functions with the New 'Green' Packaging Concerns," *SAM Advanced Management Journal,* Autumn 1992, pp. 15–23.
40. Ibid.
41. Ibid.
42. Chris Baum, "10th Annual Packaging Consumer Survey 1994: Consumers Want It All—And Now," *Packaging,* August 1994, pp. 40–43.
43. Kassaye and Verma, "Balancing Traditional Packaging Functions with the New 'Green' Packaging Concerns."
44. "Excerpt: Under the Radar," *Brandweek,* December 8, 1997 http://members.adweek.com/archive/adweek/current/brandweek.
45. Peter Breen, "Seeds of Change," *Promo Sourcebook Supplement,* October 2000, p. 18.
46. Larry Light, "Trustmarketing: The Brand Relationship Marketing Mandate for the 90s," address to American Association of Advertising Agencies annual meeting, Laguna Niguel, CA, April 23, 1993.
47. Magid M. Abraham and Leonard M. Lodish, "Getting the Most Out of Advertising and Promotion," *Harvard Business Review,* May/June 1990, p. 51.
48. Light, "Trustmarketing."
49. Larry Light, "At the Center of It All Is the Brand," *Advertising Age,* March 29, 1993, p. 22.
50. David Ghitelman, "Slotting Fees Can Top $2 Million: FTC," *Supermarket News,* Nov. 24, 2003, http://supermarketnews.com/archive/slotting-fees-can-top-2-million-ftc.
51. *The Point of Purchase Advertising Industry Fact Book* (Washington, DC: POPAI, 1997), p. 51.
52. Kelly Shermach, "Study: Most Shoppers Notice P-O-P Material," *Marketing News,* January 1995, p. 27.
53. *The Point of Purchase Advertising Industry Fact Book,* p. 39.
54. Kelly Shermach, "Great Strides Made in P-O-P Technology," *Marketing News,* January 2, 1995, pp. 8–9.
55. Angela Lawson, "The End of the Line," June 18, 2004 www.kioskmarketplace.com.
56. "NCH Annual Topline U.S. CPG Coupon Facts Report For Year-End 2012" *NCH Marketing Services, Inc., Coupon Facts Report, 2013,* www2.nchmarketing.com/ResourceCenter/assets/0/22/28/76/226/457/735949da63a14f209014dd04c27f1472.pdf.
57. "CPG Marketers Distributed 168 Billion Coupons in H1, A Slight Rise From Last Year," *Marketing Charts,* July 31, 2013, www.marketingcharts.com/wp/direct/cpg-marketers-distributed-168-billion-coupons-in-h1-a-slight-rise-from-last-year-35441/.
58. The 16th Annual Survey of Promotional Practices, Donnelley Marketing Inc., 1994.
59. "NCH Annual Topline U.S. CPG Coupon Facts Report For Year-End 2012" *NCH Marketing Services, Inc., Coupon Facts Report,*

2013, www2.nchmarketing.com/ResourceCenter/assets/0/22/28/76/226/457/735949da63a14f209014dd04c27f1472.pdf.

60. www.catalinamarketing.com/company/FAQs.html.
61. "NCH Annual Topline U.S. CPG Coupon Facts Report For Year-End 2012" *NCH Marketing Services, Inc., Coupon Facts Report, 2013,* www2.nchmarketing.com/ResourceCenter/assets/0/22/28/76/226/457/735949da63a14f209014dd04c27f1472.pdf.
62. Stephanie Moore, "Rebate Madness: How to Defend Yourself against Ruthless Rebate Scams" www.consumeraffairs.com.
63. *Washington Post,* Tuesday, February 1, 2005; Page C10, washingtonpost.com, www.washingtonpost.com/wp-dyn/articles/A52798-2005Jan31.html.
64. Lorraine Calvacca, "Polybagging Products to Pick Up Customers," *Folio: The Magazine for Magazine Management,* January 1993, p. 26.

CHAPTER 16

1. Amol Sharma, "Netflix Subscriber Growth Falls Short," *The Wall Street Journal,* July 22, 2013, http://online.wsj.com/article/SB10001424127887323829104578622213012052802.html.
2. Jim Osborne, "Getting Full Value from Public Relations," *Public Relations Journal,* October/November 1994, p. 64.
3. CSPI Newsroom, "Ben & Jerry's Fudging the Truth, Says CSPI: Nothing 'All-Natural' about Ingredients," July 30, 2002, www.cspinet.org/new/200207301.html.
4. Ben & Jerry's Homemade, Inc., press release, "Ben & Jerry's Response to CSPI Concerns," July 31, 2002, www.benjerry.com.
5. Ben & Jerry's Homemade, Inc., press release, "Ben & Jerry's Voluntarily Initiates the Recall of Pints of Karamel Sutra Ice Cream with Code 02/14/04," March 28, 2003, www.benjerry.com.
6. Sandra Moriarty, "PR and IMC: The Benefits of Integration," *Public Relations Quarterly,* Fall 1994, pp. 38–44.
7. Publisher's Statement, *Inside PR,* March 1993, p. 3.
8. Thomas L. Harris, "PR Gets Personal," *Direct Marketing,* April 1994, pp. 29–32.
9. Al Ries and Laura Ries, *The 22 Immutable Laws of Branding* (New York: HarperCollins, 1998), pp. 25–31.
10. Bill Patterson, "Crisis Impact on Reputation Management," *Public Relations Journal,* November 1993, p. 48.
11. Ibid.
12. Ben White, "Stewart's Legal Problems Hurt Firm," *Washington Post,* August 4, 2004, p. E01, www.washingtonpost.com/wp-dyn/articles/A38202-2004Aug3.html.
13. Dennis L. Wilcox, *Public Relations Strategies and Tactics* (New York: HarperCollins, 1994), p. 381.
14. "What's Your Best Marketing Tool?" *Public Relations Journal,* February 1994, p. 12.
15. Adapted from Stephanie Gruner, "Event Marketing: Making the Most of Sponsorship Dollars," *Inc.,* August 1996, p. 88.
16. IEG FAQ:"What Is Sponsorship?" IEG Network 1998, www.sponsorship.com.
17. "2013 Sponsorship Outlook: Spending Increase Is Double-edged Sword," *IEG Sponsorship Report,* January 7, 2013, www.sponsorship.com/iegsr/2013/08/12/IEG-s-Top-Sponsorship-Spenders-List-Swells-To-93-C.aspx.
18. "FIFA Secures $1.6 Billion in World Cup Sponsorship Revenue," June 3, 2010, www.sponsorship.com/news—information/news/2010/06-june/fifa-secures-$1-6-billion-in-world-cup-sponsorship.aspx.
19. Thomas R. Duncan and Sandra E. Moriarty, *Driving Brand Value: Using Integrated Marketing to Manage Stakeholder Relationships* (New York: McGraw-Hill, 1997), p. 203.
20. Ibid.; Terry G. Vavra, *Aftermarketing: How to Keep Customers for Life Through Relationship Marketing* (Burr Ridge, IL: Irwin Professional Publishing, 1992), p. 190.
21. Vavra, *Aftermarketing,* p. 192.
22. Ibid.
23. "IEG's Top Sponsorship Spenders List Swells to 93 Companies," *IEG Sponsorship Report,* August 12, 2013, www.sponsorship.com/iegsr/2013/08/12/IEG-s-Top-Sponsorship-Spenders-List-Swells-To-93-C.aspx.
24. "2013 Sponsorship Outlook: Spending Increase Is Double-edged Sword," *IEG Sponsorship Report,* January 7, 2013, www.sponsorship.com/iegsr/2013/01/07/2013-Sponsorship-Outlook—Spending-Increase-Is-Dou.aspx.
25. Ibid.
26. "Motorsports Sponsorship Spending to Total $3.76 Billion in 2013," *IEG Sponsorship Report,* February 25, 2013, www.sponsorship.com/iegsr/2013/02/25/Motorsports-Sponsorship-Spending-To-Total-$3-76-Bi.aspx and "Golf Sponsorship Spending to Total $1.6 Billion in 2013," *IEG Sponsorship Report,* September 9, 2013, www.sponsorship.com/iegsr/2013/09/09/Golf-Sponsorship-Spending-To-Total-$1-6-Billion-In.aspx.
27. Jonathan Bond and Richard Kirshenbaum, *Under the Radar: Talking to Today's Cynical Consumers* (New York: Wiley, 1998), p. 63.
28. Melanie Wells, "Going for Nagano Gold; Nagano's Remoteness Challenges Marketers," *USA Today,* February 6, 1998, p. 1B.
29. Boaz Herzog, "Let the Ads Begin," *The Oregonian,* August 13, 2004, p. B01.
30. Junu Bryan Kim, "Most Sponsorships Waste Money: Exec," *Advertising Age,* June 21, 1993, pp. S2, S4.
31. "California, L.A. a Contender to Host Next Summer's X Games," *Los Angeles Times,* October 11, 2002, www.proquest.com.
32. "Bavaria Beer website traffic rockets after World Cup stunt," June 18, 2010, www.marketingmagazine.co.uk/news/1010738/Bavaria-Beer-website-traffic-rockets-World-Cup-stunt/.
33. Lesa Ukman, "Assertions," IEG Sponsorship Report, February 23, 1998, www.sponsorship.com.
34. Ibid.
35. Wilcox, *Public Relations Strategies and Tactics,* p. 384.
36. David Fucillo, "49ers stadium naming rights details for Levi's Stadium," *SB Nation,* May 8, 2013, www.ninersnation.com/2013/5/8/4312806/49ers-stadium-naming-rights-details-name-levis-stadium.
37. John Karolefski, "The Sport of Naming," Brand Channel.com, May 13, 2002, www.brandchannel.com.
38. Paul Stanley, "Sponsownership: Sponsorships Will Become Standard for Events," *Potentials in Marketing,* June 1990, p. 64.
39. Ukman, "Assertions."
40. Vavra, *Aftermarketing,* p. 191.
41. "Corporate Advertising/Phase II, An Expanded Study of Corporate Advertising Effectiveness," conducted for *Time* magazine by Yankelovich, Skelly & White, undated.

photo credits

FRONT MATTER

Page v: © Brand X Pictures/PunchStock RF; **p. vi:** © Don Farrall/Getty Images RF; **p. vii:** © McGraw-Hill Companies, Inc./Mark Dierker, photographer; **p. viii:** © Ingram Publishing RF; **p. ix:** © Ingram Publishing/SuperStock RF; **p. x:** © Flickr.com/Jessica Spengler, http://www.flickr.com/photos/wordridden/4308645407; **p. xi:** Flickr.com/Complete Merchandise/http://www.flickr.com/photos/completemerchandise/9144838374; **p. xii:** © McGraw-Hill Companies, Inc./Mark Dierker, photographer; **p. xiii:** © flickr.com/Taber Andrew Bain/http://www.flickr.com/photos/andrewbain/1569513841.

CHAPTER 1

Opener: © NASA Jet Propulsion Laboratory (NASA-JPL); **p. 4:** © United States Government/whitehouse.gov; **p. 7:** Courtesy of AdoptUSKids and The Advertising Council; **p. 10:** © Library of Congress, Prints & Photographs, #LC-USZC4-12222; **p. 11** (top): © BananaStock/PunchStock RF; **p. 11** (bottom): © Michael Siluk/The Image Works; **p. 12:** © The Colonial Williamsburg Foundation; **p. 15** (right): © Leonard de Selva/Corbis; **p. 16** (top): Courtesy of Eric Baird and Vintage Skivvies, www.vintageskivvies.com; **p. 16** (bottom): © Classic PIO/Fotosearch RF; **p. 17:** Client: CGSS/ANPAA; Agency Luvi Ogilvy; Title: Off the hook; Creative Director; Pedro De Oliveira; Creative Director: Luis Vieira; Photographer: Laurent Diat; Photo retouch; Beefactory; **p. 18:** Courtesy of Volkswagen® Group of America, Inc., used with permission of Volkswagen Group of America, Inc.; **p. 19:** © The Advertising Archives; **p. 21:** © American Broadcasting Companies, Inc.; **p. 22** (top): © Comstock/Alamy Images RF; **p. 22** (bottom left): © flickr.com/Thomas van de Weerd/http://www.flickr.com/photos/thms/2049797897/; **p. 22** (bottom right): Courtesy of Daum; **p. 24:** U.S. Environmental Protection Agency; **p. 25:** © Stockbyte/PunchStock RF.

CHAPTER 2

Opener: © Image Source/Corbis RF; **p. 28:** © PHOTOPQR/L"EST REPUBLICAIN/Newscom; **p. 29:** © Photoshot/Newscom; **p. 31** (left): Courtesy Darty France; **p. 31** (right): Courtesy Anthony's Pizza, Berwyn, IL; **p. 32:** © PRNewsFoto/Milk Processor Education Program (MilkPEP)/AP Images; **p. 33:** © StockMontage, Inc.; **p. 34** (top): Ad Created by Devito/Verdi for Daffy's; **p. 34** (bottom): Cannes Lions International Advertising Festival Winner, 2004; **p. 35:** © D.Hurst/Alamy RF; **p. 36:** © flickr.com/fervent-adepte-de-lamode/ http://www.flickr.com/photos/51528537@N08/8521491298/; **p. 37:** © Europics/Newscom; **p. 38:** © The Advertising Archives; **p. 39** (top): The Humane Society of the United States and Maddie's Fund; **p. 39** (bottom): Ad designed by Australie Agency, France; **p. 42** (top): © Lee Snider/Photo Images/Corbis; **p. 42** (bottom): © Stockbyte RF; **p. 43:** Cannes Lions International Advertising Festival Winner; **p. 44** (top): © digital-life/Alamy; **p. 44** (bottom): Global Advertising Lawyer Alliance, Inc.; **p. 46:** Courtesy of ConAgra Foods; **p. 47:** © NC1 WENN Photos/Newscom; **p. 48:** Courtesy of Zoetis Inc.; **p. 50:** © Imaginechina/Corbis; **p. 53:** Heat & Glo®; **p. 55:** © Alejandro Rivera/Getty Images RF.

CHAPTER 3

Opener: © Kwame Zikomo/PureStock/Superstock RF; **p. 58:** Used with permission from McDonald's Corporation; **p. 60:** Courtesy of Rubio's Restaurants, Inc.; **p. 63** (top): Courtesy of DDB, Denmark, Creatives: Mikkel Møller and Tim Ustrup Madsen; **p. 63** (bottom): © Sears Brands, LLC; **p. 66:** Used with permission of General Mills Marketing Inc. (GMMI); **p. 67:** © McGraw-Hill Companies; **p. 69** (top): Courtesy of HP Canada; **p. 69** (bottom): Used with permission from McDonald's Corporation; **p. 70:** © Image Club RF; **p. 71** (top): Courtesy of ArnoldWorldwide; **p. 71** (bottom): © Pure-Stock/SuperStock RF; **p. 72:** Courtesy of DHL; **p. 73:** Courtesy of Burrell Communications; **p. 75:** Used with permission from McDonald's Corporation; **p. 78** (top): DDB Stockholm; **p. 78** (bottom): Courtesy of Outdoor Advertising Association of America; **p. 80:** © Chris Ratcliffe/Bloomberg/Getty Images; **p. 82:** Used with permission from McDonald's Corporation; **p. 86:** Courtesy of Samsung and © McGraw-Hill Companies, Inc./Mark Dierker, photographer; **p. 87:** ©Max Powers/Corbis RF.

CHAPTER 4

Opener: © Steve Allen/Brand X Pictures RF; **p. 90:** Courtesy of P&G and Wieden + Kennedy; **p. 91:** Courtesy of P&G and Wieden + Kennedy; **p. 93:** Courtesy of the Cannes Lions International Festival of Creativity, 2011 Cannes Bronze Lion Winner; **p. 94** (top): © PRNewsFoto/Virgin America/AP Images; **p. 94** (bottom): Wells & Drew Companies, Jacksonville, FL; **p. 96** (top): The PORSCHE CREST, PORSCHE, 911 and the distinctive shape of the PORSCHE 911 automobile are registered trademarks in the United States of Dr. Ing. h.c.F. Porsche AG. Used with permission of Porsche Cars North America, Inc. Copyrighted by Porsche Cars North America, Inc; **p. 96** (bottom): Courtesy of Anita Hart, flickr.com/http://www.flickr.com/photos/anitakhart/4708575874/; **p. 97:** Courtesy of P&G; **p. 99:** CKE Restaurants Holdings, Inc.; **p. 101:** Courtesy of the Cannes Lions International Festival of Creativity, 2004 Winner; **p. 102:** adidas and the 3-Bars logo are registered trademarks of the adidas Group, used with permission; **p. 103:** Courtesy of AIG; **p. 106:** Cannes Lions International Advertising Festival, 2007 Gold Lion Winner; **p. 108:** © Redfx/Alamy RF; **p. 110** (top): Cannes Lions International Advertising Festival, 2007 Gold Lion Winner; **p. 110** (bottom): Courtesy BBDO/Toronto and Chrysler Canada; **p. 112** (top): Courtesy Braun, Inc.; **p. 112** (bottom): © PRNewsFoto/Chanel/AP Images; **p. 113:** Courtesy of Kern's Nectar; **p. 114:** Courtesy of Volvo North America; **p. 115:** Courtesy of 22 Squared Agency and Southeast Toyota Distributors; **p. 116:** © Stockbyte/Getty Images RF; **p. 117:** The UPS Store Inc; **p. 118:** Courtesy Catalina Marketing; **p. 119:** © Inti St. Clair/Getty Images RF.

CHAPTER 5

Opener: © Jack Hollingsworth/Photodisc/Getty Images RF; **p. 122:** © David Cooper/Toronto Star/Zumapress.com/Newscom; **p. 124:** Courtesy of Evian®; **p. 125:** GREEN WORKS is a registered trademark of The Clorox Company and is used with permission. © 2014 The Clorox Company. Reprinted with permission; **p. 128** (top): Cannes Lion International Advertising Festival, 2009 Cannes Lion Winner; **p. 128** (bottom): Cannes Lion International Advertising Festival, Cannes Lion Winner; **p. 132** (left): Courtesy of Evian®; **p. 132** (right): © 2012 Charles Schwab & Co. Inc. Used with permission; **p. 133:** Courtesy of BMW, Canada: Agency: TAXI; Art Director: Vladimir Karastoyanov; Creative Director: Zak Mroueh, Steve Myykolyn; Copywriter: Jonathan Careless; Photographer: Richard Heyfron; Producer: Judy Boudreau: Client: BMW Group Canada; **p. 135:** Courtesy KidsandCars.org; **p. 136** (top): Tom Comunicação; **p. 136** (bottom): Avocados from Mexico; **p. 137:** © Richard Hutchings RF; **p. 138:** © PRNewsFoto/Nike, Inc./AP Images; **p. 139:** Courtesy of the United States Army; **p. 141** (top): Cannes Lions International Advertising Festival; **p. 141** (bottom): © McGraw-Hill Companies, Inc./Mark Dierker, photographer; **p. 145:** © Pixtal/Age Fotostock RF.

CHAPTER 6

Opener: © enis izgi/Getty Images RF; **p. 148:** Courtesy of the Holiday Inn® Brand Family; **p. 149:** © PRNewsFoto/The Milk Processor Education Program/AP Images; **p. 150** (top): Courtesy of TNS 2012, www.tnsglobal.com; **p. 150** (bottom): © Brand X Pictures/PunchStock RF; **p. 151:** Courtesy of the Holiday Inn® Brand Family; **p. 152:** Courtesy of Brand Asset Consulting; **p. 153:** © PRNewsFoto/No Nonsense/AP Images; **p. 154** (top): The Hive Media LLC, www.hivedoes.com; **p. 154** (bottom): © Stockbyte/PictureQuest RF; **p. 155:** The BURGER KING® trademarks are used with permission from Burger King Corporation; **p. 156:** © Stockdisc/PunchStock RF; **p. 159:** Courtesy of RDA Group, Bloomfield Hills, MI; **p. 160:** Courtesy Envirosell, Inc.; **p. 161:** Courtesy of Megan Holstine, Research Analyst, The Olinger Group; **p. 162:** © The Advertising Archives; **p. 165:** Courtesy of Volkswagen® Group of America, Inc., used with permission of Volkswagen Group of America, Inc.; **p. 169:** Cannes Lions International Festival of Creativity, 2004 Cannes Lions Winner; **p. 171:** © Robert Daly/OJO Images/Getty Images RF.

CHAPTER 7

Opener: © Kutay Tanir/Photodisc/Getty Images RF; **p. 174:** Courtesy of Pepsi-Cola North America; **p. 176:** © PRNewsFoto/Virgin America/AP Images; **p. 178** (top): © McGraw-Hill Companies, Inc., Chris Kerrigan, photographer; **p. 178** (bottom left): Courtesy of General Motors; **p. 178** (bottom right): Courtesy of P&G; **p. 180:** Courtesy BMW of North America, LLC. The BMW name and logo are registered trademarks; **p. 181** (top): © Barbara Penoyar/Getty Images RF; **p. 181** (bottom): Courtesy of Southwest Airlines; **p. 185:** Courtesy of Progressive Casualty Insurance Company; **p. 186:** Courtesy of Pepsi-Cola North America; **p. 189** (top): Cannes Lions International Festival of Creativity, 2004 Cannes Lions Winner; **p. 189** (bottom): Courtesy of Citi, ad designed by Publicis Kaplan Thaler; **p. 190:** Courtesy of Pepsi-Cola North America; **p. 191:** Angie's List; **p. 193:** © Stockdisc/PunchStock RF; **p. 195:** © Graham Bell/Corbis RF.

CHAPTER 8

Opener: © Digital Vision RF; **p. 198:** © Susan Van Etten/PhotoEdit; **p. 199:** © MHM; **p. 200** (top): © Mike Segar/Reuters/Landov; **p. 200** (bottom): Courtesy Outdoor Advertising Association of America; **p. 201:** © McGraw-Hill Companies, Inc./Lars Niki, photographer; **p. 204:** Courtesy Outdoor Advertising Association of America; **p. 205:** © Roger Walsh/Landov; **p. 206** (top):

The UPS Store; **p. 206** (bottom): © Flickr.com/Jill Cardy, http://www.flickr.com/photos/jillclardy/2997175502/; **p. 207:** Courtesy Outdoor Advertising Association of America; **p. 208:** © Halfdark/Getty Images RF; **p. 209:** © Cannes Lions International Festival of Creativity, Cannes Lions 2004; **p. 210** (top): © MHM; **p. 210** (bottom): Smith & Milton: Designer, Andy Isaac, Creative Director, Steven Anderson; **p. 211:** © Brand X Pictures/PunchStock RF; **p. 212:** Courtesy Outdoor Advertising Association of America; **p. 213:** Courtesy Cannes Lions International Advertising Festival Bronze Lion Winner 2007; **p. 217:** © Jack Hollingsworth/Blend Images LLC RF.

CHAPTER 9

Opener: © Somos/JupiterImages RF; **p. 220:** Courtesy of Peter Funch; **p. 222:** Cannes Lions International Advertising Festival Winner: **p. 224** (right): © PRNewsFoto/Deckers Outdoor Corporation/AP Images; **p. 225-227:** Fictitious ads for Florida based cruise line Imperial Majesty; ads by Tom Michael, Market Design, Encinitas, CA; **p. 228** (top): Courtesy Cannes Lions International Advertising Lion Winner; **p. 228** (bottom): © Stockbyte/Brand X Pictures/JupiterImages RF; **p. 229:** Courtesy of De Scenza Diamonds; **p. 233:** Courtesy The Allstate Insurance Company; **p. 234** (top left): Florida Department of Citrus; **p. 234** (top right): © PRNewsFoto/Carbonite, Inc./AP Wide World Photos; **p. 234** (bottom): Ad developed by Saatchi & Saatchi Romania for PSI Romania. Brand: Love Plus. Creative Directors: Nick Hine, Jorg Riommi; Art directors: Daniela Nedelschi, Florin Roman; Copywriter: Sorana Caracudovici; Photography: Octav Ionita; **p. 236:** Courtesy of Newell Rubbermaid; **p. 237:** Courtesy Campbell Soup Company; **p. 239:** Courtesy McCann-Erickson Worldwide; **p. 240** (top): Courtesy of Philips; **p. 240** (bottom): Courtesy JWT Detroit; **p. 242:** Courtesy MasterCard; **p. 243:** Courtesy Saatchi & Saatchi, Los Angeles; **p. 244:** Courtesy of 2010 FIFA World Cup; **p. 245** (top): © flickr.com/http://www.flickr.com/photos/33852688@N08/4461253561/; **p. 245** (bottom): © A. Minde/PhotoAlto RF.

CHAPTER 10

Opener: © flickr.com/Aarni Heiskanen, http://www.flickr.com/photos/27183005@N08/4957236945; **p. 248:** © PRNewsFoto/The Levi's brand/AP Images; **p. 251:** Courtesy of Procter & Gamble; **p. 252:** © The McGraw-Hill Companies, Inc./Ken Cavanagh, photographer; **p. 253:** Agencies: BUZZIN MONKEY and "die agentour"; Responsible people: Stefan Becker and Peter Linke; Contact: www.buzzinmonkey.com; Client: MINI Deutschland; **p. 254:** Sunset Publishing Corp; **p. 255:** © David Schaefer; **p. 257:** Sunset Publishing Corp; **p. 258:** Agency: Mad Dog & Englishman; Writer: Mikal Reich; Art Directors: Carol Holsinger, Gina Fortunato, David Cook; Creative Directors: Nick Cohen & David Cook, Courtesy of the Village Voice; **p. 259:** © Comstock Images/Getty Images RF; **p. 261:** © Helene Rogers/age fotostock; **p. 262:** © Flickr.com/Michel Ngilen, http://www.flickr.com/photos/20179579@N00/295637646/in/photostream/; **p. 263:** Courtesy of The Times Record/Brunswick Publishing LLC; **p. 266** (left): Newspaper National Network LP. All Rights Reserved. 2012; **p. 266** (right): © NetPhotos/Alamy; **p. 268:** © Tom Grill/Corbis RF; **p. 269:** © Fuse/Getty Images RF.

CHAPTER 11

Opener: © Design Pics/Darren Greenwood RF; **p. 272:** © flickr.com/Sam Stuart, http://www.flickr.com/photos/pasurfbird/4152407581/in/photostream; **p. 273:** © NetPhotos/Alamy; **p. 277** (top): © Comstock/PunchStock RF; **p. 277** (bottom): © The McGraw-Hill Companies Inc./Ken Cavanagh, photographer; **p. 279:** © Tony Cardoza/Getty Images RF; **p. 280:** Copyrighted image was reprinted with the permission of GEICO; **p. 283** (top): Total Gym Fitness LLC; **p. 283** (bottom): © Clay Enos/Warner Bros. Pictures/Everett Collection; **p. 284** (top): Courtesy of Wayne Fuel Dispensers; **p. 284** (bottom): © Sony Entertainment /Photofest; **p. 285:** Copyrighted information of The Nielsen Company, licensed for use herin; **p. 290:** Courtesy Radio Advertising Bureau; **p. 291:** © Glen Argov/Landov Images; **p. 292:** Courtesy Westwood One Radio Network; **p. 295:** © Hill Street Studios/Blend Images LLC RF.

CHAPTER 12

Opener: © Colin Anderson/Blend Images LLC RF; **p. 298:** Courtesy of Ikea Russia and Instinct/BBDO; **p. 299:** © PRNewsFoto/OpenTable/AP Images; **p. 300:** © Blendtec; **p. 302:** Courtesy of Pinterest.com; **p. 303** (top): © Susana Vera/Reuters/Corbis; **p. 303** (bottom): © simon denson/Alamy; **p. 305** (left): Home Page of AdForum.com, a leading website of the advertising industry worldwide; **p. 305** (right): Courtesy of comScore, Inc.; **p. 309:** © Ryan McVay/Getty Images RF; **p. 311:** Courtesy of Google; **p. 312** (top): Courtesy of Teachnology, Incorporated, www.teachnology.com; **p. 312** (bottom): Courtesy Cannes Lions International Advertising Festival Winner; **p. 313:** Courtesy Cannes Lions International Advertising Festival Winner, 2005; **p. 314:** © Photographer's Choice/Getty Images RF; **p. 317:** © Ingram Publishing/SuperStock RF.

CHAPTER 13

Opener: © Photodisc/PunchStock RF; **p. 320** (top): Leo Burnett Company Canada; **p. 320** (bottom): © Kanojuko/Dreamstime.com RF; **p. 322:** Courtesy Outdoor Advertising Association of America; **p. 324:** Courtesy Outdoor Advertising Association of America; **p. 325** (top): © TongRom Image Stock/Alamy RF; **p. 325** (bottom): Courtesy of Mattel Mexico and Ogilvy & Mather Mexico; **p. 326:** © Mark Steinmetz RF; **p. 327:** Courtesy Outdoor Advertising Association of America; **p. 329:** Courtesy Cannes Lions International Advertising Festival Winner; **p. 331** (top): Courtesy Cannes Lions International Advertising Festival Winner; **p. 331** (bottom): Las Vegas Monorail Company; **p. 333:** Courtesy of Saatchi & Saatchi Copenhagen; **p. 334:** © Brand X Pictures/PunchStock RF; **p. 335** (top): Hammacher Schlemmer & Co; **p. 335** (bottom): © Jennifer M. Blankenship; **p. 338:** Courtesy of Kantar Media; **p. 340:** Courtesy LCD Exposition Services; **p. 341:** © Fancy Photography/Veer RF.

CHAPTER 14

Opener: © Kalium/age fotostock RF; **p. 344:** © McGraw Hill Companies, Inc., Mark Dierker, photographer; **p. 346:** Cannes Lions International Festival, 2008 Grand Prix Winner; **p. 347:** Cannes Lions International Festival, 2004 Lion Winner; **p. 351:** © Photo by Eric McCandless/ABC via Getty Images; **p. 355:** Courtesy of Sports Illustrated and Time Inc.; **p. 357:** Lava® Soap is a registered trademark of WD-40 Company; **p. 359:** Courtesy Godiva Chocolatier, Inc.; **p. 360** (top): Courtesy Crownline Boats; **p. 360** (bottom): © Comstock Images/Alamy RF; **p. 364** (top): © Photodisc/Getty Images RF; **p. 364** (bottom): Courtesy of Kantar Media; **p. 365:** © Paul Bradbury/age fotostock RF.

CHAPTER 15

Opener: http://www.flickr.com/photos/47761330@N00/8284102255/; **p. 368** (top): Copyrighted image was reprinted with the permission of GEICO; **p. 368** (bottom): © Albert L. Ortega/Getty Images; **p. 369:** © 2013 Dell Inc. All Rights Reserved; **p. 370:** Courtesy Cannes Lions International Advertising Festival Gold Lion Winner; **p. 371** (top): Copyrighted image was reprinted with the permission of GEICO; **p. 371** (bottom): Courtesy of Priceline.com; **p. 372:** © Comstock/Punchstock RF; **p. 373** (left): Kroger Community Rewards and the Kroger logo are registered trademarks of The Kroger Co. of Michigan, a division of The Kroger Co. McGraw-Hill obtained permission to use the Kroger trademarks and image from Kroger's website; **p. 373** (right): © salesforce.com, Inc. Used with permission; **p. 374:** © Comstock Images/Alamy RF; **p. 375:** © Digital Vision/Getty Images RF; **p. 376:** Courtesy of L.L. Bean; **p. 377** (top): © Chris O'Meara/AP Images; **p. 377** (bottom, left to right): Courtesy of Orbitz, LLC. All rights reserved; © Hotwire, Inc. All rights reserved; © NetPhotos/Alamy; **p. 379** (top) © Fuse/Getty Images RF; **p. 379** (bottom): © David Paul Morris/Getty Images; **p. 380:** Courtesy of Nordstrom; **p. 383:** © flickr.com/Doug Kline/http://www.flickr.com/photos/popculturegeek/6764017819; **p. 385:** © PRNews Foto/GLEUKOS, Inc./AP Images; **p. 386:** SNAPPLE is a registered trademark of Snapple beverage Corp. © 2008 Snapple Beverage Corp. Used with permission. All rights reserved; **p. 389:** © 2007 Payne Heating & Cooling Systems. All rights reserved; **p. 390:** © Scott Olson/Getty Images; **p. 391:** Courtesy STK LLC; **p. 392:** Courtesy Campbell Soup Company; **p. 393:** Courtesy Catalina Marketing; **p. 394:** The Dannon Company, Inc.; **p. 395:** © S. Olsson/PhotoAlto RF.

CHAPTER 16

Opener: © Flickr.com/Anna Fox, http://www.flickr.com/photos/harshlight/7911368670; **p. 398:** © REUTERS/ Mike Cassese /Landov; **p. 399:** © PRNewsFoto/Ainsworth Pet Nutrition/AP Images; **p. 403** (top): © The McGraw-Hill Companies, Inc./Photo by Eric Misko, Elite Images Photography; **p. 403** (bottom): Cannes Lions International Festival, 2012 Lion Winner; **p. 404:** Courtesy of the Rainforest Action Network; **p. 405:** Photo courtesy of Zappos, © 2010 Zappos.com, Inc.; **p. 407** (left): Courtesy of Special Olympics International; **p. 407** (right): Sacramento Municipal Utilities District (SMUD); **p. 408:** © Comstock Images/Alamy RF; **p. 409:** © Stephen Pond/Getty Images; **p. 412:** Courtesy Campbell Soup Company; **p. 413:** Quicken Loans Arena; **p. 414:** © Dynamic Graphics/PunchStock RF; **p. 416:** Courtesy of The Home Depot Foundation; **p. 417:** © Vetta/Getty Images RF.

index

A

B

C

D

E

F

G

H

I

J

K

L

M

N

O

P

Q

R

S

T

U

V

W

X

Y

Z